The House Was My Home

My Life on Capitol Hill and Other Tales

By

Daniel M. Freeman

Cadmus Publishing

www.cadmuspublishing.com

Published by Cadmus Publishing
www.cadmuspublishing.com

ISBN: 978-1-7343644-3-9

Library of Congress Control Number: 2019916950

Dedication

This book is dedicated first and foremost to Mimi. She has made this book, and my life immeasurably better. It is also dedicated to the magnificent friends who have shone a torch to shepherd me through my life journey. You have been an essential element in my voyage (in order of appearance), Professor Eric Easton, Professor Earl Dudley, Ashley O. Thrift, Judge Leonard Braman and Dr. James P. Evans. I could not have done it without you, and I am profoundly grateful for your guidance and friendship. Each of you has provided me with intellectual stimulus and emotional support and has vastly enriched my life. Whenever I think about you and the positive influence you have been, the words of the Irish poet William Butler Yeats come to mind:

Think where man's glory most begins and ends,
And say my glory was I had such friends.

I love you all.

Introduction

There was a line in a poem written in the late '60s which resonated with me at the time and still does; "I shall live my life on the Eagle's wing". It was written by someone who wanted to serve his country by being a positive force in government. For me, that meant serving the American people through public service. That was my life's goal.

I often frustrated people I worked with and later my students by saying, "I do not do politics, I do government". I am not a politically astute person, but I do have a reservoir of knowledge and interest in crafting policy through the legislative process (sometimes with the assistance of the courts). At one point, when I was working as Counsel and Parliamentarian to the House Judiciary Committee, the General Counsel, his deputy, and I were talking about an interesting constitutional issue. I loved engaging in this kind of intellectual dialogue. I proffered a solution, and the deputy was horrified. "Geez Freeman, you don't care anything about politics; all you care about is good government". I responded, "Yes, what's your point?"

I started to consider writing my professional life's story many years ago. Since I spent the majority of my career working in the House of Representatives, I was frequently asked about strange, weird and extraordinary things I had witnessed. "The House Was My Home" is the result of my desire to share some of my experiences. Xavier Becerra, a former Member of the House, and now the Attorney General of California, wrote urging me to write this book. He said, "Don't keep all that stuff locked up in your brain". Former Congressman Jim Rogan, himself a prolific author, also encouraged me to "write it all down".

Many of these events were important historical episodes, and, frankly, some of them are funny, not always at the moment, but with the application of tincture of time, amusing in retrospect. I must confess to a minor genetic mutation which has affected my life in a good way: I am related to the comedian Henny Youngman, the so-called "King of the one-liners". He was the author of his signature punch line, "Take my wife. Please!"

One of the most gratifying comments I received during my career was from a Congressman from Illinois who said, "Dan, I always enjoy your ability to see some humor in almost any situation. What I admire the most about you is that you take your job seriously, but not yourself". In an ego-maniacal place like Capitol Hill, that was high praise indeed.

I have chosen to include some material about things that happened to me before I began to work in the House of Representatives, as well as during the short breaks I took from working on the Hill. I have also included my teaching in academia and with the Science and the Courts (EINSHAC) project. I believe this enables me to include some entertaining and educational experiences.

I spent the better part of four decades in public service, working in the White House, the U.S. House of Representatives for three different committees (for four different Chairmen from both parties, always on the majority staff) and eight general counsels, the Office of Emergency Preparedness in the Executive Office of the President, Peace Corps Headquarters and for local government in Peoria, Illinois and Washington, D.C.

The primary purpose of this book is to discuss my professional endeavors in government. The comments and opinions expressed, unless specifically attributed, are solely my attempts at candor, irony, sarcasm and humor. If anyone takes offense, so be it. I have called them like I saw them.

In my writing about some of the people I have encountered along the way, and especially about students I had while teaching at American University, I have used pseudonyms and/or limited identifying details to ensure their privacy. In some cases, I have omitted their names in order to protect the guilty. It is not my intention to make anyone regret my having written this book. There are many people who were significant in my professional life who are not mentioned or only discussed briefly. This is not necessarily a reflection of their importance.

I have always considered the opportunity to work in government to be an honor and a rare privilege. I was inspired to go to work every day (well, almost every day). I did public service and was proud to do so. I was interviewed by the Washington University Magazine in 1983, and I was asked, among other things, how would I define a successful person. I said, in my view, "it is someone who has the courage to laugh often, to win the respect of intelligent people, to earn the appreciation and trust of honest critics, to appreciate beauty, and to leave the world a little better than when he or she got here." I stand by that statement all these years later.

The Novelist Verlin Cassill said, "All wisdom is contained in stories". I hope you can absorb some wisdom from the stories I have conveyed here as well as enjoy the humor in many of them. There are, I hope, some you will consider real gems.

I am deeply grateful to many Members of Congress for their support both while I was working on the Hill, and when I was teaching at American University. I am particularly indebted to the four Members who have written comments about this book, Howard Berman, Dan Glickman, Norm Mineta and Pete Sessions. They are all people I respect and admire. I am a better person for having had the opportunity to learn from each of them.

I am indebted to my editor Morten Wendelbo for his dedication and hard work. I hope you enjoy my reminiscences.
DMF

About the Author

Professor Daniel M. Freeman (A.B. Washington University, J.D. Columbia University) is a native Washingtonian. He has had extensive experience in government policymaking. He is admitted to the bar of the District of Columbia and Federal Courts, as well as the U.S. Supreme Court. He served in the White House under an Assistant to the President during the Carter Administration.

He was Counsel to the House District of Columbia Committee during the consideration of the Home Rule Act. He was Counsel and Parliamentarian to the House Judiciary Committee under three separate Chairmen of both parties. He was the staff counsel on three judicial and one Presidential impeachment. He subsequently served as Counsel and Parliamentarian to the House Committee on International Relations, working on major foreign relations issues including authorizations for the use of military force in Iraq and Afghanistan. He is an expert on constitutional law and worked on a myriad of constitutional and legal issues within the Judiciary Committee's and the International Relations Committee's jurisdiction. He is an experienced authority on Congressional parliamentary procedure and a frequent speaker on Congress.

At the end of his tenure on Capitol Hill, Professor Freeman was invited to join the faculty of the Washington Semester Program at American University as the Academic Director of the Public Law Seminar. That program, which included students from colleges and universities all over the nation and several foreign countries, was designed for pre-law students. The seminar included meetings with Supreme Court Justices, Federal and local judges, Members of the House and Senate, Cabinet Officers, senior government officials and many distinguished speakers from the private sector.

Professor Freeman has also had considerable experience in the complex issues relating to bioethics. He taught an Honors Colloquium on "Bioethics and the Law" for undergraduates at American University, and a course in "Legal Issues in Bioethics" at the University of Baltimore School of Law. He is a frequent speaker on bioethics issues both in the United States and abroad. Professor Freeman has written extensively about science and the law, specifically on legal issues related to genetics and bioethics. He has served as a faculty member on a program to educate State, Federal and International judges on scientific and bioethics issues and how to deal with them in a judicial setting. He served as the technical adviser on the Robert Redford film "Quiz Show" for the scenes dealing with Congress. Professor Freeman is a Fellow in Residence at the American University's Center for Congressional and Presidential Studies.

Table of Contents

Appendices

I. Washington University in St. Louis

In high school, I was not focused on where I wanted to go to college. I knew I wanted to be out of Washington because I had been advised by many people that the best way to learn about life is to get away from home. I had a few options, but not a lot. My so-called "safety school" was the University of North Carolina. I did not get in.

We lived in Chevy Chase, Maryland, and there was a small semi-circular street behind our house. Senator Hubert Humphrey's house was on the corner, a few houses down was Senator Russell Long's, and down from him lived Senator George McGovern. I used to spend time on Capitol Hill whenever I could, and I tried to go to important hearings. I watched the debates about the ballistic missile gap during the Kennedy/Nixon campaign and the critical controversy over the Nuclear Test Ban Treaty, which was signed in 1963.

Having a father who was a prominent lawyer, I got to experience some interesting events. I loved going to the Supreme Court to watch oral arguments. A family friend, John Davis, was the Clerk of the Court, and whenever there was a compelling case, Mr. Davis arranged for me to get a seat.

During my senior year of high school, I got to watch my father argue an important case at the Court dealing with the rights of a naturalized American citizen, *Schneider v. Rusk*. There was a law passed in reaction to the post-World War II migration of many German nationals to the United States. To prevent Germans from moving to the U.S., getting American citizenship, and then moving back to Germany, the law directed the revocation of U.S. citizenship to any naturalized citizen who returned to their native country for more than three years. Angelika Schneider came to the United States from Germany with her parents before her fifth birthday. She acquired derivative American citizenship through them. She had grown up in the United States outside of New York City and attended Smith College in Massachusetts. After graduation, she went abroad to continue her studies where she met and subsequently married a German citizen. Schneider then settled in Germany with her husband and began a family. In 1959, when Schneider tried to renew her U.S. passport, the State Department refused her request, saying she was no longer an American citizen. If she had relocated to any country, other than Germany, the law would not have affected her.

My whole family went down to watch my father argue the case. The Court held the statute to be unconstitutional because it discriminated impermissibly against naturalized citizens who went back to their country of origin. The Court said it was a violation of the due process clause in the Fifth Amendment and ruled the statute invalid.

+ + + + + + + + +

I attended the National Conference on Citizenship that fall as the guest of a club I belonged to. The main speaker was John Glenn, the first American to orbit the earth. While there, I met the man who was my official sponsor for the conference. He was fascinating and was interested in me and my accomplishments and plans, which was very gratifying. He said he had heard a lot about me, which gave me pause, and that he wanted to know about what my future path was going to entail.

I told him candidly I did not know where I was going to college. I wanted a school with a city nearby and one which had an excellent political science program. I grew up with the advantages of being in an urban environment. Living outside Washington, D.C., I had access to all the governmental and cultural activities which the Nation's Capital provided.

I told my sponsor about the schools I was applying to, which included the University of North Carolina, Washington University in St. Louis, and the University of Wisconsin, among others. He said if I were interested, he would be happy to write me a recommendation letter for the University of Wisconsin. I did not know how much influence his letter might have, but I eagerly took him up on his offer. He wrote a beautiful letter in support of my application. I found out later his father and grandfather had both been on the Board of Regents at Wisconsin, and that he was currently a member. Needless to say, I got in.

When the time came for me to choose a school, I showed my father three postcards, one from each of the schools I had been admitted to. I asked him which school he thought I should attend. He said, "Go downstairs to your room and think about it. Then come up and tell me what you have decided".

What I decided was I could not face the prospect of living through the winters in Wisconsin. I found out no one goes outside from October to May and that there are underground tunnels which crisscross the campus. The second school was out in the country, and that did not appeal to me. Washington University had a beautiful campus on the edge of St. Louis, a large city which had pro football, pro basketball, a good symphony and a strong political science department. I chose WashU, as it is more commonly known, and I never regretted it.

✦✦✦✦✦✦✦✦✦

Washington University had been a commuter college for a long time. In the early '60s, it started to broaden its horizons in an effort to become a nationally and internationally renowned university. When I got there in the fall of 1964, there were many students from the St. Louis area in my class, referred to simply as "townies". Most of them lived with their parents and commuted to campus.

There were certain benefits to dating a "townie". One of them was Sunday dinner. The dining hall was closed on Sunday evenings, so getting something to eat was always a challenge. There were few places within walking distance of the dorms, and although there was a short-order snack bar in the student center which was open on Sunday evenings, it was always jammed. Until I started dating a townie, finding Sunday dinner was a bit of a chore.

One of the places I would go on Sundays in search of a meal was to local church groups. I would find someone who belonged to a church and get myself invited for their Sunday dinner. The churches knew the dining halls were closed, and they usually had events on Sunday evenings that included a meal. I got to know which ones had the most interesting programs, which usually consisted of a guest speaker and dinner. I also found out which ones had the best meals; steak always being the prime target [pardon the pun]. The only downside to this practice was getting trapped at a dinner which was focused on religion. I did not want to be recruited or proselytized. I just wanted a good meal.

✦✦✦✦✦✦✦✦✦

In September of 1964, there were a lot of things going on in St. Louis which interested me. One of them was the construction of the St. Louis Gateway Arch. It was scheduled to be completed that fall. It is an extraordinary stainless steel monument built in the form of a weighted catenary arch. It is like a chain hanging down from two posts, except in this case, it is upside down. It was designed by architect Eero Saarinen who also designed Washington Dulles International Airport. At the time, you could see from the stone archway in Brookings Hall on campus, through Forest Park, all the way downtown to the building site on the Mississippi riverfront. On the early morning of October 28, 1965, I happened to be sitting on the steps of Brookings. I wanted to see the keystone of the Arch go in. I understood they did it early in the morning to ensure a proper fit before the heat of the sun caused the metal piece to expand.

I could see the two stainless steel legs of the Gateway Arch almost touching each other. There was a large crane poised nearby. At around 9:30 am, I saw the crane lift the last 8-foot keystone into place. It looked like the crane was moving in slow motion. I had a perfect view from my perspective on campus. It was ethereal. Unbeknownst to me, Herb Weitman, who was the WashU photographer, captured me sitting there, a lone student contemplating life. He did not know until later what I had been looking at.

Many years later, I was at an alumni event where former St. Louis Congressman Dick Gephardt was the guest speaker. He was the Majority Leader of the House of Representatives from 1989 to 1995 and the Minority Leader from 1995 to 2003. After retiring from Congress, he founded the Gephardt Institute for Civic and Community Engagement at WashU. He was the speaker at the event, along with Steny Hoyer, who succeeded him as the House Majority Leader. During the pre-session reception, I got to talk to Dick about my attending Washington University. He only knew me as a Hill staffer. It was a strange coincidence that we both recalled where we were on the day the centerpiece of the Gateway Arch was installed. He was driving on the Eads Bridge, which crosses the Mississippi River on the way to a meeting. You can see the Arch from the bridge. He happened to be crossing the bridge at that same moment as I was watching from campus.

✦✦✦✦✦✦✦✦

Along with making sure I got fed, I also had to consider my courses. I wanted to take all the required classes and then get to the real focus of my interest, upper-level political science courses. Graduation required either hard science courses like physics and organic chemistry that were aimed at the pre-med students or some softer science courses, which included Earth Science, Botany and Human Anatomy for the rest of us. The latter was the track that most of the students who were pre-law selected. Since I was fairly sure I wanted to go to law school, it was "rocks, flowers and people" for me.

WashU had a policy of encouraging freshmen to engage in small seminars which were aimed at students who wanted to be active in what was called a colloquium. These were "honors courses" and counted for one credit hour a semester. Since I enjoyed the give-and-take of a discussion-focused class, I applied for and got into three of them; Political Science, Earth Science and Economics.

The honors class in the Earth Sciences Department was an extra credit course to go along with Earth Sciences 101. The class usually met on Saturday mornings, and we would root around in the various rocks in the Earth Sciences lab. On one sunny Saturday morning, Dr. Harold Levin, the professor, had arranged for us to get on a bus and drive to a quarry about 45 minutes away from campus to hunt for trilobites. I was not a morning person, and we had to meet at 8 am. However, since I loved being in the honors class, and Dr. Levin was a superb teacher, I made sure to get on the bus on time. We drove a long way out of the city and arrived at the quarry to hunt for fossils.

After we had done that for a while (I even found one), we got back on the bus for the ride back to campus. I was exhausted, so I made a beeline for the five seats across the rear of the bus and laid down to take a nap. I was out in .0003 seconds. I do not know how long we had been on the road when I heard a big bang and then "whap, whap, whap". We had a flat tire! We all piled off the bus and stood around like a bunch of fools staring at the tire. I said, "Well, it is only flat on the bottom", which was not well received by my classmates.

Dr. Levin asked the driver if he knew where the jack and the spare tire were. Unfortunately, he was a junior high school principal who drove the bus on weekends to make some money. It was a sorry comment on the American public education system that an obviously educated man had to take a second job driving a bus to make ends meet. What it meant to us was that he did not have a clue about how to change the tire. This bus had six wheels, two in the front and two on each side in the back. The flat tire was on the outside right rear. We were able to find the spare tire, but not the jack.

Since Dr. Levin and I were on good terms, he looked at me plaintively and said, "Any ideas?" As it turned out, I did. We had been studying igneous rocks, and I saw a big flat rock on the side of the road. It was about 15" x 20" and about 6" thick. I said, "This may not be igneous, but it may be ingenious". I got one of my classmates to help me move the rock, so it was directly in front of the inside right rear tire, the one that was still good. I suggested to the bus driver he move the bus forward about 10-12 inches up onto the rock so that the inside rear tire would be elevated onto the rock, and the flat outside tire was off the ground completely. Dr. Levin and the driver were intrigued by my resourceful thinking. Dr. Levin said (á la Henry Higgins), "By George, I think he's got it!"

Because it was my bright idea, I was tasked with trying to wrestle with a lug wrench to get the flat off and the spare on. I had done that many times on mere automobiles, but this was a first. An interstate transit-sized bus! A group of the bigger guys in the class and I wrestled the massive tire and wheel off, and then, somehow managed to hoist the spare onto the axle and secure it. I was pleased with myself, but I was done in. I told Dr. Levin all I wanted to do was "Get back to Wash U and wash me".

When we got back to campus, and before we got off the bus, Dr. Levin got on the PA system and announced, "Since Dan thinks he saved the day by finding a proper igneous rock, he expects to get an A in this class. However, since the rock was metamorphic and not igneous, that is not going to happen". I was too tired to protest.

✦✦✦✦✦✦✦✦✦

The freshman honors course in Political Science was taught by a forbidding professor, William Nisbet Chambers, who also taught the survey course in American Politics- Poli Sci 101 I was taking. He was gruff and did not seem to be interested in teaching a bunch of freshmen. I felt I could get a better experience in the smaller honors course format. I applied and was turned down without any explanation. I decided to appeal directly to Dr. Chambers. I wrote him a memo explaining to him my background, especially my interest in Congress. I told him about my going to Congressional hearings and my experiences in a whole range of government-related activities. He told me to come in and discuss it. At the end of our meeting, he agreed to let me into the class. I was intimidated by him but was glad to be able to be in the class. My term paper was about the political philosophy of Alexander Hamilton. Little did I know I was a half a century ahead of time in being interested in him. I beat Lin-Manuel Miranda to the punch! (the creator of the hit musical "Hamilton") The course was outstanding, and I got an A.

✦✦✦✦✦✦✦✦✦

The other one-credit honors course I took was in Economics, which was being taught by a young faculty member who would later become a prominent economist, Murray Weidenbaum. It was the cohort of the Economics 101 survey course. My roommate, Ron Zaba, and I took it together, but we did not get around to finishing our paper by the end of the spring semester. We asked Professor Weidenbaum if we could take an incomplete and write our paper over the summer. He agreed, and while we were working at the Bank of America in San Francisco, we managed to get the paper done.

Professor Weidenbaum was supportive when I asked him to write a recommendation for me to spend a year abroad. I had applied to the London School of Economics (LSE). He was enthusiastic about the possibility and urged me to pursue it. Unfortunately, WashU, which had many study abroad programs, did not have one with the LSE. I jumped through a lot of administrative hoops to get WashU to accept my proposed year abroad credits from the LSE. With Professor Weidenbaum's help, the powers that be finally agreed. There was one not so minor hitch; my draft board. I had a student deferment from the draft because I was attending an "accredited university in the United States". The board would allow for foreign study only if I were "engaging in a course of study in another country *while registered in an American educational institution*". All of the other study abroad programs that qualified for deferments had formal agreements between the two schools, thereby allowing students to be registered at WashU even though they were studying abroad. I could not work out anything acceptable to WashU, the LSE, and the draft board, and so I could not attend. I was very disappointed.

✦✦✦✦✦✦✦✦✦

Early in my sophomore year, I started dating a "townie", Jenny, who lived at home in a suburb of St. Louis. She was a lot of fun and being around her parents and her 10-year old sister was easy. Her mother was a terrific cook who specialized in tantalizing desserts. Sunday dinners were an active event; it was not get fed and get out.

An example of how much fun they were involved their family photos. Over the fireplace in their living room, they prominently displayed photos of the parents and each of the two girls. They were professionally done. I had injured an ankle playing football and needed to have an x-ray. This happened just before Thanksgiving, so I had it done by my doctor at home. It did not show any break, which was a relief to me. I asked the doctor if I could have the film. He gave it to me, and I mailed it to my girlfriend inscribed "From the bottom of my sole". Typical of me.

A couple of weeks later, I was invited, along with my roommate, for Sunday dinner at my girlfriend's house. When Ron and I walked in, it took me a minute to become aware of it, but I noticed the pictures on the wall had been shifted, and in the center was the x-ray of my ankle! I fell out laughing. It was her father's idea, and it showed what a fun person he was.

My roommate had a bit of a foul mouth, which living in a men's dorm probably exacerbated. I asked him to be especially careful with his language at dinner. Things seemed to be going rather well until Ron said: "Please pass the fucking potatoes". The room immediately became silent. Ron tried to recover but only succeeded in digging himself deeper into a hole by saying, "Oh shit, I'm sorry". Jenny gasped, her mother froze, the younger sister looked quizzically at Ron. She knew something was wrong but did not know what it was. This was the 60s when the "F-bomb" was not thrown around often; especially in mixed company. Jenny's father was as cool as the middle seed of a cucumber, as they say in the South. He looked at his wife and said, "You heard the man Sarah, pass him the fucking potatoes". Once again, there was another pregnant pause, and then everyone except the younger sister burst out laughing.

✦✦✦✦✦✦✦✦✦

Being on the debate team was a marvelous experience for me. I still recollect the college debate topic for that year verbatim: "Resolved that the United

States should substantially reduce its foreign policy commitments". It allowed me to travel to tournaments all over the country; we went from Boston to San Francisco (Harvard to Stanford) and all over the Midwest, including Peoria (Bradley University) and Cape Girardeau, Missouri (South East Missouri State University).

My debate partner, Michael Silverman, and I had very different personalities. On the way to each tournament, Michael was quiet and did not want to talk about anything but the debate topic and our tactics. I, however, was always animated on the way there and wanted to talk about the tournament, the city we were traveling to, the news, girls, or whatever. By the end of the tournament, I was exhausted and did not want to talk about it or anything else. He was relaxed and relieved and was chatty. This engendered some tension between us.

On the way to a tournament somewhere in Southern Illinois, our debate coach Ben Sandler, who was driving, for some reason, greeted the oncoming Greyhound bus. We heard Ben say, "Hello, bus". In my shy, quiet, retiring manner, I said, "Ben, who the hell are you talking to?" He responded that he was merely greeting the bus. All of us in the car thought that was rather strange. When we stopped for gas later that afternoon, being the devil that I was, I found a postcard that had a picture of a Greyhound bus on it. I surreptitiously bought it, and when we got to our destination for the tournament, I wrote on the card, "Hello, Ben. It was nice to see you on the road". I signed it "Your friend, the bus". I mailed it to him back at Wash U, but not until I had shown it to my teammates, who all got a big laugh out of it.

One of the girls on the debate team became a good friend. Joan Sonnenthal (now Golub) was from Houston, a hotbed of high school debate competition. She was terrific. She had the elegant ability to make persuasive arguments, no matter the question presented. She was also good to have on the team because she had a lot more personality than my partner, Michael. We would frequently debate each other for the experience it gave us. We also had a lot of fun on our travels.

During my senior year, and her junior year, we used to eat dinner together regularly. Her fiancé, Jay Golub, was at Harvard Law School, and that posed some difficulties for her. Long-distance relationships can be hard. Having her fiancé in Cambridge while she was in St. Louis was difficult. Joan had helped me get through the rough times with my first long-distance romance with a girl in Peoria, Illinois, and I tried to help her deal with a similar situation. More about Peoria later.

She was a rock as far as I was concerned. She is the most supportive person I have ever known. When I was studying for the Law School Admissions Test, I was getting a little nuttier than usual. This was, I thought, literally my whole life being put on the line. If I did not do well enough to get into a good law school, I thought my future looked grim. The night before the exam, I was tight as a drum and could not calm down. Joan and I had dinner together in the campus dining room, and I got up to get a cup of coffee. She said, "Sit down, relax, and do *not*, repeat do *not*, have a cup of coffee. That is the last thing you need". She then suggested we do the same thing she and her fiancé had done the night before he took the exam. I thought I should study, and she told me if I did not know it by then, I was not going to learn it. We went back to the dorms and sat in one of the quiet rooms. She mixed up a small pitcher of Brandy Alexanders and put on my favorite piece of music, Brahms's Symphony Number One, followed by Tchaikovsky's First Piano Concerto. She told me the thing I needed most was a good night's sleep. I went back to my dorm and slept well and scored high enough on the LSAT to get into Columbia Law School. What a fantastic friend!

She and I would occasionally get into mischief, which was almost always amusing. One day for some unknown reason, we were talking about cars. She told me she did not know how to drive a stick shift. I decided it was a skill that everyone should have. Instead of teaching her how to drive my stick shift Valiant, I decided she should learn on something better. We went to a local Renault dealer, posing as a couple who were car shopping. We told the salesman we were looking for a car for her. It had to be small and economical, and she had to feel comfortable driving it. He told us the best bet for her would be the Renault 4, one of the first front-wheel-drive cars available in the U.S. We could not have cared less about that.

I "confessed" to the salesman that my girlfriend did not know how to drive stick. "Not a problem", he said. "I can teach her in a short time". By this stage, we were both having trouble keeping it together. I sat in the back in fear for my life while Joan tried, as best she could, to make this car bend to her will. She did not do badly, but I was pleased to have the test drive over with. We had a good time, and that was the whole point.

One night, sick of dorm food, I decided to go out to a local steak house called the "Flaming Pit". I called Joan and asked her if she wanted to go with me. She told me she had already eaten and was not hungry but would go along to keep me company. Off we went. After I had perused the menu, I signaled our waitress we were ready to order. She looked at Joan and said, "What can I get you, Hon?" I piped up, knowing Joan did not want anything, and said rather sternly, "*She* is *not* having anything". Joan got teary-eyed in an Academy Award-worthy performance. I continued, "When you learn to make a decent meal, you can eat at a restaurant. Until then, you can watch me eat". The waitress was horrified, and Joan played it to the hilt. Later, she decided to have a cup of coffee and so I brusquely ordered her one. I knew she took it black, so when the waitress sympathetically brought the coffee and offered her cream and sugar for it, I told her Joan "did not need the extra calories". After leaving a generous tip, we told the waitress we were doing an experiment for our psychology class and thanked her for being so kind. "College kids. What can I say?" was her reply.

When I went off to law school, Joan was unhappy she would not have anybody to "play with". "Both of the men in my life have abandoned me for law school", she said. "What have I done wrong?" About the middle of November, I was becoming weary of law school and how difficult it was. I came out of class one afternoon and hailed a cab. I went straight to LaGuardia Airport and caught a flight to St. Louis. I got there in time to be seen walking through the student center and hear Joan scream, "It's Dan! It's Dan!" I spent the weekend at WashU, and Joan found me a place to stay in one of the dorms. We had a good time, and both of us felt better by the time I left on Sunday. I knew the next time I would see her was going to be at her wedding. In what was considered a breach of protocol at the time, Joan asked me to be one of her "bridesmaids". However, Jay, her fiancé, was kind enough to allow me to be one of his groomsmen. I would not have looked good in one of the dresses the bridesmaids were wearing.

In the latter part of her senior year, she was having some difficulties. She was facing significant life changes and was beating herself up. She was going to graduate from college and move to Cambridge to live with this man she had hardly seen over the past two years and was more than a little freaked out. I sent her a telegram which read, "Don't be dumb or else I will whup you upside your head". It was at that point I started calling her, in the most friendly way, "DJ", which stood for "Dumb Joan". That moniker stuck for years after that. We spent a lot of time talking, and for some reason, she thinks I got her through it. I am not sure what I did except listen, but I guess that is what friends are for. I was very pleased to get an email from Joan while I was completing this manuscript. She attached a photo of that telegram which, after more than 50 years, she still has!

A couple of years later, she and Jay were going to be visiting Washington, and we arranged to get together. I was seeing someone, and I had talked about Joan a lot, so my girlfriend was interested in meeting her. We were supposed to join them for dinner on Saturday night. Joan called me early that afternoon and asked me for a "big favor". Her husband was working at a giant law firm and putting in lots of time on the job. Associates at those firms are always under tremendous pressure to put in loads of billable hours. She asked me if I would mind terribly their canceling our dinner together, so she and Jay could enjoy the evening by themselves. She said they hardly got the chance to do that in Houston, and she wanted to take advantage of their being away. I understood completely, and that was it. No problem.

My girlfriend and I decided we would go out for dinner on our own. We went to my favorite Italian restaurant downtown. I had been going there since I was a kid, and I loved the food. As we walked into the restaurant, we went to the lower level where they had a series of tables for two along the wall and, in the back, a large room for bigger parties. We were told by the waiter, who knew me, to go to the backroom since they were not that busy. As we were walking to the back, I saw Jay, who was facing me at one of the small tables for two. I spotted the back of Joan's head. I stopped at the table, with my waist at Joan's eye level, and she exclaimed, "That's Dan's belt!" Can you beat that? She recognized my belt! I introduced my girlfriend and, aware of their desire to have time alone together, we left them and had dinner on our own.

Many years later, when I was working on the Hill, she and Jay were in town with their two kids. Joan and the kids stopped by my office to get House Gallery passes. When she walked in, I gave her a big hug and a smooch. Her daughter's expression of disbelief was priceless. I do not think she had ever seen that happen before. Joan would not let go of me as she introduced her kids.

We still love each other, and I know I am very fortunate to have her in my life. She has been a cherished friend.

✦✦✦✦✦✦✦✦✦

I was the unofficial travel agent for the debate team, partially because of my knowledge about airplanes. In the late '60s, all the major air carriers had "youth fares", and these programs allowed anyone under 21 to fly for half fare on a space-available basis. For every tournament we had to fly to, my task was always to find out which flights I thought would be most likely to have empty seats so we could get on. I also had to keep in mind that we were on per diem, and so any flight we could get on *and* get a free meal was a bonus. It enhanced the impact of our travel money. TWA had a central hub in St. Louis, and I was pretty familiar with their fleet. At the time, they had two kinds of four-engine aircraft, Boeing 707's and the Douglas DC–8s. These were the biggest aircraft flying at the time. TWA also flew the smaller three-engine Boeing 727s as well as the twin-engine Douglas DC–9s. Based on that knowledge, I would try to find flights going to wherever we were headed on the larger aircraft, focusing on those around mealtimes. Mostly we got on, but occasionally they were booked solid, and we would have to wait for the next flight to our destination. It was fun playing the game.

On one trip we had to fly to New York City. I noticed that there was a Boeing 707 leaving St. Louis around 5 pm. This was the perfect target for us since it was a big plane, and they were serving dinner. Because I had something else to do in New York, I left a couple of days before everybody else, but on the same flight. The plane was practically empty, so I did not even have to wait at the ticket agent's desk to find out if there was space. She told me to board immediately because she knew there would be room.

By the time we took off, I had noticed that there was nobody sitting in my row on either side of the plane, and there was nobody within five rows of me. I usually like to get up to walk around on long flights. That night I walked back towards the galley and ended up chatting with the attractive flight attendant. Since I had been flying out of St. Louis for several years, I had gotten to know many of the flight attendants who were based there. I was having a lovely, flirty conversation when it became time for Alice to start the dinner service. I reluctantly went back to my seat, but not until I had received a big smile and a batting of her eyes.

This was one of those circumstances that you dream about. I'm sure many people have come up with a perfect pithy response to someone's comment, but only have it come to their consciousness the next day. However, this time I came up with one immediately. After dinner was served to the practically empty coach cabin, with the lights dimmed so people could sleep, Alice came by with the coffee service. When she got to me, she looked at me with a twinkle in her eye and said, "Coffee, tea, or me?" Now it was the swinging '60's, with the emphasis on sizzle in advertising at the time, including Braniff's slogan of "We will move our tail for you", and I had heard that line before. This is where the magic of my twisted mind came into play. Without the slightest hesitation, I said: "Whichever is easier to make". That comment could have been met with a slap in the face, a brusque ice-cold brush-off, or as it happened in this case, a lascivious smile. I received the latter. We then made plans to get together for dinner in New York the next night.

We had a delicious dinner at a quiet Italian restaurant that was a favorite of hers, which was near where she lived in Greenwich Village. One of the topics of conversation was people that we both knew. Since the main connection we had was TWA flight attendants, it turns out that I knew several women who were at some point based in St. Louis. One mutual friend was now based in London, one was in Paris, and one was in Munich. Maybe it was her exceptional sense of humor and free spirit that inspired me, but I was able to come up with yet another perfect line on the spot, instead of having it pop into my head later.

After the main course, we enjoyed some cheese and a glass of Port. I couldn't help myself, and I looked into those baby blues and said, "I am different from most guys, I like a little Port in every girl". I was relieved that she got a big kick out of that comment.

✦✦✦✦✦✦✦✦✦

I had some difficulties with the campus cops. As I recall, there was some Missouri statute requiring campus cops to be morbidly obese and refugees from a senior citizen center. As a young college kid, they did not have much respect for me or me for them.

One night I was driving through the campus, and I came to a red light. My date was sitting in the middle of the front seat next to me, and I had my arm around her, and my left arm was on the steering wheel. A campus police officer pulled up in the lane to the left of us and looked over. His car had electric windows, and he lowered the passenger door window. He said to me, "Son, I think you better use both hands". Being the smart ass that I was, I coolly looked him in the eye and said, "But officer, how will I steer?" Fortunately, the light changed, and I turned right, hoping that he would not follow.

I had another incident with a campus police officer sometime later. These were the times when women lived in separate dorms and they had curfews. The men did not. Pretty weird. I guess that meant the powers that be felt the women were the root of all evil on a college campus. Lock them up, and there would be less mischief. Having studied with a freshman woman who had to be in by 10 p.m., I would arrange to meet my upper-class date around 10:30 pm after having supposedly "just returned from library". This tactic became known on campus as the "late-date mambo".

On this occasion, I was dropping off my early date at her dorm just before 10. I did a U-turn on the street in front of her dorm. While this was a one-way street, it was cold outside, and I thought it would be better that I drop her off immediately in front of the dorm entrance. The radio was off, the headlights were off, the engine was off, and we were just sitting there talking. At this point, a campus police officer on foot walked up to the driver's side of the car and made a motion with his finger that I should roll down the window, which I did. He said to me, "Son, you're going the wrong way". Continuing in my role as a smart ass, I looked at him and said, "But officer, I'm not even moving". He responded by pointing up to the one-way sign on the lamppost near where we were parked which pointed the other way and saying, "Didn't you see the arrows?" I said, "Arrows, hell, I didn't even see the Indians!" He was not amused.

✦✦✦✦✦✦✦✦✦

There was another benefit to the male students not having hours. Although today it seems absurd, on Saturday night, when all of the women were safely tucked away in their dorms by 2 am, the guys were free to roam. Ron Pratzel was in my class, and he was a "townie" with considerable benefits. His family ran a bakery near campus. Every Saturday night, the bakery was going full tilt to make bread, rolls, cakes and donuts for the big Sunday morning opening rush. Because I was a friend of Ron's, I got special privileges. I was allowed to go to the back of the bakery and choose whatever I wanted hot out of the oven. The ovens were churning out hundreds of goodies. I would get a small paper bag and stuff it full of tasty treats, usually glazed or chocolate donuts. I would return to the dorm to make a pitcher of Tang (which was popular since the astronauts took it with them into space). I would place the pitcher on the marble windowsill, which would keep it cool overnight. Fully prepared for Sunday morning breakfast, I would go to bed. When I woke up, I would have more than enough donuts to satisfy my hunger and a cool pitcher of Tang to go with them. I could then go back to sleep and be sure of waking up in time for lunch. What a wonderful perk!

✦✦✦✦✦✦✦✦✦✦

One of the things I enjoyed about WashU was being on what was called the "Academic Committee". The committee was responsible for bringing guest speakers to campus as "in residence" experts. The first two were the vibrant Kennedyesque Mayor of New York City, John V. Lindsay, and the U.S. Senator from Maryland, Joseph Tydings. Each of them was on campus for three days, and I was able to attend all of their sessions.

Joe Tydings was my Senator, and I enjoyed spending time with him. His visit came soon after the famous *Miranda* Supreme Court decision which required the police to inform arrestees they had the right to remain silent and the right to have a lawyer. The decision was wildly controversial and subject to much condemnation in the political world as well as in the press. Criminal rights had been a big part of the presidential election, and Richard Nixon was a tough law and order candidate. Tydings was thoughtful about the Court's decision and felt the police could handle it. It was the subject of many questions during his visit.

He was also a strong supporter of "sensible firearms control legislation". I suggested a new law to him that would require people to have a permit for the handgun they owned. I also suggested firearms dealers require proof of the kind of handgun for which the purchaser had a permit when they purchased ammunition. My thinking was if you had to have a permit to buy ammunition only for the guns you owned which were registered, there was less likelihood of people buying ammunition for unregistered firearms.

The student who was in charge of the Academic Committee was an extremely bright drone who was bereft of any kind of personality. I felt she could not be bothered to talk to me since she clearly thought I was her intellectual inferior. Her tone changed after my father's law partner, Abe Fortas, was appointed to the U.S. Supreme Court vacancy occasioned by Justice Goldberg's resignation to become Ambassador to the United Nations.

Mr. Fortas and I knew each other since I used to work at my father's law firm during college breaks. His office was next to the front desk, which I frequently staffed. He was known as a formidable force at the firm. He and I, however, got along very well.

When Lyndon Johnson became President, Mr. Fortas, a long-time confident of LBJ's, who was a very busy man, became even busier. Fortas had been one of the key lawyers who preserved "Landslide Lyndon's" 87 vote victory in his 1948 race for the U.S. Senate. Johnson used him as a trusted adviser after that, on a whole range of issues. This affected me personally since I used to drive downtown in the evenings and park in the semi-circular driveway in front of the law firm's townhouse office building. After Johnson became President, Mr. Fortas' car was frequently parked in "my place" at night.

Mr. Fortas was not ready to leave law practice, and his wife, Carolyn Agger, a tax lawyer in the firm, who was a tough cookie, was also displeased about his appointment to the Supreme Court. From what I gathered, she did not want to take the financial hit going into government service would entail.

The story which Mr. Fortas told me was he was at the White House with the President in June of 1965 when President Johnson told him the two of them were going to the press room to make an announcement. "What announcement?" asked Fortas. Johnson said he was nominating him to the Supreme Court. Fortas told the President he did not think it would go over well with his wife. "Carolyn will be livid", he told me was his reply. LBJ said, "Abe, I just sent 500,000 boys to Viet Nam, I am sending you to the Supreme Court". In essence, he was drafted.

His nomination was confirmed in August. A funny thing happened when I returned to campus that September. The formerly cold dismissive coed who was the chair of the Academic Committee called me up and, just as sweet as could be, asked me to join the committee. I knew there was something fishy about it, but I figured it would give me a fantastic chance to meet some extraordinary people. I agreed immediately.

About a millisecond later, without even pausing to take a breath, she asked if I could get Mr. Justice Fortas to come and speak. She was shameless. But, what the hell, if I could pull that off, I would be a hero, and I would also get to spend a good bit of time with a whole range of distinguished guest speakers.

I got in touch with Justice Fortas' secretary, Gloria Dalton, with whom I had always been on friendly terms. I told her a formal letter would follow if she thought Justice Fortas would consider coming. Much to my surprise, Gloria called me later that week and said to send the letter because "He would love to do it". I was thrilled! We arranged for him to come to campus in the spring.

When I was home for Thanksgiving, I used to drive my father to the office so that I could have the use of his car during the day. It was a little weird to have him sitting in the back seat reading the paper while I was driving. He even kidded about getting me a chauffer's cap. One day, I dropped him off at the office, parking his car in the law firm driveway. I took the occasion to drop in to see one of the law firm's secretaries I had gotten to know, Diane Jackson, who was Carolyn Agger's secretary. When I got to Miss Agger's outer office, Diane was there, and Miss Agger's door was closed. That suited me fine. I do not think Miss Agger knew who I was, and she had a reputation for being difficult.

While I was talking with Diane, the telephone rang. It was a White House operator; President Johnson was calling. Diane put the call on hold and buzzed in to Miss Agger and said, "The President is calling". I could hear Agger thunder in response through the closed door, "Tell him I am busy". Diane dutifully did so and hung up.

About a minute later the phone rang again, and I could hear LBJ's booming voice saying, "This is the President". "One moment Mr. President", Diane replied and then she buzzed Miss Agger again and said, "It is the President himself calling". I saw the button on the telephone line with the President's call light up and heard Miss Agger shout into the phone, "Goddamn it, Lyndon, when my people say I am busy, that means I am too fucking busy to talk with you". And then I heard the phone get slammed down. I decided it might be a good idea to leave the office.

✦✦✦✦✦✦✦✦✦

Two of the most significant academic undertakings during my college career were my senior year political science thesis about the Roosevelt court-packing fight in 1937, and my study of the legal issues relating to how alcoholics are treated by the criminal justice system. My advisor on my thesis was Dr. John Sprague, a professor of Political Science. I worked with Dr. David Pittman, a Sociology professor on the alcoholism issue following a case going to the U.S. Supreme Court that term, *Powell v. Texas*.

Dr. Sprague was a fascinating man who had boundless energy. He was wrapped up in lots of projects, but he always seemed to have time for me. Unlike many professors I have known over the years, he had an acute sense of when to listen and when to talk. The research I was doing about how FDR tried to pack the Supreme Court with Justices who would not strike down his New Deal programs was fascinating. Dr. Sprague encouraged me to dig deep into the records of the debates in Congress and to interview anyone I could who knew something about Roosevelt's plan.

One of my father's law partners was Thurman Arnold, who had been the Assistant Attorney General for the Anti-Trust Division immediately following the court-packing fight, and he knew many of the players. He was happy to consent to an interview, and his insights were keen and frequently very funny. He talked about the parallel battles between Roosevelt and the Supreme Court over his New Deal programs, and Roosevelt and Congress over his proposal to pack the Court. Since FDR felt he was losing the battle with the Court, he needed to fight Congress to overcome its reluctance to give him the authority to add new Justices to the Court. Roosevelt's proposal was to add a new Justice for every sitting Justice who was over 70 years old. He thought the newly appointed members would not be so prone to declare his programs unconstitutional. It was during this discussion I came up with the title for my thesis: "Dual Duel". Judge Arnold thought it was appropriate, and Dr. Sprague, knowing my penchant for puns, thought it was very much me.

When Arnold left the Justice Department, it was to accept a life-tenured position as a Judge on the United States Court of Appeals for the District of Columbia Circuit. This court is frequently referred to as the "second-highest court in the land" because a lot of its decisions involve the Federal Government since a majority of the Departments and Agencies are located in Washington. He left the Court after only two years, and I asked him why. He said, "I would rather be speaking to a bunch of damn fools than listening to a bunch of damn fools".

The Chancellor of WashU was Thomas H. Eliot, a former Congressman and professor at Harvard and MIT. He was a classic New Englander, proper but with a kind, almost grandfatherly manner. He loved being around students. He was also a big supporter of the debate team. He thought our going to tournaments all over the country was good for the University's reputation. This was especially important as he was trying to transform the school into a nationally recognized institution. I attended many events at the Chancellor's residence.

One day during my senior year, I was there, and I was happy to spend some time talking with Mrs. Eliot, his delightful wife. We were discussing a paper I had written about the factors involved in the selection of Supreme Court Justices. She knew of my connection to Justice Fortas. I was, and still am, very interested in the work of the Supreme Court. Mrs. Eliot asked me if she could read my paper! I was surprised and told her I would get it to her the next day. She read it and wrote me a lovely note about it with a series of comments and questions. I do not know many people at Washington University whose papers were read by the Chancellor's wife, or, for that matter, at any other college or university. It was another reason why I loved my time at WashU.

The *Powell* case, the focus of my paper on how the courts treat alcoholics, was fascinating. Leroy Powell was arrested for public intoxication, a crime under Texas law. Powell was a chronic alcoholic who contended being charged with a crime for being intoxicated amounted to cruel and unusual punishment in violation of the Eighth Amendment. He argued that being drunk in public was a symptom of a disease. The trial court upheld the conviction saying alcoholism was not a valid defense. The question presented to the Supreme Court and argued in the briefs was, "Is the conviction of a chronic alcoholic for public intoxication cruel and unusual punishment in violation of the Eighth Amendment?"

I did as much research as I could on both the legal and sociological issues which the case presented. I also delved into the medical evidence about alcoholism. I found out the American Medical Association had concluded alcoholism was a disease as early as 1956. The finding was based on the theory that alcohol addiction is caused by a disease of the brain and is not controllable by the patient. Some of the elements of the disease are an inability to control alcohol intake and compulsive thoughts about alcohol.

The theory of Powell's defense was if alcoholism was a disease over which the defendant had no control, then being publicly intoxicated could not be a criminal offense because the defendant lacked the required *mens rea*--criminal intent. Powell was being represented by Peter Barton Hutt, a young lawyer at the prestigious Washington law firm of Covington & Burling. The *Powell* case was the only alcoholism case ever heard in the United States Supreme Court. Mr. Hutt agreed to meet with me to discuss the case. Dr. Pittman said he would pay for my airfare to Washington if I could guarantee him I would get a chance to sit in on the Supreme Court argument.

Fortunately for me, I had not one, but two aces up my sleeve. John F. Davis, who was the Clerk of the Court, was an old friend of the family, and Justice Abe Fortas had been my father's law partner. I managed to get a seat for the argument which took place on March 7, 1968. It was fantastic for me to have the opportunity to sit in on a case where I had read all the briefs and knew the arguments for each side.

Justice Thurgood Marshall wrote the opinion for the Court, which was announced on June 17. It was a 5-4 decision. The Court upheld the conviction and the law, holding the record did not prove that alcoholics were unable to control their alcohol consumption. The law, according to Marshall's opinion, did not punish Powell for his alcoholism, but for his being drunk in a public location. There were several concurring opinions, and Justice Fortas dissented joined by Justices Douglas, Brennan and Stewart. I was disappointed, but I got the chance to view history being made, and I wrote a good paper about it.

After the *Powell* decision, Mr. Hutt drafted the legislation which created the National Institute of Alcohol Abuse and Alcoholism and the National Institute of Drug Abuse. As a result, two-thirds of the States have repealed their statutes that had made public intoxication a criminal offense.

Later, when I was in law school, Justice Marshall came to speak. After his main presentation, he agreed to take questions. I asked him about the *Powell* decision, and he said any other decision would have only changed the name on the door of the places where alcoholics were held from "jail" to "treatment facility", and that would be a cruel lie.

Nineteen sixty-eight was a tumultuous year all over the country, but especially on college campuses. Columbia had been at the center of the action. There were a series of student demonstrations that erupted over the University's links in support of the Viet Nam war as well as a more local issue relating to the building of an allegedly segregated gymnasium in Morningside Park near the main campus. Those demonstrations culminated in students taking over Low Library, where the University President's office was located and several other university buildings. The New York City Police were called and in and violently removed the protesters.

There was a lot of coverage of the Columbia protests on college campuses nationwide, and WashU was no exception. Many of the people who knew I was applying to law schools inquired about where I was going. On several occasions, when I told them I was going to Columbia, people responded, "Oh, that's too bad" or other negative comments. This upset me, but I was still excited about going to a top Ivy League school, student demonstrations or not. I did not think I would be involved, so it probably would not affect me.

As soon as I graduated from WashU, the draft board reclassified me as draft-eligible and ordered me to report for my physical. This was at the height of the anti-war movement, and, candidly, I was more interested in going to law school than Viet Nam. I had suffered a relatively severe back injury playing football, and my doctor told me he did not think I would pass the physical. I still had to go up to Fort Holabird in Baltimore for the dehumanizing cattle-car-like process of the exam. I spent several hours being poked and prodded and giving samples of various bodily fluids. The last stop was with a physician. He looked over all the paperwork, made me stand up while he palpated my spine, and then snapped the x-rays of my back into the lightbox. I was nervous and asked him, "Doc, do you think they will send me overseas?" He was still looking at the image and said, "Son, only if we are invaded". I did not laugh. I did not smile. I wanted to get the hell out of there before he could change his mind.

II. Affairs of The Heart #1

Although I was too young to be thinking about marriage, I had several fulfilling romances. However, by the time I came to Capitol Hill, I had had the dubious distinction of having had two rather difficult relationships, each of which involved the so-called "eternal triangle". An eternal triangle has a couple and a third party. Usually, that entails a man, a woman, and either "the other woman" or "the other man". In my case, they involved God as the third party [Affairs of the Heart #1], and the woman's mother as the third party [Affairs of the Heart #2].

Affairs of the heart #1—Peoria, Illinois

My first serious girlfriend lived in Peoria, Illinois, when I was in college in St. Louis. Her name was Cynthia, and I was crazy about her. The long-distance relationship posed some problems. I met her at Bradley University in Peoria, where I was attending a mixer during a debate tournament. We began a rather intense relationship, a lot of which took place via letters and phone calls. I got to Peoria whenever I could, but it was a three-hour drive from St. Louis. I was trying to juggle getting a degree and being active on the debate team, which required a lot of travel.

Cynthia had been involved with someone else when we met. After we had been seeing each other for a while she told me the only reason she followed up on my suggestion I come to Peoria to visit her was because her boyfriend was not treating her well, and she thought a visit from "a college man" would make him jealous. She did not even consider that anything would come of my one visit.

Cynthia's father had a fabulous baby blue triumph TR-3 convertible. The first time I visited, he asked me if I would like to take it on our date. I was tempted to say, "Hell, yes!" However, since this was my first time meeting the parents, I managed to control myself. I told him that would be terrific.

I found out some time later, Michael, Cynthia's older brother, was none too pleased with my arrival on the scene. He said, "Who the hell is Daniel Martin Freeman that he gets to drive my father's TR-3?" I am glad I did not know about this strife at the time. I was nervous enough having come from out of town to go on a date with this beautiful girl.

Fortunately, at home, I lived across the street from a used car dealer who specialized in foreign and exotic cars. He always let me drive them when he brought them home. I became adept at driving temperamental cars with stick shift. I got to drive various Mercedes sports cars, Alfa Romeo convertibles, and even a Jaguar XK-E! I was moderately confident I could drive the Triumph.

Despite all of the nervousness I had about going to visit her, the weekend was lovely. We had dinner at a famous (at least in Peoria) restaurant--Vonachen's Junction. It was a very romantic venue. The dining room was a converted railway dining car. We had our own compartment with candles and flowers on the table. It was a magical evening. Her plans to, paraphrasing Aretha Franklin, "make her boyfriend blue", had an unexpected outcome. She and I hit it off! She had not expected we would fall in love, but it happened anyway.

We continued to write and talk on the phone, and we had visits whenever school, the debate team schedule, my finances, and Ozark Airlines would permit. It was never often enough, and sometimes our phone calls were uncomfortable. I often said, "The only thing worse than making a phone call which does not go well is not making that phone call".

I managed to find a good go-between. I called Ozark Airlines so often I got to know one of their telephone agents, Caroline. Whenever I wanted to get a message to Cynthia which did not require my speaking to her, I would call the toll-free number for Ozark conveniently headquartered in Peoria and asked Caroline to call for me. Cynthia got a kick out of getting calls from "the Greater Peoria Airport".

I found a job for the summer in Peoria, thanks to Professor Bob Salisbury, the Chairman of the Washington University Political Science Department. I thought this would be a meaningful chance for me to get to know Cynthia better and for us to spend more time together. I asked Dr. Salisbury if he knew any law firms in Peoria that might need a summer law clerk or messenger. He said he would do a little research and get back to me. He called an old friend of his, Ray Tucker, who was the former Mayor of St. Louis. Mr. Tucker knew the Mayor of Peoria and suggested that I call him directly. By the time I contacted Peoria Mayor Bob Lenhausen's office, Mr. Tucker had already been in touch with him. I was offered a position as the administrative intern for the City Manager of Peoria, sight unseen. Once I got housing at the Bradley University dormitories established, I was good to go.

I was happy in the job with the City of Peoria. The City Manager, Len Caro, was a tough chain-smoking man who turned out to be a good boss. He expected a lot but was positive, with the manner of a teacher, and was always willing to give me constructive criticism. He would frequently suggest how I might have done something differently that would have enhanced both my effectiveness and sometimes his.

One time I answered a call from the wife of a City Councilman. I asked her how I could help, and she simply told me that she wanted to speak to Mr. Caro. I dutifully took that message to him next time he was off the phone. He asked me what the woman wanted to talk to him about. I responded that I did not know. He then told me, "That is an efficient use of your time as the intern, but not an efficient use of mine". He went on to say, "If you had asked her the reason she was calling, maybe I would be better prepared to deal with it, or I could have even had you take care of whatever it was she wanted". That was my first lesson in being a good staffer, and I was to learn many more during my career.

The other man in the office was Henry Holling, a warm and caring young man only a few years older than me. He was Mr. Caro's right-hand man. Henry was also interested in making sure that this was going to be a learning experience for me. He was genuinely committed to his service to the city and was the kind of "Mr. Fix-it" who knew everybody in the city government, and they all knew him. He was well-liked and adept at working with people. I admired him and enjoyed having the chance to learn from him. He also had an easy and quick sense of humor that enhanced every interaction. We both referred to Mr. Caro as the "City Mangler", but not in his presence.

There was a hamburger joint that I used to go to occasionally for dinner. The owner, Bob Clark, was also the cook. He and his wife, who also worked in the restaurant, were very kind to me, and I became a regular. One evening Mr. Clark came up to me in sort of a conspiratorial manner and asked since I worked for the city if I would be willing to talk to his son about going to college. I said yes, and was flattered, although I thought I was a little young and inexperienced to be giving out advice. However, Mr. Clark always saw me in a coat and tie as I was usually coming in after work. He thought it would be a good thing for his son to meet me in my work environment where everyone was dressed in business attire. This was Peoria, small-town America, and there were not a lot of professional role models around.

When I told Henry the next day that this young man was coming in to speak with me to gain some wisdom, he cracked up. Unbeknownst to me, Henry had plans to get another good laugh. The young man arrived in my office on time at

3 o'clock. I welcomed him and proceeded to brag on his father a bit. At about 3:10 pm, there was a knock on the door and in walked a subservient, nervous and obsequious Henry Holling. I had never seen this Henry Holling before. He timidly shuffled his feet and asked me, "Mr. Freeman, is it okay if I go for a cup of coffee? I promise I will not take too long." Henry was a rapscallion! I had a hard time keeping a straight face. I talked with Brian Clark for about a half-hour about college, and what having a college degree would mean for him. I mostly asked him questions about what he wanted to do with his life and sought to give him some guidance based on my "extensive" experience. After he left, Henry came bursting into my office and we agreed that his performance was masterful.

I managed to squeeze a little bit more out of this situation. The following week, when I went into the restaurant to have dinner, Mr. Clark was effusive in his thanks to me for spending the time with his son. I told him I was happy to do it and that I hoped that his son continued his education. As I was sitting there, reading a book and eating my dinner, it occurred to me for some reason that Mr. Clark was going to pick up the check for my dinner. When I got up to the cash register to pay Mrs. Clark, she smiled and said: "No, Mr. Freeman, we would like you to be our guest".

Clark's was not the only restaurant that I frequented that summer. There was a steakhouse near where I was staying called the Steak Shack. I used to go there every Tuesday night before the City Council meetings. The first time I went in, I asked for iced coffee. The waitress looked at me peculiarly. She had never heard of iced coffee, and neither had anybody else in the place. So, I explained to her how to make it. I told her "back East", where I come from, restaurants put some freshly brewed coffee into the refrigerator. When they poured cooled coffee over ice, it does not melt the cubes and dilute the coffee. This was pre-Starbucks. She thought that was astounding. She thanked me for educating her. When the check came, she signed it "Thank You! #7" with a smiley face. On the back of the check was a place for me to comment on the food and service. I wrote, "Number seven is the greatest!"

The following Tuesday, as I entered the Steak Shack, I saw Number Seven, and she escorted me to a table in her station and then said, "I will be right back". Within a minute, she came back beaming and promptly placed a glass of iced coffee on the table. She told me she had prepared it earlier in the shift, just as I had described it. From then on, my iced coffee was delivered as soon as I sat down. I was afraid to even think about asking for anything else. I always wrote something complimentary on the back of the check about "The always exceptional Number Seven". I also learned to be a good tipper.

Being in Peoria, a city of approximately 100,000 people, was somewhat of a shock for me. I had come from Washington, D.C., with a population of 800,000, which was the center of our government. I was known as a "big city boy" who had come to the small town. This was all brought into perspective a little later in the summer when I was talking to one of the people who worked in City Hall. She was a friendly young woman who worked in the Legal Aid office. She was the quintessential Midwestern farm girl. We got to talking one day about our commutes. She was from a small town outside of town, and she told me she was nervous about coming into the "big city" of Peoria from her little farming town. I told her that I had a bit of culture shock coming from Washington, D.C., to small-town Peoria. She thought that was funny and said she could not imagine what living in a city bigger than Peoria would be like.

One of the most interesting characters that I met in City Hall was the General Counsel of the city, a bright and interesting man named Max Lipkin, who had a gruff demeanor. I spent as much time as I could around him since I thought I could learn a lot. He had a keen sense of right and wrong, as well as an innate ability to bore into a situation, define the problem, and then concoct a good solution. While I had spent my youth around lawyers who dealt with legal issues relating to fundamental societal problems, Mr. Lipkin dealt with immediate real-life problems that affected people in their daily lives. He was always able to come up with a way to resolve them. He was, however, more than a little intimidating.

In my second week working for the city, I received a phone call instructing me to come to Mr. Lipkin's office. I dropped everything and ran upstairs to find out what he wanted. As I was ushered into his office, he was sitting behind his desk, sleeves rolled up, his tie was loosened, and he was obviously in the middle of something intense. I walked in and did not say anything. I was afraid to disturb him, and I figured he would turn his attention to me when he was good and ready. This was a practice I was to employ throughout my career. After a couple of minutes, he looked up at me and said rather abruptly, "You and your girlfriend will come to dinner on Thursday". This was not an invitation but a command performance. He then returned to whatever problem was confounding him at the time. It was not the most gracious invitation I had ever received, but I was glad to have it although I was somewhat trepidatious about going to his home. Even though I was nervous, the evening was pleasant, and I did not commit any noticeable faux pas. Cynthia and I were on our best behavior. I was relieved to have survived the evening, and Cynthia thought the Lipkins were nice.

The following week I was able to sit in while Mr. Lipkin dealt with an important issue concerning the city's contract with the local bus company. At the time, Peoria was a one-company town. It was the world headquarters of Caterpillar

Tractor. Caterpillar closed its plant for two weeks every summer so that the entire workforce would take vacations then. It was the most effective way to deal with vacations since it would be hard to run the assembly lines smoothly with different workers missing at different times throughout the year.

The city subsidized the bus company, and Mr. Lipkin had discovered that the bus company ran holiday schedules for the two-week period when the Caterpillar plant was closed. He felt that was inappropriate because other people in the Peoria workforce still had to get to their jobs, and the limited bus schedule made that more difficult. He thought that was unfair and started negotiating with the bus company about providing service to those areas of the city that served the non-Caterpillar employees on a regular schedule during the Caterpillar summer shutdown. His main bargaining chip was to threaten to withdraw the city subsidy to the bus company. It was interesting for me to watch him defending the public interest in having transportation facilities available for *all* the taxpaying citizens of the city.

As the summer proceeded, it was clear that things were not going well on the romantic front. The previous summer, Cynthia had gone on a trip to the Middle East with her church group. When she returned, she regaled me with stories of one of the people on the trip, a young priest who, it turned out, spent a good bit of time trying to talk her out of being involved with me. The issue of my not being a Catholic was the primary reason for my not being suitable in his eyes. I never did meet him, and I was pretty damn sure I did not want to. The fact that I was good to her and good *for* her did not seem important from what I heard about their discussions. I did not think he was a possible romantic rival since he was a priest, but from the way Cynthia talked about him, I still felt threatened.

One Wednesday, when Cynthia and I were having lunch, I asked, "What do you want to do this Saturday?" She looked me straight in the eye and said, "I have plans". It came like a thunderbolt. I was devastated. She did not describe the plans, and so I was left to ponder all of the worst possible scenarios.

A good friend of mine from college, Nancy, whose hometown was Peoria, was glad that I was going to be in Peoria for the summer. She was a vibrant and vivacious girl who was a good shoulder for me to cry on about my deteriorating situation with Cynthia. I talked to my buddy Nancy the day after my upsetting lunch with Cynthia, and she suggested that she and I do something Saturday night to keep me from getting too depressed. I reluctantly agreed even though I did not know what she had in mind. She thought we should go to one of the nice hotels that had a cocktail lounge that featured dancing. That was okay with me since I liked to dance.

That evening as Nancy and I were on the dance floor, I looked over her shoulder and my blood turned cold. There was Cynthia with someone who was wearing a clerical collar. I must have reacted physically because Nancy could feel me tense up. She said to me, "Daniel, what is wrong?" "We have to leave", I replied. "Why?" she asked. "Cynthia is here with dancing with someone". Nancy was steadfast. She said, "We are not going anywhere. If she wants to come over and introduce her priest friend, fine. But we are staying here". And we did. I was extremely uncomfortable, but Nancy was splendid. Cynthia did not acknowledge me, and she did not come over and introduce this man, whose primary mission in life seemed to be to make me miserable. At the time, I was not even sure she knew I was there.

Cynthia and I had lunch the following week, and she asked me if I had seen her Saturday night. I told her I had. Of course, I had! With my voice dripping with sarcasm, I asked her why she did not bring "the cardinal", who she had been raving about incessantly for months, over to meet me if he was so fantastic. I never did get an explanation.

Cynthia was someone who lived in a world outside my experience; she was a devout go-to-mass every day catholic from a small town in the Mid-West. For someone who was a city boy and a devout atheist, this raised some serious problems. Growing up in a household where being a lawyer was the epitome of success, I was used to attempting to reason through any difficulties I had in my personal relationships. I found it devastating to learn that her religion was so much more important than I was and to realize there was no way for me to question those beliefs with her in a logical way. Her default answer to a challenge to any specific belief was, "That is what I believe in my heart that God commands".

The difficulty I was facing was made starkly clear to me one weekend. She wanted to go to Sunday mass and asked me to go with her. I think she was trying to save me from myself. I was not anxious to go, but I wanted to spend time with her, so I caved.

I had only been to mass once previously. That was with my roommate, Ron Zaba, during my freshman year of college. He volunteered to let me experience a catholic service. On the day Ron took me to the church near campus, I was disconcerted at one point during the service when I could not keep track of whether I was supposed to be sitting or standing. Everyone was standing up, so I did too. Many of the participants went up to receive communion. Since I was standing, I stayed that way. No one said anything about being seated. Little did I know that after each person came back to their seats, they knelt in prayer. By the time everyone had come back, I was the only one standing. I found that embarrassing.

But I digress. I went to mass with Cynthia that Sunday morning. At the end of the service, the priest said that there was a bill pending in the Illinois State Legislature relating to liberalizing its abortion laws. He commanded everyone to sign the petition against the bill before leaving. I was highly offended because I had been doing some research about the legal issues relating to reproductive freedom, and I thought the proposed law was a good idea. At least it would be a step in the right direction. However, it was a mistake for me to consider that anyone in the church would hesitate about signing the petition. It was a direct command from the priest. This was alien to me. I did not realize that it was compulsory and was angry as we turned to leave the church. As we were walking towards the door, Cynthia said to me, "Wait, I want to go sign the petition". I was astounded but did not show it. After that, things became more and more difficult, and I realized that this was not going to work out. Except for weddings and funerals or as a tourist, that was the last time I entered a church.

As I was getting ready to leave Peoria at the end of the summer to go back to St. Louis and my senior year at Washington University, Cynthia and I had a long conversation. She said she needed some time to think about our relationship and to make some decisions. By that time, although I was not aware of it, I think I had already made up my mind. She asked me not to call her and to wait until she called me. I went back to Washington with a sense that this was not going to work out. The wait was difficult and painful, but it gave me time to make a decision. It was over. She did finally call and told me she had decided she wanted us to get back together, and we would try to work things out. Changing the subject, I said, "How is your mother?" That was the end.

✦✦✦✦✦✦✦✦✦

Little did I know that less than ten years later, I would be in a hotel room in Washington D.C. during a practice session in preparation for a Supreme Court oral argument to occur the next day in the case of *Roe v. Wade*. The woman who was going to argue the case, Sarah Weddington, was young to be arguing a significant constitutional law case. I made a casual comment to her after the mock argument that she should take special care to make sure Justice Blackmun's questions were answered completely. "Why him in particular?" she asked. "Harry Blackmun knows more about medicine than anyone on the Court. He was the General Counsel at the Mayo Clinic", was my answer. When the opinion was announced in January of 1973, it surprised a lot of people. The bulk of the first part of the opinion dealt with the history of gynecology and was written by none other than Mr. Justice Blackmun.

From then on, the issue of abortion was to be on my plate regularly when I was on the staff of the House Judiciary Committee.

III. Columbia University Law School

I applied to several law schools during my senior year of college. The rule of thumb was to apply to a couple you probably could not get into, a couple you probably could get into and a "safety" school, which you are pretty sure you can get into. Even though I had a recommendation from a sitting Supreme Court Justice (Abe Fortas), I did not get into Yale. I also did not get into Harvard. These were my pipe dream schools, and I felt sure I would not get into either. Unfortunately, I was right. Next on my list was Columbia. I thought I could get in since my father had gone there and I was a "legacy applicant". I was admitted. My safety school, Georgetown, also accepted me. Since Columbia was the highest-rated school I got into, it was the obvious choice. I never regretted that decision.

When I arrived in New York City to attend Columbia, I was enthused, and a bit overwhelmed. On a crisp, clear fall evening during the second week of classes, I remember walking across the bridge over Amsterdam Avenue on the way back to my apartment from the law school. I was intensely concentrating on the case I had been reading. It dealt with negligence and contributory negligence. Those two concepts are fundamental to tort law. I briefly looked up, and I could see the New York City skyline all the way down to the Empire State Building. The first thing that came to mind was, "What the hell are *you* doing here at the Columbia University Law School, thinking about contributory negligence?" I felt it was clear that I did not belong there. That was a rather startling revelation.

I was aware that in every law school, there were people called "gunners". These were the hot dogs who had gone to prestigious colleges, seemed to know everything about everything, and were not reluctant to tell you how knowledgeable they were. Considering the high proportion of them in my class, I was not sure how this law school thing was going to turn out for me. I was sure I was already more than two weeks behind, and it was only the second week! It was quite a distressing experience! I subsequently heard someone refer to this as "imposter syndrome"; a feeling you get that you do not belong.

My crushing insecurity about being there was elevated the next day when I found out that two of my classmates had dropped out. I had gotten to know one of them a little bit and was shocked to find out that he left. I thought he was bright, and I did not sense he felt in over his head. I do not know whether anybody noticed that I felt overwhelmed. I expect that everybody was thinking about themselves and were not tuned in to what was going on with other people. What I did not know at the time was I am moderately dyslexic. I was having a hard time keeping up because of the enormous amount of reading required.

One of the things I decided to do was to organize a study group. I knew that I did not want a five-person group made up of people who all felt the same way about the issues we were going to be dealing with. So, I picked people who I thought were engaging, committed, and fun to be around, but with markedly different perspectives. Law school can be tough, and I did not want to be spending a lot of time with drones. I wanted amiable people with a wide range of world views. The first person I picked was a self-described "conservative southern boy". The second was someone who had never in his entire life been out of Brooklyn before coming to Columbia Law School in Manhattan. I was not sure where he was on the conservative/liberal scale, but he was scary smart. The third was a quintessential left-wing liberal from Berkeley, while the fourth was from Wisconsin and was a middle-of-the-road Midwesterner. I figured with these people I would have a good balance of points of view. One of the problems I did not anticipate was that the guy from Brooklyn, who was an orthodox Jew, could not meet with us in a non-kosher venue. We often wanted to meet at a coffee shop near the law school, but he could not partake of anything there since he kept strictly kosher. We worked around that impediment. I found that studying with these people was very helpful and also kept me engaged.

One of the "gunners" in our class always had a question at the end of the class. It was usually a stupid question, but he was never shy about asking. He had come to Columbia after having served in the military and was quite proud of that. This was a time when college campuses were not the friendliest environments for military personnel. He often walked around campus in his uniform. Every Saturday, he would go off to training with the local National Guard unit. He was kind of a buffoon, and as the semester progressed, many of us were gleefully waiting for him to ask the next stupid question. He would always shoot his hand up and wave it around, trying to get the professor's attention. We thought he might split a gut if he did not get called on. Professor Hill, our torts professor, referred to him as "Lieutenant Smith", and, as the semester progressed, so did we.

On the last day of class before the final exam, Professor Hill said, "Are there any questions?" Sure enough, Lieutenant Smith's hand shot into the air. Professor Hill pointedly scanned the entire class of 150 students searching in vain for someone else to call on. A lot of us recognized what was going on; Professor Hill was desperately looking for *anybody* but Lieutenant Smith to call on. A couple of students who were possibly interested in asking a question quickly lowered their hands. Professor Hill inhaled, then exhaled dejectedly, sat down on the desk, and with a sigh said, "Okay, Lieutenant, you get the last question". Smith then proceeded to ask a completely ridiculous and inane question. We were all sitting in silence, waiting for what was to come. Professor Hill did not disappoint us. He said, "Lieutenant Smith, it astounds me that whenever you speak, you somehow subtract from the total mass of human knowledge". The room exploded in laughter.

I loved law school. I had some outstanding teachers and some brilliant classmates. There were also several classmates that I stayed as far away from as I could. I enjoyed the intellectual challenge of many of the issues that came up, especially constitutional law and criminal procedure. None of these issues was clear-cut and being able to debate them with a bunch of smart people was stimulating.

✦ ✦ ✦ ✦ ✦ ✦ ✦ ✦ ✦

By 1969, most of Columbia University had been through a year of riots, protests and police activity. Things had calmed down by the Spring, and there was a fantastic event that took place on Low Plaza, the same place where the bulk of the demonstrations had taken place the year before. A group of students known as the Kingsmen, an acapella singing group, had added 1950's doo-wop songs to their repertoire. They decided to give a concert which was a salute to that music and called it "Grease Under the Stars", also known as the "GUTS" concert. It was on May 3rd, and over 3,000 people jammed the plaza. They did not try to improve on the oldies but worked to come as close to the sound of the original records as they could. It was wildly successful. The group continued to perform for decades after as "Sha Na Na", and even performed at Woodstock. It was a fabulous evening that I enjoyed just "groovin' to the tunes". I had spent some time in high school as a disc jockey on a local radio station. That helped me appreciate the concert because I knew the words to all of the songs. I was in heaven!

Since I had always been interested in Congress and was a political science student at Washington University, I applied for a position with a well-regarded law school organization, the Legislative Drafting Research Fund (LDRF). There was a whole range of journals and organizations at the law school, but this was the one that appealed to me the most. Professor Frank Grad was the head of the LDRF, and he was a superb man to work for. We had many discussions about a whole range of topics, some relevant to the LDRF, and some not. He had a phrase that he regularly used, "That's a nice question". He was the professor who had the most profound impact on me during law school. He was always urging me to know the other side. He said that unless you understand the other point of view, you could not effectively represent yours. He felt strongly that to be an effective advocate, you had to know the strengths and weaknesses of both sides of any question.

The work of the Fund was varied; we dealt with the whole panoply of issues from automobile emissions regulations, to zoning, to working on the proposed New York State statute relating to the liberalization of its abortion laws. New York was the first state to liberalize its laws in this area. The work on this proposal was to be the initial step of many in my long-time work on women's reproductive freedom. It was the connection to the pro-choice movement, which led me later to have a small role in *Roe v. Wade*.

One of the good things about working at the LDRF was that I had an office in the law school building. My office, which I shared with several other members of the LDRF staff, was a terrific place for me to work on fund projects, as well as to study. I had everything I needed, including a coffee maker, office supplies, a typewriter (yes, we were still using typewriters in the late '60s), and even a telephone.

The working telephone was something of a luxury since I did not have access to one in my apartment. I did have a phone and a phone number and got a monthly bill, but I could never count on getting a dial tone when I picked it up, and it would sometimes cut out during a call. That used to drive me crazy. I got so aggravated by the miserable and unreliable service that I decided to write a letter to the President of the New York Telephone Company. What one would typically expect in that circumstance is either nothing or that someone in a flannel shirt with a large toolbelt would show up then try to remedy the problem.

I, however, got lucky, and three men in business suits showed up at my apartment. They came in, fiddled with the wires, and made a couple of calls to whatever central station they needed to talk to, and after that my phone was working just fine. The last thing the supervisor said to me when he was leaving was, "Next time, call us directly. Do *not* contact the President of the whole company". The lesson I learned from that was that I *should* contact the top executive in any consumer circumstance. I have invoked that lesson innumerable times since then.

I worked at the LDRF the summer after my first year. I got a nice sublet in the Yorktown area on the upper east side of Manhattan. My commute included taking the 86th St. crosstown bus through Central Park, a transfer to the IRT subway and getting off at 116th St. which was the Columbia University stop. At the time, I found New York was a tough place to be. People on the bus practically disappeared within themselves. There was no chatting with strangers. It was analogous to today's transit riders who are all glued to their smartphones.

I got the bus in the morning at the same time every day. Several days in a row, I noticed an attractive woman wholly engrossed in a Spanish textbook. She was studying Spanish, and I was studying her. One morning I got on the bus, and there was a seat available next to her, and she did not have her nose buried in the textbook. I violated the unwritten New York City law of not talking to strangers on public transit and spoke to her. "Did you finish your Spanish course?" She was at first, stunned that someone would talk to her on the bus—the no talking zone. However, we got to chatting, and she seemed nice. She worked for a national hero at the time, Walter Cronkite. She was bright and animated once she had come out of her NYC transit cocoon.

The third time I saw her on the morning bus, I got up the courage to invade the cocoon and asked her out. She knew I was a law student and, therefore, was probably harmless. We made a date, and I was to pick her up at her apartment, a few blocks from where I lived.

I have been accused of doing some weird things to enhance my social life. This was to be no exception. On the way to pick her up, I stopped at a grocery store and bought a 5-pound bag of flour. When I got there, I handed it to her, and she looked quizzically at me and asked why I had brought it. I said, "I was told it is a nice gesture to bring a woman flour on the first date". She said, "I think you mean 'flowers'" and started laughing.

While no romance developed, we became good friends, and I would see her occasionally when I was in New York, as well as when she was in Washington. She called me one day to tell me she was going to be in Washington to interview "some freshman Congressman from Tennessee; Al Gore".

The most spectacularly weird thing which happened on the famous 86th street crosstown bus occurred during the evening rush hour. I had observed during that time of day, everyone on the bus was glued to the evening paper, the *New York Post*. It was the shield behind which most people hid so as not to have to interact with anyone.

I was sitting in the middle of the bus when a very tall man got on. He was wearing a pink dress, pink shoes and a frilly pink hat, and was carrying a pink umbrella. He had a three-day growth of beard. I am not a New Yorker, and so I was gawking at this character. When he got up to the farebox, he hung his pink umbrella on the chrome bar between the driver and the passengers. He opened up his frilly pink purse, got out his tiny pink coin purse, and deposited his token.

As I looked around, I was aware that nobody was paying any attention to this extraordinary person. He proceeded to sashay down the center aisle of the bus and sat in the last row. I was mesmerized and watched him all the way. Nobody else batted an eye.

The bus driver, who was a big burly man, reminded me of Jackie Gleason's character, Ralph Kramden, in the television show "The Honeymooners". The driver looked at the chrome bar and noticed the man had left the pink umbrella hanging there. I could see the driver look up in his rearview mirror and locate this guy at the back of the bus. Still, as far as I could tell, nobody else was paying any attention. The bus driver turned around, and in a booming voice which would have done Ralph Kramden proud shouted, "Hey Cinderella, you forgot your magic wand!" Nobody on the bus seemed to notice. With some effort, I suppressed a laugh.

The man got up, pranced to the front of the bus to retrieve his umbrella. When he got there, he picked up his umbrella and tapped the bus driver on both shoulders with it as if he were the Queen of England granting a knighthood, and said in a high-pitched voice, "Poof, you may turn to shit!" I thought this was hilarious, but I do not know if anybody else did.

✦✦✦✦✦✦✦✦✦

Back to law school. I was fortunate to have a close friend of the family working as the Dean's Special Assistant. Roz Rosenthal was the sister of my mother's best friend. I would frequently visit her to chat, and she would occasionally have me over to her apartment for dinner.

One of the things which I learned in college, which served me well in law school, was to pick the courses I wanted to take based on both the subject matter *and* the professor. If the subject matter was interesting, but the professor was not stimulating, the course would not be good. An excellent professor could make even a dry subject interesting. In the second semester of my first year, I was to take Criminal Procedure from an American legal legend, Herbert Wechsler. Professor Wechsler had argued many cases before the Supreme Court, including *Times vs. Sullivan*, the famous case dealing with libel of a public official in 1964. He was also the main intellectual force behind the Model Penal Code, which was a model for all the states to use in upgrading their criminal justice laws. Although he was universally regarded as a brilliant legal scholar, I had heard from people at school that his classes were rather lugubrious. He would sit up in front of the class and read sections of the Model Code.

Fortunately for me, I chatted with Roz about this, and she told me that they had a new professor joining the faculty in the upcoming semester who was also going to be teaching Criminal Procedure. Roz said this man was a well-respected appellate litigator who had come from the office of the District Attorney for Manhattan. She also said he was a dynamic and outgoing personality who had day-to-day experience in dealing with important questions of constitutional law relating to criminal justice. Roz suggested that I might be happier in his class. Boy, was she ever right! Professor Richard Uviller was everything she had described him to be. So, instead of listening to Professor Wechsler read the Model Penal Code to the class, I got to be engaged in the give and take of the Socratic Method where the professor took us through all kinds of complex and challenging problems while constantly changing the scenario. This was much more to my liking, and I thanked Roz profusely.

Roz came to the rescue the next semester as well. I was once again faced with the choice of classes to take, one of which was a small Constitutional Law seminar, which was also taught by Professor Wechsler. Once again, I went to the font of all knowledge about the law school, Roz Rosenthal. She told me that another new professor was coming to Columbia who had just finished his clerkship with Chief Justice Earl Warren. Benno Schmidt was a young man, not much older than I was. Roz had met him, and she thought he was going to be a lively professor. Obviously, he was bright; he had come from clerking for the Chief Justice of the United States.

Professor Schmidt's constitutional law seminar was everything I could have hoped for. It was challenging because of the wide range of views among the students, and the debate could become hot and heavy. I took this course during the height of the Vietnam war, and the powers of the President were front and center in everyone's minds. President Nixon had just authorized bombing Cambodia, and there were anti-war protests all over the country.

We were engaged in the debate about war powers and what the Constitution required. One of my classmates, Peter, made sure that everybody knew that he went to Ha-vad [he pronounced it in bold with a hard H]. He was rather pretentious and wore a corduroy sport coat to school every day. He always had a Ferrari lapel pin in the buttonhole. Now he was from New York City, and I knew he did not even have a driver's license, much less a Ferrari. He arrogantly quoted to me the constitutional language, which states that only Congress has the power to declare war. His position was that since Congress had not declared war against Vietnam, we could not be at war. So there!

My response was that Congress does have the sole power to *formally declare* war, but that the President, as Commander-in-Chief of the armed forces, has the power to *wage* war, even though it legally does not meet the definition of war. When Professor Schmidt asked Peter what his response to my argument was, he turned to me with condescension and disgust dripping in his voice and spat out, "What did you say was the name of that *college* you went to?" I was incredulous but managed to respond by saying, "One where they did not teach you to be a pompous ass".

✦ ✦ ✦ ✦ ✦ ✦ ✦ ✦ ✦

The outrage over President Nixon's bombing of Cambodia resulted in student strikes all over the country. There were several demonstrations planned on the Columbia campus, and the university arranged for some law students to act as security. During the training sessions, we were given armbands identifying us as marshals, and we were told to be prepared for the New York City Police to intervene if things got out of hand. I was wary of that possibility, especially because I did not want to have an arrest on my record when I applied for admission to the bar after law school. One of my classmates, who was always in a drug-induced haze, was there. A trainer asked, "Have you ever been picked up by the fuzz (a popular term for the police at the time)? My classmate responded, "No, but I bet it hurts". That cracked everybody up.

Because of the disruptions, all on-campus finals were canceled that spring and were replaced with take-home exams that were due in September. Many of my classmates, with dreams of sugar plums and straight A's, planned to spend a lot of hours slaving away over the take-home exams and turn in a practically perfect product after Labor Day. I chose not to have them hanging over my head the whole summer, so I closeted myself in my office in the law school and spent almost four full days writing my exams. By doing that, I was done at the end of May when I left for the summer! Come September, after talking to many of my classmates, I concluded I had made the best decision. Most of them spent the same number of hours on the exams as I had, but they also spent a lot of time agonizing over them.

✦ ✦ ✦ ✦ ✦ ✦ ✦ ✦ ✦

During my third year, I took the required course in evidence, and, against my better judgment, I picked the class that met at 8:45 am even though I am not a morning person. The reason I chose to take evidence at that ungodly hour was that the professor was a sitting Federal Judge, Jack B. Weinstein. Judge Weinstein literally wrote the book on evidence. His casebook was used in law schools nationwide. He held the class early so that he could finish and drive to the Federal Courthouse in Brooklyn at a reasonable time. He issued a standing invitation to anyone in the class to join him and sit in on whatever matter he was hearing on that day. It was the luck of the draw as far as what kind of case it would be.

I decided to take him up on his offer early in the semester. That morning we were discussing a case in class concerning the complicated hearsay rule on the admissibility of evidence. As the class was coming to an end, I leaned over to my classmate Michael Moncher and asked him whether he was interested in joining the Judge in court.

Michael was one of the top students in our class, but he was very nervous. He was a voracious eater because his metabolism was so high. We were both a little apprehensive about being in the car with Judge Weinstein for the long ride to Brooklyn. As he was packing up after class, the Judge asked if any of us wanted to go with him. Michael and I went up to the rostrum and told him we were interested. We should have known something was fishy because the Judge usually did not ask. But we thought nothing of it at the time.

This was to be my maiden trip to Brooklyn. My father, who grew up in Manhattan, told me that I should keep in mind the adage, "There is no woman in the world worth traveling to Brooklyn for". We did not get much of a Brooklyn experience because we drove straight into the garage in the Federal Courthouse. We went with Judge Weinstein up to his chambers, where he explained to us what the ground rules were for our "participation" in the proceedings. The rules were pretty simple; listen, learn, and keep your mouth shut. The Judge explained to us a little bit about the case, who was suing who and for what, but he purposefully (I think) did not tell us what the specific issue was that he was going to have to rule on that morning.

After our short briefing about the case, the Judge's law clerk escorted us into the courtroom. Michael and I sat at the clerk's desk to watch the proceedings. As the Judge knew, the question before him that morning was the very *same* question we had discussed in class less than an hour before! It was on a motion to admit some testimony based on an exception to the hearsay rule. The Judge looked over at us with a twinkle in his eye as the lawyers for both sides made their arguments on whether the evidence should be admitted. We, not so quickly, realized that we had been set up. However, it was going to get worse.

After the Judge heard the arguments from the lawyers, instead of ruling immediately, he declared a recess. As the Marshall solemnly intoned "All rise", we got up and followed the law clerk back into the Judge's chambers. Judge Weinstein sat down at the conference table and said he wanted to discuss the issue with us before he ruled on the motion. (With us?)

"Well, gentlemen, how do you think I should rule?" he inquired. Michael looked at me and then at the Judge, and said with a sense of urgency, "Excuse me, Judge, I must use the restroom". The Judge pointed to the bathroom, and Michael bolted from the room.

I felt completely abandoned as the Judge turned to me and said, "Well, counselor, since your co-counsel has designated you to deal with this question, what do you suggest my ruling should be?" I started dancing as fast as I could and laid out arguments on both sides in an attempt to fill time. Hopefully, I would have Michael's assistance before I would have to suggest how the Judge should rule. My feeble attempt to avoid answering the question was quickly truncated when the Judge said, "I know what the arguments are since I just heard them from counsel. How do *you* think I should rule?"

After what seemed like a 20-minute pause, I came up with my answer. I told him I thought he should admit the testimony, although I am sure I did not sound convinced. While looking plaintively and unsuccessfully for Michael to return, I explained why. The Judge looked up at the clock and said we had to get back into the courtroom. Michael suddenly appeared, looking a bit sheepish and a little green around the gills. The Judge did not give us any indication of what he had decided. I was just happy to be off the hot seat.

As we were sitting down at the clerk's desk in the courtroom, I leaned over and said the Michael, "What the hell happened? You left me hanging out there on my own!" Michael turned to me and said, "I got so nervous I had to go to the john and chuck my cookies". I found it difficult to keep a straight face, much less avoid bursting out laughing.

Judge Weinstein then gaveled the hearing to order and began to explain his decision. I was relieved to find out he was going to rule in the way I had suggested [guessed]. The Judge decided the testimony could be admitted under the exception we had discussed. It was a fine point of law, but it was important for this case. I did not think the ruling severely prejudiced the defense's case. I thought Judge Weinstein applied the evidentiary rule appropriately.

✦ ✦ ✦ ✦ ✦ ✦ ✦ ✦ ✦

In my second semester that year, I again applied my rule about picking courses by who was teaching. I had to choose an elective, and I decided to take a course in insurance law. Professor William F. Young taught me contracts during my first year. He was a low key and taciturn man from Texas, who I thought was a terrific teacher. I asked him once about whether he read insurance policies. "Dan, life is too short to read that stuff", he replied.

Professor Young and I got to be friendly. We used to talk after class and occasionally would go for coffee or lunch. He came to my rescue during my third year when I was involved in an automobile accident. It was late on a Friday night, and I was driving back to my apartment from LaGuardia airport. The fastest way to do that was to drive across 125th St. Although that route was the shortest, it also took me straight through Harlem, which was probably not a good idea late on a Friday evening.

As I came to an intersection going West, I had a green light, and there was a New York City bus on the other side of 125th St., going East. An older woman came shooting out from behind the bus, against the light, into the middle of the street. Although I slammed on the brakes, I hit her with a sickening thud. I immediately got out to see how badly she was hurt. In the five seconds it took me to get out of the car, a large and intimidating crowd had gathered. I was the only white person in view, and I was scared, afraid that I had seriously injured this woman, and I was in fear for my own safety.

I had a blue casebook in my car on the front seat for my criminal law class. A young boy, probably no older than 12, saw the book looked at me with hate in his eyes and said, "White man goin' fast. He gonna do the law'n himself". Fortunately, two police officers soon arrived. A Harlem hospital ambulance arrived within 45 minutes. That was the longest 45 minutes of my entire life.

When I got back to my apartment, I was deeply shaken by the experience. I did something unusual for me, and that was to mix myself a drink. I then decided to call Professor Young at home for advice on what to do. He was wonderful and tried to calm me down. Although it was late, he asked me if I wanted to spend the night at his home. He and his wife lived near campus. It was a kind thing to do. I deferred on that but took him up on his invitation to lunch the next day. He talked me through what was to happen, if anything, and had already checked with Harlem hospital to find out the status of the woman. Fortunately, she was not seriously injured, and finding that out was a tremendous relief. Later my insurance company informed me she attempted to get some compensation for her injuries. They interviewed me by telephone. My lawyer mode kicked in. I told the agent there was no negligence on my part, and even if there had been, she had been contributorily negligent by crossing against the traffic light. Nothing more ever came of it. Professor Young continued to be concerned, for which I was grateful.

On the day I graduated from law school, Professor Young sought me out in the massive crowd in the Columbia University main quad, Low Plaza, and handed me a small package. It was a graduation gift, and the gesture completely caught me off guard. It was a three-piece Parker pen and pencil set, a ballpoint pen, a mechanical pencil and a rollerball pen. I carry those three writing instruments to this day.

✦✦✦✦✦✦✦✦

The most interesting and exciting thing to happen during my law school career was when I took a clinical course in appellate advocacy. Professor Michael Meltsner was an adjunct member of the faculty at the time and was an NAACP Legal Defense Fund litigator as well. The class was small. There were only seven students. Professor Meltsner was involved in a case that was going to the Supreme Court that term. Three of us were assigned to help him write the briefs and to prepare him for oral argument. The rest of the class was to work on another case.

The matter I was going to be working on was entitled *In re Burrus*. It was a juvenile justice case which posed the following question: "Does the Sixth Amendment right to a jury trial, as applied to the states by the due process clause of the Fourteenth Amendment, apply to juveniles?" This was a group of consolidated cases that included more than 40 juveniles. They had a variety of charges against them, and all had requested jury trials. The requests for jury trials were denied. We worked on preparing the briefs to be filed in the Supreme Court. It was astounding to know the Justices would be reading our work! After the briefs were filed, Professor Meltsner told us that he was going to arrange for the three of us to sit in on the oral argument at the Supreme Court, to be held on December 10. We were thrilled!

The day before, we gathered at the law school moot courtroom for a dry run. We three law students got to play Supreme Court Justices while Professor Meltsner argued the case. He had instructed us to interrupt him whenever we felt it was appropriate and to ask him some of the hard questions which we had identified during our work on the briefs. We knew Justices always interrupted counsel during arguments. Meltsner was a strong proponent of "know both sides", and we knew the weak points of our side of the case. The mock argument went on for more than two hours. It was a very meaningful experience for us, and Professor Meltsner seemed to enjoy the give-and-take.

Since I lived in the Washington area, we went to my parent's house immediately after the practice argument, spent the night there, and in the morning, we went downtown to the Supreme Court. In my excitement, I failed to take any appropriate clothes with me. I drove down from New York thinking that I would have something suitable at home. All I had was a pair of white check slacks and a burgundy sport coat. I was embarrassed but stuck.

The case was scheduled for 10 am, and the three of us went downtown early. We got there with plenty of time to spare. The argument was outstanding since both sides were represented by skilled advocates, and it was marvelous for us because we knew the case so well and could easily follow the proceedings. Although we had been warned about it, we were all a little surprised about how often the Justices interrupted the lawyers to ask questions, some of which seemed irrelevant. I thought Professor Meltsner did an excellent job, and we all nodded or smiled when there was a question from the bench which we, (and Professor Meltsner), had anticipated.

After the argument, the four of us walked down the steps of the fabulous Supreme Court West front; the same steps that Thurgood Marshall walked up the day he argued *Brown vs. Board of Education*. As we came to the bottom of the steps, there was a lot of interest from the press about the case, and they wanted to interview Professor Meltsner. He said to the reporters that he would be happy to speak with them, but first, he wanted to talk to his students. I was somewhat surprised since people are always highly motivated to talk to the press and be seen on television. The four of us walked over to the North part of the Supreme Court plaza by the fountain. Professor Meltsner said, "I hope you all noticed that I did not get any questions from the nine Justices on the Court which you had not asked me yesterday during the mock argument. Thank you. Excellent work. I am very proud of you all". It was a grand moment for a group of law students.

We would not find out the result until after graduation. The Court issued its opinion on June 21, 1971. It held jury trials were not constitutionally required in juvenile court cases. We were all disappointed but knew we had had an extraordinary experience which few lawyers, much less mere law students, ever get.

✦ ✦ ✦ ✦ ✦ ✦ ✦ ✦ ✦

I also worked on a death penalty project that was a little daunting. The law students' job was to provide representation to indigent people who had been convicted of crimes and sentenced to death and whose cases were on appeal. While most of the work could be done on campus, in the library, it occasionally required us to meet with our clients.

My first visit to any kind of jail was while working on one of these appeals. I had to drive up to Greenhaven Correctional Facility, a maximum-security prison located about 90 minutes away from New York City. I did not know what to expect, I was nervous, and also looking forward to using my (limited) legal skills to help out our client, a convicted felon who had received a death sentence.

It was a beautiful spring day as I drove through the rolling hills, around a big curve in route 216, and I saw an enormous 30-foot-high stone wall surrounding the prison which went on as far as the eye could see. I pulled into what I thought was the parking lot, got out of my car, and started walking towards the entrance. I had not walked 10 feet when I heard a booming voice over a loudspeaker. "Sir, you are parked in the wrong zone. Please move your vehicle immediately". When I looked up, trying to see who was talking to me, I saw a guard up in one of two towers that flanked the entrance. He was standing behind a large machine gun. Based on that fact, I decided it would be prudent to move my car, which I did quickly.

Sometime later, I read an article in the newspaper which described the prison. "Rising from the abundantly lush slopes of upstate farmland to disrupt the traveler's gaze, the fortress-like prison overwhelms its surrounding ecology". That is how I saw it, too. The facility was over 20 acres and could house over 2,000 inmates.

This was before 9/11 and the regular use of metal detectors for screening, so I was not prepared when an officer told me to empty my pockets and walk through the scanner. There was a loud beep that scared the hell out of me. A corrections officer said, "Sir, you need to take *everything* out of your pockets. The only thing I had left was a roll of LifeSavers, which I promptly took out. The aluminum foil around the candy had set off the alarm.

After security, I was met by one of the deputy wardens who was going to escort me to the visiting room where I was supposed to meet the client. As we were walking through, he pointed out the protocol about doors. The guards would open one door and would not open the next one until the first one was closed. There was never a time when you could walk through two doors. When we got to a portion of the prison where the cells were located, he asked me if I would like to go into a cell "to get the feel of it". I was getting the heebie-jeebies as I heard cell doors being slammed shut all the way down the corridor, so I declined his invitation. I do not recall much about the interview with the client. What I do remember is the soul-shaking sound of the cell doors slamming. From that day forward, I never entered a jail cell even though I was given a chance on several occasions.

IV. Williams And Connolly

In 1970, when I was in my second year of law school, I started applying for summer associate jobs, mostly with law firms. I was not at the top of my class, not on law review. I bombarded Washington D.C. law firms with applications. Like applying for colleges, I was told it only cost you a stamp to reach for the unobtainable, so I decided to apply to Williams and Connolly, among others. Edward Bennett Williams was the most famous trial lawyer in the country at the time. He represented many high-profile clients including, John Hinckley, Jr., Frank Sinatra, financier Robert Vesco, Playboy publisher Hugh Heffner, spy Igor Melekh, labor leader Jimmy Hoffa, organized crime figures Frank Costello and Sam Giancana, oil commodity trader Marc Rich, U.S. Senator Joseph Mc-Carthy, corporate raider Victor Posner, the Washington Post and the Reverend Sun Myung Moon. Williams successfully defended – among others – Congressman Adam Clayton Powell, Jr., the Teamsters Union, former Texas Governor John Connally, and, as one of his last clients, Michael Milken, the corrupt Wall Street tycoon. He also happened to own Washington's professional football team. Every law student in the country was dying to work there. For reasons which I will never know, I got the job.

The first case I was assigned to work on was with Brendan Sullivan (who represented Colonel Oliver North during the Iran/Contra hearings many years later). Brendan was an intense and laser-focused lawyer. He was a perfectionist. The client, Arthur G. Barkley, was a deranged man who hijacked a TWA passenger jet, which was supposed to fly from Phoenix to St. Louis. He commandeered the plane and forced it to fly to Washington Dulles International Airport. A Phoenix bakery truck driver, Barkley took control of TWA flight 486 over northeastern New Mexico, after getting no satisfaction in a long-standing feud he had with the IRS over a $471 tax penalty.

In a drama that played out in the air, and terminated at Dulles Airport, Barkley demanded millions of dollars from then-President Richard Nixon. After a smaller amount of money was delivered, Barkley shot and wounded the TWA pilot while the plane was sitting on the runway at Dulles. The pilot, treated in intensive care at Fairfax Hospital, survived, and Barkley was charged with several crimes.

One of the things I was supposed to research was the difference between being prosecuted for violations of federal law as opposed to state law. As I discovered, if Barkley had been charged under federal law and was acquitted by reason of insanity (a distinct possibility), the federal government would have to let him go free (this aberration in the law has been corrected). However, if the Commonwealth of Virginia (where Dulles Airport is located) was to prosecute him for violations of Virginal law, and he was acquitted by reason of insanity, he would be sent to a Virginia State mental hospital. The federal prosecutors and the state prosecutors decided that he was probably going to plead insanity successfully. That being the case, they wanted to make sure he was not able to walk out of jail. I did a long memo on the bifurcated jurisdiction that I submitted to Mr. Sullivan. He told me he was going to show it to Mr. Williams. Virginia took jurisdiction. Barkley was charged with the state crimes of robbery, abduction and maiming. He was found not guilty by reason of insanity in November 1971. We considered that to be a good result. The Commonwealth's Attorney, Robert Horan, visited him every year along with his lawyers and his psychologist. After a visit in 2006, Horan said, "The remarkable thing about this defendant is his mental situation hasn't changed in 35 years".

✦✦✦✦✦✦✦✦✦

I was a semi-jock in those days. In college, I played quarterback on the dorm touch football team and centerfield on the softball team. I had a much better than average throwing arm in both sports. Thus, I was invited to play on the firm's softball team. I learned quickly that this was "Ed's team", and he was *very* competitive. Part of the reason he was so successful in practicing law was because of his intensity. My game was going to be that Sunday afternoon, and I was excited about being in what I hoped would be a good bonding experience with some prominent lawyers. Williams was 51 at the time, but I was assured that he would play and that *he* would pitch. It was sort of like "it's my ball and we will play by my rules" when we were kids. They put me in center field, and I just wanted to play well and not screw up.

I was playing well. I was four-for-four at the plate, including two home runs, and I made three running catches in deep center field, including one over the shoulder catch á la Willie Mays. I had also thrown two runners out at the plate. One of the lawyers who became a good friend told me he thought the only reason I had been hired for the summer clerkship was that I could play ball.

It was the bottom of the last inning, and we were leading by one run with the other team coming to bat. The bases were loaded with one out. The batter hit a towering fly ball over my head, but I felt I could get to it. I made a good over-the-shoulder catch and whirled to throw the ball to the catcher to prevent the runner on third from scoring. Unfortunately, I overthrew him, and the ball sailed into never-never land. The runners on second and third scored easily, and we lost the game. Williams was furious. He let loose with a string of expletives that stunned me. I was ready to crawl into a hole. He instantly forgot all about my hitting and previous outstanding outfield play; all he knew was we lost the game, and I was responsible. I tried to downplay it, but it was clear to me, as well as to the rest of the team that Ed never liked to lose in *anything*, and that *he* would *not* forget.

I came into the office early on Monday, and the game was the last thing I was thinking about. I was eager to find out how my memo was received by Brendan Sullivan and what the next steps in the Barkley case were going to be. As soon as I sat down, the phone rang. It was Lillian Keats, Mr. Williams' secretary. She told me Mr. Williams wanted to see me "right away". I could not figure out why since most of my work was for Brendan Sullivan.

I raced up to Mr. Williams' office, and Mrs. Keats told me to go in. Williams looked at me and then said these terrifying words, "Shut the door". I had a bad feeling, and I felt like I was in deep trouble. I did not think he had read the memo about the Barkley case, and I could not imagine anything else he would want to talk to me about. "Dan", he said, "your performance here has not been up to our standards". I was stunned. I was not sure what he was talking about. He then picked up the phone and said, presumably to Mrs. Keats, "Send in Dan's replacement". What the hell was going on? I was unaware that I had done something so terrible that I was going to be fired and replaced so soon. I was going to need a change of underwear!

There was a knock on the door, and Williams boomed, "Come in." I could hear the door open, but I was facing the other way, staring dumbfounded at Mr. Williams. I turned to look at my replacement. I could not believe my eyes: it was Joe DiMaggio, the legendary centerfielder for the New York Yankees! I almost passed out. Under any other circumstances, I would have been thrilled to meet one of the greatest baseball players of all time. But I was so shaken up, I could not even focus on that. Williams and DiMaggio got a big kick out of terrorizing me. They were old friends who had met for breakfast that morning and decided it might be fun to mess with my head a bit. Boy, were they ever successful!

The good news was that after I recovered, they started to discuss a case,

Wong Sun v. United States, that Williams had argued before the U.S. Supreme Court acting under an appointment by the Chief Justice. This was a famous criminal procedure case decided by the Warren Court. It dealt with the question of an improper search warrant and whether contraband found pursuant to it at the *wrong address* could be admitted into evidence in a criminal trial. The warrant was obtained for a search of a Chinese laundry at *815* California St. in San Francisco. However, the police had intended to get a warrant to search *850* California St. The warrant was thus defective because of the incorrect address. The police found contraband at the *incorrect* address, which they wished to use in prosecuting Wong Sun for a narcotics offense. This case resulted in the so-called "fruit of the poisonous tree" rule. If the original warrant was improper, then the police could not use any evidence they found under that defective warrant. The evidence was "tainted" and, therefore, inadmissible.

The back story was that at 8 am on the morning of the oral argument in the Supreme Court, the ever-meticulous Ed Williams realized he did not know how many Chinese laundries there were in the 800 block of California St. in San Francisco. He wanted to know what the chances were of making a mistake in the warrant. So, he called an old friend who lived in San Francisco (DiMaggio) and asked him to go and count them. It was 5 am on the West Coast. This was the sort of mission that Perry Mason would give to Paul Drake. At the same time, Justice William Brennan, who would eventually write the majority opinion, came to the same realization. He, too, was unaware of the chances of raiding the wrong Chinese laundry. He called a former law clerk who lived in San Francisco and asked him to do the same thing; count the laundries on the 800 block of California Street. DiMaggio walked from South to North counting Chinese laundries, while the former law clerk walked from North to South doing the same thing. There is no record of how many there were, or what each of the counters found. Brennan never asked the question, but Williams was prepared, as usual, in case he did.

✦ ✦ ✦ ✦ ✦ ✦ ✦ ✦ ✦

It was during that summer I first got bitten by the "litigation bug". One of the experienced trial lawyers in the firm, David Povich, had an interesting case that was going to trial. He was defending two rather unsavory pharmacists who were charged with selling drug paraphernalia. They owned a drug store in a part of the city where drug-dealing was rampant. They were not accused of selling drugs, but with selling thousands of empty gelatin capsules. Empty capsules were used when pharmacists made up prescriptions by hand, known as compounding. The mixture would be loaded into the gel capsules for sale to the consumer. The prosecution charged these two men with selling a perfectly legitimate product, the gel capsules, in such enormous quantities that they had to know the capsules were being used to sell illegal narcotics. This was a case of selling a legal product for an illegal use. It was the sheer quantities that prompted the government to prosecute.

David monopolized the two summer law clerks to work on the case. We had an astonishing educational experience. We, of course, could not open our mouths in court, but we did a lot of the background research for the pleadings. We also got to sit in on the whole trial, which was exciting. We then met with David every evening as he went over what had happened during the proceedings for that day. We listened to him plot strategy and joined his meetings with the clients. It was a terrific experience, and I learned a lot about trial tactics. The two defendants were convicted, which seemed to me to be the correct result, but we were disappointed to have lost.

✦✦✦✦✦✦✦✦✦

As the summer went on, Mr. Williams seemed to get friendlier, possibly because of the enjoyment he and Joe DiMaggio had in giving me a hard time. In July, the football team's coach, Vince Lombardi, had been admitted to Georgetown University Hospital in serious condition with colon cancer. Mr. Williams went to visit him every day. As a devout catholic and Georgetown University graduate, Mr. Williams took some comfort knowing that Coach Lombardi was there at a Jesuit institution.

One day, as he was leaving the hospital, he hit another car as he was backing out. The other car was stationary, so it was clearly his fault. He called me in and asked me to handle the matter for him with the owner of the other car. It was a heady experience for me, as a law student, to be able to call the owner of the car and say, "I am representing Edward Bennett Williams…", even in such a minor matter. With very little money at stake and his fault unchallenged, Mr. Williams still wanted to play hardball about what he was going to pay the car's owner. There was about $400 worth of damage to her car. She needed a rental car while hers was being repaired. There was a difference in the estimates between the two repair shops, as well as a $15 difference in the cost of the rental cars from two different companies. Mr. Williams wanted to lowball her on both. I managed to get her to agree, and Mr. Williams was satisfied.

I noticed that a football magically started showing up at the softball games on Sundays. I enjoyed throwing the football around. I had a good arm and could throw a ball accurately about 60 yards, which is pretty good for someone who never played football seriously. One Sunday afternoon, I ended up throwing the ball around with, of all people, Ed Williams, the man who owned the local pro football team! I thought that was cool.

On the following Tuesday, I was in his office talking about the fender bend-er. He was pleased with the way it was going. Then he told me he had just re-turned from visiting Coach Lombardi in the hospital. He said the coach was in bad shape, and it looked like he did not have much time left. I knew how much Mr. Williams wanted a coach of Lombardi's caliber to steer the team; he want-ed them to be winners. I knew from our conversations that he thought Coach Lombardi could do that. Because of the coach's illness, it was not going to hap-pen. To make matters worse, there was a lockout/strike by the players that sum-mer. I think Mr. Williams was pulling my chain when he said, "Dan, you and I are both going to live out our football dreams. I think maybe if things continue as they are, I am going to coach the team, and you can be the quarterback!" He had a big smile on his face. I did not know whether it was because the thought of his coaching the team was a dream of his or because he knew what a ridic-ulous idea it was for me, at 6 feet and 180 pounds dripping wet, to even think about being on an NFL playing field. I thought of journalist George Plimpton's book "Paper Lion", written about the summer pre-season game when he got to play one series for the Detroit Lions as a walk-on with no real experience. I enjoyed a similar fantasy for a few minutes.

✦✦✦✦✦✦✦✦✦

I began to learn an important life lesson: "Find a mentor; be a mentor". I have been fortunate to have found three mentors and have had the joy of being a mentor to many young people.

One of the lawyers I became friendly with was Earl Dudley. He was to be my first mentor. Earl is a brilliant lawyer, a superlative writer and a warm and friendly person. He had graduated near the top of his class at the University of Virginia Law School and had been a law clerk for Chief Justice Earl Warren. I ended up house-sitting for him when he and his family went away to the beach at the end of the summer.

While I was not assigned to work with Earl during my clerkship at Williams and Connolly, we frequently had lunch and talked about some of the cases he was working on. Over time we developed a close friendship where we discussed just about everything from legal questions to politics to football.

He did give me one specific assignment while I was at the firm. He called me into his office and said, "Freeman, I want you to find out how to do some-thing which I never learned how to do in law school; how do you file a lawsuit in Virginia". Here was this extremely bright lawyer, and he did not know how to initiate a suit! I was not surprised by that since I, too, had gone to a first-rate law school, and I did not know how to file a lawsuit either. We got a chuckle out of that, and Earl said, "We both know how to think like a lawyer, but not how to *be* a lawyer".

He was an extraordinarily good writer. We often talked about his utilizing an "economy of language" in written work. He was also an articulate and persuasive advocate. I was in awe of him and frankly was surprised he found me someone worthy of his time.

After I graduated from law school, I began working at the law firm of Surrey, Karasik & Greene. (More about that firm later.) Earl and I would have our regular Friday lunch. Although he was not much older, I felt him to be wise beyond his years and certainly beyond mine. I began to rely on his advice and counsel about a lot of things, both professional and personal. He helped steer me through my first career transition. It was abundantly clear from our regular conversations that I was unhappy at the firm, and Earl was supportive in getting me through it.

Several years later, after I had left the Surrey law firm and was working on the Hill for the House District of Columbia Committee, Earl called to ask me to have lunch. I already had a lunch scheduled with a lawyer I had worked with at the law firm. His name was Hal Krents, and he was a dynamic, magnetic personality who everyone wanted to spend time with. He had been blind since he was a kid and still managed to graduate from Harvard Law School. Because he was so popular, getting a lunch date with him was a coup not to be lightly canceled.

I asked Earl if we could meet later in the week, and he said, "No, this is important, time-sensitive, and I would like your advice". Although I was reluctant to cancel with Hal, I perceived some urgency in Earl's voice. I called Hal to get a rain check and went downtown to meet Earl. I was still a little uncomfortable with the fact that Earl wanted *my* advice. I always thought that he would be the one giving *me* advice.

What he wanted to talk about was an offer he had received from House Judiciary Committee Chairman Peter Rodino, of Watergate fame, to be the General Counsel of the Committee. I was enthusiastic about the prospect of Earl coming to work on the Hill, and I had visions of my working for the Judiciary Committee myself. I said to him, "I will get you my resume immediately". Little did I know that less than five years later, I would indeed be asked to work on the Judiciary Committee staff.

After discussing the pros and cons, I encouraged Earl to take the job, and he did. I was pleased to be able to be both a good friend to Earl and someone whose advice he valued. I still considered him to be a mentor.

I liked having Earl "in the neighborhood" on Capitol Hill. We would get together frequently for lunch or coffee to chew over a personal, legislative, or legal problem. During one of my visits to the Judiciary Committee staff offices, I met the Chief Counsel of the Civil and Constitutional Rights Subcommittee, Alan Parker. I found Alan to be intriguing, funny, and interesting. As it turned out, Alan would become my boss a few years later.

Earl was a real Anglophile. He had traveled to England many times and often talked about how much he loved being there. I had never been, so we decided we would do a road trip around Southern England. We were going to visit London and then drive around some places he had not visited. It was all going to be new to me, and I was energized.

I wanted to visit the Houses of Parliament, and Earl was happy to join me. A friend of my family, Gerran Lloyd, otherwise known as Lord Lloyd of Kilgerran, was a member of the House of Lords. He offered us the chance to join him for "a beverage of your choice" in the House of Lord's tea room. Since both Earl and I worked in the American Legislature, the chance to see our British forebears was an offer we quickly accepted. Gerran was a rapscallion and a joy to be around. He had a keen sense of humor.

We met him in the Peer's Guest Room next to the House of Lords. We were having a friendly chat when Gerran popped up and got the attention of a distinguished-looking gentleman across the room. Gerran enthusiastically waved him over to meet us. This man was spot-on as a British Lord. He was tall, with perfectly coifed hair, and was dressed impeccably, with pinstriped pants and a proper waistcoat. Earl and I stood up to be introduced. With a smile on his face, Gerran said, "Earl Dudley, I would like you to meet the Earl *of* Dudley", at which point we all burst out laughing. From then on, I referred to Earl as EOD (the Earl of Dudley).

Gerran took us into the House of Lords Chamber, where we watched a bit of debate before he leaned over and said, "Let's go see what the elected rabble is doing". The "elected rabble" was the House of Commons. The tension between the lower House and the upper House, which Earl and I dealt with in Congress, was just as palpable in the English Parliament.

That evening we were invited to join Gerran for dinner at his daughter's home with her husband, who was also a lawyer. Elizabeth and Daniel Robbins were the classic English couple, very proper. However, at dinner, humor was abundant. We had a delightful evening talking about all kinds of things from esoteric legal issues to oldies music from the '50s. Elizabeth got out some old 45 rpm records. I impressed her with my almost total recall of those records. I could name a song based on the first four bars. It was because I had been a high school teen reporter/disc jockey. The biggest surprise came when she put on an old Pat Boone record, "Love Letters in the Sand" and I started to sing. Back then, I had a fairly good voice, and I knew all the words!

Many years later, my wife and I went out to Dulles airport to surprise Elizabeth and her daughter. They were between flights, and I knew which one they were taking on their way back to London. I was not sure I was going to recognize her, and certainly, I would not recognize her daughter. As we were standing in the concourse, I saw a woman who looked to be about the right age with a young woman. I went up to her and said, "Excuse me, but can you tell me who sang 'Love Letters in the Sand?'" She gave a big whoop and threw her arms around me. She was elated to see me and to reminisce about that dinner party.

Before we left London, Earl and I had a couple of things we wanted to do. First, as part of a busman's holiday, we wanted to visit the High Court of Appeals. We sat in on a couple of arguments which were, for the most part, rather dull. We both got a kick out of one barrister who kept referring to his young associate as "learned junior". I thought I might suggest that if I ever became a partner in a law firm, but Earl thought it would not go over well at home.

The second thing which I wanted to do was to buy a suit. For some reason, I had fixed my sartorial desires on a charcoal gray double-breasted suit. I had seen someone wearing one in Washington, and I thought it was elegant. We looked in a couple of places, and none had what I wanted. We walked into Gieves & Hawkes on the world-famous Saville Row. It was a very upscale shop that specialized in "bespoke" luxury menswear. There was no way I could afford what a custom-made suit would cost, but what the hell, I was just looking.

When the salesman came over to inquire if I were looking for something specific, I told him. His eyes lit up, and he asked me to stand still while he measured me. "I think I have just the thing for you, sir". He went into the back room, and instead of bringing out a bolt of cloth, which I assumed he did with most of their clients, he brought out exactly what I had been looking for; a beautiful gray, double-breasted, luxuriously soft suit. He suggested I try it on. I was reluctant to do so because I was afraid I would love it and then be unable to afford it. I had erroneously assumed at Gieves and Hawkes they would have you come in for a couple of fittings and do the cuffs and sleeves to your specifications.

However, the suit fit perfectly; the sleeves were correct, the pants legs were cuffed correctly, and the waist was comfortable. I was trapped. I asked the salesman why this suit was ready-to-wear in a shop that specialized in bespoke clothing. He said to me in a rather conspiratorial whisper that the suit had been ordered by a regular client who had "been unable to complete the purchase". I left it at that and discovered the suit was on the high end of what I wanted to pay, but it was still affordable. I decided to take it. I was pleased with how fortunate I had been. As the salesman was ringing up the sale and putting the suit into a carrying bag, I casually asked him why the original client had been unable to complete the purchase. He hesitated before answering. I did not know what I expected, maybe something about a financial setback, but was surprised when I learned he had "passed on". I was going to be wearing a dead man's suit!

One of the problems being "across the pond" was driving on the other side of the road. I was not comfortable driving or even trying it. Earl had driven in England before, so we divided the tasks; he would drive, and I would navigate. I have a superb sense of direction and have always been able to do an excellent job of not getting lost.

We were driving to see Stonehenge, and my crack sense of direction somehow failed me. We had doubled back, but I still could not find the road we were looking for. We stopped so Earl could take a look at the map. I showed him where I thought we were and said, "If we could find this blue road, we would be fine". Earl looked at the map carefully and said, "Freeman, you idiot, the 'blue road' is a river!" We did eventually manage to find our destination without going into the water.

We had a deal that whenever one of us wanted to stop and see something, we would. This was good because of our mutual interest in photography. However, I noticed there was never a church that Earl did not want to see. He loved them all, not for their religious impact, but for their historical value.

During our trip, I planned to go to Paris for the weekend. We arranged to meet at the Royal Crescent Hotel in Brighton at 7 pm on Sunday. Earl was astounded when I walked into the lobby at precisely 7 pm. "Freeman, only you could have been so punctual", he said.

Later at dinner, he asked me if he could look at my calendar book. During the trip, I was making notes of where we had been and what we had done. He was also keeping a travel log, but he had missed a couple of things. I gave him my book and did not think anything more about it.

The next morning at breakfast, he asked me about my notes. "Dan, I saw you wrote 'AFC' several times. What does that mean?" I had to confess it meant "another fucking church".

Among other things I learned from Earl was the art of photography. He had a darkroom set-up in his home, and I would regularly go over to learn the basics of developing black and white film and printing photographs from the negatives. Later he taught me a new process of printing from color slides, called Cibachrome. Before then, printing in color was difficult because you needed to have strict temperature controls; within a quarter of a degree. With Cibachrome, you had a plus or minus 3-degree window, which made it much more home-darkroom friendly. I subsequently set up my own darkroom and was printing both color and black and white photos. An interest in photography was one more good thing that my friendship with Earl contributed to my well-being.

Earl eventually left the Judiciary Committee to open a private law practice. While I missed having him on the Hill, I still made it a point to get to see him regularly for lunch. He continued to be a mentor and a sounding board for me. He seemed always to have time for me and listened carefully to what I had to say. Many people can speak eloquently, but few have become skilled in the art of listening perceptively. Earl was a master at it.

One day we met for lunch at the Tabard Inn, a charming restaurant downtown near Earl's office. He was in a fantastic mood and was bursting to tell me the "good news". "I am going to Charlottesville to teach at Mr. Jefferson's University". This was marvelous on many fronts; he thoroughly enjoyed Charlottesville, he had been teaching at the law school for several years on the weekends, and he loved it. I also think he was ready to leave private practice. I told him I was elated for him and even picked up the check for lunch.

I continue to think of him as one of the best men I know.

V. Affairs of The Heart #2

During the summer after my second year of law school, when I was working at Williams and Connolly, I started dating Virginia, whose mother, Elizabeth, worked at my father's law firm. She had recently graduated from Middlebury College and was doing temporary secretarial work at the firm, filling in for people who were on vacation, before going to study in Germany on a Fulbright Scholarship. We got to be close, and I thought it was a serious relationship. The problem was that this was eternal triangle number two; man, woman, and woman's mother. Virginia was besotted with Elizabeth, her mother, who was stern, strict, and Victorian in outlook.

Virginia and I saw each other regularly over the summer. She lived at home with her mother before leaving for Germany. That posed some problems for us because I too was living at home, so there was no place we could be alone. Whenever we were at her place, her mother always seemed to be there. Her mother was also a conservative person – in the social sense. She frowned upon any kind of physical affection between us. We could get away with holding hands as we walked along, but any cuddling, hugs, or kisses were frowned upon. Virginia and I are affectionate people, but we were always tiptoeing on eggshells so that her mother would not get upset. Every time we made plans to do something, she had to check with her mother to make sure it was okay. I found this to be irritating, and my annoyance grew over the summer as the foreboding presence of Elizabeth became more and more intrusive.

As the summer was coming to a close, I was conflicted about the relationship. I was getting lots of brownie points from her mother for being supportive and kind to her daughter. However, I think she lived in constant terror that we would end up having sex. Horrors! The fact that her mother worked at my father's firm added an extra layer of concern as her mother was afraid that "people would talk". I, frankly, like Rhett Butler, did not give a damn, and neither did my father.

My parents were utterly hands-off when it came to my social life. I would occasionally bump into them at the theater or the Kennedy Center, usually when I was with a date. I would introduce her, and my parents would be friendly, but that was all. It was never mentioned again.

The summer ended, and Virginia and I had a long talk about where our relationship was going. It was not settled in any way. She was going to go overseas by steamship from New York. The logistics of getting her mother, her mother's ex (her father), and the two of us to the city became a real nightmare. I was driving since I was going to be taking my car to New York for my last year of law school. The question then was, were we going to have to drive up to New York with her mother in my car, or was I going alone and meeting them in New York? The two of us going by ourselves was not going to be an option. Sure enough, her mother insisted Virginia and she take the train, and I would meet them up there. I never did find out where her father lived, but the final result was I would drive to New York alone, and meet them at Toots Shor's for dinner. Toots Shor's was a legendary bar and restaurant where all the famous and beautiful people wanted to be seen; people like Frank Sinatra, Jack Dempsey, Mickey Mantle and Muhammed Ali. I had never been there. It was a "special occasion" restaurant for most people.

I had never met her father, and I do not remember much about him. He was, I think, showing off by taking us to a famous New York hotspot, and he was continually pointing out various celebrities, most of whom I had never heard of. I think he had a little bit too much to drink, and he got all slobbery when he started talking about "his little girl" going off to Europe on her own. Elizabeth was constantly correcting his behavior, and I was clear about why their marriage did not work. It was a typically loud and busy New York restaurant "where the action is", but I would have preferred to be alone with Virginia at an IHOP instead of being out with "maw and paw". Virginia and I could not talk over the hustle and bustle of the restaurant and the chatter between her tipsy father and disapproving mother. The evening was, at least for me, a complete disaster. Because of the presence of her parents, a quick hug and a peck on the cheek was the only thing which was appropriate as we said good night.

We were going to meet the next day at the ship for the final farewell. I had gotten myself into a zone where I was going to ignore the parents and focus on Virginia. We babbled inanely about nothing much until it came time to leave. When the "All ashore who's going ashore" sounded, her parents had the good taste to leave us alone for our final farewell, which was a bit more passionate than the one the night before. I left the ship, said a hurried goodbye to her parents and went back uptown to Columbia.

During the semester, we exchanged many letters, lots of tape-recorded messages, and a few expensive phone calls. I was looking forward to her coming home for the Christmas holidays, and I was thrilled to see her when she did. She was going to be in Washington for a couple of weeks, and we had intended to spend a lot of time together.

I had fond hopes of most of that being out of her mother's sight as much as possible. Alas, that was not to be. She spent the majority of the time with her mother doing "girl stuff" or playing bridge. I never learned to play bridge, but I understand it can be addictive. I called her one morning at 9 am, and she and her mother were already playing bridge. Too early for me. We arranged for me to come over at 7 pm to pick her up and go out. When I got there, I was stunned to find out they were *still* playing bridge! Her mother became a bit upset that I was going to take her daughter out instead of spending the evening at home with her. Give me a break!

I did manage to tear her away from mom's clutches a few times during the holidays. You may ask yourself, why did I put up with this? That is a question I asked myself regularly, but I could not come up with a good answer. I was lovestruck; clearly, I should have entered a plea of temporary insanity.

During the Christmas vacation, we made plans for me to join her in Europe during my law school spring break. She had a car in Germany, and we were going to have an idyllic and romantic drive around Europe. I got the impression that mom was displeased about the possibility of our being together in a foreign country unchaperoned, but I simply did not care.

We proceeded to make our plans by letter and phone call. I had never been to Europe and had a bad case of what I call "language claustrophobia". I was going to be uneasy being in a place where I could not understand or be understood. Virginia spoke German, so I figured it would be ok. I slipped into my travel agent mode and found a round trip ticket for $119! I was going to fly to Paris, spend the night in a hotel and then fly down to meet her in Nice.

I was a bit apprehensive when I landed in Paris. Immigration and customs were not a problem since they were used to Americans, and most people at the airport spoke English. I was so exhausted from the long flight and anxious about being in France, that I decided to stay at the airport hotel. I did not even have to leave the building. I am sure it was expensive, but I was tired and uncomfortable. I thought the most comfortable thing would be to stay there and get my morning flight to Nice.

The next day, I got onto my flight and sat in the window seat on the left side of the plane. As we approached Nice, the plane banked to the left, and I had a gorgeous view of the Cote d'Azur in all its splendor. Since I was on a domestic flight, there would be no formalities, so I could get off the plane and look for Virginia. I came out of the jetway and saw her about 100 yards away. In my mind, we were transported into a cheesy perfume or shampoo ad; we approached each other bounding blissfully in slow motion, her long locks flowing slowly up and down. It was perfect! We flew into each other's arms, and all was right with the world, at least temporarily. We smooched and hugged and were together at last. I then heard a noise, like fingernails on a blackboard, reminiscent of Margaret Hamilton's voice in the "Wizard of Oz" when she said, "I will get you my pretty, and your little dog too!" My blood froze when I heard "Hello, Daniel". I immediately turned around without unleashing my firm grip on Virginia to see---her mother! Trapped like a rat!

We spent the next three weeks driving around central Europe—the *three* of us! We saw some fantastic things, but the romantic getaway I had envisioned was just "clouds in my coffee", as Judy Collins would say. Her mother would get pouty when the two of us wanted to be alone. I could not catch a break. I did a lot of the driving, and Mom did not even like the way I released the clutch pedal. She said I should not let it pop back up, but I should release it ever so gently. Geez!

One night, when her mother agreed to just the two of us going to dinner without her, Virginia and I made a big show of getting dressed up to go out. We had intended to sneak back into the hotel for nefarious purposes. As luck would have it, as we were re-entering the lobby, we saw her mom was sitting there. When she asked what we were doing coming back into the hotel, we made up an excuse about my needing something from my room. The two of us started towards the elevator to get whatever it was, and mom said sternly, "Sweetie, why don't you wait here with me while Daniel goes and gets his [whatever]. I am sure you do not want to be seen going into a man's hotel room". Rats, foiled again!

We got to Paris in the middle of April, and I had hopes of the romantic atmosphere being a stimulant to our getting to spend some alone time. That was not to be. Picture this. You are in Paris on a beautiful spring day, with the woman you love. The flowers are blooming, and you are up in the Eiffel Tower, though only the lower level because I do not do heights. I put my arms around my "main squeeze" and proceed to give her a romantic kiss. As a result of that, I heard, "I wish you would not do that, Daniel. After all, we are Americans here in Paris". I have no idea what the hell that meant except "get your grubby paws off my little girl, you lecher". The fact that there were many other lovers around, doing much the same thing, did not matter to her. Maybe it was ok because they were French?

We ended up in Zermatt, Switzerland, in the Alps, a gorgeous ski resort area. We had a lovely dinner and discussed the plans for the next day. I suffer from acrophobia and am terrified of heights, and Virginia knew this. Notwithstanding that, they decided we should all get up early the next morning and take the ski lift to the top of the mountain. I looked at them and said as sternly as I could, "I do not do ski lifts". Virginia tried to save the day by saying something namby-pamby like, "Oh, we will work something out". What we "worked out" was the two women did not care about my phobia: they wanted to go to the top of the mountain, so they were going with or without me. Although I did not show it, I was incensed. They then got up from the table and left. I simply sat there, astounded.

The next morning after breakfast, I could have decided to go back to my room and pound sand, but I said, "screw it" and got my bulky sweater and put on my hiking boots. I talked with the man at the desk and found out about the best hikes to lookouts. I spent most of the day on the mountain, enjoying the fabulous scenery. I was cold and tired, but I was not going to go back and be at the hotel when they returned. I was going to have a good time despite them. It was a lovely day, mostly filled with solitude and glorious vistas, and I had a pleasant interlude at one lookout.

There was a lot of snow on the ground, and the footing was not good. I had my heavy hiking books on, so I was comfortable and walking steadily. I climbed up to one of the lookouts and stood there, taking it all in. I heard footsteps behind me and saw a lovely young woman climbing up to the observation platform where I was standing. I turned around and put out my hand to help her up. She said to me, "Je vous remercie. Vous êtes très aimable". I replied simply, "De rein", in my best French accent. We stood there silently for a time when she turned to me and started to say something in French. I looked at her and said, "I am sorry, but I have almost exhausted my French". She said, "Oh, you are English. I thought you were French from your lovely accent". I told her I was doubly complimented by being regarded as French, and not being perceived as an ugly American.

On the way back to the hotel that afternoon, I seriously considered packing up and leaving. I had taken a tremendous body blow to my self-respect; I could not believe I was putting up with this situation. I got really down on myself. I planned to go to England, where I had never been, and where I thought at least I could be understood. However, the coward in me took over, and I decided to stay. When Elizabeth and Virginia got back, neither of them had any inkling how upset and angry I was, but since I did not make it evident, that is on me.

Later that day, Elizabeth wanted to wash her hair. That meant we were being asked to leave their hotel room. I said, without thinking, "Let's go down to my room and finish the crossword puzzle". Again, I was sternly rebuked with the line, "No gentleman entertains a lady in his hotel room".

Chastised, we went down to the lobby coffee shop. I still did not fess up about my anger. When we got downstairs, I think Virginia felt a bit guilty. She broached the subject of our taking some classes that summer in England, at the University of Oxford. I would have graduated law school by then and had not planned to start work until September. I looked at some of the classes that were being offered, and I was interested in several. I probably should not have, but I had to ask, "Just us, not your mother?" She smiled knowingly and said, "Yes, just the two of us, but do not mention it to mom until I have a chance to talk with her". I think she knew that was going to be difficult.

The next day, we ended up in Strasbourg, France. A girl I went to college with, Sharon Miller, had moved there after her junior year. She spent that year in Strasbourg and met a man, married him, and stayed in France. She did not know I was coming, but neither did I! Since we had been corresponding, I recalled her address. As we were driving through the city, I recognized the name of the street. I stopped the car in front of the building. It was one that had buzzers for every apartment, and I did not know which one hers was, so I pushed them all.

Luckily, she was home. When Sharon came down to see if it was me, she was astounded. She could not believe I had materialized out of thin air! She jumped into my arms and gave me an enormous hug. I introduced Virginia, and her mother and Sharon invited us up to meet her husband and have coffee. I was so happy to see her and possibly grateful not to be trapped for a little while.

After coffee, mom suggested that she and Virginia go off to Baden Baden by themselves, and I could stay in Strasbourg with my friends. That caught me by surprise, but I was strangely relieved. I still recall watching them drive off and feeling a vast weight lifted from my shoulders.

Sharon, her husband Yves, and I had a lovely time. I vented a bit about my romantic problems, and they were kind. To this day I can tell you what and where we had dinner. It was in the Strasbourg town square, at an outdoor restaurant in the shadow of the massive cathedral and I had, of all things, goat in garlic sauce and crepes for dessert.

I had made arrangements with my parents to call them during the trip because I was waiting for answers about jobs. I had several irons in the fire and did not want to miss getting back to people who might be offering me employment. Since the East coast was 6 hours behind the Strasbourg time zone, I called after dinner. I was thrilled to find out I had been offered a job with a law firm, Surrey, Karasik, Greene and Hill. The first thing I did the next morning was to send a telegram to the hiring partner which said simply, "I accept your offer".

Virginia and her mother returned the next day to pick me up, and we headed to Luxembourg, where I was to get my flight back to New York. There was some drama about what time I was going to drop my luggage at the airport. The result was that Virginia got caught, yet again, between her mother and me. I got ready to go, and she drove me to the airport. The last part of the trip was anti-climactic because I had made some important decisions about my life. We had a bit of a tearful farewell at the airport, and that was that.

✦✦✦✦✦✦✦✦

I returned to law school in New York, older, and maybe wiser, but not without some significant self-concept wounds. It took me a long time to get over that trip. As graduation approached, I began to plan a trip for the summer after the bar exam. I was lucky the D.C. exam was in early June. Many of my classmates had them later. While they were studying, I had the summer off to travel.

Just before I left on my graduation gift trip around the country, including stops in Florida, Texas and Hawaii, I got a strange call from my father. He said Virginia's mother asked him to tell me to contact her. I blew the whole thing off and told him not to worry about it. Several days later, I got a call from my father's secretary Marguerite (who was a friend of Elizabeth's) with a similar message, call Elizabeth. I said to her, "OK, you have delivered the request". I was not going to give her an opening to lecture me about how important it was for me to do so, or even to let her inquire about my plans for the summer. Elizabeth could easily get my phone number, but I suspect she was afraid to call me. I think she was terrified I would be joining Virginia overseas without a chaperone. I do not know for sure what she wanted to say to me, but I had my suspicions. That was not a phone call I intended to make.

Unbeknownst to Virginia (or her mother), I had no intention of going to England that summer. Many years later, when I bumped into her, Virginia told me she even went to the train station in Oxford to meet me! For some unfathomable reason, even though we had never discussed it or made specific plans, she was expecting me to show up there on a particular day, on a specific train! At least, I surmised, that is what she had led her mother to believe. Clueless.

Since the day I left them in Luxembourg, I had not been in touch, and I certainly had not informed her of any plans to go to England. The last thing I said to her before getting on the plane was, "I hope you and your mother are happy". I guess she did not comprehend the sardonic, sarcastic nature of that comment and the finality it represented.

Fast forward a couple of years to a lunch with an old friend. He and I had worked together and were close. Since he knew Virginia and I had broken up, he told me he had asked her out, and she had accepted. We were waiting at the bar for our table, and his revelation did not bother me at all. However, as he described the evening, I not surprised. He told me she brought her mother along! I burst into almost maniacal laughter. So much so, that other people in the restaurant turned to look at me. I laughed hysterically for at least five minutes.

But wait! There is more! Several years later, when I was working on the Hill, I got a phone call from Virginia. I had not spoken to her since the day I left Luxembourg. It was the day the singer Karen Carpenter died. The Carpenters were popular when Virginia and I were together, and their record "We've Only Just Begun" was sort of "our song". Virginia called to reminisce about the good times we had had. I did not feel any anger or resentment, but I think I was a bit cool towards her. I changed the conversation from the topic of "us and the good old days" to what she was doing now. She filled me in on her professional life; she was teaching and told me she had been engaged to be married, but that it did not work out. I did not know whether she was angling for us to get together, but I suspected as much. I did not take the bait. I did ask her where she was living. I could hardly contain myself when she told me she was living in the same building as her mother! I knew I had made the correct decision those many years ago.

VI. Before the Hill

After law school finals, I drove back to Washington to start studying for the bar exam. That was going to be the last hurdle before I could start my professional life as a lawyer. I signed up for the bar review course at the Georgetown Law School. I lived with my friend, Tim Rothermel, who was also taking both the prep course and the three-day exam. The exam consisted of six three-hour sessions of essay questions.

One of the best things I ever did in junior high school was learning to type. The class was mostly girls, but I was determined not to be distracted by them, and to avoid having to rely on my chicken-scratching handwriting. Typing was the best way to go. I had typed all of my exams in law school, so I was comfortable taking the bar exam that way. I type much faster than I write, so time limits on exams were less of a factor for me. I had a law school professor tell me I got at least half a grade higher on my exam because he could read it.

I believe Earl was partially responsible for my passing the bar exam because he let me borrow his electric typewriter. I think Earl's machine must have had some of the answers magically imbued in it. At least, knowing it was his, I had a smidgeon more confidence I could get through it successfully. At the time, not many people typed their exams. I was scheduled to take it at the old Georgetown Law School. A separate room was set up for people who wanted to type. It was June in Washington, and it was, as usual, hot. Almost everyone taking the exam was grateful the old building had air conditioning. I was not. Although the typing room was air-conditioned, it only had two settings; "on" and "off". When it was on, it produced enough cold air to compensate for 150 people with 98.6-degree bodies. There were only ten people in the typing room, and it was freezing. I had to regularly go out into the non-air-conditioned hallway to warm my hands. This was a three-day essay exam; multi-state multiple-choice exams had not yet been created. Having an electric typewriter rather than a manual meant my hands did not get cramped up from three days of non-stop typing. People tell you never to leave an exam early. Because I had typed my exam, it took me much less time than if I had hand-written it. So, I had plenty of time to retype it. I was able to correct some mistakes, both typographical and substantive. Being able to type was a boon to my exam-taking experience.

As Tim and I were driving to the exam on the first day, we were quizzing each other. He said, "What is equitable estoppel?" I remembered collateral estoppel, but equitable estoppel was not in my head. "Hell, I don't know. Look it up". He did and read the definition to me. At least we were covered in case that esoteric question came up. Sure enough, the first question on the exam was, "Define equitable estoppel". I completely blanked. I knew we had talked about it 20 minutes before, but I could not for the life of me recall it. At least with the time cushion my typing gave me, I was able to avoid panicking and resolved to return to it later. I left space on my page to do so. Fortunately, I was able to recover it from the deep recesses of my addled brain before the end of the first morning's session. I rolled down the typewriter's platen to the blank space at the top and filled in what I thought the answer was, something about barring a claim.

The other question which flummoxed me was, "What can you tell me about Judge Greene's opinion about…?" relating to some fine point of civil procedure unknown to me. I started my answer by saying, "Having attended law school in New York City, I am not familiar with Judge Greene's opinion, but here is what I know about (whatever the issue was)". It was not an auspicious way to start a three-day exam.

I refused to engage in the daily post-mortems that a lot of the others seemed to enjoy. I think some of them got a charge out of knowing they had completely nailed one or more questions. There was the usual quota of gunners who knew every answer to every question and were more than happy to fill you in. Many who engaged in these sessions came away despondent about having utterly blown a question.

The rest of the exam was a blur. I did not feel dread because I did not think I had bombed it, but I was not very confident I had passed, so I was not elated either. By the end of the first week of June, the ordeal was just a memory, and I had the summer free before starting my job with the law firm. I was looking forward to both traveling and then getting to work as a "real" lawyer. Some of the people I visited on my travels were law school classmates, many of whom were still studying for the bar exam because they were among the unfortunate people living in states which had their exams much later in the summer.

✦ ✦ ✦ ✦ ✦ ✦ ✦ ✦ ✦

Surrey, Karasik and Greene

On Monday, September 13, 1971, I showed up for work at Surrey, Karasik & Greene. I had accepted the offer from a firm called Surrey, Karasik, Greene & *Hill*, but after I signed on, there had been a nasty split, and former partners were not speaking to each other. I tiptoed around the debris, not having any idea what happened. I did not want to know, and I hoped it would not affect me.

When I arrived, the receptionist welcomed me and told me to have a seat in the waiting room, which I did. I sat there for ninety minutes, too nervous to ask what the hell was going on but feeling very uncomfortable. Finally, the secretary for the partner I was going to be working for showed up and apologized profusely. She told me they had simply forgotten I was waiting. That did not bode well.

Two other new lawyers started when I did. I ended up working with one of them, George, on a couple of matters. George was a drone. He was fond of writing 50-page memos and was not as bright as some of the other young lawyers in the firm. He was going to make up for that with dogged determination. His one goal in life was to become a partner in the law firm, working on international matters. "I love international law", he once told me. Most lawyers who are working in international law are merely dealing with domestic commercial matters, conducted by foreign companies. The binding law in most of those cases is either federal or state law. The only people who really practice "international law" are those working for governments that are subject to international treaties.

George was enthusiastic when I got assigned to research a question of New York State law because the client was an international corporation located in the U.K. I tried to explain to him it was purely a state law question. Still, he was excited for me because the client was a multi-national. To each his own, I suppose.

Late one afternoon, we were finishing up a memo to a partner due in two days. We were almost finished when, at 6 pm, I told him we would have to finish it the next day since I had to get to class. "Are you taking a tax course at Georgetown Law School?" he inquired. I was not, I said and explained that I was taking a Smithsonian Associates class in Rodin sculpture. Looking puzzled, he asked if the firm was giving me credit for it. The answer, of course, was no. "Well, then, why are you taking it?" I said, "George, if you asked me that question, you are not going to understand the answer".

Humor was not in evidence often in the law firm. Almost everyone was serious, and funny comments were not received too well. There was one incident that I thought was both funny and well-received.

We were going over our reply brief on a case dealing with the W.R. Grace shipping company. In a lengthy brief, there are almost always errors, especially in citations. As the low man in the hierarchy, it was my job to read the opposition's brief for errors so that we could point them out. I was also responsible for catching any errors in our brief.

The secretary who typed it was fantastic, but even she could make an error. As the partner, the other associate, and I were going over it, I pointed out an error that made me chuckle. In quoting something we did not agree with, we usually cited it as "page... Grace Brief". This time it read "page...Grace Grief". The partner, who was a formal "Virginia Gentleman", laughed out loud, and to my surprise, with both what he said, and the language he used, said, "Fuck it. Leave it in!" We did.

+ + + + + + + + +

Tim Rothermel and I had not been thinking about the results of the bar exam. But in early November he phoned to say he had heard the results were going to be made available that morning. You had to call the Washington Post to find out whether you passed. Tim said he would do it and immediately let me know. I sat there for the longest ten minutes of my life, staring at the telephone and holding my breath. At last, it rang, and when I grabbed it, all I could hear was Tim screaming, "We did it! We did it! We did it". I finally exhaled, but decided it was not enough to hear it from him; I wanted to hear it for myself. I called the Post and got to the man who had the results. I asked, "Do you have a Dan Freeman on the list of those who passed?" He said he did. I asked him if it was "Daniel Martin Freeman". He said it was, and I was finally satisfied that I had, in fact, passed the bar exam.

I went downstairs to the office of the partner I was working for to tell him the happy news. In the back of my mind, I remembered the offer to join the firm was contingent upon passing the bar exam. I excitedly told him, but he was completely nonchalant about it. "Of course you passed the bar," he said, "I had no doubt about it". **I sure as hell did!**

+ + + + + + + + +

One of the things I had decided about how I was going to live my life was that I was going to eat well and properly. I committed myself to learning how to cook and eating three balanced meals every day. Every night at home, I would make sure I had an entrée, a couple of vegetables, and usually a salad. This was somewhat unusual as far as my contemporaries were concerned, but I persevered and became a fairly good cook.

It came as a shock to some people. A woman who lived across the hall from me knocked on my door one evening. She looked awful and told me she was very sick. She asked if I had any food because she had not been able to get out to the grocery store. I told her I had roasted a turkey and had some potatoes and salad. She was astounded! Being able to cook was a useful skill.

✦✦✦✦✦✦✦✦✦

This might be a good place to recount what a good friend of mine has called the "weirdest thing I have ever heard of anyone doing on a date". After law school, I was making enough money to be able to take a date out to a nice restaurant occasionally. My girlfriend Carol, whom I dated for a while, loved to try out different sorts of places, and we would seek out the most interesting new restaurants. Some people object strenuously to sharing meals. "May I have a taste of your ..." is occasionally not well-received. Carol was of a different school of thought; she loved tasting. It gave her the chance to try something new. We even had a tacit agreement never to both order the same dish.

I told Carol I wanted to try a new Scottish restaurant and maybe we should make a big evening of it and go black tie. She loved that idea on two counts. She had never been to a Scottish restaurant, and she loved to dress up. I put on my tuxedo with a formal yellow shirt with black velvet vertical stripes and a cape with a white frog closure and went to pick her up. She looked smashing and told me how much she enjoyed wearing a long gown.

We drove around for a bit, chatting animatedly about things happening on the Hill. She worked for a U.S. Senator who was on the Senate Judiciary Committee, so we had lots in common professionally. She was not paying any attention to where we were going, and I had not told her where this Scottish restaurant was. After about twenty minutes, I pulled into a big McDonald's and parked the car. She said, "You're kidding…This is the Scottish restaurant?" I told her this was it. She started laughing and said, "Only you would consider doing this, you devil". I was not finished.

As we walked into the restaurant and ordered our food, we noticed a lot of people were looking at us. I guess black tie was not de rigueur at McDonald's. We picked a table in the middle of the place, and I told Carol I would be back. I went out to the car to get the other accouterments I needed for the evening. With a swish of my cape, I produced a small candelabra and a cassette deck. I lit the three candles and turned on the music; Rachmaninov's piano concerto #2, one of my favorite pieces of music. We had our big macs, our fries and some fabulous tunes. It was a terrific evening.

✦✦✦✦✦✦✦✦✦

Later in the fall, the New York office of the firm asked for an associate to be detailed to that office for three or four months to work on a case for a big client of theirs, the pilot's union for American Airlines. George and I were both considered for the assignment. I was not anxious to go back to New York City, but

I was single, and George was married. When we were approached about it by the managing partner, George could hardly contain himself. He was ready to go that minute. I said I would consider it, but I wanted to make sure the firm would pay for my travel back to Washington on the weekends. When the partner left, I asked George what his wife would say about his being gone for several months. "Dan, this could be a significant move for me in my career. I couldn't say no", was his response. It was clear to me his career was more important to him than mine was to me. I never asked him what his wife thought about it.

I eventually was the one assigned to go to New York. It was not an altogether good experience. Initially, I had to go through the hassle of finding an apartment. The first place the New York office found for me was a fourth-floor walkup with no kitchen (only a hot plate), and no visitors allowed after 6 pm. I told them it was unacceptable, and they thought I was being picky. I ended up subletting an apartment from a woman who was going to be out of town for four months. It was in the Village and close to the subway. The managing partner in New York thought I was running a scam, and that the apartment belonged to a girlfriend and I was pocketing the rent. What a jerk!

While I was in the New York office, I was in touch with some of my law school classmates who had gone to work in the "canyons of Wall Street". There were several who were working in large and prestigious law firms downtown. I would occasionally get a chance to meet them for lunch or dinner. They would regale me with stories about life in a big legal factory. It was astounding to learn of the pressure they were under. Billable hours were all that was important. At least they were not expected to bring in business as first-year associates. There was a lot of discussion about how they would try to game the system. There were strict rules about when you would qualify for the firm to pay for a car to drive you home, and when you could charge the client for dinner if you worked late.

The billable hours competition was intense. One of my friends told me he had a contest with two other associates about who could bill the most hours in a day. Even though the quality of your work would undoubtedly diminish after 12 or 14 hours on a given day, a lot of associates put in that kind of time. On the day of the bet, there were three results. One of the three had billed 20 hours. I thought that was ridiculous. The second associate had had the gall to bill 24 hours! I wanted to know how he could explain that to a partner. How could you possibly have 24 billable hours? He must have gone to the bathroom, or at least taken one non-business phone call. I was astounded his managing partner did not challenge him. However, he only came in second. The third one billed 27 hours! He had arranged the contest to take place on the day he was flying to the West Coast, so his day was 27 hours long. He won the contest, but I am not sure it was worth it.

The matter I was working on was the preparation for a formal administrative law hearing before the Civil Aeronautics Board (CAB) in Washington. Not only did we represent the Allied Pilots Association (the union which represented the American Airlines pilots) but also the machinists who worked for Ozark Airlines. The senior partner in New York, Marty Seham, was going to appear at the hearing, and I was going to be "second chair" (or maybe "learned junior"). I would return to Washington when the pre-hearing work was completed in New York. Marty, in preparing me for the hearing, reminded me that although I was going to be physically back in Washington, my priority was to still be with the New York office and the CAB matter. I understood that, and I came back to Washington, ready and raring to go.

On my first day back in Washington, I was in the office early, before going to the CAB for the hearing. Walter Surrey, the senior partner in the firm, saw me and directed me to go up to Capitol Hill immediately to get a copy of a bill he wanted. I told him I had to be at the CAB to meet Marty and could not go. He was angry. I was a little irritated that he wanted to send me on a messenger's errand, which would conflict with my first real hearing. I heard more about it later, after the hearing recessed for the day.

For me, one of the highlights of the CAB hearing came on a day when Marty could not be there, and, for the first time in my life, I was on my own representing a client. To elevate the anxiety level I felt, that was the day our client from Ozark Airlines was going to be on the stand. Opposing counsel was a partner in the big Washington firm of Covington and Burling. I knew a little bit about him, and he was pleasant in our banter before the hearing started. However, when the bell rang, he was a "take no prisoners" lawyer.

He was cross-examining our client and asked him an inappropriate question about whether his union was seeking to gain representation on behalf of the mechanics at another carrier. I formally objected to the question. The hearing officer sustained my objection and directed our client not to answer. Then, in what I considered to be a cheap shot, taking advantage of the rookie across the table (me), the Covington lawyer observed, "I notice the witness did not deny it". Much to my concealed glee, the hearing officer said, "He did not have to. His lawyer protected him". Wow, what a fantastic feeling! I still resented the fact that the experienced Covington lawyer had tried it, but I was happy with the result. I never talked to him about it, but I was tempted. I did manage to make sure Marty got a copy of the transcript, and our client approvingly mentioned the incident to him.

✦✦✦✦✦✦✦✦✦

The firm asked each of the associates to write a memo describing the kind of matters we wanted to work on. Just as important to me, they wanted to know what we *did not* want to work on. I said I was interested in litigation and aviation, and that I was definitely *not* interested in tax or securities. I had no interest in financial matters or corporate law. So, what did the powers that be decide to do with me after my CAB hearing? You guessed it, securities. Arghh!

The securities partner to whom I was assigned for my post-CAB work asked to see me the afternoon of the incident with Walter Surrey. He told me in no uncertain terms that although I was still technically working for the New York office on the CAB matter, now that I was physically back in Washington, my priority was to be working for *him* and the Washington office. I was caught in the middle between these two partners, the one I was assigned to in the New York office and the one I was assigned to in Washington. They did not like each other, which made it uncomfortable for me.

The Washington partner, Charles, was one of my least favorite people. Even his secretary told me she realized he was both difficult to deal with and not a very good lawyer. He spent a lot of time being belligerent with his clients and with the younger lawyers working for him. He loved to lord the fact that he was a partner in the firm over the associates. He would also ask us to do personal errands for him, just because he could. One day he "asked" me to go pick up his car for him. He pompously handed me his business card on the back of which he had written, "Joe, this is Dan, give him the Jag". I did it, but I was pissed off. I got to drive a nice Jaguar, but I was tempted to take it for a real joy ride before returning it to him. I was also considering telling him I had not taken the course in menial tasks in law school.

✦✦✦✦✦✦✦✦✦

While at the firm, I was doing some volunteer work for a women's reproductive rights organization. I made sure I never missed any precious firm billable hours on what Charles considered a "frivolous" pro bono matter. The only two times I left the office to work on the case were to take a couple of hours off on October 10, 1972, to participate in the dry run for the oral argument of *Roe v. Wade*, and then the next morning to attend the real thing at the Supreme Court. Charles was not happy about my going to the Court. He told me I should have arranged to deal with my "extraneous commitments" after hours. I told him I had petitioned the Supreme Court to conduct the arguments that evening, but the motion was denied. He did not think that was funny.

To demonstrate what a miserable human being Charles was, as I was walking back up 15th street towards our office after the oral argument, I noticed one of the partners in the firm, Bob, sitting on the 10th-floor ledge of the building. It looked to me like he was considering jumping. I ran into the office to make sure people knew what was happening, and they did. Bob's psychiatrist was called, and one of his good friends, Jim, went out onto the ledge to try to talk him back into the building.

Bob and Jim were standing on the 10th-floor ledge immediately below Charles' 11th-floor office window. One of the younger lawyers tried to enter Charles' office to keep track of what was happening on the ledge. He was unceremoniously thrown out of the office because Charles "was trying to work". The psychiatrist arrived and talked Bob back off the ledge and into the building. I was outraged by Charles' behavior, but being a mere associate, I said nothing. I got a call a couple of years later from someone at the firm saying, "Bob finally did it". He had died from a self-inflicted gunshot wound.

Charles loved to keep people waiting as a way of showing off his importance. He was having problems at home, so he was not in any hurry to leave the office. He was also inappropriately interested in the social life of the associates. Mid-afternoon on a Friday, he said he wanted to see me later. I told him I had a date meeting me at the office at 6. That was a mistake. To this day, I still believe he kept me waiting for more than an hour on purpose while my date and I cooled our heels. He then deigned to call me into his office and told me the matter he wanted to discuss could wait until Monday.

I woke up one morning, feeling terrible. I had a high fever with chills, was coughing, and had shortness of breath. I called my doctor, and he told me to get a chest X-ray as soon as possible. It showed I had viral pneumonia in my left lung. I called the office and told the receptionist I was sick and would not be coming in that day, and probably not for several more days until I was cleared by my doctor to resume work. Within an hour I got a call from Charles who demanded, "Why aren't you in the office?" If he knew I was not there, he must have gotten that information from the receptionist, and I was sure she would have told him why. I explained I was very sick, and he wanted to know what was wrong. I told him I had viral pneumonia in one lung. He poo-pooed my condition and told me, "I had a friend who had viral pneumonia in *both* lungs, and he was able to go to work".

Charles would frequently call me in to his office to ask me, "What do you think your father would do in this situation?" One time I said, "Why don't you call and ask him? He will probably charge you". He was not amused.

Just before I left the firm, Charles asked me about my experience working with him, and I was candid. I expect he thought I was fortunate to have been able to study at the feet of the master he thought himself to be. I told him I did not feel it was the kind of learning experience I had hoped for as a young lawyer. "Why, Dan, I thought I was being quite pedagogical", was his reply. He was clueless, and I was happy to be rid of him and, I am sure he of me. I heard later from a friend, who had become a partner at the firm, that Charles was stripped of his partnership and then asked to leave.

✦✦✦✦✦✦✦✦✦

Office of Emergency Preparedness

I got my first post-graduate government job in the Office of Emergency Preparedness (OEP) in the Executive Office of the President. The sole project was to work on the President's proposed disaster relief legislation. This was a welcome change. The people I was working with and for were friendly, skilled, and committed to the job at hand. I was treated as a professional, and I was one of three lawyers on the team. My advice and suggestions, especially when it came to drafting the proposed legislation, were welcome and taken seriously.

This was my first foray into the complex world of the interplay between statutes and rules and regulations. It was a topic I would turn to in earnest when I was teaching. The process of deciding what was important enough to go into the law and what should be reserved for implementation through the promulgation of rules was challenging. I often think rules are made up of provisions deleted on the statutory drafting table.

One of the lawyers I worked with was terrific. He was always helpful and went out of his way to make me feel part of the team. He was going to leave the government when this project was finished and go into private practice. I admired his work ethic, his willingness to consider other opinions, and the way he treated people. I have run into many lawyers over the years who simply did not respect anyone who was not a lawyer. That is shallow and counterproductive. Much to my surprise, this lawyer asked me to join him in his new law firm. I was not even a little bit tempted, considering the bad experience I had endured in private practice, but I was delighted he thought highly enough of me to make the offer. I declined after telling him how honored I was.

On my last day at OEP, there was a surprise going away party for me. I was caught completely off-guard. The Director of the Office, a wise, kind, and gentle man named Bill Crockett, broke into the celebration to say a few words. He was generous about my contribution to the work product. He presented me with an engraved citation, which included the following words: "In recognition and appreciation of your outstanding professional ability and contributions to the development of the President's proposed disaster legislation. Your aggressive approach, coupled with a sincere and cooperative manner, have contributed greatly to the success of the project and have earned you the respect and admiration of your associates".

I was stunned. Bill Crockett said: "It took a lot for us to catch Dan speechless!" It was special. I stayed in touch with Bill for many years. He is a class act.

The draft bill that we prepared became the starting point for the Disaster Relief Act of 1974 (Public Law 93-288). It was signed into law by President Nixon. It was the law that established the process of Presidential disaster declarations and was the precursor of the law that established the Federal Emergency Management Agency.

By the end of the project, I had secured what my real career goal was; a job on Capitol Hill.

VII. Chairman Diggs and the House District of Columbia Committee

Article One, Section 8, of the United States Constitution, places the District of Columbia (which is not a state) under the exclusive legislative jurisdiction of Congress. Throughout its history, Washington, D.C.'s residents lacked voting representation in Congress. The Twenty-third Amendment to the Constitution, ratified in 1961, gave the District representation in the Electoral College, which was a step in the right direction, providing its citizens a small voice in presidential elections. However, they had never had any direct impact on how they were governed.

The 1973 Home Rule Act, officially known as The District of Columbia Self-Government and Governmental Reorganization Act, provided the local government more control of its affairs, including the direct election of the City Council and Mayor. Before the enactment of the Home Rule Act, the city was governed by a Presidentially appointed Board of Commissioners. Historically, the President has, and to this day, still does, nominate all judges on the D.C. courts. Judges nominated to the District of Columbia Superior Court (the trial court), or the District of Columbia Court of Appeals (analogous to a state Supreme Court) must still be confirmed by the U.S. Senate.

In 1972, Congressional committee jurisdiction over the District was vested in the House District of Columbia Committee. The committee was, in essence, the local city council in that it promulgated legislation for the city in conjunction with its counterpart Senate committee. It was a strange formula. The argument for this structure was that the city belonged to the entire nation. It was not designed to be a place of residence for citizens, merely a temporary home for those who came to work for the government. Congress simply did not trust the city to take care of its affairs.

D.C. residents suffered through minimal home rule despite repeated attempts by some Members of Congress to grant the city an elected government. Those attempts were stymied by a coalition of Southern Democrats and conservative Republicans who alternately believed that the Constitution empowered them to govern D.C. and that D.C.'s majority black population simply could not govern themselves.

The House District Committee Chairman from South Carolina, John L. McMillan, was vehemently opposed to home rule. Many people from Washington went to his district to assist his opponent in the Democratic primary. When he was defeated, the committee literally changed from white to black with Congressman Charles C. Diggs, an African American from Detroit, taking over.

One of my father's law partners, Cliff Alexander, was well connected in D.C. affairs. He subsequently ran for Mayor after the Home Rule Act was passed. I told him I was interested in working on the newly constituted committee, and he said he would try to help me. Congressman Diggs, the new Chairman, was a shy and introverted man. He was the antithesis of what one would expect in a Congressman. It was not surprising to find out he was a mortician by trade. His family owned the largest funeral home in Detroit, which catered to African Americans. It was called "The House of Diggs".

Mr. Diggs had chosen Bob Washington as his Chief Counsel. Bob was an imposing presence. He was a tall and extremely articulate African American. He was a Howard University Law School graduate and had been a teaching fellow at Harvard Law School. He returned to Washington to serve as Counsel on the Senate Committee on the District of Columbia. He knew the city, the local politicians, and the Hill. He was a "threefer".

Cliff, my father's colleague, had talked with Bob about me, and after some back and forth, Bob offered me a position as one of the committee's new counsels. He put together a rather eclectic staff that consisted of another lawyer, who was the only holdover from the McMillan staff, an urban planner, and a fantastic budget guru.

The holdover was a man who immersed himself in the essential but devastatingly tedious task of correcting the transcripts of the committee hearings. He was a creature of habit. Every day at 11:35 am you could hear him slam his desk drawer closed, lock it up, and go downstairs to the Longworth cafeteria for lunch. He came back to the office at 12:15 pm like clockwork. He did not add much to the substance of the work of the committee staff. He was there to make sure the paperwork got done. One day when we were involved in an important meeting about strategy on the Home Rule Bill, and he stood up and announced, "I don't know about you all, but my paycheck stopped at 5 pm." He then left. Our budget staffer, Linda Smith, looked at me in amazement. She is one of the best professional people I have ever met. She is brilliant, knowl-edgeable, indefatigable, and has a large personality. She and I were around the same age, and the holdover was more than two decades older. We chalked it up to generational differences.

Linda and I became good friends and have stayed in touch for more than 45 years. She and her husband relocated to Hawaii to run a plastics company, and she ended up being one of the top assistants to the Governor of Hawaii. She continues to be an extraordinary professional. I was glad to have had the opportunity to work with and learn from her.

Chairman Diggs was, frankly, a very strange man. He was basically humor-less and seemed to lack the ability to connect with people and rarely made eye contact; he would talk to your shoes. Obviously, he was not my kind of person, and I realized soon I had to tone myself down whenever I was with him. Bob always took the lead when we were meeting with the Chairman. There were times when Bob said something strange, and the Chairman would look to me for a response or an explanation.

It is funny how you recall little incidents, but for some reason, this one sticks in my mind. Bob tended to talk in rather pompous language. One day when the three of us were in Mr. Diggs' office, Bob said, "Well, Mr. Chairman, we will just have to concretize the indices of the factors involved". Mr. Diggs looked at me, rolled his eyes, and exhaled. I said, "I think what Bob is suggesting is we weigh the strengths and weaknesses of the proposal". Diggs looked at me with a hint of a smile and said, "Thank you for the translation".

Knowing I had to dial back my outgoing personality when I was around him, I had worked out a peaceful co-existence with Mr. Diggs. I always won-dered how he continued to get re-elected. I expect all those years of being a mortician allowed him to relate to people at stressful times. I did not understand it, and while we never had a cross word between us, I think we both understood we were from different planets.

Early on in the Congress, the Chairman decided to hold a reception for the new Members on the committee and their staffs as well as ours. It was a good chance for me to meet some people I would be working closely with. The Chairman's wife was also there. I always think, if possible, it is a good thing to have the boss's wife know you. I sat down next to her and introduced myself. She, too, was reserved and came off as cold and distant. I said my name and explained I was one of the new lawyers on the staff. Her response was ambig-uous: "Yes, the Chairman has spoken of you". I thought it was strange that she referred to her husband as "the Chairman". My response was, "Was it good or bad?" thinking a little humor could not hurt. To my befuddlement, she said, "He has spoken of you". I decided to quit, even though I did not think I was ahead in any way.

I got to understand Mr. Diggs a bit more as we spent time together. I knew he hated going to receptions, and he was invited to a lot of them. As Chairman of the District Committee and a leader on African affairs on the Foreign Relations Committee, he was sought out frequently. He would often want someone on our staff to represent him at the D.C. related events.

Although I did not do well at receptions, sometimes I would go because they were work-related. Mr. Diggs and I had an arrangement. He would inquire, "Freeman, are you going to that reception at (wherever) tonight?" Unless I had something else planned, I would say, "Well, Mr. Chairman, I can if you would like me to". If he had called about it, I knew that meant he wanted me to go and represent him. What he asked me to do, which was a fascinating revelation to me, was to take his name tag off the table at the entrance. "You are an F (Freeman), and the Ds (Diggs) are not too far away on the table. When you reach for yours, grab mine, and many times the sponsors will notice my name tag is gone, and I will get the credit for having been there". So, from then on, whenever he asked me if I was going to something, I knew what that meant. We had had a meeting of the minds.

Mr. Diggs decided he should make an oversight visit to the main prison facility for the District of Columbia located in Lorton, Virginia. It had a Youth Center as well as facilities for convicted felons. The building was designed to resemble the campus of a university, and it used open-plan dormitories. At some point, older adult felons began to be housed alongside the younger prisoners. With more adult prisoners, the facility became more like a school for hardened criminals.

Mr. Diggs, like most Members of Congress, wanted to have a staffer with him when he was making any kind of official visit. I had no strong desire to see the prison. After my experience at Greenhaven, I was not interested in going. However, for some reason, the Chairman specifically asked for me. So there I was, trapped in the back seat of a car for almost an hour with Mr. Diggs. He was his usual shy, quiet self, and we did not engage in much conversation. It was an awkward and mostly silent trip. I expect he was completely comfortable with that, and I just kept quiet.

When we got to the prison, we were escorted into the various facilities, including the cafeteria, the library, the exercise area and the cell blocks. I declined the invitation to go into a cell. Mr. Diggs, however, went in, and several inmates saw him. One of them said, "Hey, that's Congressman Diggs in the cell!" The

Chairman was impressed that the prisoner knew who he was. "Thanks for the recognition," he said with a big smile on his face. I remembered that incident later when the Congressman went to prison for taking kickbacks from personal staff whose salaries he had raised.

✦✦✦✦✦✦✦✦✦

One of the jobs as committee counsel was to prepare for hearings. As we were acting as the de facto City Council, many of the issues confronting the District would be dealt with by us. Traffic congestion was a considerable problem, and there was a myriad of suggestions about how to deal with it. One of them was to build another bridge across the Potomac River. The project was known as the Three Sisters Bridge, which was proposed to run across the Potomac River north of the Francis Scott Key Bridge.

We were holding a full committee hearing on the feasibility of building the bridge, and one of the witnesses who was invited to testify was a traffic engineer who had studied the traffic flow over the Key Bridge. Mr. George Jackson had conducted his study in a professional manner and had provided it to the Committee for the hearing record. As is usual in Congressional hearings, the prepared statement is submitted, and the witness gives a summary of his testimony. Then it is up to Members and staff to ask questions. Sometimes these exchanges become heated, but more frequently, they are underwhelming. When the Members are not actively engaged in the importance of the issue, the latter is usually the case.

After Mr. Jackson had given his summary, the Chairman recognized other Members to ask questions. This was back in the days before television coverage of Congressional hearings when the staff would question the witnesses. Since no Members had any questions, the Chairman turned to me and said, "Counsel, do you have any questions for the witness?" There were a couple of minor issues about Jackson's study I wanted to get on the record and so I asked him about them. Jackson, having testified many times before, answered them clearly and cogently. It was at that point that the devil in me took control. "Mr. Jackson", I began, "Is it accurate to say the gist of your testimony is that there is too much traffic on the Francis Scott Key Bridge?" Jackson replied, "Yes, Mr. Freeman, that is correct". "In that case, maybe we should simply rename the bridge and call it the *car strangled spanner*". After a momentary pause, while the terrible pun sank into people's consciousness, the room burst into laughter, excluding the Chairman. He said, "Counsel, have you finished?" I took the hint.

✦✦✦✦✦✦✦✦✦

There was another situation later that called out to me to say something silly, but this time I managed to resist the urge. Senator Thomas Eagleton was the

Senate counterpart to Chairman Diggs. I liked him. He was down to earth and was nice to me. He was from Missouri, and when I told him I went to Washington University in St. Louis, I got a big smile from him. From that day forward, he always remembered my name and the WashU connection.

We were having a pre-conference committee meeting to try to work out the most significant details of the final Home Rule Bill. Two of the major issues were the planning authority and the judicial appointments provisions. Since I was responsible for the judiciary sections of the bill, I was included in the meeting. We met in Mr. Diggs' office; Diggs, Eagleton, Bob Harris, Eagleton's Chief Counsel, Bob Washington, and me.

We were discussing the judicial nomination process. Eagleton had a misunderstanding of what the latest draft contained which troubled him. Unbeknownst to him, since the last time Bob Harris has briefed him, the two staffs had come to an agreement that met his objections and which Mr. Diggs was comfortable with.

Eagleton raised the issue, and Diggs explained to him that Harris, Washington and Freeman had worked it out in a manner that Diggs told him would solve the problem. Eagleton was pleased and did not even ask for an explanation of the solution. He said, "Oh, if that's the case, let's leave it up to Bob, Bob and Dan". The words and music which popped into my head were the Beach Boys singing "Ba ba ba ba Barbara Ann". This time I was able to control myself.

✦✦✦✦✦✦✦✦✦

During the ramp-up to consideration of the bill on the floor, the staff was assigned to do briefings about the bill. There was a lot of misinformation being circulated by opponents of Home Rule. Bob thought we should set up a Home Rule informational roadshow, invite House Members' staff and give them an accurate explanation of what the bill did and what it did not do. I participated in a lot of these presentations and answered a lot of questions.

One of the briefings was well-attended, and I noticed an attractive woman in the front row. I immediately decided to send a sign-in sheet around, ostensibly so I could get everyone's name and whose office they were from. This frequently happened at these briefings on a whole lot of topics, so no one gave it a second thought. Being a clever person, by knowing she was the second person to sign in, I was able to get her name and find out which Member she worked for.

Her boss was Congressman Jack Kemp, a former quarterback for the San Diego Chargers and the Buffalo Bills. I called her up later that day with some fairly lame excuse and asked her out. We ended up dating for quite a while. I got to know Jack Kemp because I would frequently stop in the office to see her, and he was often there. He was always friendly, and we would frequently talk about football or what was happening on Capitol Hill. Jack once asked me about the collar bar I always wore. I told him it was a birthday present given to me by a mentor, and I had worn one every day since then. I noticed he began wearing one as well. That was my sartorial splendor contribution to his wardrobe.

✦ ✦ ✦ ✦ ✦ ✦ ✦ ✦

Going to the House floor for the first time was a thrill. Because I am always hyper-prepared, I made sure that I had answers for every question I anticipated being asked and several others, just in case. Having watched some of the debates from the gallery, I knew that frequently Members would ask the bill manager to yield and ask him a question for the record to establish some point in the legislative history. I knew these were structured colloquies which were carefully worked out in advance. The staff of the Member asking the question and the staff of the Member responding would go back and forth until they could agree on acceptable language for the colloquy. We would then prepare the final version, which the two Members would read on the floor word-for-word.

This was a lesson that was useful later when I was working for the House Judiciary Committee. Members would use colloquies to establish some legislative history about an issue during a committee markup. A markup is a committee meeting to consider proposed legislation. It is called a markup because it is when Members get to offer amendments to a bill, thereby marking it up. I was always wary of amendments that were drafted on the spot. The law of unintended consequences would often come back to bite us. Since I sat next to Chairman Rodino (and his successors Brooks and Hyde) during every markup, I could usually suggest the Chairman inquire whether the amendment's author would be willing to put language in the committee report to be filed in the House instead of in the text of the bill. After the markup, the Member's staff and the committee staff could work out mutually acceptable language to make the legislative history clear. That was always a much cleaner way to accommodate a Member who had an esoteric interest in an issue. This also helped ensure that the statutory language, which had usually been carefully worked out by the committee staff with the aid of House Legislative Counsel, was not modified in an inappropriate or unintended manner.

We were fortunate in the House to have the assistance of a group of lawyers whose only job was to draft legislation. Having people who were experienced in making sure that new legislation fit in properly with current law was necessary. They (usually) had no axe to grind; their job was to make sure the legislation was as well-written as possible.

I found out this kind of careful drafting was not always possible when dealing with Members on the floor. It was organized chaos because Members would

often come up to the Chairman asking for information about a particular provision in the bill that was of interest to them. Frequently, the Chairman was not
knowledgeable enough to handle those questions, and your job is to protect
the Members from themselves. Unfortunately, on more than one occasion, the
Chairman responded to an inquiry incorrectly because the bill had changed
during the process. For example, the language about the application of the
Hatch Act to government employees who wanted to run for office on the new
City Council had changed between the subcommittee and the full committee.
The Chairman answered a question about it correctly based on the subcommittee language. His answer was *not* accurate about the language in the bill we
brought to the floor. It was sometimes awkward, but part of the job was making
sure that people had accurate information.

In those circumstances, I would privately tell the Chairman about the error
and ask if he would like me to speak to the other Member and clarify the matter. Most Members who are managing bills do not want to leave the manager's
chair on the floor, and they certainly do not want to admit to being wrong about
something. I would usually get approval to do that, and the Member receiving
the clarification was usually grateful. Sometimes it backfired, and the initially
misinformed Member would then seek to offer an amendment to "clarify" the
bill.

The constant barrage of requests to the chairman for information and accommodations was something I was not mentally prepared for. I was surprised
by both the gamut of the inquiries and the sheer volume of them. To his credit,
by that time, Chairman Diggs had gotten comfortable enough to pass a Member on to me immediately rather than attempting to give an answer he was not
sure of. He told me once, "You know this stuff cold, and I do not, so I would
rather defer to you to give the correct answer than have me mumble my way
through it and get it wrong". I admired his candor and self-awareness.

During an electronic vote, Members gather in various places all over the
Chamber. They have a minimum of 15 minutes to get to the floor from wherever they are in the Capitol complex. I had often told guests when I was taking
them to the gallery to watch the proceedings that a lot of work gets done during
these votes, but most of it has nothing to do with the pending bill. Members
take the opening to talk with colleagues about a host of subjects, including
other legislation, invitations to visit their districts for fundraisers, and a broad
range of others.

There was a special moment for me as the Home Rule bill was passing the
House. During the electronic vote, the subcommittee Chairman, Brock Adams,
came over to Linda Smith and me when the bill had gotten to a majority, 218,

and said, "This would not have happened without the two of you. I am grateful to you". Unusual, but well received by both of us.

✦✦✦✦✦✦✦✦✦

We had finally worked out all the language, including the necessary compromises on almost all of the issues. We believed it would pass both the House and the Senate and were ready to convene a formal meeting of the conferees. The Republicans had raised a parade of horrors about what would happen if Congress gave up major portions of its control of the District. The dissenting views in the report on the bill even suggested the local government might, in a fit of pique, shut off the water to the U.S. government buildings, including the House, the Senate and the Supreme Court.

This was my first time attending a conference committee meeting, and I was thrilled to be there, but I was a little apprehensive. When the House and the Senate have passed differing versions of a bill, conferees are appointed by each house to work out the differences. The conferees meet to hammer out compromises and to discuss the explanatory statement which will accompany the legislative language. This is real law-making in action. Bob had told me that if any questions came up about the judiciary title of the bill or the other two major sections I was responsible for, the Chairman would recognize me to explain it to the conferees. I would be briefing some Members of the House I did not know well enough to say hello to and possibly several U.S. Senators! Fortunately, the only questions about my provisions were straightforward. I think I did an acceptable job. It was fascinating to watch the back and forth between the House Democrats and Republicans, mostly for public relations points, and between some of the House Republicans and the Senate Democrats.

One of the House conferees was a sour old codger from Indiana, Earl Landgrebe. He was proud of the fact he voted "No" on everything. On his last day in Congress, I heard him brag about getting "one last red one". Red signified a no vote. When he walked into the conference committee meeting room, Senator Eagleton had the grace to get up and introduce himself. Landgrebe was not very polite. He told Senator Eagleton he was not doing the citizens of Landgrebe's congressional district any favors with this "abdication of federal power" and letting the city run itself. Eagleton handled it very well. He did not let Landgrebe bait him.

✦✦✦✦✦✦✦✦✦

Going through the legislative process was a superb learning experience. As one of my friends later observed, I became a big fish in a small pond. The House District Committee was a non-major committee under the House Rules, and it did not normally handle any significant legislation. However, the Home

Rule Act was different. It was an important endeavor, and it had to go through the entire legislative process; initial drafting, introduction, subcommittee hearings and markup, full committee markup, writing and filing a report, getting a rule to permit it to be debated and voted on in the House, going to conference with the Senate, preparing both the final conference report and the important Joint Statement of Managers and, lastly, preparation for consideration of the conference report in the House. I was able to learn a lot about the business of law-making to which I would devote a significant part of the rest of my life. Although, when compared to many others, the bill was not significant, the process was the same as for every other law. It was, however, very significant to the citizens of the District of Columbia.

✦✦✦✦✦✦✦✦✦

My sense of humor was evident in many different situations. We had a committee softball team, and we were going to get T-shirts to wear during games. I did not expect Chairman Diggs to show up at any of them. With that in mind, I thought it would be fun to have a catchy name for the team. Since Mr. Diggs was a mortician by trade, I came up with the name "Diggs Deeper". We did get a chuckle or two out of that.

Speaking of a chuckle, Mr. Diggs's first name was Charles, and I would occasionally refer to him as "Chuckles", but *never* when I was around him. Most of the other staff thought it was funny, especially considering his rather dour persona most of the time. I do not know how he found out about it, but one day when a bunch of the staff was meeting with him in his office, something came up that he was not happy about. He expressed his displeasure by saying, "That's what makes Chuckles frown". I burst out laughing, and Mr. Diggs cracked a knowing smile, a rarity for him.

He never called me by my first name, and I do not know whether that is because he was being formal, or he thought it was inappropriate. I noticed that I got into the habit of referring to myself in the third person when speaking with him. I had to drop some papers off at his house on Capitol Hill one day after work. I rang the doorbell, and instead of answering the door, he stuck his head out of the second-floor window and said, "Who is it?" Without thinking, I responded, "Freeman".

✦✦✦✦✦✦✦✦✦

While we were working on the Home Rule Act, the D.C. Courts were confronted with a serious shortage of funds for the Public Defender Service under the Criminal Justice Act (CJA). If Congress did not act, there would be no lawyers available to represent indigent people charged with crimes. There was a serious legal question about whether anyone charged with a crime could have a fair trial if they did not have the assistance of counsel. It had been only ten years since the Supreme Court had declared the constitutional requirement that people charged with felonies had to have counsel, and if they could not afford counsel, the government would pay for it (*Gideon v. Wainwright*). The inability of the government to pay for counsel for indigent defendants might preclude prosecuting those defendants altogether.

Bob and I recommended to the Chairman that the committee hold a hearing on the criminal justice funding emergency. He concurred, and I was charged with the responsibility of setting it up. I prepared what I referred to as a "hearing scenario", which contained an outline of the problem which the hearing was to address, a list of possible witnesses, and a synopsis of their testimony. I would need the Chairman's approval to invite the two people I wanted to testify: the Deputy Attorney General of the United States, and the Chief Judge of the D.C. Superior Court.

The Deputy AG would testify about the Federal role in prosecutions in the District of Columbia and the terrible toll it would inflict on the criminal justice system if funding for the Defender Service was not continued. My practice was to make sure I knew ahead of time what any witness was going to say so I would arrange a meeting before any hearing. I requested a meeting with the number two law enforcement official in the U.S. government as if it were routine.

I became a little more anxious about it when I was told I could park in the Department of Justice atrium in the center of the building. I was cleared into the parking area, and then into the building. I was cleared, yet again, to go up to the hallowed halls of the 6th floor where the senior Department officials' offices were. Feeling rather insignificant, a young lawyer working for a non-major Congressional committee, and even a little embarrassed to be bothering this prominent official, I tried to put my game face on and walked in.

The Deputy AG was terrific. He greeted me warmly and thanked me for coming down to the Department for our meeting. I certainly would not have even thought of asking him to come to the Hill! We went over the problem with the funding for the CJA and who the other witnesses were going to be. He told me he would get his statement to me promptly, asked me if there was anything I wanted him to emphasize, and then "poof" the meeting was over. I was elated. I had thought it possible he would chew me out for bothering him and then unceremoniously throw me out of his office, but it could not have gone better.

The only other witness was going to be Harold Greene, the Chief Judge of the D.C. Superior Court, who I had not met. Since the D.C. Courts were beholden to Congress for their funding, I was more comfortable about asking him for an appointment. I took Polly, one of our interns, with me because I wanted her to understand why I liked to interview any witness before the hearing. She was eager to learn, and I was aware of her interest and was trying to encourage her.

When we walked into the Judge's chambers, I looked at him and complimented him on his beautiful tie. It turns out he and I were wearing the *same* tie! What are the chances? We had a productive meeting, and Polly was pleased to have been included. Judge Greene and I developed a good working relationship that endured for a long time. However, I did not foresee the possible hiccup which was on the horizon in my own backyard.

Before the hearing, we had a meeting of the staff who were working on it; Bob, Linda Smith, Mary, who was one of the other lawyers on the staff, and me. We were going over the categories of questions we wanted to ask the witnesses and what points we wanted to make for the record. We needed the testimony to make the case of the dire consequences not providing full funding of the CJA program would cause. Without it, the criminal courts in the District would grind to a halt. Things were going well until Mary suggested she had some "pointed" questions for the judge about some issue entirely unrelated to CJA funding. Judge Greene was a key witness on the CJA issue, and the point of the hearing was to highlight the emergency which faced the courts in the city, so I was surprised. This was not a time to go into extraneous matters. I thought it best that we presented a unified front on the CJA and not divert attention from that to some unrelated issue Mary was interested in.

We got into a rather intense debate about Mary's "right to cross-examine" a witness. She insisted that since Judge Greene had volunteered to appear at the hearing, he was "fair game" on anything which Mary wanted to ask him about. I was irritated. I tried to point out the sole purpose of the hearing was to raise the alarm about CJA funding and to make sure it was continued. Any divergence from that topic would diminish the impact of Judge Greene's testimony. I also pointed out the committee had invited the Judge to testify on the CJA issue, and he had graciously agreed based on my representations about what the committee expected to achieve. I thought going off on some other topic would be counter-productive, and we certainly did not want to blind-side Judge Greene with questions about some non-germane issue.

I suggested to Bob that if he were going to allow Mary to ask irrelevant questions, I felt honor-bound to let Judge Greene know in advance. I did not want him to be embarrassed by a question out of the blue, and I did not want to jeopardize my good relationship with him. After some acrimonious discussion, Bob decided to split the baby and let Mary prepare her questions and submit them to him before the hearing. If they were worth asking, we would, during the hearing, ask Judge Greene if he would be willing to answer some additional questions and submit the answers to them in writing later. That seemed to settle the matter. As it turned out, Mary could not make it to the hearing, and I was the counsel. I asked a few questions about the CJA funding emergency to clarify the record and *only* about the CJA funding.

✦✦✦✦✦✦✦✦✦

Several months later, I got a call from Judge Greene. We had a brief friendly chat, and he asked me about a case involving one of his colleagues. It was a criminal case which posed an interesting legal question about the trial judge's ruling on an evidentiary question. We talked about the issue, and I made some observations about the case. Our conversation sounded like a law school exam. We had previously talked about how I took my evidence course in law school from Judge Jack Weinstein and what a fantastic experience that had been. Judge Greene then said he would like me to represent the defendant in the appeal and to brief and argue the case!

I had never tried a case, and my only appellate experience was several moot courts while in law school. Judge Greene's request was an unexpected compliment, and I was delighted at the prospect and a little bit apprehensive about representing someone whose freedom was at stake. I told him I was flattered he thought I could do this, especially coming through a pro bono appointment from the Chief Judge of the Superior Court. I asked him for a day to think about it and to do a little research.

The first question I had was whether, as a government employee, I would be permitted to represent a criminal defendant in court. I thought I could get Bob to approve it, but I wanted to make sure there was no House rule or other legal impediment. I also wanted to read more about the evidentiary issue in the case.

When I checked out the relevant statute, there was a specific provision that prohibited any government employee from representing a client in a case where the government was a party. Since every criminal prosecution in the District of Columbia was brought in the name of the United States, that would apply to me in this situation. I was disappointed and relieved at the same time. I got up my courage to call Judge Greene. I told him if I were to agree to represent the defendant, he would have to put me in jail and fine me a large amount of money and cited the section of the code. I expressed my disappointment since I believed it would have been an extraordinary learning experience for me. I also thanked him profusely for the honor of being considered.

✦✦✦✦✦✦✦✦✦

There were always a lot of interesting characters around Congress, and I got to meet more than a few. One of my friends worked for Congressman

Mendel Davis. Davis was a young Member who was elected to fill the seat of Mendel Rivers, who had held the South Carolina seat for more than 30 years. When Rivers died during surgery, Davis, who was his godson and namesake and who worked in his office, decided to run to replace him. The special election was very close. Davis was an unknown newcomer. In a brilliant tactic, all the campaign material from bumper stickers to posters said, "Vote for Mendel". Although I never saw any data, I am sure a large proportion of the voters cast their ballots for Mendel Davis, thinking they were voting (again) to re-elect the deceased Mendel Rivers.

My friend Wayne was Davis's Chief of Staff and had a terrific sense of humor and a well-grounded world view. In the egocentric world of Capitol Hill, he was down to earth. His main life focus was his sons and their baseball fixation. When I was in the Cannon Building, I would occasionally stop in to see Wayne. I would walk directly back to his office, which was the farthest from the front door. The receptionist knew me, and I did not have to stop at the front desk to be cleared. She would smile and wave me through.

One morning I came by, and there was a new receptionist. She had a full figure, a sweater which was too small and too low cut for a professional office, bleached blond hair with dark roots, long bright red fingernails with matching bright red lipstick, way too much makeup, and a sort of far-away gaze. When I came in, she was on the phone, clearly not a business call (you can always tell), chewing gum, and doing her nails. She did not know me, and I thought she should have asked me who I was and what I wanted. Nope, she could not be bothered. I was surprised but kept on walking. I would not be so rude as to interrupt her private phone call.

When I got back to see Wayne, I said, "Who the hell is that at the front desk?" He responded, "Aw, that's Liz. Wayne Hays told us to hire her". That explained everything. Hays was a Congressman from Ohio who was a tyrant. Hayes used to yell at pages if they were sitting down while operating the elevators. He was also the Chairman of the House Administration Committee, which he had taken from being an unimportant backwater committee and developed into a considerable power base. He controlled everything from parking spaces to typewriters to offices. He was a man to be reckoned with.

A couple of weeks later, I was in the Cannon Building again, and I dropped in to see Wayne. A new receptionist smiled and asked me who I wanted to see, as a receptionist should. When I got back to his office, I asked him what had happened to Liz. He rolled his eyes and said Mr. Hays had "asked"(with air quotes) Davis to assign her to his subcommittee office upstairs in the Longworth Building. Of course, if Hays "asked", it happened that day. Liz came back to Wayne practically immediately and complained bitterly, "There's no couch in that office". Wayne explained he had called the House Property Shop, and they were out of couches. "I'm calling Mr. Hays!" was her petulant response. Wayne told me he got a call 20 minutes later from Property asking where he wanted the sofa delivered. That is *real* power.

Wayne also told me he went over to Longworth the next day to see the office. He was astounded to find there was a black negligée hanging in the closet. It seems Liz was "entertaining" friends of Mr. Hays.

A couple of months later, the *Washington Post* reported that Liz had been on the payroll of Hays' House Administration Committee as a clerk-secretary. During that time, she admitted, her actual job duties were providing Congressman Hays and other Members sexual favors: "I can't type, I can't file, I can't even answer the phone." She was done, and so was he. He resigned from Congress soon afterward.

A truly wonderful thing happened to me in an elevator in the Longworth Building. I was coming up from the basement to my office on the third floor. On the ground floor, someone got on who I did not know. I was wearing a rather vivid yellow tie. His eyes lit up, and he proclaimed with a strong Southern accent, "Wow, that is quite a yellah tie". I told him I took that as a compliment and thanked him. As it turned out, he was working for Congressman Jim Mann from South Carolina, who was on the House District Committee.

I decided to be magnanimous, and the next day with the tie rolled up in a gift box, I took it down to him in Jim Mann's office. I found my "elevator friend". Ashley Thrift and I began a remarkable friendship that day. He has been a stalwart pillar in my personal support system, and I treasure him. We have forged a strong personal bond.

He is an enthusiastic basketball fan. His never-ending devotion to the North Carolina Tarheels is in his DNA. He always knew about legendary Coach Dean Smith's recruiting and what next year's team was going to look like. He also enjoyed playing the game. He and his wife, Julianne, were living in the dorms at George Washington University because she was a resident advisor, so the university provided them with housing. Because she was on the staff, they had access to all the university facilities, including the gym. Ashley called me one day and invited me to join him at the gym for some pick-up basketball. I had not played basketball for several years, but knowing his enthusiasm, I thought it might be fun. I showed up at the gym in my fancy Pete Maravich Gold sneakers. "Pistol Pete" Maravich was a prolific scorer at Louisiana State University, for the Atlanta Hawks and the New Orleans Jazz. He was famous for his ball-handling, his uncanny shooting ability and his floppy socks. Ashley was more amazed by my gold shoes than he was by my "yellah" tie.

Because I was not a very good basketball player, I was a little apprehensive about playing with such a dedicated student of the game. He was not tall or quick, but he knew how to play ball. When you have had a layoff from participating in any sport, one of two things can happen when you take it up again. You can be just plain terrible, which is normal, or you will be uncannily good until you realize that something is wrong. On that day, I was definitely "on". I started shooting, which was not my usual mode. I was usually the one who passed the ball to other people so that they could shoot. However, for some reason, after the first two shots I took went in, I started feeling it, an unusual sensation for me. Ashley kept passing the ball to me, and I kept sinking shots, even from the top of the key. He was astounded. He said, "It's Danny, the Dunk!" That nickname stuck. Since that day, he and his wife frequently call me "Dunk", and their two daughters still call me "Uncle Dunk".

When Earl Dudley and I returned from England, I went down to visit Ashley. I was wearing my new gray double-breasted suit. When he saw me, he said, "Damn, Dunk, you look like you just walked in off of Saville Row!" I smiled as I unbuttoned my suitcoat and showed him the label which read, "Gieves & Hawkes, Saville Row". "You are too much", he responded.

Sometime later, I went over to their house after work. We were going to have dinner. I happened to be wearing that suit. When I got to their house on Lincoln Square, I was surprised to find a washing machine sitting in the living room. Ashley asked me to help him carry the damn thing up to the third floor where the water connection was. So, there I was, in my Saville Row suit, lifting a heavy and awkward load up a couple of flights of narrow stairs. That incident has lived on in the lore of our relationship. Whenever Ashley needs help with something around the house, he always reminds me not to dress up for the occasion.

He is a constant source of good advice. One of his mantras was, "You are not always going to win, but you should put yourself in a position to win". He got that from Coach Dean Smith, and he lives by it. He works harder and smarter than anyone. He had met hundreds of famous people in his years on the Hill, but he did not have an "ego wall" with photos of them. I decided the one picture he might like to have was one of Coach Smith inscribed to him. I wrote to the coach and asked him to sign it this way: "To Ashley Thrift, a man who always puts himself in a position to win". It is one of the few pictures he displayed on his office wall, and I was pleased to have been able to get it for him.

We stayed in touch when he went over to the "dark side" of the Hill (the

Senate) to work for Senator Earnest Hollings, and after he moved to North Carolina when his wife was named President of Salem College in Winston-Salem. His wife and daughters are good friends of ours. We have traditionally assembled for Thanksgiving, either in Washington at the Hay Adams Hotel or in Florida, where they are enjoying their retirement. Their younger daughter was a frequent guest speaker when I was teaching at the Washington Semester Program at American University. She works on Capitol Hill and always gave a delightful and candid talk to my students.

✦ ✦ ✦ ✦ ✦ ✦ ✦ ✦ ✦

Another fantastic thing about working on the Hill was the interesting people who showed up for speaking events or receptions in aid of one cause or another. Each committee had an ornate hearing room that was a nice venue for such events. If another Member asked the Chairman for the use of the Full Committee hearing room for an event, he almost always said yes.

In the middle of 1973, when the war in Vietnam was still raging, Congressman Ron Dellums, a liberal African American Congressman from Oakland California, asked the Chairman for permission to use the room. The meeting was for an anti-war group who were there to lobby Members to oppose the war. I did not know anything about it, because these events rarely involved the Committee or me. People would start showing up, sometimes early, and ask to be admitted to the room.

As I was walking through the front office, I saw two people sitting in the waiting area. That happened all the time. One of them smiled at me and asked me a question. She had the most mesmerizing eyes. I gazed into them and almost immediately recognized I was face-to-face with Jane Fonda! I do not recall what she asked me, or what I said in reply. Wow, Jane Fonda!

She asked me to join them, and I did. A young woman from Dellums office, whom I did not know, was tasked with getting Fonda to the meeting. They were having a fairly intense discussion about the war. Jane Fonda was vehemently against it. She was one of the most prominent public faces in the antiwar movement. She traveled to Hanoi in July 1972 and posed with some North Vietnamese troops on an anti-aircraft gun. According to the "Washington Post", that photo "probably more than anything earned her the nickname 'Hanoi Jane'". The woman from Dellums office said all of her friends were supporting LBJ and the war and were giving her a hard time about being anti-war. Fonda looked at her and said, "You need to get better friends". That stuck in my brain.

There was tremendous fallout about Chairman Diggs permitting the room to be used for an anti-war meeting. It created a big backlash that affected the policy on the use of the room. Diggs had initially said he did not want to police who used the room and for what purpose, but he paid the price for being hands-off. In the future, permission to use the room was much harder to get, even for Members of the committee.

✦✦✦✦✦✦✦✦✦

You never know when lightning is going to strike, and I had no idea how important the District of Columbia Judicial Conference of 1974 was going to be and the dramatic effect it would have on my life. It was there I would meet the second eminent mentor in my life. The conference was to be held at Airlie House, a well-known, beautiful conference center about an hour into the Virginia countryside. Because I had been responsible for drafting the judiciary sections of the Home Rule Act, Chief Judge Greene invited me to be his guest at the conference. During the lunch, I sat across the table from Ted Newman, a D.C. Superior Court Judge, who would subsequently be named Chief Judge of the D.C. Court of Appeals, and a rather elegant Superior Court Judge named Leonard Braman. While Judge Newman was a voluble, outspoken, and opinionated man, I found Judge Braman to be erudite, intellectual, precise, and rather intimidating. I would later describe Leonard as the only person I know who speaks in perfectly diagrammed sentences.

For some reason, which I have never fully comprehended, Judge Braman was to become my mentor. It was going to be a long courtship because Leonard was such a formal and formidable presence. I did not always feel comfortable being my own witty, charming and effervescent self around him. I was always concerned about my saying something stupid.

The only similar situation I ever had was with Congresswoman Barbara Jordan. You will find her picture in the dictionary, next to the definition of the words "imposing persona." She was the Congresswoman from Texas who made a name for herself during the Nixon impeachment hearings. She had a thunderous stentorian voice and a manner of speaking, which left people shaking in their boots. I did not know her, but I would frequently see her in the Capitol complex. I always had the feeling that if I were to say, "Good morning, Ms. Jordan", her response would be, "And what sir, are the meteorological bases of that observation?"

Judge Braman and I started getting together for lunch on a fairly regular basis. I continued to be astounded that he would agree to do so. He had an extraordinary curiosity about everything and was always asking me questions about things which interested him and me. He was intensely interested in my observations about legal issues that were in the public eye.

I learned through attending several celebrations in his honor, such as significant birthdays, that I was unusual in the galaxy of people who surrounded him. Most of the lawyers who attended these gatherings had worked for him, either as a law clerk or in a law firm. They all held him in awe; only the best and brightest were able to forge a continuing relationship with him. I was able to joke around with him. I do not think those other people, at least in their own minds, had the option to do that. I still, at least for the first few years, was trepidatious about disappointing him.

An example of Leonard's inquisitiveness and precision occurred during an evening Earl and I had at his home. We had returned from our trip to England and Leonard had invited us for dinner and to show him the photographs we had taken. In the most precise and detailed way, he wanted to cross-examine us each to find out how we took pictures of identical scenes, which turned out very differently. He was fascinated about how each of us had used our own "photographer's eye" with such varied results.

During my many professional trials and tribulations, Leonard was always available to talk with me and give advice. His standing in the legal community amongst lawyers and judges was extraordinary. On several occasions, he was to write letters of recommendation for me, which were models of clear, cogent and effective writing. I try to adopt his voice when writing letters of recommendation today.

We were supposed to have lunch one day in March 1977, when a group of terrorists took over the District Building and two other sites. One of the complaints the terrorists had was about the way they had been treated in a murder trial several years before. Some of the perpetrators of what was called the 1973 Hanafi Muslim massacre were prosecuted in a trial presided over by Judge Braman.

When I became aware of what was happening downtown, and why Judge Braman's secretary had called to cancel our luncheon, I was alarmed because I thought that he might be in danger. It was because of that fear I called the U.S. Marshals Service, which was responsible for security in the D.C. courts, and informed them of what I believed to be a possible threat to Judge Braman. I found out later that, not necessarily as a result of my phone call, the Marshalls had swooped in and taken the judge out of the city for his protection.

I wrote him a letter telling him that I thought he had gone way over the top to avoid having to have lunch with me. I continued that "the seizure of three buildings was completely unnecessary, one building would have been sufficient." The letter was received in the humorous tone I intended, which was a positive comment on our relationship.

For almost two years after that, Judge Braman and his family were under 24-hour guard. Whenever he and I would go out to lunch together, there was an armed security guard in front of us and one behind us. I must admit it made me a little nervous. On one occasion, we went to a restaurant that had a plate glass window. One of the security guards told us that we would not be permitted to sit at that table next to the window because of the risk of someone taking a shot at Leonard. I often felt like I had a bullseye on my back when walking down the street with him.

Judge Braman and his wife Joyce were aficionados of opera. They would prepare for every performance by studying the libretto. They drove to the West Coast to see the Wagner Ring Cycle in its entirety using the time in the car to review the music. That is true dedication.

Knowing of their addiction to Wagner, I got tickets for the three of us to go to a two-night presentation of a six-hour film at the Smithsonian about Richard Wagner starring Richard Burton, Vanessa Redgrave and John Gielgud. Wanting to make sure that I was going to get the most out of the film, I got a book from the Library of Congress about Wagner. There was a scene in the movie of the entire Wagner family being photographed. I was fascinated to see that the placement of the actors in the film was identical to the photograph in the book.

I was not a lover of opera, but since my senior year in college, I had learned to love ballet. Leonard and Joyce had never been to a ballet. We decided to have a "cultural exchange"; my wife Mimi (a classically-trained ballet dancer who I will introduce you to in "Affairs of the Heart #3") and I would join the Bramans one night to see an opera, and then they would join us for a ballet. We took them to see one of the breathtaking Tchaikovsky story ballets, and they took us to a Mozart opera. A good time was had by all at both events.

The Bramans were early "foodies". Leonard was especially interested in what I thought were weird and unusual dishes. The two of us used to go to a Washington institution for lunch, A.V., a well-known Italian joint with red-checkered tablecloths and Chianti bottles on the tables. Leonard was friendly with the owner, August, and would often go back into the kitchen to see what struck his fancy. The four of us would occasionally go there for dinner, and one of the significant birthday parties for Leonard was held there.

One of Leonard's favorite dishes at A.V. was sheep's head. Seriously? They would take a half a sheep's head, bread it and bake it. I was *not* interested in trying it. Leonard also loved all kinds of esoteric seafood. I am not a seafood lover, but he enjoys it immensely.

Mimi and I had several food events with the Bramans. The first one involved Leonard teaching Mimi the proper way to eat Maryland crabs. He loved them. I am with the Chinese people on this; you should come to the table to eat, not to fight with your food. Mimi was an adept student as Leonard took her step by step through the detailed process of getting every scrap of meat from the crab.

One weekend, Leonard decided Mimi and I should be tutored in the fine art of building a proper submarine sandwich. Talk about a broad range of culinary tastes! Since he was from the Philadelphia area, the proper name for such a sandwich is a "Hoagie". Leonard believes the essential part of such a treat is the bread. He traveled to the Italian district in Baltimore to obtain all the proper ingredients. These included the correct bread, selected cheeses, meats, and olive oil.

The proper technique in building such a sandwich was precisely laid out. First, you must cut the bread in half laterally. Then, with two fingers, you tease out the doughy center portion of the top and bottom of the loaf and set them aside. The oil goes into the troughs in the top and bottom, and you layer on the cheese and then the meats. The benefit of using this method, it was explained to us, is you do not have too much bread in the hollowed-out main sandwich. And, as a bonus, you have the roll of bread you have taken out from the top and bottom to use for a "reverse" sandwich; you wrap slices of meat and cheese around them.

We had one culinary exchange weekend at the Braman's house. The first night they were to make us a special fish dish, and the second night I was to make my version of chicken Kyiv. I am allergic to alcohol, but Leonard loves good wine. Mimi is up for trying anything. Leonard opened a bottle of Bulgarian champagne which someone had given to him. They both tasted it, and with simultaneous grimaces on their faces, they committed it to the drain.

When I had been a member of the D.C. bar for three years, I qualified for admission to the U.S. Supreme Court bar. I asked my father, who was a member, to make the formal motion before the Court. He agreed to do so, and I went about getting the necessary certificate of good standing from the D.C. bar. While that was in progress, my father mentioned it to my sister, and she wanted to be admitted as well. When it came up at the dinner table at my parents' house later, my mother said she would like to join the group. My brother Andy, an inventor, computer wiz, violin maker, and lawyer had not been a member of the bar for the requisite three years, so he did not qualify at the time.

My mother had never gone to college. However, she talked her way into the Washington College of Law at American University and received her LLB degree (Bachelor of Laws) in the late 40s. She never practiced law, but she was a member of the D.C. Bar in good standing. Therefore, she was eligible.

I got all the paperwork for the three of us completed and submitted, and we scheduled a date with the Clerk. On April 21, 1975, the four of us were in our places in the Supreme Court Chamber. One of the lawyers who went before my father moved the admission of his son and his grandson. It was a special family event for them.

The Chief Justice then recognized my father to make his motion. "Mr. Chief Justice and may it please the Court, I move the admission of Mrs. Phyllis Freeman, my wife, Mrs. Nancy Freeman Gans, my daughter, and Mr. Daniel M. Freeman, my son. I am satisfied they possess the necessary qualifications". Chief Justice Warren Burger, who was straight out of central casting as a learned jurist with his white mane of hair and his stentorian voice, was not known for his sense of humor. However, he said: "Mr. Freeman, we grant your motion and will admit Mrs. Freeman, Mrs. Gans, and Mr. Freeman and suggest you bring the rest of the family down next week". We had one-upped the lawyer who moved the admission of his son and grandson!

Later that week, I got a lovely personal hand-written note from the Chief Justice, which said, "Mr. Freeman, it was a pleasure to welcome you to the Court on 'Freeman Day.'" When I had my certificate framed, I had that note included as a special memento of that day.

Our family event became a rather popular filler for the Associated Press. A blurb about it was printed in many papers around the globe, including the "International Herald Tribune". I got notes, calls and letters commenting on it from all over.

✦✦✦✦✦✦✦✦

I used the Congressional summer recess to explore my interest in litigation further. I signed up for a two-week course at the National Institute for Trial Advocacy, in Reno, Nevada. This was an incredibly rigorous course being taught by a group of judges from both the trial and the appellate benches. Classes ran from 8 am to 7 pm with breaks for meals. The students were from a wide range of law practices. There were people from big firms which paid their way, people from small firms, solo practitioners, and me, the lone legislative type in the crowd.

During most of each day, we were "in court." The instructors always had a real judge preside. We had different scenarios we were responsible for knowing. The instructors had arranged for local citizens to play various roles, including being the plaintiff, the defendant, and jurors. We did both criminal and civil cases. While the lead lawyers for each case were designated ahead of time, during each "trial," the rest of the class were allowed to make objections as if they were opposing counsel in a real trial. The lawyers who were conducting the trial had to be able to argue the merits of any objections.

We were dealing with a case concerning a claim against a hotel where a guest's jewelry had been placed in its vault for safekeeping. The jewels had disappeared overnight, and the owner was suing the hotel for the value of the purloined items. I was not one of the lead counsels, but I was paying attention. Carl McGowan, a judge from the U.S. Court of Appeals for the District of Columbia Circuit, was presiding over our moot court. He was very formal, even going so far as to wear his judicial robe. In this course, the protocol for making an objection was usually informal. Not so before this judge. In order to make an objection, you had to stand up and say, "Your honor, I object." You had to wait until the judge recognized you, and then state the grounds for your objection. With some other judges, you could object and state the grounds immediately.

The plaintiff, the owner of the jewels, was on the stand testifying. Her lawyer asked her whether the jewels were insured and for how much. Knowing how formal the judge was, and knowing that this was an improper question, I stood up and said, "Your honor, I object, and I move for a mistrial." The second part of my motion caught many of my classmates by surprise. (Who moves for a mistrial in a moot court?) Judge McGowan recognized me and said, "What is the objection counselor, and what are the grounds." I decided to play it to the hilt and asked the judge to have the jury excused. I felt that they should not hear even the argument on my motion because it would be prejudicial to my hotel client. Several of my classmates were bemused by this request. However, the judge agreed, and "poof" we were told to assume the jury had been excused while we argued the objection. Still on my feet, I waited to be recognized. Judge McGowan asked me to proceed. I stated that any inquiry about an insurance company being involved was prejudicial to my defendant hotel since the jury, knowing the money would not come out of the hotel's pocket, might be more inclined to find for the plaintiff. I further argued that once the jury had heard the question, they would not be able to ignore the possible insurance subrogation issue. I said the mere suggestion of such compensation had compromised the jury, and therefore, a mistrial was appropriate. There were a lot of eyes rolling and snickers. I think many of the students did not consider me to be a "real lawyer," and this was a bit of "hot-dogging." Judge McGowan, after having heard from the lawyer for the plaintiff, said he was prepared to rule. He said to me, "Counsellor, in the jurisdiction where I sit, raising the possibility of insurance company reimbursement *would* be grounds for a mistrial." I was on a roll, so I said to the judge, "Your honor, I am a member of the D.C. Bar." The lead instructor, Federal Judge Prentice Marshall, gave me a knowing smile of approval. We proceeded with the "trial," of course, notwithstanding my valid objection and my valid motion for a mistrial.

The other case where I got creative was a criminal case. The issue of reasonable doubt was vital. The question was whether the defendant could have been at the scene at a specific time. The witnesses had testified somewhat contradictorily about what time they saw the defendant. I decided to stress that point and to emphasize that because of the conflicting testimony, there was reasonable doubt about my client's guilt. Before the afternoon session, when I was supposed to give my closing argument to the jury, I went into the classroom and adjusted the clock on the wall forward by 10 minutes. I then set my watch back by 5 minutes.

When I addressed the jury, I asked them to look at my watch, which said 3:*30* pm, the digital clock on the wall which said 3:*45* pm and then to look at each of their watches when they went into the jury room to deliberate. I knew everyone thinks their watch is accurate, but I was also fairly confident there would be a variation in what they showed. I concluded by stating that the issue of when the defendant arrived had not been proven beyond a reasonable doubt by the prosecution. I concluded by pointing out based on the "wide variety of answers to the question 'what time is it,'" that I had sufficiently shown reasonable doubt for them to return a not guilty verdict, which they did.

At the end of the two weeks, I was exhausted but pleased with what I had learned about being a trial lawyer. I had gained some knowledge of substantive law, a better understanding of how to prepare for witnesses, and how to do a good cross-examination. Judge Marshall and I ate lunch together on the last day. He asked me about my experience, and I expressed my gratitude for all I had learned. He told me I had the skillset to become a good trial lawyer. Wow! I was blown away. However, on the plane on the way home, in going over the whole experience, I concluded that even though it was something I might be able to become skilled at, I did not think I wanted to be a litigator. An important lesson learned.

After Home Rule was enacted and Bob Washington left, the situation on the committee staff lost its allure. While there were a few things to occupy my mind, the big mission had been accomplished, and I started looking for a new position.

VIII. Private Practice—Shea and Gould

After having loathed law practice, I made the mistake of thinking since I had more experience, maybe private practice could be interesting and fun. Bad mistake. It turned out to be neither.

I went to work for the Washington office of a large New York firm, Shea and Gould. Bill Shea was the person responsible for the creation of the New York Mets, and Shea Stadium was named after him. One of the people I went to law school with was in the New York office, so I decided to give it a try.

In the Washington office, there were two partners, two associates and two secretaries. The work turned out to be boring, and the atmosphere hostile.

I got myself into hot water almost immediately. The firm had prepared announcements about new lawyers joining the firm. I did not know who drafted these, but they were grammatically incorrect, and they implied that the two lawyers who were joining the firm were members of the DC bar as was required by the Rules of the Bar. I was a member, but the other lawyer Wilbur Mills, who had been the Chairman of the House Ways and Means Committee, was not. Wilbur had been admitted to the Arkansas bar even though he had not graduated from law school because the Arkansas legislature adopted a law deeming anyone elected to Congress to be a member of the State Bar. During his years as Chairman, the Ways and Means Committee was arguably the most powerful committee in Congress, and he was its leader. He was responsible for much of the U.S. Tax Code. There were almost no tax, trade, or government entitlement measures of the 1960s and 1970s that did not bear his mark. Measures such as tax cuts and Medicare were enacted only when he was ready.

He began a plunge from the heights of Congressional power in 1974 when his car was stopped by the police and Mr. Mills, in an obviously intoxicated condition, emerged in the company of a local exotic dancer who threw herself into the Tidal Basin! Mills subsequently reported that he was an alcoholic, lost his committee Chairmanship in 1975, and announced he would not be a candidate for Congress in 1976. When he joined the practice, he did so at the behest of Bob Casey, a prominent tax lawyer in the firm. Casey had known him for years and thought he would be an important rainmaker. Wilbur had taken on his alcoholism tenaciously and had been dry for several years.

Pointing out that Wilbur was not legally entitled to practice law in the District of Columbia was met with extreme consternation by the partner in the Washington office. However, Bob Casey, who was one of the nicest men I ever met, took the bull by the horns and asked me to find out what needed to be done to get Wilbur admitted. Bob knew that I was familiar with the DC court system and with its admissions officer from my work on the District Committee. Since Wilbur was a member of the Arkansas bar in good standing, he qualified to be admitted by reciprocity. All he had to do was show up and have somebody formally move his admission.

I took care of all of the paperwork. I arranged for Wilbur, Bob, and me to appear at the District of Columbia Court of Appeals for Wilbur's admission. Notwithstanding his meteoric fall from grace, Wilbur was still recognized as an important person. The clerk of the court, recognizing that fact, made sure that on the day Wilbur was to be admitted, the Chief Judge, Ted Newman, would be presiding. Ted Newman was one of the people I met at the conference at Airlie House when I met Judge Braman. Ted had attended Harvard Law School and was delighted to know that Wilbur had as well.

When we got to the courthouse, everything was ready except for one minor detail. The clerk asked Bob Casey, who was a name partner in the law firm and an old friend of Wilbur's, "Mr. Casey, who will be making the motion?" Typical of Bob Casey, he did not hesitate for a second and said, "Mr. Freeman will be making the motion". I thought that was an exceptionally nice thing for him to do, but as I got to know him better, I would learn that it was not out of the ordinary for him. Ted Newman made a big deal out of admitting a "fellow Harvard man" and granted my motion.

The firm had to reprint the announcements (including correcting the grammatical error I noticed). The partner in Washington I would be working for was not too happy about that. This would be the first of many bumps in the road during my short tenure at the firm.

✦✦✦✦✦✦✦✦✦

One of the partners specialized in representing small restaurants, which did not seem to be in line with the big corporate practice of the New York office. He liked to lord his importance over these clients who were small businessmen, usually restaurant owners who came from other countries. He seemed to get some satisfaction out of bullying them. One of them had lent money to a friend and had not been reimbursed. I was assigned the task of filing a lawsuit to get the money back. I drafted the complaint, and I was pleased with the fact that I had prepared a legal action seeking eight million in damages! However, it was not such a deal since the loan had been for 8 million Italian lire, not dollars.

Based on the clear documentation we had about the loan and the borrow-er's refusal to repay, I felt our case was strong enough that making a motion for summary judgment might be successful. I explained that to the partner in charge of the case, who was severely lacking in self-confidence, which made working with him difficult. He was skeptical, as he was with almost everything I proposed.

I prepared the motion and a notebook for the oral argument in case the partner decided we should go for summary judgment. In the notebook, I in-cluded all of our filings, all of the cases we relied on, definitions from legal dictionaries, and everything else which the attorney arguing the motion might need. I showed it to the partner. He flipped through it cursorily and tossed it back to me in a rather dismissive manner.

I had never appeared in court before, and I was very eager to argue the mo-tion. The partner was so insecure I was sure he was terrified about the prospect of doing it himself, which showed in the curt manner in which he said, "Do you want to do it?" The implication in his tone of voice was that someone of his stature would not deign to do something so inconsequential. Briefly, I toyed with the idea of saying, "Oh, no. This is something *you* should do. After all, you are the partner in the firm". I thought that if I had done that, he might have had a heart attack on the spot. Instead, I said that I definitely would, and he condescended to my request.

When the day came for the argument, I was nervous, but I knew we had a good case. I was not confident we would win on summary judgment, but I thought if this case ever came to trial, we would win. That was not the issue before the court; we wanted the judge to rule in our favor based on the plead-ings without having to go to trial. I made the argument and seemed to get into a rhythm and passed the low bar of at least not embarrassing myself. As I walked out of the courtroom, I bumped into a lawyer I knew who was a litigator, a real live courtroom lawyer. He asked me about the case, and we briefly discussed it. He was surprised when I told him it was my first oral argument. He told me I had done an excellent job and that I had "a future in the courtroom". I was flattered.

The judge denied the motion for summary judgment, and a couple of weeks later, we went to trial. I was designated to examine our first witness, our client, who would testify about his making the 8 million lire loan to the defendant. The partner had decided that *he* wanted to cross-examine the defendant. I think he had visions of destroying him on the stand, like Perry Mason. He wanted to show off to his client what a hotshot lawyer he could be.

As I was about to conclude the testimony of our client, the judge asked, "Counsel, is the rest of your evidence cumulative?" I immediately recognized the judge thought we had proven our case with the pleadings and the testimony of this one witness. He did not want to waste any time hearing redundant evidence. I told the judge it was, and he said, "I would like to hear from the defense". The partner was sitting next to me and did not comprehend what had happened. He was angry and said, "What are you doing?" I leaned over and whispered, "Relax, we just won". He still did not understand what had happened.

I thought the judge was ready to rule in our favor, but first, he wanted to hear from the defense. The defendant testified that he needed the money urgently, and our client was the best possible source since he had the money in lire at a bank in Italy. We did not get a chance to cross-examine the defendant because the judge asked him, "What did you need the money for?" The response was, "I wanted to buy a present for my mother". The judge was not impressed by that response, and he looked at us and said: "Counsel, I am prepared to entertain a motion". This meant we had won, and the judge did not need to hear anything more. The partner still did not get it. Based on the prompt from the judge, I stood up and moved for judgment in our favor. The defense lawyer got up to object, not to the judgment in our favor, but because the amount of the damages "had not been proven". He said we did not know how much 8 million lire was worth in American dollars. Because of that uncertainty, he argued, the judge could not enter a final judgment. I started to get up to respond because I had the answer to that question already prepared. The partner grabbed my arm and spat out angrily, "What are you doing now?" I looked at him and said, "Winning".

I stood up and asked the judge for permission to approach the bench, which he allowed. I presented the judge (and defense counsel) with notarized affidavits containing copies of the Wall Street Journal pages for the two relevant dates giving the exchange rate from lire to dollars: the date the money was lent, and the current rate along with the calculations of what 8 million lire was worth in dollars on those dates. The judge complimented me on how well-prepared I was, and he received the affidavits into evidence. I was well pleased with myself, but I knew I could not show it. We won! I never heard a positive word from the partner about how well I had handled the case.

This partner's lack of confidence and failure to pay attention to details made working under him very difficult. One of our clients had been served with a subpoena from the Securities and Exchange Commission for documents. Someone from the company, which was located in New Jersey, was going to drive down and deliver them. It was a weekend, and that was the kind of thing mere associates do; spend the day waiting around. The employee had a flat tire on the way, which ruined my Saturday plans. He finally arrived late in the afternoon and delivered six boxes of papers. I asked him if there were any smoking guns in the boxes. He said he did not think so, "but you never know, do you?" I decided to come in on Sunday and go over all of the records page-by-page. I did not know what to look for since I had not been given any guidance, but I thought I ought to go over every piece of paper and see if anything jumped out at me.

The bulk of the papers were interoffice memos about supplies and orders, and there were lots of receipts for meals at an Italian restaurant. There was one memo about a case which had been filed in federal court, not against our client, but against somebody in the same business. Our client had been called in to testify. I did not feel it necessary to take note of who had what for lunch, but I did make sure to read this particular memo with care.

On Monday morning, the partner came in and asked me if I had reviewed the materials. I took him into the conference room to show him the six boxes of papers. Six boxloads is a lot of paper! He said to me in a condescending and dismissive tone, implying there was no way I would have looked at everything, "I suppose you read every one of them". I felt *he* certainly would not have. I simply said to him, "I would never turn over anything to the government which I had not read and understood". I did not include the phrase, "You incompetent jerk", but I certainly thought it.

Things went downhill from there, and I was encouraged to move on, which I did soon after that, having learned my lesson about myself and private practice.

IX. The White House

I had been in touch with Sarah Weddington occasionally after the *Roe v. Wade* decision. She had been elected to the Texas House of Representatives. She was the embodiment of the defender of women's reproductive rights and was constantly traveling for speaking engagements. President Carter appointed her General Counsel in the Department of Agriculture in 1977. I welcomed her to Washington when she arrived and offered to help her in any way I could. She said I was an "old Washington hand", and she was sure I could be of assistance at some time in the future. In 1978 she was named Assistant to the President by Carter to handle women's issues. She invited me to join her small staff in the White House. I was eager to do so.

On my first day, all hell broke loose in the women's rights world. President Carter, who had named Bella Abzug to the National Advisory Committee for Women in 1978, fired her that day. She dared to criticize him publicly for cutting funding for women's programs in an angry exchange at a White House meeting on women's issues. During the meeting, Ms. Abzug attempted to lecture the President on the duties of the committee and its role in serving the needs of women. There was also a critical press release distributed by the Women's Committee in advance of the meeting attacking the impact of Mr. Carter's economic policies on women. Sarah's office immediately started getting torrents of angry phone calls from women who were appalled.

That night, the President, knowing what a strain the day's events had been on Sarah and her staff, invited everyone up to the White House movie theater. I was exhausted and had gone home at 9 pm. I just missed getting invited to see a movie with the President. I am not sure I would have been able to stay awake had I gone.

Firing Bella Abzug from the Women's Committee had no real upside for the President. All of the liberal Democrats were furious, and all the conservatives were elated. It hurt Carter with his base and encouraged the opposition.

Because of the flood of letters and calls, the staff started to prepare a letter for Sarah to send out in reply. We then decided on a strategy that entailed making two draft responses; one for supporters and another for opponents. Sarah got upset that we had not consulted her about the two-pronged approach. I was surprised since this situation was not that complicated. You knew what you wanted to say to each side. I thought our job was to make her job easier by preparing the drafts for both letters and then let her revise them as she wished. She wanted to know why "nobody asked me". The letters did not change dramatically with her edits. She took umbrage because we had not discussed the strategy of writing two letters with her first.

✦✦✦✦✦✦✦✦✦

I found the atmosphere at the White House to be combative. There were lots of clashes over seemingly minor matters. The President did not help by the way he managed things. He wasted his time deciding who was going to use the White House tennis courts. Geez, Mr. President, don't you have more important things to do?

There was a three-person pecking order below the President. After that, not much mattered. Sarah was down around number 42, and consequently, she and her staff did not have any influence at all. There were significant conflicts on what the President was going to say in the State of the Union Address. A substantial victory for Sarah was to get one line included. I had nothing to do with that, and I was glad of it. It did not make sense to watch these people keeping score throwing their weight around over something so relatively inconsequential. I think part of the problem was that people on the outside know you are from the White House, and they are in awe. It can give you an inflated sense of your importance. I know Sarah spent a lot of time on the road. I expect she did not get much respect in the White House, but when she traveled around the country to give speeches, people she met with fawned all over her. She was Ms. *Roe v. Wade*, and everyone, especially women's groups, were thrilled to be in the same room with her.

I recall her coming back from a trip with one of her staff. I knew the staffer well, and she told me a hilarious story, which I gather Sarah did not think was too funny. Sarah was speaking to a group of trade union members about women's rights. The audience was not openly hostile, but not that friendly either. It was, to no one's surprise, mostly men. At one point during the speech, she said, "Women are the foundation of America". Some big gruff man in the audience responded, "Yeah, and you know who laid the foundation". I am glad I was not there because I would not have been able to keep a straight face.

✦✦✦✦✦✦✦✦✦

There is something about entering the White House that makes your heart beat a bit faster. It happened to me every morning. Being able to walk through the West Wing and say good morning to the President of the United States was a rush. I never talked with him beyond that, but I did see him occasionally as I walked through the complex. I knew people on the staff who did get to meet with him, but the degree of wonder it engendered was inversely proportional to the number of times it occurred. Jimmy Carter did not inspire people, especially those who were responsible for dealing with Congress.

The President did not care about the Hill, and because of that the Congressional Leadership had an almost palpable contempt for him. Carter's Chief of Staff was Hamilton Jordan (pronounced Jer-den). Speaker Tip O'Neill referred to him as "Hannibal Jerkin". A Member who I knew fairly well told me Carter had not called him or had anyone relay to him the message about the President closing down a vital water project in his district. He found out when a reporter asked him about it as he got off a plane back home. The Member was furious both because the project had been canceled and because no one in the administration thought to at least give him advance warning. He felt he was blind-sided and was very angry about it.

One of my colleagues described Jimmy Carter as a man who was committed to doing what he considered to be the just and moral thing. Carter did not believe he needed to explain the righteousness of his actions, and he simply thought people would recognize it. There was not much room for dissent within the ranks. He thought the legislative branch was a minor and mostly irrelevant factor in governance. He was Governor of Georgia, and he was a believer in the power of the executive. He was not popular on the Hill.

✦✦✦✦✦✦✦✦✦

Because office space is such a hit-or-miss proposition in the White House, I got the office which my predecessor vacated. I was in prime real estate! It was on the basement floor of the West Wing next to the White House mess. There were lots of faces I recognized walking by, and some of them mistook me for someone important. I never disabused them and frequently would introduce myself to some relatively famous people. I was soon transferred to a much grander office in the Old Executive Office Building. It had 14-foot ceilings, beautiful tiles on the floor, and gorgeous scrollwork. However, as real estate agents say, "Location, location, location". The move was not a promotion. Out of the West Wing meant out of sight and out of mind.

✦✦✦✦✦✦✦✦✦

One of the most important events during my time at the White House was on the South Lawn when Vice Premier Deng Xiaoping of the People's Republic of China arrived to meet with the President. Everyone was waving American and Chinese flags. It was a historic day, and I felt privileged to be there.

I was frequently assigned to tour-guide duty. I knew the White House well and was often asked to give tours to important guests, or not-so-important guests of important people. I got to be known by the Secret Service officers, and I made it a point to greet them whenever I could. They have tough jobs and giving them a smile and greeting them by name was the least I could do.

One day I was asked to take someone's two old maiden aunts around. I did not mind because it got me out of the office and around the complex. After walking through the West Wing and ending up in the East Wing where the First Lady's offices are, one of the women asked me a question. I had greeted one of the Secret Service agents as we walked by his post. The question was, "Why are so many of the security people hard of hearing?" I was puzzled and asked her why she thought that. She said, "I noticed most of them are wearing hearing aids". I did not understand what she was talking about, and then a moment later, it came to me. I told her they were not hearing aids, but radio communicators so they could keep up with the whereabouts of various protectees in the White House complex.

✦✦✦✦✦✦✦✦✦

Both before and after my move to the White House, Judge Braman and I would frequently meet at his favorite Chinese restaurant in Washington's Chinatown, named Szechuan. Leonard was friendly with the owner, Tony Cheng, who was often referred to as the "Mayor of Chinatown". We would go there regularly when I was on the District Committee, and I had the time to go out for lunch. Tony and I became friendly, and he would invite me every year to his blow-out Chinese New Year's celebration. This event always included massive amounts of food, firecrackers, and the obligatory visit from a 25-foot-long dragon. It was always a fantastic event.

Working at the White House did not permit going out to lunch. I was lucky to grab a sandwich at the food center in the Executive Office Building (EOB). There was an unspoken ethic you did not leave until Sarah left, and if you could beat her into the office in the morning, you got brownie points.

One day Sarah asked me if I knew any good Chinese restaurants. One of the other people on the staff had asked her. She was new to town, and I was a native. I recommended Tony's restaurant and told her I knew the owner. I gave her Tony's name and told her to mention my name when she got there. Sarah did not think she was going but was asking for one of the "big three" in the

President's three-man pecking order, Jerry Rafshoon. I did not give it another thought until later.

The version of the story I got was that Rafshoon had gone to the Szechuan and liked it. It turns out he was on a scouting mission for the President. Soon afterwards, Tony got a call in the middle of the day informing him Carter would be coming for dinner that night. He was to expect the Secret Service to do a security screening of the restaurant. Tony went home to shower and shave and put on his best suit. When the President's party arrived, the Secret Service detail, the President, Jerry Rafshoon, and a couple of other people, Tony was waiting at the door. He was introduced to Carter, and as they were shaking hands, Tony said, "Mr. President, you know my friend Mr. Freeman who works for you in the White House". The President smiled and said the diplomatic thing; of course, he knew me. Tony was impressed, and from then on, he greeted me like a VIP. When I heard about it, I was amused.

While my time at the White House was limited, I did get a peek into how it operates and how the macro world of politics functions, as well as how the micro-world of inter-office strife comes to the fore. I think, at least for me, it was a great place to have been, but not to be. One of my friends characterized it as "better in the rearview mirror". I concur.

X. Chairman Rodino and the House Judiciary Committee

When I was in high school, I was a camp counselor at a camp in the Pocono Mountains in Pennsylvania, Camp Shohola. I spent several summers there and enjoyed it. While there, one of the campers in my charge was a very funny kid named David Nellis. He was a good kid who was skinny and hyperactive, always joking around. I got to know his father, Joe, and over the years, he and I became friendly. He even offered me a job in his firm after law school, but I was interested in a more established firm.

David and I stayed in touch. He ended up in public relations for a series of companies, including working for a local department store, the Hecht Company. He then opened up his own PR shop. His sense of humor was still evident. He got vanity license plates for his car; PRIBS, which stood for Public Relations is Bull Shit.

Joe Nellis had been an investigator for the Kefauver Senate Crime Committee. It was a special committee to investigate organized crime. Several years later, he ended up as the General Counsel of the House Select Committee on Narcotics. While in private practice, he had argued several important civil and corporate cases, including the U.S. Supreme Court's first decision on the constitutionality of antiabortion laws (*United States v. Vuitch*, 1971). He also played a role in the successful argument of *Roe v. Wade* by assisting in the preparation for the appearance before the high court. It was through Joe that I met Sarah Weddington and got invited to participate in the dry run the day before the argument.

The General Counsel of the House Judiciary Committee was Alan Parker, who I had met through Earl. He had an interesting and somewhat checkered career path. Alan did not go to college and said he almost did not graduate from high school. He said he would rather sit in the library and read than go to class.

He worked several jobs, including being a radio disc jockey and as an inheritance tax appraiser with the State of California. He had such a facile mind that one of the lawyers he met suggested he go to law school. The San Francisco College of Law had a policy of giving prospective students credit for life experience. Alan studied there for a year and then went on to complete the full three-year law school program at Santa Clara University Law School.

Alan was close to Congressman Don Edwards, who represented a district in Northern California. Edwards was a liberal Member who was prominent in the civil rights movement. He became the Chairman of the House Judiciary Committee Subcommittee on Civil and Constitutional Rights and was a key player in every major civil rights bill. He came to Congress in 1963 and had a significant role in the Civil Rights Act of 1964 and the Voting Rights Act of 1965.

Edwards asked Alan to become his legislative director and then named him to be Chief Counsel to the subcommittee. When Earl left the Committee to go into private law practice, he urged Chairman Rodino to name Alan as his replacement, which he did.

After serving as the Judiciary Committee's General Counsel for many years, Carter's Attorney General, Griffin Bell, asked Alan to become Assistant Attorney General for Legislative Affairs. As luck would have it, Alan's replacement as General Counsel was Joe Nellis, David's father. Mr. Rodino was on the Narcotics Committee and had gotten to know Joe in that capacity.

One day out of the blue, Joe called me and said, "I have just been named General Counsel of the House Judiciary Committee. Get your ass up here. I need you". I knew Alan Parker was leaving the Committee, but I did not know Joe knew Mr. Rodino at all, much less well enough to be named as Judiciary Committee General Counsel. He had spent most of his time while working in Congress doing hard-nosed investigations about some pretty tough characters, organized crime figures and drug lords.

Joe was short and stocky and was a bit rough around the edges. He had a rough gravelly voice and seemed to be a little bit out of his element. After the stressful ordeal of Watergate, the Judiciary Committee and Mr. Rodino were interested in doing some serious legislating. Joe's style and manner were not well suited to that agenda.

I was fortunate because Joe was fond of me. In many ways, I felt I was the lawyer son he did not have. I had known his family for a long time and was invited to David's second wedding. Some of the Judiciary Committee staff knew me because of my relationships with Earl Dudley and Alan Parker, but many of them considered Joe and me to be part of a package deal. That did not always redound to my benefit.

✦✦✦✦✦✦✦✦✦

The Judiciary Committee had seven subcommittees that had specific subject matter jurisdictions. The subcommittees used to be designated by numbers only; sub 1, sub 2, etc. The old system was used, and some say abused so that the Chairman of the full committee could refer bills in a way that suited him and not be constrained by subject matter. He could assign bills to his subcommittee to expedite them or kill them. The post-Watergate reforms were created to enhance the authority of the subcommittee chairs and put an end to that system. However, assigning the subcommittees specific subject matter jurisdictions based on historical structure resulted in some strange combinations. For example, the Courts and Intellectual Property subcommittee had jurisdiction over intellectual property and courts but not Federal Judgeships. Bills relating to the operation and jurisdiction of the Federal Courts were referred there. The Monopolies and Commercial Law subcommittee had jurisdiction over monopolies and commercial law and, interestingly, judgeships. This did not mean the nomination of people for a specific judgeship but increasing the number of judgeships in any particular place.

Because there were some complaints about the subcommittee organization, the Chairman established an ad-hoc committee to examine it and come up with recommendations to make the configuration more logical. Each of the subcommittees had a vested interest in maintaining jurisdiction over its significant areas of expertise.

Joe had designated me to be the lead staffer on this and to make sure it was done objectively. We prepared three different proposed structures for consideration by the Members; a five, a six, and a seven-subcommittee model. While several of these potential reconfigurations made sense from a purely structural perspective, there was going to be a lot of resistance to realignment if any subcommittee was going to lose something it considered important. Staff on some of the subcommittees and the subcommittee chairs had conniptions about some of the suggested realignments. Everyone was protecting their jurisdiction; they were happy to take on more but were protective of their turf. Moving the judgeships jurisdiction away from Mr. Rodino's subcommittee to the Courts Subcommittee was, according to Joe, a nonstarter. He told me in no uncertain terms that Chairman Rodino was not going to give up the judgeships jurisdiction and that I needed to "remember who signs your paycheck". So much for objectivity.

✦✦✦✦✦✦✦✦✦

Mr. Rodino had decided during Watergate that he needed somebody in the room who knew the House Rules thoroughly. He thought that with the high stakes involved in a presidential impeachment, things could get rather hairy, and he did not want to end up making any parliamentary mistakes on such an important matter, especially if it was going to be televised. He designated one of the lawyers on the full committee staff to become the committee Parliamentarian. Mr. Rodino was the first committee chairman in the House to do so. While the House Parliamentarians were available by telephone, you could not always get through to one of them immediately. If a Member made a point of order during a committee meeting, the Chairman had to rule on it promptly. Not being able to get the correct answer quickly could be a problem. The lawyer who had been the committee Parliamentarian when I got there left about a year after I arrived. The next morning Joe told me, "As of today, you are the committee Parliamentarian". I had strong mixed feelings because I knew that I was not up to the task, but I was motivated by the prospect.

Becoming the Parliamentarian turned out to be a significant and positive development in my career. It required me, as quickly as possible, to learn the House Rules, which enhanced my stature as an institutionalist. It also gave me the incentive and the necessity of getting to know the people in the House Parliamentarian's office. I established an excellent working relationship with each of them, which was incredibly helpful throughout my service in the House. I became friendly with Pete Robinson and Charlie Johnson. I always knew that if I was in a jam, I could call them, and they would help me. I told Charlie later I felt I had gone to the "University of Charlie Johnson" to get my degree in parliamentary procedure.

One of the reasons I was able to get through quickly was because the clerk in the office, Muftiah McCartin, and I became good friends. Muftiah had an exceptional ear for voices and always knew it was me. She was constantly ready with whatever information I needed or was able to get me to one of the Parliamentarians if I was in the middle of a markup and needed help urgently.

I made it a point to become a mentor for her. She was the first young person I knew who I felt comfortable enough with to offer advice and encouragement. I also learned from her, and I truly believe our relationship enabled me to become better at it for others later on. Muftiah taught me that offering meaningful, constructive criticism was part of being a good mentor. There were a few occasions when I was reluctant to say something to her, which could have been perceived negatively, but she always encouraged me to tell her exactly what I thought, and I knew both of us would live through it.

I am glad I was the one who urged her to go to law school and wrote her a recommendation for admission. We would often discuss issues she was studying. Strange as it may seem, to this day, I recall discussing the difference between intention and motive. She is now the chair of a practice group in the prestigious Washington law firm, Covington and Burling.

On the committee staff I had four different areas of responsibility; I was to handle certain legislation that was retained at the full committee level, act as the Committee Parliamentarian, prepare everything for full committee meetings including motions, bills and parliamentary rulings and also to help Joe stay out of trouble. One of the historical anomalies of the way the committee was set-up for full committee meetings was where the General Counsel sat. For years, the policy was to have counsel sit at the witness table during markups. The purpose of this was so he would be able to respond to questions from the Members about the bills, especially legal questions. There was a microphone at that table so that the counsel could respond on the record, and everyone could hear. That was when all of the Members of the committee were lawyers, and when Members were sufficiently comfortable with asking questions of staff during a meeting. Those days had long gone by the time I got there. No Member in the age of television would yield to mere staff on the record. If a Member had a question, it would be asked via the Member's personal staff, or directly to committee staff, but off the record. This was good news for me because that meant that neither Joe nor Alan felt compelled to sit up on the dais near the Chairman. I sat there on a small stool behind him, where I could prompt him. It was cramped enough with only me there.

One of the most important things I did in preparation for full committee meetings was to call the legislative staffer for each Democrat on the committee and say, "It's proxy time". At the time, proxies were permitted by the rules. I would usually have a proxy from every Democrat. When there was a roll call vote, and the name of an absent Member was called, I would say "proxy", and the Chairman would vote for the absent Member. Occasionally, a Member's staff would tell me how to vote the proxy on a particular amendment or on final passage of a bill. I would write the directions on the proxy. I made sure they were followed by Mr. Rodino. There were a couple of occasions where the Chairman wanted to vote the proxy contrary to a Member's specific instructions. I had to tell him that if he did not abide by a Member's wishes, I would never get another proxy.

During full committee meetings, the Members' personal staffs would sit at a table reserved for them. During a roll call, if I was unsure of how a particular Member wanted their proxy vote cast, I would make eye contact with the relevant staffer and look for a signal. It got to the point sometimes when I would get a thumbs up for an "aye" or thumbs down for a "no." That was easy. The hard part was when I looked over and got no signal either way or a shrug of the shoulders because the staffer did not know. In those cases, I would tell the chairman not to vote the proxy.

Taking advantage of the rules which permitted proxies led to a lot of roll call votes being controlled by Mr. Rodino. His predecessor, Manny Cellar, the longest-serving Chairman of the Committee, would welcome each new Member with a demand they sign a general proxy for all matters for the duration of the Congress. The rules no longer permitted that. However, it was permissible to get a general proxy limited to procedural matters only, which was good for the entire Congress. Every two years at the beginning of a new Congress, I made sure I had one of those for every Member, just in case. I only had to use them once, but because I had them, we were able to defeat a procedural motion when we did not have the votes in the room. Alan Parker was impressed by my prescient thinking. I was rather proud of it myself. I continued to get those general proxies every Congress until the rules changed prohibiting the use of proxies.

During roll call votes, before the wide-spread use of blackberries and cell phones, sometimes Members who were not present would get phone calls from their staffs who were in the committee room to alert them of an upcoming vote. Members hate to miss any recorded votes in the Committee or in the House. If they are in town, they need to be recorded. They do not like to give their opponent in the next election ammunition about "absenteeism". Often when a vote was being called, and I knew there were Members absent from the committee room but who were on the Hill, I would signal the clerk who sat at the witness table facing the dais to call the roll slowly to give Members time to get there. Frequently, when a message came through that a Member was on the way before the vote was announced by the clerk, someone who had already voted would inquire of the Chairman, "How am I recorded?" The clerk would then report that Member's vote. This was done by several Members to stall for time. As soon as I saw a straggler arrive, I would prompt the Chairman to call his or her name, that being their clue it was time for them to vote. Occasionally, a breathless Member would run into the room and look to the senior Member on their side of the aisle for a signal about how to vote.

One thing I found offensive was the superiority complex which many lawyers have because they went to law school, and it was frequently evident in meetings with people from outside. I was sitting in on a meeting with the General Counsel and two lobbyists, one of whom was a lawyer and one of whom was not but had been working in the field for more than 20 years. The first time the non-lawyer subject-matter expert opened his mouth, the General Counsel asked him, "Are you a lawyer?" I thought this was rude and arrogant. When he said no, it was clear she had dismissed him as irrelevant. It was so obvious and so obnoxious. I do not think she made eye contact with him for the rest of the meeting. I considered apologizing to him on her behalf, but I thought it might get back to her.

✦✦✦✦✦✦✦✦✦

A lesson I learned was that getting someone to do what you want, or, in current terminology, "getting to 'yes'", is an important skill in any profession. I usually volunteer to do the first draft of any document. That puts the power of inertia in your hands. It provided the chance to get my thoughts into the foundational document. People would always have their modifications or "improvements" to add, but having my words be the fundamental basis of the conversation was, I thought, an advantage. Many times, ideas which might have generated controversy were ignored to get to other concepts. It meant more work for me, but it enhanced my ability to achieve my goals. I felt it was a good practice.

✦✦✦✦✦✦✦✦✦

The Department of Justice (DOJ) Authorization Act was an important bill for which I had the main responsibility. It was extremely detailed because it included language allocating funding for all of the functions of the Department. I worked with Alan in his capacity as the Assistant AG for Legislative Affairs, so we got to know each other even better.

There were also some hot-button issues relating to prisons, message switching (at the time a new area dealing with electronic surveillance) as well as funding levels for various parts of the Department. While the bill was being considered in the committee, each of the five subcommittees had input within their subject matter jurisdictions. We took each subcommittee's recommendations and incorporated them into a new text, which we would use for the full committee markup.

We then had a full committee hearing on the bill. The witness was going to be Ed Meese, Reagan's Attorney General. Meese came up to say hello to the Chairman and then went to the witness table to testify. One of the Members came up and asked the Chairman if he were going to "put him under oath". The Chairman was not comfortable with asking Meese to be sworn in, but he did not want to treat the Republican Attorney General too gently. He asked if I had the language of the oath, and I did. He told me to inform Mr. Meese about the oath. I was uneasy delivering the news to the Attorney General of the United States that he was going to have to swear to tell the truth, but I was just the messenger. I was expecting some reluctance or irritation, but Meese was not in the least bit concerned and said, "Thank you". It all went as smooth as glass and nobody said anything about it. I had gotten agitated for no reason.

The DOJ bill was favorably reported by the committee with no substantial problems. The staff prepared the report, which I filed. We requested a rule for the consideration of the bill in the House from the Rules Committee, and the Chairman testified before that committee in support. They gave us an open rule, which meant any germane amendments were in order. We spent a couple of days on the floor considering amendments before the House passed the bill. The Senate passed its version, and we went through the parliamentary hoops of formally disagreeing with the Senate amendment (the Senate's version of the bill) and requesting a conference between the two houses to resolve the differences.

Because there were so many individual issues and potentially so many areas for mixed signals and people working at cross-purposes, I was designated to be the point of contact between the two houses. There were some issues that Mr. Rodino was interested in, and there were others that either a subcommittee chair or individual Members were concerned about. I had to juggle all of those inputs from the majority as well as work with the minority to figure out those places where we had an agreed-upon House position and those places where we had a difference between House Republicans and Democrats. We then had to reconcile those with what the Senate Democrats and Republicans wanted.

Usually, before going to conference, we would ask the Legislative Counsel's Office to prepare what was known as a side-by-side. This was a large folio type document which included the listing of the provisions in the House bill, the comparable provisions in the Senate bill, and as negotiations developed, notations of what the conferees' staffs had worked out. These notes would include comments such as "Senate recedes" meaning the House provision would be in the final document, "House recedes with an amendment" which would represent an agreed-upon compromise on a provision, "House majority/minority disagree," and "House majority/minority agree," and so on. This document was updated regularly as negotiations proceeded. We needed to have a listing of all of the items which were in disagreement between the two houses, which ones we at the staff level felt we had resolved, and which ones we needed to have direct Member input.

When we finally got to a formal meeting of the conferees, we had narrowed the issues down to 44 items. Mr. Rodino was the Chairman of the conference committee because it was the House's turn (the Senate Judiciary Committee Chairman, Ted Kennedy, had been the Chairman of the last conference). He opened up the conference by saying, "Counsel will now take us to the items". I was a little intimidated since there were several Senators there as well as many Members of the House, and I was running the show! Joe was clueless about both the conference process and about the substance of the bill.

I had established a good working relationship with both my House minority counterpart and with the Senate staff on both sides of the aisle. Out of the 44 items, I was able to inform the conferees which ones the House had a unified position on, which ones both the House and the Senate had agreement on, and which ones the staff had reserved as "Member items". I went down the list one-by-one starting with those where we had agreement on all issues. I needed to describe the agreement and have the Members concur. With each one, I asked for the verbal concurrence of the Senators and House Members. I then went to those where the House staff had a joint position, and the Senate staff had a different joint position. One staffer from the House (usually me) and one staffer from the Senate would explain the issue and what the differences were between the two houses' positions on that issue. It was up to the Members to come up with a final resolution. After that, I went to the "Member items", which was where the most controversial matters were discussed. Those discussions involved Members, and the staff was there merely to advise them.

This is also the place where a conferee might want to add some language about an issue which had not been the subject of discussion during the conference. In that case, if I knew about it, I would tell the Chairman to recognize the Member to describe the legislative history he wanted to be included in the Joint Statement. I did not want any Member or staffer trying to slip something inaccurate or inappropriate into the document.

We finally got agreement on all 44 issues, and the conference committee adjourned. That was the easy part. The next job was to prepare the final papers. These consisted of two sets of documents (a set for each house); the final agreed-upon legislative language on every issue, which is formally called the Conference Report, and the Joint Explanatory Statement of the Managers. Drafting the legislative language was usually not that difficult. I had made sure we had someone from House Legislative Counsel present to ensure he understood what the Members had agreed to. The more difficult document was the Joint Statement, which is what normal people would refer to as report language. The format of the Joint Statement is, 1) a recitation of what the House bill said on every issue, 2) what the Senate bill said on every issue, and 3) an explanation of what the conferees had agreed to on each one. When the Senate or the House had accepted the other body's language, there was no problem.

When the Conferees had agreed on something that was in neither the House or Senate versions of the bill and had reached a middle ground position, the statement had to explain what the compromise was and why they had chosen it. This was where there were some differences in various staff 's recollection of what the conferees had agreed to. There were a couple of these disputes, but we were able to reach agreement on the entire Joint Statement fairly quickly.

I was pleased with my efforts, and the Chairman complimented me on my "first-rate work" and the smoothly run conference committee. Just as important, for future reference, was the compliment I got from Jack Brooks, who at the time was the Chairman of the House Government Operations Committee. He thought I had done an outstanding job in preparing the briefing book for the House conferees. He even called me up to his office to show it to Bill Jones, who was the General Counsel of the Gov Ops Committee. I knew Bill, and I was pleased to have Chairman Brooks brag on me a bit. Unbeknownst to any of us at the time, Bill would one day become my boss when Mr. Brooks became the Chairman of the Judiciary Committee.

✦✦✦✦✦✦✦✦✦

The other major bill which I had primary responsibility for was the unitary tax bill. You would think a tax bill would have been referred to the Ways and Means Committee, but for some reason, in an agreement reached many years previously, it came to the Judiciary Committee. Taxes are not an area that I was particularly interested in, but the unitary tax, which dealt with the question of taxation of overseas income, was intriguing. After I was designated to handle it, I noticed that I started receiving a lot of phone calls from interest groups. Ordinarily, I would not have to deal with them, and I did not feel getting these calls was a good thing.

Working on this bill, which could have an enormous financial impact on a company, is where I learned the lesson of "follow the money". Since every corporation which had any operations overseas was interested in any changes to the taxation of their income and because most of them had people working for them in Washington, I suddenly became popular. I received a lot of invitations to lunches, which I always refused. I did this for several reasons. First, I usually did not have an hour and a half to spend with them. Second, although many of my colleagues enjoyed going out to fancy restaurants where the lobbyists would pick up the check, I did not. I thought it would be a much more efficient use of my time to have people coming to see me in the office and get down to business rather than squandering it other a long lunch "establishing a relationship". I know many Washington reps who felt pressure from their bosses to have lunch with senior Congressional staff as often as possible.

One day, I received a phone call from someone with whom I had spoken a couple of times previously about the unitary tax issue. He was pleasant and knowledgeable, and I was willing to listen and learn from him. On this day, however, my view changed. He invited me to spend the weekend with him and his partner in the lobbying firm duck hunting on the Eastern Shore. I was utterly appalled. This was straight out of the classic picture of big money lobbyists; duck hunting with lots of expensive food and, I expect, expensive booze. This was probably business as usual for them. I begged off saying I had plans, and from that day forward, I kept him at a distance.

I was never comfortable dealing with government affairs representatives. There were times, however, when bringing in a subject matter expert could be instructive. Since some of the areas we were dealing with were outside of my experience, such as copyrights and bankruptcy, I welcomed the chance to sit in on meetings where I could learn, still being fully aware that I was getting an advocate's point of view. The good ones, who knew their stuff, were always willing to concede points that were not in their favor and were reliable and willing to get back to you if you needed more information. One head of the Washington office told me his rule of thumb was for every five minutes he spent with a Member, he would try to spend an hour with the staff educating them. He felt most Members had the "attention span of a flea". If the Member knew the staff had been fully briefed, he felt confident their message would be conveyed appropriately. He also knew the staff could always get to him if the Member needed more information.

A lobbyist I knew would regularly come in to say hello and "touch base" with me. I was astounded by how much she knew about the personal lives of some of the people on our staff. I think she soon recognized that I was not interested in establishing a friendship with her or hearing gossip. One of the people with whom she became friendly was an attorney who worked on the Intellectual Property Subcommittee. This attorney came by my office one afternoon to discuss an issue and mentioned the lobbyist. She started telling me how close they had become. I cautioned her about how fleeting those relationships are because once you leave the committee, they will drop you like a hot potato. She disagreed because they had become such good friends. I bumped into her a couple of years later, after she had left the committee. I asked her about her "good friend", and she sheepishly confessed to me that I had been correct. They had had practically zero contact since she had moved on.

✦✦✦✦✦✦✦✦

Jack Brooks was the next most senior Democrat on the committee. On many occasions, Mr. Rodino would be unavailable to handle some piece of committee business, such as testifying before the Rules Committee or managing a bill on the floor. I would be deputized to find out if Mr. Brooks was free and willing to step in, and if so, to go up and brief him. Rodino would not call Brooks; he would have someone inform me of the need to get Brooks to do whatever it was. I would then call his Chief of Staff, Sharon Matts, explain it to her, and see if Mr. Brooks was available. Mr. Brooks was a formidable, tough character, and he could be extremely intimidating.

An example of his pinch-hitting for Mr. Rodino happened when I asked him to testify before the Rules Committee on a rule for the Department of Justice Authorization bill. I had prepared a statement for him covering all of the essential points in the bill, as well as the specifics of the rule we were requesting. I had informed the Rules Committee staff about what kind of rule we wanted, and that Mr. Brooks would be testifying in place of Mr. Rodino. Among other things, I included in the statement was a request for funding for the INS. As Brooks was reading the statement, he looked up at me and said in his best Texas drawl, "What's INS?" Although immigration was a significant issue before the committee, it was not something that Mr. Brooks was involved with, so it made sense that he simply did not know the letters INS stood for the Immigration and Naturalization Service. People who are immersed in an issue frequently are not aware that some of the jargon/and or acronyms are like a foreign language to people who are not in that particular loop. I was relieved everything went well at the Rules Committee.

I managed to establish a good relationship with Mr. Brooks. I thought that since I was going to have to work with him regularly, I should get to know him. I was up in his office one day, meeting with him and Sharon Matts. She had been with him for years and was a joy to work with, and she would often sit in on our meetings. I felt comfortable calling her whenever I needed something for Mr. Rodino. After we had completed our business and were sitting around chatting, Mr. Brooks and Sharon were talking about the local prosecutor in Beaumont, Texas, a small city in his district. He suggested buying this man a new suit. I made eye contact with Sharon. I think she knew I felt this was a terrible idea. Mr. Brooks noticed it and looked at me. I took the bull by the horns and said, "Mr. Chairman, I do not think that is a good idea". "Why not?". I said this prosecutor might someday have to make a decision about prosecuting him or someone linked to him. Having given him a gift might not look good if it became public. He looked at Sharon and said, "Do you agree?" She did, and he asked why. Her response was, "What Dan said". That enhanced my credibility with Brooks. I think he respected someone who was not afraid to say they thought he was wrong.

Later, when Alan Parker's successor was the General Counsel, I got up the courage to ask Mr. Brooks for a favor. I was being considered for a position with the Senate Judiciary Committee under Senator Kennedy. I stuck my neck out and asked Mr. Brooks to call Kennedy on my behalf. He was well aware of the difficulties in working under the new General Counsel. Notwithstanding the feeling of anxiety in approaching him, it was worth it because he agreed to do so.

A couple of weeks later, I received a call from the Senate staff saying Senator Kennedy had decided to "go in another direction", and I was not going to get the job. I was disappointed, but I wanted to cover my bases with Mr. Brooks, so I called Sharon immediately to get in to see Mr. Brooks to inform him of Senator Kennedy's decision. I went up to thank him even though his efforts were not successful. I was concerned he might be upset his recommendation was not sufficient to land me the job. Also, I wanted him to hear about it from me and not from someone else. Much to my surprise, Kennedy had already called him and told him they had decided it would be best to hire a woman. Brooks told me that and said, "I don't think you want to have that sex change operation just for a goddamn job". I smiled. He then said, "Don't worry, son, we will get you out from under that (expletive deleted)". [A reference to Alan's replacement. He was not a fan.] When he was about to become Judiciary Committee Chairman after Mr. Rodino's retirement, I was told a lobbyist asked him if he was going to keep her on. His response was, "Let me see, a nanosecond is shorter than a millisecond, right?"

✦✦✦✦✦✦✦✦✦

One of the finest men I have ever met is Congressman Norman Mineta. Norm was to be the third remarkable mentor in my life. Born in the United States, Norm is of Japanese ancestry. Unlike many Members, Norm treats everyone with kindness and respect. There is no differentiation between Members and "mere staff". He believes that the American people do not understand the bargain they receive from the high caliber professional staff on the Hill. He was aware that staff works long hours for less money than they could get in the private sector. He is an extremely warm and thoughtful person.

In the aftermath of Pearl Harbor in 1941, signs went up in Southern California, directing all persons of Japanese ancestry, "aliens", and "non-aliens" to report to train depots to be shipped off to detention centers in Wyoming. As a ten-year-old boy, when Norm arrived at the assembly point with his family, he was wearing a Cub Scout uniform and had a bat, glove, and baseball with him. The Marines took the bat away from him because it might have been used as a weapon.

Many years later, this former internee who had been elected Mayor of San

Jose, California, and then became a Member of Congress, was an original sponsor of a bill which, when finally enacted, was called the Civil Liberties Act of 1988. The law contained a formal apology by the American government to those Japanese American internees and provided each one $20,000 in compensation. The bill was referred to the House Judiciary Committee, and I had the good fortune to be able to work on it with Norm.

One of my many tasks was to introduce legislation. There is a wooden box at the rostrum in the House where bills are "dropped in", and committee reports are filed. On many occasions, when I was introducing legislation, the staffer or the Member would ask me to "get a good number". My response to that request usually was, "If the lobbyists cannot memorize a four-digit number, they do not deserve all that money".

The apology bill had been introduced in previous Congresses, but it looked like there would be enough votes to pass it in the 100th Congress. Tom Foley, who was the Majority Leader, was the original sponsor. That was an indication of how important the Leadership felt it was. The bill had 123 original cosponsors, and by the time it passed the House, it had 166. Norm wanted a specific number for the bill, H.R. 442. He had a reason for wanting that number. During World War II, there was an army unit made up entirely of Japanese Americans. They fought valiantly in Italy and other places in Europe. It was the most decorated brigade in American military history. It was the 442nd brigade, and Norm thought it would be a meaningful symbolic gesture to have the bill memorialize that.

On January 6, 1987, I went to the floor with Norm to make sure he got that number. I had alerted the Parliamentarians to the situation, and they let me know exactly when we needed to go to the floor to formally introduce the bill. He did not need me to assist him in doing this, but he kindly asked if I wanted to go with him. I, of course, said I did. It was going to be a significant moment in history. We went to the floor, and at the appropriate time, we handed the bill to the Parliamentarian on duty and were given the next number available; H.R. 442.

The bill was ordered "favorably reported" by the Judiciary Committee in August. I had the honor and pleasure of being on the floor when it was considered in September. Speaker Jim Wright, fully aware of the symbolism involved, asked Norm Mineta to preside over the House during its consideration. It was a very powerful symbol to have this former internee in the Speaker's chair.

It was the most moving debate I had ever seen in the House. When Norm Mineta came down from the rostrum and took the floor, you could have heard a pin drop:

"To me, this is a very, very emotional day, in sharp contrast to May 29, 1942, when, as a 10-year-old boy wearing a Cub Scout uniform, I was herded onto a train under armed guard in San Jose, CA, to leave for Santa Anita, a race track in southern California. And here, on the 17th of September 1987, we are celebrating the 200th anniversary of the signing of that great document, the Constitution of our great land. It is only in this kind of a country, where a 10-year-old can go from being in a Cub Scout uniform on an armed-guarded train to be a Member of the House of Representatives of the greatest country in the world".

Most of us thought that was the emotional end of the debate. Norm would be the final speaker, and then there would be a vote. It was getting late in the day, and there was a lot of restlessness in the Chamber. Many people felt there had been enough debate on the bill. Members were anxious to have the last vote of the day and get on to other things. There were some *sotto voce* cries of "vote, vote". Despite those pleas, Congressman Ron Dellums, a tall, commanding African American Member from Oakland California, sought recognition to speak.

"Mr. Chairman, I appreciate the pleas to go home, but we are here to do business, and this gentleman does not speak on the floor every day on every issue, and there are few issues… that are compelling enough that one must speak … There comes a moment when one has to speak, to tell his or her own story vis-a-vis the proposition that is before the body.

My home was in the middle of the block on Wood Street in West Oakland. On the corner was a small grocery store owned by Japanese people. My best friend was Roland, a young Japanese child, the same age. I would never forget, Mr. Chairman, never forget, because the moment is burned indelibly upon this child's memory, six years of age, the day the trucks came to pick up my friend. I would never forget the vision of fear in the eyes of Roland, my friend, and the pain of leaving home.

My mother, as bright as she was, try as she may, could not explain to me why my friend was being taken away, as he screamed not to go, and this 6-year-old black American child screamed back, "Don't take my friend."

It is about how much pain was inflicted upon thousands of American people who happened to be yellow in terms of skin color; Japanese in terms of ancestry, but this black American cries out as loudly as my Asian-American brothers and sisters on this issue.

Vote for this bill…and let Roland feel that you understood the pain in his eyes and the sorrow in his heart as he rode away screaming, not knowing when and if he would ever return".

There was stunned silence. The power and eloquence of Ron Dellums was something I will always remember.

Norm and I had established a warm personal bond. I was able to get his advice and counsel regularly since I always knew I could find him on the House floor during votes. All through the difficulties with Alan's successor, Norm was always willing to listen, give advice, and on several occasions, make phone calls on my behalf. I cherish his friendship and am proud to call him my friend.

✦ ✦ ✦ ✦ ✦ ✦ ✦ ✦ ✦

The most difficult legislative battle I ever participated in was about, of all things, bankruptcy judgeships. This is not a topic which I was inherently interested in, but Alan Parker was. Because Alan was, Mr. Rodino was. It was a simple issue that ended up spiraling into a huge endeavor. The question was whether bankruptcy judges were to get the same constitutional protections as other Federal Judges, who were Article III judges, such as life tenure. At the time, bankruptcy judges, referred to as Article I judges, were appointed for a term of 15 years. The tension between the two types of judges came to a head as a result of a Supreme Court decision relating to the powers of bankruptcy judges. The decision overruled an important labor law provision, and the unions were very unhappy. Mr. Rodino came from Newark, a very pro-union city. He was getting a lot of pressure to legislatively reverse the Supreme Court's decision with what was referred to as the "labor law fix".

This rather straightforward dispute became extremely heated and ended up involving a lot of extraneous matters, which were highly significant, including the creation of a large number of Article III judgeships, which could be appointed by a Republican President, Ronald Reagan. At the time, the Democrats controlled the House, and the Senate was in Republican hands. Alan was intent on getting Article III status for the bankruptcy judges, but the Article III judges were adamantly opposed.

The House bill, as ordered reported by the Judiciary Committee, was modified by the Rules Committee to strip out the most important provision, as far as Alan and the Chairman were concerned, the Article III status for the bankruptcy judges. It left the bill as a shadow of its former self. The Senate bill contained a lot of inconsequential matters which did not trouble the Chairman or Alan. However, it did contain the creation of a large number of new Article III judgeships. These were full-fledged life-tenured Federal judgeships that would be filled by the Republicans. The Chairman and Alan were vehemently against that.

We ended up agreeing to go to conference on the two different versions of the bill passed by the House and the Senate. That may not have been such a good idea. There was a strong push by labor to get the labor law fix enacted as soon as possible. We went into the staff conference before a formal meeting of the conferees with a clear mandate about what we could and could not agree to. The first of these was classic Alan Parker. Counsel for the Senate Judiciary Committee started off her opening salvo with, "Alan, can we talk about judgeships". Alan put on an Academy award-worthy performance of refusing to do so, and then when the Senate staffer insisted, he slammed his materials closed, got up, and walked out. A little stunned, I gathered my materials and followed him out the door.

We reconvened the next day and did not make much progress. At the staff level, we were not going to be able to work out a compromise on either of the two main issues; the labor law fix and the creation of a large number of new Federal judgeships. They were going to be "Member items". There was nothing complicated about them. We either were going to do the labor fix or not, and we were either going to add a whole slew of new Federal judgeships or not.

We were on the floor doing something else when we got word that the Senate had agreed to a formal meeting of the conferees. It was to begin in less than an hour. Fortunately, I had all my materials with me, and I scampered over to the room on the Senate side of the Capitol, where we were going to be meeting. It had always been my practice to check out the room ahead of time. When I got to the Mansfield room, which I knew was going to be packed with lobbyists, I wanted to make sure that the House Members would be facing outwards, with the Senators having their backs to the audience. If nothing else, that would serve to minimize the amount of outside interference that our House conferees would get from people in the audience. Alan came over to the room with Chairman Rodino. When he saw how I had set up the room, he said, "Good staff work Dan." He understood the nuance. I observed later that I had put our backs up against the wall. That turned out to be applicable in both senses of the words. Rodino was being pushed hard by organized labor to do the labor law fix. Whatever the price he needed to pay for that by caving in to the Senate on other matters, that was OK with labor. It was simple; judgeships in exchange for the labor law fix.

Senator Strom Thurmond was the Chairman of the Senate Judiciary Committee. He had a very short attention span and did not want to fool around with "all these trivial issues" which he felt the staff had already worked out. He said, "There is no reason to spend a lot of time going over this. It has all been worked out". As far as Thurmond was concerned, all of the judgeships had been agreed to, and he was willing to accept the labor law fix that the unions wanted in exchange for them. Alan was beside himself. During a short break, he pulled the Chairman aside and told him that the labor law fix was not worth all of these Republican-appointed Federal judges.

In the room was the labor union's top representative. All he was interested in was making sure the labor law fix became law. When the Chairman asked him whether it was worth giving the Republicans the ability to appoint a large number of conservative Federal judges, he did an impressive dying Cassandra move putting his hand to his forehead and solemnly shaking his head, "Yes, Mr.

Chairman, we think you have to do it." That was it. It was over.

Alan was apoplectic, and we walked back to our offices in the Rayburn Building without saying much. The Members of the conference committee had agreed on the broad outlines of the compromise; that job was finished. The next thing that had to be done was the preparation of the final version of the text of the legislation. The all-important Joint Explanatory Statement of Managers also had to be drafted and agreed to everyone's satisfaction.

The Chairman knew Alan was upset, but he still called to tell him to get to work on the Joint Statement language. Alan threatened not to do it. It was extremely tense for a while. After he cooled down a bit, he got down to writing. I was in charge of preparing all of the other paperwork.

I assembled everything, including the required signature sheets, which, as usual, was a pain. I was responsible for tracking down all of the Members who wanted to sign the conference report and get their original signatures. Many Members did not attend the meeting of the conferees, so I had to find them wherever they were in the Capitol complex. You need to have a majority of the conferees sign to complete the report. I managed to get all of the necessary signatures, and once all of the legislative language and the Joint Statement language were done, we went to the floor to formally file. This has to be done on the floor by a conferee. That meant getting the Chairman to the floor when there was a window during legislative business for him to be recognized to do it. It was a logistical challenge, but I managed to pull it off.

The legislative ping-pong that is required on a major bill includes making sure the official papers are transmitted back and forth between the House and the Senate. A clerk from the House or the Senate, after having been formally directed by their respective body to do so, enters the other Chamber and is recognized by the presiding officer to deliver a message. The clerk then intones, "Mr. Speaker (or Mr. President). I am directed by the House (or Senate) to deliver a message in writing".

There is no requirement about which house has to go first in consideration of a conference report. There are political considerations which sometimes supersede the normal procedure. Once you have decided which house should go first, the staff from that house takes possession of the official papers. The staffer in charge has to make sure the official papers are either at the Senate desk or the House rostrum. The protocol is that the house which is in possession of the official papers surrenders them to the other house at the conclusion of the conference committee meeting. In this case, when the conferees met, it was not clear which house would go first. The Senate staff had the official papers, and I had neglected to retrieve them before the day we were supposed to go to the floor because of that uncertainty.

Under the House rules, there is one hour of debate time allotted for the consideration of a conference report. Using the script I had drafted, the Chairman was recognized to call it up. We had just begun, when suddenly I realized I did not have the official papers. I went up to the rostrum to talk to my friend Pete Robinson, who was the Parliamentarian on duty, and asked if he had them. He did not, and we looked at each other and said, "Whoops". Normally the clerk at the rostrum would have to have the papers in order to report what legislation was being considered. Somehow that "minor" matter did not come up. I told Pete I would be right back. I ran to the cloakroom to call the Senate staff to get them to me ASAP. In the main rotunda of the Capitol Building, there is a small piece of white marble, which is literally the center of the Capitol and the center of Washington DC. I arranged for the Senate staffer to meet me at that spot, where I took custody of the papers and ran back to the House. I stopped at the door, caught my breath, and casually sauntered up to Pete and handed them to him. That minor emergency being taken care of, I went back to my seat behind the Chairman. As far as I know, nobody was the wiser, and I learned yet another lesson in Congressional procedure.

✦✦✦✦✦✦✦✦✦

There was one funny thing that occurred during the otherwise bitter fight over the bankruptcy court judgeships. Chairman Rodino was invited to speak about the issue at the American Bar Association national convention to be held in Atlanta in August—Atlanta in August? Not a good idea. For some reason, the Chairman decided not to go, and Alan was the designated substitute to give the Chairman's remarks. The topic was one which Alan felt strongly about, and he was very enthusiastic about going. He invited me to go with him. I was willing to do so. However, at the time I agreed to go, I did not know Alan suffered from aviophobia—fear of flying.

I later learned from Alan about his intense fear of flying when he told me about the last time he had flown several years before, with Congressman Norm Mineta. Norm was used to taking the red-eye flight from his California district back to Washington. Alan knew Norm from his Northern California political roots. Alan's flight with Norm was a complete disaster, to hear Alan tell it. He thought that Norm was going to engage him during the flight and "help me keep the plane in the air". Much to Alan's dismay, Norm proceeded to do what every right-thinking person does on a coast-to-coast red-eye flight; he went to sleep. Alan was horrified and outraged that Norm would do that to him. As far as I know, that was the last time Alan flew, and he never forgave Norm for abandoning him at 30,000 feet.

So, with that background, I was informed Alan and I would be taking the overnight train to Atlanta. Arghh! Instead of a nice 2-hour flight [before TSA], we would endure a 14-hour overnight train trip.

I agreed to go because I had a plan. My father loved going to lawyers' conventions; the American Bar Association meeting was one of his favorites. I knew my mother was going with him and would celebrate her birthday in Atlanta. I told my father to take her to a restaurant called The Abbey for her birthday dinner, and I would make reservations for them. He agreed, not knowing what mischief I had planned.

The Abbey was a gourmet restaurant in a gorgeous old converted monastery where all the waiters wore heavy monk's robes with peaked cowls. There were lots of stained-glass windows around, and the lighting was at a fairly low level. I spoke to the owner and asked him to be a co-conspirator for this birthday event. I told him I wanted to be my parents' waiter. He was a fun-loving person and readily agreed. My mother had just had cataract surgery, so I knew her vision would not be too good in the low light.

There was one possible hiccup in the plan. Since I was attending the ABA meetings with Alan, I had to be on the lookout for my parents. I did not want to inadvertently run into them and spoil the surprise I had planned. I did see them coming out of a meeting room on the second day, and I skedaddled.

When my parents arrived at the restaurant and were seated, I approached them as their waiter in my heavy monk's robe with the cowl pulled over my head. I put on my best southern drawl and said, "Good evenin' folks. Would y'all like to have a drink before dinner?" My father looked up, but I do not think he realized it was me. They declined beverages, and I proceeded still incognito. I explained the specials, and then stopped and looked at my mother and said (continuing my southern drawl), "Well, I unnerstan today's your birthday young lady. Is that a fact?" She perked up and said, "Yes, it is." I paused because I had been told the most important part of telling a joke is timing. I said, "Damn, you look like you are old enough to be my mother!" My father almost laughed, and my mother looked at me like she was trying to decide whether to be offended or amused. I then whipped the cowl off my head and said, "Damn, you **are** my mother!" It took her several moments to come to grips with the fact that I was actually there. We had spoken by phone earlier when I called to wish her a happy birthday, and she "knew" I was in Washington. She could not reconcile that with my presence in front of her.

The owner then came over and informed me that, "Due to your offensive behavior towards one of our guests, you are fired!" So, given my notice, I chose to sit down and have dinner with my parents. It was not until halfway through dinner that my mother finally accepted that I was really there. She kept reaching over and touching my arm just to make sure I was not a figment of her imagination. It was fun.

Members were always full of ideas that they thought were brilliant, which they felt the Chairman should know. They would often say, thinking I was a direct pipeline to Mr. Rodino, "You tell the Chairman…", but I was uncomfortable in delivering such a message. My response usually was, "Believe me; it is more effective if you tell the Chairman yourself". They rarely took that advice.

One particular incident was different. This time the Member did deliver his message directly to the Chairman. One morning before a full committee meeting, I was at my desk, and Mr. Rodino was sitting in one of two guest chairs across from me. In walked Mike Synar, a young and aggressive Member from Oklahoma. He was always bellicose, opinionated, and was not susceptible to being reasoned with. He came in and sat down and started to lecture Mr. Rodino about how to handle a piece of legislation, "Pete, this is what you have to do…". The Chairman just sat there and listened with a wry smile on his face. When Synar left, the Chairman shook his head in disbelief and said, "Can you believe that is how a young whippersnapper talks to the Chairman of the committee?" I chose not to respond.

That was the first time I heard the chairman say something negative about another Member. He told me he held Synar in "minimum high regard". A catchy phrase that said a lot.

The Chairman's wife had been quite sick with brain cancer when I joined the committee staff. I had not met her, and I knew her illness was taking a toll on the Chairman. I was aware they spent a good deal of time with doctors, including a trip to the NIH. The day she died, I was in the Rayburn cafeteria with Jack Brooks. I told him Mrs. Rodino had died, but he already knew. He would be leading the delegation to the funeral in Newark. There was going to be a military aircraft to take Members to attend. Mr. Brooks asked me if I was going. I was a little surprised; the thought had never occurred to me. I told him I did not know Mrs. Rodino and I did not think I would be attending. He said to me, "If *my* boss's wife died, I sure as hell would go to the funeral." This was coming from the man who might someday be my boss.

I hurried up to see the Judiciary Committee's Staff Director, Jim Cline, who was responsible for all official committee travel. I told him what Mr. Brooks had said and asked him if it would be possible for me to go with the official delegation. I was relieved to find out he agreed with Mr. Brooks, and I got to go on my first military flight.

There were a lot of Members on the plane, and I found out seating was determined by seniority, which meant I sat near the back. Up front was Jack Brooks, who was leading the delegation and his special guest, Ben Civiletti, the Attorney General. Mr. Civiletti and Mr. Rodino had been friends through their Italian American connection. While we were airborne, I went up to thank Mr. Brooks for his "suggestion" and to give him credit for allowing me to come on the Congressional plane. He, in his Texas manner, said to the Attorney General, "Ben, you know Dan Freeman, one of our legal eagles..."

✦ ✦ ✦ ✦ ✦ ✦ ✦ ✦ ✦

Pat Schroeder was a pioneer Member of Congress. She was at the forefront of the women's rights movement, and she is a warm and cheerful person. However, I felt there were times when her view of the legislative process verged on the absurd. One morning during a full committee meeting, we were marking up a proposed constitutional amendment calling for a balanced budget. Passage of this proposal would have had dramatic negative impacts on both the federal and state governments and the American people. It was being pushed by fiscal conservatives and had a lot of support among Republicans. Most Democrats were strongly opposed.

During a break in the markup, Schroeder came up to Mr. Rodino and said, "Peter, let's really fix them and pass the worst possible text and send it over to the Senate." Rodino looked at me and said, "What do you think of that, Dan?" I said, "I do not trust the Senate not to do something stupid, by taking it seriously and actually passing it. This is important stuff; after all, we *are* talking about the Constitution here". That was the end of Schroeder's idea.

✦ ✦ ✦ ✦ ✦ ✦ ✦ ✦ ✦

There are lots of interesting things that happen on the House floor. As a mere staffer, you have to be very careful about what you say. I almost put my foot in it one day with a Member who I admire, Steny Hoyer. There was a roll call vote about something dealing with government employees. I was looking at the electronic scoreboard during the vote. The scoreboard keeps a running numerical tally with the bill number, what the vote is about, and the number of Members voting "yea," "nay," or "present." The House also has an electronic scrim up above the Speaker's chair, which shows how each Member has voted; there is a green light for "yea," a red light for "nay" and an orange light for "present." I had not looked at the scrim. The bill was going to pass overwhelmingly, but curiously, there was one Member who was recorded as "present," which was unusual. I assumed some Member had hit the wrong button inadvertently. However, I was *thinking*, "I wonder what knucklehead voted present".

What I *said* was, "I wonder who voted present". Steny was sitting behind me, and he heard me. He said, "I did" and proceeded to explain why. Whew.

On another occasion, Steny demonstrated his knowledge of the legislature. He had been the President of the Maryland Senate before he was elected to Congress. He knew his way around. A roll call vote had been demanded on a simple motion, which was usually agreed to by unanimous consent or a voice vote. The Republicans were upset about something not related to the motion itself, and I did not know what that was. The demand for the roll call vote was a protest about something else. Steny was sitting next to me, and a Member came in and asked him what the vote was about since it was not evident. Steny's response was clear, crisp, and to the point. He said, "This is about who controls the House". I thought that was a good lesson.

Steny was a player in another incident. Late one evening, we were on the floor, killing time waiting until the Majority Leader, Dick Gephardt, came to the floor to announce the schedule for the rest of the day. Members were filling time by giving one-minute speeches about anything and everything to keep the House in session while the Leadership decided how to proceed. In the well of the House, speaking about something (which he obviously considered to be important), was Marty Russo, who is a tough Chicago bully. He is mean, and he did not "play well with others". During his "important" speech, there was a low-level chant of "Gephardt, Gephardt" from people anxious to hear from the Majority Leader about the schedule. No one was listening to Russo. He got very angry, and when he finished, he charged Dennis Eckart, one of the Members who had been chanting. Russo grabbed Eckart by the throat and started to strangle him. I thought he was going to do some serious damage. Fortunately, Steny Hoyer and Barney Frank leaped in and physically restrained Russo. Eckart, looking like a whipped puppy, slithered away to a far corner of the Chamber. That was the closest to a real "floor fight" I ever saw.

✦✦✦✦✦✦✦✦

When we were working on the House floor, one of the staff's jobs was to provide information to Members, especially during roll call votes. Frequently Members would not know a lot about whatever was being voted on. This was especially true in the days when bills were considered under open rules, which permitted any Member to offer any germane amendment to a bill. When roll call votes were being taken by electronic device, often, Members would come up to the manager's table and ask the staff what the vote was about. I had a four-step mantra, which I used to explain the situation which I taught to all of the committee staff. Members would frequently approach me first because they were more likely to know me.

I would go through the steps one-by-one, depending on how much information the Member needed. The idea was to keep things as simple as possible and give the Member only as much information as was necessary to allow them to decide how to vote. Staff working on "their" bill were all too frequently so eager to talk to Members about the bill they had been working on for months, they got carried away. I tried to teach them to keep it simple.

Here is my four-step mantra when talking to Members about a vote:

1. The Chairman is voting yes (or no)—frequently, that is all they need to know.

2. It is Member X's amendment and the Chairman's voting yes (or no)—they usually had been briefed by their staff on the amendment. Using the sponsor's name usually made it clear.

3. It is the Member X's amendment changing the requirements for a visa (or whatever) and the Chairman's voting yes (or no).

4. If the Member needs more information than that, then I would turn them over to the subject matter staff handling the bill.

It was rare that I had to go through all four. Just knowing how the Chairman was voting was usually sufficient. The Members can look up at the electronic voting scrim to check and see how others in their state delegation, political party, or the so-called "litmus test" Members have voted; such as Hyde on right to life issues or Ed Markey on telecommunications questions.

One day when we were on the floor, a staffer for Congressman Bruce Morrison, who was the Chairman of the Immigration Subcommittee, was responsible for the bill. It was an important and somewhat controversial immigration bill, and there was a lot of interest. During the consideration of an amendment that Morrison had offered, there was a demand for a roll call vote. During votes the Members who were managing the legislation would be assigned to "whip the doors", which meant they were to go to the entry doors and inform incoming Members of how they should vote. It was rather silly in some cases because you would have a Democrat and a Republican at each door saying diametrically opposite things as Members walked in. Frequently it would just be "vote aye" or "vote nay", and that would be enough to guide the Members.

The staff would stay at the majority manager's table. During the commotion of a roll call vote, a Member approached the majority table and asked the Morrison staffer, "What is the argument against this amendment?" Much to my dismay, she gushed her answer, which was, "There isn't one. This is Bruce's amendment". Bruce was her hero and could do nothing wrong. I was dismayed and made eye contact with the Member and pulled him aside to answer his question. I then had the unpleasant task of informing the staffer there was *always* an argument against an amendment. Members want to know what their opponents will say about it in the next campaign. They still might vote with you, but they want to know what to expect about the vote. This oozing over the fabulousness of "Bruce's amendment" was not her mission; it was to give Members the information they needed. Making sure Members are not blindsided is an important part of the job.

✦ ✦ ✦ ✦ ✦ ✦ ✦ ✦ ✦

When Jimmy Carter lost the 1980 election to Ronald Regan, Chairman Rodino asked Alan to come back to the Judiciary Committee as General Counsel. Alan inherited me, and Joe was pushed aside and became a "consultant". Although Joe was physically around, he was not involved in any committee work. Getting used to Alan as a boss was easy, although he and Joe did many things differently. Since Joe did not know much about legislation, I always assembled the documents when going to the floor. The first time I had to get ready under Alan's tenure, I did my usual preparations. He was surprised, and I think a little disappointed. He said, "I always used to do that". I simply told him it was another thing he did not have to worry about.

Alan was a wonderful man and a terrific boss, and I thoroughly enjoyed the time I spent working for him. Because we had known each other for a while before he became my boss, we had a good relationship from the beginning. That allowed me to be able to say things candidly, which might not have been appreciated in a different situation.

✦ ✦ ✦ ✦ ✦ ✦ ✦ ✦ ✦

I was assigned to be the point person on a major bill relating to the Legal Services Corporation and several other matters all within the jurisdiction of the Courts Subcommittee, which was chaired by Congressman Bob Kastenmeier. I had gotten to work with him on several matters, including the Harry Claiborne impeachment, the first impeachment in over 50 years. Kastenmeier was a smart, tenacious, and stubborn man who was not always of a cheerful countenance. His staff assistant, who was the one I would call when I wanted to talk to him, would let me know whether it was a good time. She always knew that when he was wearing a particularly unattractive green suit, that meant he was in a bad mood. She used to refer to it as a "green suit day". I always relied on her judgment.

In the consideration of this bill prior to going to conference, most of the legislative work had been done by the subcommittee staff. Still, Mr. Kastenmeier had assigned me to handle all of the negotiations in the conference committee with the Senate. That meant that I was to be in regular contact with the Senate staff as well as our staff. The woman who was handling the matter on the Senate side was often difficult, both in her manner and in my ability to get in touch with her. She was going to law school at night, and she frequently left the office early. I also got the feeling that she was not very senior on the Senate Judiciary Committee staff and did not have a close working relationship with her Chairman, Senator Ted Kennedy.

At one point during the negotiations, one of our subcommittee staffers, who was a Nervous Nelly, was in my office discussing one of the issues in the conference. I had been instructed by Alan Parker, who was the General Counsel and my direct boss, not to discuss the negotiations with anyone outside the conferees. He told me there were a lot of outside folks who wanted to be perceived as "players", but that if anybody asked me what was happening with any particular item, I was to respond, "It is in conference". That meant, "I am not talking to you about it". I received a call from a lawyer for one of these good-government groups who considered herself to be an important actor on this bill. She asked me about the state of the negotiations on the issue of importance to her organization. She said she needed to know so she could "weigh in." As instructed, I said, "The bill is in conference". She persisted and wanted to know exactly what was being discussed by whom and who was supporting what. I repeated, "The bill is in conference". She was flabbergasted and said she had never been treated this way in all of her years working the Hill. I said, "My boss told me not to discuss it with anyone, and that is what I am going to do. The bill is in conference".

She immediately called Nervous Nelly, who was upset that her friend from one of the groups did not seem to be able to get any information from me about the state of the negotiations. I think Nelly was also frustrated that she did not know the status either. She scurried back to my office, complaining to me about it when my phone rang, and it was Chairman Kastenmeier. She immediately picked up the extension phone and blurted out, "I am here too, Congressman". Kastenmeier took the opening, without any prompting, to tell me how glad he was that I was handling the negotiations. I think he had talked to Alan Parker about Alan's desire to keep the negotiations closely held. The phone call was short, and I expect it was because Nelly was on the call. She got no relief from her frustration during the call.

Several days later, I was walking with Chairman Rodino through the Capitol, when we bumped into Senator Kennedy in the rotunda. Kennedy wanted to talk to Chairman Rodino about one of the issues in the bill. There were just the three of us standing there talking as the tourists flooded by. Kennedy kept looking at me and talking directly to me. He knew I was handling the bill for the House, and that I was familiar with the issue. I kept shifting my eyes to try to get him to speak to Mr. Rodino, but he continued to talk directly to me. Rodino listened. Kennedy then pointedly asked the Chairman whether he could agree to his proposal. Rodino asked me whether we could do what Kennedy wanted. "If that is the result you want, Mr. Chairman, I can make it happen". Rodino said, "OK, Ted, consider it done". Although we reached an agreement on that one issue, I was uncomfortable about the dynamics among us, with Kennedy's speaking mostly to me. I do not think Rodino or Kennedy noticed, which was a good thing.

Later that afternoon, I got a call from Kennedy's staffer, and I told her what I had been instructed to do by my Chairman. She emphatically said, "Senator Kennedy will *never* agree to that". I told her it was exactly what Senator Kennedy had asked Mr. Rodino and me to do not three hours ago. "You talked to Senator Kennedy?" she exclaimed. She had not talked to him in more than a week. I was more current on Kennedy's thinking than she was.

✦✦✦✦✦✦✦✦✦

On Mr. Rodino's birthday one year during the Reagan administration, Alan and the Chairman were in the Chairman's office. They were notified that William French Smith, Reagan's first Attorney General, and Bob McConnell, the Assistant Attorney General for the Office of Legislative Affairs were in the reception area and wanted to see Mr. Rodino. This was a surprise visit, but the Chairman said to ask them to come in. As they walked into the office, the Chairman and Alan both stood up to greet them. Smith and McConnell were there to deliver a birthday cake and to sing "Happy Birthday" to Mr. Rodino. He loved it. From the way Alan described it to me, he was grinning ear to ear.

Mr. Rodino picked up a knife, cut a slice of cake and handed it to the Attorney General, cut another slice and handed it to the Assistant Attorney General, and then cut a slice for himself. That left Alan standing there with no cake, which nobody but Alan seemed to notice.

When Alan got back to our office and told me the story, he was in high dudgeon. He was outraged that the Chairman would leave him standing there as if he did not exist. I said as I rapped my knuckles on his desk, "Alan, we are just furniture around here". He sort of smiled and said, "Boy, you got that right".

✦✦✦✦✦✦✦✦✦

One of the projects I was assigned to work on was getting Mr. Rodino to make an oral history. I understood that several people had tried to do this, but Mr. Rodino never seemed to get along with the interviewer. When Alan asked me to see what I could do about getting him to talk about his life and Watergate, I thought of the Oral History Project, a highly regarded program at Columbia University's School of Journalism. I contacted them, and they were very enthusiastic about the possibility.

One of the significant benefits of working on Capitol Hill was that, during recesses, we could avail ourselves of the opportunities to visit all of the fabulous museums and other cultural resources Washington has to offer. I used to go down to the National Gallery of Art regularly. One day I took my friend Muftiah with me, and we went through the Impressionist exhibit, which is magnificent. One of the other places I used to go regularly was the National Archives. Not only did they have original copies of the Constitution and the Declaration of Independence on display but occasionally exhibited a thirteen-foot-long parchment, which was an original copy of the Articles of Confederation. This was shown only once every decade because the document was so fragile. The Archives also had a terrific speaker series, and I used to take advantage of that as often as possible.

While we were in the middle of trying to get Mr. Rodino to do the oral history project, I had gone to the Archives during lunch. I was supposed to meet with Mr. Rodino at 2 o'clock to talk about it. When I went in to see him, I told him I had just been to the Archives and what a thrill it was for me to see an original copy of the Constitution. I naïvely asked the Chairman how he had reacted the first time he saw our founding document. He sheepishly admitted to me that he had never been. I offered to arrange for him to go, but there never seemed to be a good time. Indicative of the luck we had had with the oral history project, the interviewer the Chairman had approved died of a heart attack at the airport on the way down to Washington. Unfortunately, Mr. Rodino's full oral history was never recorded.

✦✦✦✦✦✦✦✦

Martin Frost was in my sister's law school class. He used to call me occasionally to get campaign contribution information for him from the Clerk of the House. He had been a newspaper reporter and a commentator on a Dallas television station. He was not endowed with a warm personality and was fairly stuffy, to say the least. After he lost in his first run for Congress, he was elected in 1978. I thought he had immediately caught a bad case of "Memberitis," which is a disease that some people get when elected, which makes them feel superior to mere mortals.

During his first term, I would run into him occasionally on the House floor. At one point, he invited me to have lunch. We set a date, and I showed up at his office. We were going to go over to the House restaurant. When I walked into the office, I told the receptionist who I was, and she buzzed in to Martin to tell him I was there. This was back in the day when the hold button used to light up in red, indicated when the boss was on the phone. I saw the light go out, so I knew he was not on the phone, but he kept me waiting. This was a tactic some people use to impress their guests with how busy (and important) they are.

When he finally appeared, he made a big show of introducing "my Congressional staff" to me. He emphasized how diligent he was in keeping up with events in his district. He pointed to the fax machine and told me he had staff in Texas send him everything of importance from newspapers in Dallas. I guess he did not realize I knew *every* Member did that. He then announced, "Mr. Freeman and I are going over to the House restaurant".

As we were walking over to the Capitol, we were talking about the proposed constitutional amendment to ban school busing for desegregation purposes. This was a matter pending before the Judiciary Committee, and it was going to be coming to the House floor soon. It was one of the bills I was working on. Martin proceeded to tell me in his pompous, condescending way, "I have talked to Tip about this…" I was supposed to be impressed by the fact that he had talked to the Speaker. I did not think Tip O'Neill spent a lot of time talking to freshman Members. Martin then told me that he always took it "very seriously" when he came over to the House to vote. Yeah, what else is new?

There was an uncomfortable exchange when we got to the Members Dining Room. Over the years, I went there frequently for lunch and knew the maître'd, John, and most of the waitstaff by name. As we walked up to the entrance, John, who always wore a tuxedo to work, smiled at me, reached out to shake my hand, and said, "Hi, Dan, who is your friend?" Martin was displeased about not being recognized as an important person. I never asked John about it, but I would not be surprised if he did it on purpose just to bring Martin down a peg.

✦✦✦✦✦✦✦✦✦

There was a young Member from Cleveland, Ohio, Ed Feighan, who was interested in trying to do something legislatively regarding handgun control. He was an active Member who was bright and wanted to learn the ropes. The committee's Staff Director, Jim Cline, took an immediate dislike to him because Feighan was the nephew of a former Member who had made Jim's life miserable. I counseled Jim against vicarious liability. I liked the Congressman a lot, and I found him to be eager to get some type of legislation passed to curb the scourge of handgun violence in America's cities.

Feighan was one of the Members who came to Congress with the goal of trying to make a difference. He was always ready to learn and listen, and never tried to be a publicity hog. The House was populated with many show horses, but Ed was a real workhorse. He was a veteran of state and local government and had an excellent understanding of how Federal law affects people on those levels. For me, he was the best kind of Member.

Along with his other credentials, he was always willing to listen to other Members, and even to staff! His attitude was that he was the rookie, and he wanted to soak in as much knowledge as possible from the veterans. He also had a very gentle and warm persona. I enjoyed working with and being around him. We could have used a dozen like him, if not more.

His Judiciary Committee staffer was a young, fresh-faced former Rhodes scholar named George Stephanopoulos. George was inexperienced, but, like his boss, easy to work with. He and I regularly talked about the gun control issue. I put him in touch with Doug Bellis, who was the man in the Office of Legislative Counsel in charge of Title 18 of the U.S. Code, which contains most of the criminal laws. I thought those two should work together to make sure whatever bill he finally came up with was drafted correctly. George was pleased to find out he had access to Doug. I told him what I told my students at American University twenty years later: "Legislative Drafting is the second hardest kind of writing. The hardest is good poetry, and not much of that is done anymore".

Feighan introduced a bill in the House, and a companion bill was introduced in the Senate by Howard Metzenbaum. The "Handgun Violence Prevention Act." The purpose of the bill was to require the chief local law enforcement officer in any jurisdiction to perform a background check on all handgun purchasers and to provide a waiting period before the purchase was completed. George and I talked a lot about what kinds of things would be sufficient grounds to deny the purchaser a gun.

This was something I would revisit with my students at AU. Would a criminal record be sufficient, or would it have to be a criminal record of a violent crime? Would a history of mental illness be grounds for denial? There are a lot of privacy issues involved. Also, we had to consider the length of the waiting period, which would have two functions. First, it would possibly prevent crimes of passion, which included both murders and suicides by providing a "cooling off" period. Second, the waiting period would have to be long enough to allow the local law enforcement official to perform a meaningful background check.

The bill, which became known as the Brady bill (named for Jim Brady, Reagan's press secretary who was seriously wounded when the President was shot), went through many iterations over the almost 2,500 days it took to get it enacted. It finally became public law in November of 1993. George left the Hill to work on the Dukakis campaign in 1988, but he returned after Dukakis lost and went to work for the House Majority Leader, Dick Gephardt. I would see George regularly on the floor until he told me one day in 1991 he was leaving the Hill to "work for Governor Clinton." After Clinton was elected, George became the communications director. I did not see him during those years, except on television. He left the White House in 1996 and took a job with ABC news.

The Supreme Court fascinated me. The committee had legislative jurisdiction over the Court, and that was part of my portfolio of issues. It is near the Rayburn Building, so I went often, and I got to know many of the people there. It helped that I was a member of the Supreme Court bar. They were almost always accommodating to my requests for a seat, even for major cases.

The next time I saw George was on January 13, 1997. I was sitting in the Supreme Court Chamber, waiting for the Justices to come out from behind the velvet curtains at the stroke of ten o'clock, reminiscent of the Wizard of Oz. The Marshalls were filling in the last few empty seats with people who wanted to watch the oral argument in the *Clinton v. Jones* case. We chatted briefly and then listened to the argument.

✦ ✦ ✦ ✦ ✦ ✦ ✦ ✦ ✦

One of the most incredible people I met while working on the Hill was Chuck Schumer. He is a hyperactive, aggressive, indefatigable, and persistent Member from New York City. He is a combination of workhorse and showhorse. The funny line at the time was that the most dangerous place in Washington was between Chuck Schumer and a microphone. I had also heard that there was an unwritten rule when you were in his office, never stand on the small oriental rug in front of his desk. The reason for this was not that the rug was so valuable, but because, back in the day when telephones were connected to the base with a cord, if you were standing behind the rug you not get hit when he threw the handset at you, which I heard he often did.

Although he was very high maintenance and hyperactive at all times, he and I got along well, and he frequently came to me for parliamentary advice. One of the things I taught him early in his service was about the difference between debate that took place in the House and in the Committee of The Whole House on the State of the Union. The Committee of the Whole, as it is called, is the parliamentary sub-group of the House where debate on major bills takes place. Every Member of the House is a member of the Committee of the Whole. When we are in the House, the presiding officer is referred to as "Mr. Speaker", and when we are in the Committee of the Whole, the presiding officer is referred to as "Mr. Chairman".

Chuck asked me one day how you could tell the difference, so he could use the proper term when addressing the chair. I explained that there was an easy visual test. The Mace of the House of Representatives also called the Mace of the Republic, is a ceremonial scepter and one of the oldest symbols of the United States government. It represents the governmental authority of the United States, and more specifically, the legislative authority of the House of

Representatives. It has thirteen ebony rods, representing the original thirteen states of the Union, which are bound together by silver strands, crisscrossed over its length. Atop this shaft is a silver globe upon which sits an intricately cast solid silver eagle. At the beginning of each session of the House, the Sergeant at Arms carries the Mace of the House in front of the Speaker in a procession to the rostrum. When the House is in session, the mace stands on a 3 feet high cylindrical pedestal of green marble to the Speaker's right. When the House is in the Committee of the Whole, the mace is lowered to a position on the floor next to the Parliamentarian's chair, more or less out of sight. I told Chuck, all he had to do before he started speaking was to turn and look at the mace. By noting its position, up or down, he could know whether we were in the House or the Committee of the Whole. From that day forward, whenever Chuck went to the well of the House to speak, he would grab the lectern, and just before starting his remarks, he would turn to look at the Mace, and he would know how to address the presiding officer correctly. I always got a kick out of seeing that.

I had heard there was another unwritten rule in Chuck's office; he had to be on the front page of the New York Times at least once a week. There had been extensive coverage in the Times of a series of raids by the New York City Police Department on "chop shops", which were garages or warehouses where stolen automobiles were disassembled to salvage parts, which could be sold. I learned that the most frequently resold part of a stolen car was the airbag from a Honda. That made sense to me since Hondas were the most popular cars in the country, and I assume that the replacement market for airbags was robust.

Because of all the publicity in New York City, Chuck decided to hold hearings on the "chop shop" problem in the Crime Subcommittee, which he chaired. Vehicle identification numbers (VIN) are required to be placed in the dashboard of every car sold in American. Chuck was going to introduce legislation to require they also to be stamped on *all* major parts of new cars, including the transmission, the engine block, and of course, the airbags. The bill which he had drafted made it the responsibility of the Secretary of Transportation. He came into my office to talk to me about it to make sure Chairman Rodino would refer it to his Crime Subcommittee. After carefully reading it, I told him that Mr. Rodino would not be able to do that because it would not even be referred to the Judiciary Committee, much less to his subcommittee. He exclaimed, "You're crazy". I responded, "I may be, but I'm not wrong". "What the hell are you talking about? This is about crime; of course, it has to come to my subcommittee".

I explained that because the bill mandated the Secretary of Transportation have the duty to ensure the numbers were placed on the parts, the Speaker would refer the bill to the House Transportation Committee and *not* to the Judiciary Committee. The Transportation Committee has jurisdiction over the Department of Transportation and its Secretary. Any bill establishing a new duty for the Secretary of Transportation would go through the other committee.

Chuck was beside himself because he had already prepared a press announcement and was beginning the process of scheduling hearings. He asked me if there was any way to fix this. I told him there was a way to correct the referral problem, but that it was bad drafting and bad policy. He did not seem too concerned about the latter as long as he could have the hearings in his subcommittee. I told him all he had to do was to change the official who was given the new duty from the Secretary of Transportation to the Attorney General. That would cure the referral problem. The Department of Justice and the Attorney General were within the jurisdiction of the Judiciary Committee.

I told Chuck there was another way around the problem. Instead of having a legislative hearing on the bill he had drafted concerning the VINs, he could have an "oversight" hearing about the Justice Department's efforts to combat interstate transportation of stolen property, i.e., the airbags and other "chopped" parts. Since auto theft is mostly a local problem, having the hearing only on the "chop shops" did not have enough of a federal nexus to make it a federal issue. By making the hearing about the interstate commerce in stolen property, it would have the appropriate jurisdictional hook. Chuck was very enamored of his bill, so he said he would think about it.

At the time, I kept a large pitcher in my office, next to the chairs where visitors would sit. I would fill it as needed with snacks. On this day, I had just filled it with yogurt covered raisins. By the time Chuck and I had finished our conversation, I noticed all the raisins were gone. He had scarfed up an entire pitcher full! I made some comment to him about how keeping up with him was difficult, especially when it concerned snack food. To his credit, the next day, someone from his staff showed up with a whole bag of yogurt covered raisins to replenish my supply.

Chuck is an extremely bright man and a hard worker. He throws himself into every issue with boundless enthusiasm. Because of that, he figures he knows more than anybody else about everything and that he should be included in every decision-making event. During the consideration of the Simpson/Mazzoli immigration bill, we had reached the point where we were about to go to conference. The House had passed a bill, and the Senate had passed its version. It was time to try to reconcile the differences between the two bills to see if we could come up with something which would pass both houses. We were on the floor taking up a relatively minor bill. Then, Chairman Rodino and Immigration Subcommittee Chairman Ron Mazzoli were going over to the Senate to meet with Senator Simpson, who chaired the Senate Immigration Subcommittee. Schumer came up to the Chairman and told him, "Mr. Chairman, you should not be meeting with the Senate without me being there. I know that stuff". Now, I expect in Chuck's mind that would apply to every subject matter under the sun. Mr. Rodino somehow decided the meeting could proceed without Chuck.

✦✦✦✦✦✦✦✦✦

Since I have always been a rules-oriented person, it made sense that I became the Parliamentarian. Even as a kid, I was always the go-to guy in football games, baseball games, or anything else when a question about the rules came up. The House rules are published in a thick volume called "Jefferson's Manual and Rules and Practice, House of Representatives". Every Member gets a copy, and every year the Parliamentarians provide certain staffers with leather-bound copies with their name embossed on the front. I got one every Congress when I worked on the Hill, and I am pleased to say, I have received one every new Congress since I left, as a token of appreciation and, I hope, respect.

Most Members do not know much about the rules and do not care about them. It was my job to make sure they were applied correctly, and that the Chairman was prepared to rule appropriately in any parliamentary situation. I was also to understand them well enough to use them to our advantage.

During Watergate, the Chairman had a telephone installed in the committee room next to his chair. The phone did not ring, but there was a light that would blink to signify an incoming call. Charlie Johnson, who was Deputy Parliamentarian of the House at the time, had responded to an inquiry from Dan Cohen, my predecessor as Committee Parliamentarian, about the effect of a motion to table a proposed amendment to the impeachment resolution. The information that was initially given to Dan was incorrect, and Charlie was at home trying frantically to get through to either Dan or Mr. Rodino to correct the error. Contrary to the initial information Dan was given, if a motion to table a proposed amendment was adopted, the entire underlying resolution would also be tabled, thereby killing the entire impeachment resolution. As Charlie tells the story, he was watching the proceedings on television at home. As he was trying to complete the call, he could see the little light blinking on the phone in front of Mr. Rodino, but nobody was answering it. This went on for almost 5 minutes until Dan finally realized the blinking light meant there was an incoming call. Dan answered it and handed it to Mr. Rodino for Charlie to give him the correct answer. This is another one of those backstories about how things accidentally go right or wrong. In this case, Charlie was able to save the day.

Several Members were knowledgeable about the rules, and that was not always such a good thing for me. For example, we were marking up a major crime bill. After the subcommittee had conducted its hearings and completed the amendment process, a new version containing all of the modifications was ordered reported to the full committee. This was the normal process, and I would always include in the Chairman's call-up motion a unanimous consent request that the new version be considered as read and used as the base text for amendments. With that request having been granted, the committee could proceed to use the subcommittee-reported version as the target for any perfecting amendments. The reported text frequently differed dramatically from the introduced version of the bill.

Jim Sensenbrenner was one of the Members who knew the rules well. He was adamantly opposed to the bill and was trying to use the rules to slow down its consideration. When the bill was called up, he objected to the normally pro forma unanimous consent request to waive the reading of the subcommittee product. Under the rules, if the reading was not dispensed with, the whole thing had to be read out loud. It was over 150 pages long. Waving the reading was not subject to a vote; it could only be done by unanimous consent. So, the Chairman was required to direct the clerk to read the entire text of the subcommittee reported text.

The Subcommittee Chief Counsel, Tom Hutchinson, was a savvy veteran of the Hill and was also someone with a good sense of humor. As he was reading this thick document out loud over the microphone, Sensenbrenner was sitting in his seat reading the newspaper. It was clear that demanding the reading was a delaying tactic, but we were stuck. As Tom was reading, he started skipping every other line, which most people did not catch. However, at one point, Sensenbrenner put down the sports page and notified the Chairman that the clerk was not reading properly. With a smile, the Chairman directed the clerk to read correctly. The real question then was, what did Sensenbrenner want in exchange for withdrawing his objection to waiving the reading? That question was answered (although I do not remember how), and he withdrew his objection to the unanimous consent request. The bill and the substitute were then considered as read and open for amendment.

During the markup of an important bill, a question was raised about what language would be in the final text being ordered reported to the House. One of the minority Members of the committee raised a parliamentary inquiry about the procedure. Larry Smith, a Congressman from Florida, who was extremely bright, was speaking on the question. He said, "Procedure is crucial in every legislature. You give me control of the procedure in any situation, and I will beat your brains out every day". It was not subtle, but it certainly made the point.

✦✦✦✦✦✦✦✦✦

One of my favorite Congressional characters was Senator Alan Simpson. He was a tall, lanky man from Cody, Wyoming. He had a very dry wit and was lots of fun to be around, although at times his rapier-like comments drew blood. I had gotten to know him because he was the main Senate sponsor of the immigration bill. He was somebody who, unlike many Members, did not treat the staff like second-class citizens. He knew everybody's name, and he was not reluctant to talk to the staff. He and I got on very well.

One day he was coming out of the White House during the Reagan Administration at a time when he felt the press was being unfair to the President (Imagine that!). In speaking with reporters outside the West Wing, he took them to task and assumed a Hamlet-like corkscrew posture as he raised his hands in front of his face, cupped his fingers into claws, and twisted his face looking like a snarling animal. He said, "You're asking things because you know he's off-balance, and you'd like to stick it in his gazoo". The photograph, which Diana Walker of Time Magazine took at that moment, appeared in newspapers nationwide. It was a brilliant image. I decided to call her and ask her for a copy of the picture which I wanted Senator Simpson to sign for me. She said she would do it "on one condition"; I would get Simpson to sign one for her. Later that afternoon, I saw Simpson in the Capitol and told him of my deal with Diana. He said he would sign one for me and one for her "on one condition", that being she sign one for him. The deal was struck, and all three of us were happy. His inscription on my copy of the photo was extremely gracious, and included, "You are a great 'hand' in this operation. A real pro. Thanks for your kindness to me".

✦✦✦✦✦✦✦✦✦

Although I had been on the debate team in college and had done moot court in law school, I was still not comfortable speaking in public. To remedy that, I decided to get as much practice as possible. I knew it is something most people fear, second only to snakes and spiders. The committee got lots of requests for meetings with foreign officials and presentations about the committee's work from student groups. The people in our front office were aware that I was almost always willing to meet with these groups. Because of that, a lot of requests came my way.

I enjoyed these exchanges because I got to share my knowledge and love of Congress. People who made the effort to come were usually interested in what I had to say. I would usually meet groups in the full committee room because that enabled me to talk about the history of the room, including the impeachment hearings concerning President Nixon, the confirmation hearings for two Vice Presidents of the United States (Ford and Rockefeller), and the important legislation which had been considered there.

The meetings with foreign officials were a mixed experience because frequently, my guests did not speak English, and an interpreter would accompany them. I always found that difficult to deal with because it took twice as long for me to say what I needed to say, and then have it translated. I was often unsure the nuances of what I was saying were being correctly translated. On several occasions when the guest was French, or Italian, I could tell when the translator was adding their spin to what I had said. I got so irritated in one meeting, I finally told the interpreter to, "Please, just translate what I say".

One of the guests I met was a judge from South Africa. This was during the time of momentous transition in that country, and I was looking forward to the meeting. The General Counsel told me to take the meeting because she could not be bothered to deal with "some racist judge". Based on that comment, I was surprised when the black judge walked in. I am certain that during the meeting, I learned more about his country than he did about mine. The General Counsel later asked me if I confronted the judge about apartheid. I told her he was black and when he was leaving, I said that what I wished for his country was peace. He responded by saying, "We need peace with justice". That had an impact on me.

I used to speak regularly to students from the Georgetown University Government Affairs Institute (GAI) about the legislative process. The Institute's primary function was to educate government affairs professionals from Federal Departments and Agencies about Congress. I regularly did two presentations: one on legislative bills and resolutions, and one on conference committee procedures. As I would make it my practice later when teaching at American University, I always tried to engage the students and to inject a little humor whenever possible. The folks at GAI seemed to enjoy my sessions, and I continued to speak to their classes after I left the Hill.

One of the people at GAI who I became friendly with was Sue Lagon. She was a knowledgeable teacher and was also warm and funny. One day, when I was walking past one of the meeting rooms in Rayburn where they have educational sessions and lunches, I saw her speaking to a group. I waved as I went by and I saw this look of panic on her face, which then morphed into relief. She beckoned me into the room. When I went in, she told me she had a Member of Congress scheduled to speak to the class who had canceled at the last minute. When dealing with Members of Congress, you always have to be prepared for that eventuality. Roll call votes, committee meetings, foreign dignitaries dropping in, constituent groups, and a whole range of other random occurrences frequently disrupt planning.

She asked (begged) me to speak to them. I agreed and proceeded to wax adequate about Congress. I told several funny stories and answered some questions. Since this was an advanced legislative process class, and the students were experienced professionals, their questions were excellent and thoughtful. As I usually do in these situations, I told them I would be happy to take questions but that, "I do government, not politics. I will leave speculation about what Congress was going to do about any particular matter up to the pundits".

When Sue told me time was up, I thanked the group for their attention, got a hearty round of applause, and went over to say goodbye to her. Sue thanked me and said I had come to her rescue. When I got to my office the next morning, there was a gift bag sitting on my desk with a note from Sue thanking me for being willing to help her out and being her "lifesaver". When I looked into the bag, it was filled with LifeSaver candies.

Another good thing about working on the Hill was I got to witness some important events. In August of 1981, I was in the lobby of the Rayburn Building, known as the "horseshoe entrance". I had heard that Egyptian President Anwar Sadat was going to be visiting, and I wanted to see him. On March 26, 1979, on the White House lawn, Israeli Prime Minister Menachem Begin and Sadat signed a peace agreement, known as the Camp David Accords, ending the state of war between their two countries that began in 1948. The Accords had been forged over 13 long days at the presidential retreat in the Catoctin Mountains. It was a major step towards peace in the Middle East. There was lots of optimism about it.

As I stood in the foyer with a few of my colleagues, someone said, "There goes a real diplomatic hero". I said I agreed, but I hoped he would not become a martyr for peace. Little did I know that less than two months later, he would be assassinated, not by anyone linked to Israel or Jewish interests, but by fundamentalist Egyptian Army officers.

Having floor privileges gave me the option to go into the Chamber whenever something interesting was happening. I took advantage of that on many occasions. One of the more memorable days was October 2, 1980. The FBI had conducted a sting operation trying to entice Members of Congress to take bribes from an undercover FBI agent posing as an Arab Sheik. It became known as Abscam. More than thirty political figures were investigated, and six Members of the House and one Senator were eventually indicted and convicted.

One of the Members who was convicted was Michael "Ozzie" Myers. He was videotaped accepting a bribe of $50,000. On that tape, Myers is recorded saying that "money talks in this business and bullshit walks." His criminal conviction did not automatically remove him from office. The House had to go through the formal process of expelling him.

The House Committee on Standards of Official Conduct, usually called the Ethics Committee, had done the investigation of the Myers case. Myers had claimed he was conducting his own probe; he argued he was merely "play-acting" during the meetings with the "Sheik". The Committee report stated: "The evidence in this case—a case based not on hearsay, conflicting eyewitness accounts, inferences, and the like, but upon the Representative's own words and acts, recorded and in-person, is clear and convincing. That evidence demands the strongest possible Congressional response". The Committee recommended the House adopt a resolution that expelling Mr. Myers.

Ethics Committee Chairman Charles Bennett reiterated Myers' declaration of guilt during the debate on the expulsion resolution. "He admitted in that testimony he received $50,000 in cash, thinking it was $100,000; that he believed this money was coming from a real sheik..."

One of the Members who was also targeted, but who did not succumb to the attempted bribes, was Bill Hughes, a Member of the Judiciary Committee. He made an important point during the debate, which I thought about later during the impeachment of Judge Harry Claiborne. Hughes argued that the criminal conviction itself should not be relied on by the House in making its decision to expel. He said, "... our findings *can be totally divorced from a conviction in a criminal court*. That basically is irrelevant... I intend to support the committee and its finding". (emph. added) The question of whether the House should be bound by the findings of another branch of government would come up in the impeachments of three Federal Judges in the mid-1980s. Interestingly, Bill Hughes would be a manager on the part of the House in the Senate impeachment trial of Judge Harry Claiborne.

I was interested in this part of the debate, which was conducted in a very solemn manner. It came down to a serious constitutional question, which I had studied. There was a relevant Supreme Court decision in 1969, *Powell v. McCormack*. Adam Clayton Powell was a senior Member of the House who was involved in a financial scandal. Powell was *re-elected* after he had refused to pay a judgment ordered by a New York Court. The Speaker asked Powell to refrain from taking the oath of office, and the House adopted a resolution *excluding* him and declaring his seat vacant. There was a significant difference between the House *preventing* a duly-elected Member from taking his seat, thereby *excluding* him, and the House *expelling* a duly-elected Member after he had been elected. In the *Powell* case, the Supreme Court had ruled that Congress does not have the power to establish additional qualifications for election to the House beyond those specified in Art. I, § 2, cl. 1-2 of the Constitution. There are only three requirements: the candidate must be at least 25 years old, must be an inhabitant of the state (not the Congressional district) in which he or she is elected, and must have been a citizen of the United States for the previous seven years. The Court ruled the House could not *exclude* Powell from taking office since he fulfilled all three qualifications, but it could *expel* him once seated.

Chairman Bennett, "in all fairness" yielded half of the debate time to the respondent, Congressman Myers. I was caught off-guard by that, but it was the appropriate thing to do. It was clear Myers was going to be expelled, so why not give him some of the time. Mr. Bennett was the Congressman responsible for putting "In God We Trust" on the currency. I was tempted to show him the words in the first amendment about Congress not making any law "respecting an establishment of religion."

Floyd Spence, who was the Ranking Republican on the Ethics Committee, spoke in a somber tone:

"Mr. Speaker, the basic point is that there is nothing unique about people who are not without fault sitting in judgment of others who have been judged or charged with wrongdoing. We can find no one who is entirely without fault to do the job that we must do. We must ourselves sit in judgment of our colleague. Otherwise, we would be living in a jungle where no law or rule of civilized behavior could be enforced because no one could qualify to sit as a judge or a jury. This is your House and my House. We hold these seats as custodians for the people we represent. No one else is responsible. No one else can vote for us. No one else, no person, nobody, no branch of government, no agency, no organization, can determine this question for us. No one else can police this House but those sitting here today at this time in this place".

When Myers was recognized to speak, the House became very quiet. Myers attacked the method by which the Justice Department had gone about the sting operation. He claimed that "the conduct of the Government was so outrageous that the Government should have been precluded from bringing the charges." Several Members were genuinely concerned about the tactics the FBI had used in enticing Members. There was also some discussion about the fact that Mr. Myers' conviction was on appeal, and therefore it was not final. It was clear, however, that this was a *fait accompli*. Myers said as much: *"…obviously I am not going to change anybody's mind on how they are going to vote, but I would like to start off first of all and say I am sorry I put the House in this position. I do not feel good about it. I told that to the committee, and certainly, I owe this House an apology for my actions. …*

In closing, I guess there is not much more I can say, and I do not think anything I have said today is going to change anyone's mind, but in closing, I just want to say this. When I walked over here today, when I was sitting on the floor, I know what it feels like now to sit on death row. In a way, I am awaiting execution, and you, the Members of this body, are the ones who will decide my fate. As you go to that voting machine to put your cards in, keep in mind, use a comparison when you hit the button when you vote to expel, that it will have the same effect as hitting the button if I were strapped in an electric chair in this well. That is all I have to say".

Myers was expelled from the House of Representatives by a vote of 376 to 30, becoming the first Member of the House to be expelled since 1861. It was a solemn undertaking. I felt I had been present for an important historical event. I was privileged to have been there.

+ + + + + + + + +

One of the people I got to meet and talk with was Lee Iacocca. He was going to testify before the Monopolies Subcommittee, which Mr. Rodino chaired. The hearing was about the internationalization of the auto industry. At the time, Mr. Iacocca was the Chairman of the Chrysler Corporation. This was after he left Ford. The hearing was going to take place in the full committee room adjacent to my office. Mr. Rodino decided to let Mr. Iacocca wait in my office before the hearing. I have always loved cars and was very interested in having the chance to talk with him. Mr. Rodino introduced us and left him with me, saying he would send for him when it was time to testify. We talked for about 20 minutes about the Ford Mustang, which was his initial claim to fame. He confirmed my understanding that it was a rather boring Ford Falcon with a sexy body. He told me about some of the new cars that Chrysler was building and the types of buyers they were targeting. He was easy to talk with and was receptive to my questions. I do not know whether it was because of the way Mr. Rodino introduced me to him or the fact that I had a nameplate on my desk, but he always addressed me as Dan. I think that is an example of his remarkable people skills.

Mr. Rodino came back to get Mr. Iacocca, and as they were leaving to go to the hearing, Mr. Iacocca turned to shake my hand and said to the Chairman, "Dan and I had a nice chat. He knows his cars". That brought a big smile to my face.

I went in to watch the hearing. After Mr. Iacocca's testimony, there was a short break, and Mr. Rodino asked me to escort Mr. Iacocca over to the Capitol. As we were walking through the Rayburn Building, I told him that I had promised myself if I ever get a chance to speak with him, I would ask him about the Plymouth turbine cars and what had happened to them. He told me a total of 55 were built: five prototypes and a limited run of 50 for a public-user program. After the conclusion of the user program in 1966, Chrysler reclaimed all of them and destroyed all but nine; Chrysler kept two, five are displayed at museums in the United States, and two are in private collections. He also explained why it failed; the engine was not able to meet the necessary performance requirements, it had sluggish acceleration, as well as subpar fuel economy, and it was relatively noisy. One other complicating factor was the high temperature of the exhaust. If someone was standing on the sidewalk next to the car, the almost 200-degree exhaust gases could be dangerous. It was a fantastic experience to be able to have an easy and interesting conversation with somebody I had watched on television for years who had become an American icon.

✦✦✦✦✦✦✦✦✦

Not only am I fascinated with cars, but I am also very interested in aviation. One of my trips to Europe involved seven separate flights, and I made sure that I was on a different type of aircraft on every leg of the journey. I was intrigued when I found out Richard Branson, the Chairman of Virgin Atlantic Airlines was coming to the committee offices for a meeting with the Chairman. It was going to be held in the private conference room next to my office.

Mr. Branson, the billionaire owner of the airline, is an extraordinary man. He is an English magnate, investor, author, balloonist and philanthropist. He and a couple of people who were with him were sitting in the conference room waiting for their meeting, and I went in to meet him. Mr. Rodino always allowed me to do this unless there was some sensitivity to the meeting. I spoke with Branson about the history of the committee room, and then I started asking him questions about the aviation business.

We discussed the difference between wide-body and narrow-body jets, the ever-increasing efficiency of jet engines, and the ETOPS waivers which were being granted by the FAA. ETOPS stands for Extended-range Twin-engine Operational Performance Standards. This waiver permits twin-engine aircraft to fly routes, which at times are more than 60 minutes flying time away from the nearest airport suitable for an emergency landing. Previously, fuel-efficient two-engine aircraft were prohibited on those routes for safety reasons. To get certified, a plane had to be able to fly on one engine long enough to get to an airport more than an hour away.

Branson is a man who oozes excitement and confidence. He was very animated and could easily talk about a whole range of topics. I explained some of the significant things that happened in the Committee hearing room; the Watergate hearings, Vice Presidential nominations, and major antitrust and crime legislation. I thought he was very knowledgeable. He knew enough to ask perceptive and thoughtful questions. It was an extraordinary privilege to speak with him.

✦✦✦✦✦✦✦✦✦

I love professional football. One of the things my wife had to get used to when she moved to "the colonies" was my addiction to watching what she calls "the matches". Monday Night Football was a ritual with me, and she learned to deal with that. I prefer announcers who are actually watching the game they are covering and not rambling on about irrelevant things. I loathed the way Howard Cosell handled these broadcasts. During the games, even in the middle of a play, he would babble on and on about who he had dinner with and what they said about the current controversies involving the NFL. Occasionally, he would interrupt his monologues with the observation that someone had scored a touchdown (during the game he was supposed to be covering). It used to drive me crazy, and Mimi knew how I felt about him.

One Monday night, I was watching a game, and Mimi was down the hall where she could hear the television. At one point, Howard was babbling away, and I heard her say in a most un-British manner, "Shut up, Howard". I cracked up. She certainly was becoming Americanized.

As luck would have it, the next morning, the Monopolies Subcommittee was holding a hearing on the antitrust exemption for baseball. The chief witness was going to be none other than Howard Cosell! I went into the General Counsel's office when we were ready to start the hearing because I knew that Mr. Rodino was there. I knocked on the door, entered, and there was Mr. Rodino with Howard Cosell. I had trouble keeping a straight face because as soon as he opened his mouth, I wanted to say to him, "Shut up, Howard".

He was brilliant with an encyclopedic knowledge of sports history. During his testimony, he reeled off the Brooklyn Dodgers' opening day lineup in 1947, which was Jackie Robinson's major league debut with him playing first base. One of the "know-it-all" Members tried to correct him, "Mr. Cosell, didn't Jackie Robinson play second base?" Cosell informed him in his usual haughty manner that the brilliant Eddie Stanky was playing second base at the time, and so Robinson was playing first. I rather enjoyed seeing the arrogant Congressman getting corrected publicly. But the fact the ultimate know-it-all, Howard Cosell did it, diminished my pleasure.

✦✦✦✦✦✦✦✦✦

There were rare occasions when Mr. Rodino would say something humorous. Although they were few and far between, every once in a while, he did. We were having another hearing about major league baseball's antitrust exemption. None of the other professional sports had such an exemption. This was a result of the Supreme Court ruling in 1922, which largely insulated the business side of baseball from antitrust suits.

One of the witnesses at this hearing was Ted Turner, the multimillionaire owner of the Atlanta Braves. During the question and answer period after his testimony, Mr. Rodino asked him why he thought baseball enjoyed the antitrust exemption, unlike all other professional sports. Mr. Turner's response was, "I guess it is because they play it with wooden bats". Mr. Rodino turned to me with a smile on his face and said, "I guess you do not have to be that smart to make a lot of money". No one understood what Turner meant. It was bizarre.

✦✦✦✦✦✦✦✦✦

I had an interesting encounter one afternoon with someone I did not know. A tall man walked into my office unannounced and said, "Hi Dan, can we talk for a minute?". He was from the Diplomatic Security Service in the Department of State (DSS). I had no idea who he was or why he was there. He told me he needed to "secure" my office for another committee's hearing the next day in the Judiciary Committee hearing room. I was unaware of this hearing, but I later found out Chairman Rodino had given the other committee permission to use the room for its hearing. The main witness was going to be Alexander Haig, then-Secretary of State. That explained why the security agent from DSS was checking out the space. They were going to use it as a holding room for Secretary of State Alexander Haig prior to his testimony. I was informed in no uncertain terms I needed to vacate the space during the entire morning. I was a little miffed to be so unceremoniously thrown out of my own office.

I had been sitting in that very spot when John Hinckley tried to assassinate President Reagan in March 1981. Soon afterwards, Secretary Haig appeared in the Press Room in the White House. He announced, "Constitutionally, gentlemen, you have the President, the Vice President and the Secretary of State, in that order, and should the President decide he wants to transfer the helm to the Vice President, he will do so," Haig, apparently "forgot" that the Speaker of the House and the Senate President Pro Tempore come before the Secretary of State in the line of succession under the terms of the Presidential Succession Act. In a dozen words that would become infamous, he said, "As of now, I am in control here, in the White House". At the time, Vice-President George Bush was on an airplane en-route from Texas. While Haig got a lot of grief about it, technically, he was correct if what he meant was that he was the senior official in charge **at the White House**. Most people did not give him the benefit of the doubt since he was not universally loved.

I decided that before I vacated the office for Secretary Haig, I would leave something for him to peruse if he was interested. I happened to have a report from the Congressional Research Service entitled, "Presidential Succession". I thought he might like to look it over while he was at my desk. I made sure to leave it open to the page which outlined the order of succession. When I returned to my office, there was no evidence that he had taken advantage of the occasion to learn about the law.

✚✚✚✚✚✚✚✚✚

One of the things you have to do as a staffer is to clean up after a Member who has made a mistake. All too frequently, Members would get wound up in their rhetoric and would speak about Americans having constitutional rights including, the right to "life, liberty and the pursuit of happiness". That language is nowhere in the Constitution; it is in the Declaration of Independence. There were several times when I had to approach a Member who had made this mistake and point out the error and suggest correcting their remarks in the Record. More often than not, the Member would ask me to do it, and I would go up to the rostrum where the Congressional Record clerks sat and take care of it. Since I spent a lot of time on the floor, I got to know all of the floor staff, and they were always fantastic in helping me out.

Funny things happened on the floor regularly. One Monday morning, we were there to consider a couple of non-controversial bills under the suspension of the rules procedure, which provided limited debate time and did not allow amendments. There were more than 20 bills on the schedule. They were flying by fast and furious. A Member whose first name was Robert was recognized and went to the well of the House to speak. He really got into it and was vociferously arguing against the bill. After a minute or so, one of his colleagues yelled out, "Wrong bill, Bob". It was hard to keep a straight face. Bob hurriedly asked permission to "revise and extend" his remarks, and I am sure some clerk in the Congressional Record office moved his remarks to the appropriate place.

✚✚✚✚✚✚✚✚✚

One of the most unusual people I met was a Jesuit priest who was a Congressman from Boston. He was a liberal Democrat and was simply frenetic. He was always on the go at sixty miles an hour. It was difficult to keep up with him. He also had a very short attention span. I did not know him well, but at least well enough to talk with him about the work of the committee. I was friendly with his personal office staff. They would always be understanding when I would describe something weird he had done.

I do not think he had much of a sense of humor and did not have many opportunities to find out. One day he was walking down the hall in the Rayburn Building munching on a bag of Fritos. He was rapidly scarfing them down. It was rather amusing to watch. He stopped to speak with me and offered me some Fritos. I declined, but I could not resist the temptation to make a joke.

I said, "Father Drinan, you like those a lot, don't you?" "Yes, Dan, I do", he replied. "Does that make you a chip monk?" was my reply. He did not get it. So be it.

✦ ✦ ✦ ✦ ✦ ✦ ✦ ✦ ✦

Mr. Rodino was not a man endowed with a vibrant sense of humor. He was not overly serious but did not seem to enjoy (or get) a funny remark. As I got more comfortable with him, I allowed myself to inject a quip or two into our private conversations.

At the beginning of October of 1979, we had a full Committee meeting scheduled. As Mr. Rodino and I were sitting in the hearing room waiting to begin, we were talking about the witnesses who were going to testify. Mr. Rodino was a devout Catholic and was a member of the Order of Malta, an important lay religious order of the Catholic church. I knew Pope John Paul II had celebrated mass the night before during his visit to New York City. The mass was held at Yankee Stadium, which was large enough to hold the 80,000 plus people who attended. Mr. Rodino was there and sat in a VIP section close to the man he always referred to as "the Holy Father".

I asked the Chairman about it. "Mr. Chairman, I understand you were at Yankee Stadium last night". "Yeah, Dan. There were lots of people there". I could not resist, so I said, "Was it the Cardinals against the Angels?" Another Member was sitting next to us, and he laughed out loud. Rodino did not get the joke.

✦ ✦ ✦ ✦ ✦ ✦ ✦ ✦ ✦

The Chairman was enormously proud of his Italian heritage. He spoke Italian fluently and did so often with Italian dignitaries who visited and with some Americans of Italian descent, such as Justice Antonin Scalia. While we sometimes had difficulty in getting him to reach out to people about legislative business, if something came up related to the Italian American community or his family, he was very proactive.

An example was when his granddaughter came to visit Washington with her high school class. Mr. Rodino pulled out all the stops and called several Italian American Members personally and asked them to speak to the group. They were in the full committee room, seated in the Members' chairs on the dais. The Chairman's granddaughter, Carla, who had been a page on the House floor the previous summer, was sitting in the Chairman's chair in the center of the group. Mr. Rodino was speaking to them about Congress when an Italian American Member he had "invited" to come speak to the group came in. This was, in reality, a command performance.

Romano Mazzoli was a man I knew well since he had been on the District

Committee when I was there and was also on the Judiciary Committee. He was complying with Mr. Rodino's summons and was going to speak to the group. As he was waiting, I walked up behind him and whispered, "The one in the middle is Carla, the Chairman's granddaughter, who worked as a page last summer on the floor". He did not acknowledge me, and I withdrew.

The Chairman introduced him, and without any hesitation, he greeted the group armed with the information I had supplied. "Carla, it is nice to see you again. We certainly miss you on the House floor". Both Carla and the Chairman beamed. It was an example of good staff work. The only thing missing was a thank you, but I had grown used to Members not thinking of that. I helped make Mazzoli look good in the Chairman's eyes, and Carla was elated.

✦✦✦✦✦✦✦✦✦

One day my cousin, Henny Youngman, the famous borscht belt comedian, was in town, and we had lunch. After lunch, I asked him if he would like to meet Congressman Rodino. He was enthusiastic about it. I knew Mr. Rodino was a big fan of Henny's, so I called to make sure he was in his office. We went upstairs, and as we walked in, Henny looked at the Chairman and said, "Wow, that's Peter Rodino, who saved the country!" That happened to the Chairman often since this was not too far removed from Watergate. However, Mr. Rodino's response was not the usual one. He said, "Wow, that's Henny Youngman! Please come in and sit down".

Henny sat down next to the Chairman and started talking to him in his usual rapid-fire manner. Henny was the kind of person who would put his hand on your arm and look you in the eye. He said, "Mr. Rodino, Mr. Rodino, I understand you are Italian. Is that true?" The Chairman loved it and beamed and said, "Yes, I am." Henny replied this way: "O k a y, -- I-- w i l l-- t a l k—s-l-o-w-e-r." I had to restrain myself again, but I do not think Mr. Rodino got the joke.

✦✦✦✦✦✦✦✦✦

Richard Bolling was a Congressman from Missouri who was the Chairman of the House Rules Committee until 1983. His Chief of Staff was a friend of mine, and I knew Mr. Bolling well enough to have a friendly conversation with him. He had a reputation of being the smartest man in the House, but he was also a difficult, prickly person who did not suffer fools gladly.

Rep. David Obey, a Democrat from Wisconsin, said of Bolling, "He was the most brilliant legislator in this century who never became Speaker." Bolling was known for an acerbic style and a reluctance to put up with some of his colleagues who did not measure up to his high standards. That did not make him the most popular man in Congress. He was known as a supreme legislative tactician and was an expert in parliamentary procedure.

He once told me a story about being a witness to history. One day in April of 1945, he was in what was known as the "Board of Education" room on the South end of the Capitol, H-128. The room was called that because it is where a few select Members would regularly gather to get an education from Speaker Sam Rayburn. Rayburn would meet there with the Democratic leadership to plot their strategy as well as for drinks and poker games. The regulars in H-128 included Lyndon Johnson (who was a Member of the House from 1937 until he was elected to the Senate in 1948), House Parliamentarian Lewis Deschler, and Harry Truman, who would spend lots of time there as both a Democratic Senator from Missouri and later as Vice President.

In the room that afternoon were Harry Truman, Johnson, Rayburn, and Bolling. The telephone rang, and as per protocol, Bolling, as the junior Member present, answered it. He turned to Truman and said, "Mr. Vice President, it's for you". It was Mrs. Roosevelt, summoning him to come to the White House "immediately". Truman ran back to the Senate to get his hat and rushed to the White House. As he entered the family quarters, Mrs. Roosevelt delivered the stunning news. She said, "Mr. President, the President is dead". That was the first time Truman had ever been addressed as "Mr. President" (except in the Senate where he was its President), and that is how he found out FDR was dead, and he had become President of the United States! It may be hard to comprehend today, but Truman had been Vice President for only eighty-two days and knew nothing about the Manhattan Project or the atom bomb. That was a compelling story.

On one of the last days of the session, before Bolling retired, he was managing the rule for consideration of one of our committee's bills. I was on the floor getting ready. During one of the roll call votes, which was being taken by electronic device, there was an opening for me to approach him and wish him well. I perceived he was not in his all too frequent "biting off your head" mode, so I thought it was safe. I told him I had researched the Rules of the House and determined you did not have to be a Member of the House to be elected Speaker. I suggested he consider that possibility. For the first time in all the years I had known him, he broke into a smile and thanked me for the compliment.

✦ ✦ ✦ ✦ ✦ ✦ ✦ ✦ ✦

My dicey relationship with the press began early in my career in the House`. I was not well enough known for the press to call me directly, and the front office would usually send press calls to Mr. Rodino's press secretary. There was a reporter who worked for one of the small newspapers that covered the Hill, who would call me occasionally to ask about certain provisions in the bill or some other bill pending before the committee. I would never say anything about what I thought would happen but give her only factual information.

She called me one day to ask about the referral of a bill to subcommittee. It was part of my job to review bills that the Speaker had referred to the Judiciary Committee and make a recommendation about which of our subcommittees should get the bill. This was usually straightforward, although there was a bit of overlapping jurisdiction among some of them. Frequently there was some jockeying going on to either secure referral to a particular subcommittee or to avoid it. The subcommittee staffs were very aggressive about protecting their jurisdictional turf. The reporter was trying to gin up a story by seeing if she could generate an intra-committee dispute.

She was interested in a bill concerning judicial review of cases relating to abortion. In the wake of *Roe v Wade*, this was highly controversial. I told her the decision had not been made on the referral. She then called a staff attorney on one of the subcommittees to which the bill might be referred and told him that I said it was not going to be referred to his subcommittee. He got upset and came down to my office to complain first about the referral, and second about the fact that he had to find out from the press. I told him exactly what I told the reporter. The final decision had not been made. She had not been truthful and was merely trying to create some controversy and possibly a story.

I was angry and called the reporter. I informed her that I had found out that she had lied about something I had said and that she should not call me again. She replied she had not lied, but merely posed a hypothetical. I had more confidence in our staff than I did in her and reiterated my intention not to talk to her in the future. She whined that it was not a newsworthy story the way I had described it. I told her my job did not involve making sure she had a "good" story to print.

✦✦✦✦✦✦✦✦✦

When Alan Parker left the committee to lead the Washington DC office of the Association of Trial Lawyers of America (ATLA), this idea of keeping up with other lobbying groups came up. The trial lawyers had a considerable lobbying presence in Washington and always had high-level trial lawyers available for an overnight fly-in. Trial lawyers regularly make a lot of money and are also frequently active in political campaigns, including fundraising. Alan always complained about people out in the hinterlands who were used to being movers and shakers in their hometowns wanting to fly into Washington and "straighten out" Members. He said there were many times when he counseled them that the best thing to do was nothing. Sometimes, against Alan's advice, these bigwigs flew into town, expecting Senators and senior staff to fall all over them. Alan felt this frequently did more harm than good.

Alan was aware of how silly the concept of "Everybody is doing it, so we have to just to keep up" was. He was aware, but he was not immune to it. Soon after Alan left, he decided ATLA should have a reception to "honor" Members of Congress. I was shocked when he told me how much they were going to spend on this event. Some Members would attend, briefly, and they were the people who would immediately afterward be calling for campaign contributions. Members attended because they knew ATLA had lots of money to donate to their political campaigns. Because of my friendship with Alan and because Mr. Rodino liked having staff around to insulate him at these kinds of events, I attended, although I thought it was a foolish waste of time and money. I expressed that to Alan but not in those terms.

✦✦✦✦✦✦✦✦✦

In the spring of 1987, what became known as the Iran–Contra investigation began. A Joint House-Senate committee consisting of 15 Members of the House and 11 Members of the Senate was established for it. The hearings were held from May 5 through August 6. Mr. Rodino was a member of the joint committee, and this took up most of his time, as well as the General Counsel's. She was with him from gavel to gavel and afterwards. She would frequently call from the hearing room with bizarre questions relating to the Watergate hearings. I felt like Perry Mason's private detective, Paul Drake.

One of the calls I got from her was to provide some information to a well-known journalist/columnist for Newsweek magazine. She told me I would be getting a call from this person with some specific questions about Judiciary Committee history. Within five minutes, I got the call from a gruff and self-important woman who wanted answers immediately. Several of her questions were susceptible to simple answers, which I provided. Some dealt with more complex topics that I was reluctant to answer in haste without doing some research. Others involved requests for speculation about what Mr. Rodino would do in the event certain things happened. I certainly was not going to answer any question of that kind. I refused to become engaged in a debate with her about what my responsibilities were to her publication. She then pulled out what I am sure she figured to be her trump card and asked me, "Do you know who I am?" I was not going to give her the satisfaction of telling her I knew how important she was (at least in her own mind). I merely responded, "Yes, you are someone who wants my help". She was none too happy with my failure to genuflect. I told her I would have to call her back with a couple of the answers I did not know off the top of my head. She said, "You don't seem to understand that I am on a deadline". I was tempted to tell her that **I** was not on a deadline, but I did not. I told her I would get back to her only when I had *complete* and *accurate* answers, notwithstanding her deadline. She slammed the phone down and did not take my call when I tried to give her the answers she sought. I guess she got them from someone more susceptible to her bullying techniques.

There were educational opportunities available all the time on the Hill, lectures, seminars, and frequent health fairs run by medical specialty groups, all trying to get Congress to do their bidding. The range of screenings you could get for free was tremendous. If I had the chance to have a non-invasive screening test performed for free at one of these sessions, I would always volunteer. I went every year when the dermatologist's association ran skin cancer screenings. I had a bone density test done. I also volunteered to be the one person in the audience learning about aortic aneurisms to have the scan done, once again, for free. The Red Cross ran regular blood drives, and I frequently went down to the health unit to donate.

It was the guest speaker sessions I enjoyed the most. The panoply of speakers ranged from foreign policy to prison reform, to the frontiers of medicine. They were always given by top people, and most of the sessions were fascinating. Each group wanted to put their best foot forward before Congress, so the sessions were almost always interesting.

The Biomedical Research Caucus Briefings, which were held every month, were particularly interesting for me. The initial goal of the organization was to double the budget of the National Institutes of Health (NIH) within five years, and that was accomplished. The speakers included household names such as Anthony Fauci, the famous NIH researcher who we see and often hear on TV and radio, Dr. Thomas Starzl, the renowned transplant surgeon and Dr. Francis Collins, who at the time was the Director of the National Center for Human Genome Research. Dr. Collins later became the head of the NIH. These sessions began in 1990 and continue to this day.

One session was particularly memorable. Dr. Dennis Selkoe, a Harvard researcher who specialized in Alzheimer's disease, was introduced. He stood up and turned to look at the clock on the wall. The was a brief pause as he watched the second-hand sweep around to straight up and said, "Ten years ago, to the minute, I spoke to this group about what we knew about this terrible disease. I am now here to tell you everything I told you that day we no longer believe to be true". He then went on to discuss the latest research. Congressman George Gekas was the Chairman of the caucus which hosted the event. I was the most senior staffer who regularly attended these sessions. Because of that, I would always get to ask the first question. George recognized me, and I asked the researcher, "How much of what you have told us today will turn out to be inaccurate ten years from now". He smiled and said it was a good question, and he did not have the answer to it.

One of the most fun events was sponsored by National Public Radio (NPR), which was facing vast funding cuts by the budget hawks. They decided to pull out the big guns. They brought in Tom and Ray Magliozzi, who were known as "Click and Clack, the Tappet Brothers". These men hosted a weekly show on NPR called "Car Talk", where, according to the NPR web site, "America's funniest auto mechanics take calls from weary car owners all over the country and crack wise while they diagnose Dodges and dismiss Diahatsus". They were hysterically funny. It was worth listening to the show each weekend to hear them crack each other up. The night they spoke in the Rayburn cafeteria, they had the place in stitches. It was better attended by Members of Congress than many other "serious" policy-centric events. At the end of the session, they made their pitch for funding. I do not know if the program that evening affected how any Member was going to vote, but it sure got a lot of them laughing.

Other types of sessions took place off the Hill and were also designed to enhance the reputation of the host group. Sometimes they had another purpose. Several of us from the committee were invited to go out to the Secret Service training facility in suburban Maryland, to participate in a protectee attack scenario training session. The Service does this regularly, and they are always looking for volunteers to make up a crowd to simulate a real-life situation. We went to what looked like a Hollywood set of a downtown main street. We were all given protective glasses since they were going to be using live explosives. We got to watch a "President" exiting a building and walking towards the "beast", which is what the presidential limousine was called. At some point, which neither the trainees nor we knew, there would be an attack. It could have been by someone with a gun, a grenade, another type of incendiary device, or something else which posed a threat.

I found it fascinating and a bit unnerving. Everyone knew there would be an assault of some kind, but it was disturbing to be waiting for it to happen. I felt greater empathy for the Secret Service trainees after the short time I was "on alert". Those people live that 24/7. We watched several different scenarios play out. What was especially interesting was the post-event evaluation. I asked if I could sit in. The Service does not always allow this, but for some reason, they said yes. It was analogous to a medical morbidity and mortality conference. The purpose was to discuss what went wrong, as well as what was done well. Practice, Practice, Practice.

Another kind of educational experience that was frequently available was in emergency medical treatment. When I first arrived on the Hill, I signed up immediately for a course in CPR. I figured it might be handy to know how to do it since I was surrounded by a lot of older people, mostly men, who were possible candidates for a heart attack. I took refresher courses whenever they were offered. I am pleased to have the knowledge, and also pleased I have never had to use it.

I got training in the use of the Heimlich maneuver. That was simple, and the training was short. Again, it was something I have never had to use.

I also learned about recognizing stroke symptoms. We were given the "FAST" stroke warning signs; Face drooping, Arm weakness, Speech difficulty, and Time to call 911. I was taught how to do a neurological test by asking the person I was trying to help to squeeze my fingers on both hands. By doing that, you can tell if someone is weaker on one side, which can be a sign of stroke.

The only time my neurological testing skills came handy was one day when I was coming back from the Capitol through the Rayburn subway tunnel. I saw an older woman collapse. Her husband was stunned and simple froze. He did not know what to do. I went over to see if she had any of the FAST symptoms and did my neuro check. I folded up my suit coat and put it under her head. She was coherent, and, I think, more embarrassed than hurt. Unfortunately, we were in the basement of the Capitol, and there was no cell phone coverage. Three people from the Capitol physician's office finally showed up. I decided to do my "Lone Ranger" act and said my work there was done and went back to my office. The most disheartening thing about this incident was this woman was a constituent of a Member of Congress who amazingly happened to come upon the scene as I was trying to assist. He got completely flustered and said he had to get to an appointment and disappeared. He told me later he felt I had the situation well in hand, so he was comfortable leaving.

✦ ✦ ✦ ✦ ✦ ✦ ✦ ✦

One of the most talented staff people I got to know was Tim Keating. I met him when he was a youngster working in the House Democratic cloakroom. Tim was a master of information about each of the Members. He knew their districts and what kinds of things interested them and could always predict what was going to happen on the floor. He was a tremendous asset in helping me do my job and was an exceptionally cheerful and dedicated member of the team.

One day I was given a pair of tickets to the Washington D.C. opening of a major motion picture. Because the Judiciary Committee has jurisdiction over intellectual property, people from the movie industry were frequent visitors and often invited our staff to their events. I did not like going to those things, and I thought I should give the tickets to someone else. Since it was going to be a large event, I knew no one would miss me, and no one would be able to casti-gate me for giving the tickets to a "mere staffer".

I went over to the Democratic cloakroom to find Timmer (as I called him, and still do). As usual, he was there doing his thing. I said I had these tickets and I thought maybe he and Ann, his wife, would like to go. He urged me to find a Member who could use them. "Screw the Members; you are the one who helps me do my job. I would like you to have them", I replied. I think he was surprised, but he took the tickets, and he and his wife had a marvelous time. It was something I was happy to do, and it did not hurt to have Tim as a friend.

After he left the Hill, he ended up in the Clinton White House and was always helpful to me. He even scored me tickets in the Presidential Box at the Kennedy Center on several occasions. Those tickets are usually reserved for Members when the President was not going to use them. Mimi danced in the Washington National Opera production of "Amahl and the Night Visitors", and I wanted to take some friends to see it. I asked Timmer if he could get me a couple of seats in the box for New Year's Eve. I knew there would be no Members in town. He called me back and said, "Not only can I get you a couple of seats, but I can also get you the whole box". I took seven friends, and we had a great time.

After Tim left the White House, and after I left the Hill to teach at American University, he would regularly speak to my students. During the decade I taught at AU, he worked first at Honeywell, then with a prominent lobbying firm and later as a Senior Vice President for Boeing. Tim is a very busy man, but he al-ways made time for us.

✦ ✦ ✦ ✦ ✦ ✦ ✦ ✦

The humorist in me came out during one of the subcommittees' hearings on criminal justice matters. Several witnesses were called to testify, including a social psychologist, Dr. Stanton Samenow, who worked as a clinical research psychologist for the Program for the Investigation of Criminal Behavior at St. Elizabeth's Hospital in Washington, D.C. Stan had been the head counselor at the summer camp where I worked when I was in college, Camp Shohola. There was a big sign in front of the lake where the camp was located, which said, "Shohola, the Indian word for beautiful waters". I had not seen him for more than 20 years, but I decided to go sit in on the hearing. When it was over, Doctor Samenow was surrounded by a multitude of people wanting to speak to him. I joined the gaggle, and then I asked him a question, "Doctor Samenow, can you please tell me what the Indian word for beautiful waters is". His eyes opened up like saucers, and he exclaimed, "Who are you?". He knew I was someone from his Shohola past but did not know who. After I told him who I was, we laughed, and the rest of the people standing there did not know why.

✛ ✛ ✛ ✛ ✛ ✛ ✛ ✛ ✛

My doctor, Fred Gill, during an annual physical, had suggested I should get more exercise. When he asked me what I did to keep in shape, I told him I played racquetball. He was not familiar with the game, so I invited him to play one day to see if he liked it. He did, and we ended up playing twice a week regularly. He became a dear friend in addition to being my physician. We would talk about everything under the sun when we were relaxing in the sauna or the whirlpool afterward.

One night, Fred's racquet slipped out of his hand. It was tethered to his wrist, so it flipped back and hit him square in the mouth. He began bleeding profusely from his split lip. We decided to go to the emergency room because he felt he would probably need a couple of stitches. He was holding a towel to his lip as we drove to Suburban Hospital, where he was on staff. Everyone there knew him. He told me there was one doctor who worked in the emergency room who he "would not let touch my body". Fred was hoping that doctor would not be working that evening. No such luck.

Fred asked me to check him in and take care of the paperwork, and he went straight back to the treatment area. In filling out the forms, I came to the blank for religion. I put "equestrian" in. Fred then appeared and asked me to come back to the treatment area. Of course, the doctor he wanted to avoid was on duty. Fred was not going to refuse treatment because that would have caused a big stink at the hospital. When we got back to the suture room, he introduced me. "This is Dan Freeman. He is my lawyer". I could almost feel the doctor inhale in apprehension. Fred had made his point, and I was laughing inside.

While he was being stitched up, the triage nurse from the front desk came in. She said, "Dr. Gill, in the religion box on the form your friend filled out, it says, 'equestrian'. What did he mean?" Fred looked at me quizzically, and I said, "Oh, I was just horsing around".

XI. Affairs of The Heart #3—I Finally Got It Right!

In December of 1981, I got a call from my father's former secretary, Marguerite Glicksman, a larger-than-life personality who was rather controlling and domineering. She was quite British and called everybody "Luv". She had been my father's secretary for a long time and was usually very nice to me. She called to tell me that an old friend of hers, with whom she worked in Vienna after World War II, was coming to Washington. He was bringing his daughter, who was a ballet dancer with a Belgian ballet company. Marguerite wanted me to take the daughter out while she was in Washington. I politely refused. She persisted, saying her guests would be here for three weeks, and she was sure I could spare some time to take her out. Knowing Marguerite as I did, I knew she would push me to entertain this young woman, especially since it was around the holidays. Congress was not in session, so I was not that busy. I stood my ground and refused the blind date. One reason was that I hate blind dates, and especially in this case, because there was no future in it as she lived in Belgium. The other reason was that I was concerned about my being able to communicate with her since she was living in Belgium, and I assumed she only spoke French.

Marguerite then asked me if I would at least show her around the Capitol. I had become experienced at doing this, and I loved sharing this special place with people. I agreed to take her on the tour, but *only* the tour. We arranged for her to come to my office at 10 am on Thursday.

On Wednesday, Mimi Legat called to tell me in her formal British accent that she had found a ballet class on Thursday morning, which she wanted to take. As a professional dancer, it was not unusual for her to want to take a proper ballet class as often as possible to stay in shape, even while on vacation. She asked if we could reschedule her tour of the Capitol, and I told her I was free Friday afternoon. We agreed to meet at my office at 2 o'clock as I had a lunch date with my cousin, Henny Youngman. Being with Henny was always a fabulous experience, and I wanted to make sure I had plenty of time.

I had become a lover of the ballet before I met Mimi. The first ballet I attended was the New York City Ballet's performance of "Jewels", which was choreographed by George Balanchine. I saw this in the summer before my first year of law school at the Post Pavilion in Columbia, Maryland. I was enthralled by it. While I was in law school in New York, I would take the subway from the Columbia campus directly to Lincoln Center to see the New York City Ballet as often as possible. I could usually get the $2 "nosebleed" seats in the upper balcony. I thoroughly enjoyed Balanchine's choreography, and loved the Jerome Robbins ballet danced to the exquisite Debussy piece "Afternoon of a Faun".

After I graduated from law school and came back to Washington, one of the first things I did was to buy a subscription for the ballet series at the brand-new John F. Kennedy Center for the Performing Arts. The series included ballet companies from all over the world, the New York City Ballet, the American Ballet Theater, the Stuttgart Ballet, the Bolshoi Ballet, and many others.

My fondness for the New York City Ballet and especially the Balanchine ballets led me to a false assumption about my upcoming meeting with Mimi. As far as I knew, Balanchine ballerinas were all very tall- 5' 10" to 6 feet and slim, without a lot of curves. So, that is what I was expecting on Friday afternoon.

Boy, was I wrong! At 2 pm in walked a beautiful 5' 3" woman with a lovely figure. Being British, she was reserved and formal but had a fantastic smile with delightful dimples and pretty blue eyes.

We got acquainted for a few minutes and then began the tour of the Capitol complex. I first took her to the House Judiciary Committee hearing room, where the Watergate hearings were held less than ten years before. I was working on the Hill at that time, and like everyone else in Washington, and most of the country, I was utterly engrossed in what was going on. Watergate was not on her radar. She was a dancer in a Belgian ballet company, and she was not that impressed to be getting the up close and personal look at one of the main venues for that historical event.

We went over to the Capitol using the Rayburn Building shuttle tram. It has only one stop, but most tourists get a kick out of riding on it. When we got to the Capitol, I took her into the House Chamber and explained a bit about the history of the House. I described what I did when the House was considering legislation. She seemed genuinely interested. We then went into Statuary Hall, which was the original House Chamber before the House relocated to its current home in the South end of the building. I then demonstrated the "whispering well". I placed her on one side of the hall and walked about fifty feet away and whispered down towards the marble floor, "Mimi, can you hear me?" She was able to hear me clearly. She knew it was me since I was the only person in the area who knew her name.

The whispering well was the result of an architectural anomaly, which, after it was discovered, was used for political espionage. The ceiling has an unusual parabolic shape. Without the architect's intention to create one, it serves as an acoustical dome; people whispering on one side of the room can be clearly heard on the other side. Back in the day, John Quincy Adams used to pretend to be asleep with his head on his desk so that he could eavesdrop on politicians across the aisle without their knowledge. There is a plaque on the floor, which marks the spot where Adams' desk was located.

We entered the Main Rotunda of the Capitol, which is truly impressive. I told her this was the place where America honors its heroes. I pointed out the white marble spot where the catafalque bearing the coffins of Abraham Lincoln and many others, including John F. Kennedy, had lain in state. I also showed her some of the fabulous artwork which adorns the building, including the extraordinary Apotheosis of Washington by Constantino Brumidi, which is the fresco in the oculus of the dome.

We walked over to what I called "the dark side", which, to me, is the Senate. People who work on the House side are suspicious of the Senate (and vice versa). We sometimes refer to it as the "legislative hospice where House bills go to die". We visited the old Senate Chamber, which is where the Supreme Court used to sit after the Senate moved into its current location at the North end of the Capitol. We went downstairs to the old Supreme Court Chamber, where the Court originally sat. It was in this room that I believe the American Civil War started because this was where the infamous *Dred Scott* case was argued. The Supreme Court's decision holding Dred Scott to be his owner's property led directly to the war.

I love showing off the Capitol, and Mimi seemed to be enjoying herself. I asked her if she wanted to go out for a drink, and she agreed. We went to a nearby Capitol Hill restaurant and spent a couple of hours talking. My stalwart commitment about not taking her out began to weaken.

For the next three weeks, while she and her father were in town, I completely monopolized her. This was frustrating to Marguerite because she had lassoed several other men to take her out. Their loss. We visited a lot of the tourist sites in and around Washington, including the most important memorials and even Mount Vernon. We also went to Annapolis and Baltimore; she got the complete royal treatment.

While I was successful in fending off any other possible suitors, there was no way I could get around the fact that she was here with her 80-year-old father, Sam. She felt strongly she had to spend a good bit of time with him. He told me he had been "fileted" many years ago, referring to back surgery that resulted in his having trouble walking, which was why he used two canes. Because of his limited mobility, and because we had a bit of a struggle getting him in and out of my two-door Toyota, I ended up borrowing my father's car several times during their stay. My father had a huge Lincoln Town Car. My siblings and I referred to it as "the Milt Marshmallow". It handled like a sofa, but it was big and comfortable enough to take Mimi, her father, and on one occasion, Marguerite and her sister Lieba as well, on an excursion.

Mimi and I joked years later about the fortuitous timing of our going out to my parent's house (known to the family as "the Milton Hilton") to borrow the car. It was football season, and my parents were avid fans. They were watching a game when Mimi and I walked into the house. During a commercial break in the game, I introduced her to them, and 12 seconds later, I had the keys, and we were gone. As I noted previously, my parents, thank goodness, stayed out of my social life.

Mimi and I went to the ballet and the theater at the Kennedy Center while she was here, and I took her to several fun places to eat, including a couple of my favorite dives. The Charcoal Grill in Bethesda had the best burgers in town, and so I drove her out to the 'burbs for dinner. There was also a terrific local pizza joint we visited.

By this time, Marguerite was getting a bit concerned that I was hogging Mimi's time, and she was not able to go out with some other fine fellows who she had lined up. It was time for a serious warning. She told Mimi that American men were "fast", and Mimi should be careful about spending too much time with me. As Mimi described it to me, it was quite funny.

✦✦✦✦✦✦✦✦

My commitment to eating properly and knowing how to cook came in handy. I invited Mimi over for dinner. I laid on an impressive feast. We had what I called "Chicken Daniél", chicken breasts sautéed in garlic butter covered with sliced mushrooms and shredded gruyere cheese. I also made noodles Romanoff and a simple salad with my lemon juice and dill dressing. For dessert, I made flambéed Bananas Foster over vanilla ice cream. She was impressed.

✦✦✦✦✦✦✦✦

Mimi and her father were scheduled to leave on a Sunday. The plan was for them to fly from Baltimore to London together. Mimi's dad lived at the former ballet school, where Mimi grew up in Southeast England. He had a car waiting for him to get from Heathrow to his home. Mimi would catch a connecting flight to Brussels. She lived in the Belgian city of Charleroi, which is an hour outside of Brussels. I, too, had travel plans. Starting the following Monday, I was going to take a week off in the Caribbean. December is not my favorite month since I loathe cold weather. I regularly traveled to somewhere warm at that time, since Congress was usually in recess.

However, notwithstanding my carefully made plans, I had another idea. On Saturday, I asked her, "Are you free for dinner next Tuesday?" She replied in her usual proper British tone, "Yes, Daniel, but I shall be in Belgium where I live". I looked her straight in the eye and said, "Okay, I will meet you there". She was a bit shocked, to say the least. I thought at that time it would not be difficult to get a flight at a reasonable price on short notice. Airfare to Europe in December is notoriously cheap.

She was pleased with the idea, and we planned the logistics. She would fly to London with her dad on Sunday, get her connecting flight to Brussels, take the train to Charleroi, have time to clean up her apartment and do some grocery shopping and then meet me at the airport in Brussels when my flight arrived on Tuesday. We made a tentative backup plan, which was to meet at the hotel "nearest the airport in Brussels" if there were any travel difficulties. This was in the days before cell phones. However, neither one of us was sufficiently familiar with the airport to know there were dozens of hotels in the area. There was no way to know which hotel was "nearest the airport".

We decided not to say anything to her father and especially not to say anything to Marguerite about our intended rendezvous. On Sunday, I drove them to Baltimore Washington International Airport (BWI) and bid them a fond farewell as they got on their flight to London. On Monday, I flew to JFK airport in New York to catch my flight to Brussels. That evening before my flight, I tried to call Mimi in Charleroi several times from JFK. I had expected her to have arrived home by that time. As they say in England, "No answer came the stern reply". I never did get through to her, and later I found out why. The weather in Europe was terrible, and Mimi had a very difficult time getting from London to Brussels. By the time she got there, trains were not running because of the snowstorm, and all hotels nearby were full. She could not even get out of the airport. Unbeknownst to me, the weather was affecting my flight as well.

When I got to the plane in New York, I went to my assigned seat, and somebody was sitting there. I asked the flight attendant about it, and she said, "Why don't you go sit up in the forward cabin". I was pleased to do that since I thought that the "forward cabin" meant first class. That was not the case since this was the intercity bus version of a Boeing 747; the whole front section was coach. However, I was the only one in the forward cabin. I took advantage of the situation and was able to lay down flat across the four seats in the center of the plane.

Mimi, meanwhile, was sleeping on a bench at the airport in Brussels waiting for me. The airline staff in Brussels told her my flight was delayed due to either sleet or something I never heard of, "freezing fog". She was told that there was a distinct possibility that it would be diverted to Amsterdam. This did not make her happy since I'm sure she was exhausted after having spent the night at the airport. However, at the last minute it the fog had lifted, we were going to be landing in Brussels.

As I was wending my way through the cattle chute to immigration and customs, the man behind me tapped me on the shoulder and pointed to the gallery above us. There was Mimi waving to me! I think she was relieved that my flight had landed and was in the correct city.

After we collected my luggage, we went to the train station, which is adjacent to the airport. This was a typical European railway station which had an announcement board containing letters and numbers which flipped over, "clack, clack, clack, clack" as new times and destinations were posted. Since it had snowed heavily while I was in the air, ground transportation was helter-skelter. Hordes of people would wait in the central hall looking up at the information board anxiously awaiting notice that a train going to their destination was ready for boarding. As soon as the newest information came up, the mob would rush towards the designated track. It was a complete zoo! After about an hour of waiting, we finally managed to get a train. It was like scenes I had seen of the Tokyo subway. We had to be physically forced into the car by railway staff because the cars were so jammed.

Once we had arrived at Mimi's apartment in Charleroi, she decided to call her father and tell him that she had arrived safely and to make sure he had as well. She then informed him she had a visitor – me. Her father could not understand why I was there. Being British, a major focus in his life was the weather. He knew of my planned trip to the sunny Caribbean and could not fathom why I would go to Belgium, where it was cold and snowing instead. "He is in Belgium? I thought he was going to the Caribbean. The weather in Belgium is terrible". Mimi said, "Daddy, he did not come for the weather".

The next morning Mimi went off to the theater for her regular ballet class. One of the women she shared a dressing room with asked her if she brought anything interesting back from her trip. Mimi said, "Yes, an American lawyer!" Since I was only the second lawyer she had ever met, it was an astounding development.

We spent the next few days in Charleroi getting over jetlag and visiting various parts of the city. She introduced me to several of her friends, many of whom did not speak English. My French is practically nonexistent. A lot of smiling and nodding sufficed as communication.

We then decided to make the 2-hour railway trip to Paris for the weekend. One of the marvelous things about Europe is you are only a short train ride away from a lot of interesting places. On our last night in Paris, we were looking for a place to have dinner and asked at our hotel for a recommendation. The concierge gave us the name of a place that seemed reasonably close and sounded ideal. Mimi, who spoke fluent French, called the restaurant to make a reservation and then innocently asked them where the nearest Metro stop was. We had done most of our sight-seeing using the excellent Paris Metro system. I gather the man she was talking to was a little perplexed by that since people who eat at this restaurant *do not* ride on public transportation.

We walked to the restaurant which was near our hotel. It was on the Place de la Concorde at the end of the Champs-Elysées. It was in a free-standing building on some of the most expensive real estate in the world. As we entered, we looked warily at each other, thinking this might not be what we had in mind. However, the staff swooped down on us, took our coats, and were escorting us to our table before we had time to reconsider what was probably a mistake and almost certainly out of our price range. As we walked into this extremely beautiful restaurant, I saw two men sitting across the way who looked familiar. Lo and behold, there were two of my father's law partners. I knew them, but not well, and I chose to ignore them and go straight to our table. We had a delicious meal.

On the way out of the restaurant, the two lawyers were still there, and we made eye contact, so I figured it would be rude not to stop by and say hello. We chatted briefly, and then one of them asked us, "What are you doing here in Paris?" Mimi responded innocently, "Oh, we came for the weekend". She did not realize that these men, who knew I lived in Washington DC, would assume we had probably come over on the Concorde and were having dinner in this very expensive restaurant as part of the lifestyle of people who jet off to Paris "for the weekend."

After I returned from Europe, my father told me that one of them had spoken to him about our meeting and expressed his admiration. He was still under the false impression that I had flown over to Paris from Washington for the weekend. My father, who knew nothing about my trip to Belgium, told me later that he simply said, "Some people just know how to live!".

After returning to Charleroi from Paris, we spent the next few days enjoying ourselves until it was time for me to go home. I told her I had to catch a flight the following Saturday. One morning when she was in ballet class, I found the nearest florist and went in to order her roses for Valentine's Day, which was about three weeks away. I thought it would be a nice romantic gesture and gave the florist a handwritten note to be delivered with the flowers. My bumbling French, combined with the florist's bumbling English, did the trick. I asked her if she knew Mimi Legat, and she responded: "Ah, certainment, la danseuse". One of the benefits of being in a small town is a lot of people know who you are. With that seen to, I reconfirmed my flight. The reason I had to leave that Saturday was because the Super Bowl was Sunday. I was not about to miss the most important football game of the year. Mimi had no idea about the game, and I decided to leave it that way.

We were in regular touch by telephone and letter and planned to meet in Italy in April. We spent three weeks there traveling seeing Rome, Florence and Venice. It was a spectacular trip!

✦✦✦✦✦✦✦✦

Mimi's contract with the ballet company in Charleroi ended that summer, and she had not yet decided what she was going to do. We talked about whether she would be interested in coming to live with me "in the colonies". She was intrigued by that idea, and we decided to have her come for a month in May when I would be working, as Congress was going to be in session. This would be a glimpse of realistic day-to-day life and would give her a taste of what living in America would be like. That experiment worked out well. We decided that when her contract expired, she would pack up her things in Charleroi and go to visit her father in England. Then at the end of August, she would come to Washington, and we would begin our lives together.

She got work teaching ballet at Georgetown University and a few other small ballet schools in Bethesda, Potomac, and Reston. I continued to work on Capitol Hill, and things were fantastic.

Her father was in his 80s and was more than a little parsimonious. He very much liked to visit us, and he enjoyed being fussed over. However, we lived in a two-bedroom, one-bath apartment in the city, and it got a little cramped when he visited. Because he figured he was flying all the way from England and paying airfare, he wanted to get his money's worth. He had no commitments in England, so he could stay for a good while. I have talked to friends and colleagues about visits from their relatives, and none of them had had the experience I had. Mimi's father would come to visit us for 4 to 6 *weeks* at a time!

Not unrelated to her father's semi-annual invasions, we decided that our apartment was too small, and we needed to start looking for a house. Our real estate agent called me one day to tell me she had found a marvelous garden for Mimi, which happened to have a beautiful house on it. It also had the number of bedrooms we wanted and room for a darkroom for me. We ended up buying it. It is in Chevy Chase, five blocks from the house where I grew up and where my parents still lived! Having the house with all the extra room made Sam's visits a lot easier to deal with.

We did find that in order to purchase a house, we were going to have to deal with the realities of Mimi's immigration status. The simplest way to deal with that was to get married, and so we decided to do that. Neither of us felt any strong need to get married; we were very happy the way we were. However, as I have pointed out, we "had to get married" because of the INS and the IRS. For us both to contribute to the purchase price and to avail ourselves of the tax benefits of homeownership, including tax deductions for mortgage interest, it turned out we needed to be married. Also, since she did not have a green card, working could have become a problem. Getting married would remove both difficulties. I did not feel any change occasioned by being married, but Mimi felt people treated her a bit differently.

Neither one of us was interested in having a big wedding, so we decided to do it as simply as possible by going to the courthouse in Rockville. In attendance were the court clerk, her assistant, Mimi, and me. We went from the courthouse to my parent's house, where my mother greeted us at the door. She was fond of Mimi and was pleased but a little surprised to see us at 11 a.m. I asked my mother, "How many daughters-in-law do you have?" She thought for a few seconds and then said, "I don't have any". I then said, "Wrong answer! You now have one". It took her a minute or so to realize the implications of my statement, but when she did, she threw her arms around Mimi with utter joy. She then disappeared and rushed back with a bottle of champagne that she had been saving for a special occasion.

She then said to Mimi, "You have to call your father". Mimi picked up the phone and dialed her dad in England. Her father was very interested in the garden and plants. So, when the call went through the first thing he said was, "I'm glad you called, I wanted to talk to you about the hibiscus". Mimi tried to interrupt him to tell him the news, but the line started crackling and then died. My mother said, "You have to call him back". I suggested Mimi try the operator. She got an operator on the line, who thought there might be some problems with the overseas lines and asked her to try again later. "I just got married, and I need to tell my father", was her response. The operator was sympathetic and placed the call herself and said she would wait on the line to make sure it went through. When her father answered the phone, he started rabbiting on about the damn hibiscus. Mimi finally was able to cut him off by saying, "Daddy, we just got married!" There was a long silence on the line. From then on, I referred to myself as the man who married Sam's daughter and ruined his life. We also called my sister, Amy Malone, who lived in the area, to tell her the news. I could hear her shouting in the store where she worked, "My brother just got married!" repeatedly.

Congress was not in session, but I called the office to tell my boss we were running late and that we would go directly to the restaurant where we had planned to have lunch. Before I had a chance to do so, she said, "You're late for work", and not in a friendly way.

Mimi and I arrived at the restaurant and were waiting for Alan, his wife Odette, and my boss, Alan's replacement, in a private room upstairs, which I had reserved for the occasion. As the three of them walked in, I said to Odette, "You may kiss the bride". Odette immediately understood and hugged Mimi. My boss seemed upset that she did not know we were plotting to get married. She and I had been shopping during lunch the day before, and I bought a new tie to wear for the occasion. She said somewhat angrily, "I should have known!"

✦✦✦✦✦✦✦✦✦

The next day was Thanksgiving, and we decided to sleep in. However, the phone rang at 8 am. It was my enthusiastic friend George with whom we were supposed to have dinner the night before. We had canceled the dinner because we had gotten married and wanted to spend the evening on our own. In his usual gregarious manner, George said, "Hey Dan, we're downstairs. Buzz us in." Mimi and I threw some clothes on, and we heard George and his wife Connie coming down the hallway, fully laden with packages. He was carrying a big box with a ribbon on it, which turned out to be a wedding gift, and she was carrying a grocery bag full of food. George said, "We brought you a wedding breakfast, go back to bed!" So, we did.

They disappeared into the kitchen, and a few minutes later appeared in the bedroom with a lovely white wicker breakfast tray filled with goodies including a tiny vase with a rose in it, a split of champagne, a quiche, a small white (wedding) cake with a candle in it as well as the appropriate implements. That was wedding cake number one. As the four of us tucked into breakfast, Mimi and me in the bed and George and Connie on chairs, I said, "This is the first time I have ever entertained more than one person in my bedroom".

A short time later, they disappeared, and we went back to sleep. When we woke up, and Mimi told me that she had the strangest dream that George and Connie had shown up at our place and made us wedding breakfast. I informed her it was not a dream.

✦✦✦✦✦✦✦✦✦

As it was Thanksgiving Day, most of my family was going to gather at the

Milton Hilton for dinner. My brother Andy, my sister Amy and her husband John, and my parents were there. There was the appropriate excitement about our marriage, and we had a nice traditional Thanksgiving meal. When it came time for dessert, Amy leaped up, went into the kitchen, and came out with a stunning tiered three-layer wedding cake. That was wedding cake number two. Since she is a cake decorator, I was not completely surprised, but for her to whip up a lovely cake like that overnight was special.

Later, my father pulled me aside and said, "Your mother thinks Mimi has gotten shortchanged by not having a big wedding celebration. So, if your mother asks if you would like to have a party to celebrate your wedding, *the answer is YES!!*" While neither of us was particularly interested in having such a party, obviously it was important to my mother, so we agreed.

In January, my parents gave us a lovely party for us at the Milton Hilton. The gathering included friends of mine, friends of ours, friends of Mimi's, and a smattering of friends of my parents, some of whom we did not know. Amy had done her thing again and produced yet another spectacular wedding cake beautifully decorated and, just as important, it was delicious. That was wedding cake number three.

The following summer, we went to England to visit Mimi's father and a whole gaggle of her relatives and friends. It was a beautiful summer day, and we had a party outside in honor of our wedding. Mimi's cousin Beryl greeted me by saying, "While it may be after the fact, this is still our chance to check you out". Beryl is a hoot, and that was the beginning of a long and close relationship. In order to celebrate the occasion properly, Ada, the woman who had been the cook at the Legat School for decades, decided she wanted to make us a wedding cake. Mimi readily agreed. She always says "yes" to cake.

What I did not know at the time was that British wedding cakes are different from American cakes. An American cake has a sponge cake on the inside and a soft buttercream frosting. British wedding cakes are a whole other animal. The inside is similar to a brick; it is made of the kind of leaden fruit cake which Americans re-gift every Christmas season. It is soaked with brandy or rum and covered with marzipan. Then it is covered with a special icing, which is very hard and brittle and cracks when cut. Wedding cake number 4 was a British cake. Ada had made the top tier without alcohol since I am allergic to it. However, when she prepared the top layer of icing, the stiff British version (called Royal icing), I think she put in a couple of cups of Portland cement. It was rock solid, and we had a difficult time trying to cut it. There is a photo of us holding onto a large knife, which is bent almost in a semi-circle. Ada was mortified. I hate fruitcake anyway, so I did not feel deprived and begged off tasting it. What the hell, it was my fourth wedding cake! Mimi loved it.

Mimi adapted easily to almost everything about living in "the colonies", with the possible exception of strong southern or New York accents and some peculiarities concerning American professional football. As I mentioned previously, I am an avid football fan, and Mimi has been tolerant of that. There are two things to which she is vehemently opposed; the "two-minute" warning and overtime. It took her a long time to get used to the fact that the "two-minute" warning only meant there was probably less than a half-hour left before the game ended, not two minutes in real-time. She considered overtime to be a personal affront.

She has the incredible ability to sit in the room and read while I am watching a game. I do not have those powers of concentration. I would occasionally interrupt her and point out an exciting play, and she would look at the replay and be minimally impressed and return to her book.

She showed her football stuff the year the Washington football team went to the Super Bowl. The city was in a fever! A local concrete company even painted one of its trucks' mixing drum to look like a football (the shape was pretty close) with the team logo on it. Before the game, we went to the local deli to get submarine sandwiches. Having subs was practically a legal requirement in order to properly watch the game. Most of the people in the sandwich line were wearing some type of team paraphernalia. It was, as we used to say in the 60s, "a happening". The man who was in front of us was not paying attention when his sandwich was handed to him, and it fell to the floor. Mimi yelled, "Fumble!" Everyone cracked up, and I loved her even more.

Since we were married, it became much easier to get her immigration situation straightened out. All that was required for her to get her green card was for us to fill out a bunch of paperwork and go to the Immigration and Naturalization Service for an interview. They were cracking down on marriage fraud for immigration cases at the time. Mimi does not do well in official settings, and she was nervous about having to go through the interview. However, it went well, and she soon got her green card.

Gene Pugliese was my best friend on the committee staff, and he was the Chief Counsel of the Immigration Subcommittee. He suggested that we should get Mimi her American citizenship as soon as possible. He said, half in jest, "If Mimi gets stopped for going five miles an hour over the limit, with the way these people are looking at the immigration laws, she could be deported. You better get her naturalized pronto!"

Because we were married, that should not have been difficult. To qualify, you must take an American citizenship examination. However, Mimi is uncomfortable with officials, and the thought of having to show up and take her citizenship exam was not something she was looking forward to. I tutored her on American government, including using a pneumonic (Jell-O) for the three branches of the federal government; J-judiciary, E-executive and L-legislative. By the time she was ready to take the exam, I think she had a good handle on anything they could possibly ask her, including who her Senators were, or her Member of Congress was, and even the Justices of the Supreme Court. We had to drive to Silver Spring, a nearby suburb, for her to take the exam. On the way, I was giving her some last-minute questions. Finally, as we were getting near the building, I said, "Okay, here is your last question. What are the last two words of the national anthem?" She looked at me and smiled and then said, "Play ball!" She passed the exam with flying colors.

Once your paperwork has been approved, you have to take an oath to become a citizen. This is usually done by a Federal Judge. I had asked a former Member of Congress whom I knew quite well, Abner Mikva, to administer the oath. He had left Congress to take a Federal Judgeship on the United States Court of Appeals for the District of Columbia Circuit. He was very gracious and agreed to do it, and I thought it would be nice for Mimi to have a simple, quiet private ceremony. However, about a month before her swearing-in, she got a notice from the INS informing her that the day she was to be sworn in was Citizenship Day in the State of Maryland, and they were going to be swearing in everybody who was in the pipeline at the time.

We found out that on the day of the ceremony, George Hudson, the former Headmaster of the Legat School of Ballet, who Mimi was very fond of, was going to be in town visiting us. The three of us went up to Baltimore, where the ceremony was being held, in of all places, Oriole Park at Camden Yards. Instead of the intimate ceremony in Judge Mikva's chambers, she was going to be sworn in at a baseball stadium along with 4400 other people!

When we got there, we were greeted by a heaving wave of people, which included all the citizenship applicants and their friends and families. It was a complete zoo! George and I sat in the right-field stands, while Mimi and the rest of the new citizens-to-be were gathered in the stands along the third base line. This was Mimi's first and only visit to an athletic stadium. Fortunately, George brought his camera with a long telephoto lens, and Mimi was wearing a rather striking sundress, which enabled us to pick her out. A Federal Judge swore them in en mass. The event was quite moving.

✦ ✦ ✦ ✦ ✦ ✦ ✦ ✦ ✦

While Mimi enjoyed teaching, she longed to be back in the theater dancing. She decided to audition for the role of the Spanish Princess [a dancer] in a production of Jules Massenet's opera "Cendrillion". She got the part and was thrilled to be performing again. This opera role turned out to be the first of a long series of engagements with the Washington National Opera (WNO).

Placido Domingo was one of the Artistic Directors at the Opera, and she got to work directly with him as a choreographer on several operas, and also to perform with him. He is a delightful man and was lovely to work with. I got a chance to get to know Mr. Domingo a bit, and I thought he was wonderful. She worked with some other famous people in the opera world, including Jose Carreras, Frederica Von Stade, Ava Marton, and Alessandra Marc. She even went to Japan with the WNO to perform in the opera "Sly" with Mr. Carreras.

I had a photo of Mr. Domingo and Mimi doing an "apache" which is what you and I would call a "dip" when a couple is dancing. I had written to Mr. Domingo to ask him to autograph the photo. I did not receive a response. I met him at an opening night party for one of the operas, and I said, "Mr. Domingo, you owe me a letter". He, of course, had no idea who I was or what I was talking about. I explained it to him, and he said he would get to it promptly. Less than a week later, the photo arrived in the mail. He had inscribed it this way: "To Mimi, with my very best wishes. It takes two to tango". From that point on, he always referred to me as "Daniel, Mimi's husband".

✦✦✦✦✦✦✦✦✦

To me, one of the high points of Mimi's career with the Washington National Opera was her performance as Madame Butterfly's mother in the famous and moving Puccini opera. They made her up to look like a 100-year-old woman. She was covered in white makeup, had a long shaggy grey/white wig, and looked ancient and decrepit. I did not recognize her when I saw her backstage before the opening night performance.

She was concerned about the ending of the first act. It is the wrenching and heartbreaking scene where the mother is releasing her daughter's blood into the earth. The director decided the best way to show it was to have Mimi's character softly toss a bright scarlet silk scarf into a hole in the stage floor. It is a poignant moment, but Mimi was very concerned about throwing the scarf; she did not want to miss the hole in the floor because of air currents on the stage when there was an audience. She agonized about it. I said, "Do what Michael Jordan does; practice, practice, practice". I also suggested a National Football League official's trick; put some un-popped kernels of popcorn in the material to give it a little heft to make it easier to throw. What they finally decided to use was sand sewn into one corner. She went to the theater each day and did her practice "free throws" with the loaded scarf and felt much better about it. The opera company had also connived to make sure the scarf disappeared into the earth (hole in the floor); they had a stagehand underneath the stage with a long black glove on. He would stick his hand up through the opening to snare the scarf in case Mimi's aim was off. It worked out well.

The second time I saw the performance, I took a dear friend of ours, Vee Gill, who is married to our extraordinary doctor and friend Fred Gill. Tim Keating managed to get me two seats in the Presidential box! We even got the combination to the refrigerator where they had soft drinks and splits of champagne. Vee was delighted to be there. When the curtain came down at the end of the first act after Mimi has softly tossed her daughter's blood into the earth, everyone sat there in stunned silence. As the lights came up, I looked into the box next to the Presidential box, and there was Mr. Domingo. He thrust his hand out towards me to shake and barely missed the nose of the man sitting between us. He said, "Ah, Daniel, Mimi's husband!" As I shook his hand, I said, "Mr. Domingo, how could you make my beautiful young wife into an old hag?" He smiled and said, "We had to do it for the sake of art!"

I then looked at the man who was sitting between us whose nose Mr. Domingo and I had nearly clipped and recognized him. I put out my hand to greet him and said: "Hello, Senator Kennedy, it is nice to see you again". He stood up and shook my hand and said candidly, "I know I know you, but I don't remember how". I explained that we had met often when I worked for Mr. Rodino on the House Judiciary Committee staff. He said, "Oh, yes, of course. You attended many meetings with Peter and me".

Another special evening was the opening night of "Romeo and Juliet". Mimi was the choreographer for the chorus. There was to be a black-tie party after the performance. Mimi was wearing a lovely off-the-shoulder gown, and I was appropriately dressed like an Emperor penguin. I was on the aisle, and Mimi was to my right. We had decided to switch seats after the second act because Mimi had to be backstage after the final curtain to take a bow as the choreographer. There would not be enough time for her to scurry up there after the final curtain. I turned to the stunning woman sitting next to me who was wearing a smashing red dress. I leaned over to her and told her why we had switched seats. I opened the program, showed her Mimi's photo, and said, quite proudly, "My wife is the choreographer, and she has to be backstage to take a bow". This woman was so sweet. She gently put her hand on my arm and said, "How nice for you. My husband is Romeo".

XII. Chairman Brooks and the House Judiciary Committee

Anytime you start a new job, you will have to get used to a different supervisor. When Jack Brooks became the Chairman of the House Judiciary Committee, it was not a completely new job for me, but it certainly was a new boss. Not only would I have to get accustomed to working for Mr. Brooks, but I would also have to learn how to work with the staff people he brought with him from the House Government Operations Committee.

I knew Mr. Brooks had a practice of requiring every candidate for a position on the staff to be interviewed by him personally, Democrat or Republican, full committee, or subcommittee. If you passed muster during the interview, he would give you a cheap plastic Jack Brooks key chain. It was a rite of passage. However, I never went through that. I was never interviewed nor offered a job. I simply kept showing up for work and kept the same office. No one ever said anything to me about being hired, so I let inertia take over and hoped for the best.

While Brooks brought a lot of his staff over from the Government Operations committee, there were a lot of Judiciary Committee staff, especially the nuts and bolts administrative staff, who were going to be retained. They knew the ropes. The financial clerk, Jim Farr, who had been with the committee for years, was one of several people who was kept on.

Brooks' General Counsel from Government Operations, Bill Jones, came over. He and Brooks had worked together for years. He was impressive. Very steady and unflappable. He knew how Brooks wanted to work and tried to make sure things were done the way the new Chairman was used to. Saying "Chairman Rodino did it this way" was not a successful strategy.

✦✦✦✦✦✦✦✦✦

Another example of jargon and Mr. Brooks came up when we were han-

dling a bill called the Freedom of Access to Clinic Entrances law, the so-called
FACE bill. This was a highly controversial bill dealing with access to abortion
clinics, and it was not something that Mr. Brooks was familiar with. It was being
handled by the Subcommittee on Civil and Constitutional Rights, which was
chaired by Congressman Don Edwards. Mr. Edwards was a leader in the civil
rights area, and reproductive freedom was a key issue for his subcommittee.
Anything dealing with abortion was highly contentious, and although the bill
came through Mr. Edwards' subcommittee, it was a full committee measure as
it went to the floor.

The House and the Senate had passed different versions of this bill. To reconcile the differences, a conference committee was appointed. The conference
was held, and a compromise was reached. The House Rules dictate that any
conference report can contain only matters "within the scope of the matters
committed to conference". If it includes something that was not in the Senate
bill and not in the House bill, nor somewhere in between, the conference report
would be subject to a point of order. If such a point of order was made, it could
not be considered in the House.

The House and Senate staffs had done a good job of merging the two bills
and came up with a satisfactory compromise. Because they were aware of possible legal challenges to the legislation, being careful lawyers, they decided to
add a savings clause to the final language. A savings clause provides that if any
provision of the law is determined to be unenforceable, the remainder of the
statute is still valid. While this was good lawyering, it was bad legislating. Neither
the Senate bill nor the House bill contained a savings clause. Although including
it was a prudent thing to do, because it was in neither the House bill nor the
Senate bill, it meant that the conference report would be subject to a point of
order for a scope violation, thereby killing it. A conference report is a privileged
matter, and it can be called up at any time by a conferee. The inclusion of the
savings clause precluded calling it up without a protective rule.

To get around this problem, we had to get a rule from the Rules Committee
that would waive the scope point of order. I had the unenviable task of calling
Chairman Brooks at home to explain to him the necessity of getting a rule to
take the FACE bill up on the floor. The first question he asked me was, "What
the hell does FACE mean?" I explained it to him, and he said, "Freeman, you
sumbitch, (his normal way of addressing me) why does the staff waste time
making up these goddamn cute names for bills?" I did not answer that rhetor-
ical question. He then asked me, "Do we really need a rule for this?" I simply
said, "Yes", and he told me to "get it done and go home and get a good night's
rest". Before he hung up, he said, "Say hello to your bride".

I contacted the Rules Committee staff and prepared the required written request for a hearing on a rule. I told them I wanted a simple rule that would waive the possible point of order. Mr. Brooks had to go to the Rules Committee and testify, which was an extra step that should not have been necessary, but we successfully dealt with it. Bill Jones told me Mr. Brooks was pleased I had prevented his being subjected to the embarrassment of having a sustainable point of order raised against the conference report.

✦✦✦✦✦✦✦✦✦

The people who came over with Chairman Brooks seemed to be terrified of him and would never engage him in normal conversation. Brooks had the reputation of being a mean SOB. Years later, when I was teaching at American University, CBS News anchorman Bob Schieffer, a Texan himself, who was a guest speaker, told me, "Jack Brooks was the only man Lyndon Johnson was afraid of". I was not afraid of him, but I certainly was wary. The Gov Ops staff were astounded when I would talk to him like a normal human being. One day when Bill, his deputy, Bob Brink, the Chairman and I were in the Rayburn cafeteria having lunch, Mr. Brooks asked me in his normal style, "Freeman, you sumbitch, how is your bride doing with those azaleas?" Bill and Bob were astounded that I would talk to the Chairman about gardening. We chatted back and forth about what kind of plants Mimi had selected and whether we needed to amend the soil, etc. As Bob and Bill and I were walking back to the committee offices, Bob said, "I cannot believe you talked to the Chairman about that". He had a reputation around the committee for being a bit stiff. Many of us referred to him as "Ollie" because he reminded us of Oliver North. I was surprised that he was surprised.

There were other things I had to get used to working for Jack Brooks. His practice had been to sign letters only on Fridays. Since Gov Ops worked on a limited number of pieces of legislation, that was sufficient. On the Judiciary Committee, things frequently came up that were time-sensitive, so the Chairman had to get used to being presented with correspondence at any time during the week.

I found out the hard way about violating the Brooks "elevator rule", which I did not know existed. If you got onto the elevator with the Chairman and he was going back to his office, it was bad form to push the button for any floor other than four, which was where his office was located. Even if you were getting off on the 1st floor, which was where the committee offices were, you always let the Chairman go up to the 4th floor first. Not knowing that, I got on the elevator with Bill and the Chairman on G3, and since I was going to my office, I pushed 1. I heard a throat clearing and got a glare. I learned my lesson.

There was another thing that the staff on the Judiciary Committee did differently. We talked to Members. Soon after Brooks took over, I got a call from Congressman Don Edwards. He was an extremely nice man, and frequently called staff with questions. I went in to tell Bill about the call because I thought it was something the Chairman should be aware of. Bob, who was sitting there, as usual, looked at me in amazement and said, "You talked to a Member?" I was informed that Gov Ops staff never talked to Members; a Member would get his or her staff to call the Gov Ops staff who would then get an answer from the Chairman and relay it back. I told them Judiciary Committee Members were used to and comfortable with, calling staff directly, and it might be difficult to enforce that on our Members. It was an alien concept to them.

Jack Brooks could be cold as ice. We were on the floor one day, managing a bill. A Member came up to talk with him, and I was sitting there behind him. I knew the other Member's mother was in the hospital, but I did not have a chance to tell the Chairman. They talked briefly about whatever, and then the other Member left the floor. I told the Chairman about his mother, and he said, "I don't give a shit about his mother *now*. If I had known that 5 minutes ago, I would have said something".

One of the people who came over with Brooks was his chief investigator. He was just plain mean. He loved being able to lord his power over people and tell them he would subpoena them to testify if they did not cooperate with him. His office was next to mine, but I stayed as far away from him as possible. He would occasionally stop by my office on the way to his.

One afternoon he started to tell me about some subpoenas *he* was going to issue. I was rather surprised by that since, under the Judiciary Committee rules with which I was very familiar, any subpoena had to be authorized by a vote of the Full Committee. He was livid. Under the Gov Ops rule, the Chairman had the authority to issue subpoenas on his own. He told me he was "not going to have any Members of Congress fuck up my investigation".

Occasionally, I would say the perfect thing in front of the Chairman. My office was situated directly off the committee room, and Members frequently used it during meetings or as a holding room for witnesses. One day I came around the corner and turned into my office where I saw Mr. Brooks and John White, a Texas politician and former Chairman of the Democratic National Committee, sitting in the two guest chairs. I was going to do an about-face and not interrupt them when the Chairman saw me and said, "Come on in, son". I knew he liked to show off his staff to visitors. He said, "You know John

White". I did not, but I shook his hand and said I was pleased to see him. Mr. White asked me, "Is this your office, Dan?" I had a lot of my photographs displayed on the walls, not the normal ego wall pictures of me with famous people which most politicians have, but landscapes and portraits I had taken and printed. I said, "No, sir. It belongs to Mr. Brooks, and he lets me use it". That brought a smile to the Chairman's face.

I do recollect another time when the Chairman was showing off his "toys" (the staff). Soon after he became the Chairman, he stopped into the committee offices with an old friend. It was clear that he was flaunting his new committee digs and staff. The professional staff of the Judiciary Committee consisted mostly of lawyers. That had been an unwritten rule for years since the committee was dealing with legal matters most of the time. I happened to be standing there in the front office when they walked in. The Chairman introduced me to his friend as one of his "legal eagles". The guest asked the Chairman, "Jack, how many lawyers you got working for you?" The Chairman took a drag on his ever-present cigar and replied, "About half". I could not help but laugh.

✦✦✦✦✦✦✦✦✦

My good friend Gene Pugliese and I used to have lunch together regularly in the Rayburn cafeteria. As we were sitting there one day, we saw the Chairman. In violation of the unwritten rule about talking with the Chairman, I invited him to join us. He said he only had five minutes and sat down. I did not see any reason to talk to him about business. I knew that he had been in the motorcade in Dallas on November 22, 1963, so I decided to ask him about it. "Mr. Chairman, what was it like in Dallas?"

For the next hour, Gene and I were privileged to learn about things that happened on that terrible day from someone who was there. Mr. Brooks is in the famous photo of LBJ taking the oath of office on Air Force One. He told us some stories that had never made it into the press and gave us his insights. He was at the hospital when President Kennedy was pronounced dead. He told us that Lyndon Johnson took command immediately and was ordering people around. Mr. Brooks was told, "Jack, you take care of Bird". That was the new president's way of putting Mr. Brooks in charge of making sure Mrs. Johnson got to the plane. At that time, no one knew whether there was a conspiracy afoot to take out other members of the American government.

As Brooks told us the story, it got more and more fascinating. It was evident that the moment John F. Kennedy had been declared dead, Lyndon Johnson was the President of the United States, and there probably was no legal or constitutional urgency for him to take the oath of office. Johnson understood the importance of the symbolism of his taking the oath and insisted that it be done before Air Force One took off. Brooks told us that Johnson was aware of every little detail and orchestrated everything down to where Mrs. Kennedy and everybody else was going to stand. He was not going to take the oath of office until Mrs. Kennedy was available to witness it and to be photographed doing so.

Johnson was not above retaliating against Attorney General Robert F. Kennedy for what he perceived to be the terrible way Kennedy had treated him going back to LBJ's days as Senate Majority Leader. Johnson felt that Robert Kennedy had marginalized him as much as possible, was openly hostile, and made him grovel even though he was the Vice President of the United States. Johnson loathed him.

One of the things Johnson did to rub salt in the wounds of Robert Kennedy was to ensure that the Federal Judge who would administer the oath of office on Air Force One was someone whose confirmation Kennedy had initially held up. LBJ thought he did so because she was from Texas and because Johnson supported her. Brooks told us about another thing LBJ did to stick it to Robert Kennedy, which I thought was particularly cruel. He insisted on getting the language of the Presidential oath of office directly from the Attorney General. The oath is in the Constitution, and they could have gotten it from any one of 100 places, but Johnson insisted his staff get it directly from Kennedy.

This was an extraordinary window into history which Gene and I were permitted to look through. Brooks was a protégé of Lyndon Johnson's; we were fortunate to be able to hear about what happened from an eyewitness. I am sure that had Bob Brink or Bill Jones been around, we would not have.

The fact that Johnson and Brooks were close was no secret. I was told by a good friend who worked in the Clinton White House, that when Chairman Brooks came to the Oval Office to meet with President Clinton for the first time, the White House had been declared by Hillary to be a smoke-free zone. Jack Brooks was an inveterate cigar smoker. When he got to the Oval Office, President Clinton offered him a cigar. Clinton said, "Mr. Chairman, you were smoking cigars in this office with LBJ when I was still in college, so please feel free to light up".

✦ ✦ ✦ ✦ ✦ ✦ ✦ ✦ ✦

Mr. Brooks had a series of pithy sayings that I frequently use. One of those is when referring to overly flattering introductory language about a guest speaker, "That is the kinda crap only your mama would believe". Having been a Marine, he was not opposed to using some strong language. However, you got used to it and ignored it. One day we were on the floor to take up a piece of legislation at the beginning of the proceedings. We had to wait while the House went through its usual opening formalities. This was after Michael Dukakis was resoundingly defeated in the presidential election. One of the byproducts of that campaign was the new practice of all of the Members and staff having to recite the Pledge of Allegiance at the beginning of each session. Mr. Brooks thought it was ridiculous that he should have to recite the pledge. He said he had already taken an oath of office to "support and defend the Constitution of the United States", and he thought to require Members to recite the pledge was "political tomfoolery". After the pledge that day, he said, "Thank *you*, Michael Dukakis".

During a full committee markup of a fairly controversial bill, we knew there were going to be several amendments offered which might be subject to points of order. My job was to prepare rulings for the Chairman if any of them was offered. I was able to find out about 14 amendments various Members intended to offer which would be subject to a point of order. I was ready with rulings for each one. As the committee went through all of the amendments, a point of order was raised on each. After a short debate, the Chairman had to be prepared to rule. In every case, he would stick out his hand, and I would give the written ruling to him. I took it as a compliment that the Chairman never wanted to review them ahead of time; he relied on me to make sure they were correct. He would just read them as I had written them. We got into a good rhythm, and I was ready for each one. However, near the end of the markup, someone offered an amendment that I had not seen or heard about. A point of order was made, and the Chairman simply reached out for the ruling he expected. I leaned over and whispered to him that I had not seen this amendment, and I would have to give him a ruling "off the top of my head". He looked at me and my practically bald head and said, "Well son, there ain't too much there, is there?" I did not take offense since his haircut was very similar to mine.

Mr. Brooks was pleased to find out about my practice of getting proxies before every full committee meeting. He would always check to make sure I had them. He was scrupulous about complying with any instructions which came with them. As the roll was called, I would say either, "Proxy" if there were no instructions, "Proxy Aye (or Nay), depending on what the Member has specified. He would vote a proxy differently than he voted if I told him that is what the Member wanted. He would always honor the Members' wishes, including going so far as not to vote the proxy if he even suspected exercising it would create a problem for the other Member. "I think we will just let that one go", he would say. I respected his honoring those instructions.

There were two significant pieces of legislation the committee processed during the Brooks years. Probably the most important, as far as the effect it would have on the American people, was the landmark Americans with Disabilities Act (ADA). That law, which is a key piece of civil rights legislation, has had a dramatic effect all over this country. Anyone who has seen braille signs on the Metro or used a wheelchair accessible ramp can understand that. The bill was referred to five separate committees in the House, including Education and Labor, Energy and Commerce, Public Works and Transportation, Ways and Means, as well as Judiciary. This was highly unusual. The enactment of that law took a lot of heavy lifting by a lot of people. Steny Hoyer was the main sponsor. He became Majority Leader in the House in 2019. He used all of his skills to make the ADA a reality. I was initially surprised to see him during our committee's consideration of the bill. Most Members do not attend meetings of committees on which they do not serve. At our markup, he was busy behind the scenes answering questions and urging Members to support the legislation. He was a hands-on legislator and knew the bill inside and out. He attended all five of the different committees' sessions when it was being considered. He was very pleased to find out that Chairman Brooks had one of our lawyers who was fluent in American Sign Language there to sign during the meeting. There were several people following the legislation who needed that accommodation.

Steny was instrumental in getting the bill ready to go to the floor in a form that was both meaningful for the disability community as well as acceptable to the business community. He labored tirelessly to make sure it was both effective and realistic. He worked closely with committee chairs, the Leadership, and, all along the way, with the staff. He recognized, better than most Members, the importance of making sure the staff understood his goals. It was a legislative tour de force by a master of the legislative process. I admired his dedication to ensuring the passage of this important law.

✦ ✦ ✦ ✦ ✦ ✦ ✦ ✦ ✦

The other major bill that went through the committee was The Violent Crime Control and Law Enforcement Act of 1994. It implemented many crime-fighting provisions, including a "three strikes" mandatory life sentences for repeat offenders, the money to hire 100,000 new police officers, $9.7 billion in funding for prisons, and an expansion of death penalty-eligible offenses. Most significantly, it included a prohibition on the manufacture for civilian use of certain semi-automatic firearms that were defined as assault weapons, as well as certain ammunition magazines that were defined as "large capacity." These magazines were known as "banana clips" because of their shape. It was those provisions that many people believe were responsible for the defeat of Speaker Tom Foley, and Chairman Brooks in the 1994 elections, and were important factors in the Republicans taking control of the House for the first time in 40 years.

The crime legislation took a tremendous amount of work and started as a series of five smaller bills that were ultimately combined into one. We did this purely for parliamentary reasons. If we had put everything into one bill, at the markup, a whole range of issues would have been considered germane. We wanted to avoid a criminal justice free-for-all.

We had prepared reports on all five, and I filed them with the Clerk of the House on the day before we went to the floor. Usually, the House rules require the committee reports to be available before a bill could be called up. A Member had complained about not having copies of the reports. The Rules Committee provided a rule for their consideration waiving that requirement. They had not been printed by the time the Chairman had started speaking about the rule. As the Chairman was in the well talking about the reports, one of the staff in the cloakroom brought them to me. Bob was so terrified of the Chairman he was afraid to interrupt him. I thought the timing was perfect for me to get them to him. I took copies of the reports and walked into the well and handed them to Mr. Brooks. He took them like a relay runner accepting the baton; he did not hesitate for a second. He never said a word about it, so I figured I did the right thing. I am sure I would have heard about it if Mr. Brooks was displeased at being interrupted.

We had decided to introduce a new version of the crime bill, and we were going to have to keep the House in recess late into the night while the final drafting was done. I spent the evening in my office, preparing to go to the floor. The bill was not ready until after 2 am, and we got to the floor around 2:30. My wife had awakened about that time, and seeing I was not there, like an excellent Congressional staffer's wife, she decided to find out where her husband was by turning on the television coverage of the House on CSPAN. Sure enough, there I was on the floor with Mr. Brooks. She was relieved to see me and promptly went back to sleep.

The bills bounced back and forth between the House and the Senate. The Congress.gov website shows that 168 separate actions were taken on this legislation, from its introduction in the House on October 26, 1993, to its being signed into law by President Clinton in September of 1994. Things got very complicated, and the original conference report on the bill was recommitted to the conference committee to work out the final language.

The Speaker appointed nine conferees from the Judiciary Committee. He subsequently appointed secondary conferees from other committees. The Judiciary Committee had jurisdiction over the lion's share of the bill. We would whenever possible, work with the staffs of secondary committees on their provisions. The last thing we wanted was for secondary conferees to show up and take time to discuss their provisions. We would ascertain what they wanted and try to accomplish those goals. Fortunately, the Senate rules do not provide for conferees from secondary committees.

The conferees met in late August in our hearing room. In some ways, it was a parliamentary nightmare. I had to be on top of which Members got to vote on which provisions. The non-Judiciary conferees had a limited role. The main issues concerned criminal justice matters, especially extra cops on the beat, federal funding for prison reform, and the elephant in the room, the assault weapons ban. The secondary conferees would not be able to vote on those core issues.

One evening while working on the crime bill, Chairman Brooks and I were having dinner in the House restaurant. Senator Joe Biden, the Chairman of the Senate Judiciary Committee, suddenly appeared and sat down. Biden said, "Jack, I just do not understand your rules over here". Mr. Brooks looked at me and smiled and said, "You tell him, Freeman". I looked at Biden and said, "Senator, over here, we do not understand *your* rules". He responded by explaining what happened to him when he was first elected to the Senate. He told us he was on the Senate floor early in his first term, reading the Senate rules. Lawton Chiles, a Senator from Florida, came over and told him not to waste his time trying to learn the rules. "Joe, it is easy. All you have to know here is unanimous consent or 60 votes". Biden smiled at us and said, "So that is all I know".

The standard process of deciding who will be the Chairman of the conference committee is simply that it alternates back and forth from the House to the Senate. In this case, Mr. Brooks was going to be the Chairman of the conference committee, because it was the House's turn, but that was of no serious import. It only meant that he was responsible for recognizing people to speak and for moving the adoption of compromises on behalf of the House and, when appropriate, formally accepting proposals from the Senate. There were several occasions during the meeting of the conferees where House Members would have to vote on a proposed House position to offer to the Senate. That is where it became difficult for me. I had to know ahead of time which committees had jurisdiction over which provisions to call the roll for any recorded votes. I needed to ensure all the Members who were entitled to vote on an issue were called on, and those who were not were not.

The conference went very late. It was about 2 am when we got to the point where we believed we had everything nailed down. The procedural posture we were in was that the Senate needed to make a motion to wrap things up. As the Chairman of the conference committee, Mr. Brooks recognized Senator

Biden to make a motion on behalf of the Senate conferees (he was the only one there), proposing the final compromise language on all of the issues which the House would then formally accept. Biden and Brooks were sitting on opposite sides of the committee room, about 50 feet apart. I think all of us were tired, and it was clear that Biden did not know exactly what to do. Mr. Brooks leaned over to me and said, "Freeman, you sumbitch, go tell that dumb bastard what to say". So, I got up and slowly walked from one side of the room to the other and said to Senator Biden, "The Chairman would like you, on behalf of the Senate, to move the final language and request the concurrence of the House". C-SPAN was broadcasting the conference committee live. (I could not imagine who could possibly have nothing else to do at 2 am but watch this).

Most of the eyes in the room were on me. However, I did not know whether the cameras had tracked me as I tiptoed across the big room from Brooks to Biden. I was fairly sure they were on Biden at the time. He listened to me dictate the required motion and then said, "Dan, that is too complicated. Write it out for me". Everyone waited while I picked up one of the notepads on the table next to him and, in my legendary chicken scratching, wrote out the language and handed it to him. After being formally recognized by Chairman Brooks, Biden began to read it out loud into the microphone. He got about 1/3 of the way into it when he stopped, unable to read my handwriting, and said, "Dan, what the hell does this say?" There were lots of guffaws in the room among those who were awake. This went out over the live broadcast, and I was somewhat embarrassed but too tired to care. We got this minor hiccup resolved and had reached final agreement on the conference report.

As I mentioned previously, I had been trained, when dealing with live conferences, to get as many of the conferees as possible to sign the papers *before they leave the room*. Once they have departed, tracking them down for the required signatures can be extremely difficult, especially if a conference ends in the middle of the night. I was prepared and had the conference report signature sheets with me because I knew some of the conferees would slip away if I did not pounce on them immediately. I always did that because you never know when a conference is going to end quickly. I did not want to have to run back to my office to get those sheets. Usually, I would get my Senate counterpart to provide the required Senator's signatures. Senator Biden was authorized by Senator Kennedy and the other Democrats to sign for them. Biden, his Chief Counsel Cynthia Hogan, and I sat down in the hearing room for him to sign the papers. Senator Biden asked me if I had other pens to use besides the 29¢ Bic ballpoint he had. I gave him both my blue ink ballpoint and my black ink rollerball pens which Professor Young had given to me at my graduation from law school.

He was impressed with my preparedness. He said he wanted the signatures to look different, and having different writing instruments with different ink colors seemed to do the trick.

When it came time to take the conference report to the floor, there was a lot of heavy-duty lobbying going on. President Clinton was deeply involved in the process. I understood that he had called a lot of Members who were wary of antagonizing the NRA, which was opposing the entire bill based on the inclusion of the assault weapons ban. Once again, we were working late and waiting for word from the Leadership about whether we had the votes. It was not clear.

I was in my office going over some language when the Chairman walked in. He said he wanted to use the phone. I started to get up and leave him alone in the room for his private phone call. He put his hand on my shoulder and said, "Sit tight". He then proceeded to call his wife, and I tuned out. While he was on the phone, Leon Panetta, President Clinton's Chief of Staff, who I had gotten to know a little bit when he was a Member of the House, stuck his head into my office and said, "Dan, my boss wants to talk to your boss." With more than a little apprehension, I tugged on the Chairman's sleeve, interrupted his call, and told him the President was calling. I recollect it clearly, since the first thing Mr. Brooks said to the President when he got on the phone was, "Mr. President. Happy belated birthday". The President's birthday was the day before.

The conference report passed the House on August 21, and the Senate on August 25. I was invited to the signing ceremony on the South Lawn of the White House on September 13, along with all of the staff who had worked on the bill. Little did I know the dramatic effect this law would have on me.

✦ ✦ ✦ ✦ ✦ ✦ ✦ ✦ ✦

One of the more interesting issues that came up during my time working for the committee was flag burning. The Supreme Court had ruled in a Texas criminal case (*Texas v. Johnson*) that the Texas state law prohibiting the burning of an American flag was unconstitutional. The Court held flag burning was protected free speech; "Johnson's conviction for flag desecration is inconsistent with the First Amendment". I have frequently said Congress reacts to events in two ways; hysterically or glacially. In this case, it reacted hysterically.

Texas v. Johnson was decided on June 21, 1989. Chairman Brooks introduced H.R. 2978 "the Flag Protection Act" to overturn it on July 24. The committee considered the bill and filed its report on September 7, a mere 78 days later. The bill was initially debated in the House on September 12, under the suspension of the rules procedure, and it passed 380-38.

Just before the vote in the House, I had a conversation with Congressman Bill Hughes, who was the Chairman of the Crime Subcommittee, which initially processed the bill. He supported the bill and spoke in favor of it on the floor. In a private conversation, he asked me whether I thought it was constitutional. I deferred, saying, "You are the Member, what do you think?" He said they had considered the Supreme Court opinion when drafting the bill, and he thought it would pass constitutional muster. Noticing I had cleverly not answered his question, he said, "Dan, you are a constitutional scholar, what do *you* think the Supreme Court will do?" I replied I did not like to guess about what the Court would do. He then pushed and went to the heart of the matter, "Do you think this bill is unconstitutional". I said, "If you want to know what I think the Court will do, read *Texas v. Johnson*. That contains the latest insights into the Court's thinking. Granted, it was a 5-4 decision, so who knows". He then challenged me. "I will bet you dinner the Court will uphold it". I told him I did not like to wager on things I could not control, and I was not able to control much. He insisted, and I relented.

The bill became law when President George W. Bush refused to sign it within the constitutionally mandated 10-day layover. He had decided to allow it to become law without his signature, an option which the Constitution expressly permits. In his non-signing statement, he said he was not going to sign it even though he supported protecting the flag. The Department of Justice had determined "the only way to ensure protection of the flag is through a constitutional amendment". The statement said the law's constitutionality "must ultimately be decided by the courts". That was the Department's way of saying they were not sanguine about it. If the President had vetoed it, the veto would have been immediately overridden by Congress since it had passed both houses with large veto-proof margins. If he signed it, he would look bad when and if the Supreme Court threw it out as unconstitutional.

The bill became law at noon on October 28, 1989, and within minutes, it was challenged in Seattle and Washington, D.C., where men burned American flags in protest. They were charged with violating the new statute. Their lawyers argued the law was unconstitutional. U.S. District Court Judges in both cases ruled the law violated the constitutional rights of the defendants under the controlling Supreme Court precedent of *Texas v. Johnson*. (Judge Barbara Rothstein, the trial judge in the Seattle case, would become a regular speaker to my Washington Semester classes.) Since Congress had provided for expedited review because of the important constitutional issue involved, there would be no U.S. Court of Appeals consideration. The case went directly to the Supreme Court.

The two cases were consolidated and argued on May 14, 1990 and were decided on June 11, 1990. Pretty quick turn-around! The Supreme Court said to Congress what I thought they would: "See what we said in *Texas v. Johnson*, you knuckleheads". (That is not a direct quotation from the opinion, but only my paraphrasing of it.) I was correct, and Bill Hughes lost the bet. He took Mimi and me to dinner fairly soon after that. Well, not so soon; I had to bug him for several years, and in the waning weeks of his last term, he finally took us out.

✦✦✦✦✦✦✦✦✦

In early 1989, during the committee's closed Democratic organizational caucus, there was a coup in the selection of the Chairman of the Immigration Subcommittee. The sitting Chairman, Romano Mazzoli, was defeated in a secret ballot. The new Chairman was Bruce Morrison, a Congressman from Connecticut. Mazzoli was caught completely off-guard. Morrison got to name some of the staff on the subcommittee, but Mr. Brooks, as the full committee Chairman, had the authority to name the Chief Counsel. He was not that sure of Morrison, and he said to Bill Jones, "I think we will just keep old 'Puglesee' (as he pronounced it)". He wanted to make sure he had someone he could trust to keep anything untoward from escaping the Immigration Subcommittee. Although Mr. Brooks got to name the Chief Counsel, Morrison was able to move somebody from his personal staff to the subcommittee staff. That did not always work out well.

✦✦✦✦✦✦✦✦✦

One afternoon the Chairman, Bill, Bob, and I were in the Rayburn cafeteria (again), and the Chairman began talking about a repair he had to do to some drywall in his home. One of his kids had done something which had caused an irregular 3 or 4- inch hole in the wall. He was complaining about how difficult it was to match the irregular opening when repairing it. To the other's horror, I explained to Mr. Brooks a relatively easy way to make that kind of repair. You had to enlarge the hole to make it into a square or rectangle and cut a piece of drywall as a patch to fit in the newly formed hole. Then you would insert a backer for the patch using a paint stirring stick and secure the patch with drywall screws through the stick. Bob and Bill looked at me again in amazement. I was talking to the Chairman as if he were a normal person about repairing some drywall. The Chairman seemed to be impressed and said, "What are you doing this afternoon, son?" I perceived this to be a not so veiled "invitation" to come to his house and assist him, or probably do the repair. My quick response was that my direct boss (Bill) had a lot of work for me to do, and I did not think I could get away. Fortunately, that ploy worked.

✦✦✦✦✦✦✦✦✦

Jack Brooks was a wealthy man. I understood he had interests in several banks. For some reason, he took an interest in my father's financial situation and how it was going to affect me. I always deferred answering his questions about this topic. I explained to him that my father never discussed his finances with me.

Brooks would regularly ask, "Is your daddy distributin'?" This was a reference to a perfectly legal tax-avoidance practice of diminishing the amount of your taxable assets by distributing them through tax-free gifts. One day, when it was just the two of us, he asked again, and then proceeded to proudly tell me that he was distributing $10,000 to each of his three children every year. That was the IRS limit on tax-free gifts at the time. I told him if he was seriously interested in moving money to his children tax-free, he could give them each up to $40,000. "What are you talking about?" he asked brusquely. I said I was not a tax lawyer, nor was I an accountant, but as I understood it, he could give $10,000 to each child, his wife could give $10,000 to each child, and they could each give $10,000 to each child's spouse. I suggested he talk to his financial advisors about this. He thanked me somewhat warily. Much later, he told me I was correct.

✦ ✦ ✦ ✦ ✦ ✦ ✦ ✦ ✦

Jack Valenti was in the motorcade in Dallas and is also in the photograph of LBJ taking the oath that day. He did not know Lyndon Johnson well, but Johnson took him on that long sad flight back to Washington, and from that day forward, Valenti was on his staff. He became Johnson's first Special Assistant and even lived in the White House for the first two months of Johnson's presidency.

Valenti left the White House in 1966 to become the President of the Motion Picture Association of America (MPAA). He became a prominent lobbyist and was a key player in Democratic political circles. His ability to get things done on Capitol Hill was legendary. One of the implements in his toolbox was a private movie theater in downtown Washington. He would invite Members of Congress and other important people to come to the MPAA for dinner and a movie. It gave him access to many Members and key people in the executive branch.

When Mr. Brooks became the Chairman of the Judiciary Committee, Valenti was elated. The Judiciary Committee had jurisdiction over intellectual property law, including copyrights, which were the lifeblood of the movie industry. Any changes in copyright law could have a direct impact on film studios, and Valenti was tenacious about protecting them.

Valenti threw a "Salute to the House Judiciary Committee" dinner and invited all the Members of the Committee and a few senior staff. My wife and I were, for some reason, included. As is usual when Members of Congress are around, those of us on the staff hung back to the end of the line for the buffet, and then scoped out the best and most unobtrusive place to sit. Bill and Bob were looking around for the staff table, which they expected would have been set up. The idea of their socializing with Members was alien to them.

Mimi and I had fixed our plates and were waiting for an indication of where we should sit by following Bill and Bob. I knew that they would never do anything untoward or inappropriate when the Chairman was in the room. The only likely place was a table where only one person was sitting. Unfortunately, it was a Member who was not someone you would want to have dinner with. He was dull as dishwater, and no one wanted to join him, neither his colleagues nor staff.

While we were standing there deciding, Jack Valenti came swooping down and corralled us, saying, "Dan, Mimi, the Chairman would like you to sit with us". There was no way to get out of it, so we ended up sitting at the head table with Mr. and Mrs. Valenti, Mr. and Mrs. Brooks, and several other Members. I was a bit uncomfortable, not knowing where Bill and Bob were. I thought they might be aghast about our sitting at the head table with the Chairman. I do not think they wanted to be at that table, but I am sure they thought it was inappropriate for Mimi and me to be there.

You never know what would be perceived as unacceptable behavior on the part of staff; Members can get upset at the most insignificant thing. I tried to be on my toes with Brooks being there. Poor Mimi got trapped sitting next to Congressman Bob Kastenmeier, who spent the entire evening asking her questions about ballet. He was interested, and I heard him ask her about a difficult step. I do not think she enjoyed the evening being in the spotlight, but she soldiered through it.

✦✦✦✦✦✦✦✦

One Friday afternoon, I went into Bill's office to tell him I was going to leave a bit early to go to the funeral of a family friend. The former staff director of the committee had also recently died, and I had taken time off to go to that funeral as well. Bill said to me, "I'm glad I am not a friend of yours. Your friends keep dying". I said I considered him to be a friend and went off to the funeral.

Saturday morning, Bob called to tell me Bill had died in his sleep. He was only 50. I was completely shocked. Bill was universally held in high regard, and it was a terrible loss to the committee, the Chairman, and, of course, to Bill's wife and kids. It also had to be an enormous blow to Bob, who spent his entire day glued to Bill's hip.

Although nobody I knew talked about it at the time, the prospect of having Bob named to be Bill's replacement as General Counsel was horrifying. Fortunately, I was not around during the transition. Mimi and I went to the funeral home for the wake on Sunday evening, and then on Monday, we left for our long-planned vacation. We were going to be gone for three weeks.

While we were away, I got a call from my friend Gene telling me that Mr. Brooks had decided to name Jonathan Yarowsky to fill the position. To me, that was good news because Jon and I had worked together closely while he was on the Monopolies Subcommittee staff.

Having been by-passed, Bob became even more difficult to deal with, and he tried to keep me from talking to Jon. He even went so far as to block me from entering Jon's office one day. Bob was a pain for the rest of his time on the committee staff. Much to the delight of many, Mr. Brooks arranged for him to be named to a position in the Department of Justice. Although it was an open secret among the staff that this move was in the works, Bob, in his going away remarks, said it had been a "surprise".

✦✦✦✦✦✦✦✦✦

One Tuesday morning, as we were preparing to convene a full committee meeting, the Chairman and I were chatting. He asked about my weekend. I told him Mimi and I had gone up into the Pocono Mountains for the 50th anniversary of the summer camp where I worked as a counselor. He wanted to know what we had done there, and I told him that I taught Mimi how to shoot a rifle and a bow and arrow. He asked me how she did, and I told him she did very well. He looked at me with a devilish grin and inquired, "Did that worry ya a bit?"

✦✦✦✦✦✦✦✦✦

Jack Brooks could be caustic. I tried not to be the target of those barbs, and I was mostly successful. I did see them launched at other people, and sometimes it was funny, but sometimes it was just plain vicious. Jerry Nadler was elected in a special election to fill the seat of Ted Weiss, who died before the 1992 Democratic primary election. Nadler was, at the time, morbidly obese. He was not a shy man and was imbued with an exaggerated sense of his own intelligence. Brooks had a private meeting with Speaker Foley in his office adjacent to the floor to talk about the assault weapons ban. In the meeting were Brooks, Foley, and staff from both offices. The door was closed, and Foley and Brooks had begun. Jon Yarowsky and I were standing up against the wall, staying out of the way. All of a sudden, "Bam" the door was slammed open and in stormed Jerry Nadler. "Are you talking about guns?" he asked. He assumed we were and that he should be included. Brooks looked at him over the top of his reading glasses as he frequently did, and with a mixture of sarcasm and humor said, "Jer, come on in. Pull up a couple of chairs". It was difficult to keep a straight face.

✦✦✦✦✦✦✦✦✦

That night, after almost everybody else had left, Brooks, Foley, and I were sitting in the Speaker's private office in the Capitol. It was late, and they were telling war stories. The Speaker, who I did not know well, asked Mr. Brooks if he had ever told him the story about his first conversation with then-President Johnson when Foley was a freshman Member of the House. Mr. Brooks said no, so the Speaker proceeded to tell us about it. He was at Dulles Airport to catch a flight back to his district in Washington State. A woman from Northwest Airlines stopped him and said, "Excuse me, are you Congressman Foley, Tom Foley of Washington?" The freshman Congressman was surprised to be recognized, but he said he was, indeed, Tom Foley of Washington. The ticket agent said, "You have a telephone call from the President in our office. Please come with me". He was stunned by this. He had never met or talked with President Johnson. He could not understand why the President would be calling him, a mere freshman Member of the House. He was escorted to a private office and told that the line on the telephone with the blinking light was the one with the White House operator. He picked up the phone, pushed the blinking button, and said, "Hello, this is Tom Foley". The White House operator said, "Is this Congressman Foley, Tom Foley of Washington?" "Yes, it is", he responded. The White House operator said, "Please hold for the President". A moment later, Foley heard LBJ's booming voice saying, "John?" He replied, "No, Mr. President. This is Tom Foley. Tom Foley of Washington". The President shouted into the phone, "Goddammit, Shit, I told them to get me John Fogarty of Rhode Island", and he slammed down the phone. Foley was stunned. He gathered himself and hung up the telephone. He hurried out of the office because he was concerned he might miss his flight. The woman from Northwest said, "Did you finish your conversation with the President?" Foley, still a bit flummoxed, said, "Yes, I did". "Don't worry about missing your flight. We will hold the plane for you because you were delayed by your important telephone call". Foley told us he did not fess up to the truth.

✦✦✦✦✦✦✦✦✦

As the committee Parliamentarian, I worked closely with the House Parliamentarians. There were several lawyers in that office with whom I had a superb working relationship. Charlie Johnson, who was the Deputy Parliamentarian, was a big fan of my cousin, comedian Henny Youngman. Charlie always called me Henny, and I always called him CJ. I got signed copies of Henny's joke books for Charlie. I regularly accused him of using the Henny Youngman joke books instead of the House Rules and Manual when deciding parliamentary questions. Charlie subsequently became the Parliamentarian of the House when Bill Brown, a warm and delightful man, retired.

I could always count on Charlie to help me out when dealing with complex parliamentary issues and with difficult Members. Charlie is a true professional, and there was no question when the Republicans took control of the House that the entire Parliamentarian's staff would be retained. This was not true in the Senate, where a switch in party control would result in the naming of a new Parliamentarian. The House Parliamentarians always enjoyed a reputation for being nonpartisan, experienced, and excellent.

In the summer of 1993, Charlie called and told me that he had the proverbial "offer I could not refuse". Robert Redford was going to be making a movie about the quiz show scandals in the 1950s. During that time, quiz shows were very popular, including "21" and "The $64,000 Question". In order to build suspense and increase the number of viewers, the producers of those shows were giving the answers to some of their contestants. One of the most popular contestants was Charles Van Doren, the scion of a prominent New York family.

Redford had planned to film recreations of the Congressional hearings that were held about the scandal. The producer had invited Charlie Johnson to be a technical advisor on the film to ensure the scenes portraying the hearings were accurate reflections of the events. He couldn't do it since he and his wife had planned to go on vacation during the days those scenes were going to be filmed. He originally asked Muftiah McCartin if she wanted to do it, but her husband was about to undergo back surgery, and she declined. She suggested to Charlie that I might be a good person since I was a committee Parliamentarian, and I would be very familiar with how committees worked. Charlie agreed, and he asked if I was interested, which I took as a fabulous compliment. Things were a little dicey at the time because I was not sure whether Congress would resolve yet another budget crisis in time to adjourn for the August recess. I had several phone calls with the assistant producer, Susan Moore, telling her that I would love to do it, but I could not be sure when or if I could get away.

Fortunately, Congress managed to reach a deal on the budget and adjourn in time for me to get to do this. I was asked to come to the New York State Historical Society Building on Central Park West in New York City, where the congressional scenes would be shot. When I got there, I introduced myself to Susan, and she began to describe the set-up and what would be required of me. Out of the blue, Robert Redford walked over and asked her, "Where is the Congressional consultant?" She said, "He is right here" and introduced me. So, there I was, face to face with Robert Redford! I told him how much I admired his work and how especially moving I thought his Oscar-winning film "Ordinary People" was. He was gracious, asked me to call him Bob, and showed me into the Historical Society's hearing room, which they were using for the congressional scenes. He asked me some specific questions about how people would move around, who would sit where, and about some of the dialogue. He also encouraged me not to be shy and said that if I saw anything which was not correct or had any suggestions to enhance the accuracy of the film to let him know.

I must admit, after all of the things I had heard about movie stars, I was pleasantly surprised. Everyone who I talked with, (I was on the set five days) was open and friendly. I got to meet Paul Scofield, one of my very favorite actors, who played Charles Van Doren's father. I also met Mira Sorvino, who played Goodwin's wife, and she was very friendly. The only person who I found to be a "Hollywood type" was Rob Morrow, who played the Richard Goodwin character. Goodwin was one of the committee counsels during the hearings.

I made sure to get to the set early every day and have conversations with a lot of interesting people. One of the most fascinating was Michael Ballhaus, who was the cinematographer. He was working with his son, Florian. I think both of them were pleased that I was intrigued about how they were doing their jobs. Because of my interest in photography, learning about the cinematography was a treat. Michael discussed camera angles, depth of field, and color saturation, among other things. I was like a kid in a candy store, and Michael was my host.

One of the people I also liked was Kathy O'Rear, the costume designer. She and I got talking one day about how she went about making sure all of the costumes were absolutely period-accurate. She even made sure all the characters were wearing correct 1950s underwear. I was impressed by both her professionalism and how warm she was. I did not know until the second day that she was Bob Redford's significant other. She enhanced the experience for me.

When I was talking to Bob about the hearings, he was impressed that I had reviewed all of the still photographs I could find as well as the few film clips available of the actual 1950s hearings. I had gone into the archives in the Library of Congress to see all the original material. I told him one of the quandaries I had was what to tell him about how many stars there were on the flag in the hearing room. These hearings took place over several months about the same time as Alaska and Hawaii were admitted to the union. Therefore, the number of stars on the flag changed. Unusually my review of the photos of the hearings showed there was no flag in the hearing room, so the issue was moot.

On the day we were filming the Van Doren testimony, Bob directed Ralph Fiennes, who played Charles Van Doren, when he finished his testimony to get up from the witness table, turn around and walk slowly towards the exit in the back of the hearing room. He had told the people playing the photographers who were waiting at the door, to start taking pictures as soon as Charlie got up. They started snapping away with flashbulbs popping. Since Bob had told me not to be shy if I saw anything wrong, I told him the photographers would not have been able to take multiple pictures that quickly with the equipment they had at the time. The Speed Graphic was standard equipment for most American press photographers until the mid-1960s. This camera took outstanding pictures, but it was big and unwieldy. Today, photographers can take lots of pictures in a few seconds. In 1959, a Speed Graphic had to be reloaded and have a fresh flash bulb inserted for every shot. So, I told him they could not be clicking away like crazy. Bob said, "Sort of like a six-shooter, right?" "No", I said, "more like a single-shot derringer". He thanked me and went over to talk to the actors to change how they would play the scene.

He asked whether Members and staff would be moving around while people were asking questions, or when a witness was testifying. It seemed strange to him to have all this hustle and bustle while the hearings were going on. I told him it happens all the time. He also asked me to look over the dialog of the scene where the witnesses were sworn in.

Charlie Johnson and his wife Martha were able to visit the set on their way to their vacation spot. They were escorted up into the hearing room between takes, and the three of us were talking about the set. Redford walked up to us and said, "Excuse me, but I would like to talk to Dan for a moment". I introduced Charlie and Martha and let him know that Charlie was the one who was responsible for my being there. Charlie said to Bob, "Do not believe a word he says". I bragged on Charlie a bit, telling Bob that Charlie had taught me everything I know about congressional procedure, "although that might not be saying much".

One day while I was sitting on the set with one of the producers, a young intern came up and breathlessly said, "Mr. Freeman, you have a telephone call". I was surprised since I did not think anybody knew where I was, and Mimi was in England. I took the phone call and lo and behold, and it was my former Chairman, Peter Rodino.

Since leaving Congress, Mr. Rodino was having a hard time. He used to complain to me bitterly about how poorly people treated him; some would not even take his calls. When he was "The powerful Chairman of the House Judiciary Committee", everyone treated him with exalted deference. Those days were gone. He called me frequently, and I always made it a point to speak with him. Sometimes he would call just to chat and reminisce, and sometimes he had a specific favor to ask. Once, he asked me to get Paul Tagliabue's telephone number. Tagliabue was the Commissioner of the National Football League, and I expect the Chairman wanted the number so he could ask him for Super Bowl tickets for his son. He also called me after the Supreme Court ruled in the Pledge of Allegiance case. He was on the committee when the pledge was amended by statute in 1954 to include the words "under God". He wanted a copy of the committee report. Although I was no longer on the Judiciary Committee staff (I had gone over to International Relations with Chairman Hyde), I managed to get a copy of the document from the clerk at the Judiciary Committee for Mr. Rodino.

He was calling me on the movie set to ask me to do him a favor, and I said, "Certainly, Mr. Chairman, whatever you want". I always called him "Mr. Chairman" since I knew he loved it. The favor he wanted was for me to take someone to lunch. I asked him why, and he said, "I think he could benefit from talking to an experienced Congressional lawyer". I thought that was a nice compliment coming from Mr. Rodino, and I readily agreed. I then asked him who he wanted me to take to lunch. I was shocked when he told me it was Bernie Nussbaum. Bernie had been the Deputy to John Doar on the House Judiciary Committee's impeachment staff during the Nixon impeachment investigation.

Bernie was White House Counsel in the Clinton White House. He had gotten to know Hillary during her work as one of the junior lawyers on the Nixon impeachment staff. One night in 1973, when Bernie was giving Hillary a ride home, she mentioned her boyfriend from Yale Law School was visiting the next day. "What is his law firm?" Nussbaum inquired. "No law firm", she responded. "He's moving back to Arkansas to run for state Attorney General". She continued, "Well, he's thinking about running for Governor because one day he's going to be President of the United States". As I heard the story years later, Bernie's response was, "Bullshit, Hillary".

I did not know what I could possibly say to Bernie which would be helpful to him. I had heard stories about his being a tough New York lawyer who was frequently unpleasant. However, I called him at the White House and said Mr. Rodino had asked me to take him to lunch. I said I would be happy to meet him wherever it was convenient. Because Congress was in recess, I had the time to come downtown to the restaurant of his choice. He rather brusquely said he would get back to me, and I left it at that.

About a week later, after I had returned from New York, his secretary called me to set a date for lunch and to tell me that Mr. Nussbaum was "inviting me to join him in the White House mess". From what I heard about Bernie Nussbaum, I expect this was his way of showing off how important he was. I said to his secretary, "Fine, I know where that is because when I worked at the White House, my office was next to it". That was my way of letting him know I was not going to be bowled over by being there.

I dutifully went down to the White House and waited for him in the West Wing lobby. I know many people like to have others wait for them to reinforce how important/busy they are. I did not react to that tactic and greeted him cheerfully when he finally showed up. During our lunch, we spoke briefly about why Mr. Rodino had asked me to meet with him, but I did not tell him Mr. Rodino thought I could be helpful to his navigating the "Washington scene". I am sure Bernie thought there was nothing he needed help with. He seemed preoccupied during lunch. I think eye contact is very important; I had more eye contact with Abraham Lincoln during that lunch than I did with Bernie! He was continually scanning the White House Mess to see if somebody important walked in. This is a typical Washington habit which frankly kind of irritated me. As we parted, I thanked him for lunch (since he had to pay), and I went upstairs to the second floor of the West Wing to visit my friend Tim Keating who worked in the Office of Congressional Affairs.

Tim and I had a nice chat. He asked me what I was doing at the White House. I told him I was there to meet with Nussbaum. His comment was, "Bernie's a great lawyer, but having him here is like having a left-handed first baseman when what you need is a shooting guard". It was clear to me he thought Bernie was highly skilled at being a tough New York litigator, but navigating the shark-infested waters of Washington was not only a whole different ball game but an entirely different sport.

✦✦✦✦✦✦✦✦

The Quiz show crew was going to be filming a scene on the East Front of the Capitol. Somehow Redford had convinced Heather Foley, the Speaker's wife, to allow them to shoot there after they wrapped up the Congressional scenes in New York. Although I did not have anything to contribute, they invited me to come down to watch and to bring Mimi.

We started walking from the Rayburn Building, where my parking space was located over to the East Front, when one of the Capitol Police officers who I knew, stopped us. He said, "Sorry, Dan. Only people with movie ID are allowed on the Plaza this morning". I smiled and showed him my "Quiz Show" badge. He chuckled and let us go.

When I looked onto the Plaza, I was amazed to see an old D.C. Transit bus from the 1950s and several classic cars parked there. They were recreating the scene. It was fun to see. The main thing which was out of place was the Statue of Freedom, which usually sits on top of the Capitol dome. It was resting on the ground at the far end of the Plaza. The statue was being refurbished, and to complete the work, it had to be taken down using an enormous helicopter. The film crew had to make sure it did not appear in any scenes they were shooting.

We got a chance to talk with Bob and several of the film crew. I also introduced Mimi to Paul Scofield. We spent a good part of the morning there and then left.

A lot of people on the Hill were excited to learn about my "Hollywood career". Many wanted to know what it was like to work with Robert Redford. I described my terrific experience. I explained what I did, and how impressed I was with both Redford and most of the people on the set. Someone asked me what the difference was between working on a movie and working on Capitol Hill. My response was, in Congress, you do not get a chance for do-overs. Making a movie, you can always say, "Cut; take two".

The following fall, the postproduction work on the movie was completed, and the release was scheduled for September. There were going to be several previews, and one of them was to be at the spacious Warner Theatre in Washington. As part of the motion picture industry's presence in Washington, movie premieres were a very popular type of event. Because I had worked on the film, Mimi and I were invited. Also on the list were many Members of Congress, including most of the members of the Intellectual Property Subcommittee of the House Judiciary Committee. Funny thing about that.

Mimi and I took our seats, and I slipped off to go to the men's room. As I came back up the stairs, I saw a couple of Members whom I knew well. I was about to greet them when this attractive woman and I made eye contact, and she exclaimed, "It's Dan!" She barreled between the two Members, dragging the man she was with along and gave me a big hug. It was Kathy O'Rear, and the man she was dragging with her was Robert Redford! I loved it, but I think those two Members were not pleased. I was about to introduce them to Bob and Kathy, but I decided against it. I thought it might not go over too well that Robert Redford knew who I was but did not know who they were.

I got a call a couple of months later from the Vice President of the Motion Picture Association of America, telling me they were going to be showing "your movie" at the MPAA theater and inviting me to attend. It was going to be the same kind of event which Mimi and I had gone to in honor of the Judiciary Committee, where we sat at the table with Jack Brooks. I knew the MPAA Vice President because he was married to somebody on our staff. He told me I could invite some friends. I asked him how many. I did not want to get greedy, and I knew that the MPAA was paying for the dinner. I also knew that their private theater held 75 people. He said I could ask up to 40 people to come to see "my movie"! I was stoked!

This was a splendid occasion for me to see lots of my friends and, frankly, to be the center of attention for once. I have been to several of these events before, but this time a lot of people would know who I was. It was very amusing to see what happened at the end of the film. As soon as "The End" came up on the screen, half of the people got up to leave. The others (my friends) stayed glued to their seats, watching the credits roll. After a long, long list of people, including I think, the man who provided the bagels, there it was in massive letters, *"Technical Advisor—Daniel Freeman"*, which triggered an enormous round of applause from all of my fans. It was a lot of fun!

✦✦✦✦✦✦✦✦✦

Having a good relationship with Members sometimes causes them to ask for strange things totally unrelated to your position. Lamar Smith used to call me for humor to put into his speeches back in his home district. He would frequently ask for "good lawyer jokes". I always helped him out because he is such a nice man and had always treated me well.

When he was the Ranking Republican on the Judiciary Committee's Immigration Subcommittee, there was a hearing which had several witnesses. His counsel on the subcommittee, Cordia Strom was a good lawyer and a thoughtful woman. At the end of the hearing, one of the witnesses literally dropped dead. Cordia was very upset, and Lamar sat with her for over an hour, not as her boss, or as a Member of Congress, but as a caring human being who wanted to help her deal with that traumatic event.

Cordia and I got along from the get-go. She was a new Republican counsel, and I was on the Democratic staff, but I always strove to treat people with respect, no matter which side of the aisle they were on. At one point during a negotiation about an immigration bill, one of the Democratic lawyers attempted to take advantage of her in a clearly underhanded way. It was a cheap shot he tried just because Cordia was new to the committee and did not know the ropes. I put a stop to it immediately and told the offending staffer in no uncertain terms that "We don't do things that way". I think he was a bit miffed (probably because he got caught), but Cordia was pleased. She came up to me later and asked me, "Can I give you a hug?". I said, "Sure, but why?". She said she thought I was a "good professional and a fair and kind man".

✦✦✦✦✦✦✦✦✦

It was during Mr. Brooks' Chairmanship of the Judiciary Committee that I met a young woman who I would mentor. We had four summer interns from Mr. Brooks' district who were assigned to work on the committee staff. Three of them were fairly bright and thrilled to be here in Washington for the summer. The fourth, Ann Johnson, was not only bright and cheerful, but it was her declared intention to learn as much as possible about Congress while she was here. I took her under my wing and made sure she had as full an experience as possible. Ann always volunteered to stay late and was an intellectual sponge. She was constantly looking for ways to learn more.

Although interns are technically not permitted on to the House floor, I made a point of taking her with me whenever interesting things were happening. This included Judiciary Committee bills and also some unusual parliamentary situations. She could not get enough. I always accused her of having "B positive" blood because she was the most positive person I had ever met.

Her father was a lawyer and her mother a judge, and I thought that there might be some pressure for her to go to law school. After she decided she wanted to, I wrote a letter of recommendation for her which, to be perfectly candid, was spectacular. She later told me the Dean of the South Texas College of Law in Houston, kept my letter on his desk as the gold standard of what a good letter of recommendation should be.

At the end of the summer, I was sad to see her leave, but I was pleased she was going to go back to Texas to complete her undergraduate work. Ann came to me and asked if I knew anyone in the Clinton White House because she wanted to work there before returning to finish her degree. My friend Tim Keating was there, and I called him about Ann. I said, "Timmer, I am about to do you the best favor anyone ever did for you". I told him Ann was pure gold, and he should snap her up immediately. He did and has always been grateful to me for recommending her.

In May of 1995, Ann began as an intern in the Office of Intergovernmental Affairs in the White House. At the end of the summer, she went to work as an intern in the Office of Legislative Affairs, working for my friend Tim. She was then given a permanent position as a staff assistant in the House Liaison Office. Tim was ecstatic about her work and her attitude. He thought she was terrific. She was then given a job at the Clinton/Gore campaign, and after the election, she went to work on the Inaugural Committee. By that time, I thought she had had enough and threatened to throw her out of town if she did not leave after the inauguration to finish her education.

She went back to Texas and received her law degree and has become a prominent attorney in Houston. In a case before the Texas Supreme Court, Ann made Texas legal history representing a 13-year old girl who had been prosecuted for prostitution. Ann successfully argued that under Texas law, a minor could not legally consent to sex and therefore could not be charged with the crime of prostitution. Ann won a landmark decision protecting a child victim of sexual exploitation.

She is an extraordinary woman who I am proud to know and humbled that she considers me to have been a mentor to her. We keep in touch, and I am glad to know how well she is doing. She is currently running for a seat in the Texas legislature.

✦ ✦ ✦ ✦ ✦ ✦ ✦ ✦ ✦

Near the end of the 103rd Congress, Chairman Brooks and a couple of other Members were gathered in my office adjacent to the committee room. One of the Members asked the Chairman if it was his private office. That gave him a thought. After the informal gathering, when the other Members left, Jon Yarowsky, the Chairman, and I were talking. The Chairman said to Jon, "We need to get Dan a better office". A couple of days later, I had been set up in my new office at the other end of the committee suite, and a sign reading "Chairman" had been put up on my old office door. I do not think this was about getting me a new office at all. It was about getting the Chairman an office in the committee suite. Ironically, Mr. Brooks never got to use it.

✦ ✦ ✦ ✦ ✦ ✦ ✦ ✦ ✦

The horseshoe entrance to the Rayburn House Office Building is the main entrance where people used to get out of their taxis. One day when I was walking back to my office from lunch, I saw a cab pull up, and a young Member of Congress got out. Maria Cantwell was a wealthy former Silicon Valley executive who ran for Congress with a good-sized war chest and won. Members of Congress, especially those who have money, are frequently oblivious to the necessity of paying for everyday things like meals and taxis. There is always a staffer around to deal with those mundane things.

On this occasion, however, she was alone in the cab. The driver told her how much she owed. I was standing next to her when she said told him she did not have any money. She assumed, I guess, it would somehow be taken care of, and she did not have to worry about such things. I stepped in and offered to lend her the $5 she needed. I made a point of saying, "I would be happy to *lend* you the taxi fare". She thanked me, and I gave her my card, so she would know where to send the money. I foolishly thought her first order of business when she got to her office would be to send an intern down with the money, possibly with a note of thanks. That did not happen.

More than a week later, I was on the floor working on a bill. There was a roll call vote, so all the Members came streaming in to vote. I saw Ms. Cantwell and decided to gently point out the fact that as her knight in shining armor, I had not been reimbursed. She blanked out a bit, not recalling the incident. I refreshed her recollection about my coming to her rescue. I then told her, "You owe me five dollars for the taxi fare". It finally came to her, and she pulled out a $5 bill and gave it to me. Seeing that one of my friends came up and asked me why a Member was giving me money on the House floor. I told him it was an instance of remedying a case of "shell-out falter". He thought it was a terrible pun but confessed later on that he had used it himself.

✦✦✦✦✦✦✦✦✦

May 31, 1989, was another day when, having free access to the Chamber, I was able to be a witness to history. That was the day Speaker Jim Wright gave his moving resignation speech. He had been the subject of an intense investigation by the Ethics Committee about allegations of financial improprieties which were led by a then back-bencher Newt Gingrich. His address went on for more than an hour. Members paid rapt attention.

Speaker Wright spent part of the time defending himself against the charges that he had taken gifts in exchange for special treatment on legislation. His tenor during the speech ranged from defensive, to angry, to bemused and certainly to emotional. He loved the House, and it was a devastating blow for him to have to leave.

At the end, he was speaking to a thoroughly engrossed audience.

"And it is grievously hurtful to our society when vilification becomes an accepted form of political debate, and negative campaigning becomes a full-time occupation; when members of each party become self-appointed vigilantes carrying out personal vendettas against members of the other party. In God's name, that's not what this institution is supposed to be all about. When vengeance becomes more desirable than vindication and harsh personal attacks upon one another's motives and one another's character drown out the quiet logic of serious debate on important issues, things that we ought to be involved in. Surely that's unworthy of our institution and unworthy of our American political process. All of us in both political parties must resolve to bring this period of mindless cannibalism to an end!! We've done enough of it!"

There was a standing ovation. It was an incredibly powerful moment.

He confessed to making "many mistakes" and then offered himself as a kind of human sacrifice.

"Let me give you back this job you gave to me as a propitiation for all of this season of bad will that has grown among us". He urged both Democrats and Republicans to end the rancor. *"Let [my resignation] be a total payment for the anger and hostility we feel toward each other. Let's not try to get even".*

He urged the Republicans not to try to get even over the defeat of the nomination of Senator John Tower to be Secretary of Defense, and he urged the Democrats not to try to get even about his resignation.

Later, on the way back to my office from the Capitol, I saw him walking alone. He and Jack Brooks were fellow Texans and close friends. He knew I worked on the Committee under Mr. Brooks. Respectfully, but cautiously, I approached him. Under the circumstances, I did not know what kind of mood he would be in. I said he had given a magnificent oration, and I admired his courage and his citizenship. I told him I would never forget his eloquence and his dignity. He said warmly, "Thank you, Dan, for those kind words. And thank you for your service to the nation and my good friend Jack Brooks". I was honored by his words.

Photographs from My Hill Years

With Chairman Henry Hyde
To Dan Freeman, with much esteem and admiration.

With Associate Justice Stephen Breyer
To my friend Dan with best wishes and admiration

With Speaker of the House Tip O'Neill
To Dan Freeman, Best Wishes.

With Associate Justice Sonia Sotomayor
Dan, you are amazing!!

With Chairman Peter W. Rodino
To Dan Freeman—
Is it germane or not germane—That is the question--!
With warm regards and best wishes

A great moment with former Secretary of Transportation and Secretary of Commerce Congressman Norm Mineta with the replacement bat I had made for him with the logo "Citizen--Norm Mineta--442".

Dan: You're the all-time big slugger!! Thanks a million for all your help in seeing the Civil Liberties Act of 1988 into reality!! Eternally grateful,

With Civil Rights icon Congressman John Lewis
To Dan, Keep the faith

 Congresswoman Ileana Ros-Lehtinen
Proudly Representing Florida's 27th District
April 16, 2013

With House International Relations Committee Chair Ileana Ros-Lehtinen
Dear Dan—It is a delight to be your friend! Thanks, professor!

With Speaker of the House Nancy Pelosi
To Dan—best wishes

With the Dalai Lama

Senator Alan Simpson—the famous "Gazoo" photograph
Courtesy Diana Walker/TIME

To Dan—You like this?! It is a dazzler isn't it? Enjoy! You are great "hand" in this operation. A real pro. Thanks for your kindness to me. My very best,

AL SIMPSON
WYOMING

United States Senate
Assistant Republican Leader
WASHINGTON, D.C. 20510

August 9, 1988

Daniel M. Freeman
Counsel and Parliamentarian
Committee on the Judiciary
U.S. House of Representatives
2137 Rayburn House Office Building
Washington, D.C. 20515-6216

Dear Dan:

You rascal, you! I see you have obtained these
dazzling photos from Diana Walker of Time magazine. I
have come to know her during my time here, and she is a
special lady. On the day she took that remarkable picture,
I turned around after I heard all the clicking, and she
said, "You'll never guess what I have in here." And I
said, "Oh, yes, I will!" I knew!

It is, as you say, "a hell of a photograph." At
least, my mother thought that it was!!

I have inscribed one for you, and one for Diana for
her "rogues' gallery." And then, I have added a trick
here! I am returning to her the one that she had signed
which is not scribbled on, and I will ask her to sign
that for me and return it for my "rogues' gallery." That
I would enjoy! So you have triggered a nice, mutual
result, and I am sending a copy of this letter to Diana.

Dan, thank you for your courtesies and kindnesses
to me over the years, and especially for your fine work
with regard to the long conference committee activities on
the immigration reform legislation. Your office was,
indeed, the scene of many famous, or as you say, "infamous,"
informal immigration conference committee activities. You
were very generous with your time and with your talents.
Thanks so much -- you have truly "made a difference." I
always enjoy seeing you in this fascinating arena, and I
look forward to seeing you in the future. Please always
let me know when I can be of proper assistance.

My best to you, Dan.

Most sincerely,

Alan K. Simpson
United States Senator

Simpson "Gazoo" photograph letter to me

With Director Robert Redford on the set of the film "Quiz Show"
Thanks for your help, Dan

Polaroid photo from the set of "Quiz Show" and my film crew ID badge

XIII. Science and the Courts (Including "Small World" #1)

During my service for Mr. Brooks on the Judiciary Committee staff, I got a chance to get involved in a fascinating project dealing with science and the judiciary; The Einstein Institute for Science Health and the Courts (EINSHAC). It provided training on the scientific, legal, and ethical implications of the Human Genome Project to judges in the United States and many foreign nations which had independent court systems. America's state and federal courts experience constantly evolving developments in science and technology, resulting in a higher degree of case complexity as well as novel forms of evidence in entirely new areas of law.

I became a member of the board and the teaching faculty, which had many people in the burgeoning field of bioethics. This was a fantastic opportunity for me to broaden my horizons, travel to interesting places, and meet prominent people in both the scientific world and the judiciary. Nearly 500 judges participated in case-related scientific method topics and emerging legal issues.

One of the people on the teaching faculty who I got to know was Ananda (Al) Chakrabarty, a microbiologist. While working at General Electric, he developed a genetically engineered organism which would eat oil. This organism did not exist in nature. Al cleverly put together some bits and pieces of DNA and created a brand-new life form. He attempted to patent his new organism, but the U.S. Patent Office denied his application because it decided you could not patent a living thing. Dr. Chakrabarty appealed the Patent Office's decision all the way to the U.S. Supreme Court. The Court, in the famous *Diamond v. Chakrabarty* case, found that the organism was indeed patent-eligible since Dr. Chakrabarty created it; it had not existed previously. I got to travel with Al all over the U.S., including to Hawaii, and to several foreign countries, including Italy. He was an ideal traveling companion who has a grand sense of humor and a brilliant scientific mind.

Ming Chin is a Justice on the California Supreme Court with a razor-sharp intellect, and in a non-judicial setting, a keen sense of fun. He was EINSHAC's main representative from the California courts and was also on the Board of Directors. I learned a lot from him about law, judging, and civic responsibility. His wife, Carol, is a pharmacist who often joined him at our sessions. One of the many things I admire about Ming is that he owns an original Datsun 240Z sports car. I keep asking him to leave it to me in his will, but his son seems to have beaten me to it. Ming and I became good friends through our work on this project.

At one of the sessions, we were meeting at the University of California, Riverside. Ming was scheduled to give the keynote address. As a member of the states' highest court, his speech was highly anticipated since a large number of judges from the California judiciary were attending. He is an extraordinarily gifted speaker who manages to keep people's attention, as well as entertain and teach them. His presentation was well received.

When I made my way to the reception afterward, there was a large gathering around Ming. If you are a California lawyer and you get a chance to meet a California Supreme Court Justice, you take advantage of it. Ming was a rock star in this forum. Everyone was enthralled to be in his presence. I had seen how people fawn over politicians, so this was not new to me, and I was happy to let his fans revel in his aura.

When I approached the gaggle surrounding him, I caught Carol's eye, and she whispered to Ming that I was there. Ming came over and warmly welcomed me. He then offered to get me a drink. I deferred since I thought the crowd was anxious for him to stay. He insisted and went to the bar and returned with my drink. I then stepped back to the outer edges of the group while Ming continued to dazzle them. I heard someone say, "I don't know who the bald guy is, but he must be important because Justice Chin went and got *him* a drink". I had trouble keeping a straight face, and Ming laughed when I told him about it afterwards.

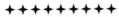

Later that year, I was able to join Ming and several other members of the EINSHAC faculty for a judicial education meeting in Rome. There was a large contingent of the Italian Judiciary in the audience. I was scheduled to speak about the legal and bioethics issues presented by a famous case in Florida, concerning an infertility clinic. This clinic was performing in-vitro fertilizations with the client's eggs and donated sperm. Tragically, one of the donors, who they used regularly, carried a genetic mutation that could cause a serious kidney disease to the babies that often resulted in early death. Many of the embryos created with this sperm would be born with this condition. The Florida clinic had utilized this donor very frequently. The question in the litigation was whether the clinic knew, or should have known, of the deleterious genetic mutation and stopped using that donor's sperm.

I was giving this presentation in English, but at least half of the audience were jurists who only spoke Italian. We were fortunate to have simultaneous translation. I had learned in the past to speak more slowly in those situations. I was told that the Italian language has 30 percent more words than English, so you had to give the translators plenty of time. I had also been warned not to try to tell a joke to a multilingual audience. Frequently, it just does not translate well. However, I was going to give it a shot. I was prepared for this situation. Between sessions, I went into the translator's booth and gave them an outline of my presentation. I specifically pointed out where I was going to attempt humor. The two translators thought the line was funny, but that did not necessarily mean it would go over well with the judges. The joke was that the sperm donor had donated to the clinic more than 300 times [wait for it], ...but not on the same day! Half of the audience (the English speakers) laughed immediately, and it took a very long several seconds before the Italians were let in on it by the translators. I had to pause while waiting for them to catch up. All in all, it went over well. One of my American colleagues said, "You really are Henny Youngman's cousin".

+ + + + + + + + +

Another fascinating person I got to work with, who has become a dear friend, is Andre Davis, a Federal District (trial court) Judge from Maryland. Early on in the EINSHAC seminars (1996), we were giving a "boot camp" to educate judges about scientific evidence and how to treat it during trials. At this time, there was a roaring debate about what standards the courts should use to determine the reliability of scientific evidence. DNA evidence was just beginning to come into its own as a reliable tool in the courts. The session was being held at the Lawrence Livermore National Laboratory. We had access to the labs, and I was showing Judge Davis how to do a test for DNA matching purposes. Electrophoresis is a technique commonly used to separate DNA according to size. You put samples into a gel and run an electric charge through it. The charged DNA molecules move through the gel. Different lengths of DNA move at different speeds. You can distinguish DNA fragments and match identical samples. This technique was fairly new at the time. Judge Davis said, "Dan, this is very interesting, but I don't think I will have many DNA cases in my courtroom". Little did he know at the time how important this would become.

He told me several years later that the exercise we did was helpful in cases where scientific testimony, including DNA evidence, was being proffered. Judge Davis was subsequently elevated to the 4th Circuit Court of Appeals and then left the bench to get back into the trenches as the City Solicitor of Baltimore.

✦✦✦✦✦✦✦✦✦

EINSHAC had a conference in Berkeley, California, for members of the California Judiciary. A lot of trial judges, as well as a good number of appellate judges, including my friend California Supreme Court Justice Ming Chin, participated.

I was going to be the opening speaker on the second day of the conference at 9 am. Getting up early was not difficult for me since my body was still on East Coast time. However, I could see many people dragging their way into the large conference room for my presentation with coffee in hand. I decided to start with a little humor, which is not always a good idea early in the morning.

I was introduced and went to the lectern. As I began, I said I understood there were a lot of judges in the room. I asked them to stand up and to do a few arm stretches and twists. I then told them why; the stretches were to get their blood pumping and help wake them up. I stated the other reason I asked them to stand was because as a lawyer, I always had to stand whenever a judge entered the room when the clerk says, "All rise". I thought it was time the judges had to stand up for me. It got a good laugh, which was the point.

✦✦✦✦✦✦✦✦✦

Another EINSHAC conference gave me the chance to experience the proverbial "small world" phenomenon. An advantage of being on the teaching faculty is that all the participants know who you are because you have been introduced, and they have heard you speak. The downside of that is people come up to talk with you, and you have no idea who they are. At a conference in Banff, Canada one summer, I spoke about the newly enacted Genetic Information Non-discrimination Act (GINA), and, as usual, I included some humor, which I was relieved to know went over well.

During the lunch break, I was wandering aimlessly looking for a good place to sit. The faculty were encouraged to spread out and sit with participants and not all gather with other EINSHAC faculty whom they knew. A woman who I did not know invited me to sit with her and some of the other participants. We all introduced ourselves, and, as usual, I promptly blanked on the names. Fortunately, everyone had name tags on, so I surreptitiously glanced at the name tag on the woman who invited me to join her. She was Linda Dalanis, a Justice on the New Hampshire Supreme Court. She was engaging, and we spoke a bit about GINA. She was complimentary about my presentation and told me having a good sense of humor was a great attribute for any public speaker. I told her my sense of humor was a result of a genetic mutation since I was related to the famous borscht-belt comedian Henny Youngman. That piece of information seemed to stun her. "Where are you from originally?" she asked. I told her I was from Washington, D.C. "Do you have a sister who lives in the Boston area named Nancy Gans?" she asked incredulously. I replied, "Guilty as charged". She then revealed to me she had been my sister's secretary eons ago when Nancy was in a law firm. They even shared maternity clothes. It was my sister who urged her to go to law school! What are the chances of our meeting? She subsequently became the Chief Justice of the New Hampshire Supreme Court. "Small world", indeed!

✦✦✦✦✦✦✦✦

One of the best conferences I attended was in Concepcion, Chile. Judges from all over Latin America attended. The session was held in conjunction with the Global Biotechnology Forum (GBF), which drew more than 2000 delegates world-wide. We were able to do the entire judges' program about science and the courts as well as actively participate in this major international conference. The GBF was organized by a UN organization and the Chilean government. It brought together representatives from the scientific community, and the public and private sectors as well as high-level governmental decision-makers to review opportunities and challenges posed by biotechnology in the developing world.

Dr. Yang Huanming, also known as Henry, was a delegate to the GBF. He is one of China's leading genetics researchers. He is the Chairman and co-founder of the Beijing Genomics Institute. I had met Henry on several other occasions, some of which were on his regular visits to Washington. He is a member of the prestigious American National Academy of Sciences and is a world-renowned scientist. His main work includes the mapping and cloning of human genes, the sequencing and analysis of the human genome, and examining human genomic diversity. He is a warm, brilliant, and humorous man who enjoys the stimulation of bright people.

I would frequently get an email from Henry informing me that he was coming to Washington the very next day! Unfortunately, sometimes these communications were couched in a panic mode because he was having some problems obtaining a visa to enter the United States. Denying a scientist of Henry's prominence a visa to enter our country was preposterous. We were *almost* always able to resolve the problem.

Henry liked to gather a bunch of his American friends together in Washington DC's Chinatown for a grand dinner. These dinners were sometimes overwhelming because of the large number of people, the amount of alcohol involved, and the high decibel level. Mimi and I found that the best approach was to arrange for a private dinner with Henry and whoever he was traveling with. That gave us a chance to converse with him, and since we were able to select the restaurant, we could choose someplace quiet. With only the three of us, or possibly one of Henry's assistants, it was a much better way to enjoy his company. One of the places we used to go had private tables called "snuggeries". Each table was in a separate area with partitions and a velvet curtain. The tranquility enhanced our ability to talk. Henry speaks with a heavy accent, and the low noise level made it easier for us to understand him.

Henry's commitment to using the tools of science to better humankind is extraordinary. Among other things he accomplished was the identification of the virulent virus, called SARS (Severe Acute Respiratory Syndrome), which caused worldwide concern because of its ability to spread rapidly. It was first reported in Asia in February 2003. Over the next few months, it proliferated to more than two dozen countries in North America, South America, Europe and Asia before it was contained. Henry was an important player in the effort to identify and treat the virus. During one of our dinners, he told me that he would have felt personally, criminally liable if any of his research staff contracted the virus. They took all the biohazard precautions possible, but he was still afraid that someone would get sick.

Mimi and Henry got along well. She thought he was a lot of fun and very interesting. In my experience, there are many situations where the inclusion of a spouse at a gathering changes the dynamic. There have been situations where Mimi would choose to go to an event without me because she felt I would not enjoy it and vice versa. A perfect example of this is high school reunions. I never even considered putting Mimi through the ordeal of being introduced to a whole bunch of people from my youth who I did not know anymore. However, dinner with Henry was always exceptional.

Mimi did not go with me to Chile for the judges' conference and the Global Biotechnology Forum. Because Henry was going to be there, Mimi wanted me to give him a gift from us. We knew how much he enjoyed time in Washington and decided to give him a coffee table book called "Above Washington". It is a fabulous photography book of pictures of various places in Washington DC, taken from the air. Some of the extraordinary photographs give you a view of a place you know well but from a different perspective, such as looking at the Lincoln Memorial from 100 feet above it. I initially thought this was a marvelous idea and bought a copy for Henry. It did not occur to me that such a high-quality photographic book was going to weigh a ton! I ended up lugging it all the way to Chile.

Henry was not going to attend our Judge's Boot Camp, but I knew I was going to see him at the Global Biotechnology Forum. The day finally arrived for the opening plenary session of the GBF. With book in hand, I waded into the throng looking for Henry. The most logical place for me to go was to the Chinese delegation. When I got there and inquired as to Henry's whereabouts, one of the Chinese delegates told me that he was across the way with the Korean delegation. This was no surprise since Henry was quite gregarious and knew just about every scientist in the world of biotechnology. I found my way over there and was able to make eye contact with Henry and saw him break into a big smile. We greeted each other warmly, and I told him that I was "Mimi Legat's messenger" with a special present for him. I opened my backpack and bestowed it. He loved it!

We were standing near the center aisle of the massive assembly hall and saw someone coming towards us. I had no idea who he was, but having spent my career in Washington, I recognized the VIP treatment this man was being given, including being surrounded by security agents, who I assumed were armed and dangerous. The VIP made a beeline for Henry with an outstretched hand and a big smile. Henry spoke to him in Spanish with his heavy Chinese accent. He then presented me as "My dear friend from the United States Congress, Daniel Freeman". I did my best to be friendly and practically exhausted my command of Spanish by saying, "Con mucho gusto!" He shook my hand, patted me on the shoulder, and then was whisked away.

Soon the business meeting of the Forum was called to order. According to the program, the President of Chile, Ricardo Lagos, was going to open the session. I thought the fact that the President was going to give the opening address spoke volumes about how important biotechnology was going to be in Latin America. When President Lagos was introduced and came forward to speak, I was stunned to realize that he was the man to whom I was introduced by Henry, not 20 minutes before!

In addition to the plenary sessions, there was a myriad of breakout sessions on a whole range of topics. There were many meetings about the judicial process in dealing with the new biotechnology questions. There were also several devoted to discussions of the complex bioethics' issues involved. I was asked to speak at two. There were over 100 people in each, and I was more than a little nervous. I reworked my presentation several times, including on the day I was to give it. My dear friend Jim Evans was there helping me with the computers and with suggestions of things I needed to do to make my presentation more effective.

The most meaningful talk I gave was on bioethics and the rapidly evolving science in genetics. I spoke of my expectations for the future, including my desire for the "magic genie" of the human genome to be utilized for the good of humankind. I spoke about possible issues that could be raised in judicial forums and my hopes that future judges would be well-equipped to deal with the complex scientific, technological, and legal problems which they would present.

I took a gamble and decided to end my presentation (which was presented in PowerPoint in Spanish) with the following: "I would like to paraphrase Dr. Martin Luther King Jr. by saying that I, too, have a dream. My dream is that the fantastic scientific advances which we are witnessing today and will see in the days, months, and years ahead, will be robust, valuable and will be treated with the respect and care which they deserve by scientists, judges, elected officials, doctors and all of us who will become patients". I then flashed the last slide up on the screen, "Tengo un sueno", which is Spanish for "I have a dream". I got a warm round of applause and was pleased with my presentation.

✦✦✦✦✦✦✦✦✦

Not everyone you meet is worth your time. There was a very conservative Federal Judge who was not able to keep his political opinions to himself. When he found out I worked for the Democrats on the House Judiciary Committee when they were in the majority, and then for the Republicans when they gained control, he was constantly giving me grief, calling me a "closet Democrat". He irritated the hell out of me. Unfortunately, he was chosen to be on the teaching faculty for the EINSHAC meeting to be held in Concepcion. My rule was that domestic politics stops at the water's edge. When you are an American citizen, especially if you are in a foreign country in your official capacity, you should not be critical of the American government. That rule was obviously not one he believed in. During the Clinton administration, he took every occasion to bad-mouth the President. When we were in Chile, this jerk even called the President "the biggest liar in the history of the country". I was outraged that he did this in front of a group of Chilean judges. It was not relevant to the scientific evidence issues we were discussing, nobody asked him about it, he just decided to open his mouth. At the time, he looked like a clown because he was wearing flashy red Walt Disney suspenders and a loud Mickey Mouse tie. (That is not my characterization, it was a violently colored tie with Mickey Mouse on it.) I was embarrassed that he was representing our country. At one of the receptions, he came up to the group of people I was speaking with, including several Chilean judges. He, once again, started to give me grief. I looked him straight in the eye and said, "Do not ever talk to me again! *Ever!*" I am glad to say he never did.

✦✦✦✦✦✦✦✦✦✦✦

Because of my work with EINSHAC, I also got to co-teach a course on Healthcare Policy at the Graduate School of Public Policy at Georgetown University. One of the other lawyers from the EINSHAC faculty and I taught an evening course that focused on how healthcare policy is formulated by the executive branch, the legislative branch, and occasionally, by the judiciary. It was the first time I had taught night school, and the students were excellent. If a student is working full time, and also taking classes at night, they are usually dedicated to maximizing the experience. I dealt with most of the issues that came up about the legislative process, and my colleague handled most of the matters relating to the executive branch. We also had a Delaware Supreme Court Justice, who discussed the judicial questions.

One of the students and I were talking one night about working on the Hill. Her father-in-law was a Vice President for Congressional Affairs for Trans World Airlines. Since my wife and I flew TWA regularly to visit her family in England, I thought it might be helpful to meet him. I offered to take him to lunch. He was surprised to have a Hill staffer offer to take *him* to lunch. He told me it was usually the other way around. I enjoyed our lunch, and we talked about aviation.

Several months later, I got an offer in the mail from TWA relating to my frequent flier miles account. The promotion was to bid miles for the chance to spend time at the TWA training facility at JFK Airport, which included a session with a training pilot in a jet aircraft simulator. I was enthusiastic about that possibility, but I did not have enough miles to win the bidding.

I figured, nothing ventured, nothing gained. I called my new friend at TWA and asked him if there was any way he could get me into the simulator. He did not know about the facility, but he promised he would check about it for me. He called me the next day and asked me when I would be available in New York. Mimi was going to be out of town, and I had planned to go up to New York while she was away. He set it up, and off I went to learn how to fly!

When I got to the facility, I was met by one of TWA's training pilots who escorted me into the mammoth building, which housed what was at the time a state-of-the-art trainer/simulator for the Boeing 727. He asked me if I was a pilot, and I said no. He told me to sit in the left-hand seat anyway (where the pilot sits). He then asked me where I would like to go. I did not have a quick answer to that question, so he said that since I was from Washington, DC, "Let's go to Dulles". He pushed a few buttons on his control panel, and I looked out the front, and there was Dulles Airport!

He explained the various controls I would need to know how to use, including the throttles, the yoke, and the foot pedals, which controlled both the brakes and the steering. I was a little overwhelmed. We got "clearance" from the tower, and he talked me through taxiing out and take off. It was exhilarating, and I quickly forgot that this was only a simulator. He was a brilliant teacher and clearly enjoyed that role.

One of the remarkable things about the training simulators is they could be used to take pilots into dangerous situations and teach them how to get out of trouble while never getting off the ground. For the next hour, he took me through some situations which had resulted in crashes; and taught me, as he had taught many real pilots, how to fly through them. He showed me how to do an aborted takeoff, an aborted landing requiring a go-around, and how to fly through a violent wind shear. Wind shear had recently caused a fatal crash of a Delta jet in Dallas. He described the weather conditions there at the time of the crash and then taught me how to deal with them successfully. I have to admit it was stressful. He told me not to worry because "Only a hundred and thirty-eight people are sitting behind you". I think I lost about 10 pounds sweating through that, but I had a ball!

✦✦✦✦✦✦✦✦✦

Serendipity struck again when we had a conference scheduled at Washington University, my old stomping grounds. I was on the teaching faculty for this event and was pleased to be back at WashU. I had heard about a new organization on campus related to bioethics. It was the Center for the Study of Ethics and Human Values. Since I had some free time between sessions, I went over to the Center's offices to see if I could meet Dr. Ira Kodner, the Center's Director. Dr. Kodner was an Endowed Professor of Surgery at the WashU School of Medicine. The Center's mission was to become a forum for examining some of the important ethical issues confronting society as well as to serve as a resource for studies of human values by faculty, students, and the community.

Dr. Kodner was in his office, and he welcomed me as both a WashU alum and someone interested in bioethics. We had a long discussion concerning the necessity of doctors being educated about the principles of bioethics. Ira is an engaging and interesting man who I liked immediately. He invited me to his home for dinner with his family, which I readily accepted. When we got there, I found out the Cardinals baseball team was playing that night. For the Kodner family of rabid baseball fans, having the game on during dinner was mandatory. I was used to that since I grew up in a home where the Washington football team's schedule dictated what time Thanksgiving dinner was to be served. Ira's wife, Barbara, and their two daughters joined us for dinner. It was a very warm and friendly evening. I was almost disappointed when I had to get back to the conference.

That was the beginning of a good friendship. Ira invited me to co-author an article about bioethics and emergency surgery with two other doctors from the WashU Medical School faculty. I was the only lawyer on the team, but that did not seem to pose any problems. It was published in a book, "Acute Care Surgery," in 2007 and an updated version in "The ASCRS Textbook of Colon and Rectal Surgery" in 2011, with a renowned bioethicist Dr. Mark Seigler from the University of Chicago Medical Center as an additional coauthor. I have joined Ira regularly when he comes to Washington for medical meetings, and have been a guest speaker on occasion. He has invited me to come to events at WashU, which I do whenever I can. I thoroughly enjoy his company and the intellectual stimulation it provides.

I was fortunate to be in St. Louis for another event and managed to get some time to have lunch with Ira. There was going to be a special session at the medical school that afternoon, and Ira asked if I would like to go with him as his guest. The speaker was Dr. Thomas Starzl, a world-famous pioneer in the field of organ transplantation. It was going to be his last public lecture. I had read his book, "The Puzzle People: Memoirs of a Transplant Surgeon" and was enthusiastic about attending. I think Ira was pleased to find out how interested I was in hearing Dr. Starzl. It was a fascinating event, and I was thrilled I was able to be there.

Ira had arranged for a car to take me to the airport afterwards. We were not far from the WashU campus. I asked the driver to stop at the steps of Brookings Hall. I walked up the steps and sat for a few moments in the same place I had sat all those years ago as the Gateway Arch was completed. It was a lovely bit of nostalgia for me.

✦✦✦✦✦✦✦✦

My wife and I were vacationing in Maui before EINSHAC meetings which were to take place in Honolulu and Kona. I was to fly over to Honolulu and meet up with some of our faculty, including Justice Ming Chin. We were going to address a plenary meeting of the Hawaiian judiciary, with judges from all levels. I looked very out of place when I got on the inter-island flight. I was in my work uniform, double-breasted suit, tie with collar bar, and cufflinks. I do not think I have ever seen anyone on Maui wearing a suit. But I thought since I was addressing the judges, I should be properly attired. When I got to the place where the meeting was to be held, I saw Ming and the two other members of our faculty who were going to participate. No one from the Hawaii State Courts was there to greet us, so we all decided to walk over to a nearby restaurant for lunch.

After our informal lunch, we went back to the convention center. I thought all of our presentations went well and flew back to Maui while the others flew over to the Big Island, where a separate EINSHAC "boot camp" for judges was to be held. Along with many judges from the Hawaiian courts, there were judges from several other countries and many courts across the United States attending. There was a series of meetings on a wide range of topics. We planned to spread out the workload among the faculty. Each of us would be on a panel once in the morning and once in the afternoon.

When I arrived the next day on the Big Island of Hawaii, everything seemed to be in good shape. One of our faculty had brought her fantastic administrative assistant. All of the paperwork for reimbursements and travel arrangements was done, and everything was ready for the conference to begin. After Mimi and I checked in, we went down to the opening cocktail hour. The people from the Honolulu meeting were there, as was the rest of the faculty. I was mingling and saying hello to some old friends when I bumped into one of our group. She told me she thought I was a "glutton for punishment." I did not know what she meant. I had looked at the schedule, and I told her I was slated to speak on one of three panels in the morning. She said I should look at the new and revised schedule. I had gotten used to these things being somewhat flexible, but I was shocked to find out I was listed on *all three* panels for the morning. I did not find out until later that our fearless leader was incensed when he found out no one from the Hawaiian judiciary was there to greet us before the Honolulu meeting. I was not offended, but he was very upset that the judges on our panels were not treated with the respect they deserved. In a fit of pique, he dealt with this by pulling all of our judges from all the panels for the morning sessions. The result was I was thrown into the breach. It was pretty weird, but I dutifully went on.

✦ ✦ ✦ ✦ ✦ ✦ ✦ ✦ ✦

One of the best things that ever happened to me in my entire life was meeting Jim Evans at that meeting. Dr. Evans (he is both an M.D. and a Ph.D.) gave a good presentation on genetics. He knew he was going to be speaking to a group of lawyers/judges and was able to dazzle us without confusing us with jargon. His talk was filled with genetic terminology, which he explained as he went along. I am sure the fact that I was interested had something to do with my reaction to his presentation.

I was sitting with him at lunch, and he asked the group where the term "gerrymandering" came from. As I was Counsel to the House Judiciary Committee and reapportionment was a topic within the committee's jurisdiction, I happened to know the answer. I explained it came from the early 19th century and was based on a famous editorial cartoon in the *Boston Weekly Messenger*. The cartoon portrayed the similarity between a salamander and the shape of the new voting district, which was drawn when Elbridge Gerry was the Governor of Massachusetts. The new district map was designed to be favorable to Governor Gerry's party. Jim was suitably impressed. I would rather be lucky than good. He happened to ask a question to which I knew the answer.

We got to talking about the venue. The meeting was being held at the Mauna Kea Resort, which seemed like it was beamed in from Mars. There were three big resorts on the Kona coast, and they all had pristine white sand beaches. We were told the natural conditions at the site were just lava rock. The developers of the resorts had tons and tons of white sand brought in to make the beach more attractive to tourists. I told Jim about the breathtaking snorkeling directly in front of the hotel. He said he was so nearsighted that a fish would have to bump into his mask for him to see it. I asked him to give me his glasses, which, upon inspection, looked like they had come from the bottom of a Coke bottle. I put his glasses on, and I could see fairly well. I told him to stay put, and I would be back. I went up to my room and got my mask, which has corrective lenses. Since my prescription was probably close to his, I thought he might like to go snorkeling and actually see the fish. He was grateful. Later that evening, he called me and enthusiastically explained he had just had a "practically religious experience", seeing all the beautiful Hawaiian fish clearly. That was the beginning of a deep and meaningful friendship.

Jim has been my go-to source for anything medical as well as for a whole range of other topics. I am always in awe of the breadth and depth of his knowledge on matters medical/scientific, as well as government, politics, and many other topics. Not only is he well-informed, but he is thoughtful in the contemplative connotation of the word. He has an insatiable thirst for learning. I have had many fantastic opportunities to engage him in discussion and debate. I think we both come away from those discussions with a little less certainty about our positions. They force us to rethink. He is not unengaged and silent until it is his turn to talk. He is taking in what you have said and examining it under his intellectual microscope. He is a joy to be around.

Jim was always traveling to conferences and giving presentations about genetics. He was invited to speak at the St. Francis Hospital Conference on Bioethics in Honolulu. He could not attend and suggested me as a substitute. I was on two panels at the conference in Jim's place and found it interesting. While I was there, I met Jim Pietsch, who is a professor at the University of Hawaii's William S. Richardson School of Law.

Several years later, I spoke to Pietsch's bioethics class on the *Gonzalez v Oregon* case dealing with physician-assisted suicide. I was pleased to learn that the former Chief Justice of Hawaii, William S. Richardson, for whom the school was named, was in the audience. One of the students, a former army officer, opined the case was about the 10th amendment, which I enthusiastically said was exactly correct. Most people had misinterpreted the decision and believed it dealt with the Equal Protection Clause. I thought it concerned federalism and the power of states to regulate medical practice. I enjoyed the class immensely.

✦✦✦✦✦✦✦✦✦

Mimi and I were traveling to Cape Cod to attend an EINSHAC conference where I was to be the opening speaker that evening. Our travel plans called for us to fly from Washington to Boston, and then change planes. The short hop to Cape Cod was on a puddle-jumper, a small twin-engine turboprop aircraft operated by one of the regional carriers.

We took our seats on the plane in plenty of time and found the flight was oversold. They were looking for one volunteer to be bumped. The airline would provide the volunteer with a limousine to the airport on Cape Cod. Knowing how Mimi would much rather be on the ground than in the air, my genetic mutation leaped out. I looked at her, and she nodded her assent. I then said in a humorous tone, "Take my wife, please". Several people, who obviously knew the Henny Youngman line, laughed. The flight attendant came down the aisle to see if I was serious. I told her my wife would be more than happy to volunteer. The attendant was relieved, and Mimi got off the plane.

When I landed, after a very bumpy flight, I was glad to think Mimi had avoided it. She would have been very uncomfortable. At the inn where we were staying, I tried to unpack. There was one minor problem; the keys were on Mimi's key chain. I ended up wearing the same clothes I had traveled in to the meeting that evening. Since it was a fairly casual event, that was fine.

By the time the pre-conference cocktail reception was wrapping up, and we were getting ready to start, I still had not seen Mimi. About three minutes before I was to begin, she walked in, looking calm and relaxed. She told me she had a lovely drive from Boston to Cape Cod. She was supposed to be dropped off at the airport but asked the driver to take her directly to the meeting site. She gave him a nice tip, and everyone was happy. We spoke briefly, and then it was showtime.

I began my remarks with the story of Mimi's travels. A lot of the people at the conference knew me well enough not to be surprised when I related that I had said on the plane, "Take my wife, please". It was an entertaining way to begin.

XIV. Chairman Hyde and the House Judiciary Committee

Congressman Newt Gingrich was the mastermind of the Republican drive to take over the House in the 1994 elections. He was the brains behind the "Contract with America". This document, drafted mostly by Gingrich and his colleague Dick Armey, was released just six weeks before the election. The contract specified actions the Republicans were going to take if they took control of the House of Representatives, something they had not done in 40 years. The contract was extraordinary in that it provided for speedy House consideration of specific legislation to address what the Republicans viewed as the foremost problems facing the country.

The contract provided for legislative action on the *very first day of the session* to immediately:

1. Require all laws that apply to the rest of the country also apply equally to the Congress.
2. Select a major, independent auditing firm to conduct a comprehensive audit of Congress for waste, fraud, or abuse.
3. Cut the number of House committees and cut committee staff by one-third.
4. Limit the terms of all committee chairs.
5. Ban the casting of proxy votes in committee.
6. Require committee meetings to be open to the public.
7. Require a three-fifths majority vote to pass a tax increase.
8. Guarantee an honest accounting of our Federal Budget by implementing zero base-line budgeting.

The Contract went further in promising to bring to the House floor for a vote a wide range of reforms within the first 100 days, each with a short, catchy name. These included:

1. The Fiscal Responsibility Act calling for a balanced budget and line-item veto for the President
2. The Taking Back Our Streets Act, an anti-crime package including stronger truth-in-sentencing, "good faith" exclusionary rule exemptions, effective death penalty provisions and additional law enforcement funding
3. The Personal Responsibility Act to discourage teen pregnancy along with cutting welfare spending
4. The Family Reinforcement Act to provide for child support enforcement, tax incentives for adoption, and to reinforce the central role of families in American society
5. The American Dream Restoration Act to provide for a tax credit for children and repeal of the marriage tax penalty
6. The National Security Restoration Act to provide for the restoration of national defense and prohibit the placing any U.S. troops under UN command
7. The Senior Citizens' Fairness Act to raise the Social Security earnings limit, and repeal the 1993 tax hikes on Social Security benefits
8. The Job Creation and Wage Enhancement Act to create small business incentives strengthening the Regulatory Flexibility Act
9. The Common-Sense Legal Reform Act to enact tort reform
10. The Citizen Legislature Act to enact term limits to replace career politicians with citizen legislators

Those of us on the staff were aware of the Contract, but no one I talked with thought a Republican takeover of the House was a realistic possibility. I do recall one of the Republican lawyers on the Constitution Subcommittee with whom I worked very well, saying to me, "You know, when we take over, we should keep you on". We both laughed. We did not think about the effect the new Republican majority and its Contract would have on the workload and operation of the Committee because we did not believe it could happen.

Lightning did strike, and there was a tectonic plate shift in Congress. When the dust had settled on Wednesday morning, November 9, 1994, there was a stunning net gain of 54 Republican seats and, with its new majority, control of the House. The Speaker, Tom Foley, lost his election as did my boss, Jack Brooks, the Chairman of the House Judiciary Committee.

One of the shocking logistical manifestations of the changeover was the delivery early on the Wednesday morning after the election to Chairman Brooks' Congressional office of a pallet of banker boxes to be used to pack up 42 years-worth of Congressional files. He was the most senior Member to be defeated, so the dominos of assigning offices for the 104th Congress began with him vacating his. It was a slap in the face being told, in essence, to "pack up and get out immediately". I was told he was angry about the abruptness of it. There were a lot of offices to be changed, with some of the more junior people who won their elections getting newer and better digs, thereby making room for the incoming freshmen. Some of the senior people who had been defeated were being forced to vacate promptly to make room for the new Members.

A lot of us on the staff realized we were going to have to start looking for jobs. There were a few people on the administrative staff who we thought were going to be kept on, but most of us were drafting resumes on Wednesday. I had not given much thought to what I was going to do. I did not think that whoever the new ranking minority Member for the Democrats was going to be would need somebody with my parliamentary experience. The Parliamentarian's job is to assist in getting legislation done, not in trying to slow it down. Sure, it made sense to have someone familiar with the rules to make sure you did not get steam-rolled, but mostly the job was focused on legislative action.

Carlos Moorhead was a Congressman from Glendale, California, and a very pleasant man. He was not a firebrand; just a "steady as she goes" kind of person. As the senior Republican on both the Energy and Commerce and Judiciary Committees, he seemed well-positioned to get a Chairmanship on one of the two. However, Gingrich, the new Speaker, did not think Carlos was enough of a red-meat Republican to serve in either position. When Gingrich approached Henry Hyde (the next Republican in seniority after Moorhead) about the Judiciary Committee Chairmanship, Henry, being the good man he was, told the Speaker he would not take the job until he talked to Carlos. Moorhead told Hyde, "If they are not going to give it to me, there is no one better than you. Go ahead and take it".

Moorhead was to tell me later in a private conversation that "Newt screwed me, and there was nothing I could do about it. I am glad Henry met their litmus test and became Chairman". He said it without the bitterness that I thought would have been appropriate. I felt sorry for him, but he did get the Chairmanship of the Intellectual Property Subcommittee as the second prize.

Alan Coffey, who had been the Minority Chief Counsel, would be the new General Counsel. He called me on Thursday with an intriguing invitation. He said, "Dan, we know where we want to take this policy bus, but we do not have anybody on our staff who knows how to drive. Would you be willing to stay on as the Committee Parliamentarian?" I was pleasantly surprised by the offer. Based on my experience working with Alan and with Henry Hyde, and, not inconsequentially, the fact that I did not have a job, I said yes. He told me to show up in Henry's office on Monday morning, and we would discuss it. I thought it was an idea to be worked out, not a done deal.

On Monday morning, Henry, Alan and I met for what I expected to be a rather intense interview about whether they would feel comfortable having somebody who had worked for the Democrats for all those years working for them. I was pleased to find out as far as Henry was concerned this was a *fait accompli*. Having established a good working relationship with him, especially during the Claiborne impeachment, seemed to have made this an easy decision. "You are an institutionalist, and I expect you to continue to be one", Henry said to me. Alan was a little less confident about how it was going to be perceived by both Democrats and Republicans.

Henry had offered me the job and I accepted. Before the new Congress with its Republican majority began, I was my office when Sharon Matts came down to the committee offices to collect some of Mr. Brooks' things to be shipped to his office in Beaumont. She congratulated me on the job and asked if I wanted to call Mr. Brooks and tell him about it. I think that was her kind way of telling me Mr. Brooks should hear about it from me. With all the upheaval, I had not thought of it, and, in retrospect, I think he might have been upset had he not heard about it directly from me. Sharon placed the call for me to make sure I got through to the Chairman. He was very friendly and congratulated me. He said he appreciated my calling him to let him know and wished me luck working with "those people". Sharon knew Mr. Brooks well and had done me a good deed by suggesting I call him. I told her how grateful I was.

One of the first things I did after securing the job with Henry was to go around the committee offices and scavenge for furniture. With almost all of the Brooks staff leaving, no one was there to object to my appropriating things to furnish the "better office" that Mr. Brooks had provided me so he could take over my old office. I was able to find a large sofa that I dragged into my new digs. It was a nice three cushion leather couch, which was long enough for me to lay down on. This turned out to be a good find since there were many late nights ahead. I also grabbed what was called a "Member's Chair". These are large tufted button chairs with brass nail heads. These were hard to find since they were originally issued to Members only. I also scored a couple of brass lamps for the end tables by the sofa and a similar brass standing lamp, which I placed near the Member's chair. I used these for the next six years, while Henry was the Chairman of the Judiciary Committee. Unfortunately, when we went over to the International Relations Committee, my office was not big enough for any of my purloined acquisitions.

✦✦✦✦✦✦✦✦✦

Under the Contract with America, the Judiciary Committee was going to be processing the bulk of the legislation, and we were going to be extremely busy. Two days before we were to go to the floor with the first piece of legislation, I was meeting with Alan and Henry to discuss the parliamentary procedure. Alan suggested that it might be a prudent thing to have me waiting in the cloakroom as opposed to being visible on the floor sitting behind Henry as he was managing the bill. Henry said, "We hired him, we should use him. I do not see any reason to hide him". That was that.

Not only were we going to have to deal with some controversial matters, but the cutting of committee staff and the prohibition on proxy voting were going to have a considerable impact. The elimination of proxy voting simplified my life a bit. I no longer had to contact Members' offices before each full committee meeting or wrestle with questions about whether to vote an absent Member's undirected proxy. Included in the problems which the Contract would raise was the fact that Henry Hyde was vehemently opposed to term limits. He had made that clear to the Leadership, and he knew they would not deny him the Chairmanship because of it. They did not require him to agree with every part of the Contract.

✦ ✦ ✦ ✦ ✦ ✦ ✦ ✦ ✦

As I began work for the new Republican majority, the pressure was intense on me for two reasons. First, I was being scrutinized closely by the Republican staff. Most of the people who had been on what was the minority staff knew me, and I think I had a good reputation for fairness. A lot of the new people who joined the majority (Republican) staff were suspicious of me because I had worked for "them" (the Democrats) previously. Some of the new people simply did not trust any Democrat. Secondly, a lot of the Democrats, both staff and Members, were upset that I had chosen to stay on. Someone said to me that Chairman Hyde's decision to keep me on was evidence of my being either "totally morally bankrupt or very good at my job". My response to that comment was that those two were not mutually exclusive. Some people did not think that was funny, but those who knew me smiled.

Staying on as the Parliamentarian for the new Republican majority was the cause of one ugly scene on the House floor. Fortunately, I was not there to witness it. Dick Armey, who was the new Majority Leader, had a staffer who was his committee liaison. I did not know her, and she did not know me. However, she was described to me as "rabidly partisan". I found out later that she was sending out scathing memos to the Republican committee staffs, telling them not to trust any of the Democrats and certainly not to be seen having lunch with them. I do not know what prompted that particular memo, but I expect she saw some Democrat having lunch with one of her trusted Republicans (or at least formerly trusted Republicans). Henry was on the floor in the first month after Republicans took control, and this woman approached him and, as it was relayed to me, excoriated him for hiring a "goddamn Democrat" and demanded he fire me immediately. "You cannot trust those people", she raged. Henry, who was a kind and gentle man, told her in no uncertain terms that he was the Chairman, and he would hire whomever he wanted to. He told her *he* would be the judge of that person's competency. I made it a point to stay as far away from her as possible, although we did end up being on speaking terms. I found out later where she got her animus towards Democrats. Her husband was Clarence Thomas. Considering what he went through during his Senate confirmation battle, I was not completely surprised she felt that way. I was willing to cut her some slack, but not much.

✦ ✦ ✦ ✦ ✦ ✦ ✦ ✦ ✦

While knowledge of the rules can be a good thing, inaccurate knowledge can lead to confusion. One of the Members of the committee from New York City was not tolerant of being educated, especially by a mere staffer like me. He knew what he knew, and there was no correcting him. During one of the first markups of legislation, the committee worked from a new text of the bill— called a substitute. When all the amendments to the new text were disposed of, the Chairman called a vote on the substitute. This motion was agreed to. The next step was for the committee to adopt the original bill *as amended by the substitute*. After the first vote, the New Yorker started to object to the second vote. He insisted another vote was not required. I went over to him to explain that the second vote *was* necessary under the House Rules. He told me in no uncertain terms that he had been in the New York legislature for 14 years, and you do *not* need a second vote. I told him as far as I knew, the New York State Legislature used Roberts Rules of Order, and that the House rule was different. I explained the House rule required a separate vote because a Member might prefer the substitute to the underlying bill, and therefore vote for it, but might be opposed to the original bill. A Member might think the substitute to be "less terrible" than the original bill. He could vote for the substitute and against the bill. He was not swayed. His response was, "Well, that is a stupid rule!"

✦ ✦ ✦ ✦ ✦ ✦ ✦ ✦ ✦

Henry had a fabulous sense of humor, which made him a pleasure to be around. I enjoy a laugh, and early on, I was comfortable enough with him to feed him a good line. One of the first actions the committee had to take in the new Congress was to set up a plan for what it was going to do for the next two years. This had to be in a formal document that outlined the committee's legislative and oversight agenda. The plan did not have any binding effect, and as anyone who had worked in Congress knows, things change all the time, and this document was not going to have much of a half-life. However, as required, the staff put together a draft proposed committee agenda for the new Congress, and it was circulated to the Members before the first full committee meeting.

The proposed plan was merely a vehicle for discussion, and for Members to bring to the committee's attention things which they thought should be addressed during the new Congress. With the change in majority/minority status, Republicans were seated on Henry's right and the Democrats to his left. It was funny to see him frequently looking to his left when he should have been looking to his right and vice versa. For as long as he had been in Congress, it had been the other way around. I, however, was the only one whose seat did not change. I sat on my stool directly behind the Chairman.

As we were getting ready to conclude, Henry recognized one of the junior Members from New York City, José Serrano, who had a gravelly tough from "Da Bronx" accent. Congressman Serrano's insisted a new item be included in the plan. He wanted the Committee to hold public hearings on the denial of one of his constituent's First Amendment rights to free speech. He complained that this constituent, a radio talk show host, had been "banned from airwaves". He contended that by banning the broadcast of the radio show, his constituent's "free speech rights had been taken away". Serrano was outraged about the terrible precedent this would set. He then revealed the name of the constituent. It was Howard Stern, a so-called "shock-jock", which the dictionary defines as a "radio talk show host who expresses opinions in a deliberately offensive or provocative way". Serrano was adamant that the Committee convene oversight hearings "to expose the travesty of the banning of his broadcasts". I leaned forward from my position behind the Chairman and whispered to him, "Tell him we could have such hearings, but we would be banned from broadcasting them". Henry was not fazed, and he turned on his microphone and said, "Well, I will tell the gentleman we could hold such hearings, but we would be banned from broadcasting them". The room exploded in laughter. Henry turned, rocked back in his chair, pointed to me, and said, "That is why I kept you on".

I had gotten to know Congressman Howard Coble since he joined the committee in 1985. He was the classic "good ol' boy" from North Carolina. He had a down-home accent and manner. He certainly did not come across as the polished urbane person some Members try to project. He, too, had a wonderful sense of humor. We had enjoyed many good laughs over the years. Howard always called me, "Dan, Dan, the parliamentary man". After the committee meeting that day, he came up to me and said with a big grin on his face, "That line had 'Freeman' written all over it". I accepted that as a compliment but made an expression which said, "Who me?" It was the first of many times Howard would catch me feeding a good line to someone.

++++++++

Something I learned a long time ago came in very handy in working with Henry Hyde. Long before going to law school, I found that it is hard for people to read and listen at the same time. I know these days with all the electronic devices around, multitasking is the norm. However, I was taught early on if you are presenting a document to somebody, and you want to discuss it with them, you should always make sure they have the opportunity to read it first. That means either you make sure they have it sufficiently in advance to read and absorb it, or if you are delivering it just before you are about to discuss it, you should sit there while the boss reads it. Do not start explaining it! Just shut up. You will know when it is time to talk when the boss stops reading and looks at you or asks you a question. Most people do not do this. As I got to be more senior and people were presenting me with papers, I would ask them to be quiet while I went over them. Some junior staffers would be so excited to describe their crucial and fabulous work they would not give me a chance to take in the material.

The first three or four times I went in to brief Henry about something, I approached it as I normally would. I would tell him what I was there to discuss, a subpoena, a bill going to the floor, or a meeting that was about to happen, hand him the briefing memo, and then sit there without saying anything while he went over it. The next time I went in to see him, I did the same thing. He looked up at me, and he said, "It is very rare to find someone smart enough to sit there quietly while I have a chance to review the material. I want you to know how much I appreciate your always doing that for me".

++++++++

There was another incident where my sense of humor was demonstrated. We were in a full committee meeting and during the lull between witnesses, I told Henry a rather long and complicated joke. He thought it was terribly funny, and I knew him well enough to know he would want to use it later. The punch line was complex, and he asked me to repeat it slowly so that he could write it down. I did, and he did.

Later that afternoon, I was on the floor with him during a series of votes. I would frequently go over to the House during votes just to spend time with him. I knew where he usually sat, and since I had permanent floor privileges, I could go whenever I wanted. Sometimes we would discuss committee business, sometimes we would talk about what was going on in the government, and sometimes we would chat about philosophy or sports. I loved being able to do that and having him be comfortable enough with me to engage. As we were sitting there, several other Members came over to join in a general bull session. Among the participants were Dick Armey, the Majority Leader, who was quite a character, Lamar Smith, Howard Coble and Barbara Cuban. Henry decided this was the perfect time to tell that joke. He started, and when he got to the end, he reached into his pocket to pull out his written version. At the last second, rather than mangle it, Henry said: "Dan, it is your joke, you tell it". I would never have done that if he had not asked me to. The standing rule is the staff never up-stages the Member. After I delivered the punch line, the gaggle of people burst out laughing much to Henry's glee (and mine). Dick Armey started to respond in kind by telling a joke of his own. He got part of the way into it and stopped. He looked at me and said, "I ain't going there because my daddy always told me, 'Don't ever try to bullshit a bullshitter.'" I took that as a compliment.

✦✦✦✦✦✦✦✦✦

Henry was always good at injecting a little humor into any situation. During a full committee meeting, one of the liberal Democrats was rambling on and on about something. What I remember about it was Henry saying, "You know Dan, their nuts are just as nutty as our nuts". While I agreed with him whole-heartedly, I just smiled.

✦✦✦✦✦✦✦✦✦

With the Republican takeover of the House, there were a lot of new staffers. Many of the more conservative Members of the House came from fundamen-talist Christian backgrounds and, not surprisingly, they brought like-minded staff with them. I have always been a separation of church and state purist, so much so I object to having references to God on our money. Because of that, the oath for swearing in witnesses which I had prepared and used for years did not include the words, "so help me God". Under the new Republican regime, the first time I was asked for the oath, the subcommittee chairman administered it as I had written it. I do not think he even noticed the difference. One of the new subcommittee lawyers almost had a stroke because I had used an "incom-plete" oath. I told her it was sufficient for federal perjury prosecution purposes and had been cleared for use in Congressional committees. We had used that version across-the-board for all witnesses. Therefore, we did not have to change the oath to accommodate the situations where witnesses were not willing to use the sectarian reference. I do not know if she changed it when her boss was swearing in witnesses, but I would not be surprised.

We were in a break during a recorded vote in the House during a subse-quent committee meeting. A bunch of staff was sitting around chatting when the question came up about whether the office was going to be closed the following Monday for a religious holiday. I do not recall what the holiday was, and I did not know whether we would have the day off. The same woman who complained about the oath happened to be there. In an attempt at humor, I said, "Henny Youngman says the main problem with being an atheist is you do not get any religious holidays". She looked at me in horror with saucer-sized eyes. "Did you say you were an atheist?" she asked incredulously. I certainly was not going to get into a discussion about this with her, so I responded, "What I said was that *Henny Youngman* made the comment about being an atheist. I was quoting him". I think she suspected I was the devil incarnate for even suggesting there was such a thing as an atheist. I kept my distance from her from then on.

✦✦✦✦✦✦✦✦✦

One of the Members I had fun getting to know was Steve Largent, who had been an All-Pro wide receiver for the Seattle Seahawks. I assume I was one of many people who wanted to talk to him about football. Although that was an easy opening subject for him, he was more interested in talking about government. I was on the floor with Henry one day, and Largent approached to ask him a question about the proposed constitutional amendment to require a balanced budget. Largent mentioned he was planning to sit in the gallery to watch the Senate debate on the amendment. I said, "Steve, you are a Member of Congress. You have floor privileges in the Senate". He was very pleased to know that and was relieved he would not have to get over to the gallery early to make sure he got a seat.

✦✦✦✦✦✦✦✦✦

One of the most significant issues in the Contract with America was "The Citizen Legislature Act". H.J. Res. 2 was a proposed amendment to the Constitution that would have imposed 12-year term limits on Members of Congress (i.e., six terms for Representatives, two terms for Senators). Henry was adamantly opposed to term limits. During the committee's consideration of the resolution, there were several different versions offered, including varying limitations on the number of terms, on the number of years of service, and combining House and Senate service. Henry believed strongly that being a "careerist" as a legislator was a *good* thing. He spoke about how important it is to have people who know what they are doing representing constituents. Henry opposed every one of the multiple iterations of term limits offered during the Committee markup. He did the Leadership's bidding by having a markup and sending a bill to the floor for a vote. The Contract said only that the House would *vote* on it within the first 100 days. It did not (and could not) guarantee it would pass.

The Committee met on February 28 and, after substantial debate, ordered the resolution H.J. Res. 2, reported to the House *without recommendation* by a recorded vote of 21-14. Normally the committee would order legislation *favorably* reported to the House. The fact that Henry voted "aye" on the motion to report was only because the report was to be filed "without recommendation". He had made his position abundantly clear. The report was filed on March 6, 1995. After much discussion amongst the leadership, another constitutional amendment was proposed by Congressman Bill McCollum, H.J. Res. 73. It provided a limit of 2 terms for the Senators and six terms for Representatives. The McCollum resolution was called up for debate on March 29, 1995.

Henry's statement was described by one Member, as "one of the best speeches I have ever heard on the House Floor that I know the Member wrote himself". It was clear, he felt strongly, and his speech was later referred to as a "stemwinder". High praise indeed.

"I just cannot be an accessory to the dumbing down of democracy…. defending experience against ignorance is certainly obvious. Being called a 'careerist' is not pejorative, it is a compliment… When the neurosurgeon has shaved your head, and they have made the pencil mark on your skull where they are going to have the incision, and he approaches with the electric saw, ask him one question, are you a 'careerist'?"

"And I will tell you; I will not surrender. I will not concede to the angry, pessimistic populism that drives this movement because it is just dead wrong…I have one piece of advice: Trust the people".

As he came back to the floor manager's seat to rousing applause, I complimented him saying, "All that stuff we write for you is never as powerful as your own words".

The bill got only a bare majority (227–204), falling short of the two-thirds majority (290) needed for constitutional amendments. Three other term limit proposals failed to get more than 200 votes.

✦ ✦ ✦ ✦ ✦ ✦ ✦ ✦

There were a couple of terrific young lawyers who joined the committee staff when Henry became Chairman. Both Dan Bryant and Mitch Glazier were bright and eager young men who were thrilled to be working on the Hill. The single characteristic they possessed that made them easy to work with was they understood how little they knew. They had both come from strong academic backgrounds, and they were superb writers. Early on, Mitch and I were discussing something elementary about putting together a legislative hearing. He told me he felt so stupid and out of his comfort zone. I used one of my favorite lines. "There is a difference between ignorance and stupidity. Ignorance is a lack of specific knowledge or training. Stupidity is the inability to learn. Ignorance is remediable; stupidity is forever".

They readily acknowledged their ignorance of the Congressional process and were comfortable asking for my help. I made it a point to answer their questions, as well as to warn them about potential problems that they might not have anticipated. I always felt teaching new staffers was part of my portfolio. Putting together hearings, drafting legislation and amendments, recognizing pitfalls in the potentially complex amendment process, and getting reports written are not skills in the normal toolbox which young lawyers get in law school. Adding to that, there can be the overwhelming pressure from some very self-important Members of Congress to do their bidding and do it immediately, even though sometimes it is either the wrong thing to do or it is the right thing, but it is being attempted in the wrong way.

While there were other new staff who came in with a superiority complex and a chip on their shoulder, Dan and Mitch were a joy to work with. They knew I had their best interests at heart, and both said they learned from me. They became very good at their jobs and went on to stellar careers, Dan in both government and the private sector, and Mitch in the private sector.

A lot of working on the Hill is simply knowing how to deal with people. As a fairly senior staffer, most Members knew they could rely on me because I knew what I was doing, and very few would challenge me. I was told by Henry after I had gotten yelled at by a Member who threatened to have me fired, "Dan, consider yourself bullet-proof". It was nice to have that kind of support, which many staffers did not get.

Dan Bryant brought a special kind of life awareness to his working world. While he understood the importance of what he was doing on the job, his intellectual and moral view of the world was broader. Dan was always thirsty to discuss, analyze, and learn. I was especially impressed by something he did during a fairly important meeting we were holding in the conference room behind my office. We were conferring with Senate staff to try to hammer out a compromise on a controversial issue. We had almost reached an agreement when I saw on the TV in the conference room a bulletin about a shooting at the Capitol. Two Capitol Police officers had been killed, and there was a live camera shot of the East Front. I called for a short recess. One of the other staffers objected to the recess. "Let's wrap this thing up", he insisted. I explained I wanted to call home and make sure my wife was not worried. This jerk called me a "wimp". Dan responded to him by saying, "If he is a wimp, so am I because I am going to call *my* wife as well, to put her mind at ease". I did not need his support, but it spoke volumes to me about what kind of person he is.

✦ ✦ ✦ ✦ ✦ ✦ ✦ ✦

I got to hone my mentoring skills with a young lawyer-to-be who came to the committee staff as a legal intern. Nicole Nason joined the committee during the summer after finishing law school. She was assigned to the Crime Subcommittee and fit in quickly. I found her to be bright, interested in the work of the Subcommittee, anxious to learn, and dedicated. She also possessed an acerbic sense of humor, which I found to be a positive attribute. She could do the best imitation I have ever heard of Margaret Hamilton as the Wicked Witch of the West from the Wizard of Oz: "I'm melting; I'm melting".

She and I hit it off well. We spent a good bit of time together in preparing for and sitting through committee hearings and markups. I would make a special effort to include her when I was going to be on the House Floor. I gave her my famous tour of the Capitol, and we even went to the Supreme Court. Her fiancé was going to be working in Washington, so we also frequently discussed careers.

Nicole was in my office one day talking about her professional options after her internship ended. She told me she would love to come work on the Committee staff. She was well regarded by everyone who had dealt with her. I told her to march herself into Alan Coffey's office and ask for a job. She was terrified of Alan, who could be quite gruff and intimidating. I gave her the proverbial "Dutch Uncle" lecture and a verbal kick in the butt. She rather reluctantly went in to see Alan. She came back to my office and told me he had said "yes", as well as informing her, "I just made your career". She was ecstatic. I was pleased for her and happy I had been able to help.

She became Counsel to the Crime Subcommittee and did an outstanding job. During the Clinton impeachment, she was the Deputy Director of Communications. She then worked for a short time in the private sector before returning to the Hill to work for a Member from Florida, Porter Goss. She was his Counsel and Communications Director. At the time, Goss was the Chairman of the House Intelligence Committee. We kept in touch both when she was downtown and after she returned to the Hill. Mr. Goss was then named to be Director of the Central Intelligence Agency. He asked Nicole to come with him and work in the General Counsel's office of the CIA. She asked me to have lunch with her to discuss it. She had children, and I was concerned she might not ever see them again if she took the job at the CIA. She told me Goss had promised her that she could leave at 5 o'clock every day. I looked at her and said, "Bullshit. That just is not going to happen". I then said that if she accepted the job, I would kill her before she had a chance to report for duty. She decided not to take the job.

She has often told me what superb advice I had given her, the murder threat notwithstanding.

In March 2003, she had the good fortune to be asked by Transportation Secretary Norm Mineta to be the Assistant Secretary for Governmental Affairs. She was part of Norm's kitchen cabinet, and she got the extraordinary experience of working with him practically every day. After a couple of years, she had tentatively decided to leave government and spend more time with her children. She drafted her letter of resignation addressed to the President and took it in to show Secretary Mineta. As she tells the story, Norm tore the letter up, much to her consternation. She said, "Mr. Secretary, you cannot do that. That is my letter to the President". He told her he had something else for her to do. She was immediately nominated to be the Administrator of the National Highway Transportation Safety Administration (NHTSA). With Secretary Mineta's support, she was quickly confirmed by the Senate. She did a terrific job there and still managed to make it a point to speak to my classes regularly. More about that later.

Nicole relocated to Connecticut when her husband took a job there. When Rex Tillerson was named Secretary of State, she was asked to come down to Washington four days a week as a Counsellor to the Secretary. Because she was such an asset to the running of the Department, she was named Assistant Secretary of State for Administration. Nicole had a hand in everything that was going on in the Department. She had the lead role in negotiating with the Israelis about opening the American Embassy in Jerusalem.

As things happen in Washington, she was at a reception at the State Department, where she was introduced to Elaine Chao, the Secretary of Transportation. From that casual meeting, she was asked by Secretary Chao to become the Administrator of the Federal Highway Administration. Former Secretary of Transportation Norm Mineta testified on her behalf before the Senate Commerce, Science and Transportation Committee. She was confirmed by a vote of 95-1. She told me she could not figure out what she had done to Bernie Sanders to make him be the only "nay" vote.

✦✦✦✦✦✦✦✦✦

After the forced march of the Contract with America, Alan Coffey decided that it was time for him to leave the Hill. I was pleased when I found out that Alan's replacement would be Tom Mooney. Tom was the Chief Counsel of the Intellectual Property Subcommittee and was a very experienced and well-respected Hill staffer. Henry was comfortable with Tom, as was everyone I talked to. He was not an attention seeker and was not anxious to be out front or in the news. Like me, he thought it was a Members' job to be in the press, not the staff's. We joked we liked to let the Members put their own feet in their own mouths. Tom and I had worked together well under both the Democrats and the Republicans, and I thought working with him would be a pleasure. I had referred to him as "Moon Man" for as long as I had known him.

Over the years, I had worked for many people. Some of them hired me, and some of them inherited me. Tom inherited me and was pleased about it. Of all the bosses I had over my career, the one I enjoyed working for the most was Tom. It was a fabulous working partnership. Tom had Henry's complete confidence and support, and I felt I had Tom's. He had a wonderful sense of priorities, and serving the Chairman was number one. He also had a good sense of humor, which allowed me to express my own. I loved every minute working for him, and he went out of his way to make sure I knew he appreciated my work. He and I continue to stay in touch, and I feel grateful for having him as a dear friend.

Tom only had one rule: "No blindsiding the Chairman". The rule was especially important considering the large degree of autonomy that Tom gave to the staff. He believed in hiring good people and letting them do their jobs. Tom did not micromanage and did not feel a need to be in on every decision. What he did want to ensure was that important information got to him, and through him to the Chairman, so Henry would not be caught off guard. His hands-off approach made it much easier for the staff to work, but it came with two imperatives; be responsible and keep the Chairman informed. I was very comfortable with both.

✦✦✦✦✦✦✦✦✦

While working for Chairman Hyde on the Judiciary Committee staff, I continued to do guest lectures on the legislative process. One of my regular engagements was with the Government Affairs Institute (GAI) at Georgetown University. I frequently did a session for them about the different kinds of bills and resolutions and how they are utilized. One I used as an example of both how important the form can be, and how Members always kept their constituents in mind, was an "H.Res.". These are frequently used for non-controversial matters, and when passed, they represent the sense of the House. They have no binding legal effect.

The specific example I used for these classes was a resolution introduced by John Shimkus, a Member from Illinois. He was a friend of Henry's and was an easy-going man. H.Res. 970 in the 110th Congress was a resolution to express the sense of the House in support of the designation of June 30 as "National Corvette Day". I would use this example because it was clearly insignificant in the grand scheme of things, but it demonstrated how important it is to keep the folks at home happy. I found out from Shimkus that he had had dinner with a big supporter the night before introducing this earth-shattering resolution. This man happened to be one of the largest Corvette dealers in the country. I then pointed out to the GAI audience who the cosponsors of the resolution were because it was instructive. All of the cosponsors had GM/Corvette plants in their districts. Automobile manufacturing plants employ a lot of people, and all of those people can vote. Happy voters equals reelection.

I used the occasion to poke a little fun at John Shimkus. I would tell the GAI group that this resolution honoring a sports car that gets about 5 miles to the gallon was debated on the noncontroversial calendar the same day that an important energy conservation bill was considered. I thought the timing was ironic, and when I mentioned it to John Shimkus, he grinned sheepishly.

✦✦✦✦✦✦✦✦✦

The Ranking Republican Minority Member of the committee for a long time was Hamilton Fish IV. He came from a long line of politicians who had served in Congress, including his grandfather and his father. When he died in 1996, there was a memorial service at the National Cathedral. Mr. Fish had always been nice to me, and I decided to attend. At the end of the service, a lovely young woman in a long white dress sang two hymns. They were beautifully done and moving. She did it *a cappella* and elegantly. When she was finished, most of us were leaving to join the family for a reception in another building. I noticed Henry going up to say something to the singer. He was a deeply religious person. I wondered what he said to her.

Later that day, he and I were alone in his office in the committee room, and I asked him about it. He told me he said, "Thank you for that beautiful performance. You gave each of us a glimpse of what heaven must sound like". That brought a tear to my eye. I put my hand on his shoulder and said, "You probably made her day. I know you just made mine".

✦✦✦✦✦✦✦✦✦

I had told Henry the story about how I met Mimi, and he was gracious to her the first time they met. He asked her about her background as a ballet dancer. "Mimi, Dan tells me you are a ballet dancer. Do you often dance on your toes?" Mimi said she did. Henry then said, "Why don't they just get taller dancers?" It was cute.

Over the years, Henry would sometimes tell visitors *his* version of the story of how Mimi and I met. It was not accurate, but I never corrected him. Frequently when I was with Henry at an event, he would introduce me. Maybe just to fill time, he would say, "Let me tell you the story of how Dan met his wife". He would tell them I was at the Kennedy Center watching a ballet when I saw this beautiful girl dancing on stage and decided I had to meet her. He continued by telling them I went backstage and found her and asked her out. That was the beginning of a romance that resulted in our getting married. He always got a charge out of telling the story, and I did not have the heart to set him straight.

✦ ✦ ✦ ✦ ✦ ✦ ✦ ✦

I was always grateful to Henry for telling new Members what an excellent resource I could be for them, but there were times when it got to be a bit too much. For example, I was on the floor one day, helping a Member manage a bill. I was frequently the only committee staffer on the floor when some relatively non-controversial piece of legislation was being considered. A page brought me a message that I had a phone call in the cloakroom from Congressman Sonny Bono. I had no idea why he would be calling me. The first time there was a break in the action, I left the floor to take the call.

Sonny was a new Congressman from Southern California who everybody knew had been part of the famous singing duo Sonny and Cher ("The Beat Goes On"). He had been friendly to me whenever the committee was meeting, and I was happy to try to help him out whenever I could. When I picked up the phone, he said, "Dan, thanks for taking my call. Henry said you know everything about Capitol Hill and Washington DC". I told him that was probably hyperbole, but I was born and raised here. He then asked me for driving instructions from his new townhouse to the Capitol! I chuckled to myself and gave him the answer.

Although Sonny was not the brightest Member, and he was not a lawyer, which handicapped him when we were dealing with complex issues of constitutional law, he was a warm, down-to-earth man. He brought his children to a committee meeting on "Take your kids to work day". He was delightful with them.

After his singing career ended, he had been a restauranteur in Palm Springs and brought some things he had learned from that experience with him. One day, we were in a markup which had lasted for hours and gone into the early evening. People were getting tired and grumpy, but we still plowed ahead. Sonny ordered pizza for everyone, including (gasp) the staff. When the pizzas arrived, the Chairman called a recess, and everyone went back to the conference room to get something to eat. Everyone left, except Congressman Martin Hoke and me. Martin and I spent the entire break debating whether what he considered to be his "very important" amendment was in order. I had told him it was not germane, and if a point of order was made, I would have to advise the Chairman to rule it out of order. We debated this rather arcane matter for the entire break, so I did not get any pizza, but I did stick to my guns on the amendment.

Not too long after the break, it seemed clear people were wearing down, and we would be able to finish the bill and adjourn. Hyde told me later that Sonny had ordered the high carbohydrate food because he knew it would make people sleepy, which would enhance everyone's desire to bring the committee meeting to a close. Clever, I thought.

After Sonny died in a skiing accident, his widow, Mary, took his seat in Congress. I had met Mary on several occasions. She was wonderful to me and was completely unpretentious. I got to know her better when she became a Member. She was one of the people who would come to me instead of "bothering the Chairman". She knew I could be a conduit for messages she needed to get to Henry. She would also come to me for advice on legislative matters.

On October 24, 2000, the Leadership had scheduled a Judiciary Committee bill for consideration under the suspension of the rules procedure. The bill dealt with some esoteric question of Administrative Law. It was my responsibility to get a Judiciary Committee Member to manage the bill. Fortunately, I found out Mary was going to be available, and she agreed to meet me on the floor.

Since it was her birthday, I wished her a happy birthday, and then briefed her on what she was going to have to do. She had never managed a bill before, and she was clearly nervous. I introduced her to Rob, who was the staff attorney on the bill. I gave her the parliamentary motions she would have to make. I told her I could either give her a three-page statement which she could simply read, or a three-inch-thick briefing binder on the topic which Rob had prepared and was eager for her to use. Rob was fired up and raring to go. This was his first piece of legislation to go to the floor. He wanted to go into agonizing detail with Mary about the intricacies of section 553 of the Administrative Procedure Act. I asked Mary which document she wanted to use.

She looked at Rob and then me, and said, "I think I will take the short version". She asked what she should do if someone asked her a question. I told her not to worry; we did not have any reason to believe there would be any questions. If there were, she could pause briefly while one of us filled her in. I noticed she was sniffling, and I asked her if she was OK. She said she was, but her nose ran when she got nervous. Ever the diligent staffer, I went back to the cloakroom and got her a package of tissues. She was grateful.

I was sitting behind her, and Rob was next to her. Just before she was recognized to call up the bill, I leaned over, and like a baseball manager said, "OK kid, just throw strikes". She got a kick out of that and seemed to relax a bit.

She handled it well. She made the motion, read the prepared statement, and relaxed while the minority manager read his statement. She then did the wrap-up motions I had prepared. The Speaker Pro Tempore called the question on the passage of the bill, and it passed on a voice vote.

Mary was utterly relieved. She turned around and gave me an enormous hug and a big fat kiss right on the lips. I was surprised, to say the least. She then left through the back door. I gathered my materials and walked towards the door in the front. Presiding that day was Congressman Jim Hansen from Utah, who I knew. As I was leaving, he crooked his finger, motioning me to approach him up on the rostrum. When I got within whispering distance, he looked at me and said, "Freeman, you dog!" I expect he was envious of the big smooch I got. I replied, "Eat your heart out!" You have to understand the Member and the situation to know what you can get away with. I got away with that comment.

After I left the Hill, Mary was always thoughtful about making time for my students and me. On a particularly busy day, she told the class why she was making time to meet with them. "I have lots of invitations to speak to a wide range of groups. I always made it a point to speak to this class because I love Dan Freeman, and I will always be grateful to him for being such a warm and wonderful resource to me as a new Member". Wow!

✦✦✦✦✦✦✦✦✦

One of the adages I recall is from a book by Alan Mulally. He was the Chief Executive of Boeing at the time I read it and went on to lead the Ford Motor Company. The quote is, "The main problem with communication is the illusion it has actually occurred". This kind of thing frequently occurred when two Members had a conversation, and each walked away with wildly different perceptions about what had been decided. I saw this regularly when staff would get together after conferees had met and try to draft the Joint Explanatory Statement of Managers. Everyone who was charged with putting together the final language had been in the room when the Members decided what they wanted to do. People's recollections were, as far as I was concerned, not always congruent with the discussion which I witnessed, and sometimes differed dramatically.

I had this failure to communicate happen often enough, so I learned to be extremely careful. Whenever I would get the Chairman to approve something orally, I would specifically ask him, "Do I have your approval to do this?" and in some circumstances, "Do I have your approval to sign for you?"

✦✦✦✦✦✦✦✦✦

One of my responsibilities was to be present for every subcommittee mark-up in case parliamentary issues came up and to make sure all the I's were dotted, and the T's were crossed. We had five subcommittees with differing numbers of Members. You need a working quorum of 1/3 of the Members to start the amendment process, but you need a majority of the Members to be present to constitute a reporting quorum for final passage of any legislation. Frequently we would go through the amendment process in one of the Rayburn Building hearing rooms, with only a working quorum present. If we did not have a majority present to take the vote on reporting the bill to the full committee, we would recess the subcommittee. I was always ready for this scenario and had the statement prepared for the Subcommittee Chairman to declare the subcommittee in recess to reconvene in the Rayburn Room in the Capitol adjacent to the House Chamber immediately after the next vote in the House. We knew we could grab Members from the floor because if they were in town, they would definitely be there to vote. Once we had the reporting quorum present in the Rayburn Room, I would hand the Subcommittee Chairman the motion on final passage prefaced with, "The Chair notes the presence of a reporting quorum". On some occasions when we did this, I would add to the motion that we have a roll call vote. I would always do this if the bill was significant, such as an impeachment resolution.

My normal insistence on clarity escaped me one day when the Crime Subcommittee had a markup. I was doing something else and ran up to the markup without my copy of the House Rules and Manual, which I usually carried with me. In my Manual, I had printed out the total number of Members on each subcommittee, the number needed for a reporting quorum (a majority), and the number needed for a working quorum (one third). As I walked into the room, I asked the subcommittee counsel who was handling the bill, "How many do we have". She said, "We have eight". That much math I could do and deduced we needed at least five Members to constitute the necessary reporting quorum to take final action on the bill. Much to my surprise, when it came time for the motion on final passage, we had seven Members there, but I realized the subcommittee had a total of *fifteen* Members, not eight. I had to stop the subcommittee Chairman from putting the question until we had eight Members (a reporting quorum) present. When I asked the subcommittee counsel later, "Didn't you tell me 'We have eight'?" She explained "we" to her meant Republicans, and "we" to me meant the total Members on the subcommittee. Each of us thought we had communicated, but…

✦✦✦✦✦✦✦✦✦

It was during that markup I had a very unpleasant encounter with Congresswoman Sheila Jackson-Lee. She was one of the most difficult Members of Congress I have ever had the displeasure of dealing with. She came to Congress in 1995 and rapidly gained a reputation as both ineffective and unpleasant. She sought time to speak on everything, whether she was involved or not. She would be recognized for the normal 5 minutes, per the House rules, and would continue to talk after her time had expired. It was rude and disrespectful because other Members wanted to speak, but she simply did not care. She would keep on talking, on the floor or in committee, even after having been gaveled down and told her time had expired. After she had long gone past her allotted time, she would frequently say, "I yield back the balance of my time". Henry, normally a very patient man, finally had had enough during a committee meeting. He said to her on the record, "The gentlelady has no time to yield back".

Early in her career on the Hill, I overheard a Member talking about her. He said, "We have had Democrats talk to her, women Members, Black Members, to try to tell her to limit her verbosity. She has been told she is completely ineffective, and her insistence on talking about everything is frequently counterproductive, but she either does not care or does not believe them".

The "Daily Caller", a Capitol Hill newspaper, said of her, "Capitol Hill is famous for its demanding, insensitive bosses. Yet even by the harsh standards of Congress, Sheila Jackson-Lee stands out. She may be the worst boss in Washington". I was told that she had the highest staff turnover of any Member of the House. She was frequently characterized as abusive, and I had witnessed that often. On many occasions, I had told her my name. She always addressed me with the hiss, "Sssst", which I found insulting. Whenever she did that, I would again remind her, "My name is Dan." That never seemed to get through to her.

During a subcommittee markup, the Chairman offered a rewrite of the bill, which is called an amendment in the nature of a substitute. The operative language was to "strike all after the enacting clause and insert in lieu thereof the following:" The language to be inserted was the new version of the bill. It was this substitute which Members would debate, and to which they would offer their perfecting amendments. While it was pending, several Members offered individual perfecting amendments which were debated and voted on. The Chairman asked if there were any further amendments, and no one spoke up. At that point, the Chairman put the question on the substitute. That was adopted by a voice vote. With a reporting quorum in the room, the next step was to vote on the motion to report the bill favorably to the full committee in its amended form.

Ms. Jackson-Lee had become confused and sought to offer an amendment at that point. The subcommittee Chairman asked me whether an amendment was in order. I told him it was not unless she was got unanimous consent. Lacking that, the only thing left to do was to vote on final passage. He informed her of the parliamentary situation and called for the vote on final passage of the bill. Ms. Jackson Lee was furious, and instead of talking with the subcommittee Chairman, she came over to confront me. One of the Legislative Counsels was there, and he confirmed my understanding of the rule. She demanded to see the text of the rule. I showed it to her, and she was not in the slightest bit mollified. The rule was clear, and her lack of knowledge had cost her. The enmity she had generated among the Members made any attempt at a unanimous consent request by her problematical. She did not apologize for the temper tantrum.

When the bill was called up at full committee, she sought to offer her perfecting amendment, which, at that stage, was in order. I had told Tom and Henry about the incident at the subcommittee markup per our "no blindsiding" rule. Ms. Jackson-Lee took the opportunity to take a shot at me by saying in an accusatory manner, "I had proposed the amendment at subcommittee, but the Parliamentarian ruled it out of order". Henry was magnificent. He said, "I am sure it was the subcommittee Chairman who ruled it out of order, and I have boundless confidence in the committee Parliamentarian who advised the Chairman".

Late one Friday afternoon, when the House had adjourned, I was in the front committee office, and I saw her sitting there. I did not attempt to speak to her as she was berating someone on the phone. She slammed the phone down. She saw me walking by and wanted to ask me something. As usual, she addressed me--"Sssst". I was tempted to walk on but did not. I, again, told her my name, which she ignored. She mentioned a message I should give to the Chairman about something she wanted. I suggested to her that message would be more effectively delivered Member to Member. I then ventured into dangerous territory and asked her why she regularly kept on talking when her time had expired. She answered venomously, "No white man is going to tell *me* when to shut up".

✛✛✛✛✛✛✛✛✛

My first experience with Tom Lantos was during a joint hearing. A subcommittee from the Government Operations Committee and the Judiciary Committee's Crime Subcommittee were holding the hearing. These joint sessions are frequently difficult because of questions about who gets recognized and in what order. Sometimes there is some jostling about who is going to chair. It was agreed that Congressman Bill Zeliff, Chairman of the Gov Ops subcommittee, would preside. I did not know him, but he said he was told I would be there to help him out if need be.

There was some tension between Lantos and Zeliff because a relative of Lantos's ran for Congress against him. Lantos was displeased with a ruling Mr. Zeliff made about a proposed subpoena. He ruled the request to issue a subpoena was not in order since the joint subcommittee gathering was a hearing and not a meeting for the transaction of business. Lantos took the unusual step of formally challenging the ruling. Mr. Zeliff asked, "Mr. Lantos, are you appealing the ruling of the chair?" Lantos said that he was. Chuck Schumer, a Member of the Judiciary Committee's Crime Subcommittee, posed a parliamentary inquiry. "Can we ask the Parliamentarian (Dan Freeman) who has been very fair. In fact, he was our Parliamentarian before we lost him, and he may be again". Lantos rescinded his request. I was glad to have that kind of public affirmation from Schumer, especially considering the difficulties I had had previously from some Democrats about my staying on as Parliamentarian under the Republicans.

✦✦✦✦✦✦✦✦✦

One of the big problems we dealt with was Federal Judges' compensation. Judicial salaries were directly linked to those of Members of Congress. When voting to raise their own pay, Members could use the argument they needed to raise judicial salaries. Congress was under a lot of pressure from the judiciary about it. Judges would have law clerks leave and start at some of the big firms being paid more than the judge they clerked for. Many people were reluctant to apply for judgeships since the salary was low compared to what they could receive in private practice. It used to be that getting appointed to a Federal Judgeship was the capstone of a career. Judges are now appointed in their 30s and 40s. However, the salary question gave some lawyers pause before accepting a Federal Judgeship.

Henry was always sympathetic to the appeal for raising judicial compensation. He thought the federal bench was a crucial part of our government. As Chairman of the committee, he was fully supportive of de-linking Members' and judges' salaries. This would permit Members of Congress to vote to raise the pay of judges without having to face criticism about raising their own. One of the first bills that came out of the committee contained this de-linking language. The Leadership went crazy. They were concerned that if this were enacted, there would never be another pay raise for Members of Congress.

The Rules Committee, in crafting the rule for floor consideration of the bill, took out the committee-reported de-linking language. It was extraordinary for the Rules Committee to delete language which the committee of jurisdiction had recommended. They simply deleted the provision altogether and refused to allow any amendments to the bill relating to judicial salaries.

Henry was angry and told Tom Mooney and me to see if we could figure out a way to make that delinking amendment in order on the floor. Tom called the best parliamentary wizard he knew to try to figure out a plan of attack. Billy Pitts had been Bob Michel's top floor assistant and was brilliant and talented. After Michel left the Hill, Billy also went on to other things. It was pretty clear someone with Billy's institutional love of the House would not fit in with the Gingrich crowd. I felt he was a great resource, and it was a shame not to have his expertise be used by the Republicans when they took over in 1995. Like me, Billy is a car guy. He owned an old late 1940s Hudson and had restored it. I was in awe of it and Billy.

Billy had a role in the movie "Dave", which came out in 1993. In the big scene near the end, when the imposter President is to address a joint session of Congress, he played the role of the Doorkeeper who intoned "Mr. Speaker, the President of the United States". As a Hollywood veteran, he came over to talk with Chairman Brooks about my working on a film with Robert Redford. At the time, Brooks did not know about it, and Billy blew my cover. Typical of the way he treated people, he apologized, but he thought it was amusing.

The text that the Rules Committee had made in order was very narrow, and purposely so. The de-linking amendment would not have been germane to it. If offered, the amendment would have been subject to a fatal point of order. We were sure the Rules Committee and the Leadership had done this on purpose. We decided on a strategy of having the subcommittee Chairman, Howard Coble, offer a series of what were called "cut and bite" amendments, which would, in parliamentary terms, broaden the base of the bill, thereby making the amendment in order. Each of the "cut and bite" amendments was innocuous and did not raise any red flags. This was "inside baseball" parliamentary maneuvering, and I thoroughly enjoyed it. The Rules Committee staff were buzzing around the floor vigilantly and anxiously trying to protect the text from the delinking language. After several of these inconsequential amendments were adopted, the Parliamentarians gave us the go-ahead that the amendment would then be in order.

As soon as the Rules Committee staff became aware of this, they alerted their Chairman, Gerry Solomon. He was a tough, disagreeable, mean man. He was extremely upset and came raging up to confront Henry. He insisted Henry promise not to offer the amendment even though it was now in order. The Leadership was opposed to it and did not want it even considered. Henry, being ever gracious, told him, "If the Leadership does not want me to, then I will not offer it". That was not good enough for Solomon. "Give me your word", he demanded. Henry was offended, and frankly, so was I. He did not offer the amendment, but he was steamed about the way in which Solomon confronted him.

✦✦✦✦✦✦✦✦✦

Blaine Aaron worked tirelessly to make sure Henry always had the proper accommodations to get where he needed to be and was as comfortable as possible in doing so. I admired his effectiveness, loyalty and team spirit. He was not interested in getting public or even private credit for all he did. I know both Henry and Tom Mooney were grateful to him for his superb support.

He asked me to speak to his son's junior high school class about government in general and Congress specifically. This was a bright group of students, and I was not surprised they were well prepared for the meeting. After having discussed the Congressional legislative process, I turned to a hot topic at the time; music piracy and copyrights. There had been a lot of publicity about students downloading music from the internet without paying for it. I explained the copyright laws and the fact that it was illegal to steal someone's intellectual property. I quoted Lamar Smith in saying downloading copyrighted music without compensating the owner was the same as going into a store and stealing a CD. This was back when people bought music on CDs.

I like to take questions from students. I find it interesting to know what concerns them. These students had a lot of questions, and most of them were good. I did get one question that threw me for a loop. A student got up and said, "My father told me Paul McCartney was with another rock and roll group before Wings. I'm almost certain that is not true. Do you know the answer?" I looked at Blaine and said, "This student has just demonstrated how old I am." I responded to the student this way: "As hard as it may be to believe, your father is correct. The group was called the Beatles, and they sold more records than any group in history". One of the students asked, "What's a record?". I just smiled and shook my head.

✦ ✦ ✦ ✦ ✦ ✦ ✦ ✦

Henry called me one day and asked me if I would be willing to take one of his big campaign supporters to lunch in the House restaurant. I understood this man had been a supporter of Henry's for a long time and had donated a lot of money to his campaigns. I readily agreed and went over to the Chairman's office to pick up Ron Gidwitz, his wife and two sons.

As we were walking through the Rayburn Building, one of the custodians pushed his cleaning cart filled with supplies from the men's room out into the hallway. He was a large man dressed in a blue-collar outfit with his name embroidered on a shirt. I knew him, and we briefly greeted each other. I called him Dave, and he called me Dan. I asked him about his son and how he was getting along at school. The son had been having some difficulties with reading, and I had purchased an illustrated dictionary for him. The conversation was brief, and then the Gidwitz family and I took the subway over to the Capitol. The two boys loved riding on the subway train. It was always a big hit when I gave my Capitol tour, especially with kids.

As we entered the elevator, the Chairman of the House Appropriations Committee, Bill Young, got on. Mr. Young was one of the Members I knew well enough to sit and chat with. I would often do that during votes. He always sat in the same place. Members knew where they could find him in an area I called "deep left field", in the back row to the Speaker's left. When he saw me, he reached out to shake my hand and greeted me by name. His wife had been ill, and I asked about her. He said he appreciated my inquiry.

We got off on the first floor where the House restaurant was located, and Mr. Young stayed on. Henry's office had called ahead, and the maître d', John, was expecting us. He sat us at a lovely table underneath the Brumidi fresco of George Washington accepting the British surrender at Yorktown, which ended the Revolutionary War. I love showing this piece of art because it is unique. When most people see it, they do not realize it is a fresco; it is painted onto the plaster of the wall. At some point, the architect of the Capitol decided to make it look like a painting hung on the wall and placed an elaborate gold frame around it. The other interesting thing about it is that in the lower right-hand corner, there is a briefcase with a long sash draped over it with the following letters painted onto it: "C Brumidi a citizen of the US". Constantino Brumidi was so proud of being an American citizen that he memorialized it in a painting in the Capitol!

The family seemed to enjoy the historic setting with all of the Members around as I pointed them out. As they were leaving, Ron said to me, "Dan, do you realize what you did today?" I did not know what he was referring to. He continued, "You treated the man who cleans the toilets and the Chairman of the Appropriations Committee with the same human respect. I admire you immensely for that". I had not noticed, but I was glad *he* did. He sent me a lovely thank you note which included the following quotation: "No matter how educated, talented, rich or bright you believe you are, how you treat people is the true test of your humanity". I was very touched by the warm note.

+ + + + + + + + +

One of the new Members during Jack Brooks' Chairmanship of the Committee was a bright young man, who was chock full of charisma, Xavier Becerra from Los Angeles. He was a rising star in the Democratic Party and was the first Latino to serve on the House Ways and Means Committee. He also served as Chairman of the House Democratic Caucus. He was another Member who was not too proud to learn from a "mere staffer". I include him here because of a touching incident which occurred during a markup of an immigration reform bill under the Republicans. As a minority Member, he was dedicated to making sure the new majority did not damage the immigration system to the detriment of many of his constituents.

During the debate, he sought recognition. He was an extremely articulate speaker and was a strong proponent of family values. This commitment to family was demonstrated when he walked into the room with his baby daughter in his arms. She was being fussy, and so, as he was speaking, he got to his feet and started to rock her. It was a powerful image, and I was struck by its tenderness. The reporter of debates was disgruntled because Becerra was standing up. He was away from the microphone, which made it difficult for her to get every word. It got even more special when one of his colleagues who was sitting next to him put his arms out to take the baby. Xavier did not miss a beat. He handed the baby over to Mel Watt, an African American Member from North Carolina, and kept speaking.

The baby started to cry. Mel told me later he thought the baby did not recognize his black face, and that was the problem. Becerra did not win the debate, but I was impressed with his grace under pressure.

He would also speak to my classes every semester when I taught at AU. I appreciated his kindness, especially since I knew how busy he was. He later resigned from Congress to become the Attorney General of California. I hear from him occasionally. The student who sat next to me in law school, Brian Frosh, is the Attorney General of Maryland. These two AGs are involved in several lawsuits. Xavier wrote to me saying that I was keeping good company with Brian. He urged me to write this book.

✦ ✦ ✦ ✦ ✦ ✦ ✦ ✦ ✦

There was a situation at the end of a Congress where I cleverly got Rep. Gerry Solomon to help me out. There were very few Members in town, and I needed someone to call up a couple of noncontroversial bills on behalf of the Judiciary Committee. Henry was not around, and I could not find any other Member of the committee to make the unanimous consent requests necessary to consider the bills. I found out that Solomon was in his office, and I thought I might coax him to step in. I knew that he and Jack Brooks were both Marines and were proud of it. I decided to use that to my advantage.

I called Solomon's office, told the receptionist who I was, and asked to speak to the Chairman. I told her I was calling on behalf of Chairman Hyde, which was enough to get me through. When Solomon got on the phone, his tone of voice was not inviting. Not unusual. However, I had an ace up my sleeve. I said to him, "Mr. Chairman, Jack Brooks told me that if I ever needed something done, I should get a Marine". I had him! His response was, "What can I do for you?" We arranged to meet on the floor to call up the two bills. I was successful in getting the committee's business done. It may have been a bit Machiavellian, but it did not hurt anybody, and I did my job.

Official Travel—Codels and Staffdels

There are two types of official travel; Congressional Delegations (Codels), which include Members of Congress, and Staff Delegations (Staffdels), which are made up of staff traveling on official business.

Codels

In all the time I had worked on the Hill before the Republicans took over, I had never been invited to go on a Codel. A Codel is a Congressional delegation made up of at least five Members and a few staff who travel abroad, frequently on military aircraft, for purposes of oversight investigations. The oversight responsibilities of Congress are a large part of the job to make sure that government programs are being properly run. I had always heard these trips referred to as "junkets" and was not that interested based on some of the horror stories I heard. From what I gathered, many Members treated the staff like gofers on these trips, and so the glorious depictions of traveling internationally on a military jet were frequently misleading. Not having to touch your baggage or go through customs and immigration, sounded enticing, but the idea of waiting on Members did not appeal to me.

Early in 1996, Tom Mooney, called to tell me Carlos Moorhead, the new Chairman of the Intellectual Property Subcommittee, was going to travel to South America to meet with leaders in several countries, to talk about intellectual property issues. American copyrights, patents and trademarks are our most valuable economic resource, and they are frequently violated in other countries. Mr. Moorhead was going to lead the delegation. Tom asked me if I wanted to go. I was surprised, especially knowing the tight lid which had been kept on who got to travel under Mr. Rodino.

I told him I would love to, but I did not see what value I could bring to such a delegation. Tom said not to worry about that. He said I was always helpful to Mr. Moorhead, and him, and it would be a good thing for me to get to know more about the intellectual property issues. I said I would have to check with Alan, who was my direct boss, but I was "rarin' to go".

I did not know all the hoops one would have to jump through to go on such a trip, but I was willing to learn. I was surprised to find out the Capitol Physician's office would provide me with any necessary immunizations at no cost, and any food allergies or special requirements I had would be taken into account. There would be a military doctor on the trip as well as senior military officers who would be in charge of logistics. I was happy to be included and was willing to say "Yes, Sir", and do what I was told.

You never know which Members are going to be on a Codel. There are cases of Members who say they would like to go, and then bail out at the last minute. There are some difficult Members who one would try to avoid, and there are some who are a real pleasure to be with. I got lucky on this trip. One Member, who could be difficult, decided at the last minute not to go. There were three Judiciary Committee Members who I knew and liked, and one Appropriations Committee Member, Tom Bevell, who I did not know but who turned out to be splendid.

Colonel John Wilson was our military escort, and it was clear from the beginning he knew what he was doing. He was on top of everything. There was another military escort assigned to us, an Air Force Major. The two of them made a good team, and I did my best to be low maintenance.

One evening we were sitting in the control room, which was the room in the hotel we were staying in where all of the logistics and communications were located and where people frequently gathered. Pat Schroeder, a Congresswoman from Colorado, Rick Boucher, a Congressman from Virginia, and several staffers were sitting around chatting. I felt I knew Mrs. Schroeder well enough to call her Pat, and I also felt comfortable calling Congressman Boucher by his first name, Rick. There was a lull in the conversation, and Pat Schroeder said, "Somebody tell a funny story". Usually, that is a clue for a Member of Congress to amuse the group with a yarn. Since things seemed fairly relaxed, I decided I could probably get away with it, and I told the story from my law school days of the man on the crosstown bus. It went over well, and everybody thought it was hilarious.

I got to spend a good bit of time with Tom Mooney while we were traveling and developed an abiding affection for him. He is a stocky Irishman with a wonderful sense of self and, unlike many congressional staffers, not prone to self-aggrandizing behavior. Tom loves beer; he even owns an Irish pub. We got into a routine while traveling, where I would ask him if he would like a "malted beverage". I do not think he ever said no to that offer.

Flying on a military plane was terrific! Everybody got their own row, and the military escorts were excellent. The flight attendants were considerate, and it was a very comfortable way to travel. I tried to keep a low profile.

The first stop was Panama City. I was interested in seeing the Panama Canal. I had heard it was something you had to see to comprehend its massive size. I did some reading about it and was astounded by the magnitude of the operation. The amount of cargo going through each year is astronomical.

We were flying on an old Boeing 727, which was a three-engine jet that had a stairway in the tail, so you did not need to be at an airport with a jetway or even a rolling staircase. As per protocol, the head of the Delegation, Congressman Moorhead, was the first person off the plane, followed by the other Members, and then the staff. I was still a bit uncomfortable about being there, so I waited until the very end; I was the last one off the plane. What I had not realized was the American Ambassador to Panama would be there to greet the delegation. It was my old friend, former Congressman Bill Hughes. He and his wife Nancy, who had been with us at the flag-burning bet payoff dinner, were on the tarmac along with several high-ranking military officers. When I got to the Ambassador, he greeted me with a big smile and a "Dandy Dan, how nice to see you". I certainly felt welcome.

The next day, we got the full tour of the Miraflores lock in the canal. It was fascinating. The antiquated mechanisms had not been updated for decades, but they still worked. The lock is a two-step configuration. The original gate machinery consisted of an enormous drive wheel, powered by an electric motor, to which was attached a connecting rod, which in turn was attached to the middle of the gate. The mechanism was due to be replaced in 1998, so we saw the original. The process is operated from a central control room, which is located in the partition between the locks. The mechanisms were designed to minimize the chance of operator error. There is a complete miniature model of the locks, with moving components that mirror the state of the actual lock gates and valves. The operator can monitor the mechanism in real-time and see exactly where the components are during the process of opening or closing. Mechanical interlocks are built into the controls to make sure that no component can move while another is in an incorrect position.

To get to the control room, we had to maneuver across the canal on top of a set of locks. The walkway was somewhat precarious, and you could only cross when the gates were closed. Each gate has two leaves, 65 ft wide, which close to form a "V" shape with the point upstream. The force of water from the higher side pushes the ends of the gates together tightly. The gates can be opened only when the water level on both sides is equal.

As we were crossing, I was following Mrs. Bevill. She was having some difficulty, and as she got to the apex of the V, she stumbled. I reached out and grabbed her hand and got her stabilized. She was very grateful and thanked me profusely. She and her husband were from Alabama and were steeped in Southern gentility. Later that day, Mr. Bevill came up to me and said, "Sir, I appreciate your taking good care of my bride today".

One of the people on the trip with us was Andrea Camp, who worked for Pat Schroeder. Andrea is bright and was easy to work with. We were seated in the same row on either side of the aisle. We had been talking before boarding the plane. Since she became a parent, she had become uncomfortable about flying. Because my mother had a serious case of fear of flying, I had sympathy for her. Instead of being alone in her row, as the rest of us were, she was sitting with a woman she worked with. I had a hunch about why. I thought she probably felt better with her friend there.

I was aware that the takeoff roll from the Panama City airport would be extremely long due to the heat and the atmospheric conditions. As we started to taxi out, I engaged Andrea in a rather animated and detailed conversation about her family. I was rabbiting on and on. After what seemed like an agonizingly long time, we finally became airborne, and I decided I could shut up.

Andrea's friend leaned over and said to me, "Dan, what the hell were you doing babbling away like that?" Andrea looked at her friend and said, "I know *exactly* what he was doing. He was being kind by trying to distract me". She turned to me and said, "Dan, thank you for being so thoughtful".

Colonel Wilson and I had chatted about my interest in aviation. He was not particularly impressed when I told him my total flight time in the cockpit was 90 minutes in a TWA 727 simulator. On the penultimate day of the trip, when we were getting ready to take off from Rio de Janerio, he came back to where I was sitting and told me to get up to the cockpit quickly. I unbuckled my seat belt and scrambled up to the front. I was thrilled. We were going to take off directly over the Christ the Redeemer statue on the mountaintop above Rio, and I was going to be in the jump seat! I heard the pilot go over his checklist with the copilot, including, "If we get into trouble, I will take fly the airplane". That was a bit surprising, but when I asked him about it later, he told me it was standard operating procedure for the two pilots to decide ahead of takeoff who was going to take command in an emergency. Frequently the copilot will be flying the plane. They usually alternate each leg of the journey. I had headphones on and had been told our call sign, "Boxcar 39", so I knew when air traffic control gave instructions to our aircraft. I had a ball listening and watching. It was a thoughtful thing for Colonel Wilson to do, and I had a fantastic experience.

✦ ✦ ✦ ✦ ✦ ✦ ✦ ✦

If you love the Capitol building as I do, the chance to take a tour of the dome is something you cannot pass up. You need to be a Member of Congress to be permitted to take guests up there. Rick Boucher invited several of us who had been on the Codel to South America to go as a way of thanking us. It was a lovely gesture from a nice man. I even got to bring Mimi. It is quite an ascent; you have to climb up between the outer shell of the dome and an inner shell on scaffolding-like stairs. When you get outside at the top, you have a spectacular view of all the Congressional office buildings, the Library of Congress, the Supreme Court, and all of downtown Washington D.C. It was breathtaking!

✦✦✦✦✦✦✦✦✦

StaffDels

I met a Chilean doctor in Washington one evening at a dinner for the EINSHAC faculty which included some foreign dignitaries who were interested in, among other things, bioethics. I sat with Dr. Martin Zilic, who was a doctor and an academic. All I knew about him was he was the chief bioethics officer at a hospital in Concepción. We had an interesting conversation about the intersection between medicine and law. He said he was impressed by how well-schooled I was about medical issues. We talked a lot about organ donation and how best to maximize the impact an individual organ could have when transplanted. We discussed the issues of transplanting a liver into someone who was an alcoholic, and also the difficult problems about whether to transplant into the sickest patient, or those not as sick so that the organ would have a more extended life. We also talked about definitions of death; cardiovascular death and brain death.

Dr. Zilic told me he was the main organizer of the First Global Biotechnology Forum (GBF), which was to be held in Concepción, Chile, in 2004. (I discussed this previously in the Science and the Courts section.) He invited me to attend. I thought there might be some possibility of EINSHAC participating in the Forum, so I told him I would stay in touch and try to arrange it.

Fortuitously, there was a group of staff people from the committee who were going to Santiago, Chile to meet with both American and Chilean officials about a whole range of issues, including drug trafficking and intellectual property. Tom, who occasionally participated in the EINSHAC program, asked me if I would be interested in going on this Staffdel. I said I would love to go and, if it were appropriate, I would like to visit Concepción while I was in Chile. He agreed, and I left all of the planning for the Santiago portions of the trip to the lawyer on our staff who was going to be leading the delegation. I contacted Doctor Zilic and told him I would be "in the neighborhood" and would like to see him while I was there. He responded enthusiastically, telling me he would meet me at the airport. I was somewhat surprised by that but happy to know that I would get to spend some more time with this fascinating man.

The people on this trip were lawyers on the committee staff, both Republicans and Democrats, a couple of whom were fluent in Spanish, which was very helpful. We met first with people from the American Embassy and discussed what we wanted to see. I was still not used to the fact that when visiting foreign countries on official business, a car and driver would be made available to us whenever we wanted. As I was going to be leaving early the next morning to fly to Concepción, I asked our driver if it would be possible for me to get a ride to the airport. I told him I would be happy to take a cab, but he would not hear of it. What I did not understand was that the embassy drivers wanted all the extra hours they could get to enhance their incomes. He said he would pick me up at my hotel at six the next morning in plenty of time for me to get my flight. After a long day, I was ready to go back to the hotel and get some sleep. Unfortunately, I was trapped. The rest of the delegation and our (not so fearless) leader wanted to visit a statue of Christ the Redeemer, similar to the one in Rio de Janeiro, but on a much smaller scale.

The next morning the driver picked me up as promised, and I flew down to Concepción. I was pleased to see that Doctor Zilic was there to meet me. The airport looked new and was impressive. I casually mentioned something about it to Martin, and he said, "I did that". The import of that comment did not sink in immediately. As we walked out of the terminal, Martin's car was parked at the curb. He and I and the other two people with him hopped in, and away we went. It also did not dawn on me that it was unusual to be able to just leave your car parked right in front of the terminal.

We drove into downtown Concepción and pulled up in front of what was obviously a government building. Standing at the curb were two soldiers with automatic rifles. We got out of the car, and I looked at Martin and said, "Is it okay for you to park here?" He said, "Yes, it's fine; they know me".

We entered the building, went upstairs to an ornate conference room, and were seated there waiting for who knows what. A couple of minutes later, a rash of photographers showed up and in walked a distinguished-looking gentleman with a mane of white hair and a warm and friendly face who was obviously some important government official. I stood up, and Martin introduced me, and we shook hands amid a barrage of cameras flashing, but I had no idea of what was going on.

He and I chatted through an interpreter about my trip to Chile. I spoke about our Staffdel and the work I was doing with EINSHAC. After a few minutes, he got up and wished me well and vanished. I found out later the man I met with was the Mayor of Bio Bio, one of the most important administrative divisions in Chile, which are analogous to American states.

Martin, his colleagues, and I left, and took me around Concepción, showing me many of the facilities which would be used during the upcoming Global Biotechnology Forum. He had done a tremendous amount of work. It looked like it was going to be a fabulous event. I was glad to know EINSHAC would be holding a judicial training conference contemporaneously so that I could participate in some of the GBF sessions.

I was then dropped off at the airport to fly back to Santiago to rendezvous with my colleagues. I was tired, but I was glad I had made the trip. Martin was a dynamic man, and I thoroughly enjoyed spending time with him.

The next morning, we went to the embassy for a debriefing. I let the rest of the staff speak first because I thought I would have the least to say, and what I did say would probably be of minimal interest to the embassy staff. When the others finished, the head of our group recognized me. I said I had been in many of the meetings in Santiago, which they had already heard about, but I had also taken a side trip to Concepción. I was then asked to elaborate. Cluelessly, I started as follows: "I spent yesterday with Dr. Martin Zilic…" There was an immediate stirring among the embassy staff. I had obviously said something significant but was clueless as to what it was. "You met with Martin Zilic?" I was asked incredulously. "Yes, I spend the whole day with him", I replied. The embassy staff wanted to know why they had not been informed about the meeting. I was then told that Martin Zilic had been the Mayor of the Bío Bío Region of Chile and was one of the most important political figures in the country. Who knew? I just thought he was a university-affiliated doctor who knew about bioethics. The word got out that I had friends in high places.

Our final meeting was with a group of Chilean legislators. I sat back and let the rest of the staff talk about drugs and intellectual property cooperation. I was afraid to say anything about my meeting with Martin since it had caused such an uproar at the embassy. The Chilean legislators mostly did not speak English, so one of our lawyers from the Democratic staff, Paul Oostburg Sanz, did the translation. I liked and respected Paul. He is a rather serious person, but smart and good to work with. I was a bit irritated later on when I overheard the head of our delegation who was a Republican say she would have felt more comfortable if a "Republican had been doing the translation".

Near the end of the session, the head of the Chilean delegation presented each of us with a lovely medallion in a blue velvet box to "help us remember our visit to their country". The medallions were embossed with the symbol and name of their legislature, "Camara de Diputados Chile". Everyone on our side of the table just sat there silently. I thought it would have been rude not to thank them. Since no one made a move, I took the initiative. I stood up and said, "We are grateful to you for all of your hospitality, good citizenship, and your commitment to a better world. While these medallions are beautiful, and I know we will each treasure them, we will not need them to remind us of our visit. Your warmth and hospitality have been memorable. It has been a superb experience for each of us". Paul translated, and I assume he did not make any serious mistakes which a Republican certainly would not have made.

✦ ✦ ✦ ✦ ✦ ✦ ✦ ✦

I was asked by Tom to go to Bangkok on a Staffdel to meet with the American embassy staff on some issues relating to international organizations. I would also be able to meet people about the Science and the Courts program. I was grateful to have the opportunity. There were several memorable parts of the trip. I had talked with Brian Taylor at the American Embassy, who would be my control officer and would help me with any arrangements. I had explained to him what I wanted to accomplish. He told me the DEA officer at the embassy, Alan Jones, was from the Washington area. When I talked to Alan, I found out he went to Walter Johnson High School, which is near where I live. Before leaving, I went to the school and got him a WJ baseball hat. He was ecstatic when I handed it to him upon my arrival at the embassy.

Brian told me I had to be careful about the combination of jet lag, heat and humidity. The air quality in Bangkok is not good, so lots of people wear face masks. He warned me no matter how used to Washington, D.C. heat and humidity I was, I would "hit the wall" within 58 minutes on the first day. I thought he was being a bit over-cautious. But, bam, the next day, after less than an hour, I had to go back to the hotel to get some rest and cool, clean air.

The embassy had provided me with a car and driver, which still made me a bit uncomfortable. I did not think I rated that kind of special treatment. I was mindful of how the drivers wanted to be on-call so that they could get paid. My driver was an interesting, well-spoken man who encouraged me to call whenever I needed him.

I took some advice from my friend Ashley who had traveled extensively on official Congressional business. He suggested I ask one of the embassy drivers to give me a tour of the city. I was always early for my appointments, so I urged my driver, Pravat, to show Bangkok to me while we were on the way. He always referred to Thailand's ruler, whose image was displayed on practically every lamppost as "My King". It was very endearing. The King was the longest-serving monarch in the world. He was beloved. I always sat in the front seat of the car to better connect with Pravat, and so I would not have to lean over a divider to hear him.

I got to see a lot of beautiful and significant sites. The most impressive were the stunningly gorgeous Buddhist temples. Pravat escorted me to the most famous temples, and then, the local insider he was, he took me to some which were not well known but were spectacular. He refused to let me pay him for the extra time. He said it was his duty as an embassy driver to get me to my appointments, and his duty as a Thai citizen to show me the beauty of his country.

I had a midnight flight out, and I was told by my control officer to have my bags ready to go at 10 pm. They would be taken through customs beforehand. I was not going to be picked up until 11 pm! I found it hard to believe that would give me enough time to catch my flight. However, Pravat showed up at 11, and sure enough, he whisked me to the airport in plenty of time.

When I was departing, I again offered to pay Pravat for taking good care of me. He declined and then said something which surprised me. He told me he had been driving "VIPs" around Bangkok for more than 25 years, and I was the only one to sit in the front of the car and talk with him as an equal. He was honored I had done that. I told him I would not have had it any other way.

I knew I had a long flight ahead, which would give me plenty of time to prepare a report about my trip. I had time for two cups of coffee at the airport and was wide awake. I was pleased to be flying in the upper deck of a Boeing 747, which was quiet and only half full. There were a couple of built-in desks in the cabin, and I was able to set up my computer at one of them. By the time we landed, I had finished the first draft of my report, watched a movie, and even had a short nap.

XV. Four Impeachments--Three Judges and A President

Judge Harry Claiborne

Early in 1986, it became clear the Committee was going to have to deal with the issue of impeachment of a Federal Judge. For the first time in history, a Federal Judge had been convicted of a felony (tax evasion) and refused to resign. He had been sentenced to two years in prison. Under the Constitution, the judge had life tenure, which applies "during Good Behavior". He would remain a judge, drawing his salary, notwithstanding his felony conviction, unless and until he was impeached by the House and convicted by the Senate and thereby removed from office.

The Constitution, Article I, Section 3, provides the penalties. "Judgment in Cases of Impeachments shall not extend further than to removal from Office, and disqualification to hold and enjoy any Office of honor, Trust, or Profit under the United States..." There had not been an impeachment for more than 50 years. Previously, ten Federal Judges had been impeached. Of those, four were convicted by the Senate, four were acquitted, and two resigned before an outcome at trial. All four who were convicted were automatically removed from office, and two of them were disqualified from further federal office.

The last impeachment was in 1933. Judge Halsted Ritter, a U.S. District Judge in Florida, was impeached by the House, convicted by the Senate and removed from office. Since that time, Congress had enacted the Judicial Conduct and Disability Act of 1980, which provided procedures for the filing of complaints against Federal Judges. Under that law, if a complaint was made against a sitting judge, there can be an investigation conducted by the local Judicial Council.

The Council of any circuit can refer its findings on any complaint to the Judicial Conference of the United States, which is the governing body of the U.S. Courts. The Conference can certify its findings to the House of Representatives with the suggestion that "consideration of impeachment may be warranted".

The impeachment process, as outlined in the Constitution, is relatively simple. The House has the "sole power of impeachment". It acts like a grand jury and decides whether to impeach (charge) a civil officer of the government. If the House, by a simple majority, adopts a resolution of impeachment containing specific charges, known as articles of impeachment, the matter is sent to the Senate, which has the "sole power to try" all impeachments. In a Senate trial, Members of the House, who are called Managers, act as prosecutors, and the Senators act as jurors. It takes a two-thirds vote in the Senate to convict on any article. Conviction results in immediate removal from office.

With this staring us in the face, the General Counsel (Alan Parker's replacement) directed me to prepare a memo on the history of judicial impeachments. I spent a good bit of time going over the House Precedents, which had been written, for the most part, by my friend Pete Robinson in the Parliamentarian's Office. I prepared a long and detailed memorandum on the subject for the Chairman, which I gave to the General Counsel. I happened to be up in the Chairman's office sometime after the memo had been submitted to him, and I noticed it on his desk. As far as I could tell, the only change in the memo was the name of the author. My name had been deleted, and I knew that that was not a good sign.

While the Chairman intended to hire an experienced trial lawyer to handle the impeachment because it was tantamount to a real trial, I was assigned to be the lead counsel on the staff. Mr. Rodino told me he wanted to have someone knowledgeable about the Congressional process actively engaged to ensure the prerogatives of the Committee, and the House were protected. I also think he wanted to have someone directly answerable to him in charge.

Since the new Judicial Conduct and Disability Act had come from the Courts Subcommittee, which was chaired by Congressman Kastenmeier, Chairman Rodino decided to refer the impeachment resolution there. As I had gotten to know Kastenmeier reasonably well by that point, he told me he was pleased to have me assigned to assist him and his subcommittee.

Chairman Rodino and I had discussed the advisability of relying solely on the findings of another branch of government in impeachment cases. There had been a suggestion that a criminal conviction on its face was sufficient grounds to impeach. The argument was, since he was convicted of a crime, *ipso facto*, he should be impeached. I asked, "Doesn't separation of powers come into play?"

I argued the House should not be bound by the findings of another branch of government, and it should do its own investigation, and apply its own standard of proof and take into consideration some critical questions:

a) What if there were irregularities in the trial where the conviction was improperly obtained, and the judge was found guilty, but later evidence reveals he should not have been convicted?

b) What weight should the House give to a "not guilty" verdict?
The House should not be bound by an executive branch finding because it might want to impeach a judge who was acquitted [this turned out to be prescient] because of:
i) suppression of illegally seized, but relevant *inculpatory* evidence,
ii) inadequate or improper prosecution

c) Should the House be bound by criminal law burden of proof "beyond a reasonable doubt," or should it use another, lesser standard since the respondent's "life, liberty or property" are not at risk?

The Chairman decided we should at least start the fact-finding process. He introduced a simple resolution of impeachment in the House which stated: "Resolved that Harry E. Claiborne, Judge of the United States District Court for the District of Nevada, is impeached of high crimes and misdemeanors". There were no specific charges or remedies in the resolution; it was just the basis to start the process in subcommittee. The resolution was referred by the Speaker to the Judiciary Committee, and Chairman Rodino referred it to the Kastenmeier subcommittee. After receiving testimony, the Subcommittee would amend the resolution to include the specific charges in Articles of Impeachment, as well as the penalties the House was requesting.

The subcommittee convened an executive session to hear testimony about Judge Claiborne's crimes and his conviction. The Judge was still in the federal penitentiary. He had wanted to come to the hearing and testify. I expect he was probably an excellent jailhouse lawyer, but I did not think it was appropriate to say that to anyone. Arrangements had to be made with the U.S. Marshals Service to transfer the Judge to Washington for the hearing. I must admit I was taken aback when the Judge was escorted into the hearing room in handcuffs.

His lawyer, Oscar Goodman, was a colorful character straight out of the movies. He certainly was a showman during this impeachment and trial, and it came as no surprise to me that he became the Mayor of Las Vegas some years later.

When Mr. Kastenmeier called Claiborne to take the witness table, he declined to testify. I whispered to Kastenmeier that he should get Claiborne on the record demurring, which he did. It seemed strange that Claiborne had requested the chance to appear, had traveled to Washington, but then he decided not to. Goldman asked to make a presentation to the subcommittee on behalf of the Judge instead of Claiborne's testifying. This was allowed, although I did not think the subcommittee was required to. Counsel's testimony does not have the same impact as that of the respondent. Claiborne was a convicted felon, and the chances of the House not impeaching him were zero. I thought the same was true of conviction in the Senate; it was a foregone conclusion.

After the hearing, but before the subcommittee had its formal markup when it would consider specific articles of impeachment, I met with Doug Bellis of the Office of House Legislative Counsel to draft proposed articles. Doug is one of the brightest people I have ever met. He is omnivorous in his continuing quest for knowledge. The subject he was most interested in was physics. He reads "*Le Monde*" in French every day. He is also a talented lawyer and drafts-man.

Legislative Counsel's job is to help translate Members' ideas into legislative language. The office has specialists on every title of the U.S. Code. Doug's particular area of expertise was criminal law. I never did anything legislative without running it past Doug. I used to tell my students that legislative drafting is the second hardest kind of writing, good poetry being the hardest. Doug had a comprehensive knowledge of the criminal code and the most up-to-date case law in the field. The difference between using the word "knowingly" and the word "willingly", while not evident to a lot of people, could make a substantial difference when a judge was reviewing a new statute. If Congress inadvertently used one term instead of the other, it might signify, at least in a judge's mind, a purposeful intention to change the law. Without Doug's careful eagle-eye, something like that could slip through, and some judge would later interpret it (incorrectly) as a change in Congressional intent.

While Doug and I were preparing for the Subcommittee markup, we discussed whether we should include both penalties (removal and disqualification). We were aware of the fact that two judges in prior impeachment convictions had also been disqualified by the Senate. Since Federal Judges were being ap-pointed at younger ages, we thought it would be prudent to include the second penalty of disqualification, in the resolution. We knew even if we included it, the Senate could decline to vote on it, or they could simply ignore it. We also were aware the Senate could elect to invoke disqualification on its own motion even if the House had not included it. Doug, being a stickler for precise drafts-manship, felt it was prudent to include it. I concurred.

As we were drafting the complete resolution, including articles of impeach-ment and the penalties, the General Counsel walked in and demanded to see the draft. She looked it over and said to me, "You must be the stupidest person I know". I could not resist the smart-aleck answer. "That may be true, but why do you raise it now?" Her response was, "He is 72 years old. He will never get another federal job". I tried to explain to her the Senate could ignore it, but it had invoked it on at least two occasions. Presciently I then said, "You never know who the next one is going to be". Her response was similar to what parents often say to their children ("Because I said so"), "I am the boss, and I say take it out". So, I did.

There was an interesting occurrence during one of my meetings with Congressman Kastenmeier about the Claiborne impeachment. He and I were meeting in his Congressional office to go over the next steps in the process. There was a knock on the door, and his longtime assistant, Ann Marie Feeney, using her most proper and formal tone, said, "Congressman, do you have a few minutes to meet with some constituents?" My experience had been that no matter what you are doing as a Member of Congress, you *always* have time to meet with constituents who are visiting Washington. Recognizing that imperative, I stood up and prepared to leave. I told Kastenmeier I would be in my office, and as soon as he was ready to resume our discussion, I would come back. However, much to my surprise, he asked me to stay.

The serious, stern and humorless Bob Kastenmeier I knew evaporated before my eyes, and an outgoing smiling person appeared. He greeted the constituents warmly and then introduced me to them! I was caught completely off-guard. He described me as a "very bright constitutional lawyer" who was his counsel in the impeachment proceedings of Judge Claiborne. He explained in detail that his chairmanship required him to take on this "important constitutional responsibility". As I thought about it later, it occurred to me that he was showing off to his constituents and making a point of his important responsibilities. Having me there also gave him a good excuse not to spend too much time with them. I expect he hoped they would be impressed by the significant work he was doing and would report that back to as many people in the district as possible. The visitors were voters, after all.

The Subcommittee conducted hearings in executive session and heard from the Chief of the Public Integrity Section of the Department of Justice, Charles Wiggins, a former Member of Congress who was a judge on the 9th Circuit Court of Appeals and Mr. Goodman. Once the hearings were completed, the Subcommittee met to consider specific articles of impeachment. The record of the executive session was made public by voice vote. The Subcommittee debated and favorably ordered four articles to the full committee.

The Judiciary Committee had had a long-standing unwritten rule that all the Members were lawyers. As far as I know, the first Member to be named to the committee who was not a lawyer was Larkin Smith from Mississippi, who was elected in 1989. He had been a law enforcement officer before serving in Congress. After that, there were several Members who did not have law degrees. This occasionally became a problem since the entire staff was, with one exception, exclusively lawyers, and almost all the issues we were dealing with had public policy ramifications relating to legal questions.

In the Claiborne impeachment, the benefit of having lawyers on the committee became evident. At the full committee markup, one of the Members suggested that rather than going through the complex process of impeachment in the House and trial in the Senate, the House should just "reduce this judge's salary to zero". Mr. Hyde, who was to become a Manager (prosecutor) in the Senate trial, gently informed the Member of the constitutional prohibition against doing so. He had the language of the Constitution at hand and said, "I would remind the gentleman of the text in Article III of the Constitution concerning judicial compensation. It reads, 'The judges, both of the supreme and inferior courts… Shall, at stated times, receive for their services a compensation *which shall not be diminished during their continuance in office*'" (emph. added). He did not say, "You moron", but his response immediately put an end to the idea of cutting the judge's salary to force him to resign.

The committee voted unanimously (35-0) to adopt the four articles of impeachment and recommend them favorably to the House. Soon after that, there was a unanimous vote in the House (406-0) on the impeachment resolution. Immediately, the House then adopted a series of housekeeping resolutions. These named nine Judiciary Committee members, led by Mr. Rodino, to be Managers to represent the House as prosecutors in the Senate trial, provided for funding for that effort, and authorized formal notification to the Senate of the impeachment. The Lead House Manager was William J. Hughes, who was the Chairman of the Crime Subcommittee and an experienced prosecutor. Among the other House Managers was Henry Hyde. It was in working on this impeachment that I got to know him.

Immediately after the vote on the impeachment, and the adoption of the three housekeeping resolutions, I joined a solemn procession of the nine Managers. We walked from the well of the House, through the north doors, straight through the Capitol into the south door of the U.S. Senate. We were surrounded by officers from the House Sergeant at Arms Office, who parted the Red Sea of tourists for us through Statuary Hall, the old House Chamber, through the main rotunda, past the old Senate Chamber and directly into the Senate. When we got there, the Senators were all sworn in as jurors in the matter of the impeachment, and Chairman Rodino was recognized to formally present the articles of impeachment.

Charlie Johnson did me a big favor. He arranged for the Speaker to present me with the gavel which he used on the day the House impeached Judge Claiborne. The gavel now hangs in my office, along with the picture of Speaker Tip O'Neill and me. It was typical of Charlie to do that.

Chairman Rodino had asked his old friend Bert Jenner, who was the Minority Counsel to the Judiciary Committee during the Nixon impeachment proceedings, to recommend a lawyer to be Special Counsel to the House Managers for the trial in the Senate. He wanted an experienced trial lawyer to assist the Managers. Jenner recommended an elegant and polished law partner of his, Nick Chabraja. Nick was a powerhouse, and he quickly gained the respect of the Managers.

The Senate established procedures for the impeachment trial, including the use of a committee to hear evidence, the so-called Rule XI committee. Instead of having a full trial in the Senate, they chose to have the evidence taken by a 12-member committee. Under a rule first adopted in 1935, the special committee was to receive testimony and other evidence and report its findings to the Senate. Previously, impeachment trials had been conducted in their entirety before the full Senate, including the testimony of witnesses. The use of the Committee process permitted the Senate to continue to conduct legislative business during the evidentiary stage of the impeachment trial.

The Rule XI committee met in the famous Russell Senate Caucus room. This was the room where the Watergate hearings took place, and where both John F. Kennedy and his brother Robert F. Kennedy announced their presidential candidacies.

The Committee began seven days of televised hearings. The House Managers, acting as prosecutors, were on one side of the room. On the other side was Judge Claiborne, again escorted by federal marshals, and his lawyer Oscar Goodman. The Senate Impeachment Trial Committee examined the evidence and heard testimony before reporting its findings to the full Senate.

I was impressed by "Mac" Mathias, who was the Chairman of the Committee. He had been a Member of the House and was a well-respected Senator. I thought Senator John Warner came across as a bit pompous. He asked long, complicated questions, trying to impress everyone with his legal background. He had obviously gotten some staff person to get copies of Judge Claiborne's opinions and made a big show of pointing to them. Those opinions are published in bound volumes called Federal Reports. They have the identifying numbers on the bindings. The only way you can tell which volume contains a particular opinion is by looking at the bindings. Warner's prop set-up made clear he was not going to be referring to any particular opinion since he had the bindings facing outwards towards the audience (and the television cameras, of course). He could not see the numbers, but the viewers could. It struck me as showing off.

The House Managers were given the use of a separate holding room to store our materials and have private meetings. An awkward situation came up when Mr. Rodino, Congressman Hughes, and I were in the holding room the day before Judge Claiborne was to take the stand. Hughes, the former prosecutor, felt he should be the one to cross-examine the judge. Rodino said, "No, Bill. I think I am going to get Nick to do it". All of a sudden, it got very cold in the room, and I promptly excused myself. I did not want to be there to see Hughes, who I admired, be humiliated by Rodino's passing him over for the plum assignment of cross-examining Judge Claiborne.

Nick did a stellar job and had almost finished when he asked the judge a final question. "What was the reason you cheated on your taxes?" Claiborne looked at him and said nothing. Chabraja then thrust the knife into him by saying, "I think it is clear. It was greed". Most of the Members were used to the more civil Congressional-type discourse, and they bristled at the harshness of the comment. One of them said softly, "Gees, I would not have said that". I think a lot of people in the room felt the same way. Claiborne responded that there was nothing to indicate in "my whole professional life or my personal life that I have been greedy. I will tell you, sir, your remark wounds me, and I am sorry for that. Because I think you are a very fine lawyer, and it is regrettable that you would engage in such conduct, particularly in view of the fact that I have been a good judge". It certainly was an extraordinary exchange.

The Committee filed its report on September 30, 1986, and on October 7, 8, and 9, the Senate convened as a "Court of Impeachment" to hear final arguments. Claiborne had objected to the use of the committee to hear the testimony, insisting that the *full Senate* should be required to hear evidence since the Constitution says, "The Senate shall have the sole Power to try all Impeachments". The Senate did not agree. This issue of the constitutionality of the Rule XI committee would come up again in both the Hastings and Nixon impeachments.

Each side made its closing arguments. The Senate then met in closed session to deliberate. We were not permitted to be present during their deliberations, but we were confident that Judge Claiborne would be convicted.

On the afternoon of October 9, the Senate was to convene as the Court of Impeachment for the votes with Vice President George H.W. Bush presiding in his role as President of the Senate. Nick and I were standing next to the Vice President and the Chairman as they were chatting before the session began. Bush and Rodino were on a first name basis as they had served together in the House. Rodino turned to us and said, "George, I want you to meet my Special Counsel, Nick Chabraja". They shook hands as I waited to be introduced. It did not happen, and I flashed back to my comment to Alan Parker about the staff being "just furniture". I was disappointed but not crushed.

During regular votes, Senators say "aye" or "nay", and they can vote from anywhere in the Chamber, sometimes literally giving the clerk a thumbs up or thumbs down as they are milling around. When voting on an impeachment, each Senator is to respond to the President of the Senate who poses the question, "How say you, 'guilty' or 'not guilty'?" Each Senator is required to stand at their desk and respond. It is a solemn process. I found it particularly impactful when Senator John Stennis, who had lost a leg, gripped the arms of his chair, struggled to stand, and in a deep, formal stentorian tone with a bit of a southern drawl said, "Ah say, guilty, sir". Getting the final vote was anti-climactic.

There were four Articles of Impeachment, and three of them were adopted by the required 2/3rd vote. The adoption of any one of the articles was sufficient to remove Claiborne from office. The vote on the third Article of Impeachment was important for future impeachments. Article III stood for the proposition that Claiborne's conviction in the criminal courts *on its face* proved that he was guilty of "misbehavior" and "high crimes" and should be removed from office. If the Senate adopted that article, it would be accepting the judgment of another branch of government. With a vote of 46 to 17 (35 voted "present"), Article III was the only Article not adopted. Some of the Senators were concerned about the troubling precedent of having a judicial conviction being automatic grounds for conviction in an impeachment trial. There was also concern about the opposite result; that an acquittal in a criminal court might arguably dictate acquittal in an impeachment trial. This was the very separation of powers tableau which Mr. Rodino and I had examined. There was no discussion about the second remedy, disqualification.

Judge Alcee Hastings

U.S. District Judge Alcee Hastings was indicted for bribery. He was tried and acquitted in the Federal criminal court, although his co-defendant was convicted.

Under the new Judicial Conduct and Disability Act of 1980, three of Judge Hastings' colleagues on the bench filed a complaint against him, alleging he had lied in the trial to escape conviction. An investigating committee of the 11th

Circuit began its inquiry led by John Doar, who had been the Special Counsel to the Judiciary Committee during the Richard Nixon impeachment. It took three years! The investigators concluded that Hastings did indeed commit perjury, tamper with evidence, and conspire to gain financially by accepting bribes. It found there were grounds for the House to consider impeachment.

The committee reported to the Eleventh Circuit Judicial Council, which voted unanimously to support that recommendation. The same procedure then was followed by the Judicial Conference of the United States, over which the Chief Justice presides. It unanimously concurred and, pursuant to the statute, referred the matter to the House saying, "consideration of impeachment may be warranted".

During a closed organizational caucus of the Judiciary Committee Democrats at the beginning of the new Congress, the matter came up. John Conyers, an African American member of the committee and Chairman of the Crime Subcommittee, said, "I will not condone the impeachment of a black judge". Race was a big issue, and Mr. Rodino had been challenged by black opponents in primaries. Reverend Jesse Jackson, Sr. came to Newark to support Rodino's opponent, a black businessman. Jackson said, "It is time to make room for new people". The clear message was that the new person should be black since the Congressional district attained a majority black population after court-ordered redistricting in 1972.

Possibly in an attempt to avoid the race issue, the Chairman referred the matter to Mr. Conyers' subcommittee. I think he did that in order to kill it, so it would not be an issue in his Congressional campaign.

A well-known litigator and criminal defense attorney, Alan Baron was appointed as Special Impeachment Counsel. Alan is a careful and talented lawyer. He had represented a Watergate defendant, L. Patrick Gray, the former Director of the FBI. Alan's skillful representation resulted in Gray being the only person indicted in the Watergate scandal who was acquitted. Alan put together an excellent team of lawyers and investigators and proceeded methodically to assemble the facts. He had no personal animus towards Judge Hastings. He was a complete professional. Alan was new to the vagaries of Capitol Hill, but he managed to do his work and stay under the radar as far as the politics were concerned. Mr. Conyers had complete confidence in him, and those of us on the committee staff were also impressed.

After an intensive and lengthy investigation, which involved some Federal court litigation about access to grand jury transcripts, Mr. Conyers was convinced impeachment was indeed warranted. This was a stunning turn-around.

I remember the subcommittee markup of the resolution of impeachment vividly. After having taken the disqualification remedy out of the Claiborne resolution, it was abundantly clear we could not include it in the Hastings resolution. As one of the Members said during a closed caucus, "If you didn't put it in for the white judge who was convicted and incarcerated, you sure as hell cannot put it in for the black judge who was tried and acquitted". Hastings was 50 years old.

The first thing which had to be done at the markup was the reading of the articles of impeachment. I was given the clerk's duties that day, which included reading the proposed resolution and the 17 articles in their entirety as well as calling the roll for the votes. I am moderately dyslexic, and I knew I would probably have a problem reading the roman numerals which were used in the text of the resolution. I went through the 17 articles and wrote the Arabic numerals in place of the roman numerals. I did not make any mistakes.

In his opening statement, Conyers spoke of his life-long battle against racism and the time when civil rights lawyers knew "they could not expect to receive a fair hearing" from certain Federal Judges. He said, "We did not wage that civil rights struggle merely to replace one form of judicial corruption for another. A black public official must be held to the *same standard* as every other public official. A *lower* standard would be *patronizing*. A *higher* standard would be *racist*. Just as race should never disqualify a person from office, race should never insulate a person from the consequences of wrongful conduct"(emph. added). He voted "Aye" on all seventeen articles of impeachment. The subcommittee voted unanimously in agreement.

With Conyers having taken the race issue off the table, the full committee voted 32-1 on all the articles. I helped draft the committee report and then filed it before House consideration. The subsequent debate on the impeachment in the House was relatively anti-climactic because Conyers spoke in support.

During the 15-minute recorded vote, which was taken by electronic device, as usual, Congressman John Bryant approached the Chairman. He knew that the next order of business was for the House to consider the three "housekeeping" resolutions, the most important of which was naming the Managers. I had prepared the three resolutions and had them at the Speaker's desk. The Managers named in the resolution (per the instructions from the Chairman) were, Peter W. Rodino, Jr., John Conyers, Jr., Don Edwards, Hamilton Fish, Jr., and George W. Gekas.

John Bryant was a tough guy. His preferred form of recreation was riding Brahman bulls. With the General Counsel sitting next to the Chairman and me directly behind him, Bryant came up and asked if he could be one of the Managers. The General Counsel knew I had prepared the resolution as directed, and it was at the rostrum with the names printed in it. Without being asked, she turned to the Chairman and said, "No, you cannot add anyone at this late stage". The phrase, "frequently wrong but never in doubt" came to mind. There was an icy glare from the General Counsel as I sat there saying nothing. Mr. Rodino looked at me and said, "Dan, could we still do it?" I told him all I had to do was go up to the rostrum and add Mr. Bryant's name. Without looking at the General Counsel, he said, "Okay, Dan, do it", and I did. That is how John Bryant became a Manager, and it was a damn good thing because he did the lion's share of the work in the extensive hearings before the Senate Committee and in the presentation to the full Senate.

As with the Claiborne impeachment, the formal procession through the Capitol occurred, and the Articles of Impeachment were officially presented to the Senate. The Senate voted to reject Hastings' claim of double jeopardy. We had dealt with this in the House, and since the Judge's life or liberty were not at stake, we argued the double jeopardy clause in the Constitution did not apply. The Senate agreed, and they referred the matter to a newly appointed Rule XI Committee to take the evidence.

John Bryant was tenacious. He was like a bulldog. Although he was only one of the Managers, he and Alan were the heart of the effort. They spent long hours preparing for the hearings and were ready for anything Hastings and his lawyer Terry Anderson might do. They made a formidable team. I was very mindful of the fortuitous incident on the House floor when I had written John Bryant's name into the resolution naming the Managers. I think it was the most crucial factor which made conviction in the Senate possible.

The Rule XI Committee was chaired by Senator Jeff Bingaman. The hearings were held in the new Hart Senate Office Building hearing room, which was designed for radio and television coverage of important hearings. They went on for 18 days between July 10 and August 3. The committee heard testimony from 55 witnesses, including William Borders, Hastings' co-defendant in the criminal case, who was convicted and incarcerated. The House Managers presented evidence to support the conclusion that Hastings had conspired with Borders to solicit the bribe. Since Hastings and his lawyer were experienced trial tacticians, they sought to include a lot of evidence which we thought should not be admitted. The Managers had numerous formal objections to the admission of evidence proffered by Judge Hastings and his lawyer. However, Chairman Bingaman rarely sustained any of them.

Hastings, who appeared in his own defense, objected to the use of the Rule XI committee, insisting that the *full Senate* should be required to hear evidence since the Constitution says, "The Senate shall have the sole Power to try all Impeachments". This was the same argument that Claiborne had made previously, and which Walter Nixon would make subsequently. The objection was not sustained. We will get back to this argument later.

One day during the lunch break, I was almost alone in this massive hearing room. The only other person there was Senator Conrad Burns, a member of the Rule XI Committee. He had been a professional auctioneer before coming to the Senate. He had the disgusting habit of chewing tobacco and spitting the juice into a cup. The two of us were standing in the front of the empty room. He asked me, "What do you think, counsel?" I am very circumspect in those situations, so I turned it back on him. "It's up to you, Senator, what do you think?" He spit into his cup again and smiled and said, "I think there's gonna be lots of due process and then we will hang his ass".

After the hearings were completed, the Rule XI Committee filed its report. The Committee was simply to report to the full Senate on contested and uncontested facts. The committee was *not* tasked with making a recommendation on guilt or innocence.

We knew we did not have an overwhelming case. We also recognized it would be that much harder to convict after the Chairman of the Rule XI Committee Senator Bingaman, *and* the Vice-Chairman, Republican Senator and former prosecutor Arlen Specter, both announced they were going to vote against conviction. Senator Specter said he would like to have invoked the Scottish legal rule, which provided for a "not proven" verdict. With the two top members of the committee who had heard all of the testimony announcing they were going to vote "not guilty", we were disheartened, to say the least.

The Senate heard final arguments by the Managers and by Hastings and Anderson. The Senate then met as a Court of Impeachment in closed session to deliberate. The House Managers and their staff were excluded. We had no idea how it was going to go until the next day when the Senate was to meet in open session for the votes. As Alan, John Bryant and I were sitting in the well of the Senate, Senator Al Gore came over and said, "You all did a great job, but with the Chairman and Ranking Minority Member of the Committee announcing they would vote 'not guilty,' I do not think you have the votes." We were extremely disappointed. It was a telling statement about what the other Managers thought of the possibility of an embarrassing acquittal that none of them bothered to come over to witness the votes.

Senator Robert Byrd was the President Pro Tempore of the Senate. He directed the clerk to call the roll. As we sat there, I was nervous because after all the work we had done, I was afraid we were going to lose. I had a Senate roll call sheet with me, and I was keeping track of the total for and against conviction as the vote was conducted. About two-thirds of the way through the list, I spoke softly to Alan, "I think we've got this guy". Alan raised his eyebrows and smiled. Hastings was convicted with the necessary 2/3rds vote on the first two articles by votes of 69-26 and 68-27. He was eventually convicted on 8 of the 17 articles.

After the announcement of the vote on the second article, Senator Mitchell, the Majority Leader, rose and asked unanimous consent that the respondent (Hastings) and his counsel be permitted to leave. During the short break as they were leaving before the Senate was to continue the voting on the other articles, I got up and approached Senator Mitchell. I did not know him, but I wanted to tell him, "Senator, that was one of the kindest things I have ever seen". I thought that Hastings and his lawyer would want to leave and lick their wounds. Little did I know that immediately after Hastings left, he talked to the press on the steps of the Senate and announced he was running for Governor of Florida!

The Senate voted on most of the other articles of impeachment and convicted him on eight. Alcee Hastings was removed from office but not "disqualified from holding another office of honor trust or profit under the United States", as per the Claiborne precedent. Disqualification was never raised by anyone.

There was a press conference upstairs in the Senate Press Gallery immediately after the votes, and John Bryant answered questions. On the way, we were told about Hastings' plans to run for Governor. John asked me whether Hastings would be barred from that. I responded that the disqualification clause did not apply to any *state* office. It read: "disqualification to hold and enjoy any office of honor, trust or profit **under the United States**". I also told him it was a moot point since the disqualification clause was not included in the seventeen articles of impeachment, nor did the Senate choose to invoke it. Disqualification could have been invoked on any Senator's motion by a simple majority roll call vote. John Bryant asked me later on why the disqualification clause was not included. I did not tell him the whole story. I just said it was a "staff screw up".

As an historical note: From that date forward, disqualification was never included in an impeachment resolution that passed the House. In the impeachment of Federal Judge Thomas Porteous in 2010, the Senate, after voting to convict, did vote to bar him from any future federal position, notwithstanding the fact the House had not included the disqualification remedy in the resolution of impeachment. He was only the third impeached official to be sanctioned that way.

Judge Walter Nixon

Walter Nixon was the Chief Judge of the United States District Court for the Southern District of Mississippi. He was indicted, tried and convicted of perjury and sentenced to five years in prison. His conviction was based on false grand jury testimony and false statements he made to federal officers concerning a prosecution in the state courts of the son of someone Nixon knew.

I have always contended that Judge Nixon was convicted of simply being stupid or arrogant. During his grand jury testimony, he was asked whether he had anything to add. The smart thing to say was, "No, y'all have a nice day" and then getting the hell out of there. Instead, he denied his attempt to intervene in the state drug case. What he was accused of doing (talking to the state prosecutor) was probably unethical but *not* illegal. Lying to the grand jury about it *was*.

The Nixon case went through the same Judicial Council process as the Hastings case and was then referred to the Judicial Conference of the United States. The Conference certified and transmitted to the House a determination that impeachment might be warranted.

Chairman Rodino referred the matter to a different subcommittee chaired by Congressman Don Edwards. I understood neither Mr. Kastenmeier nor Mr. Conyers wished to handle another impeachment. The subcommittee held hearings on the Nixon case and adopted a resolution of impeachment containing three articles which were ordered favorably reported to the full committee. Because of the Claiborne precedent, only the single penalty of removal was included. The full committee ordered the resolution of impeachment reported favorably to the House unanimously. The House voted unanimously to impeach Judge Nixon. Managers appointed by the House were Mr. Brooks, Mr. Edwards of California, Mr. Cardin, Mr. Sensenbrenner, and Mr. Dannemeyer.

In a rather woeful footnote to history, one of the Judiciary Committee Members was incensed a sitting judge would be so imprudent as to be caught by a wiretap talking about potentially illegal things he had done. "No Member of our government, especially a Judge, should be foolhardy enough to talk on the telephone about such clearly illegal activity" pontificated Congressman Pat Swindall. He was outraged that the judge had done it, but also because he talked about it on the telephone. In October of 1988, Swindall was himself indicted for perjury related to a money-laundering scheme. A significant portion of the evidence cited in the indictment came from recorded telephone conversations he had had with an undercover IRS agent.

The new Chairman of the Full Committee, Jack Brooks, as was the standard practice, presented the Articles of Impeachment to the Senate. The Senate then, as it had done for the two previous impeachments, referred the matter to a Rule XI committee for the purpose of taking testimony.

The Nixon hearings in the Senate Committee were not as stressful as the other two. Claiborne was the first one, and we were not sure how it was going to occur, although we were confident an imprisoned felon was going to be convicted by the Senate. The Hastings hearings were much more lengthy, involved, and contentious. The Nixon case was straight-forward. Furthermore, Alan Baron was the Special Impeachment Counsel, and he had done this before. With a different team of lawyers, he marshaled the necessary evidence to get the impeachment through the subcommittee, the full committee and the House in relatively short order. He maintained his high level of professionalism and was so well regarded he was asked to handle two more judicial impeachments after I left the committee. Alan was the go-to person on impeachment.

When the hearings were over, we were fairly confident we had the votes in the Senate, and the Judge would be convicted. We then prepared for the presentations to the full Senate, making sure everything was in order.

After closing arguments, the Senate went into closed session for six hours of deliberations, which we were not allowed to attend. The next day, in open session by the required roll call vote, Nixon was convicted with the necessary 2/3rds vote on the first two articles by votes of 89-8 and 78-19. Senator Robert C. Byrd, the President Pro Tempore of the Senate, after conducting the roll call vote in his most stentorian tones, said, "It is hereby ordered and adjudged that the said Walter L. Nixon Jr. be removed from office".

We thought that was going to be the end of it, and we could return to legislative business. All of the Members and the staff felt we had done our jobs well and represented the House admirably. The ensuing judicial and electoral happenings did not directly involve the House, but we were certainly watching.

Post-Impeachment Judicial Proceedings

Nixon filed a challenge to the Senate's Rule XI Committee procedure in the Federal District Court in Washington, D.C. He alleged the Constitution required the Senate to "try" him, and the delegation of the task of taking testimony to the Committee did not comport with that duty. He alleged the full Senate did not see witnesses and hear their testimony, which denied him his constitutional right to a trial by the Senate.

Judge Hastings had also filed suit on identical grounds before his conviction. Judge Gerhart Gesell, in his opinion in the Hastings case, said: "The impeachment clause of the Constitution simply 'does not say that the *full* Senate must try all impeachments'." *Hastings v. United States Senate* (emphasis in original). The Court of Appeals affirmed the dismissal on the ground that Hastings' challenge to the Senate proceedings was premature.

In the *Nixon* case, Federal District Court Judge Louis Oberdorfer, in granting the motion to dismiss, ruled the matter to be non-justiciable:

"in light of the Senate's constitutionally granted rule making power, the authorities now available, and the deference due to the views of respected colleagues, it is difficult to conclude that the Senate's denial of plaintiff's motion for a hearing before the full Senate, while according him an opportunity to present and cross-examine witnesses before the Committee and the opportunity to argue both personally and by counsel before the full Senate, resulted in the dimension of departure from the Constitution's textual commitment to the Senate of the "sole Power to try all Impeachments" as to make this controversy justiciable and the claim meritorious." Nixon v. United States

Judge Nixon appealed the decision to the U.S. Court of Appeals, whose decision would be a binding precedent on any similar case brought in any U.S. District Court in the D.C. Circuit. The Court of Appeals affirmed Judge Oberdorfer's ruling saying, *"The district court held that his claim was non-justiciable...and we agree. Today we refuse to embark on setting limits for the procedures the Senate may choose for the trial of impeachments; the Constitution excludes us. Walter Nixon's claim is not justiciable". Nixon v. United States*

The Courts of Appeals "grades the papers" of the trial courts and tells them when they made a mistake by failing to follow its precedents in similar cases. Hastings filed a new lawsuit based on the same argument raised in the *Nixon* case, which the Court of Appeals had thrown out. Hastings suit was assigned to Judge Stanley Sporkin, and not Judge Oberdorfer. Most lawyers would have told you any subsequent suit in the D.C. Circuit challenging the Rule XI Committee would be thrown out based on the *Nixon* precedent.

Curiously, Judge Sporkin decided since the *Nixon* case had been appealed to the U.S. Supreme Court, it was not a final judgment. Therefore, he reasoned, the Court of Appeals ruling was somehow not binding on him in the Hastings case even though he conceded the issues were identical. *"In view of the grant of certiorari on the identical issue presented in this case, the Court believes that the Nixon case does not preclude it from reaching a decision in the Hastings case". Hastings v. United States* I thought it was an extraordinary ruling.

Judge Sporkin opined that Judge Hastings was denied a trial before the full Senate as was guaranteed by the Constitution.

"Without depriving the House or the Senate of one iota of their exclusive constitutional powers to impeach, try and convict "officers" of the United States, this Court has jurisdiction to interpret what the Constitution says about impeachment. It states that the accused officer is entitled to a trial. **This means a trial by the full Senate.** *Judge Hastings did not get*

a trial by the full Senate. He is entitled to have one. (emph. added)

The Court having found that Judge Hastings was entitled to a trial by the full Senate, his impeachment and conviction must be overturned and remanded to the Senate for a trial that comports with constitutional requirements. This being the decision of the Court, judgment will be entered in favor of Judge Hastings".

I could not understand why Judge Sporkin would go so far out on a limb. As a friend of mine said at the time, "Sporkin felt poor Alcee got screwed". The other fascinating part of the story is that Hastings, not encumbered by the disqualification clause, had decided to run for Congress!

Timing is everything. The Sporkin ruling was issued two weeks before the Democratic primary in Florida. The headlines in the local papers were, if not plain wrong, at the very least misleading. I have heard reporters say they have no control over the headlines for their stories because they are written by other people. The headlines were, according to everything I have read about this case, a crucial factor in the primary election. In this Congressional district, which was a heavily Democratic area, winning the primary was tantamount to winning the general in November.

The New York Times headlines said on September 24, "Impeached Judge Feels Vindicated—With Conviction Overturned, Sights are on House Seat". Also, on September 24, the Miami Times, a newspaper whose readership was predominantly African American, said, "Judge Invalidates Impeachment of Hastings; Campaign Gets Boost". In another article in the same paper, the headline was, "Vindication Long Overdue".

After the Sporkin ruling, but before the Supreme Court ruled in the *Nixon* case, Hastings placed second in the initial Democratic primary. He then scored an upset victory over State Representative Lois J. Frankel in the runoff and went on to win the general election easily. I expect the Sporkin ruling, and publicity surrounding it were significant factors.

The Supreme Court ruled in the *Nixon* case on January 13, 1993 (after Hastings had been sworn in as a Member of the House). A unanimous Court held that the question of whether the Senate's use of the Rule XI violated the U.S. Constitution was nonjusticiable." *Nixon v. United States*

The *Nixon* case was sent back to the Court of Appeals which had affirmed District Judge Oberdorfer's ruling that the case was nonjusticiable. The Hastings case was also sent back through the Court of Appeals to the District Court. Judge Sporkin wrote, in dismissing the case as he was directed to by the Court of Appeals,

"This case is before this Court on remand from the Court of Appeals for the District of Columbia Circuit for reconsideration in light of the Supreme Court's

*ruling in Nixon v. United States... As strongly as this Court believes that Judge
Hastings' fundamental rights were violated, the Court recognizes that the Nixon
decision compels that Judge Hastings' case be dismissed".*

Judge Sporkin was not a happy camper, but Alcee Hastings was a Member
of Congress. And it all goes back those many years ago when the Claiborne impeachment resolution was being drafted. Funny to think, I inadvertently played
a role in making Alcee a Member of Congress.

✦✦✦✦✦✦✦✦✦

Flash forward a few years, and Congressman Hastings and I are getting
along just fine. We would run across each other regularly in the Capitol complex, and as a Member of the Rules Committee, I saw him frequently when
our committee was requesting a rule for floor debate on a bill. Everything was
cordial and friendly. I admired his ability to let the past be the past.

Justice William Brennan died in July of 1997. There was a bus for Members
of Congress who wished to attend the funeral mass at St. Matthew's Cathedral in downtown Washington, which was where the funeral mass for President
Kennedy was held. I had spent a lot of time in law school studying Justice
Brennan's work, and I wanted to go. I asked if I could hop on the Members'
bus, and since it was not full, I was permitted to do so. As I got on, I saw Alcee
Hastings sitting by himself in the front row. His face lit up, and he asked me to
join him. So, I did. It was then when he finally got the answer as to why we did
not invoke the disqualification clause when we impeached him. I told him the
full story. He was intrigued.

As we were talking, another Member got on the bus. Seeing Hastings and
me together, he said, "Al, why are you talking to that son of a bitch? He did
your impeachment". Without any hesitation, Alcee said, "This man is a true
professional, and I respect him. The House is fortunate to have him". The
other Member said nothing and slithered down the aisle. I wrote Alcee a note
thanking him for his kind remarks.

After the 2006 elections, when the Democrats retook the House, there was
some speculation incoming Speaker Pelosi would appoint Hastings to chair the
House Permanent Select Committee on Intelligence. There was a lot of discussion about what a bad precedent it would be to name an impeached and
convicted Federal Judge to the Intelligence Committee chairmanship. However,
Nancy Pelosi and the other front-runner, Congresswoman Jane Harman, did
not get along.

Parenthetically, I had had my own problems with Jane Harman. She was an
associate in my first law firm. We worked on a case together and became good
friends. She always called me "Dan baby", a diminutive which I did not like, but

tolerated. She left the firm to go work for Senator John Tunney from California. We would speak occasionally, but she was spending a lot of time in California.

Many years later, in 1993, she was elected to the House. I saw her in the Speaker's lobby during the first week of her term. I went up to her and said, "Congresswoman, may I give you a hug?" She looked at me quizzically for a second and then recognizing me threw her arms around me and said, "Dan, baby, am I glad to see you! This is so overwhelming; I am really going to need your help". I told her I would be happy to help her in any way I could. Unfortunately, she soon got the disease called "Memberitis", which, when caught, separates Members from mere staff. She was cool and aloof from that point on, and I think it irritated her that I called her Jane.

However, things got much worse when Henry asked me to stay on and work for the new Republican majority. Jane was actively hostile to me whenever I saw her and seemed to take pleasure in ignoring me. The last straw came when I was walking through the Rayburn Building, and I saw her with two of her staff. I said "Hello, Jane" and she decided to introduce me to them. She said, "This is a *former* friend, Dan Freeman". I was furious but did not make a scene. Later that day on the floor, our paths crossed and told her in no uncertain terms that referring to me that way was insulting, and she should never do that to me again. She said she was only kidding, and I told her it was *not* funny. That was the last time I ever spoke to her.

Back to Alcee and the Intelligence Committee. I was walking from the Capitol to the Rayburn Building one day, through the underground tunnel. At the Rayburn end of the tunnel, I saw Alcee having a rather intense discussion with someone holding a tape recorder who I assumed was a reporter. I waved, and Alcee said to the reporter, "You see that guy over there", pointing to me. "He knows more about my impeachment than four hundred and thirty-five Members of Congress. Isn't that right, Dan?" he bellowed. I could not resist, and replied, "No, it is *five hundred* and thirty-five Members of Congress", thereby including the Senate. He laughed, but I am not sure the reporter got the nuance.

✦✦✦✦✦✦✦✦✦

President William Jefferson Clinton

There was a good bit of newspaper chatter about the possibility of impeaching President Clinton beginning at least a year before any formal action in Congress took place. It had always been my practice to avoid speculating about what Congress would do. Things could change in a heartbeat, and it did not do me any good to be the source of any educated (or uneducated) guessing. That did not stop everyone, and it did not stop people from asking.

The press, ever-mindful of needing to feed the 24-hour news beast, were always looking for some way to gin up a story. I would not take calls from the press and would refer them to Sam Stratman, the Chairman's press secretary. Sam and I continued to have a love/hate relationship.

If he received a press call that required specific procedural answers, he would occasionally patch me in for a 3-way conference call. He would, when introducing me to the reporter, preface the conversation by saying, "This is Dan Freeman, the Committee Parliamentarian. He hates the press". It was kind of irritating, but it kept them at bay a bit.

People who work in television cannot imagine anyone not wanting to be on. I got a call from someone at a national TV network early in 1998 asking me to appear on its national Sunday morning political talk show. He said he had heard I was the most experienced House staffer in impeachment matters, (I had worked on three). They were planning to do a segment on the topic and wanted to have someone knowledgeable to talk about the process. My response was abrupt and simple. I just said, "No." The producer was astounded and could not believe I would decline. "No, seriously? This is a chance for you to be on *national television*. Everyone will see you". Since I realized he was not getting it, I said, "Oh, 'national television,'" then paused for effect, "Then the answer is still No."

He pushed harder, implying that only a fool would refuse such an offer. Once again, the devil in me took over. I explained to him I had appeared on television before. When I was in elementary school, I was on the "Hoppity Skippity" show, a popular local children's show at the time. I had been picked to be Royal Crown King, (an honor named for the show's sponsor Royal Crown Cola). I said it could not get any better than that, so I was going to decline his offer. I am sure he did not understand.

✦ ✦ ✦ ✦ ✦ ✦ ✦ ✦

When we started gearing up to conduct a formal impeachment inquiry later that year, it became incredibly difficult for me. I found there to be three types of people on the staff: the rabid red-meat Clinton haters, the rabid red-meat Clinton defenders, and those who thought impeachment of a President was momentous, and it was something which we needed to take seriously and do carefully. I found I was suspect in both of the first two camps. The anti-Clinton staff always considered me to be suspect because I had worked for "them" (the Democrats). Whenever I would preach precision and deliberate compliance with the House rules, I was castigated for not being "with the program". That meant being on board a railroad train which Newt Gingrich was driving. He was determined to get the President. However, whenever I would assist the Republican majority in finding the proper and responsible way to do something, the pro-Clinton folks considered me to be a traitor.

There were some people, both Members and staff, who considered me to be an experienced, steady hand and who welcomed my participation. Those who viewed me positively referred to me as an "institutionalist"; someone who cared about and respected the House as an institution. They thought of me as an honest broker who took my job seriously. Many of them would seek me out privately to get my opinion of how things needed to be done and where the potential land mines were. Chief among those on the staff was an earnest young man who was new to the committee in 1995. Dan Bryant, who I have mentioned previously, was on the Crime Subcommittee staff and had been instrumental in getting some of the important crime legislation passed. He was, and is, a sober and careful lawyer. Dan has a seriousness of purpose in everything he does. I felt comfortable working with him, knowing he wanted to understand the process, and my observations about possible parliamentary difficulties were to be taken seriously.

Others on the staff who were the Clinton haters took those observations as obstructionist and evidence that I was not sufficiently in support of the main goal, which was to get the President. Some of the pro-Clinton staff were also wary of me. Any parliamentary rulings I made or advice I gave were in the context of a palpably hostile atmosphere.

One example of this was the criticism to which I was subjected after the committee voted to conduct the impeachment inquiry at the first formal meeting on impeachment. This was subsequently called the "vote count error" photograph episode, which came about because of a picture that appeared in the Washington Post the next day.

During the committee meeting to consider a resolution to begin a formal impeachment inquiry, there was a Democratic motion to limit the length and scope of the investigation. After debate on the motion and a request for a recorded vote, the clerk was directed by the Chairman to call the roll. To no one's surprise, it was a party-line vote, and all of the Republicans voted "nay", and all the Democrats voted "aye". As usual, at the end of the roll call, the Chairman said, "The clerk will report". The young man who was the clerk that day incorrectly reported the vote by transposing the outcome as follows: "Mr. Chairman, there are 21 ayes and 16 nays". (It was actually 16 ayes, the Democrats, and 21 nays, the Republicans) The Chairman announced the motion was not agreed to, which was the correct result, but the announced tally did not reflect the actual votes.

Several Members immediately pointed out to the Chairman that the clerk had incorrectly reported the vote; it was 21 nays and 16 ayes; the **opposite** of what was announced. The Chairman was asked to have the clerk re-report the vote. The clerk then again announced the vote, but in exactly the same way, incorrectly *again*! He clerk was thoroughly embarrassed and put his hands to his face, and several Democrats said, "That's OK, we accept". On the third attempt, he got it right; the motion was not agreed to.

Chairman Hyde, a man with an impish sense of humor, then said to the clerk, "See me after class". The room exploded with laughter from both Democrats and Republicans. The poor young man put his head down onto the table wholly mortified. It was at that point the Chairman gave the clerk the OK sign with his hand and cracked a big smile. I thought it was funny and was smiling as well. That is the moment a photograph was taken, which was printed in the Washington Post the next day. The caption which said the Chairman was "signifying his satisfaction with the tally on the vote defeating a Democratic substitute to the committee resolution" was a bit misleading. He and I were merely showing our amusement at Henry's humor.

I was roundly criticized for being caught on camera smiling at the result; the Democrats had lost the vote, which came as no surprise. Several people who became aware of the rash of criticism directed at me said everyone thought it was an amusing situation, they felt for the clerk, and my smiling in the photograph was not something improper that reflected some anti-Clinton bias. I was tempted to ask those kind people to talk to those who criticized me, but I knew I needed to put on my psychological suit of armor for the duration.

The investigation continued for a long time. It seemed like we were in a state of siege. People were working late, tempers were short, and the atmosphere around the offices was palpably tense. I had disagreements with several staffers about questions of procedure, and about the impeachment process. No one working on it had ever done an impeachment before, but my experience did not always count for much except with Henry and Tom, who were the two most important players as far as I was concerned.

One of the Republican staffers who was partially responsible for press liaison got angry at me for pointing out the committee had decided to keep some matters which had been received in executive session private; they were not to be released to the press or the public. In brushing my observation aside, he told me in an angry tone that he would "speak to me about that later". His meaning was clear; he would talk to the press about whatever he wanted, and my admonition about executive session material was not well received by him. He intended to "straighten me out". My insistence on complying with the secrecy vote would be dealt with by him sternly. To him, I was an obstructionist and should stop being picky about enforcing the rules. This was clearly getting to be a two-front clash; the committee deliberations, some of which were done in secret, and the public relations battle in the press. My view was we were bound by the rules relating to matters discussed in executive session. Others thought they could pick and choose what to talk with the press about. Whatever helped the mission was OK, the end justified the means; get the President, no matter what.

One of the pro-Clinton staffers, Bob, got very angry at me, and he said the investigation was just a cooked-up plot to crucify the President. In that "discussion", I was accused of being blind to reality. He admitted the President had lied before the grand jury, but it was "just about sex", and that was not a valid reason to impeach him. Dan Bryant was there observing Bob trying to take me down. In the kindest and most pointed and supportive way, Dan asked, "Weren't you the lead counsel on an impeachment and removal of a Federal Judge who was convicted and imprisoned for lying to the grand jury?" I said yes, and was grateful to Dan. (I thanked him later privately). I told Bob that as I read 18 USC §1001, it is a crime to make any materially false statement under oath, and there was nothing in there which said, "except for statements about sex". Bob was not mollified, and I just walked away.

Interestingly, one of the Members who treated me with the most respect and kindness was Rob Wexler. He was the most vociferous defender of the President and could regularly be seen on TV and heard on the radio in a booming voice attacking the entire impeachment "fiasco". He and I continued to have a good relationship during the impeachment and for several years after.

Most of the Members viewed me as someone who was doing my job. While the whole process engendered a lot of hostility and hard feelings, I tried to stay out of that. Tom realized how difficult it was for me and said to me one day, "You just continue to do your job in the professional manner you always have and try to ignore any grief you get". I took some comfort in that.

The investigation into the Clinton land deal known as Whitewater grew to include matters relating to the White House Travel Office, and Paula Jones' allegations of sexual harassment by the President when he was Governor of Arkansas. After a four-year investigation, the Independent Counsel, Ken Starr, had the 445-page report ready to be delivered to the House on September 9, 1998.

The report was supposed to be kept confidential unless and until the House voted to release it to the public. The committee had prepared secure facilities to keep it under wraps in the Ford House Office Building several blocks from the Capitol. On the day it was going to be delivered, I was in a meeting in a conference room behind my office which had a television on. As I understood it, the Independent Counsel had informed the Speaker he was prepared to submit his report.

I was disgusted with the manner in which it was delivered. As we were sitting in the conference room, the television coverage switched to a live shot of the East Front of the Capitol. The vehicles from the Independent Counsel's office drove up and were met by two Capitol Police SUVs. The officers then unloaded the boxes from the Independent Counsel's vehicles into their SUVs for transfer to the Ford Building. I was appalled that the transfer was staged in such a dramatic fashion, clearly done solely for the television cameras. I made the mistake of saying something about it. "You know, I could have told the Independent Counsel's office where the Ford Building is". That comment was not well-received. I later learned Speaker Gingrich was responsible for that bit of stagecraft.

✦✦✦✦✦✦✦✦✦

On November 19, 1998, the Independent Counsel, Kenneth Starr testified before the Committee. He alleged that President Clinton engaged in "an unlawful attempt to thwart the judicial process". The room was jam-packed, the TV lights were on, and there was electricity in the air.

As noted previously, I had "minimum high regard" (as Mr. Rodino used to say about people he disliked) for the press. I avoided them like the plague and let Sam Stratman, the Chairman's press secretary deal with them. Members could engage with them however they wished. If asked by a Member about what they could say to the press, I simply advised them not to talk about matters which had come up in executive session. That question did not come up often since lots of Members and staff were taking advantage of the occasion to be "important" and were talking to the press both on and off the record. It was a feeding frenzy.

If I ever got questions from the press when I was in the committee room, I would tell them to talk with Sam. The same was true of phone calls. Although the front office would try to screen my calls, it was so busy some calls inevitably got through to me.

My job as Counsel and Parliamentarian (I was both) required me to sit directly behind the Chairman on his right. I did so to quietly be able to tell him anything he needed to know about the rules, who was to get recognized, and in what order or to discuss any legal or constitutional issues.

The committee room was full, and every member of the committee staff was in the room. It was an historic occasion. During Starr's testimony, around 11 am, the bells rang for a roll call vote in the House. The Chairman announced a recess, and all of the Members left to go to the floor. Most of the staff went to other places in the committee complex. I had been up all night and was exhausted. The glare of the television lights did not help matters.

I was too tired to move, so I just sat there. An eager young man came up to me and said: "Mr. Freeman, I am from ABC news". He spoke with an air of importance, which simply did not resonate with me. I sighed and replied: "Talk to the press secretary". I did not say it in a friendly tone. He obviously did not know me and my bias. He persevered, "No, I don't need to talk with Sam. This is just a purely logistical matter". I responded rather rudely, "What part of 'Talk to the press secretary' did you not understand?" Unfazed, he persisted: "This is only about logistics". He had worn me down, and with exasperation and a sigh, I said, "Okay, what is it?"

Every profession has its jargon. Being someone who stayed away from the press, I did not understand when he said, "We are having a problem with our shot from camera 5", as though any idiot would immediately comprehend his problem. "Camera 5?" I replied, not having a clue. He rolled his eyes at my incredible ignorance. Undaunted, he told me that was the small lipstick camera pinned between the curtains behind the Chairman, which provided a direct shot of the witness, Ken Starr. "The problem is, when we go to camera 5, we are getting a lot of glare off your bald head. We would like you to move away from the Chairman and out of the range of that camera". He said it with a nonchalance which belied his understanding of the significance and outrageousness of what he was asking. My response was as follows: "Let me see if I have this straight. You want the Chairman's chief parliamentary and constitutional law advisor to move to a position where he cannot advise him on those matters so you can cover the hearing the way you feel is most visibly advantageous to you. Is that correct?" He nodded eagerly, pleased I understood. I will not repeat what I said to him.

✦ ✦ ✦ ✦ ✦ ✦ ✦ ✦

Although the run-up to the House vote was intense, some of the Members made it a lot more bearable. The one I remember especially well was Jim Rogan. Jim is a political junkie. By the time he had gotten to Congress, he had had a full political life. He started collecting political memorabilia as a kid. Jim often went to radio and television stations in the San Francisco Bay area where he grew up to meet important political, sports, and entertainment figures of the day. He subsequently wrote a book about this passion entitled "And Then I Met... Stories of Growing Up, Meeting Famous People, and Annoying the Hell Out of Them". Although the book was not published until after he left Congress, I got a large dose of those tales when he would regale us with them during some of the late nights we put in. Spending time with him was always a joy. He was not the type of Member who was impressed with his own importance, and he was always quick with a kind word.

He was another Member who Henry sent my way. Based on Henry's comments about my being "an experienced man of the House", Jim decided getting to know me could be helpful. We had regular talks about the House, Congressional procedure, and some of the characters I had met. While he had been a Member of the California State Assembly (being elected Majority Leader in his freshman term), unlike some other Members with state legislative experience, he did not come to Congress as a pompous know-it-all. He was always open to suggestions, observations and assistance.

He was a hard-working Member who took his role in the Clinton impeachment process seriously. He was, however, able to maintain his delightful sense of humor. He subsequently wrote a book about the experience, "Catching Our Flag: Behind the Scenes of a Presidential Impeachment". He told me he was concerned the white-hot atmosphere surrounding the impeachment and the salacious sexual content of the accusations, would lead to a distorted history of the proceedings. He decided to keep detailed notes of everything that happened as well as his perceptions about them. He chronicled every meeting and significant event. He is quoted as saying he wanted a complete and accurate historical chronicle of both the meetings, many of which were held in public and the behind-the-scenes machinations, to ensure an accurate account was written.

Jim is a combination of a serious legislator, historian, raconteur and rapscallion. His marvelous sense of humor lightened the mood on many occasions when things were getting grim. He always had an interesting story to tell. Sometimes they were even appropriate!

As Henry would say, he was a "good soldier". He dug in and did the hard work necessary to make sure the House Managers were taken seriously and represented the House well. His role as a Manager in the Senate impeachment trial almost certainly cost him his Congressional seat, and later a Federal Judgeship. He was defeated in what was then the most expensive House race in history.

I have kept in touch with him since he left Congress. He was named to be the Undersecretary of Commerce for Intellectual Property, becoming the Director of the U. S. Patent and Trademark Office. President Bush nominated him to a vacancy on the U.S District Court in California. He received strong bipartisan support, including a high rating from the American Bar Association, and California Senator Diane Feinstein's judicial nominee review committee. Unfortunately, the Senate Judiciary Committee did not even give his nomination a hearing, since California Senator Barbara Boxer put a hold on the nomination because of his role in the impeachment.

The reporters and photographers were constantly around. You could not move anywhere outside our offices without being hounded. I did my level best to avoid them. However, when we were in open session in the Committee room, and I was sitting behind Henry, photos of him often included me. There was nothing I could do about it.

When the Committee was meeting in October to consider the initiation of the formal inquiry, Howard Coble came over to ask Henry something. As he was speaking to Henry, Jim Sensenbrenner leaned back to listen in. I was in the middle. That was the moment a photographer chose to take the picture, which was subsequently called "The Mount Rushmore" photo. It was an interesting image, but what made it memorable was the Associated Press made it available to newspapers worldwide. It was printed in the New York Times, the International Herald Tribune, the Washington Post, and the Honolulu Star-Bulletin, among others. The amusing thing was how many different titles I was assigned by the various newspapers. I was referred to as, depending on which paper you looked at as unnamed staff, Rep. Dan Freeman, Dan Freeman, majority Parliamentarian, and even Jon Dudas (one of the other lawyers on the staff).

Near the end of the year, I got very sick and was not well enough to return to work until after the Senate trial. I had mixed feelings about missing that historic event, but I was glad to be on the mend and not literally in the glare of the events. I kept my own counsel about the conduct of the impeachment and what I would have done had I been in charge. No one asked me, and no one elected me.

Four Impeachments

With Chairman Bob Kastenmeier during the Subcommittee hearings on the
Claiborne Impeachment

*To Dan Freeman—Ever the power behind the Chairman's chair on the historic
occasion of judicial impeachment, With fond appreciation.*

Hastings Impeachment House Managers and staff

(Left to Right—Rep. Mike Synar, Ray Smietanka, Associate Counsel, Rep. Hamilton Fish, Peter Levinson, Counsel, Chairman Jack Brooks, Bill Jones, General Counsel, Dan Freeman Counsel and Parliamentarian, Rep. George Gekas, and Rep. John Bryant)

To Dan Freeman with best wishes, Jack Brooks

With Lead Manager John Conyers during the Senate Trial on the Hastings Impeachment (CSPAN)

(Cong. John Bryant— with Alan Baron and me keeping track of the vote)
Senate Chamber during the vote on the Hastings Impeachment (CSPAN)
(Note: Only one House Manager present)

With Lead Manager Don Edwards in the Senate Trial on the Walter Nixon
Impeachment (CSPAN)

With Chairman Hyde in the House during debate on Clinton Impeachment Inquiry (CSPAN)

With Chairman Hyde after the vote count error correction during Judiciary Committee Inquiry on President Clinton Impeachment (Rich Lipski Washington Post 1998)

Clinton Impeachment Inquiry--Ken Starr Testimony— the infamous Camera 5 image (CSPAN)

XVI. "Small World" #2—Double "Small World"

In 1991 Stephen Rayner, a prominent London solicitor (as they are called in England), was at a conference in Dublin about business in the European Union. Stephen was a family friend of Mimi's and did some legal work for the family concerning the Legat School. He was the only lawyer Mimi had met before me.

At the time, I was Counsel and Parliamentarian to the House Judiciary Committee. I had worked on impeachment inquiries and Senate trials of three Federal Judges, all of whom were impeached, convicted and removed from office. At the conference in Dublin, Rayner met a lawyer from New York, Steven Harvis. For some strange reason, they got to talking about the American impeachment process. Steve Harvis was a lawyer I worked with in the New York office of a law firm in 1972. According to Rayner, he told Harvis, "If there is to be another American impeachment, I know the man who will draw the papers". [I expect "draw the papers" is very English.] Steve asked who that would be, and Mr. Rayner told him it would be, "One Daniel Freeman". Steve replied, "Would that be Daniel Freeman married to Mimi Legat?" Wow, it really is a small world. But wait, that was just part one of the story.

The next time we were in London, Mimi and I had lunch with Stephen, and he regaled us with the story. I was astonished and told him I would be in New York soon and was going to have lunch with Steve Harvis. Rayner told me his son was living in New York with a woman named Alicia Glen. He said Alicia's mother was "a Federal Judge". I started to laugh as I corrected him, saying, "Her mother is Kristen Booth Glen, and she is not a Federal Judge, she is a New York State trial judge, and I know her well". "Small world" indeed!

XVII. Chairman Hyde And the International Relations Committee

In December, after the 2000 elections, Henry was going to be term-limited out of his chairmanship of the Judiciary Committee. Normally the chairmanships of the various committees in the House are decided very soon after the November elections. In this case, there were a lot of pieces to the puzzle of who would chair which committees, and things were murky for a long time. Henry considered asking for a waiver of the six-year term limit rule in order to continue as Chairman of the Judiciary Committee. Jim Sensenbrenner was next in line to take that position, and he was not interested in Henry getting a waiver. Henry was next to become Chairman of the International Relations Committee, but Ben Gilman, who was term-limited as chairman of that committee, was also seeking a waiver so that he could continue. There was a lot of uncertainty, and rumors were flying. This cascaded down to the committee staffs since none of us knew whether we would have jobs. Going to International Relations was something that many staffers who were subject matter experts on Judiciary Committee issues did not think was in the cards.

One afternoon in early December, not knowing what lay ahead for me, I was driving home when the phone rang in my car. At the time, I had a cell phone hardwired into the car but never used it while I was driving. Very few people had that number, so I pulled over to take the call. It was Henry calling to tell me that he had been named Chairman of the International Relations Committee and asking me to join him. I was thrilled and accepted immediately. It meant that I could continue working with Henry and Tom Mooney. That was something delightful to look forward to.

Tom had to go through the agonizing process of assessing Ben Gilman's International Relations Committee staff to determine who was going to be kept on, and who was going to be let go. I did not envy Tom that task, and fortunately, I did not have to participate in any of those discussions.

Once the transition was completed, and the staffing questions had been re-solved, we settled into a nice groove. Things were not as high pressured as they were on the Judiciary Committee, and we did not anticipate the kind of frenetic activity we had endured there. One day when we were on the floor, Henry told me, "Dan, this is going to be a pleasure, and we are not going to have any more of those late nights". Those words would turn out not to be accurate.

✦✦✦✦✦✦✦✦✦

Early in the new Congress, I attended a meeting with Henry, Tom Mooney, and three of the subject matter experts from the Gilman staff who had been retained. I knew all of these people, but not well. I knew Kristen Gilley from her days working as a legislative assistant for Congressman Bill McCollum, who had been a Member of the Judiciary Committee. Kristen is one of the best people I ever had the pleasure of working with.

Her portfolio focused on the State Department. She was an inspiration be-cause she was interested in doing good work for the American people. She is smart as a whip and has solid common sense. She is also one of the kindest and warmest people I know. I was pleased she was on the staff. I knew she and I would not have any problems working for whatever the Hyde agenda was. This was not true of some of the other senior staff. I sensed animosity emanating from at least a couple of them. It made it more difficult because Ben Gilman was still on the committee. They were used to doing things Mr. Gilman's way. Hyde had a different manner. Gilman wanted to speak on every bill and every issue at each full committee meeting. Henry felt the only people who needed to make opening remarks, especially for a hearing, were the Chairman and Rank-ing Minority Member and the subcommittee chair and ranking Member. There was overt anti-lawyer animosity as well. I heard "You lawyers..." as a criticism way too often. I never got that from Kristen, and she was glad to have lawyers around. She was always willing to listen, unlike some of her colleagues.

As we walked into Henry's office that day, I greeted him as I always did in an informal situation by saying, "Bonjour Henri" to which he replied, "Bonjour monsieur". I could see the three staffers looking rather quizzically.

As the five of us sat down, Henry said, "Dan, did I ever tell you the story about...?" and he proceeded to tell me a very funny yarn. It was hilarious. I could see the new folks being a little surprised. They were there to talk to the new boss about a serious policy issue. "What the hell is going on?" was written over their faces. I then violated the rules as far as Member–staff relations were concerned; I began to tell Henry a joke. The two men were aghast. Even Kris-ten, who knew me and my sense of humor, was bemused. Staff is not supposed to tell Members jokes; Members tell the jokes, and staff dutifully laughs.

After I delivered the punch line, which Henry enjoyed, Tom Mooney decided to break up the party saying, "If you two are finished fooling around, let's get to work". At that point, we started talking about the subject of the meeting, which was an interesting foreign affairs/constitutional question. The other three staffers made some observations about the issues. Tom and I basically just listened. Henry assessed the discussion and then said, "This is what I am going to recommend…" and he outlined his position. His discussion was well-thought-out, clear, and persuasive. He then asked, "Am I wrong?" This is something he would often do. The three others sat there, not saying anything. I thought he wanted our candid opinions, so I spoke up and said, "Yes, I think you are, and here is why…" I made the argument for the other side of the issue. The three sat there, horrified that I would contradict the Chairman.

With that, the meeting adjourned, and we five staffers got up to leave. Henry said, "Dan, can I see you for a minute". As the three holdovers and Tom left the office, they were certain I was going to get a reprimand or even get fired. You do not tell a joke to a Member, and you certainly do not tell them they are wrong. They had never seen a mere staffer take on a Member so boldly. When the door closed, and it was just Henry and me, he smiled and said, "Thank you. That is why I pay you the big bucks. I appreciate your challenging my thinking".

✦✦✦✦✦✦✦✦✦

When we got over to the International Relations Committee, Tom and I talked about how different things were going to be and that Henry would be relying heavily on me as far as getting legislation done. Tom said there were a lot of sensitive foreign policy issues on the horizon, which were not going to be dealt with legislatively. However, I was to be principally responsible for any legislative matters that came up. My job was to, as Tom phrased it, "Commit legislation". He said that he and the Chairman had discussed it, and they both felt that I would do what Henry would do 95 percent of the time. Henry wanted to have the luxury of not having to worry about the nuts and bolts of day-to-day legislation. Tom said having the comfort of knowing almost everything was going to be done as Henry wished was worth his not controlling the other 5%. This gave me a tremendous vote of confidence and a lot of leeway to do what I thought was best. That boiled down to making sure that Committee legislation was handled appropriately on the floor, keeping in mind that Henry would always be kept informed and manage floor debate on any significant legislation.

With that charge, I was able to enlist Members to manage bills on the floor in any way which got the Committee's business taken care of. I established a comfortable working relationship with Ileana Ros-Lehtinen, who was a firecracker Member from South Florida. She was the first Cuban-American, and first Latina elected to Congress. She was also more fun than a barrel of monkeys. I came to rely on her as my go-to Member whenever Hyde did not want to, or was unavailable to, manage legislation on the floor.

Ileana's Chief of Staff, Yleem Poblete, had been with her from the beginning of her service in Congress. Yleem could be difficult to deal with, and she was always ready to be offended on Ms. Ros-Lehtinen's behalf. I managed to scale that mountain of mistrust to the point where Yleem was comfortable enough with me to allow me to work with Ileana without her being present. That was rather nice, and it made getting things done for the committee much easier.

Frequently when I would recruit Ileana to manage committee legislation on the floor, we would meet in the Chamber to go over the parliamentary motions and the subject matter of the various bills. She would begin those briefings with, "Okay, Dan, tell me two jokes; one that I can tell in front of constituents and one that I can't". She was always a pushover for a good joke, and we usually had a lot of fun. She always referred to me as "Lieutenant Dan" with a twang in her voice straight out of Forest Gump.

I had become well-schooled at knowing what individual Members needed. With Ileana, I knew this was Diet Cherry Coke and hand cream. We could not take drinks onto the floor, but I provided her beverage of choice whenever possible. When she was managing legislation, I would always go to the Republican cloakroom to get her some hand cream. There was a marvelous young woman who worked there, Christina Jenckes. She kept a large bottle of hand cream on her desk. I would get a paper towel and squirt out a couple of inches of cream and have it ready when Ileana arrived. She would goo up her hands and then be ready to rock. Ileana came to rely on the hand cream being there. Knowing the Members' predilections helps.

Christina was dedicated and hard-working. She was a pleasure to work with, and I relied on her to make sure I knew what was happening on the floor. Members do not like to waste time waiting, and if you get a Member to agree to manage a bill, you need to have them walk in and be ready to go with less than two minutes to wait. Judging how long things ahead of your bill will take is difficult. Christina was exceptional at it. She and I discussed her career options frequently. I encouraged her to take advantage of the opportunity to go to England for a special Master's program in foreign policy. She had a brilliant experience there and partially based on that. Upon her return, she applied for a job with the International Relations Committee. By that time, Ileana had become the Chair, and I put in a good word for her. She did a terrific job there. She was one of my favorite people on the Hill.

✦✦✦✦✦✦✦✦✦

This is probably a good place to explain what the House and Senate cloak-rooms are. Although you might think it is where Members hang up their coats, the cloakrooms are simple non-majestic spaces adjacent to the respective Chambers, one for each party. They have a multitude of telephone booths, a bare-bones snack bar, and a few sofas which Members use to read the newspapers or take a nap. There are a couple of staffers in each whose job it is to make sure they have up-to-the-minute information about what legislation is being considered and when votes are expected. Members always want to know when the last vote of the day will be, so they can go off the Hill and "dial for dollars" (raise campaign money) or get to the airport, which is referred to as "smelling jet fumes". A lot of work gets done in the cloakrooms when Members get to interact face-to-face.

✦✦✦✦✦✦✦✦✦

When major legislation was called up, the floor manager always had a staff person who was responsible for keeping track of a list of Members who had requested time to speak on the bill, and how much time each one would get. I was frequently that staffer. One day Ileana was managing a bill dealing with Iraq, which was very important, and there were a lot of requests for time. However, since we only had one hour of debate, and the majority only controlled 30 minutes of that, time was at a premium. Most Members knew that the power behind the throne rested with the staffer who had the list.

A Member was in the well speaking on the bill, and Ileana was on her feet at the floor manager's spot waiting to yield time to the next Member. Yleem was standing facing her. They were talking to each other while I was sitting one seat over with the list of requests for time. A Member, who I did not know, came rushing over and asked in a rather belligerent and self-important tone of voice, "When I am going to speak?" He said that his staff had reserved five minutes for him. I told him that I had instructed our staff the time was limited, that no one would be given five minutes, and I was not sure that he would get recognized to speak at all. He got angry and said, "Where am I on the list?" I made a show of flipping the pages on the pad I had in front of me with the Members' requests for time. I informed him that it was likely that he would not get recognized since we were running out of time. He got angrier and repeated that his staff had reserved time for him. I pointed to two members of the Leadership and at least five members of the International Relations Committee who were sitting on the floor patiently waiting to be recognized. I said that those Members had priority over him. That made him furious, and he said to me, "This is fucked up!" In my most subservient and obsequious voice, I said, "Yes, it may be". He replied that it was a good thing we were, "out here in public, or there might be some fisticuffs". I looked him straight in the eye and stated, "Congressman, threatening to commit physical violence on a man who possesses a black belt and who might be able to help you is not a good idea".

Off to my right, I noticed Yleem and Ileana face-to-face intensely engaged in their conversation. They were clearly hiding in plain sight, and I heard Ileana say *sotto voce*, "Dan's got this, don't move". They were hanging me out to dry! Ignoring them, I told the disgruntled Member I would be happy to take his prepared remarks and submit them for the Congressional Record. He angrily tossed them at me, and I could not resist tweaking him a little bit more. I noticed that he had not signed them. I informed him that the House Rules require Members to sign their remarks. He grumpily signed them, tossed them at me again, and stormed off.

After he left, Ileana turned to me and said, "Dan, that was stupendous!" I replied sarcastically, "I appreciate your having my back. That is about all you had!" The three of us laughed and got back to business. Ileana leaned over and said, "Lieutenant Dan, I did not know you had a black belt". With a smile on my face, I replied, "Oh, yeah, I do. Here it is", pointing to the black leather belt I was wearing.

Later that afternoon, after I had returned to the office, I got a call from Tom Mooney. I could tell he was using a speakerphone. He said, "Dan, I understand you had a bit of trouble on the floor today. Something about a floor fight". I explained what happened and told him it was no big deal. I had handled the situation. Henry and Tom had always made sure I felt complete job security, and no complaint from a Member was going to threaten that. Tom asked who the Member was, and I said it did not matter, I had taken care of it. At this point in his career, Henry was over 80 years old and had serious mobility problems. I then heard Henry's voice (they were obviously calling from Tom's car). He said, "Dan, **I** want to know who it was because **I** want to take **him** outside for some fisticuffs". Good old Henry.

✦ ✦ ✦ ✦ ✦ ✦ ✦ ✦

Another situation occurred where having Henry's and Tom's complete confidence was an advantage. We had gone to conference on an authorization bill for the State Department with the Senate Foreign Relations Committee, chaired by Senator Joe Biden. One of the Democratic Members of the House who was on the conference committee had an amendment he wanted included in the final bill. He raised the issue at the formal meeting of the conferees. Both Hyde and Biden agreed to it, and no one opposed its inclusion. As far as I knew, the Member's staff was going to make sure that it made its way into the final language.

The staff stayed up late to prepare all the necessary papers to enable us to go to the floor the next day. As we were nearing the end of the debate on the conference report, I became aware of an error; the failure to include the Member's amendment in the legislative language. I immediately started to prepare the necessary papers to correct the problem. Henry would have to get recognized by the Speaker to call up a correcting resolution directing the clerk to put the inadvertently omitted language into the final version. This would have to be done through a unanimous consent request. While that request and the text were being prepared, I saw the Member come storming across the floor in high dudgeon. There were several staff people there, but I took a step forward because I was the designated javelin catcher. The Member said, "You all screwed me!" I did not flinch and responded, "Congressman, nobody screwed you, but the staff made a mistake". (I did *not* tell him that it was *his staff* who had made the mistake.) I told him Chairman Hyde was going to correct the error, but he would need unanimous consent to do so. Unanimous consent requests are frequently used in wrapping up consideration of legislation. If they have been cleared by both Republicans and Democrats, they usually go through easily. What I did not want was for someone on the other side of the aisle to either object or reserve the right to object to inquire about the purpose of the request. I wanted to make it happen as quickly as possible and under the radar. I told the Congressman that it was going to be taken care of. I asked him to go back to the Democratic side, and if anybody was going to object to Henry's unanimous consent request that he should "tackle him immediately". That took the air out of the possible problem, and the Member smiled at me and went back to the other side. He did come over after the bill passed to thank me and to apologize for having lost his temper. Not all Members would have apologized.

✛ ✛ ✛ ✛ ✛ ✛ ✛ ✛

With the situation in the Middle East heating up, and in the wake of the 9/11 attacks, the House was faced with the necessity of going through the formal process of authorizing the President's use of military force (AUMF). The bill sanctioned the use of United States Armed Forces against those responsible for the attacks on September 11, 2001, and any "associated forces." It granted the President the authority to use all "necessary and appropriate force" against those whom he determined "planned, authorized, committed or aided" the September 11th attacks, or who harbored those persons or groups.

The Joint Resolution was called up at about 6 pm, and the rule giving the resolution floor time provided for five hours of debate. I asked Henry a couple of hours later, "What happened to the concept of we were not going to be on the floor late at night"? He smiled and said it sure was less frequently than on Judiciary.

At that point, he asked me to "get someone else to drive", because he was going downstairs to get something to eat. What that meant was I needed to get Members of the Committee to take over managing the time on the resolution. It was not rocket science, but I needed to make sure I could find some willing victims to pitch in. All the floor manager has to do is to yield time to other Members. In these circumstances, I would pick people who knew and trusted me, and I would tell them who to recognize and for how much time. I would shuttle back and forth across the Chamber to talk with the staffer for the Democrats so that we could balance time. Frequently, one of us would burn off a bunch of time while the other staffer's Members were not around. I had a good working relationship with the people on Lantos' staff, so it usually worked out fairly smoothly. I would also notify the presiding officer of our plans, as well as the timekeeper and the Parliamentarian on duty. I racked up a lot of steps on my pedometer on those days.

With no votes scheduled and it being dinner time, I thought I might have problems finding someone to manage the time. I knew where Henry was going to be in case I needed him. Several Members were likely candidates, even though it was getting late. I usually corralled Members from the West Coast, because I was aware it was prime time in their districts, and they loved getting the airtime on CSPAN. Darrell Issa, a Member from California, was usually ready to help.

We went through a similar exercise in October of 2002 when enacting the Iraq Resolution (the Authorization for the Use of Military Force Against Iraq). Every Member feels compelled to speak, and many of them feel their passionate one- or two-minute oration will be the turning point.

We would occasionally get a question from a Member about why we did not just declare war. When Henry was asked, he would usually turn to me for the long explanation. I would tell the Member that under domestic law, a Congressional declaration of war automatically triggers possibly thousands of standby statutory authorities, conferring extraordinary powers on the President with respect to the military, foreign trade, transportation, communications, manufacturing, and alien enemies. It would also have the effect of nullifying many insurance policies which have an exclusion for "acts of war". The answer was simply: it was just as effective to authorize the President to use military force, and we did not open up a can of worms trying to figure out all of the possible domestic ramifications.

One evening when we were scheduled to take up a measure on the floor,

Henry asked me to get someone else to manage. It was about six o'clock again, but this time Tom had given me a heads up that Henry would be in his Capitol office because his beloved Chicago Cubs were on television, and he wanted to watch the game. I did my job and got another member of the Committee to manage the bill.

++++++++

Another example of what a fabulous boss Tom Mooney was occurred when Chairman Hyde was scheduled for a sit-down with his Senate counterpart, Joe Biden. I had spent a good bit of time with Biden when he was the Chairman of the Senate Judiciary Committee, and Tom knew that. He told Henry about it as well. At the beginning of the meeting, which was convened to discuss important matters of foreign policy, which were out of my scope of knowledge, Tom had Henry re-introduce me to Chairman Biden. Henry said, "Joe, this is Dan Freeman, our long-time Parliamentarian and can-do guy. He will always make sure we are procedurally perfect. You can rely on him". Biden turned to me, and possibly recalling the crime bill said, "Oh, I remember Dan. He has kept me on the straight and narrow many times, and I am glad to know he is still on board". I showed Senator Biden the pens I always carried, which he had used to sign the crime bill conference report, and that made him smile.

++++++++

Most of the Members I dealt with were usually pleasant, but not all. After leaving some of the more difficult ones on the Judiciary Committee, I had hopes of not having to work with obnoxious characters on the International Relations Committee. However, I was disabused of that notion rather quickly.

The International Relations Committee rule about order of recognition during committee meetings states that Members are recognized by seniority, based on who was in their seat *when the meeting started*. If a more senior Member came in 30 minutes later, he or she would not get recognized to speak until more junior Members who were in their seats at the beginning of the meeting, had spoken. This occasionally resulted in some petty behavior. At one point, a Member, known to be an unpleasant character, who had come in fairly late to the hearing, got angry *at me* because Henry did not recognize him immediately. Henry correctly passed him by a couple of times to recognize Members under what we called the "butt in the chair" rule. At one point, this Member got so upset he flung his microphone with such force it came off the connection and hit me in the stomach. "Goddammit, I am next", he yelled at me. As calmly as I could, I went over to him and pointedly returned his microphone and explained the rule to him. He did not apologize for hitting me with the microphone nor for his childish and petulant behavior.

I saw him later that day on the floor, and I asked to speak with him about the incident. I told him that although I was a staffer, I expected to be treated with respect and would not tolerate such mistreatment from him or anyone else. I pointed out that he was a repeat offender. He explained he had been abused as a child, and sometimes his anger came out. I said that was not an excuse for his cruelty others. "You could learn two lessons from being abused; the wrong one is that ill-treatment of others is a way to survive, but the more humane lesson is never to inflict abuse on anyone else because you are very aware of how much it hurts". I was clearly out on a limb and probably out of line, but I did not regret it.

Some staffers tried to manipulate the "butt in the chair" rule on behalf of their Members. Yleem tried it on several occasions, telling me Ms. Ros-Lehtinen was "in her chair" when the gavel went down. As evidence of that, she would say, "Her materials are there", or her ubiquitous Coke can was there. I knew they had been placed there by Yleem. That ploy did not work; since one of the committee staffers, Jean Marter, was responsible for giving me a roll call sheet with the list of Members who were present when the gavel went down. Jean was someone we referred to as "Jean, the machine". She was a dynamo, and always on top of everything. Thanks to Jean, I always had written proof of who was in their seat when the meeting started.

✦✦✦✦✦✦✦✦

One of the truly wonderful things about working for Henry Hyde was the way he treated the staff. He knew that a lot of us were interested in what the committee was doing and also that it was a thrill for us to meet national and international public figures.

One day I had some letters which I needed to get to him, and I knew he was over in his hideaway office in the Capitol. When I got there, I knocked on the door, and I heard him say, "Come in." As I opened the door and started to walk into the room, I saw that he had a guest. Much to my amazement, he was sitting there talking with the Dalai Lama. I apologized profusely for interrupting him and told him I would leave the letters on the table and turned to disappear, but Henry said, "Dan, please come in. I would like you to meet his Holiness". Well, I was not going to turn that invitation down! Henry introduced me and referred to me as his "wise counsel". The Dalai Lama smiled, shook my hand, and said it was an "utter pleasure" for him to meet me. "Every man needs to have a wise man to advise him", he said. I was more than a little stunned to have the Dalai Lama refer to me that way. I started to excuse myself and leave.

Henry then said, "Dan, please join us and have a seat". With that once in a lifetime invitation, I fully intended to sit there and say nothing and listen to these two brilliant men discuss *anything*! What a fantastic opening this was, and I was prepared to be the fly on the wall.

Much to my surprise, Henry asked me to explain to the Dalai Lama the bill we were about to debate concerning the authorization of use of force in Afghanistan. I thought this was more appropriately discussed by the Chairman and attempted to defer to him. However, he was perfectly happy to have me engaged in the conversation.

I asked the Dalai Lama about the conflicts he was perpetually involved in. I continued to enjoy a fascinating discussion with this internationally renowned figure. I had never met a Nobel Prize winner, and I was having a wonderful time soaking in as much knowledge as possible.

A few minutes later, there was a knock on the door. It was one of the House photographers who, unbeknownst to me, Henry had called. He had asked him to come and take a photo not of himself, but of *the Dalai Lama and me*. My litmus test for having my picture taken with somebody famous was I would only do so if they knew my name. So, thanks to Henry, I now have a memento of my meeting the world-famous practitioner of peace. This was typical of the way Henry treated me. I will always be grateful to him for his kindness.

✦✦✦✦✦✦✦✦

During an upcoming Congressional recess, Mimi and I were going to visit Bryce Canyon and several other National Parks. We would start our trip by flying to Las Vegas. Neither of us had been there. We decided to spend a couple of days and see the city. We had heard lots of stories about how incredibly strange and weird it was. Shelley Berkley was the Congresswoman from Las Vegas, and she was on the International Relations Committee. She and I were talking one morning before a hearing, and I told her I was going to be going to her district. She asked for my business card because she wanted to arrange for us to have a private tour of the over the top Bellagio Hotel and Casino.

I told Henry about my conversation with Ms. Berkley, and he asked me where we were staying in Vegas. I said we had reservations at the Stardust Hotel. Later that afternoon, Henry phoned me and said I should call Billy Sullivan, an old friend of his who was a big wig at the Stardust. Henry had contacted him and asked him to make sure we were treated well. I called Sullivan, and he told me to get in touch with him when we arrived. Sure enough, he was expecting us and made sure we had a lovely room overlooking the Strip. He bragged on Henry, and I concurred. It was such a typically Henry sort of thing to do.

Ms. Berkley's Chief of Staff had arranged for us to tour the Bellagio. Mimi and I were enthusiastic because we wanted to see the Chihuly glass sculpture in the ceiling of the main lobby. Behind-the-scenes tours are something we enjoy.

We arranged to meet in the lobby of the Bellagio with someone I thought was going to be a Berkley staffer. I was surprised to find out we were meeting with a lobbyist who represented the gambling industry in Washington. I was more surprised and frankly rather appalled to find out there were several other Congressional staffers who were on a junket joining us, or we were joining them. The organization had paid for their travel to Nevada, including stops in Reno and Las Vegas. They had managed to get them all seats for some of the most popular shows in both cities! Those tickets were very hard to get, I was told. Although I was irritated by the largess, the tour was not paid for by the lobbyist.

We went to see the hotel's main liquor-dispensing room. Every drink in every bar in the *entire hotel* is pumped through plastic tubes from this room and has exactly 1.5 ounces of liquor. We also saw the "high roller" suites, which came with a butler and his and hers marble bathrooms. I asked our host how much these suites cost per night. He said he did not know because they are always "comped" to high rollers who gamble vast sums. Next was the security room with all of the closed-circuit cameras which cover every inch of the casino. There was a private showing of the fountains in front of the hotel. They were set up to sync with the music chosen by someone in the group. While the tour was interesting, I was not comfortable about being with them. I declined the invitation to join in a private (and probably lavish) lunch in their executive dining room.

✦✦✦✦✦✦✦✦

The full committee had a hearing scheduled on a Tuesday morning, and I was looking forward to it. Doctor Henry Kissinger was the only witness. Many years ago, the practice among committees was that every Member would give an opening statement for five minutes, and then the witness would make his or her statement. After their testimony, witnesses would answer questions from Members. That practice changed, so witnesses would not have to sit for a couple of hours listening to boring and usually repetitive opening statements. I have always felt the purpose of a hearing was to hear from experts, not for the Members to give orations. The new practice was the Chairman, and the ranking minority member would each give an opening statement, and then the Chairman would recognize the witness for their testimony. The written version would be submitted for the record, followed by their oral statement. Then, they would take questions from the panel.

Doctor Kissinger was completing his opening statement when the bells rang, signifying a roll call vote on the House floor. Committees regularly meet when the House is in session, and the Leadership tries to arrange floor votes to accommodate them. Members always do everything they can to make sure they do not miss any roll call votes. Their opponent in the next election will always use missed votes against them with charges of "absenteeism". Congressman William Natcher was famous for never missing a vote. In his long Congressional career, he cast over 22,000 consecutive votes, never missing one!

Even though Doctor Kissinger was in the middle of his testimony, the Chairman recessed the committee so that all Members could go over to the floor to vote. I was in my usual seat behind the Chairman, and I asked if he would like me to escort Doctor Kissinger to his hideaway office adjacent to the committee hearing room during the break. Mr. Hyde said, "Thank you, Dan. That is a nice idea. Please do".

I went down to the witness table, introduced myself to Doctor Kissinger, and told him, "The Chairman would like me to escort you to his private office until the committee reconvenes". Kissinger did something which I have found many successful people do. He picked up my name immediately and used it. We chatted briefly on the way, and I thought to myself, "Wow, I am going to have 15 minutes alone with Henry Kissinger!" When we sat down, he asked me how long I had been with Chairman Hyde. I wanted to ask him about Nixon's last days, about prospects for peace in the Middle East, about the weapons of mass destruction fiasco, and a lot of other things. However, before I got a chance to ask him anything, the door (which I had purposely closed to ensure Dr. Kissinger's privacy) burst open, and Congressman Darrell Issa barged in.

Darrell Issa is a man who invented an automobile anti-theft device, and he was worth over $100 million. He also was someone who could not stop talking. On a Codel I was on, several Members and the staff were on the bus at Joint Base Andrews, which was taking us to our aircraft. Being an aviation aficionado, I was looking at all of the planes on the tarmac, and I noticed that one of them was an Airbus. I thought that was strange because I did not think that any of America's Armed Forces would be using planes built by Airbus, which is a European consortium. Our bus was stopped by an MP before we could get onto the tarmac. The soldier told the bus driver there was a "tarmac hold", and we would have to stay where we were until the "all clear" was given. In those situations where there is a VIP protectee around, security will never tell you who it is.

Issa was one of the Members on the trip, and he was getting irritated because we were being delayed. He went to the front of the bus and demanded to know why we were being held. The MP again said that we were in the "tarmac hold". Issa was getting hot. He informed the MP that he was a Member of the US House of Representatives, and he did not appreciate being delayed "for no apparent reason". The MP did not flinch, and we stayed where we were. (He did have a gun.) As Issa was walking back to his seat, he said, "You have no idea how important I think I am." He was not kidding.

Issa blew into the little office where Kissinger and I were, sat down, and began to lecture Henry Kissinger about what should be done in the Middle East. He did not ask questions. He did not give Kissinger a chance to answer; he just pontificated. Fortunately, one of our staff stuck her head into the office to give me the signal that the committee was about to reconvene. I told Doctor Kissinger that I would be happy to escort him back to the witness table. Issa ran out to get to his seat in the hearing room, and Doctor Kissinger looked at me and smiled. I am not sure, but I think there was an implied eye roll.

I walked Doctor Kissinger back into the committee room and became the point of a flying wedge to clear the way for him to get back to the witness table. Before he was able to sit down, three young women approached him squealing like fans at a rock concert, asking him if they could get their picture taken with him. Kissinger loved it! As they huddled around him, I glanced up and made eye contact with Chairman Hyde. He gave me a rolling finger gesture, meaning, "Let's get going". I leaned over and said, "Doctor Kissinger, if you are through playing with the girls, I think Chairman Hyde is ready to begin". He looked at me with a smile and said, "Dan, I am *not* through, but I *will* take my seat". I laughed and could not wait to go up and tell the Chairman what Kissinger had said.

John Negroponte is an experienced diplomat. He served at eight different Foreign Service posts in Asia (including the U.S. Embassy in Saigon), Europe, and Latin America. He had also held senior positions at the State Department and the White House. He was the United States Ambassador to Iraq for a short time before he was named to be the first United States Director of National Intelligence. He came to brief Members on June 9, 2004, in a closed Members-only meeting. Chairman Hyde presided, and those Members who were interested came and sat in chairs in what was normally the audience for committee hearings. I was sitting behind and between Mr. Hyde and Mr. Negroponte. Henry introduced me to him, and then Mr. Negroponte began to take questions. It became clear to me rather quickly the Ambassador did not know who many of them were. As I said to him later, "I am sure every Member who met with you during his or her 'crucial' meeting in Iraq feels you could not help but remember it". I decided to pitch in. I knew most of the people in the audience, and as a Member would raise his or her hand to ask a question, I would whisper to Negroponte the name and where they were sitting. For some reason, I chose a baseball diamond for my frame of reference. I would say, "Howard Berman, second base". The Ambassador knew that meant Berman was sitting about halfway back on the right side. I went on to point out Members in "deep left field" or "shortstop". Negroponte handled it so smoothly no one knew what I was doing. I expect many of the Members were tickled pink that he remembered their name.

When the meeting broke up, the Chairman and Ambassador Negroponte escaped out the side door. I walked behind them. As they were parting, the Ambassador said to Henry, "I am glad you had your baseball coach in there". Again, it was good staff work, but this time I got credit.

✦✦✦✦✦✦✦✦✦

My job entailed, among other things, preparing the scripts for the Chairman to use when the committee was considering legislation. On major bills, the process was for the Chairman to call up the bill "for purposes of amendment", declare it considered as read, and recognize himself for his opening statement. He would then go to Mr. Lantos, as the Ranking Democrat, for his opening statement, and after that, we would begin consideration of any possible amendments to the bill.

We would often have a list of bills on the agenda, which Henry referred to as "nothingburgers", which were headed for the floor on the non-controversial agenda. When we were considering a bunch of these, the scenario would be what came to be known as a "Freeman Special". The Chairman's script, which I prepared, would have him call all of the bills up *en bloc* by unanimous consent and order them favorably reported to the House. Since they had been cleared by both the minority and majority staffs of the full committee and the relevant subcommittees, the process regularly went efficiently and expeditiously.

One morning during a full committee meeting, the markup of the one significant bill had been completed, and the minor bills were ordered favorably reported *en bloc* via a "Freeman Special". The Chairman gaveled the meeting adjourned, and everyone started to leave. Members are usually quick to depart because they always have two or three other places to be. I noticed one of the junior Members was still sitting at his seat reading the newspaper. I said something about how unusual his not having to be somewhere else was. He then told me he was there to object to the consideration of one of the bills which already had been ordered favorably reported through the "Freeman Special". I had to tell him the committee had completed its business and had adjourned. Because there was so much noise in the room, and he was reading the paper, he did not notice the bill being called up or that the committee meeting was over. Oops.

✦✦✦✦✦✦✦✦✦

I would try to forge a connection with Members with whom I would have to interact, especially with notoriously difficult Members. To call Bill Thomas "difficult" would be a mild understatement. He was a terror, and his staffers and other Members frequently bore the brunt of his wrath. Somehow, I found out he was a car nut. I do not recall how I discovered that, but whenever I was around him, I would try to turn the conversation to cars. He was knowledgeable and always seemed willing to engage about the newest cars and, my special interest, the older classics.

One day I was over in the Capitol, showing our new Senior Counsel around and introducing him to people. I made it a point to take rookies to the floor before they had to be there to work on a bill. I would literally tell them where the bathrooms were, where they would sit, and what kinds of things they would be asked about. A dry run is always a good thing.

We were on the first floor getting off the elevator, and I saw Chairman Thomas (He was the Chairman of the Ways and Means Committee). I took my new colleague over and started to introduce him. Thomas abruptly interrupted the introduction and said, "Dan, what is the difference between the '63 Avanti and the '64?" I paused for dramatic effect, even though I knew the answer. "The '63 had round headlights, and the '64 had square ones", I responded. "Damn, you are good!" was his reply.

My cordial relationship with him enabled me to get away with murder. His staff was always terrified of him, as he was a demanding boss. They were amazed I was able to talk with him the way I did. One day, Henry and I were on the floor to call up a non-controversial bill. Chairman Thomas was managing a similar bill from his committee. Hyde asked me to go find out how long Thomas' bill was going to take since we were to follow him. I waited until someone was in the well of the House speaking and Thomas was not engaged. I went up and said, "Mr. Chairman, my Chairman would like to know how long *your* stupid bill is going to take so we can take up *our* stupid bill". I thought his staffer sitting next to him was going to have a stroke. Thomas was not fazed by my language and told me they only had one speaker left, and it would be five minutes. I thanked him and went to tell Henry. Bill Thomas, after both of us left the Hill, came up to AU to speak to my students.

✦✦✦✦✦✦✦✦

Henry and I were on the floor one morning in July of 2006. We had a couple of bills to take up under suspension of the rules. Prior to consideration of legislation, the practice in the House is that any Member could come to the floor and ask unanimous consent to speak for one minute about anything. This happened every day, and the subject matters ran from issues of national importance to commending a hometown sports team for winning a championship. The World Cup Soccer championship match was held the day before. The French had played the Italians. In a rather bizarre incident near the end of the match, France's best player, Zinedine Zidane, turned and head-butted the Italian midfielder in the chest. Zidane was ejected immediately, and Italy wound up winning the match on penalty kicks.

Before the House convened, people were gathered in the Chamber, and there was a lot of idle chatter. A Congressman from New York City whom I knew, Vito Fossella, a proud Italian-American, came up to me and asked for my help. He told me he was going to give a one-minute speech about the Italian soccer team and its magnificent victory in the World Cup. Vito said to me, "Dan, I need a good ending line. What have you got for me?" I literally did not have a minute to think about it. I said, "How about, 'The Italians were the superior team, no ifs, ands or head-butts'?" He wrote it down, gave his one-minute speech using my suggestion verbatim, and lots of people laughed. I guess he simply forgot to come over and thank me for not only helping him out but for giving him an excellent punch line for which he took full credit.

✦✦✦✦✦✦✦✦✦

The House Chamber is set up with long tables on each side for the majority and minority floor managers. There are microphones at each of these places, and there is plenty of room for both the Members and staff. I always sat behind the floor manager so that I could move around without having to crawl over him or her. I would regularly go up to the rostrum to tell the presiding officer how the Chairman wanted the debate to proceed, if he was going to ask for a roll call vote, and whether there were any parliamentary problems in the works. I would also go up to talk to the Parliamentarian on duty about process questions. Frequently I would have to go to the cloakroom to call a Member who was scheduled to speak to make sure they knew their turn was fast-approaching.

One day when I was sitting in my usual seat behind Henry, one of the women on our staff came up and asked if she could sit in my seat for a few minutes. I thought it rather unusual, but I said okay. She sat there for about 15 minutes, and I did my thing from the second seat in. After we had concluded debate on the bill and were packing up our materials, she sheepishly explained to me why she wanted to sit there. She had never met her fiancé's parents, and since the person sitting in that spot behind the Chairman got a lot of TV time when the cameras were focused on him, she wanted them to be able to see what she looked like on television. I was amused. She thanked me profusely.

On July 14, 2006, Henry and I were in the Chamber handling a bill. All of a sudden, there was a commotion, and everyone's attention turned to the aisle going back towards the Republican cloakroom. I then heard people singing

"Happy Birthday". I saw a man walking down the aisle towards the well of the House. He stopped and greeted Henry and then said to me, "Nice to see you again". It was the former Minority Leader of the House, former Vice President, and former President of the United States, Gerald Ford! It was his 93rd birthday, and he had decided to come "back home" to the House. I was under no illusion he knew who I was, although we had shared a lovely 4-minute conversation when he was Vice President.

✦✦✦✦✦✦✦✦✦

When we were on the Judiciary Committee, most of us had private offices where we could close the door and concentrate or have a private phone call. When we got to International Relations, there were just open cubicles with no doors and dividers which did not go to the ceiling. There was no privacy nor solitude. There were many times I needed quiet so I could concentrate. I would frequently go into the cavernous committee hearing room when it was empty to get away from telephones and people talking.

I caused a big kerfuffle when I asked Tom for a door. The problem for me was people were used to shouting back and forth down the hall, which I found disturbing. Also, the Deputy Staff Director, John, who was a difficult person, had a habit of listening to his voicemail on the speakerphone. Everyone could hear his messages, and I found the noise irritating.

There was one instance where it worked to my advantage. John received a phone call from the representative for Gulfstream Aerospace which manufactures some of the most sophisticated private jets in the world. The committee was involved with the company because of the possible dual-use of its aircraft and advanced avionics. Federal law requires dual-use export licenses in certain situations involving national security, foreign policy, nuclear non-proliferation, missile technology, chemical and biological weapons, crime control, or terrorist concerns. The license requirements are dependent upon an item's technical characteristics, the destination, the end-use, and the end-user. Gulfstream frequently needed such licenses to sell its aircraft abroad.

The call I could not help overhearing was from the top lobbyist for Gulfstream. He was inviting John and a couple of other staffers to Savannah to tour their factory. Since I love airplanes, and they were going to be flying on a Gulfstream IV private jet, I wanted to go. I went down to John's office and asked him if I could. I had an ace up my sleeve. Gulfstream is a subsidiary of General Dynamics (GD). My good friend from the Claiborne impeachment, Nick Chabraja, was the CEO of GD. John said he would have to check with the guy from Gulfstream, who would probably want to check with his boss, Nick.

As I heard the story, when the Gulfstream guy walked into Nick's office to ask whether it would be permissible to include me, Nick pointed to a photograph on his wall. It was of Nick, me, and a couple of the other lawyers who worked on the Claiborne impeachment. Nick always called me, "Danny Boy", which I loathe in most situations. However, coming from him, it was a friendly diminutive. "By all means, take 'Danny Boy' along. We are old friends".

On the day in question, we went out to the general aviation terminal at Dulles International Airport and boarded the plane. The aircraft was lavishly appointed, and there was lots of food and beverages available. Before takeoff, I stuck my head into the cockpit to look around. I introduced myself to the pilot and copilot. One of them asked me if I would like to sit the jump seat for the flight. Hell, yes, you did not have to ask me twice! So, while all my colleagues were sitting in the back luxuriating, I got to sit up front and have a tutorial on this very sophisticated aircraft. I do not know whether the rest of the people on the trip thought I was being snobbish by not sitting with them, but I did not care. I learned a lot about air traffic control and the capabilities of this airplane. It was terrific!

When we got to the Gulfstream plant, we were treated to a tour of the entire facility, including a Gulfstream V trainer computerized simulator. They asked if anyone wanted to go for a test flight, and I leaped in, anxious to try it out. After all, I had already had a full 90 minutes in a 727 simulator on my "flight log", so I was mentally prepared to "fly" their simulator. I got to spend about 20 minutes "flying" the G V simulator. It was a lot of fun, and possibly because of my previous experience, I did not get too rattled. It was worth the trip to try piloting another plane!

✦✦✦✦✦✦✦✦✦

After I got my door installed, I still often found it difficult to concentrate. The noise level was frequently a problem for me. The good thing about the closed-door was it served as a "do not disturb" sign. Tom, being aware of my aversion to excess noise, asked me if I wanted an office in the Capitol. He said the Chairman had access to an office on the West Front of the Capitol, which was very private. On September 10, 2001, he gave me the key and suggested I go over and check it out. I walked through the bowels of the building and found the office. It was a nice space with lots of room for a desk and a couple of visitor's chairs. Although it did not have a window, that was not a problem for me. I frequently kept my window shade down when we were on Judiciary because the glare from the white marble was too much for me. If I could have duplicated this office in the International Relations Committee suite in the Rayburn Building, it would have been perfect. However, the old saw "out of sight, out of mind" popped into my head. A big part of being able to do my job was being accessible to everyone and knowing what was going on. I felt I would be easily forgotten and out of the loop if I took the Capitol office. I thanked Tom but told him I would stay where I was. The next day was 9/11, and there was speculation the plane which went down in Shanksville, Pennsylvania, might have been headed for the West Front of the Capitol. It gave me pause.

I don't think anyone will forget where they were on 9/11. I was on a conference call at home between 9 and 10 am. Mimi had a cold and was staying in. After I concluded my call, I got into the car to drive down through Rock Creek Park to the Rayburn Building, just like any other day. Soon after I left, one of the women I had been talking to earlier that morning called my home. She, who has become a dear friend, told Mimi she had just heard there was a bombing at the Pentagon, and she thought I should know. Mimi called me in the car, which was unusual, to let me know. I called the office since I assumed Tom and Sheila would be there. Sheila told me they were evacuating the Capitol and not to try to come in to the office. With the mass exodus from the city, it took Tom over three hours to drive the Chairman home. It was a devastating day. I knew one of the women who was on the plane which crashed into the Pentagon. She had worked on the Hill for many years.

The no-door policy resulted in a rather amusing incident. Kristen Gilley's office was across from mine. She was talking with a couple of people about Richard Chamberlain, the actor who had been in several television shows. As I was walking by, I heard the conversation as Kristen confessed she had had a terrific crush on him when he played Dr. Kildare. I stopped and told her he also had a hit record, which she did not recall. I pulled the song "Three Stars Will Shine Tonight" up on her computer and put my hand out in a gesture asking her to dance. She leaped up, and the two of us tripped the light fantastic as I sang along. I have no idea what the other people in her office thought of it, but it was a glimpse into what a fun person Kristen is. We laughed about it later, wondering about how that incident would be related to other people. We did not know whether our dancing or my singing would be the central point.

Because of my interest in aviation and my enjoyment of factory tours, my friend Tim Keating who works at Boeing, arranged for Mimi and me to have a tour of the Boeing 777 factory in Seattle while we were on vacation in the Pacific Northwest. It was an extraordinary day as we got to watch them building this gigantic airplane. It was hard to believe that the complex assembly of millions of parts would fly. It was a fascinating day!

The following summer, we were going to be in France, flying into Toulouse, where Airbus has its international headquarters. I decided to see if I could arrange a tour of the factory where they build the new Airbus A-380, which is the largest commercial airliner. It is a double-decker airplane that can hold over 800 people.

I called my friend Ashley who used to work for Senator Fritz Hollings, the Chairman of the Committee on Commerce, Science and Transportation. Ashley worked on aviation issues and knew someone in the Washington D.C. office of Airbus. The Washington representative then contacted somebody at Airbus headquarters in Toulouse with the request. Within a couple of days, Ashley called to tell me he had arranged the tour. What I expected was we were going to be on a group tour of the plant, and if possible, we would grab lunch at the company cafeteria, before we flew out of Toulouse on our way home.

We got off our flight in Toulouse and located a shuttle that would take us to the Airbus factory, which is adjacent to the airport. Airbus is a major employer in the area with a large workforce. We took the bus to the main entrance of the facility. We gave the woman there the name of the person we were to meet, who would take us to our tour. After what seemed to be some rather frantic phone calls, it turned out that the Airbus official went to the arrival gate at the Toulouse airport intending to meet us as we came off our flight. He soon arrived at the reception area and apologized profusely for not meeting us. I assured him that it was not a problem and that we were just pleased to meet him. He handed me his card, which I did not immediately look at, as he was escorting us into what we thought was going to be a giant hangar where the assembly line was located.

As we got to the building, we became aware that we were not going into a normal factory, but into a Hollywood-style set which had mockups of two of the new aircraft Airbus was marketing– the A-380, and the new A-350. Somehow the message had gotten garbled. Our host was the Airbus Vice President of Sales, and he was under the false impression that we were important! We were not being given the junior varsity group tour of the assembly line. We were being treated to the VIP tour of the fully and extravagantly decked-out models of these two new planes. We chatted while waiting for our time slot to visit the mock-ups. These viewings were at a premium. While we waited, they were showing them to an Arab sheik and the Transportation Minister of a Middle Eastern country. The tour was obviously aimed at buyers, not mere tourists like us. We were a little boggled by all the red-carpet treatment but were afraid to blow our cover and reveal that we were not people who could influence anyone to buy one of these airplanes.

The mock-ups were extraordinarily outfitted since they were being used to sell the aircraft to wealthy nations for their flag carriers. The double-decker A-380 was set up in super-luxury class configuration. There was a grand staircase from one level to the next, and the interiors were so lavish that they looked like they had been copied from the Orient Express. There were gold fittings in the lavatories and even blue marble on some of the surfaces. It was astonishing. I was beginning to feel a little uncomfortable that we were taking so much of this man's time.

We were then taken for a tour of the factory floor. Having been to the Boeing plant, and seen and heard people riveting pieces of sheet metal together, we were prepared for a rather noisy environment. Much to our surprise, when we got to the assembly line, it was incredibly quiet. Our host told us that all their work was done using lasers, and so even though it did not sound like a real factory or that the workers were "out for tea", they were in the process of constructing one of these gigantic airplanes. It was awe-inspiring.

When we finished looking at the assembly facility, our host suggested that we could go to lunch. I said we would be happy to stop in at the company cafeteria and let him get back to work. But no, he would not hear of it. "I would like you to join me in the executive dining room".

We went to a small triangular room where we were outnumbered by the waitstaff. We had a lovely meal, and I enjoyed talking to our host about airplanes. Since we could see the airfield from the dining room, we even got to see what they call "the Beluga", a modified freighter version of an Airbus A-300. It is shaped like a Beluga whale, and it is gigantic! It is big enough to carry sizable sub-assemblies such as wings and fuselages from where they are manufactured worldwide to Toulouse, where the final assembly takes place.

Then came the part of the event which upset my wife tremendously. Having lived in Belgium for ten years, she had become a chocoholic. One of the waiters arrived with a triple-tiered dessert dish filled with petits fours. Mimi's eyes lit up at the thought of all of these tasty treats. However, before she got to indulge her sweet tooth, our host said, "Well, I know you have to get your flight, so we should be leaving to get you back to the airport". Mimi was prepared to sweep the entire contents of the dessert dish into her purse but resisted the temptation. Even though she was devastated, she agreed to return with me to the airport. She has never forgotten it.

I sent our host a nice note thanking him profusely, but still not revealing to him that we were not the VIPs he thought we were.

✦✦✦✦✦✦✦✦✦

Jim Sensenbrenner is a bright but prickly man. He occasionally has periods of good humor, but sometimes is difficult to deal with. When the Democrats were in the majority, I was frequently confronted with parliamentary inquiries and points of order posed by him. He was a stickler for the rules and knew them well.

I put my foot in it one day when he was the Chairman of the Judiciary Committee. I had gone over to watch an Administrative Law Subcommittee hearing about the Supreme Court because the two witnesses were Justices Antonin Scalia and Stephen Breyer. They were both experts in the intricacies of administrative law, and I thought it might be interesting, which it was. Sensenbrenner had a standing practice of swearing in all witnesses, no matter who they were. He expected all of his subcommittee chairs to do so. Chris Cannon, the subcommittee chair, is a mild-mannered man from Utah. He did not make these two Supreme Court Justices take the oath, which seemed eminently reasonable to me. I casually mentioned it to Sensenbrenner later that day when I saw him on the floor. He went crazy. He was incensed that Cannon did not swear them in. From what I heard later, Sensenbrenner gave him an earful. I apologized to him for getting him into trouble.

✦✦✦✦✦✦✦✦✦

Most of the senior people on the staff had to have security clearances so we could read sensitive materials which the State Department couriered over to the committee regularly. When they were updating Tom's security clearance, one of the investigators came in to interview me about him.

Once again, I let my sense of humor get away from me. The interviewer asked whether he used alcohol. I said he did, and I would frequently get him a "malted beverage" when we traveled together. I am not sure she knew I was referring to beer. I told her he owned a bar and was around alcohol all the time. Then she finally got around to asking whether his drinking diminished his ability to keep secrets. I, of course, said no.

She then asked whether he "advocated the overthrow of the United States Government by force or violence". I said, "You know, he just cannot decide which…" She did not get it, so I had to explain my "joke" to her, which she did not think was funny. She kept droning on with the questions she asks probably several times a day. In the end, despite my interview, Tom got his clearance.

✦✦✦✦✦✦✦✦✦

The Oil for Food Program and the UN

One of the most challenging assignments I ever received was to be the lead counsel on the committee's investigation of the United Nations Oil for Food Program. The Program was established in 1995 to allow Iraq to sell oil on the world market in exchange for food, medicine, and other humanitarian needs of Iraqi citizens, without allowing Iraq to boost its military capabilities with the profits. It was introduced by the Clinton administration in 1995. It was a response to the argument that ordinary Iraqi citizens were being inordinately affected by the international economic sanctions aimed at the demilitarization of Saddam Hussein's Iraq. These sanctions were imposed in the wake of the first Gulf War.

Amid wide-ranging allegations of fraud, kickbacks, "sweetheart" deals, and other financial misdeeds, Kofi Annan, the UN Secretary General, launched a full independent investigation of the Program. The inquiry was headed by Paul Volker, the former Chairman of the Federal Reserve System.

A whistleblower, Robert Parton, who had been an investigator with the Program, had managed to remove 16 banker boxes full of records. He claimed they showed rampant fraud and abuse, which was being covered up. Somehow our staff had gotten word of this and urged the Chairman to subpoena them. We understood Parton was willing to turn them over to Congress pursuant to a subpoena.

I was responsible for the issuance of any subpoenas. Congressional subpoenas were, to me, serious business. There was a series of hoops you had to jump through to issue one properly. I had to clear them with the House General Counsel's office and have them certified by the Clerk of the House. I was strict about making sure everything was done correctly. The Chairman authorized subpoenaing the documents, and I completed the process and had them ready to serve. They called for all of the documents in Parton's possession relating to the Oil for Food Program and required them to be turned over "forthwith", meaning immediately

This was where my love/hate relationship with the Chairman's press secretary, Sam Stratman, reared its ugly head again. My instructions from Tom about the subpoenas were explicit. He said I was to show them to no one, not the press and not even people on our staff. Sam had an animus towards the UN. He had close relationships with a lot of reporters and especially with one who was working on a story about the Oil for Food Program. I had the subpoenas on my desk when Sam came in and demanded to see them. I refused as per Tom's instructions, and Sam went ballistic. I told him the only reason I could fathom for his wanting to see them was so he could reveal them to his friend, the reporter. Sam called me a lot of names and shouted, "You have no respect for the importance of a free press". He then stormed out of my office.

Late that Friday afternoon, two of our staff, Jock Scharfen and Greg Rickman, were in the office of Lanny Davis, a well-known lawyer who was representing Parton. They were there to serve the subpoenas and take custody of the

documents. But when Jock and Gregg got to Davis' office, there was some resistance to turning over the materials. Jock called and asked me to come downtown to help because he was not getting the compliance from Davis which he
anticipated even though a valid Congressional subpoena had been served.

By the time I got there, no progress had been made. Davis, on behalf of
Parton, insisted there was a lot of material in the boxes which were not responsive to the subpoena, and he was reluctant to turn the whole batch over. The
subpoena had been deliberately tightly drawn for the limited purpose of getting
evidence of misdeeds in the program.

Davis and I did some back and forth about whether the Congressional subpoena power trumped the language in the Constitution on international treaties.
Fortunately, I had had some time to research that issue and was prepared to deal
with the legal/constitutional questions when I arrived in Davis' office.

There were several questions which we had to answer:

*1) Does the United Nations Convention on Privileges and Immunities have the effect of
constitutional authority which might preclude Congress from subpoenaing UN documents?*

I told Davis, and the other two lawyers from his firm who were with us in
the conference room, that American treaty commitments are "equivalent to
an act of the legislature". Therefore, the constitutional Article I powers of the
Congress, including the exercise of its investigative powers, were superior to
any international agreement.

*2) Does the confidentiality agreement between the UN and the former investigator (Par-
ton) preclude Congress from issuing and enforcing a subpoena for UN documents in the
possession of a former employee?*

My assessment was that the agreement in question was between the former
employee and the UN. The UN could pursue any remedy it wanted to against
the former employee directly. However, that agreement had no legal effect on
Congress' Article I investigative authority, or its power to issue subpoenas.

3) Would a court grant a UN motion to quash a Congressional subpoena?

I stated that in my opinion, it would not. The UN would have to go to a U.S.
District Court for relief. A Federal Judge would almost undoubtedly rule that
the Speech or Debate Clause of the Constitution, which precludes Congress
from being "questioned in any other place" for its legislative actions would
govern, and no court would grant such a motion. I also said it was not clear that
the UN would have standing in Federal Court to move to quash a Congressional
subpoena served upon a *former* employee.

After I had outlined my opinion of the legal landscape on these issues, Davis
asked his two colleagues what they thought. One of them said he would like to
speak with him privately. Davis said not to worry about my being there, "Just

tell me what you think about what Dan said". The other lawyer then said, "I think he is right". I was pleased but did not let them know.

We knew the people at the UN were acutely concerned about some of the materials because, in the wrong hands, they could result in serious problems and possibly harm to some of the people involved. They were distressed about the committee having them because of what they perceived as the threat of their being leaked.

Davis informed us some of the material in the boxes was not covered by the subpoena. He and Mr. Parton wanted to refuse to surrender any of those. He wanted the opportunity to examine all the documents and withhold anything they deemed not to be responsive to the subpoena. I told him (Parton was not there), all I wanted was what we had specifically subpoenaed. I emphasized to him the subpoena required production "forthwith"; meaning immediately.

Jock and Gregg sat there and watched me do what Jock later called "some brilliant lawyering". In the middle of our discussion, Davis got a call from his wife. It was clear he did not want to talk to her then, but it was also apparent that she was insistent. He finally said, "OK, I will have the Kung Pao chicken". It was a funny injection of real life into this very heavy legal negotiation. To add a bit of humor, I added, "Don't forget, no MSG." Davis laughed and repeated it to his wife.

We then got back to business, and I suggested *all* of the materials should be turned over to us immediately, and I would guarantee the committee would keep them in a secure room where no one would have access to them. I thought this was a good compromise which would give us all of the materials and give Parton and Davis the chance to screen them before we looked at them.

Jock and Greg were happy with that proposal. I asked Davis if that met the security concerns the UN had expressed, as well as Parton's goal of only giving us access to those documents he felt were appropriate. Davis said he thought the "Freeman solution" was brilliant but that he wanted a few days to go over them with his client. I made a big show of resisting any delay in compliance with the subpoena "forthwith". However, I did not think an immediate response was that important. I then proposed a compromise that they deliver all 16 boxes to us the following Tuesday, and we would give them access to the secure room to conduct whatever review they wished and do a final culling.

Davis tentatively agreed to that proposal but wanted to check with his client. I also wanted to check with my client, Chairman Hyde. Davis volunteered to talk to Mr. Hyde, but I suggested that he talk to his client, and I would talk to mine. Both of our clients agreed, and we had a deal.

When we were done with business, Davis took me into his office to show me his "ego wall". He had photographs of himself on Air Force One during both the Clinton and Bush administrations. He had been an Assistant Counsel to the President under Bill Clinton and had gone to college with George W. Bush.

Jock, Greg, and I walked out of the building content with the result. I did not know that this was just the end of the beginning of a long and torturous negotiation which was to include Paul Volker and his lawyers, Davis/Parton, and three Congressional entities. The Members of Congress we ended up working with included, from the House International Relations Committee, Chairman Hyde and ranking minority member Tom Lantos, from the House Subcommittee on National Security, Emerging Threats and International Relations of the Committee on Government Reform, Chairman Chris Shays and his ranking minority member, Dennis Kucinich, and from the Senate Permanent Subcommittee on Investigations of the Committee on Homeland Security and Governmental Affairs, Chairman Norm Coleman, and his ranking minority member Carl Levin.

As per our agreement, the so-called "Freeman solution", the 16 boxes of papers were delivered to our secure office in the Ford Building the following Tuesday. I never looked at them. I did not have a need to know, and I was happy about that. Once Davis and Parton had completed their screening, our staff was ready to start examining them.

Having to coordinate among six different Members and their staffs, along with Volker and his staff in New York, was going to be a logistical nightmare. Added to this mix was going to be Kerry Kircher, Deputy General Counsel of the House, a brilliant lawyer and a steadfast resource who was immensely helpful to me, and Volker's Washington Lawyer, Todd Stern, who was with the prominent Washington law firm of WilmerHale.

Soon after the documents were surrendered, Tom Mooney and I had a meeting with Henry to discuss the investigation. I explained to them how difficult it was going to be to get six Members and their staffs on the same page. There was always the possibility of back-channel communications between and among all of the players. Tom said to Henry, "What we need is the meanest, toughest son of a bitch we can find to represent us and to be the sole Congressional point of contact, so everything goes through him". Henry said, "Oh, good idea", as he paused to consider and then said, "That would be Dan." I never asked Tom about it, but I think it was a set-up, and I took it as a compliment.

One of the more difficult people to deal with was Susan Ringler, who was Volker's Counsel on the UN Independent Inquiry Committee. She thought the people on the Hill had no understanding of how important and sensitive the documents were. She kept repeating that "lives were at stake", and she did not feel comfortable with Congress having them. I recognized her concerns, but we had done everything necessary to keep them secure and to prevent any leaks.

On Wednesday, she had requested a meeting of her staff and all the relevant congressional staff at 10 o'clock on the following Monday morning on the Hill. Getting all of the players from the six Congressional offices to agree to meet at one particular time and place was going to be extremely challenging. Miraculously, I was able to set it up. Fortunately, I managed to get a room in the Capitol for the meeting. Senators, and by osmosis their staffs, are prickly about having to come "all the way over to House office buildings". I thought the Capitol would be acceptable, and it was. After getting all of my ducks in a row, I let Sue know we were set for 10 am in the Capitol. She said she and some of their people would come down from New York for the meeting.

She called me late on Friday afternoon and informed me they could not make the 10 am meeting. She wanted to reschedule it for one p.m. I told her that moving the meeting time was not feasible since it would be almost impossible to get all of the Congressional parties involved to agree to the change. She said, "Well, what happens if we cannot be there?" I replied, with I am sure more than a little irritation in my voice, "We will meet at 10 am *as requested by you*".

She and her people showed up for the meeting at 10 am on Monday. She began by going into a tirade about how outraged she was that these highly sensitive and potentially life-threatening materials were in our possession. She underscored how important it was that *they* (the UN) have exclusive custody of them. She reiterated that they had maintained tight security over them because of their sensitivity, and she would only feel comfortable if the UN "maintained control of them". I am not usually a nasty person, but I could not let that go without saying, "If your security is so good, how is it we ended up with 16 boxes of them?" There was a stone-cold silence in the room until she said, "I would rather not discuss that". I resisted the temptation to say, "I am sure you would not".

Lengthy and agonizing negotiations ensued. There were three sets of parties involved; 1) the majority and minority from three congressional committees, 2) Davis/Parton, and 3) the UN investigating committee staff both in New York and Washington. I was fortunate to have cooperative staffs on all three Congressional committees to work with. There was no partisan bickering, and for the most part, they left me alone to work out an agreement. After scores of drafts of proposals concerning when and how the materials would be released, if at all, it came to crunch time, and we had to decide whether to go with a two-party agreement between Congress and the UN or a three-party agreement which included Davis/Parton. My preference had always been for a three-party agreement. There was considerable back-and-forth, and for a time, it looked like we were not going to be able to get all three parties to agree.

I was getting frustrated with the recalcitrance of Lanny Davis. I had come to the conclusion we were going to have to go with the two-party agreement; Congress and the UN. We had the documents, and we did not need Davis/Parton to go forward. Shortly before we had to finalize the agreement, I had a telephone conversation with people in Todd Stern's office. I informed them that I was prepared to recommend we proceed with the two-party agreement because we could not seem to get Mr. Parton on board. I then called Lanny Davis to inform him that we were going on without them. There was a pregnant pause on the telephone, and I sensed that Lanny was not happy. The conversation went on for a while, and I could tell that Davis was anxious to have the final agreement include all three parties. Faced with the possibility of being excluded, Davis finally capitulated on the last roadblocks, and we had a deal. I was relieved but also a little irritated that it had come down to last-minute brinksmanship.

The resulting 12-page agreement needed to be signed by all the parties. I was able to secure all of the Congressional signatures (a monumental logistical undertaking itself). I asked Sue Ringler to get Mr. Volcker to sign and send his signature sheet to me as quickly as possible. She agreed to do so overnight by Federal Express. Getting Parton's signature was not difficult since he was in Washington, DC. I agreed to Ringler's suggestion because I was unaware of the fact that every piece of mail that comes to Congress had to be tested for bio-hazards and was subjected to quarantine. Unfortunately, this included Federal Express packages. I tried every way I could think of to see if we could intercept the package. I did not have any luck. It did not make a hell of a lot of difference, but I was anxious to have the signed document in my hands. If I had known about the quarantine, I would have asked to have it sent to my home.

As it turned out, all of the precise timelines we had so scrupulously and agonizingly negotiated were immediately ignored by the UN. There was nothing I could do about that. There was no way to enforce anything. The overall purpose of the exercise was for us to be able to obtain and review the documents and then make some pragmatic judgments about what deficiencies, if any existed, in the Oil for Food Program. The bottom line was we were able to look at all the materials, and the Members and Senators would get a chance to weigh in.

Jock, Greg, Tom, and I were in briefing the Chairman one afternoon when the receptionist buzzed to tell Mr. Hyde that an old friend of his from Chicago had arrived to see him. We got up to leave, but Henry wanted to introduce us first. We said hello and headed back to the committee offices.

No sooner had we walked into the office when Tom's assistant told us the Chairman had called and wanted us to come back immediately. The "old friend" was on a mission for Mr. Volker, who had sent him to "reason" with Henry. The UN people had probably searched far and wide to find somebody Mr. Volker knew well enough to send on such an errand who also knew Mr. Hyde well enough to be able to get in to see him.

As we returned to the Chairman's office, all hell broke loose. The fire alarms went off, the claxons sounded an alert, and we were directed to evacuate immediately. Henry was having mobility problems, and we all tried to assist him in getting to the emergency exit. Blaine Aaron, from Henry's personal office staff, a former military officer, was exceptionally impressive as he took control. When we got outside, we saw people running everywhere. We had no idea what the emergency was, but it seemed like a good idea to get away from the building. As soon as we got to the exit, Blaine commandeered a Capitol Hill Police car and, in a strong authoritative voice pointed to the officer who was driving and said, "You, put the Chairman in your car and get him out of danger. Now!" The officer did not hesitate and immediately got Henry, Jock, and Henry's old friend into the car.

We heard that an unidentified aircraft had penetrated the no-fly zone around the Capitol, which had been established after 9/11. The rest of us uneasily but rapidly went down the street getting away from the Rayburn Building. After half an hour, we got the all-clear and were permitted back in. The encroaching aircraft belonged to the Governor of Kentucky, and his pilot had simply forgotten to turn on the transponder, which would have identified the plane to air traffic control.

When we reconvened in the Chairman's office, we found out the message had been delivered by the mutual friend while he, Henry, and Jock were in the police car, and we were excused. I do not know if the special messenger ploy worked, but it did not hurt. This was just the opening salvo to get to Henry about the investigation.

A couple of days later, we were informed that Paul Volcker himself had called and asked to have a one-on-one meeting with Henry. Volcker was a prominent man with a long history of distinguished government service. Henry was more than amenable to such a meeting since he respected him very much. We had the opportunity to brief Henry about what we thought Volcker was going to say and get him up to speed on where we were in our investigation. One of the things Henry asked about was whether the other two Congressional committees had been kept up to date. Tom told him I had been scrupulous in making sure that both minority and majority of each of the committees involved knew what we were doing on a regular basis. He told the Chairman that no one could complain about not being kept in the loop. Good old Tom told Henry, "Your mean son of a bitch was exactly the right one for the job". It was typical of Tom not only to compliment me in front of the Chairman but also not to take any of the credit himself.

Volcker, Sue Ringler and their chief investigator flew down from New York for the meeting. The investigator was a rather self-important jerk who kept checking his blackberry and telling us, "I have important investigations I am running". I decided to join Henry and Paul Volcker rather than sit in the outer office making small talk with these two relatively unpleasant people. When it was time for Hyde and Volcker to talk privately, I left the room.

Jock, Greg and Minority Counsel David Abramowitz had gone over the materials. Fortunately, my role in the investigation did not require my reading them. Jock and Greg thought that they did show some maladministration and potentially some serious wrongdoing. The UN folks thought they reflected no such thing.

While I have my own thoughts about what went on in the conversation between Hyde and Volcker, the result was they decided it was a "jump ball". Volker was 6 feet 7 inches tall, and Hyde was 6 feet 3 inches. They had both been basketball players, and the term "jump ball" was familiar to them. What it meant was that we had not found enough evidence to substantiate the whistleblower's claims of widespread abuse. It did not mean that the UN was blameless. It only meant Congress was not going to pursue the investigation any further.

I think Jock and Greg were disappointed, but I did not have any strong feelings either way. Tom felt I had done an excellent job managing all of the rather robust personalities involved. As long as Henry was satisfied, Tom thought it was a good result. It ended with a whimper instead of a bang, but it was an extraordinary ride for me for several months.

Throughout the entire process, I relied heavily on Kerry Kircher, the Deputy General Counsel to the House of Representatives. Kerry is a superb lawyer, an exceptional writer and a talented tactician. His advice was crucial in making sure the prerogatives of the House were protected. He and I developed a close working relationship. I admire him tremendously. After I left the Hill to go to American University, Kerry regularly spoke to my classes. Interestingly, another result of this massive undertaking was that Lanny Davis and I worked together well, and he, too, became a frequent speaker in my AU seminar.

✦✦✦✦✦✦✦✦✦

As Henry got older, he gained a substantial amount of weight and was experiencing a lot of back pain. He was having difficulty standing up and sitting down. Those of us on the staff did everything we could to ease that burden. When we were in the committee room, and it was time for Henry to get up and leave, one of us was would always be there to give him a helping hand literally. When managing bills on the floor, the manager's job is to stand up and yield time to other Members. House protocol is that the floor manager must be on their feet at one of the microphones, be recognized, and formally yield time to the next Member to speak. While it was frequently important to have Henry there to manage legislation, his needing to get up and down was getting to be a problem. I talked to the Parliamentarians about it and asked if it would be acceptable if we arranged for Henry to be sitting on a couple of thick cushions. I hoped that would constitute his being "on his feet" in order to yield time. Charlie Johnson was exceedingly accommodating and said that would suffice. The first time we did this, Henry was pleased and very appreciative. That became the normal process whenever we went to the floor.

When there is a roll call vote in the House of Representatives, Members record their votes by electronic device. There are 13 voting stations in the Chamber, and Members come in, slip their cards into one of the machines and push the button for "yea", "nay", or "present". The voting machine closest to the floor manager is directly behind him. Ordinarily, it would not be a problem for the manager to stand up, turn around, and insert his card to vote. However, it was difficult for Henry. We got into a routine where he would hand me his voting card, and I would physically cast the vote for him. Unless I were dead certain, I would double-check how he wanted to vote. I made sure his vote was cast immediately. It is important for Members coming in to know how the Chairman of the committee had voted. This made things easier for Henry, and I felt it was yet one more thing I could do to make his life a little more comfortable. At one point, Charlie Johnson raised the issue of my voting for Henry because a Member had mentioned it to him. My response to Charlie was, "If I cannot help an older man who I admire by doing a simple thing like that, then something is definitely wrong in this place". I urged Charlie, tongue-in-cheek, to suggest to the Member who had a problem with it that he mention it to Henry directly. I continued to do it.

There was another issue that came up where I tried to pitch in to make life less stressful for Henry, and that was his declining hearing. I arranged with the House Administration Committee to have a hearing loop installed in the committee room. With this new technology, Henry could adjust his hearing aid so that he would be able to understand everything being said over the microphones clearly. It worked well for the most part. I would sometimes have to remind him to switch the setting on his hearing aid to the frequency of the electronic system. I got a big laugh out of him one day when a committee hearing was getting a little tiresome, and I suggested he switch over to ESPN, which I thought might be more interesting.

Since the hearing aid loop technology been so effective in the committee room, I urged the Speaker's staff to have it installed in the House. This was a resounding success, and I learned that many Members were pleased to be able to hear debates in the House clearly. The only downside to the system was when Henry was tuned into the loop, it made it difficult for him to hear us when we were sitting next to him. We got to the point of jotting down notes and showing them to him, which worked.

✦✦✦✦✦✦✦✦✦

Being able to go to the Chamber whenever I wanted allowed me to indulge my sense of history, and also gave me the chance to meet some extraordinary people. One of those people I was very interested in meeting was a new Congressman from Georgia, John Robert Lewis. Mr. Lewis was an icon of the civil rights movement. He was one of the original Freedom Riders who challenged segregation in public transportation in the South. He had been beaten, arrested, and jailed during that ride, but he was still committed to achieving integration through non-violence.

He had been one of the speakers during the March on Washington in 1963 when Dr. King gave his famous "I have a dream" speech. In 1965, as the Leader of the Student Nonviolent Coordinating Committee, he was involved in the "Mississippi Freedom Summer". He became a national figure when he took a prominent role in the Selma to Montgomery march. On March 7, 1965, he led the procession across the Edmund Pettus Bridge in Selma, Alabama. He was brutally beaten by Alabama State Troopers in what came to be known as "Bloody Sunday". The images of that confrontation were seared into the American conscience and into my mind.

On the day he was sworn in, January 3, 1987, I made sure to be in the House so I could meet him. I was thrilled to be able to introduce myself. I told him I wanted to shake his hand and thank him for all he had done for our country. It was an extraordinary occasion for me and was also the start of a meaningful working relationship.

I interacted with him regularly because of my position on the Judiciary Committee staff, and then as a professor at American University. He spoke to my students frequently, indeed, almost every semester. I always introduced him as "John Robert Lewis" because that is what he wanted Dr. King to call him on the day they met.

✦✦✦✦✦✦✦✦✦

Henry was always gracious to everyone from Members, to staff, to the wait-ers in the House Restaurant. If a Member asked him for something, his answer was almost always yes. Frequently, Members would entreat him to co-sponsor a bill, which might pose a problem for him. Alan Coffey had to get him to prom-ise not to agree immediately when asked and to defer until we had had a chance to look at the bill. Alan said Henry decided to play "good cop, bad cop", with Alan being the bad cop. It seemed to be effective.

One day we were on the floor doing a relatively minor bill when Congress-man J.C. Watts approached Henry. J.C. was an impressive African American Member from Oklahoma. After a stellar college football career, which included quarterbacking two Orange Bowl victories for the University of Oklahoma, he entered the pros. He went to the Canadian Football League and played for the Ottawa Rough Riders, who he helped reach the 1981 Grey Cup game, which is the Canadian Super Bowl.

I liked him a lot; he was an engaging and interesting man. He was not shy in asking questions about how things worked on the floor, and he was a quick study. He was going to be the Republican floor manager for a bill dealing with the commemoration of an important event in the history of the civil rights movement. It was on the non-controversial calendar, but he had not had much experience managing legislation. He asked Henry if he could "borrow" me while the bill was being debated. Henry, of course, said "yes", and then, our committee business having been completed, he left.

I stayed on the floor with J.C. waiting for him to call up his bill. As we were waiting, my hero, John Lewis, approached us and said a few words to J.C. about the bill. Mr. Lewis was the Democratic floor manager. They were both strong supporters, so it was not going to be a problem. Mr. Lewis noticed I had been "borrowed" by J.C., and he asked me if I would be willing to go over to the Democratic side and assist him while he was managing time as well. I would walk through fire for John Lewis, and readily agreed, and Watts was fine with it.

I went back and forth, sitting with Watts when he was managing time, and with Mr. Lewis when he was. There was no controversy, and there were no parliamentary issues raised for me to deal with for either Member. When the debate was over, J.C. and Mr. Lewis each walked from their respective managers' tables towards the center aisle, shook hands, and thanked each other. They both then turned to me, as I happened to be standing there, and thanked me for my help. I thought it was very kind of them. To me, it was a significant thing that two African American Members were managing a bill in the U.S. House of Rep-resentatives. I mentioned that said I felt it was an honor to be there. I followed with, "The fact that this has occurred makes me proud to be an American, and a bit ashamed because it has taken so long to happen". Lewis gave me a big hug and said, "Dan, you are my brother". That was a very special moment for me.

✦✦✦✦✦✦✦✦✦

The Terri Schiavo Case

One of the most interesting matters I dealt with while on the International Relations Committee staff had nothing to do with foreign affairs. Terri Schiavo was a young woman who had a cardiac seizure and was in a persistent vegetative state. After 13 years of enduring this agonizing ordeal, her husband, Michael, petitioned the Florida courts for permission to remove the feeding tube that was keeping her alive. It became a cause célèbre for the right-to-life movement. This private and tragic situation became a substantial public controversy when Teri's parents opposed Michael's petition in the Florida courts.

The case spent years in litigation. The Florida trial court found that Terri would not have wished the life-prolonging measures to be continued and authorized the husband to order the feeding tube removed. The matter went through fourteen appeals in the Florida courts and many filings in the federal courts. When the final decision in the Florida Supreme Court affirmed the husband's right as the surrogate healthcare decisionmaker for his wife to terminate life support, many people believed that was the end of the controversy. The feeding tube was removed.

The Florida Legislature then got involved. In an emergency session, it passed "Terri's Law", which gave Governor Jeb Bush the authority to intervene in the case. The Governor ordered the feeding tube reinserted. Amid the many machinations regarding where Terri was to be treated and who was to represent her, the Florida Supreme Court held "Terri's Law" to be unconstitutional and null and void. The result was the Governor's authority under the law was rescinded.

The case had gone through the state legislative, executive, and judicial branches, with the final result being Michael Schiavo was determined to be the designated decisionmaker for his wife. Governor Jeb Bush, his options at the state level having been exhausted, called a Member of Congress he knew who was a physician to ask him for help. Congressman Dave Weldon then proposed federal legislation aimed at preventing the withdrawal of life support.

This was where I got involved. The minority staffer on the House Judiciary Committee handling the issue was David Lachmann, who worked for Jerry Nadler. David is a man wise beyond his years, with a sardonic sense of the absurd and a caustic sense of humor. He thought this tragic and futile effort was solely a matter of state law and that Congress should not get involved. He asked me for advice about how to approach the hearing which was being contemplated.

The Weldon bill, which changed many times before the hearing, was not the version that was finally adopted. David was aware of my interest in bioethics, and that I understood some of the nuances about the procedures that were being considered.

We discussed it in-depth, and I suggested a first-rate witness, the well-known bioethicist Art Caplan, whom I knew. David was astounded by the variety of desperate options being considered, which included giving the parents standing to file a habeas corpus proceeding to have Terri turned over to their custody. Habeas corpus cases are almost exclusively limited to criminal proceedings. David was also wrestling with the threat of someone filing a federal Medicare fraud case against the husband since Terri was in hospice, which is supposed to be limited to cases where the patient had less than six months to live. Terri's life expectancy was unknowable.

The option the sponsors finally decided on was within the jurisdiction of the Judiciary Committee. The bill would give the parents the ability to bring an action in federal court. It would authorize a Federal court to hear the case *de novo*--a brand-new trial from the beginning. This was extraordinary.

The Senate was to take the bill up late at night with practically no one there. The colloquy between Senator Frist, a physician who was the Senate Majority Leader, and Senator Levin, who was the ranking minority member of the relevant committee, was an interesting dance. Levin asked if the bill mandated that the Federal court issue a stay of the Florida Supreme Court ruling while the new federal case was pending. This was crucial since the Florida court had ruled the husband was the legal decision-maker, and therefore his decision to withdraw the feeding tube was legally binding. When the bill was called up in the Senate, the feeding tube had been removed at Michael's direction under the authority of the Florida court's decision.

Senator Levin had made it clear he would object to the consideration of the bill in the Senate if it mandated the Federal judge issue a stay. He felt that such a direct command to a Federal judge by Congress would be an unconstitutional incursion by the legislature into the authority of the judiciary and would be a violation of the doctrine of separation of powers. Congress, he contented, should not be dictating what Federal Judges should do in any individual case. In the colloquy leading to the Senate passage of the bill by unanimous consent there was this exchange:

Mr. LEVIN: Although nothing in the text of the new bill mandates a stay ... (of the State court decision) Does the majority leader share my understanding of the bill?

Mr. FRIST: I share the understanding of the Senator from Michigan... Nothing in the current bill or its legislative history mandates a stay. I would assume, however, the Federal court would grant a stay based on the facts of this case because Mrs. Schiavo would need to be alive in order for the court to make its determination. Nevertheless, this bill does not change current law under which a stay is discretionary.

Mr. LEVIN: In light of that assurance, I do not object to the unanimous consent agreement under which the bill will be considered by the Senate… Because the discretion of the Federal court is left unrestricted in this bill, I will not exercise my right to block its consideration.

The final version of the bill passed the Senate by unanimous consent on Sunday, March 20, 2005, was sent over to the House that night and was debated into the early morning of March 21, which was Palm Sunday. The House Majority Leader, Tom Delay, called it the "Palm Sunday Compromise. The House passed it and sent it to the President. President Bush flew back from Texas to sign it at 1:11 am. There was some talk about his signing it in his pajamas.

The law granted the parents the right to a new trial in the United States District Court for the Middle District of Florida with all the accompanying procedures that would entail. That court would have jurisdiction to hear any lawsuit on behalf of Terri Schiavo "relating to withdrawal or withholding of food, fluids, or medical treatment necessary to sustain her life". At that time, the feeding tube had been removed. Terri's parents would need to begin the litigation by getting the Federal Judge to issue a stay or Temporary Restraining Order (TRO) of the Florida Supreme Court ruling. This would enable them to have the feeding tube reinserted. Absent such a stay, Terri would surely die before the Federal case got to trial. This was clear to all concerned and was the basis of the colloquy about a stay in the Senate.

As soon as the law was passed, Terri's parents filed a motion in Federal Court for a TRO. The Federal District Judge denied the parents' request because they had not met the necessary legal standard. As he pointed out in his decision, under federal law, the party seeking a stay would need to show four things:

"A district court may grant a preliminary injunction only if the moving party shows that: (1) it has a substantial likelihood of success on the merits; (2) irreparable injury will be suffered unless the injunction issues; (3) the threatened injury to the movant outweighs whatever damage the proposed injunction may cause the opposing party; and (4) if issued, the injunction would not be adverse to the public interest".

In his ruling, the Judge held that the parents had shown three of the four requirements but had failed to provide sufficient evidence of a substantial likelihood of success on the merits, the first prong of the 4-part test.

I have always been a footnote reader, and in footnote 2 of the trial judge's decision, he basically says to Congress (I am paraphrasing), "Hey Congress, if you wanted to change the requirements for a TRO you could have. You talked about it, but you didn't, so I am bound by *all four* requirements".

Footnote 2 reads as follows: *"The (Congressional) Act does not address the traditional requirements for temporary injunctive relief. Accordingly, these standards control whether temporary injunctive relief is warranted, notwithstanding Congress' intent that the federal courts determine de novo the merits of Theresa Schiavo's claimed constitutional deprivations".*

Even though Congress had demonstrated its intent for the court to hear the merits of the parents' case, it did not change the well-settled law regarding the grounds for a stay, even though it was within its power to do so.

The trial judge's ruling denying the TRO was appealed to the 11th Circuit Court of Appeals, which upheld the trial court's decision. The Court of Appeals said the trial judge's ruling was correct on the TRO issue; he was bound by the existing traditional requirements for granting such an order. The Court of Appeals also said Congress could have modified those requirements in the law for this one case, but it did not, although the issue had been raised in the Frist/Levin colloquy.

"When Congress explicitly modifies some pre-existing rules of law applicable to a subject but says nothing about other rules of law, the only reasonable reading is that Congress meant no change in the rules it did not mention.... It is on this point: the language of the Act clearly does not purport to change the law concerning issuance of temporary or preliminary relief.

However, we are called upon to make a collective, objective decision concerning a question of law. In the end, and no matter how much we wish Mrs. Schiavo had never suffered such a horrible accident, we are a nation of laws, and if we are to continue to be so, the pre-existing and well-established federal law governing injunctions as well as [the new federal law] must be applied to her case".

As a result of the Court of Appeals' decision, no TRO was issued, and without the feeding tube in place, Terri died soon after that.

It is the only case I have ever heard of in which both the State judicial, legislative, and executive branches and the Federal judicial, legislative, and executive branches were involved. It was an extraordinary sequence of events.

It was after this when Tom Delay and I had a little talk. The Committee was doing something unrelated on the floor, and Mr. Delay had requested time to speak. As the Majority Leader, his time did not count against the floor manager's total time allotment, and we would always give him time whenever he wanted it. As a courtesy, when he arrived, I went over to find out whether he wanted to speak immediately or be given some time to go over his remarks.

He privately made a comment about that "goddamn activist judge". I knew exactly who he was talking about. My definition of an "activist judge", which I did *not* share with him, is a judge who rules contrary to your wishes. I said something about the "legal status" of Teri Schiavo at the time the Federal Judge ruled; she had been disconnected from the feeding tube by *order of the Florida Supreme Court*. He replied bitterly, "Her status was she was alive, and the fucking lawyers killed her". I did not respond and tip-toed away.

I had learned early on not to tangle with Tom Delay. He was not called "the Hammer" without justification. One day I was on the floor before we were to take up a resolution in the committee that afternoon to authorize the use of military force in Iraq. One of the senior Republicans had publicly indicated he was going to vote "no", and the leadership was scrambling to make sure they had the votes to pass it in committee. I was talking to Congressman Ron Paul, a member of the committee, who was in a quandary about how to vote. He wanted to vote "no", but the pressure from the leadership to support the President was intense.

As we were talking, Mr. Delay came up and gave Mr. Paul an earful. Delay was really hot and came out with a stream of expletives worthy of a drunken sailor. Paul tried to make his argument by pointing to the text of the Constitution, which he had with him. Delay said, "Fuck the Constitution! This is about supporting the President". I decided the cloakroom looked very inviting and left the floor.

✦✦✦✦✦✦✦✦✦

I got a call from Kerry Kircher, my friend who was the General Counsel of the House, about a friend of the court brief (*amicus curiae*) he was trying to get a Member to sign. It was about a case relating to an employment discrimination complaint that had been filed against the Office of Congresswoman Eddie Bernice Johnson. The case arose under the Congressional Accountability Act (CAA), and it presented significant constitutional Speech or Debate Clause issues in the context of the CAA.

The General Counsel's office did not represent the Congresswoman; the Office of House Employment Counsel (OHEC) did. OHEC was responsible for defending Members of Congress and committees in lawsuits. The General Counsel's office felt the position OHEC was taking concerning the Speech or Debate Clause question was problematic. After the case had gone to trial, been appealed and ruled on by the U.S. Court of Appeals for the D.C. Circuit, a motion was filed to have the case heard by the entire D.C. Circuit, known as an *en banc* hearing. That motion was granted, and Kerry had prepared an *amicus* brief for the Bipartisan Legal Advisory Group of the House (BLAG) to be filed before the hearing of the full D.C. Circuit. The BLAG has been a standing body of the U.S. House of Representatives since 1993. Comprised of five members of the House Leadership (the Speaker, the Majority and Minority Leaders, the Majority and Minority Whips), it directs the activities of the House Office of

General Counsel in representing Congress in the courts.

The position the General Counsel's office wanted the House to take was that the Speech or Debate clause provided immunity from suits against Members' offices in certain employment discrimination cases. That position would not sit well with the public or with many Members, so the BLAG was not comfortable filing a brief.

Since Kerry thought the constitutional issue was important, and he could not get the BLAG to sign on. He asked me if Chairman Hyde would be willing to do so. Kerry had served the chairman and me exceptionally well over the years, especially in the Oil for Food Program investigation. I told him I would ask Henry.

I prepared a one-page memorandum about the case and attached the brief which Kerry had written. The memo explained the grounds for wanting the House to be on record that the Speech or Debate clause provided immunity from employment discrimination cases. I went in to see Henry and, following my usual practice, handed him the memo and sat down quietly while he read it. He clearly understood the position Kerry was asking him to take. He said, "You want me to sign on to take a position protecting the constitutional prerogatives of the House, right?" I said, "yes", and he responded, "Of course I will sign it". I told him the final version of the brief would be ready later in the week and asked him if he would authorize me to sign for him. This was a brief to be filed in a federal court, and I wanted to make sure he was comfortable. He said I was "fully authorized". I was pleased with Henry's confidence in me. Always looking for a good line to depart with, I said, "It could cost you your seat". He smiled and said, "That is one of the comforts of being a lame-duck".

✦✦✦✦✦✦✦✦✦

A last Codel

I got to travel with Chairman Hyde on a Codel to Oslo, Helsinki, and Moscow. I had not traveled with Henry before. He invited me, and frankly, I was a little uneasy once again because I did not think there was much I could add. Tom Lantos and his wife, Mel Watt and his wife, and Darrell Issa and his wife were all on the trip as well. Tom Mooney's wife, Melinda, and his secretary, Sheila Klein, who had been Tom's personal assistant for forever, were also going. They used to joke about the fact that Tom had one job, one wife, and one secretary for all his years in Washington. Sheila was wonderful, and I was glad she was along.

The first stop on the trip was Oslo, and I was eager to visit Stortinget, the Norwegian Legislature. I tried to learn as much as possible about the legislative bodies of the countries we visited. I frequently had to clear up the confusion about my title. My formal title was "Counsel and Parliamentarian". In most countries, "Parliamentarian" means an elected official.

When we got to Oslo, I checked with Tom to see if there was anything he wanted me to do. I would regularly volunteer to be "on duty" and give Tom the evening off. He put in a lot of hours because he was the top staffer. He was a trooper.

I tried to be available for anything Henry or Tom wanted. I would pitch in whenever they needed help. I did that because he was my boss, because he was my elder, and because I loved him for the way he treated me.

On the second day in Oslo, I found out I would not be needed that evening, so I called an old friend of Mimi's who lived in Oslo. Paul Podolski had been a student at the Legat School, and he and Mimi had both taken their first jobs as dancers with the Norwegian Opera Ballet. Paul stayed in Norway, working in the theater. He and his wife, Sissel, live in Oslo, and he was an administrator in the Norwegian National Ballet. We had seen him occasionally when he came to the United States, and he and Mimi were very fond of each other. I enjoyed his company immensely.

He traveled extensively, and we never knew where he would be when we called him. With cell phones becoming more ubiquitous, he could have been anywhere. The last time we called, he was in Trieste, Italy. I took a gamble and called him from the hotel in downtown Oslo. I always start my calls to him by saying, "This is the executive secretary for Miss Mimi Legat calling". He would respond by saying, "Hello, Dan." I asked him if he and Sissel were free for dinner that evening. He said, "Yes, but we are in Oslo". I responded, "Funny thing, so am I."

It was surreal when they showed up at the hotel to meet me. Paul kept touching my arm to make sure it was me and that I was really there. We went to dinner at a place Mimi and he had been to a long time ago, next to the famous ski jump at Holmenkollen. We had a lovely evening.

Our next stop was Helsinki. The city was beautiful, and we were met by the staff at the American Embassy. As usual, I visited the legislature. I talked with several members, who offered to take me into their unicameral legislative chamber. I enjoyed the tour and was fascinated by the differences between our two systems. They were very interested in what I had to say about our system.

That evening, we went to a reception at the American ambassador's house. It was a splendid home, which I spent some time exploring. When I got to the ambassador's library, I perused his collection of books. I am always interested in finding out what other people are reading. While I was there, Tom Lantos walked in, and he was doing the same thing. He said to me, "I am ready to go, but there is still so much to read". I assumed what he meant was that he had lived a long life and was prepared for death, but there was so much more reading he wanted to do before then. I thought of that incident when he died three years later.

The next leg of the journey would take us to Moscow. While we were in the air, Henry came down the aisle of the plane to ask me something. Had I known he wanted to talk with me, I would have gotten up and come forward to where he was sitting. I had my nose in a book and was listening to some music and did not notice him. When he got back to my seat and leaned over, I took my earphones out and asked him what I could do for him. All he said to me was, "Dan, are you having a good time on this trip?" I assured him that I was and told him I was grateful that he asked me to come along. That was typical Henry, and it was a little glimpse into how he treated people generally.

When we got to Moscow and were checked into our hotel, we got to visit Red Square. I had, of course, seen video of St. Basil's Cathedral with its multicolored onion domes and Lenin's mausoleum, with various belligerent Soviet leaders standing there, watching military parades. I was surprised at how small the area was, but I was thrilled to be there.

I was looking forward to this part of the trip because two people on the trip had visited Moscow previously. They volunteered to show me some of the more interesting parts of the city. Sam Stratman, Henry's press secretary, promised to show me the famous Moscow subway system. He told me the stations were fabulous works of art. The reason for this was fascinating. The Minister of the Interior at the time the subway system was built was an ambitious young politician who was trying to make a name for himself. The minister's name was Nikita Khrushchev. Sam knew the system well, and he picked subway lines and stations to maximize our limited time. Every station we visited has a unique design reflecting the ethos of the time it was constructed. The stations are lined with marble and decorated with chandeliers, intricate mosaics, heroic statues and gilded trim. It was a breathtaking tour!

I was able to arrange a visit to the Federal Assembly which includes the State Duma, the lower house, and the Federation Council, which is the upper house. I met with several staff people and had an interesting exchange about the differences between our governments. I felt privileged to have been able to visit all three legislatures during this trip.

✦✦✦✦✦✦✦✦

Henry's birthday was April 18, and every year I made it a point to find him to wish him a happy one. The last time I did that was in 2005, which was his

81st. It was also the day he announced he would not run for reelection in 2006. I was saddened to know that he was going to retire, but I was not surprised. His health was declining, and he was having trouble getting around. Another factor was that he was term-limited out of his chairmanship of the International Relations Committee. I did not think he would have enjoyed being in Congress as a rank and file Member after having spent 12 years as a full committee chairman.

On that day, I went over to sit with him and talk during votes. It was always fun to chat with him on his own, or with a gaggle of other Members. I tried to look on the bright side, and I said he could now look forward to doing all the other things he wanted to do. With melancholy in his voice, he said, "What I would really like to do is to be here".

Henry had had an extraordinary impact on my life. He was directly responsible for my continued employment in my beloved House of Representatives. He always treated me with professional respect and personal warmth. While we worked together for more than 25 years, the last 12 of which he was my boss, I never heard a cross word from him. He was a giant in many ways, as a careful lawyer, legislator, mentor, deep thinker and leader. He was a master orator. Whenever he took the floor to speak, the Chamber became hushed. He had an astonishingly positive attitude, even during trying times, of which there were many. He always looked for the best in people, and he brought that out in them. His ability to see the humor in almost any situation certainly made working for him fun. Although I did not agree with his positions on many issues, I respected his careful decision making, his willingness to hear arguments on the other side, and his ability to defend his stances clearly. I am a better man for having known him.

I recall vividly the last time I saw him. It was the closing day of the session, and I was in the Chamber. I saw him arrive in a wheelchair as he was going to vote at one of the low-level voting card stations, which had been recently installed for Members with disabilities. I went up to him, feeling sentimental and thankful, leaned over, and said, "I love you". I then kissed him on the cheek. He smiled and hugged me warmly and said, "You have been a good friend and a highly respected member of the staff. You served with distinction, humility and civility, and established a reputation which earned you the respect and trust of others. I am grateful".

I think of that touching exchange often.

XVIII. Joint Sessions of Congress

I could almost always get in to Joint Sessions of Congress. I never attended a State of the Union Address because most Members attended them, and the Chamber and the galleries are always full. When foreign dignitaries were given an invitation to address Congress, it was normally during the daytime, and there was usually room for me to get in. There were many situations when a guest was scheduled to speak, and only a few Members wanted to attend. In those cases, the floor staff would scramble and get as many pages (back when the House had pages) to pack the floor so as not to embarrass the foreign leader. This was particularly true when the speech was going to be given in another language. Those speeches always took twice as long because they would be delivered in the speaker's native language, paragraph by paragraph, and then translated into English. Printed versions of the speech in English were handed out. See Appendix 1 for a list of the Joint Sessions of Congress I was able to attend.

XIX. American University-- Washington Semester Program (WSP)

What to do after the Hill?

I was going to be out of a job at the end of the Congress, and I had to figure out what I wanted to do. I was sure I did not want to lobby, and private practice I had not found rewarding.

For more than 25 years, while working on the Hill, I had volunteered as a guest speaker for students enrolled in the Washington Semester Program at American University. This once prestigious and robust program brings students from colleges all over the nation, and frequently from foreign countries to Washington to learn about a variety of subjects. I would speak to the classes on American Government with an emphasis on the legislative process. The groups would range from 20 students to 50. I would usually meet them in the House Judiciary Committee hearing room. I received a Distinguished Service Award for Teaching from Dean Dave Brown for my contributions to the program at one of its annual dinners.

In November, being aware of the fact that Chairman Hyde was retiring, I was, as people say, "exploring my options". One possibility was to stay on the International Relations Committee staff under the new Democratic Chairman, Tom Lantos. I had switched from the Democrats to the Republicans when the Judiciary Committee changed hands in 1995, so I thought there might be a chance I could do the same kind of maneuver again in 2007. I had a reasonably good working relationship with Tom Lantos, and, for the most part, with his staff. However, as they were preparing the incoming committee staff, one of the counsels with whom I had worked with closely, advised me I should not count on it. Message received.

My wife and I were going to celebrate our 20th wedding anniversary with a trip to Australia. This trip had been planned long before the election, so the necessary task of looking for a job would have to wait. On the day before we were to leave, I got a call from Professor Rick Semiatin, one of the people whose AU classes I used to speak to regularly. He told me one of his colleagues who taught the Public Law Seminar was retiring. He wanted to know if I was interested in taking over for him.

I had a longstanding desire to teach constitutional law in an undergraduate setting, so this seemed right up my alley. Rick told me to contact Dean Brown to express my interest. I called him, and we discussed it. He told me he had heard terrific things about me and made it reasonably clear the job was mine if I wanted it. However, University policy dictated I had to be interviewed by the WSP Faculty Committee. I said I would be happy to meet with them, but I was leaving town the next day and would not be back until Christmas day. Since they needed someone to start at the beginning of the new semester in January, an in-person interview would not be possible. He asked if I was willing to have my interview over the phone from Australia. I agreed, and we planned a day and time for the call.

We were in Sydney at the appointed time. It was strange since the committee was going to call me at 3 pm Washington time, on a Tuesday, which was 6 am on Wednesday in Sydney. On the phone were Dean Brown, Professor Semiatin, and another faculty member whom I had never met, Bea Siman. We discussed my interest in the position. Since the course was about American government, the fact I knew so many people in Congress was a big plus. Getting guest speakers was a prime focus of the program. At the end of the conversation, Dean Brown told me he would discuss it with the committee and let me know their decision. We arranged for a call the next day.

The next morning at 6 am, I waited for the phone to ring. There was a slight miscommunication on the timing. He called at 7 am and asked if he had gotten the time correctly. I, of course, said he had. He offered me the position and told me I should come in to see him when we got back. I was happy about having a new job, although I was fairly clueless about what exactly was expected of me.

✦ ✦ ✦ ✦ ✦ ✦ ✦ ✦ ✦

I then had to make a rather uncomfortable phone call. Under the new committee alignment with Democratic Chairman Lantos at the helm, the Ranking Minority Member was going to be Ileana Ros-Lehtinen. She and I had a long conversation on the floor before Mimi and I left for Australia. As I have explained previously, we had a wonderful working rapport. Ms. Ros-Lehtinen and I talked about my coming to work for her when she became the ranking minority Member. We had a candid conversation, and I explained to her that my role as committee Parliamentarian was not well suited for someone in the minority. She said she appreciated my candor and understood completely. Unfortunately, I did not have a chance to talk to Yleem before we left.

After accepting the job at AU, I checked my messages, and Yleem had called. I was under the false assumption that Ms. Ros-Lehtinen would have talked with Yleem and explained my lack of suitability for a role on the minority staff. Unfortunately, she had not. When I called Yleem, she offered me a job with the committee. I told her I had just accepted the AU position and would not be returning to the Hill. There was a long silence at the end of the line. She was noticeably disappointed. I told her I had discussed it with Ileana, and we had agreed I would not be joining her staff.

My last day in the House

Before my teaching duties formally began, there was one last thing I wanted to do; go into the House and watch Nancy Pelosi be sworn in as the first woman Speaker of the House. I was able to walk onto the floor even though I was technically off the payroll. I still had my ID, and all of the security and floor staff knew me, so getting in was not a problem.

There was an exuberance in the House because the Democrats had regained control, and there were lots of hugs and kisses. I was talking to one of my heroes, Former Congressman Norm Mineta when Nancy Pelosi walked in to thunderous applause. Our eyes met, and since we had worked on a lot of bills together, especially dealing with immigration, she came over and gave me a big hug as I congratulated her. It was a lovely moment, and the House photographer was there to take a photo. Although I would return to the House with my students frequently, that was the last time I would do so when they were in session. It was a fitting coda.

I had a second reason for going to the floor; to ask Members to speak to my classes. I knew that one of the most important tasks involved in teaching in the Washington Semester Program was getting guest speakers, especially Members of Congress. I took a Member list with me, and I spoke to as many of them as I felt I knew well enough to approach. I told them I was leaving and that I would invite them to speak to my classes sometime in the future. I would only ask people with whom I had a good working relationship. Not every Member fit that description, but there was a surprisingly large number. If they consented, I would quote Chairman Hyde and say that he taught me whenever you got a Member of Congress to agree to do something, you should ask them, "What is the name of the person on your staff who makes you look good?" When I would get a quizzical look from a Member in response to that question, I would simply tell them that I wanted to know who in their office I should call to arrange it. One of the younger Members from Illinois, Jesse Jackson Junior, who always called me "Sir", said, "You call me". That was a nice compliment and unusual.

Jesse and I talked about the day I threw him out of the staff gym. After many years of staff agitating for a place to exercise, the powers that be had finally converted the Rayburn Office Building carwash into a gymnasium for the staff. The Members had a gym. One day when I was in the new staff facility, I saw Jackson looking around. As I knew him well enough to joke with him (since he and Chairman Hyde and their staffs worked together on Illinois-related matters), I said, "Jesse, you are not allowed in here. You have the Members' gym". Several of the staffers in the gym were freaked out that I was speaking to a Member so irreverently and flippantly. That happened to me frequently as I was regularly kidding with Members. Jesse laughed and soon left.

Coincidentally, later that day, I was on the way to the floor and was taking the escalator up from the Rayburn subway. At the top, I saw Jesse Jackson Senior, the famous civil rights leader. As is true of many political figures, if you make eye contact and stick out your hand, they feign recognition and smile and shake your hand. I looked him in the eye and said, "Excuse me, but aren't you Congressman Jackson's father?" He smiled and said, "Yes". Several people nearby looked at me incredulously. I expect they were asking themselves, "Doesn't that idiot know that's *the* Jesse Jackson?"

On to American University

When we got back from our trip, I went over to the campus to meet with Dean Brown to get a better idea of what was going to be expected of me. Dave was the heart of the Washington Semester Program. He was the real driving force during its formative years, as well as during those years when it had matured and become a prestigious program. My familiarity with the program was limited to the different American Government classes I had spoken to over the years.

I had expected Dean Brown to describe to me the structure of the program and the curriculum as well as the kinds of class discussions I would be having, including what subjects I should cover. I also thought that he would be able to give me an understanding of the types of students I was going to encounter. This did not happen. When I met him, he grabbed his coat and walked me over to Dunblane Hall to show me my office. It was spacious and comfortable and had belonged to my predecessor. However, it was still jammed with all of his research materials. It did have the only two things I really needed, a computer and a telephone.

With those two essentials, I started planning immediately. I was to have classes mornings and afternoons on Monday, Tuesday and Wednesday. Each semester was 15 weeks, so that meant I had to schedule at least 45 class sessions. They could be my teaching classes on campus about subjects which interested me, having guest speakers come to campus, and, most importantly, meeting with guest speakers on the Hill and other places downtown. You could not get Members of Congress or Judges to agree to come to campus because it would take too much time out of their schedules. However, since we were near a metro stop, getting downtown was relatively easy.

I must admit to being somewhat overwhelmed to be staring at an empty 3-month calendar on my wall. I knew I would be juggling schedules all semester long, and I also knew I had to get myself in gear asking people to be speakers. I would sprinkle my own sessions in and around when guest speakers were available. It was an exercise in on-the-job training. I also had to learn how to use the technology which American University used, which was not always easy for me. This came up regularly when I had to post reading materials and the schedule for the following week on Fridays. Fortunately for my technological-ly-challenged mind, we had outstanding support on campus.

Dean Brown also showed me around the classrooms in the building and the all-important class book where professors would sign up for classrooms in des-ignated timeslots. There was always a premium on getting rooms in Dunblane Hall because it meant you would not have to go outside to get to your class. There were a few other rooms available on the Tenley campus, but as soon as you got confirmation from a speaker willing to come, you had to rush upstairs and make sure to secure a room. I also had to get rooms for the sessions I would be conducting. The time slots for my own classes I could easily change when necessary to accommodate a guest speaker's changing schedule.

I was always greedy when it came to class time, and I did not like to be limit-ed to a specific class length. While most college classes have a set length, I could reserve a room for back-to-back time slots and have the luxury of going until I finished. The first thing I would do at the beginning of each class was to walk in and take the clock down from the wall. I quoted my seventh grade English teacher who had taught me, "The clock watcher is rarely the man of the hour". It always annoyed me when students started to pack up before class was over. If they did not know precisely when class was going to end, they would not do that. I told them that class was over when I was satisfied we had finished the material. Since the students had no other classes to get to, they were a captive audience. Class ended when I said, "Class dismissed".

After my initial meeting with Dean Brown that first day, I would stop by his office regularly to chat. He was always amiable and supportive of anything I wanted to do. At that time, the students lived on the Tenley Circle Campus and ate in the cafeteria in the same building as Dave's office, where they could interact with him and his staff. It was nice to learn from Dave that my students were saying good things about the course. There were five staff members, a few senior administrators, an Assistant Dean, and that was it. Everything seemed to function smoothly, and anything you needed was just a phone call or a drop-by away.

Dave was always protective when there were any difficult questions from students or their parents. That happened rarely, but when something did come up, he was very supportive. I was pleased to know that. It struck me as a bit strange since he had no way of knowing what I was doing in the classroom on a day-to-day basis. He did not see our class schedule and did not get a list of the guest speakers. The only time he asked me about speakers was one day when I stopped by on the way back from the Hill. "Did you do anything interesting today?" he asked. I responded, "We had five Members of Congress, including Senator Richard Burr, Representatives John Lewis, Steve Rothman, Mel Watt, and Tom Tancredo, who was a presidential candidate. Dave was only moderately impressed.

I am a firm believer in having a good relationship with the boss's top assistant. It is the professional equivalent of the marital command "happy wife, happy life". The Assistant Dean under Dave Brown, Donna Chapman, referred to me as the "lowest maintenance faculty member" she knew. I tried not to bug her with trivial things, and when I did come to her with a problem, it was something that I had not been able to work out on my own. She was a problem-solver and was very helpful to me. I will always be grateful to her for all she did to make my transition to AU smooth. She is one of the best professionals I have ever had the pleasure of working with.

✚✚✚✚✚✚✚✚

Washington Semester Program—The Public Law Seminar
The Public Law program was one of nine that included foreign policy, international business, American politics and international organizations. I felt strongly that I would teach government and not politics.

I designed the seminar to enhance the students' knowledge of the public law-making process and the factors that influence it. This allowed me to give the students a taste of legal issues, and it gave me a chance to sink my pedagogical teeth into constitutional law. It would be different than teaching at a law school because I could weave into legal discussions the historical context of the cases as well as their public policy ramifications.

In the classroom, students engaged in a wide range of activities, including analysis of judicial opinions, debates on public policy issues, and even a mock legislative session. I utilized the Socratic Method, which is standard in law schools. During debates, I would often assign my students to support an argument contrary to their beliefs. This was to encourage them to analyze and understand both sides of an issue. This concept was an often-repeated theme among the guest speakers and by me.

A major component of the course consisted of meetings with prominent professionals in the public policy world. The students met with Supreme Court Justices, Federal Judges, Members of the House and Senate, current and former Cabinet Officers, as well as other people in the private sector who participate in the law-making process. Students got the opportunity to interact with the speakers in small groups and ask them questions.

To get to know each student, I sent out a "Greetings" email about a month before the semester began. I asked them for some background as well as a headshot photograph of themselves. I liked to be able to recognize students by name on the first day.

The "Greetings" email discussed the internships, which were an important component of the seminar. It also gave them information about how they would get reading materials and schedules, which I would post on the AU electronic Blackboard. It described in some detail the topics we would study, and the activities and debates we were going to have. See Appendix 2 for a list of topics covered in the Public Law Seminar.

On the first day of class, the professors would meet with their incoming students in what we called the "Ice Breaker". I would give an outline of what I hoped to accomplish over the semester and describe some assignments they would be getting.

I encouraged students to "squeeze it" while in Washington. This meant that they should try to get the maximum benefit from any occasion. I urged them to explore the city and all of the incredible educational opportunities it presents.

Class Assignments

The Scavenger Hunt

On the first weekend of the semester, I assigned the students a Washington D.C. scavenger hunt. I broke them up into groups of 4 or 5 who did not know each other. They were to go to 10 different locations in the city and have someone take a photograph of them. The locations included places where they would be going during the semester: the Hill, the courthouses, the gym on campus, the Kennedy Center, and the White House, among others. The students always enjoyed this. They could use the day to get to know each other and also have some experience in getting around the city, including acquainting themselves with the Metro system.

Constitution Quiz

In the "Greetings" email, I told them they should always have a pocket-size copy of the Constitution with them. To reinforce how important that would be, I told them there would be a quiz on the Constitution on the first day of class. I urged them to read it slowly and carefully to be prepared.

During the "ice-breaker" meeting, I handed out the quiz, which contained 25 true/false questions. All of the answers were true! It was fun to see them look at me quizzically as they took the test, some of them recognizing but not believing they could all be true. It gave them a bit of insight into my diabolical nature. I did not grade the quiz; I told them they could use it as a study guide.

Internship Expectation Papers

Since they would spend two full days a week at their internships and I wanted them to do some thinking ahead of time about possible organizations where they might want to work. I required them to write a 2-4-page essay describing what types of internships they were considering, and what they expected to gain from them. This was a way for me to get them writing as soon as they got here, and to encourage them to focus on their job search.

Observations

The students were required to attend at least two public hearings during the semester and write a paper about each one. They could attend a Congressional, judicial, or regulatory hearing. The testimony is usually available ahead of time. I encouraged students to prepare by reading it and as much as possible on the subject of the hearing. I urged them to get out of their comfort zones and go to a session on an unfamiliar topic. These papers constituted an essential portion of their grades, plus attending such hearings could be a good learning experience.

Dinner Guest Presentations

Each student was to select a prominent public figure, living or dead, with whom they would like to have dinner. During the semester, I would call on students to discuss their selection and to explain to the class why they chose that person and what they hoped to learn from their "guest".

Before giving any oral presentation, I suggested they do at least one dry run, if not more, and record it. I had regularly done this and found it very useful in making me more comfortable with my presentation, as well as to catch any distracting mannerisms.

My friend and mentor, Earl Dudley, was the lawyer who introduced me to this very helpful practice. He was preparing to make an oral argument to the U.S. Court of Appeals for the District of Columbia Circuit. He decided not only to do a dry run but to record it. He handled the legal issues in the case well. However, when he reviewed the recording, he noticed he was frequently pushing his glasses back up the bridge of his nose. He found that distracting and thought the judges might as well. He decided to get contact lenses, at least for the argument.

The dinner guest exercise was always interesting to me. I was intrigued by the broad range of people the students selected. Some of them were people I had not heard of, and some were famous people who were picked for unusual reasons. For example, one of the students selected Walt Disney, and her reasons were intriguing. She wanted to know the basis of his anti-Semitism. Another student picked Timothy McVeigh, the Oklahoma City bomber. She wanted to inquire about his political philosophy and whether he thought his desire for societal change justified the use of violence. I expect he never thought about it in those terms, but her presentation was thought-provoking.

Over the years, students selected athletes, politicians, captains of industry, and historical figures. They usually enjoyed this exercise, both their own presentations and those of their classmates.

One of the best was by a student from a small Southern town who chose baseball player Jackie Robinson. Her reason for selecting him was to find out why he was picked to break the color barrier in major league baseball. His talents as a ballplayer were extraordinary, but she wanted to know about his character and how he lived through the psychological stresses that he encountered.

In all of the semesters I had students do this exercise, I had less than a handful of repeat guests. FDR, JFK, and RFK, as well as President Obama, were chosen more than once. But my students selected over 300 different "guests" over the years.

The Internships

Each student interned two full days a week in a law-related organization. Students worked in law firms, Congressional offices, interest groups, non-profits, and many other government organizations.

The jewel in the crown of the Washington Semester Program is Amy Morrill-Bijeau, the internship coordinator. She always had the students' best interest at heart and was tenacious in helping them all find positions.

The internships were varied. Some were excellent, and some were just plain terrible. I was usually the internship professor for the students in my Public Law seminar. Since I was with the students three days a week, I got to know them well, and most of them felt comfortable coming to me with problems with their internships

I did not have a lot of situations with bad internships, but there were a few. Two students came to Washington (in different semesters), having already secured their internships. They were thrilled because they had landed internships at the White House, which they thought would be a wonderful experience as well as be good for their resumes. I was distressed to find out that they both had jobs in the Office of Presidential Correspondence. All internships had to be approved by me before they started. I told these students that I was not going to approve them. They were both crushed and disappointed. Each thought that being able to work in the White House was the most exciting thing that could happen and that having the White House on their resumes would be a big plus. I had to explain to them that working in the Correspondence Office entailed processing routine letters to the President, the rest of the First Family, and probably to their dogs. It meant opening and counting the thousands of letters that flow into the White House every day, but it did not involve any substantive work.

One of the students took my advice to heart, and I helped her get a position on the Hill working on campaign-finance legislation. She had a marvelous experience, learned a lot, and got to meet some interesting people.

The other student was adamant that she wanted to work in the White House. I told her I wanted to talk with her supervisor before I would approve it. In speaking to the supervisor, I expressed my concern that my student would not have a challenging and rewarding learning experience. I said I did not want her spending the semester answering letters "written to Bo"(the Obama's dog). I hoped that she would understand my attempt at humor, but I was to be disappointed. She replied in a huffy manner, "She would not be doing that. Those letters go to the First Lady's office". I told the student that I was extremely reluctant to approve her internship, but I would if she promised she would push hard to get some substantive work.

Unfortunately, as the student gave her final internship presentation at the end of the semester, she confessed that she had been wrong, and all they were doing in that office was opening and counting letters. She did not even get to draft any possible responses. She did make a joke by saying she never got to answer a letter to a dog. I hope that was a life lesson learned.

I did have one other disappointing internship situation to deal with. One of my students was interning at a law firm. It was a small firm that had regularly pounced on students in my class at the beginning of every semester. Since the partner in charge knew my students were mostly pre-law, she thought they were likely to be interested in working in a small legal practice. Another factor that came into play was the fact that most students came to Washington without internships. As the semester began, they frequently would begin to panic. The pressure was exacerbated by the knowledge that some of their classmates already had jobs. Some of my students had worked in small law firms and had good experiences.

In this case, however, the student was so thrilled to have an offer that she accepted immediately. She did not explore any other options. This firm was not very busy, and the student was given a lot of menial tasks. She was not being given a chance to learn about being a lawyer. I was disappointed by that. I was angry when I found out my student had been assigned to research the best deal on leasing a Porsche sports car, and finding out what permit was required to build a swimming pool at the lawyer's house. I was ready to pull the student immediately after finding that out. Amy suggested we talk with the lawyer first. The three of us spoke, and the lawyer told me her practice was experiencing some problems. I rather curtly said, "I do not give a fig (I actually said that) about your practice. All I care about is that my student has a good internship experience". The situation did not improve much, but it was too late in the semester to make a change. I make it a point not to permit any other students to work there despite aggressive efforts to recruit them.

Internship Journals

Each student was required to keep a journal about their internships. I urged them to make their entries every working day, so their impressions would be as fresh as possible. I wanted to know about their on-the-job experience and what ideas they had to make their offices more effective. I emphasized the journals, as well as every other paper submitted to me, should be letter-perfect, sufficient to use as a writing sample for graduate school, submit to an internship supervisor, or a boss on a job after graduation.

The students had been cautioned about not using the office computers for their internship journals (or anything else of a personal nature, like Facebook or shopping, etc.), especially if they were in government positions. I got a call one Friday afternoon from a student, Nadine, who was in panic mode. She was working in a Congressional office and had prepared her journal on the office computer. To her shock and surprise, her supervisor had access to it. Her boss had read her journal, including Nadine's candid comments about some problems with the way the office was run. The supervisor was upset when she read these criticisms.

Interestingly, she was most concerned that I would read the journal and talk to the press about the office. I instructed Nadine to assure her supervisor that I would never do that. Nadine was relieved, and her boss was not only mollified but thought some of the comments were valid.

Later I told Nadine that she was a "knucklehead", and I reminded her I had specifically warned the class not to use the office computer for anything personal. She said, "Yes, I know it was a stupid thing to do, especially since you alerted us to the danger. I *am* a knucklehead". I still hear from Nadine, who is now in law school. She signs her emails, "knucklehead".

✦✦✦✦✦✦✦✦✦

My goals for the students

My goals for each student were threefold; to elevate their level of analytical thinking, to elevate their writing skills, and to elevate their level of oral presentation. I was frequently astounded that college students could come to American University without the ability to analyze issues, with abysmal writing skills and an incredible poverty of language. To say some of them were unprepared would be an understatement of considerable proportions.

I steered them to the Writing Center at AU, which is a free service. I had someone from the Center come to address the class at the beginning of the semester to explain how they could help students with papers. The Writing Center staff always emphasized the need for clear, concise, and cogent writing.

Justice Scalia, whenever we met with him, always emphasized the importance of good writing. He would tell the class the story about when he was working at the Department of Justice in the Office of Legal Counsel. He turned in a ten-page memo to his boss saying if he had had more time, it would have been five pages.

I also gave the students a "cheat sheet" from the Writing Center entitled "Eliminating Empty Words" to demonstrate the importance of simplifying their writing. As an example, I would put on the chalkboard the full text of a very powerful short story by a well-known author which was only one sentence long; "Unused, the baby's shoes were sold".

There were five banned words in my class. These words, when used improperly, would subject the student to being called out. Those words are: "like", "awesome", "amazing", "totally", and "literally". The use of "like" as a spacer would be noted as a "Like violation". This bad habit had become rampant among college students. My pointing it out would unnerve some students, but over time they got used to it. Many of them got to the point where they would say it, and quickly correct themselves. They became so sensitive to it they would end up correcting their siblings when home on school breaks.

✦✦✦✦✦✦✦✦✦

I had two special assignments which I made during the first week of the semester. One student would be designated to respond whenever I pointed to him or her with the following mantra: "Freeman's First Law", which meant "Get reelected". This would come up many times during the semester when discussing Congress, and I would reinforce it frequently when appropriate by pointing to the student who had been assigned the task and have them respond with the mantra. Sometimes it was shortened to "FFL".

The second was to answer the question "What are the first five words in the First Amendment?", I would ask this often. Those words are, "Congress shall make no law". I did this to emphasize the fact that the First Amendment does not guarantee rights; it is only a prohibition on what *government* can do. I would explain to the students that references to so-called "guarantees" of free speech, and religious freedom only operate as a prohibition on governmental institutions. There is no general right to free speech. As this would come up regularly during the semester, I would ask the designated student to recite the words to reinforce the concept.

✦✦✦✦✦✦✦✦✦

I decided I was not going to permit any electronic devices in my classroom. This was in 2007, and all the students had cellphones and laptops. I was told by a colleague about a study which showed that when students take notes on a keyboard, they are more likely to simply transcribe what the professor has said, instead of taking it in and synthesizing it. As I witnessed for myself one summer when I was auditing some classes at the law school, laptops can be a serious distraction. I saw many students doing other things during the classes; Facebook, email, shopping and one student was watching a movie! I read an article about a study concerning electronics in the classroom. The study of both undergrads and law students had found that those who used laptops in class had something unrelated to the session up on their screens around 40 percent of the time.

When I started teaching, there was a split in academia; some professors welcomed technology in the classroom, and many prohibited it. I felt I was on solid ground with my choice and spelled out my policy in every syllabus to give the students fair warning. I only got pushback about it from two students over my decade at AU.

I started out my technology policy with a bang. There was a Best Buy electronics store a block away from the campus. In the first week of classes, I ran into a friend of mine there. He told me his cell phone had died, and he was there to replace it. I asked him if I could have it. He said, "Dan, the thing is dead. I am going to throw it away". I replied, "A dead phone will do just fine".

As I was leaving my office to get to class every day, I would put the dead phone in the left pocket of my jacket. I always wore a suit to class to set a professional tone. About a week later, I was discussing the six prohibitions on Congressional action contained in the First Amendment. Near the end of class, as I was walking around the classroom (which was my normal practice), I had gone over the first four guarantees when a loud cell phone went off with the "Are you ready for some football?" jingle as a ring tone. Without missing a beat about the First Amendment, I walked up to the culprit and put my hand out, silently asking him to hand me the offending device. He sheepishly surrendered the phone. I took it and put it in the *right* pocket of my suit. I then completed my comments about the First Amendment.

As I walked to the front of the room, I reached into my *left* pocket and pulled out the dead phone. I turned and threw it as hard as I could against the cinderblock wall. It broke into a zillion pieces. There was an audible gasp from the class. I then asked, "Are there any questions?" There were none. I then said, "Class dismissed", and the students raced out of the classroom.

The story about "wild man Freeman" spread like wildfire through the dorms. I had established a "rep." After everyone else had left, I gave the student his undamaged phone, which was still in my right pocket. He was visibly relieved.

I enjoyed having my office in the classroom building since it made it easier for students to drop in. My ban on technology applied in my office as well. There was one funny situation when a student walked in with earbuds in his ears. The music was so loud I could hear it from across my desk. I expect this young man will be hearing-impaired later in life. As he stepped into my office, he asked me a question. I was surprised he was not aware his music was blasting away, and he probably could not hear my response. I decided to test him. When he finished his question, I began moving my mouth but made no audible sound. It took him a full ten seconds to realize he could not hear me. "What?" he said. I continued my pantomime of speaking. He pulled out the earbuds. Until I explained to him what had happened, he did not have a clue he was in his electronic bubble. I suggested he be more aware of the effects the electronic devices were having on his ability to interact with others. He was appropriately embarrassed and said he had learned his lesson.

✦ ✦ ✦ ✦ ✦ ✦ ✦ ✦

My excellent and gratifying experience in law school taught me about its educational benefits. Most of the students in my class were considering it. By using the Socratic Method, rather than straight lectures, my students could get a taste of what law school would be like, and, candidly, it made the class more fun and more interesting for me.

When students would ask me about whether law school was best for them, I would give them a caveat that although most people considered the process to be analogous to a three-year kidney stone expulsion, I enjoyed it immensely. I told them that having a law degree did not necessarily mean you had to end up practicing law. There is a broad range of interesting and challenging careers for people who have law degrees that do not involve the actual practice of law. As far as I was concerned, there were two significant benefits of going to law school; enhancing the ability to think analytically (which requires knowing both sides of any issue) and learning to write clearly and convincingly.

I always emphasized how important writing is to being an effective advocate. Judge Andre Davis used to tell my students, "There is no such thing as good writing, there is only good *rewriting*.

✦✦✦✦✦✦✦✦✦

Interesting Class Exercises

Moot Appellate Court Argument

We conducted a mock oral argument of an actual case that was pending before the U.S. Supreme Court, *Snyder v. Phelps,* an important freedom of speech case. The plaintiff, Albert Snyder, was a sympathetic figure, the father of Mathew Snyder, a Marine who was killed in Iraq. The defendant, Fred Phelps, was the leader of the Westboro Baptist Church whose followers regularly picketed military funerals. The members of the church believe that God punishes the United States for its tolerance of homosexuality, particularly within the military.

Westboro picketed Matthew Snyder's funeral displaying homophobic signs. Snyder sued Phelps and the church, claiming that their actions caused him severe emotional distress. In his defense, Phelps argued that his speech (the picketing and the signs) was protected under the Free Speech Clause of the First Amendment. The jury awarded Snyder millions of dollars in damages, and the appeal went to the Supreme Court. I divided the class into three groups; attorneys for the plaintiff Albert Snyder, attorneys for Fred Phelps/Westboro Baptist Church, and three students who would be judges.

I asked the Chief Judge of the District of Columbia Court of Appeals, Eric Washington if he had a courtroom I could use. He and I had worked together in the EINSHAC program, and he had been a regular speaker to my classes. He asked me if I would like to use the "big ceremonial courtroom". That was a no-brainer!

The next morning, I made the assignments. The most urgent question was from one of the students I selected to be a judge. She wanted to know, "Are we going to get robes"? I must admit I was a little disappointed that that was the first question that came up. I, however, had thought about that. I called the Chief Judge of the DC Superior Court, Rufus King, to see if I could borrow a robe from him. The reason I chose him was that the student I had selected to be the Chief Judge of the moot court was tall, and Chief Judge King is also tall. I secured two more robes from another judge. The oral argument went reasonably well, with some students doing better than others. For many, it was the first time they had been in a moot court. I thought this was a good experience for them especially being able to conduct it in a real courtroom.

Legislative hearing and debate on a proposed law gun control law—H.R. 1234

One of my favorite exercises was the mock legislative hearing and debate on a proposed bill to require people to have had firearms safety training before purchasing a handgun. The class would meet as a Congressional committee to hear testimony on the bill, debate its merits, and vote on its passage. All of this would be done with facsimiles of real documents. The hearing notice, the parliamentary scenario, and the witness format were identical to things I had prepared for real committee meetings on Capitol Hill.

I drafted a bill, "H.R. 1234 Safety and Firearms Training Effectiveness Act (SAFTE)", which required the Attorney General to promulgate regulations for the establishment of firearms training classes. To purchase a handgun, the buyer would have to submit proof of having taken an approved firearms safety course.

I would frequently get the full House Judiciary Committee hearing room for this exercise. I thought this added to the experience. I had spent hundreds of hours there during hearings, markups, conference committees and private meetings. It was the historic room where impeachment hearings, confirmation hearings for Vice Presidential nominees Gerald Ford and Nelson Rockefeller, and major civil rights bills had been debated.

I told the students they would be randomly assigned to be either a witness for or against the bill or to be a minority or majority Member of the Committee. Since we had met with speakers from both the National Rifle Association and handgun control groups before this exercise, I could usually tell what any student's feelings about the Second Amendment were. I would "randomly" assign students to the other side to stretch their minds. In picking witnesses, I tried to select students who had a dramatic flair. I would suggest, at least to the witness supporting the bill, he or she should testify with appropriate distress and drama about a young niece or nephew who was accidentally killed in a drive-by shooting. We had some superb acting over the years. One of the student-witnesses put together a video of his delightful niece who would not get to go to the prom or get married. He got choked up. He really got into the part! It was a terrific presentation. At the end of the semester, I presented him with a special award for the best performance by a distraught witness.

When setting up this exercise, I tried to make sure I selected a student to be the chair who was confident enough to go with the flow of the give and take of the debate. By the time we got around to this each semester, I had a good idea of who could do it well. One of the students who did an especially good job was a young woman from California, Amanda. There were some problems during the debate as to who would speak when, and she handled them with ease. Being able to make sure every argument from the minority was countered at the appropriate time required some flexibility, and she was up to the task. Amanda went on to Georgetown University Law School and is now practicing law. After the "hearing", the students would debate the bill and then have a vote on "final passage". The students would really get into it. It was almost always done well. The only exception was one semester when a student who was assigned to be opposed to the bill started to support it in his statement. A minute into his presentation, someone on his side of the aisle pointed out, "Hey, you are supposed to be *against* this bill!"

The Mosque at Ground Zero

Another exercise I enjoyed was a debate on whether the New York City Council should grant a permit to build a mosque at "ground zero" in lower Manhattan. The students were given materials about the plans for the mosque and told they would be required to vote as members of the City Council on the application for the permit. This was based on an actual situation.

The students had to determine what the issues were, such as the free exercise of religion, and what the pragmatic effects might be of building a mosque in such a sensitive location. They had to understand the facts about the proposed building, as well as the potential legal and constitutional law issues involved.

Each student would either be assigned or would choose a New York City constituency to represent. I had an exceptional student one semester who was a Latino from California. He was always good at role-playing and was able to tailor his arguments accordingly. I asked "Rabbi Rodriguez" to explain his position on the permit. He clearly understood that meant he was representing a Jewish precinct, and he made his argument from that perspective. To this day, that young man, now a practicing lawyer, signs his correspondence to me as "Rabbi Rodriguez".

Stolen Valor

Every semester there was only one case when I told the students how I felt about an issue. That was when we were discussing the "Stolen Valor" law, which made it a federal crime to lie about having received a military decoration. There was a challenge to the law based on the argument that it deprived people of their First Amendment right to freedom of speech.

Xavier Alvarez was indicted and tried for violating the statute. His lawyer moved to dismiss the indictment on the grounds that the law was unconstitutional. That motion was denied by the trial judge, and the case eventually went to the Supreme Court. His lawyer was candid in his brief to the Court. The opening paragraph says: "Xavier Alvarez lied". (This is *his lawyer* writing.) "He lied when he claimed to have played professional hockey for the Detroit Red Wings. He lied when he claimed to be married to a Mexican starlet…He lied when he claimed to be an engineer. He lied when he claimed to have rescued the American ambassador during the Iranian hostage crisis… But none of those lies were crimes". The brief also quoted Mr. Alvarez's statement at a municipal board meeting, "I'm a retired Marine of 25 years…Back in 1987, I received the Congressional Medal of Honor…". There is no such thing. There is only the Medal of Honor.

Alvarez never served in the military. There was no evidence his lies caused any harm, but as a result of this non-defamatory lie about himself, he was prosecuted for violating the Stolen Valor Act.

The students were given the Supreme Court opinion striking down the law and told to be ready to debate it in class. At the beginning of the class, I randomly split the class in half. I put up two tent cards on the tables in front of the classroom. One said, "United States", and one said "Alvarez". Half the class would represent the United States, and the other half, Mr. Alvarez. I sent them to separate rooms to organize for the argument and decide who was going to take which specific issue. I met with each group and helped them to prepare for the debate.

When we reconvened, and before we started, I told them I had something to disclose. "I usually do not tell you how I feel about any issue we discuss. I want you to make up your own minds. But in this case, I feel so strongly I think I must tell you I was a Marine, and I was awarded a Distinguished Service Cross, a Silver Star, and two Purple Hearts. I try to be objective in this class, but on this issue, I simply cannot".

I would then make the exercise a little more challenging by switching the tent cards, so the students had to argue the "other side". Sometimes a student would exclaim, "I knew you were going to do that!" The oral arguments on this case were frequently excellent. Occasionally, the combination of my disclosure and flipping sides was too much for them to handle, and the arguments did not go well.

After the debate, I usually asked for a show of hands as to what the outcome should be. I would also "clarify the record". I told them I had never served in the military, I never received any decorations, and I had just violated the Stolen Valor Act.

Washington College of Law Programs

Since American University's Law School, the Washington College of Law, was nearby, I tried to keep current on programs they were having that might interest my students. These were frequently held in the middle of the day with lunch provided. Free food is always very attractive to students.

These programs usually dealt with current issues of national importance. While most of the audience was made up of law students, the presentations were usually not so esoteric that my undergraduate students could not follow them. One program dealt with the issue of same-sex marriage. This was before the Supreme Court ruled on the issue. One of the panelists was a member of the Law School faculty and a member of the Maryland Senate, Jamie Raskin. He is now a Member of Congress. He told the story of the debate in the State Senate about legalizing same-sex marriage in Maryland. His opponent on the bill had cited the bible's teaching as a reason not to pass the bill. Raskin said to her that when he took the oath of office, he "swore on the bible to protect the Constitution, not on the Constitution to protect the bible". It was a good line and made the point very well.

One semester the Supreme Court was going to be hearing oral argument on a case about copyrights relating to cheerleader's uniforms. There were two big manufacturers, and one had sued the other for violating its copyrights on its designs. While copyright cases can sometimes be difficult to follow, this was straightforward, and it was one which college students could relate to.

Fortuitously, the law school had planned a symposium on the case the afternoon of the oral argument. I managed to get seats for my class, and we went to the Court and watched. The students were well prepared since I had supplied them with the briefs to read beforehand. It was a stimulating experience, and they got to watch the give and take between the advocates and the Justices. Some of the students were surprised about how much of the argument involved questions from the bench.

That afternoon we joined the seminar at the law school. There were panelists from both sides of the case, and it was an interesting session. By happenstance, the professor from the law school, who was the intellectual property expert, was someone who was in my high school class.

DNA Extraction

One of my guest speakers was Jennifer Luttman, a forensic evidence examiner who was the senior FBI official in charge of its DNA evidence unit. Luttman, who had testified in many criminal prosecutions, was recognized as an "expert in forensic serology and forensic DNA analysis". She provided background information about DNA, how it is analyzed, and how genetic profiles are created. She explained that this type of testing is performed by teams consisting of examiners, serologists, and biologists.

She came to talk to the students about the uses of DNA in the FBI's forensic work. I had all the solutions, test tubes, and other materials necessary for the extraction since I had done it with her before in an EINSHAC session. She took them through the process. What the students eventually got to see was some gooey glop at the bottom of the test tube, which was the strands of their own double helix. It was an interesting and fun class exercise.

✦✦✦✦✦✦✦✦✦

Guest Speakers

The guest speakers were the heart and soul of the program. My students got to meet in small groups with some very high-level officials, as well as exceptional subject matter experts. Although most of our meetings were limited to just my class of about 15-20 students, I would occasionally invite other professors' classes to join us. This was reciprocal among all of the different WSP sections, from my course in Public Law, to American Politics, Foreign Policy, and International Business courses. My colleagues on the faculty were very well-connected in their respective fields and were able to provide access to a splendid variety of outstanding speakers. See Appendix 3 for a list of guest speakers.

After every meeting with a guest speaker, I would assign a student to write a thank you note on behalf of the class. The note had to be hand-written in cursive! I told them a note written in block letters looked as though it had come from a teenager. A note in cursive makes a much better impression. Most students these days do not learn it in school. One semester one of the students had beautiful handwriting. The class quickly found that out, and she was regularly asked to do the final version of notes. I made the students send me the first draft of their note for my review. I was sometimes horrified by them! It was frequently a case of students not having had a fundamental education in writing.

Since we were mostly meeting in a small group, my practice was to require the students to stand up and to introduce themselves to the guest speaker by stating their name and their home school. I made it a point to tell the students to speak slowly and clearly. They were frequently in such a rush to get their introduction completed that it came out as an unintelligible mishmash. I also asked them to write their questions out in advance. I offered to review the questions with them. One student wanted to ask a "gotcha" question to a Member of Congress about a 5-year-old ethics complaint. She asked me if it would be an acceptable question. I said, "Not if you want to get a passing grade in this course". There was no reason to try to embarrass the Member. If she was rude to him, his staff would never grant my requests for future meetings. She was not seriously interested in the answer. I think she just wanted to get a rise out of him. I explained she should prepare a question that would provide a learning experience for her and not squander the opportunity by trying to make the speaker look bad.

The bane of any WSP professor's life was scheduling. We had to prepare for classes, seminars, and guest speakers morning and afternoon three days a week, but each of our meetings was just one of many our speakers had on any given day. It was a bit easier to be flexible if it was to be a presentation on campus, but most of my speakers were off-campus.

Speakers downtown, such as Members and other officials, were used to having to modify schedules, so cancellations and rearrangements were a regular occurrence. If someone was running late and wanted to delay for an hour or two, I had to scramble to find things to do to fill the time. The National Archives was my go-to forum in those cases. It was always open during the day, was convenient, and students could see original copies of the Constitution and the Declaration of Independence. There were regular lunchtime programs that I would let the students know about.

My students got to meet with many significant speakers during my career at American University. Many of them are friends who were doing me a favor, some of them were people I had worked with, and others were people I cold-called who agreed to meet with a group of college students. I had some turn me down, but my batting average was excellent. Occasionally I would be contacted by a speaker asking to be included again because they enjoyed the types of interactions they had had with my usually well-prepared students.

Supreme Court Justices

On the opening night of the opera "The Marriage of Figaro" at the Kennedy Center, Mimi was the choreographer and we were invited to attend a gala at the Italian Ambassador's residence. The President of the Washington National Opera Board was Kenneth Feinberg. He and I worked together closely when he was Senator Ted Kennedy's Chief Counsel on the Senate Judiciary Committee. As Ken's House counterpart, we would meet regularly to plan legislative activities.

This black-tie event was well attended. At one point during the festivities, I was speaking with Ken and someone who had also worked with him on the Senate Judiciary Committee staff. Ken said to us, "Stephen, you and Dan are doing the same kind of work now". Stephen looked at him quizzically, "What do you mean?" "Well, you are both grading other people's papers", Ken explained. Associate Justice Stephen Breyer and I just chuckled. I told Stephen I did not consider the papers I was grading to be as well-written as the Court of Appeals' opinions he was "grading". He said, "Don't be so sure".

Later I found myself standing next to Justice Samuel Alito, whom I had not met. I told him my wife was the lovely woman in the fuchsia dress who was the choreographer. He said he would be pleased to meet her. I offered to introduce him to her on one condition. He asked what that was, and I told him I wanted him to speak to my class. For some reason he agreed, and then I asked him the Henry Hyde question, "What is the name of the person who makes you look good?" He understood what I was asking and gave me her name. He spoke to my classes on several occasions.

Justice Alito was an engaging speaker and was receptive to student questions. He had written the lone dissent in the Westboro Baptist Church case *Snyder v. Phelps*. One of my students got up, and after introducing herself, said, "Mr. Justice Alito, it is an honor for us to have the opportunity to meet with you, and I want you to know how grateful we are". Justice Alito was heartened and thanked her. I think it was that kind of gesture which led to his being willing to meet with us in the future. She then asked him a very intelligent question about his dissenting opinion in that case.

✦✦✦✦✦✦✦✦

If one of my colleagues on the faculty had a "heavy hitter" agree to speak, they would frequently invite the other classes to join. This led to an exceptional experience for me. Bea Siman, who taught the Criminal Justice Seminar, invited my class to join hers and a couple of other non-WSP groups for a meeting with Justice Sonia Sotomayor. I eagerly agreed because I knew the students would love it, and I was anxious to meet her.

My class was one of five groups attending this session. I do not know how Bea got her class invited, and the other three were a strange mixture; one was made up of foreign judges, another was five graduate students, and one consisted of six civil rights lawyers.

Justice Sotomayor has a practice of having her picture taken with the groups she meets. Many of our speakers do this, but she is the only one I have ever met who would have the pictures taken *before* she speaks. I thought she would do this, and I spoke to the Supreme Court photographer, Steve Petteway, ahead of time to make sure he had my card so that he could send me the photo of my class with her.

The Justice had told Steve she would do separate pictures with each of the five groups. There was some confusion about who was going to get their picture taken and when. Amid the chaos, I thought Bea would not mind if I stepped in. I walked to the front of the room and took control. I said, "My class will be; first, Professor Siman's class will be second, the judges will be third, the attorneys will be fourth, and the grad students will be fifth. When I call your group, hustle across the hall, speedily so we can have the maximum amount of time with the Justice". Everyone seemed OK with my taking charge.

I learned Bea had a special guest with her. One of her regular speakers was a DEA agent who she had invited to join the session with Justice Sotomayor. Bea introduced me to him, and we chatted briefly. He told me he had testified in front of then-trial-Judge Sotomayor many years ago. The defense lawyer who was cross-examining him got too close and ended up accidentally spitting into his face. Judge Sotomayor unobtrusively reached under the bench and slid a box of tissues to him so he could clean up. He never forgot it.

When Justice Sotomayor arrived, she announced we would have the photos taken first, and she would speak afterward. I stood up and said, "OK, my class, let's move to the other room swiftly". They did. Between groups one and two, I quickly told the Justice the story of the DEA agent and what had happened to him in her courtroom. I then called for Bea's class to go making sure the DEA agent was seated next to her, and I introduced him. Her eyes lit up, and she shook his hand and asked him, "Didn't you once testify before me?" I felt he had died and gone to heaven! She sneaked a look at me and smiled. I thought to myself, "Good staff work".

I summoned the other three groups, in order, for their photos at warp speed. I then asked Justice Sotomayor if she would be willing to have a photo with me, and she readily agreed. Afterward, when we were walking back into the main room, she said, "Wow, Dan, that was a superb exercise in organization".

She was an impressive speaker, lively, and full of fascinating stories. She was also receptive to the students' questions. She did something which I have re-counted frequently to subsequent classes because I thought it was extraordinary. One of my students was recognized and asked a thought-provoking question. Justice Sotomayor looked and her and said, "That is a very interesting question. Let me think about it". And she did just that... for 62 seconds! I timed it. It was a superb lesson for the students about thinking first, being careful, and not blurting out the first thing that pops into your head. When we were leaving, I told the Justice that that was the best lesson she could have given them; think before you speak.

I asked Steve to give the photograph of the two of us to her staff so that she could inscribe it for me. I was thrilled when I received it about a week later. The inscription was, "Dan, You are Amazing!!!, Sonia Sotomayor". I framed it and put it up on my wall.

✦ ✦ ✦ ✦ ✦ ✦ ✦ ✦ ✦

We also had the opportunity to meet with Justice Stephen Breyer on several occasions. Since he and I had worked together on the two Judiciary commit-tee staffs, and probably because he knew that Ken Feinberg and I were good friends, he was always gracious to me.

Knowing about my time on the Hill, one of the students asked Justice Brey-er a question about the relative importance of legislative history. As he had written lots of it when working for Senator Kennedy, it was not a surprise to learn he felt it could be informative and instructive for judges who were trying to interpret the congressional intent of statutory language.

On one occasion, when he was discussing report language, he was trying to quote the Fifth Amendment and could not come up with precise language off the top of his head. As I was sitting in the front and I always carry a copy of the Constitution with me, I stood up and gave it to him, opened to the language of the Amendment. He read the quote from the Constitution and then looked up at the class and said, "I could always count on Dan to be well prepared". I rather enjoyed that.

✦ ✦ ✦ ✦ ✦ ✦ ✦ ✦ ✦

On several occasions, we got to meet with Justice Antonin Scalia. He was a terrific speaker. He was animated, exciting, and a hell of a lot of fun. He would always thank me if the students asked good questions. His description of origi-nalism was important for the students to hear because we had discussed the two main theories of constitutional interpretation in class.

One of my students, who had previously asked a question about legislative history of Justice Breyer, asked Justice Scalia about his view. He was blunt in his reply. He said, "Legislative history is a bunch of crap, cobbled together by a bunch of teenagers in the back room, unbeknownst to the Members of Congress whose intent it is supposed to represent; the sort of thing that your professor did for Chairman Rodino. Some of us up here give that the minimal deference which it deserves". He looked at me with a twinkle in his eye. I was flattered he remembered I had worked for Mr. Rodino.

✦✦✦✦✦✦✦✦✦

Members of the House and Senate

I was fortunate to have many Members agree to speak to my classes. It was not the same people every semester, although some did speak every time, like Lamar Smith, Jeff Flake, John Lewis and Pete Sessions. All of them did so as a favor to *me*. I took some pride in that. I thought of it as a compliment. I would make sure if a Member's constituent were in my class, they would be sitting in the front row, and I would introduce him or her to the Member at the beginning of the session. I would get a photograph of them and get it signed. The Members recognized it as good staff work on my part (many still considered me to be staff), and the students were usually thrilled.

I got to know Senator John Boozman, another frequent speaker for my classes when he was in the House and on the International Relations Committee. He is a taciturn and quiet man who makes you wonder how he relates to people on the campaign trail.

He was one of the Members who approached me soon after he was assigned to the committee and told me the Chairman had informed him I was an old hand, and I could be helpful to him in learning the ropes. I was impressed with new Members who did not come in with the attitude that they knew everything.

When my class met with Senator Boozman, one of my students thought he could embarrass him. This meeting occurred after the Supreme Court decision in *Obergefell v. Hodges* legalized same-sex marriage. The student asked him what the Senator thought about the issue in light of the Supreme Court decision. It did not fluster Boozman at all. No college student was going to catch a U.S. Senator off guard on such a significant and controversial issue. After all, he is from Arkansas, a conservative Bible belt state, and I was sure he had dealt with this issue many times before. "The overwhelming majority of my constituents oppose it, and I concur", he replied.

✦✦✦✦✦✦✦✦

Howard Berman was a member of the House Judiciary Committee when I was on the staff there. Howard was approachable and easy to work with, and he also had a good sense of humor. During one caucus discussion, he leaned over to me and asked, "What is the knee-jerk liberal position on this so that I can take it?"

Howard was also a senior member of the House International Relations Committee, and so I continued to work with him when I changed over to that committee with Henry. Howard never gave me any problem about my working for the new Republican majority. When I began teaching at American University, he regularly agreed to speak to my classes. His approachable demeanor and broad range of knowledge impressed the students. It was clear he took his responsibilities as a Member, and later as a committee chairman, seriously, however, he was always able to see the irony and humor in any situation.

He was the ranking Democrat behind Tom Lantos when Lantos became ill and died in early 2008. Howard had to make the transition to becoming a committee Chairman in the wake of all of the strong emotions surrounding Lantos' fairly sudden death. The last time Howard spoke to my students, he was obviously rushed, and he apologized for not being able to spend longer with the class. He told them he was running late for a condolence call to Mrs. Lantos, "But meeting with Dan Freeman's class is important to me". I certainly was heartened by that, and I wonder how many of the students understood how significant that was.

+ + + + + + + + +

Senator Richard Burr was on the International Relations Committee when he was a Member of the House, which was where I first met him. He knew my dear friend Ashley Thrift quite well. Richard represented the Congressional district where Salem College was located. Ashley's wife had been the President of Salem. Richard was subsequently elected to the Senate and became Chairman of the Intelligence Committee.

He always made time for my students; at least an hour each semester, which was extraordinary. One of the more interesting, and frankly scary, things he would do was to show how invasive electronic devices can be. When he was talking about how the students could be tracked through their cell phones, he would demonstrate it. He would ask a student for his cell phone and get him to enter the password. Senator Burr then tapped in a few letters and would announce to the class where that student had been during the previous 24 hours. It was for me a chilling revelation about how cell phones, which are an integral part of every college student's life, can pose a real threat to their privacy.

+ + + + + + + + +

Congressman John Robert Lewis is one of the most important people I have ever met. Over the years I spent on the Hill, I got to know most of the Members of the House I worked with well enough to call them by their first names. John Lewis was the exception to that practice. He always told the students about his first meeting with Dr. Martin Luther King. When Dr. King asked him, "Are you John Lewis, the boy from Troy?" He responded by saying, "Dr. King, I am John Robert Lewis". I always introduced him that way. I never felt comfortable calling him by his first name. He is an icon of the civil rights movement and has had a dramatic effect on our country during my lifetime. He has been a power in the House since his election in 1987.

Mr. Lewis spoke to my students practically every semester I taught in the WSP. He is a compelling speaker. I feel it is important for college students to learn about the struggles in the civil rights movement in the '60s. When Mr. Lewis showed them the photographs from Bloody Sunday in Selma, Alabama, and of the burned-out bus which he rode in as a Freedom Rider, it has a significant impact.

My friend Ashley says that he would rather be lucky than good. I wholeheartedly concur with that, and on two separate occasions with Mr. Lewis, I was fortunate as far as the timing of our meetings. In January of 2008, I was able to secure a meeting with Mr. Lewis for Wednesday, February 28, the day after the Georgia Democratic Presidential Primary election on Super Tuesday. Mr. Lewis had been a supporter of Hillary Clinton and had formally endorsed her the previous October.

Senator Obama handily defeated Mrs. Clinton 66 % to 31% in the primary. Mr. Lewis, when meeting with my students, told them one of the most difficult telephone calls he ever had to make was to call the Clintons and tell them he was going to endorse Senator Obama. It was a classic example of reflecting the sentiments of your constituents. Mr. Lewis was candid with the class, telling them Bill Clinton was angry, but Hillary Clinton handled the awkward phone call with grace. Mrs. Clinton was quoted as saying about Mr. Lewis' endorsement, "I understand he's been under tremendous pressure. He's been my friend. He will always be my friend". For the students to have an opportunity to hear about this significant development in American politics from a key player was a fabulous experience. I hoped it made an impression on each one of them.

Early in the spring of 2011, I arranged with Mr. Lewis's staff for us to meet with him Wednesday, February 15. I did not know that President Obama was going to honor Mr. Lewis with America's highest civilian award, the Presidential Medal of Freedom, the day before we were to meet. When I got dressed that morning, before looking at the newspaper or hearing the news, for some reason, I decided to wear the cuff links that I was given when I worked in the Carter White House. They had the Presidential Seal embossed on them. I guess since President Carter was from Georgia, and so was Mr. Lewis, I thought it would be appropriate.

When Mr. Lewis walked in, he greeted me as he usually did; he gave me a big bear hug and reminded me, "You are my brother". I always considered that to be the highest accolade I have ever received. I was profoundly moved by the warmth of his greeting and the significance of his receiving the Medal of Freedom just the day before. At that moment, with a tear in my eye, in front of my students, I took off the cuff links and gave them to Mr. Lewis to show him how proud I was to know him. He hugged me again and said, "I will treasure them". The following semester when my students met with him, he was wearing them.

✦✦✦✦✦✦✦✦✦

Congressman Bobby Scott was on the Judiciary Committee, and I worked with him often. He is an articulate and precise man and was always able to get to the core of any issue the committee was debating. He had a high opinion of the staff and was someone who was easy to brief. He caught on quickly. He was one of my go-to Members to handle floor debate.

He spoke to my classes regularly and always made sure he took enough time to answer questions. One day he was speaking to the class in the Judiciary Committee library, which is next to the hearing room. He had asked to meet with us there because he was scheduled to testify before one of its subcommittees that afternoon. He had been speaking for about 15 minutes when an aide told him it was time to go. He asked the students and me to join him for his testimony. We would then return to the library to continue the session. It gave the students the chance to watch him testify about an important issue and then ask him about it.

When we walked into room 2141, the main Judiciary Committee hearing room, Scott went straight to the witness table and was getting ready to speak. The Subcommittee Chairman, Howard Coble, an old friend, said, "Mr. Scott before you begin, I would like to point out the presence of the former Committee Parliamentarian who has just joined us. We are pleased to see you, Sir". The class got a big kick out of it, and I smiled my appreciation to Howard.

✦✦✦✦✦✦✦✦✦

One day I was to meet my students in what is known as the "horseshoe" entrance of the Rayburn House Office Building. My practice had been to gather the class 15 minutes before any meeting downtown in the lobby of the building. That gave me a cushion to find out who was missing and whether they were on the way. As I was waiting for the last student to show up, I saw Congressman John Conyers, who was, at the time, the Chairman of the House Judiciary Committee. I had worked closely with him for years. We spent a good bit of time together during the Hastings impeachment. When he saw me in the lobby, he came over and asked me what I was doing there. I told him my class of college students was going to meet with a couple of Members. Surprisingly, he said,

"Can I speak to them?" I replied, "Sure, that would be fantastic". "How about today?" he asked. "What time?" I replied. Getting a full committee Chairman to speak would be a real coup. I told him we had a meeting with another Member at 2 pm in the House Judiciary Committee hearing room. I would have willingly tried to change the time for the other speaker if Mr. Conyers was available. He told me he would wait until the other Member was finished and would come into the room after that.

Our 2 pm meeting with Congressman Bobby Scott went well. Mr. Conyers was sitting in the back room, patiently waiting. As soon as Scott left, I hustled back to the committee offices and asked Mr. Conyers to join us. The students had been sitting in the chairs in the audience, and I assumed Mr. Conyers would stand in front of the witness table and address them there. He surprised the students *and me* by asking them to go up and take places on the dais where the Members sit during committee meetings. The students loved it. Mr. Conyers and I were sitting at the witness table facing them. The first thing he did was to get them all to stand while he administered the oath of office that all Members of the House take when getting sworn in. He knew it by heart. He then sat down and was going to speak to the class as if he were a witness testifying before a Congressional panel. As he began, I decided that it would be appropriate for me to leave him alone at the witness table. As I started to get up, he put his hand on my arm and said, "Do not go anywhere, counselor. I may need a lawyer".

It was an exceptional session, which was enhanced tremendously by Mr. Conyers' sense of theater. The students enjoyed his interest in them and their questions, as well as the chance to "cross-examine a witness" in the House Judiciary Committee hearing room.

✚✚✚✚✚✚✚✚

One of the people who spoke to my class every semester was Jeff Flake. Jeff was a Member of the House, where I first got to know him. He served there from 2001 to 2013 and was then elected to the Senate. He was a member of the Judiciary Committee until 2007 when he was unceremoniously removed from the committee by House Minority Leader John Boehner because of Jeff's perceived verbal attacks on the Republican leadership on the Appropriations Committee. Jeff had always taken a strong position against separate line item expenditures, known as earmarks, which were often included in the spending bills. He felt strongly that this kind of spending should not be done in secrecy. Boehner had promised that "bad behavior" by House Republicans who voted against their Leadership would not be rewarded. He considered Jeff's public condemnation of the earmarking process to be "bad behavior". Boehner punished Jeff by taking away his seat on the Judiciary Committee. Even though Jeff was no longer on the committee, I would see him regularly. After he was elected to the Senate, he always made time for my class.

Jeff was candid about what was wrong with our government. This was especially true after Donald Trump was elected. He was upset when the President criticized Senator John McCain. Trump said, "He's not a war hero. He's a war hero because he was captured. I like people that weren't captured." In speaking to the President soon afterward at a meeting of Republican Senators, Jeff referred to himself as the "other Senator from Arizona—the one who didn't get captured—and I want to talk to you about statements like that". The President was not happy about that exchange.

One of my students interned in Senator Flake's office and had a fantastic experience. Frequently, students who intern for Senators do not get a chance to interact with them since the staffs are so large. Because of the way Jeff runs his office, he gets to know everyone, including the interns.

I became friendly with Pete Sessions, a Congressman from Dallas when he was first elected to the House in 1996. As a Member of the Rules Committee, I would frequently see him at the Committee meetings when the Judiciary Committee was requesting a rule for floor consideration of a bill. He was easy to work with and was not infected with "Memberitis". He told me he could learn more from an experienced staffer than he could from most Members of Congress. I promised never to repeat that line to any Members. We continued to have a good working relationship while I was on the Hill.

Pete was a very involved and thoughtful legislator. He cares deeply about his country and takes his responsibilities as a Member of Congress very seriously. This was made evident to me one morning when I was on the Hill in the horseshoe lobby of the Rayburn Building. I was gathering my class together before going to a meeting. While we were waiting I saw Pete come in. I went over to greet him, and he looked terrible. I thought he might be sick or was exhausted. I told him he "looked like hell". (Interesting what you can get away with). He told me he had not had much sleep because he was thinking about the Federal budget and trying to come up with a way to balance it. He kept turning it over in his mind and was not able to come up with a solution It bothered him terribly, and he was not well rested. He said he appreciated my candor. I thought that spoke volumes about what kind of Congressman he was.

After I left and went to AU, Pete was marvelous to my classes and me. He told me he considered me to be "a man on a mission". He said he wanted to support my goal of educating these young people in any way he could. He would regularly give us at least an hour, which was unusual. When he became Chairman of the House Rules Committee, he would meet with us in the small and intimate Committee hearing room. He was interested in what the students thought, as well as what he could teach them.

During one session, Pete began to talk about what the future holds. He then did something unexpected; he looked at me and asked if it was okay for him to give them a written assignment. I readily agreed, not knowing what the task was going to be. He assigned each of them to write a 2 to 3-page paper on what they expected their country (I had several international students that semester) to be like in 20 years. He gave them his personal email and asked them to submit their papers to him through it. Members do not give out their email addresses often, and I was surprised, to say the least. He gave the students the weekend to write their papers and send them in.

A week after the students had completed the assignment, Pete sent all of the papers to me. He had taken the time to read each one and added his hand-written comments. I was astounded he took the time to do that and was pleased for the students. Not all of them understood the assignment or how unusual it was for a Member to do something like that. Some of them wrote good papers.

One semester, after a meeting with Pete, one of my students came up to complain to me about him. She felt he disrespected her when talking about the hot button issue of immigration. I wanted to tell her to "grow up" but resisted the urge. She felt his characterization of people who violated our laws by over-staying their visas or who entered the country illegally was not appropriate. She thought he should have recognized there were Latina students in the class who might be offended by his remarks. I tried to explain to her that he represented a Congressional District in Dallas and strengthening our immigration laws and their enforcement was a highly significant matter with his constituents. Back to Freeman's First Law.

Pete's practice was to have an individual photograph taken with each student. He would sign them and send them to me to give to the students. Being the ever-prepared staffer, I would have a list of the students ready. Pete's staff knew I could be relied on to give them this list and to call the students up in alphabetical order to have their pictures taken with him. This almost always worked out well.

The chance to have their picture taken with a Member of Congress was usually well-received. However, one semester I had a student who was adamantly opposed to having her picture taken with this conservative Congressman with whom she did not agree. I did not want Pete's staff to know about her attitude because I relied on them to arrange for him to meet with my classes every semester. I told the student that when I called her name, she had better get up there and have her picture taken. She could burn it later for all I cared, but she was not going to embarrass me by refusing. She did have her picture taken, but there was a fairly emotional scene in the hallway afterwards. She was frustrated and angry and was reduced to tears. I thought her behavior to be petulant and childish and was not very sympathetic.

✦✦✦✦✦✦✦✦✦

One of the Members who spoke to my class regularly was none other than former Federal Judge Alcee Hastings. He would start the class by saying, "I know your professor did not tell you how we met. I used to be a Federal Judge. Hadn't been for your professor, I would still be one. He was the Chief Counsel on my impeachment". He would speak candidly about it. He is an African American from a liberal district, and his policy preferences were clear. He is a dynamic and lively speaker. The students always enjoyed the session, but many were a little surprised to know how we met.

✦✦✦✦✦✦✦✦✦

Another frequent speaker was Congressman Dan Lungren. He was doing his second tour of duty in Congress starting in 2005. He had been a Member from 1979-89. He then served as California Attorney General from 1991-1999. He ran for Governor after that. Dan and I went back to his first stint in the House when he was in the minority, and we got along very well. He used to have pitched battles with Alan Parker, but they respected each other. Dan showed up one afternoon to speak with my class without any staffer tagging along. Most Members have a staff person with them to take pictures, to "assist" them, and to call "time" when they have another appointment, which they always do. He told the class, "Only for Dan Freeman would I agree to speak on an afternoon after I had a colonoscopy". I took that as a big compliment and avoided the too-easy joke about my being a "pain in the ass".

✦✦✦✦✦✦✦✦✦

One of the subjects I covered in detail was the Administrative Procedure Act, which most students had not encountered in college. I asked them whether anyone in the class had a sibling or relative who was still in a crib. Invariably at least someone did. I asked how far apart the balusters in the crib were spaced. Some people knew the practical answer; narrow enough so a baby cannot put its head through. I asked how that requirement was established. No one knew. I would then explain that it was mandated by an administrative rule promulgated by the Consumer Product Safety Commission through the process called administrative rulemaking. I told them that for every law passed by Congress, there are 17 rules or regulations issued by the executive branch. This always astounded the students since most of them had never heard of the rule-making process. I made sure it came up regularly during the semester, most pointedly when we were discussing food safety, which several of my best speakers did.

✦✦✦✦✦✦✦✦✦

I would always ask the students to let me know if they had any connection with somebody who would be a good speaker. This frequently happened with students who were interning on Capitol Hill. It was usually not difficult to get the intern to speak to the scheduler about getting their boss to meet with my class. Occasionally there would be a family relationship that we could tap.

One of my students went to Clemson University, and he was interning for a Member of Congress from South Carolina, Trey Gowdy. He was a lawyer who came to Congress on the crest of the tea party wave. I urged the student to get me in touch with the scheduler to get the Congressman to speak. My student did the easy part, which was to convey the invitation. I had to do the hard part, which was getting a room on the Hill for the meeting. I continued to have good relationships with people on both the Judiciary and the International Relations Committees, so I would usually be able to score one of their rooms.

Mr. Gowdy spoke about the responsibilities of being in Congress and some of the important issues which he, as a member of the House Judiciary Committee, was dealing with. In response to a question about administrative rules and regulations, he went off the rails. Gowdy complained bitterly about Congress abdicating its responsibilities to the executive branch, "across the board". He said Congress should not be delegating its authority over a whole range of issues. He was adamant. "On just about any subject matter you can mention, *Congress* should be making the decisions, not some faceless unelected bureaucrats".

After Mr. Gowdy left, the students wanted to discuss the rules and regulations question; who should regulate, the agencies or Congress? I asked them when they thought Congress should be doing the regulating, and when they thought it was acceptable to delegate that responsibility to an executive agency. One of the students' grandfather had recently had a cardiac pacemaker implanted. I asked if he thought that Members of Congress, like Mr. Gowdy, should be making the decisions about whether to approve a specific manufacturer's cardiac pacemaker or should it be left to a panel of healthcare professionals. It was food for thought for many of them.

✦✦✦✦✦✦✦✦✦

The most unusual speaker connection was from a student, James, who was a serious poker player. He entered a poker tournament one weekend and ended up in the final. He was sitting across the table from a pleasant middle-age man. James won, but since James was underage and his opponent was a government employee with restrictions on his outside income, neither of them could take the prize money. James asked the man what he did which limited his outside income, and he was told his opponent was a United States Senator! As a prize for beating him, James had the foresight to extract from Senator Mark Begich of Alaska a promise to speak to my class.

✦✦✦✦✦✦✦✦✦

Senator Ed Markey frequently spoke to my classes. Ed was a Member of the House for many years and was then elected to the Senate. He is an expert in telecommunications matters and is a dynamic and large personality. Since I used to work with his staff on telecommunications issues, I got to know him well. The last time we met with him in his Senate office one of the students asked what had prompted him to become a lawyer. He said watching Atticus Finch in the movie "To Kill a Mockingbird" was the most significant event in his life in pointing him towards a career in the law.

Ed is a captivating speaker and usually gave us a lot of time. Some Members will only give you 15 or 20 minutes; Ed always gave us a full hour. After the last session where his favorite movie came up, I sent him a DVD of the film which I thought he would enjoy having.

✦✦✦✦✦✦✦✦✦

Congressman Ted Poe, a former judge who liked being referred to as "Judge Poe", was also a regular. He, too, made it a point of getting to know me because Henry said I could be of help to him as a new Member. He treated me with respect and friendliness. Poe liked to speak to the students on the steps of the House side of the Capitol building. He would usually allocate 15 to 20 minutes and would also pose for a photograph with the Capitol in the background. The students loved having that photograph and enjoyed the fact that he was thoughtful enough to make sure one of his staff was there to take the picture.

✦✦✦✦✦✦✦✦✦

One of the more emotional incidents came during a meeting we had with Congressman Mel Watt. He is an African American Member from North Carolina. He and I had a warm and friendly relationship. He was another Member who always made time for my students and me. He is a powerful speaker and talked about race in America in a perceptive and meaningful way. The sessions were always memorable. The one I recall most vividly took place the week after we had met with John Lewis. One of the students asked Mr. Watt what role he had played in the civil rights struggles of the 1960s and whether he was there with Mr. Lewis on the Edmund Pettis Bridge on "Bloody Sunday". He paused to gather himself, and I could see he was genuinely emotional. With a tear in his eye, he confessed to the students he had not been active in the movement.

When he got to the University of North Carolina in 1963, he was one of only 17 black students. His mother had warned him about missing classes. If he missed more than three, he would not get credit for the course, and would not graduate. He decided to focus his energies on academics and graduated Phi Beta Kappa. He went on to Yale Law School, where he was on the Law Journal. He said he still felt guilty about "letting John Lewis take the blows instead of me".

When I was on the floor on my last day on the Hill, I saw Mel, and he complimented me on my tie. Just before I walked out of the Rayburn Building for the last time as a Congressional employee, I stopped by his office and told the rather befuddled intern at the desk I had something for the Congressman. I took off my tie, rolled it up, and said, "Please give this to Mel". Mel just happened to walk into the office at that moment. He smiled, gave me a warm embrace, and wished me well.

✦ ✦ ✦ ✦ ✦ ✦ ✦ ✦ ✦

Cabinet Officers, Agency Heads and Senior Government Officials
I have written about Norm Mineta previously. Norm had become a good friend. As a former Member of the House, he had lifetime floor privileges. He was on the floor on my last day, January 4, 2007, the day Nancy Pelosi was elected Speaker of the House. When I saw him that day, I greeted him and asked him to speak to my classes. He said he would be happy to. Norm would regularly make time to meet with my students, and he would always bring the baseball bat which I had given him. He has a marvelous way with students, and the session with him is one I looked forward to the most.

✦ ✦ ✦ ✦ ✦ ✦ ✦ ✦ ✦

Dan Glickman was a Member of Congress from Wichita, Kansas, who was a casualty in the 1994 Republican wave. He had been a Member for eighteen years, and he was the Chairman of the Administrative Law Subcommittee on the Judiciary Committee. I got to know him well in that capacity since I was always present during any subcommittee markups. He was a first-name basis kind of person, smart, and not too full of himself. He was another Member who recognized the value of staff and who would listen to advice.

After his defeat, President Clinton named him Secretary of Agriculture. Dan was from Kansas and was well-schooled in agriculture issues, which were very important in his district. During President Clinton's February 4, 1997, State of the Union address to Congress, Dan was the Cabinet Official who was tapped to be the "designated survivor". This is someone in the presidential line of succession who is physically distant, secure, and in an undisclosed location when most of the rest of the Cabinet, the entire legislative branch, and many of the

Justices of the Supreme Court are in the Capitol Building. This is to guarantee continuity of government in the event of a catastrophic event wiping out a large portion of our national leadership.

Dan would tell my students about his experience that night. He was in New York City visiting his daughter, and he was surrounded by Secret Service agents. He said he felt "almost important", but that feeling dissipated quickly as soon as President Clinton was out of the Capitol on the way back to the White House. As Dan described it, "almost like magic, the Secret Service disappeared".

He then told them about his time as the Chairman and CEO of the Motion Picture Association of America. He replaced a Washington legend, Jack Valenti. In preparing to meet with him, my students and I would cover intellectual property issues, including copyrights, which were extremely important to the motion picture industry. During his tenure at the MPAA, Dan oversaw what was referred to as "the war on movie piracy".

The next phase of Dan's life was dedicated to working with think tanks. He taught at the John F. Kennedy School of Government and held senior positions at the Bipartisan Policy Center and the Aspen Institute. He has had a phenomenal career and is also good with students. He answered their questions honestly. The class always enjoyed this session.

I was glad to see one of my students bringing in concepts from previous sessions. Dan was talking about his involvement in general aviation policy, including his work on controversial landmark legislation providing product liability protection for small airplane manufacturers. When I asked the students why they thought a Congressman from Kansas would be interested in general aviation, one of the bright ones said, "Freeman's First Law". Glickman asked him what that was, and when he was told it meant "get re-elected", he said that was "exactly spot-on". Wichita, Kansas, is the small airplane manufacturing capital of the United States, and his constituents were directly affected by anything Congress did relating to general aviation.

✦✦✦✦✦✦✦✦✦

Ray LaHood was a regular speaker. He had been the Chief of Staff for Congressman Bob Michel from Peoria, Illinois until Michel retired, and Ray ran for the seat and won. I got to know him for two reasons. As long-time staffers, we would see each other regularly. Since I had worked in Peoria, we also had some mutual friends, including my former boss in the Peoria City Government, Henry Holling. Henry went on to become a senior official at Caterpillar, the large construction equipment company which has its world headquarters in Peoria. "Freeman's First Law" applied to Ray as a Member of the House. What Caterpillar wants is very important to him.

Ray is an elegant and formal person. He was the rare Member of the House who knew the rules well. The Leadership often asked him to preside over the House during important debates, including the Clinton impeachment. He presided more often than any other Member.

After he retired from the House, President Obama nominated him to be the Secretary of Transportation. He had been a member of the House Transportation and Infrastructure Committee for five years. He had also served as a member of the House Appropriations Committee.

When I introduced him, I would try to make a point. One of Ray's main foci as head of DOT was distracted driving. I took a poll of the class on the day before we met with him about how many of them used their cell phones while driving. Invariably, I was able to introduce the Secretary to a group of students who were "100% distracted drivers". Ray would then launch into his description of the devastating effects of using electronic devices when behind the wheel.

On one occasion, my class was meeting with him at the Department of Transportation. Two of my colleagues' classes were going to join us, and so we had a total of about 60 students in a large meeting room. Ray would regularly leave enough time to take questions from students. At the end of this particular session, after several of my students had asked good questions, LaHood's Chief of Staff came up to me and said, "Dan, I can always tell which of the students are yours because of the polished way they stand up and introduce themselves. That's very impressive, and the Secretary has noticed it".

✦✦✦✦✦✦✦✦

My colleague, Rick Semiatin, knew Andrew Card well enough to get him to speak to our classes. Card had been a Special Assistant to President Reagan. He had been Secretary of Transportation under George H.W. Bush and was White House Chief of Staff under President George W. Bush.

He is a calm and impressive man who is approachable and took the students' questions with candor, humor and humility. The most riveting part of his presentation was about the events of 9/11. Most of the students were too young to remember that day, but Rick and I sure did.

Mr. Card told the class how he informed President Bush about the attacks. Bush was in Sarasota, Florida, reading with a group of elementary school students. Card went over and whispered in his ear, "America is under attack". Bush took that in and purposely did not get up and bolt from the room. According to Card, Bush's Press Secretary Ari Fleischer was in the back of the classroom, holding a pad on which he had written: "Don't say anything yet." Card told my students the President thought it was better for him to stay in the room and not upset the children.

He then filled the students in on the frenetic and sometimes scary things that followed as the President got back to Air Force One. Transportation Secretary Norm Mineta had directed all commercial aircraft to land at the nearest possible airport. The President and his staff debated between returning to Washington or staying away in case there were threats to the President.

Ultimately, the President's plane remained airborne to avoid making it a reachable target for any remaining attacks. At least one hijacked plane, which was possibly headed for the White House or the Capitol, was still in the air. Due to the lack of proper communications equipment on board, the President struggled to contact his family and to reach Vice President Dick Cheney in the secure White House bunker known as the PEOC, the Presidential Emergency Operations Center, which is below the well-known situation room in the basement of the White House. Mr. Card's session was spellbinding.

✦✦✦✦✦✦✦✦✦

One of the immense thrills of my life is when I see someone I have mentored come into their own. My dear friend Nicole Nason is one of my mentees who has done particularly well. After taking my advice and not going to work at the CIA, she became the Administrator of the National Highway Transportation Safety Administration (NHTSA). This is the job that Secretary Mineta put her into when she attempted to resign from her position as Assistant Secretary for Legislative Affairs at the Department of Transportation.

She would come to AU to meet with my classes. She is an American University alum, so she knew her way around the campus. She was running a few minutes late one morning, and I had started class. She came dashing into the room, and with a flourish, she flung her cape off onto a chair and gave me a big hug. Without letting go, she told the students, "Whatever you do in your life, make sure you get a mentor like this wonderful man". I decided she needed no introduction after that.

Nicole spoke to the class about the benefits of a career in public service. She also spoke about the importance of rules and regulations, which by then they were familiar with. One of the students noticed her large purse and asked her about it. Questions concerning fashion are usually not relevant to the class, but much to my amusement Nicole explained it was made of woven seat belts. She thought that was a good statement of her belief in their importance in minimizing injuries in automobile accidents.

✦✦✦✦✦✦✦✦✦

One of the jobs I coveted when I was in law school was working in the office

of the Solicitor General of the United States (SG). The SG is the third-rank-
ing official in the Department of Justice. Many people do not know about the
Solicitor General but will know about the famous "Saturday Night Massacre"
during Watergate. President Nixon ordered Attorney General Elliot Richardson
to fire Special Prosecutor Archibald Cox, who was investigating alleged official
misconduct on the part of the President and his aides. Richardson refused and
resigned in protest. Deputy Attorney General William Ruckelshaus also refused
and resigned. The next ranking official in the Department of Justice was Robert
Bork, who was the Solicitor General, and he is the one who formally fired Cox.

I had always wanted to become involved in Supreme Court litigation. I got
a taste of it when I was in law school with the juvenile justice case *In re Burrus*,
and as an undergraduate in the alcoholism case *Powell v. Texas*. The SG's office
is responsible for all Supreme Court litigation where the Federal Government
is a party or has an interest in the outcome. The office prepares all the briefs on
behalf of the government.

When I started teaching at American University, I made a cold call to the
Solicitor General's office to see if I could find someone willing to speak to a
group of college students. I did not have high hopes because I knew people in
that office are incredibly busy. I hit the jackpot when Deputy Solicitor General
Malcolm Stewart responded to my inquiry and said he would be more than happy to speak to my class. The Department of Justice is a highly secure building,
and I liked the fact that everyone had to be prescreened, have a photo ID with
them, and go through a metal detector to get into the building. It emphasized
to the students how important the Department is and how tight the security
needs to be.

Malcolm Stewart had a fascinating career path which he described to us.
He had been a junior high school teacher and felt that had equipped him well
to speak to nine, sometimes unruly, Supreme Court Justices. He described the
functions of his office, which is responsible for deciding which cases should be
appealed and what the position of the United States Government should be in
each. Most of the cases which the office handles are a result of what is known
as a "circuit split". This is when two different United States Courts of Appeal
have rendered decisions that are materially different on the same legal issue. He
explained that one of the primary roles of the office was to serve as a central
clearinghouse to ensure nationwide consistency in the legal positions which the
United States government was taking in the courts.

We heard about how lawyers in the office prepared for appearances before
the Supreme Court. He outlined the process known as "murder boards", which
are the mock oral arguments. The lawyer who will be arguing the case does a

practice session in front of a number of the other lawyers in the office. This frequently goes on for more than two hours, even though oral arguments in the Court usually only last for 30 minutes. Mr. Stewart said the "murder board" is far more stressful than the real thing.

Drafting briefs for the Supreme Court is a labor-intensive and intellectually challenging exercise. He emphasized the importance of clear, crisp, and persuasive writing. I was always grateful to him for making that point so emphatically.

Mr. Stewart spoke to my classes every semester while I was teaching. His presentation was always excellent and thorough. It gave the students the real inside look into how important issues of constitutional law are considered by the highest American court. He would mention the historical tradition of representatives of the SG's office always wearing a formal morning coat with tails when arguing before the Court.

Our meetings took place at the Robert F. Kennedy Building, also known as "Main Justice". Afterward, Mr. Stewart would escort the students on a tour of the building, which was erected during the 1930s. He took us to see the offices of the Attorney General and the Solicitor General and would show us the Department's beautiful law library. He would describe many of the Works Progress Administration Depression-era artworks which are displayed all over the building. He pointed out the symbolism of the more interesting paintings, including one representing the majesty of the law with a judge holding off a mob, and another showing significant aspects of life in the 1930s, including depictions of medical breakthroughs and of Jesse Owens running in the 1936 Olympic Games which were held in Berlin, in front of Adolph Hitler.

The last place we visited was the Great Hall on the main floor, which is an ornate, two-story room that the Department uses for ceremonies and other special events. One of the most interesting stories was about a briefing in that hall, which was conducted by Attorney General John Ashcroft. The Attorney General was a conservative man and a former Senator. He was holding forth about the Department's efforts to stem the tide of obscenity. However, behind him was a large partially nude female statue. There was a huge uproar because of the "bad optics", which did not die down when it was revealed the Department later spent $8,000 on a blue drape covering the torso to make the statue "less offensive".

✦ ✦ ✦ ✦ ✦ ✦ ✦ ✦ ✦

Bill Corr is a lawyer I knew when he worked for Congressman Henry Waxman as Counsel to the Health Subcommittee of the important House Energy and Commerce Committee. Bill is a real professional who has a southern gentleman's approach derived from his Appalachian mountain roots. He went to

Vanderbilt Law School and has spent the bulk of his career advocating for better healthcare access for all Americans. He went over to the Senate to work for Senator Howard Metzenbaum and then took a job with Senate Minority Leader Tom Daschle. After working for the Campaign for Tobacco-Free Kids, President Obama named him to be Deputy Secretary of the Department of Health and Human Services. As the number two official at HHS, his main responsibilities included the unbelievably complex and detailed work of writing the rules and regulations necessary to implement the mammoth Affordable Care Act.

Bill's presentation to the students was always clear and polished. He is a dynamic speaker and had a comprehensive knowledge of the complexities of healthcare delivery in the United States. He gave thoughtful answers to students' questions.

He, too, spoke about the importance of good writing. He took the opening when meeting with my classes to put in a pitch for public service. He described the exciting and fulfilling jobs that he and I were fortunate to have had. He also spoke about the duties of citizenship, and the significant influence one could have by working in the public sector. This meeting always had an impact on me and, I think, on many of the students.

✦✦✦✦✦✦✦✦✦

Judges

Through my work on the Science and the Courts program, I got to know a lot of local, state, and Federal Judges. Many of them were gracious enough to speak to my classes.

I am very interested in reading about bioethics cases that come up in courts. I try to dig a little deeper whenever possible, to educate myself. In November 2008, I read in the Washington Post about a case where Children's National Medical Center was seeking a court order from the D.C. Superior Court to permit it to take a 12-year-old boy who was brain-dead off of the machines which were keeping his heart beating. The parents objected to the hospital's request. They were devout Orthodox Jews whose religious beliefs forbade the withdrawal of life support. They refused to give their consent. The hospital went to court to seek a protective order which would authorize the withdrawal and insulate it from both civil and criminal liability. I was intrigued and thought it might be a compelling case for my class.

I was not sure about the propriety of calling the judge handling the case, so I called another judge I knew and asked her whether it would be permissible for me to call her colleague directly. She assured me that he was "a lively fellow" and would probably take my call. Somewhat to my surprise, D.C. Superior Court

Judge William Jackson did so. I told him I had three questions for him:

1) Could he talk to me about this case? Since it involved a minor, I thought there might be a confidentiality issue.

2) If he could talk to me about the case, could I see the pleadings and show them to my students?

3) If the answer to the first two questions was "yes", would he be willing to meet with a group of college students to discuss it?

He was completely candid and said that he did not know the answers and would get back to me.

He called me the next day after checking with the judicial ethics officer of the Superior Court and told me the answer to all my questions was "yes". I was enthused for both the students and myself. I thought this would be a rare opportunity to have a behind-the-curtains look at a judge's decision-making process.

I prepared the students for the session with Judge Jackson. I included in the reading materials the pleadings from both parties, the definition of death from the D.C. Code, and some other background materials. By law in the District of Columbia, death is defined *either as*,

(1) irreversible cessation of circulatory and respiratory functions; or

(2) irreversible cessation of all functions of the entire brain, including the brain stem;

I wanted to make sure the students understood why this case was in court. While the hospital had determined the boy was legally dead under the terms of the D.C. Code, it was concerned about a civil lawsuit for damages for wrongful death or even a criminal prosecution. Getting a court to authorize the withdrawal and bar any subsequent civil or criminal legal action was the protection the hospital was requesting.

The day before we met with Judge Jackson, we discussed the case in class. The next day we went to the courthouse to meet with the judge. It was fascinating! The judge did not, of course, tell the class how he intended to rule, but he did a marvelous job of laying out the issues and the questions which he felt needed to be answered before he ruled. It was most instructive for the students and me.

The students got into it, and the questions were perceptive. I was pleased they acquitted themselves so well in front of a judge whom I did not know. When one of the students asked the judge, "What are you going to do, Your Honor?" he turned it back on the students asking each one what they would do. It was a big surprise for them to be confronted with this tough decision and a superb educational experience for both the students and me.

As a footnote, the following week, the judge called to tell me the case had been resolved. "Resolved, how?" I asked. The child had died, and the case was moot.

✦✦✦✦✦✦✦✦✦

Eric Washington was the Chief Judge of the District of Columbia Court of Appeals, which is the highest court in the Washington D.C. court system. Eric and I met through the Science and the Courts program, and he, too, became a regular speaker to my classes. He would always meet with us in one of the courtrooms and describe how the Court of Appeals functions.

In an arrangement with the law school, the D.C. Court of Appeals was going to hear oral arguments in a real case at the law school. Law students were going to be the bulk of the audience. I asked if I could bring my students. I got the OK, and we met in the moot courtroom. I had prepared the students about the issues in the case so that they could follow the argument. They enjoyed the experience.

Judge Washington has a marvelous sense of humor which showed itself that day. After the arguments, he gaveled the court into adjournment, and he and his two colleagues in their judicial robes formally left the courtroom in a dignified procession walking up the main aisle. Most of my students were sitting near the aisle as the judges walked by. As he came up to me, Judge Washington whispered, "Hi there, Mimi's husband", loud enough for my students to hear.

✦✦✦✦✦✦✦✦✦

Judge Barbara Rothstein is a US District Court Judge who I also met through the Science and the Courts program. She was a trial judge in Seattle at the time. She wrote the opinions in two important cases which I liked to cover in my class. The first was the challenge to the Washington State law concerning physician-assisted suicide, and the second was the federal flag burning statute, which I had worked on in the House.

Sometime later, she was offered the position of Director of the Federal Judicial Center (FJC), which is the education arm of the US court system. I was happy when she took the job and relocated with her husband to Washington, D.C. It meant that I would get to see them more often, and I could ask her to speak to my classes. She was a regular and told some fascinating stories.

She met the class in her courtroom and would have the students sit in the jury box, which they enjoyed. Early in the semester, I explained about caseloads in American courts. Local Courts handle 95% of the litigation nationwide. The Federal Courts (which you hear and read about more often) handle only 5%.

I gave the students my visual identification keys for understanding what kind of court they were in simply by looking around. If you walk into a courtroom and see one judge—you are in a trial court—state or federal. Trial courts have witness stands and jury boxes. The party with the burden of proof [plaintiff or prosecutor] sits closest to the jury. If you walk into a courtroom and see three judges, you are in an appellate court—state or federal. There is no jury box and no witness stand. Appellate courts' only job is to decide whether the judge in the trial court committed error. They do not receive witness testimony. Appellate courts are bound by precedents set by their state Supreme Courts, or in the case of Federal Courts, the Circuit Courts of Appeals, and the Supreme Court. Usually, if one sees more than three judges, you are in a state or Federal Supreme Court.

Judge Rothstein would always reinforce those concepts before talking about specific cases. She told them that courts, unlike the other branches of the federal government, were designed to be both independent and anti-majoritarian. That meant that the judges have life tenure (unless impeached and convicted – a high bar) and were there to protect the rights of the minority against the majority. Most of the students had not considered that concept, and it made a strong impression on them.

She told the story of the trial of the young man who burned an American flag in Seattle to protest the then newly enacted Flag Protection law. Mark Haggerty was arrested and charged with the crime of violating the new statute, which is what he wanted.

When Haggerty was scheduled to appear before Judge Rothstein, the U.S. Marshals, who were responsible for security in federal courtrooms, informed the Judge the defendant was not "suitably attired" for his appearance in court. Judge Rothstein told the students she assumed this young man was going to be in an orange prison jumpsuit and not a coat and tie. Lawyers frequently make their defendants clean up a bit for court, but not always. Haggerty was being represented by the famous activist lawyer William Kunstler.

As the Judge walked into the courtroom, she had to struggle to maintain a somber demeanor, considering how the defendant was dressed. He was wearing scruffy jeans, no shirt, and some kind of animal skin vest. At that time, when tattoos were not so popular, he was covered with them. He had a medieval dog collar around his neck and sported a Mohawk haircut dyed blue. As the clerk intoned, "All rise", Haggerty did not move. Kunstler grabbed him by the dog collar he was wearing and yanked him to a standing position. The Judge told the class she could have strangled the Marshall. "Not suitably attired" was the understatement of the year!

Notwithstanding the unsavory appearance of the defendant, Judge Rothstein told the students it was an easy case for her. She granted the motion to dismiss the charge of violating the Flag Protection Act because she deemed the Act to be an unconstitutional infringement of Haggerty's First Amendment right to free speech, albeit symbolic speech. She told the class that her opinion could be summarized as, "Hey, Congress, read *Texas v. Johnson*". The Supreme Court upheld her decision, thereby throwing the law out.

✦✦✦✦✦✦✦✦✦

Andre Davis, a Federal District Judge in Baltimore, was a frequent speaker. As I mentioned previously, we met in Berkeley, California, during a Science and the Courts program in 1999.

He volunteered to speak to my classes. His discussion covered a broad range of topics, including what it is like to go through Senate confirmation for a life-tenured position, which he referred to as a "pre-death postmortem". He said the process was agonizing.

His presentations were always lively and, in one case, went on for almost 2 hours. There was a broad range of questions, and he made it a point to engage the students when answering them. As I frequently do, he would turn the inquiry back on the student and say, "What do you think?"

✦✦✦✦✦✦✦✦✦

One of the more meaningful sessions we had with a judge was a lesson in respecting the people who come before you. Judge Jose Lopez is a D.C. Superior Court Judge who I also met working on the Science and the Courts program. Judge Lopez agreed to meet with my students to describe the duties of a trial judge and to explain who the various players in the courtroom are and what they do. We were supposed to meet with him at 2 pm in his courtroom. He was running a bit late, and so we walked in and sat down to watch him conduct a series of almost identical requests for temporary protective orders. These are judicial orders which give the applicant the court's protection by forbidding someone who might pose a threat of harm from going near them.

There were several of these that day, and we sat and listened to Judge Lopez go through the required formalities to establish the necessary grounds for the issuance of such an order. Judge Lopez would swear in the applicant and conduct a direct examination on the record. He would establish who the order was against and why the petitioner felt it was needed. He would ask what the underlying facts were and even ask, "Do you want him to stay away from you and have no contact with you?"

Satisfied of the necessity for an order, he would then state:

'We have jurisdiction over this case because you are related by blood and/or share a residence in the District of Columbia. There is probable cause to believe that an intrafamily

*offense has occurred and that the actions of **** are a danger to your safety or welfare and that without a temporary protection order, you lack adequate protection. Accordingly, we are going to grant you a temporary protection order.*

*Under this order, **** shall not assault, threaten, stalk, harass, or physically abuse you or your children or destroy your property.*

He shall stay at least 100 feet away from you, your home, workplace and vehicle".

Judge Lopez went through this process several times, and he would say the same thing to each applicant. After all of the cases were dealt with, the judge adjourned court and came down from the bench to speak informally with the students.

One of them asked whether it got boring to go through the same routine every time. He responded by telling the students, "I have recited it hundreds of times, and you heard it multiple times today. However, I must be very aware that it is probably the only time the *applicant* will ever hear it, and I need to ensure they feel their case has been taken seriously by me as a judge". It was an important lesson for the class.

✦ ✦ ✦ ✦ ✦ ✦ ✦ ✦ ✦

Other Speakers of Note

Ken Feinberg was Counsel to the Senate Judiciary Committee in the late 1970s when Senator Ted Kennedy was the Chairman. He and I would meet regularly to plan legislative strategy and to make sure our bosses were on the same page. While we occasionally had our differences on some of the legislation, we rarely had any significant disagreements, since Rodino and Kennedy were usually of like minds.

Ken had gone on to forge a stellar career as an arbitrator/mediator. As he tells it, it started as pure serendipity. My former evidence professor Judge Jack Weinstein was looking for someone to deal with the hundreds of cases relating to the use of Agent Orange during the Vietnam War. He asked Ken to take it on, and that was the beginning of a long string of matters of national importance which he handled. He was named the Special Master for the Congressionally-mandated 9/11 Victim Compensation Fund, the BP Deepwater Horizon Disaster Victim Compensation Fund, the compensation to the family of Abraham Zapruder who took the famous film of the President Kennedy assassination and many others.

He is a giant personality, and with his booming voice and strong Boston accent, he fills the room. The basic concept that I asked him to get across to the students is the difference between arbitration and mediation; arbitration is binding, and mediation is not. The most interesting and heart-breaking stories that he conveyed dealt with the 9/11 Fund. Ken does nothing halfway. He interviewed *every one* of the people who lost a loved one on September 11. He would have the students mesmerized in describing the types of claims that were made.

The situation that he called "Mr. Mom" was almost beyond belief. A woman whose husband was a firefighter and a first responder who died at Ground Zero came in for an interview. The wife described what a fantastic father he was and how he made the three children's lunches and helped them with their homework. Ken said it was an upsetting story to hear, and he authorized the full amount of compensation, $2 million. A couple of weeks later, another woman came in with a surprisingly similar story. Her husband, also a firefighter, the father of her two children, was a marvelous man who doted on their kids. He helped them with their homework and made their lunches for school every night. Although he worked long hours, he was a devoted father and husband. As it turned out, *it was the same man!* Ken told the class he authorized the full amount for her as well.

One of the students asked whether he told the women about each other. He said he had not because he would not have been able to bear the burden of the pain that would have caused. Both women lost a husband, all five children lost a father, and Ken said, "I could not make a Solomon-like choice. I did not split the baby".

Ken wrote a book about his work on the 9/11 Victim Compensation Fund called "What is a Life Worth?". It is a very moving and sometimes emotionally devastating description of the tragedies and the practicalities of trying to do justice in the face of horrible pain and suffering. Many of the students had read the book before the meeting, which helped them in asking questions. Ken inscribed a copy to me, which brought feelings of both pride and humility: "To Dan Freeman- With respect and admiration for all he has done (and is doing) for our Nation." It is one of my most treasured books.

✛ ✛ ✛ ✛ ✛ ✛ ✛ ✛

I was fortunate to have lawyers from the Office of House Employment Counsel (OHEC) regularly speak to the students about on-the-job sexual harassment and hostile work environment, as well as employee and employer rights and responsibilities under the Family Medical Leave Act (FMLA). These are federal laws that will probably come up in some way during each student's working life. I thought it would be a good experience and get them to understand how federal law can directly affect them.

Victoria Botvin was one of the lawyers in the office who had been extremely helpful to me in my role as Committee Counsel. She is a bright, razor-sharp attorney who knows her stuff and can be very practical in giving advice. Part of the Contract for America in 1995 was to make all of the federal civil rights and employment laws apply to Congress. This was not the case before then, and the Hill was referred to as the "last plantation".

I relied on her extensively, especially when preparing the Employee Manual for the committee. The Manual spelled out the employees' rights and responsibilities as well as those of the committee as the employer. Having such a document enabled the committees to avoid problems by making sure the staff was on notice about their legal rights. Each new employee was required to acknowledge receipt of the manual by signing for it on their first day.

Victoria came well-prepared for her talks to my students. She had an engaging manner and punctuated her presentation with real-life examples. Describing what constitutes sexual harassment and a hostile work environment in the abstract is not easy. Being able to give students concrete scenarios based on cases she had worked on was very powerful and effective. Talking about how to deal with the constituent who came into a Congressional office and was inappropriately physical with the receptionist, especially if it was a big campaign donor, makes a strong impression. Hostile work environments also were discussed in practical detail. It was always an exceptional session.

Victoria informed me she and her husband were moving to South Korea for his job at the World Bank. I was happy for her and her family but disappointed she was not going to be around to have coffee (which we did regularly) or to speak to my classes. I got an email from her the day before her last presentation telling me she had fallen and broken her nose and was not sure she would be able to speak to my students. Another lawyer from her office would do it if necessary. I told her not to worry and stay home and rest.

She is a trooper, and she felt well enough to meet with the class, although she did have a nasty bruise and a large bandage on her face. She told the class, "Only for Dan Freeman would I do this". I was gratified. After taking all of the students' questions, she made some final comments. She pulled out all of the thank you notes she had received from my students and me over the years. She told them they should, "Cherish the time you get to have with a fabulous teacher like Dan." Wow!

One of the other lawyers from the office who spoke practically every semester was Ann Rogers. Ann's specialty is the Family Medical Leave Act (FMLA). She did a fabulous job of explaining how important this law is, and how everyone in the class would probably avail themselves of its provisions at some point.

She explained how the law required employers to give unpaid leave to people who had a personal or family situation, which required them to take time off.

The most critical situations occur when welcoming a new child to the family, or when taking care of oneself or a family member during an illness. She told them about the problem I had had with the Deputy Staff Director of the International Relations Committee concerning allowing one of our staff to have FMLA time off every Friday morning to take a parent for dialysis. Language describing this type of "intermittent" leave is contained explicitly in the law as well as in the committee's staff manual. He did not like it one bit. He said, "That medical leave crap is just for people having babies". He was wrong, of course, and Ann backed me up.

Her talk was punctuated by real stories from circumstances she had been asked to deal with on the job as an attorney to Congressional offices. She also spoke about her personal situation regarding her mother, who had had some health problems, including a broken hip. Ann talked about using her FMLA leave to take care of her mother. That made it very real for the students.

Ann also was good at hitting the points I wanted her to emphasize. She knew most of the students were considering law school. She told them how important good writing is to anyone, but especially to a lawyer. "You want to make sure people notice that your writing is clear". I would then comment, "I don't think you want them to notice your writing at all. They should be focused on the content, not the form". She agreed with that perspective. We did that one-two drill every semester.

✦✦✦✦✦✦✦✦

One of the women who occasionally takes ballet classes as my wife does at the Maryland Youth Ballet was a lawyer with the Center for Science in the Public Interest (CSPI). Caroline Smith DeWaal is an internationally recognized expert in food safety. She was actively involved in all of the relevant legislation while she was at the Center and is a passionate advocate for ensuring the food chain is safe for all consumers. She was a very popular speaker who demonstrated a comprehensive knowledge of the laws in the field. In a very understandable manner, she described how Congress deals with the task of ensuring the laws are adequate. She has a wonderful way with students and was able to establish a rapport with them, which led to an open and free-flowing dialogue.

She discussed the initial ground-breaking food safety law, which was prompted by Upton Sinclair's book, "The Jungle". This novel was written in 1904, and it described the horrific conditions in the Chicago stockyards where meat was butchered in the most unsanitary conditions imaginable. The novel was credited with triggering the movement demanding better and safer methods of processing meat, which led to the enactment of the Meat Inspection Act and the Pure Food and Drug Act in 1906.

Caroline talked about the split in jurisdiction between two federal agencies over the foods Americans eat. The Department of Agriculture handles all meat products, including poultry. The Food and Drug Administration (FDA) is responsible for basically everything else. She described the convoluted delineations between the two, including the fact that cheese pizza is regulated by the FDA and pepperoni pizza, which contains meat, is regulated by the Department of Agriculture.

Caroline went on to a senior position in the international division of the FDA, and she turned us over to Sarah Klein at the Center. Sarah is a vivacious and fascinating speaker who got down and dirty when talking about food safety. She told the classes there were three things that she would not let her family eat; warm water oysters, sprouts, and raw unpasteurized milk because of their susceptibility to harboring pathogens. One of my students was highly offended because she had been raised on a dairy farm and grew up drinking raw milk. Sarah was clear in describing the evidence about why it was better to avoid those three products, but my student was still miffed.

In subsequent meetings, Sarah explained the FDA Food Safety Modernization Act of 2011, which was designed to combat the problem of foodborne pathogens, which cause an enormous number of people to get sick every year. In the United States, almost 50 million people get sick, over 100,000 are hospitalized, and over 3,000 people die each year from these illnesses. Sarah described the new responsibilities which are given to the FDA in the Act, which enables it to focus more on preventing food safety problems instead of merely reacting to them. It gives the FDA new enforcement powers to achieve higher rates of compliance and gives it the authority to hold imported foods to the same standards as domestic foods.

This session was always first-rate because it was something that affects everyone in the room. Sarah was excellent in dealing with students and in applying their questions to everyday situations. I always felt this was time well-spent, and it was another opportunity to emphasize the importance of rules and regulations.

One of my liveliest sessions every semester was with Ricardo Carvajal. He had worked in the General Counsel's office at the Food and Drug Administration. He is a practicing lawyer with a major law firm specializing in food and drug matters. I did not know him before I started teaching, but his name was given to me by Caroline Smith DeWaal, and he readily agreed to speak to my class. He and I developed an excellent rapport, and I enjoyed the sessions as much as the students did.

Mr. Carvajal would supply soft drinks, coffee and cookies for the students, which made him a big hit immediately. He and I were on the same page in a lot of ways. We would wear identical ties each time he met with us. At my first class session with him, I had worn a tie that had a vibrant blue background with spectacularly colorful microphotographs of the six most deadly food pathogens. He loved it, and I sent him one. The students were tickled when we walked into the conference room, each wearing the same brilliant tie.

Ricardo usually led off the seminar by asking the students a question. He would go around the table for their answers. The questions varied each semester, from what television shows do you watch, to what is your favorite thing about being in Washington DC, and one semester he asked what you enjoy the most about Professor Freeman's class. In response to the latter question, one young woman said, "All of our speakers are very personable, and they all seem to love Professor Freeman, and we are the beneficiaries of that". It was a special moment.

Ricardo was aware of my emphasis on the importance of rules and regulations. My students knew the section number of the Administrative Procedure Act (§553) under which they are promulgated. That impressed him. I always reminded him to bring three documents to the session, a) the Food and Drug Act which is in Title 21 of the U.S. Code, which is about 100 pages long, b) Title 21 of the Code of Federal Regulations (CFR), which is several hundred pages long, and c) the non-binding guidelines to accompany the regulations which were even longer. This visual aid was effective in pointing out the difference between laws and the regulations and how important the rule-making process is. He also would bring in examples of different types of tobacco products, including strawberry flavored cigars, nicotine-laced drinks and electronic cigarettes. We would have an open discussion about which of them should be regulated and which should not.

✦✦✦✦✦✦✦✦✦

Two of the speakers who gave their time to my classes are people I worked with on the Judiciary Committee. Dan Bryant and Mitch Glazier were young lawyers who I had the chance to mentor.

Dan left the Committee and went to work at the Department of Justice and became a Counsellor to Attorney General Ashcroft. He went on to a series of jobs in the private sector, including two major corporations and an international law firm. Dan is one of the most thoughtful people I know; I mean that in both connotations of the word. He thinks profoundly about his life and the people who are important to him and frequently assesses the significant parts of his existence and tries hard to ensure he is up to his high personal standards of

conduct. He is also thoughtful in the other connotation of the word; in the kind
and gentle way he treats people.

His meetings with the students were unusual. He talked to them about life
goals, how to forge them, and how to accomplish them. He also talked about
the responsibilities people have to their communities and their colleagues in
the working world. It was a deep and thought-provoking session, and I always
enjoyed it. Dan is someone who I feel has gone from being a mentee to being
a mentor. Those people whose lives he touches are fortunate. Dan has told me
he feels lucky to have found significant mentors (including me), and he feels an
obligation to "pay it forward". He is a good citizen of the world.

✦ ✦ ✦ ✦ ✦ ✦ ✦ ✦ ✦

Mitch Glazier is another one of the young lawyers who came to the Committee in 1995. He worked on intellectual property matters and was someone
else who was eager to learn about how Congress works. He was a quick study.
Whenever meeting with my students, he would preach the gospel of mentor-
ship. He, too, would stress the importance of good writing. His judicial clerkship was a one-year crash course in what he calls "precision in message". He
would tell them that "verbose legal jargon" does not do the job.

Mitch left the Hill to work for the Recording Industry Association of America (RIAA) to help with its legislative presence on the Hill. When he joined the
organization, they were trying to combat internet piracy of music. It was during
the heyday of Napster, Grokster, and other file sharing software that was used
to download copyrighted material, especially music, illegally. One of Mitch's
first assignments when he got to the RIAA, was to go to college campuses and
speak about the evils of stealing music. He would tell my classes about wearing
a garbage bag on some campuses as protection because the students would
throw tomatoes at him. He became the public face of the RIAA's campaign to
sue college students who had illegally downloaded music.

It was only a matter of time, but one semester I had a student in my class
who the RIAA had sued. I made her sit up front, next to Mitch, and introduced
them as "fellow litigants". Both of them handled it well. The student told the
class her parents settled the lawsuit for $3000, which was a lot of money at the
time. She said she never illegally downloaded another file. That made Mitch
happy.

✦ ✦ ✦ ✦ ✦ ✦ ✦ ✦ ✦

Another terrific speaker was someone from my past on the Judiciary Committee staff. Stuart Ishimaru had been one of the counsels on Congressman
Don Edwards' Civil and Constitutional Rights Subcommittee. Stuart is a bright
lawyer with palpable personal warmth. I always enjoyed working with him. He

has an eagle-eye for details, and always tries to make the world he lives in a better place, especially for disadvantaged people.

At the time I began teaching at American, Stuart had left the Hill. He had been appointed as a member of the Equal Employment Opportunity Commission (EEOC). He later became the Acting Chairman. During our meetings, Stuart would cover two separate topics. First, he would explain to the students how the EEOC functions and the types of cases that fall within its jurisdiction. The Commission is responsible for enforcing federal laws that make it illegal to discriminate against a job applicant or an employee because of the person's race, color, religion, sex (which includes pregnancy, gender identity, and sexual orientation), national origin, age, disability, or in the most recently added category, genetic information. The Commission also has jurisdiction over claims of retaliation by employers against employees who have filed a complaint. The laws apply to all types of employment situations, including hiring, firing, promotions, harassment, training, wages, and benefits. This covers a broad range of cases, and Stuart was able to explain in real-life terms what this could mean for someone who felt they had been discriminated against. Not only does the EEOC handle formal complaints, but it also works to prevent discrimination through outreach and education programs.

Stuart also discussed the importance of public service. In a warm and caring manner, he would describe his career and the benefits he derived from his various jobs in the public sector. In an evenhanded way, he dealt with the pros and cons of going to law school (an important issue for many of my students). He also discussed the question of whether to go straight from college to law school or to work between. His concern for the problems that the students were facing about important life decisions was evident. He handled these questions with the seriousness which they deserved as well as the empathy he always evidenced.

Stuart left the EEOC to move to the Consumer Finance Protection Bureau (CFPB) in 2012. He headed the Office of Minority and Women's Inclusion. The CFPB was created to provide a single point of accountability to enforce federal consumer financial laws and protect consumers in the financial marketplace. When Stuart was named to head the Office, CRPB Director Richard Cordray said, "Mr. Ishimaru's extensive experience in promoting diversity makes him the perfect person for the job". During his discussions with my classes, he would always emphasize how important it was to include women and minorities in the workplace. It was good for both businesses and their customers. His sessions were always well-received by the students.

✦✦✦✦✦✦✦✦✦

In dealing with the widely misunderstood "guarantees" in the First Amendment, I would explain that there are exceptions to all of them. And, as I have mentioned, I always had a student ready to recite the first five words of the First Amendment, "Congress shall make no law". The First Amendment is only a limit on what *Congress* can do in the areas it covers; establishment of religion, free exercise of religion, freedom of speech, freedom of the press, right to peaceable assembly, and the right to petition the government for redress of grievances. For example, American University, being a private university, is not governed by the First Amendment. I would explain there are exceptions to the First Amendment in every category. Having "in God we Trust" on our currency does not violate the Amendment, libel in the press is not protected, certain religious practices, such as animal sacrifice, are not protected.

While at AU, questions relating to the press were at the forefront. I would often get asked about how the press could get away with some of the outrageous things they printed. To discuss the First Amendment's "guarantee" of freedom of the press I invited Professor Eric Easton of the University of Baltimore School of Law to campus to speak about the most important Supreme Court decision relating to libel and freedom of the press in the history of the United States, *Times v. Sullivan.* I have known Professor Easton since high school and he is a treasured friend.

The New York Times had been sued for libel in the Alabama state courts for printing an advertisement. The ad was placed in an attempt to raise funds for the defense of Dr. Martin Luther King, Jr., who had been jailed in a civil rights protest in Montgomery, Alabama. It contained language about "Southern violators" but did not name Sheriff J.B. Sullivan specifically. Sullivan argued that the inaccurate criticism of actions by the police was defamatory *to him* because it was his duty to supervise the police department. He demanded a massive amount of money damages.

Professor Easton painted a vivid picture of the atmosphere in the South during the civil rights movement in the '60s and the very real and serious threat to the future of the New York Times posed by the libel suit. Losing could possibly have put the Times out of business. He also did a superb job of portraying the charged environment at the trial in the state court in Alabama. It was analogous to a lynch mob. As evidence of the feelings in Alabama about the suit, he quoted someone who said: "There was no way a New York newspaper was going to get away with badmouthing our Sheriff". The Times lost at trial and was ordered to pay $500,000 in damages. That was big money in 1964.

Professor Easton described the oral argument in the U.S. Supreme Court. He fleshed out the Court's decision, which held newspapers could only be liable for libel against a public official if they printed material which showed "actual malice". Justice Brennan acknowledged that the actual malice standard may protect inaccurate speech, but that the "erroneous statement is inevitable in free debate, and ... it must be protected if the freedoms of expression are to have the 'breathing space' that they need to survive." He discussed the language in Brennan's opinion dealing with the profound American commitment to the principle that "debate on public issues should be uninhibited, robust, and wide-open, and that it may well include vehement, caustic, and sometimes unpleasantly sharp attacks on government and public officials." The decision was viewed as ensuring a rigorous free press would continue to thrive without the sword of Damocles of ruinous lawsuits hanging over it. Its effect was not limited to coverage of the civil rights movement.

Professor Easton was very popular with the students. He had a wonderful way of weaving the facts and the law together, which had a significant impact on the class, especially since these young students had no way of relating to the tensions during the civil rights movement. I feel fortunate to have had him as a guest speaker practically every semester.

✦ ✦ ✦ ✦ ✦ ✦ ✦ ✦ ✦

Tim Keating had moved on after the Clinton Administration. He had worked in a prominent lobbying firm, as Senior Vice President of Government Relations for Honeywell, and as Executive Vice President of Government Operations at the Boeing Company. No matter where he was working, he managed to carve time out to meet with my classes. He did a wonderful job of disabusing the students of the widely held perception of lobbyists as evil. He and his staff made the class feel welcome. It was always an outstanding session.

Above and beyond his willingness to speak to my students, Tim knows how interested I am in aviation. As I mentioned previously, Tim had arranged for Mimi and me to have a tour of the Boeing factory where they build the 777 wide-body aircraft.

When the new Boeing Dreamliner, the 787, was going to be making an exhibition stop at Washington National Airport for a VIP event, Tim invited my wife and me. The 787 had not yet entered commercial service. This was an occasion for Members of Congress and other officials to see it. I had read a lot about the airplane and was excited about getting to tour it. The plane had all kinds of 21st-century innovations, some of which you could see and some you could not.

We got the full tour, and Tim's assistant made sure we saw everything. She also introduced us to one of the engineers on the design team who explained some of the nuances of the cutting-edge technology used. The cabin is pressurized to a level of 6,000 feet, unlike other aircraft which are pressurized to 8,000 feet. The flight attendants we talked to said that made a tremendous difference over a long flight. The oxygen saturation is higher, as is the humidity level. The result is less dehydration of the passengers and crew, who feel much better. One of the flight attendants who was assigned to the 787-tour told us she had recently flown on a 777 and could feel the difference. We got to sit in the cockpit and be astounded by all of the fly-by-wire equipment. It was very different from my 90 minutes in a 727 simulator!

Since this plane can fly up to 8,000 miles, there has be to room for the crew to rest, and we saw their sleeping quarters. They are squeezed in just behind the cockpit, above the galley in the front for two pilots, and for the other crew members, they are in the back. These aircraft carry a second set of pilots on long flights because under Federal Aviation Administration regulations the pilots are only allowed to fly a specific limited number of hours.

The wings were the most interesting part, at least to me. They are made from composite materials and change shape in flight depending on the amount of lift required. The cross-section can be modified. I asked the engineer about the length of the wings. He said they were 120 feet. I smiled and told him the Wright brothers' first flight was 119 feet. I thought it was a lot of fun to see this plane and talk to the proud people who had a part in creating it.

✦✦✦✦✦✦✦✦✦

One of the issues we dealt with was the progression of the legal conflict over same-sex marriage. In the Spring semester of 2009, the law was in flux. Several states had passed legislation permitting either civil unions or same-sex marriage. Congress, however, had passed the Defense of Marriage Act (DOMA), which said for any *federal purpose*, only marriages between a man and a woman would be recognized. Under this bifurcated scheme, a same-sex couple could file joint state tax returns in a state which recognized their marriage but be prohibited from filing joint federal returns.

It was an interesting constitutional question that was made more intense by the decision of the Department of Justice not to enforce the law. Kerry Kircher, the General Counsel to the House, with whom I had worked closely on the Oil for Food matter, spoke to the class about the issue. In the DOMA case, the Republican majority on the Bipartisan Legal Affairs Group directed the House General Counsel to challenge the Department's position in court. This was Congress filing suit to direct the executive to enforce the law. It was a very unusual conflict in the context of separation of powers.

Kerry discussed the implications of the executive branch asserting its authority to pick and choose what duly enacted laws it would choose to enforce. On one side of the argument, under the specific language of the Constitution, the President (and the executive branch) are required to "take care that the laws be faithfully executed". If Congress passes a law and the President signs it, the executive branch should not be permitted to ignore that fact and choose not to defend the law in court. The other side of the argument is that the executive branch should not be required to defend a statute which it deems to be unconstitutional. The fact that this debate arose in the context of the highly volatile consideration of same-sex marriage clearly affected the debate.

✦✦✦✦✦✦✦✦✦

Since all of my students were doing internships, I asked Laura Thrift, my friend Ashley's daughter, who worked on the Hill for a Congressman from North Carolina, to speak to the students about internships in general, and working on the Hill specifically. She would regularly bring a good friend of hers, Katy Siddall, who worked for a Congressman from Iowa.

This was a helpful session as far as I was concerned because I could rely on these two young women to say things candidly to students which might not have been appropriate for me to say. They talked about making sure you address everyone formally unless you are told to call them by their first name. In some Congressional offices and others off the Hill, people are very casual, and first names are okay. In other situations, it may be deemed rude to refer to a superior by their first name. Hearing that advice from people close to their age has a more significant effect on students than my saying it. Laura was aware I felt uncomfortable talking to the women in the class about inappropriate attire. She would tell them, "When you are sitting down, and the male boss comes over to talk to you, make sure you cover your lady parts. No cleavage, no bra straps, no short skirts". She would also talk to the men in the class about wearing suitable business clothes and making sure their facial hair was fitting for the office. They could also talk to the students bluntly about not using office computers for personal use.

Laura especially emphasized how important it was that students take advantage of being in Washington, DC. She talked about all the extraordinary museums and cultural events which were available and what an exciting place it is to work. She would also say failure to get around the city and check out all the exciting things going on while here in Washington is "just plain stupid and a wasted opportunity".

✦✦✦✦✦✦✦✦✦

Major Site Visits

U.S. Supreme Court

When I was on the Judiciary Committee staff, there was always a seat waiting for me in the Supreme Court unless there was a highly controversial case being argued. I continued going to the Court whenever possible after I left the Hill. Over the years, I had become friendly with the Clerk of the Court, Bill Suter. He had been the Judge Advocate General of the Army, its top legal officer before he came to the Court. He was gracious and would always talk with my classes. It was an impressive thing for students to be permitted to enter the inner sanctum of the Supreme Court and meet with one of the few men in the government who wore a morning coat to work.

Every semester, we would go to the Court to meet with Bill or his successor Scott Harris. I would ask (beg) for seats for my students to attend oral arguments. It was a thrill for them to be able to get into the Supreme Court Building and be ushered into the Lawyers' Lounge and see some of the other splendid conference rooms. The majesty of the Court is impressive.

Bill has a relaxed, down-to-earth manner and a terrific sense of humor. He would tell them about one of his first assignments in the army in Germany. One of the soldiers he served with was Elvis Presley.

Bill or Scott would give them an outline of how the Court functions. While they would never discuss pending cases, they would describe how cases are selected for oral argument and how the conferences where cases are discussed and decided are conducted. Questions from the students were dealt with in a receptive manner.

I would also arrange for a docent to give the class a tour of the building. We got to see the Supreme Court library, which is extraordinarily beautiful and adorned with gorgeous wood carvings. I would tell the students about the basketball court, which was directly above the Supreme Court Chamber, and refer to it with the most repeated Supreme Court joke as, "The highest court in the land". It was not to be used while the Supreme Court was in session since the bouncing ball can be heard in the massive courtroom below.

I had hoped to get a seat for the oral arguments in the same-sex marriage case *Obergefell v. Hodges*. When I asked Scott Harris if I could be "put on the list" for a seat, Scott promised to do so. He then added, "That would make you number 784!" Obviously, I did not get in.

U.S. House of Representatives Chamber

One of my "musts" every semester was to visit the House floor. Anyone can get into the gallery by getting a pass from their Member of Congress, but I was able to get my students onto the floor. I could only do this when the House was not in session, and I would ask a former Member or one of the House Parliamentarians to meet with us.

When I could get one of the Parliamentarians, especially Charlie Johnson, the session would be even better. Having the students get a glimpse into the importance of Congressional procedure helped them to understand the role I played when I was on the Hill. Charlie would regale them with tales about the different characters with whom he had worked. He would tell the story of the day he had to rule Speaker Tip O'Neill out of order when one of the Members objected to the language the Speaker had used.

Since I had spent a lot of hours on the floor, I was able to explain to the students how things worked. I would describe where the Republicans and the Democrats would sit. I also pointed out where I would sit during debates. I gave them some history, including showing them the "Dutchman" repair of one of the tables that was damaged when some terrorists started shooting from the gallery in the 1950s.

I demonstrated how the electronic voting system worked, and how the scrim above the Speaker's chair would light up during roll call votes. They could see how each Member's name was lit up, and Members coming in could see what the tally was, who had voted, and how.

There was a sound engineer on duty at all times while the House was in session. The appropriate microphones were turned on at the precise time, including the two in the well, and the two at the managers' tables. The microphone at the Speaker's desk was almost always on. There was a switch next to the Parliamentarian's chair that could temporarily cut off the microphone, so the Parliamentarian could advise the Speaker, or whoever was in the chair, about what to do. Frequently inexperienced Members were presiding, and the Parliamentarians had to give them guidance.

I had lots of stories about being on the floor, and depending on how much time we had, I would tell some of them. One of the best was about the sound system. During debate one day, Speaker Tip O'Neill was presiding, and a Member who was semi-affectionately known as "Bullet Bob" was seeking recognition. The Parliamentarian on duty had pushed the kill switch that turned off the Speaker's microphone. The small red light which had been installed into the side of the wooden rostrum would go off to indicate the mic was off. The Speaker turned to his left to ask the timekeeper, "Do I have to recognize that nut?". Unfortunately, the kill switch only turned off the sound inside the Chamber. The feed over the CSPAN broadcast was still live. Someone in "Bullet Bob's" office was watching and heard what the Speaker said. She called her boss and told him what she heard. Bob came racing up to the rostrum. He asked the Speaker, "Did you just call me a nut?" The Speaker looked to his right (not to the timekeeper on his left), and asked the Parliamentarian, "Did I say that?" The Parliamentarian on duty said he did not hear him do so. The Speaker replied, "I don't know if I said it, but I certainly was thinking it". The very next day, the switch was modified to turn off both signals, and a second indicator light for the external feed was installed in the rostrum.

I always enjoyed this visit. It was a bit nostalgic, and it gave me the chance to share my love of the House with a new group of students.

The Old Supreme Court Chamber

During the tour of the Capitol, I always made it a point to visit the old Supreme Court Chamber. The Supreme Court sat in this room in the basement of the Capitol from 1810 to 1860. Most people will tell you the Civil War started at Fort Sumter, South Carolina. To my mind, the war started in that very room, where the Supreme Court heard oral arguments in the infamous *Dred Scott* case. Scott was a slave who had fled the state where he had lived (Alabama), where slavery was legal and relocated to a free state (Missouri) where slavery was prohibited. He filed a lawsuit to gain his freedom in a Missouri state court in St. Louis, on the grounds that his presence in a free state had freed him from the bonds of slavery. The Supreme Court, on March 6, 1857, ruled (7–2) that a slave who had moved to a free state, where slavery was prohibited, was not entitled to his freedom. Scott was deemed to still be the property of his owner, no matter where he resided. The Court held that slaves were not and could never be citizens of the United States. The decision added fuel to the sectional controversy and pushed the country closer to civil war.

U.S. Senate Chamber

A visit to the Senate Chamber was a little more difficult for me to arrange as I only knew a few people with access. Sometimes I could get people from the Parliamentarian' office or the Sergeant at Arms staff to escort us. I tried to do the Senate after having visited the House. Due to the smaller membership in the Senate, it is more intimate. Students would frequently comment about the relative size of the Senate since it looks much bigger on television.

I described the events which I had witnessed while I had been on the Senate floor during impeachment trials. Whenever possible during site visits, I tried to make it personal and describe what my role was in any particular venue. I would point through the main doors of the Senate, which, if open, would give you a view all the way through the Capitol to the House, showing the class the route we would follow from the House when presenting Articles of Impeachment to the Senate.

The Senate Parliamentarian, Alan Frumin, and his deputy, Pete Robinson, were always very gracious in spending time with my classes. They would describe interesting things, which were really inside baseball, such as Senator Ted Kennedy's desk that had been the desk his brothers John and Robert Kennedy used. There was a tradition of Senators writing their names in the bottom of their desk drawers. Alan would frequently show the Kennedy's signatures to the class. He would also pull out the drawer in the desk that Hillary Clinton had signed.

A not well-known curiosity was the "candy drawer". It had been the desk of John Heinz from Pennsylvania. It was located near the door closest to the elevators adjacent to the Senate subway. This is the door that the majority of the Senators use when coming over to the floor from their offices. Among the major corporate citizens in Pennsylvania, which Senator Heinz represented, was the Hershey candy company. His desk was always well-stocked with a variety of mini Hershey's candies. Senators would frequently stop on the way in and grab a few goodies. The staffer who failed to keep that drawer well-stocked was in trouble! The tradition continues to this day.

The Vice President's Office in the Senate

The Vice President of the United States is, under the Constitution, the President of the Senate. He has an office adjacent to the Senate floor. Whenever possible, I would arrange for someone from the Senate Historian's Office to escort us into the office and discuss the history of the furniture there.

I would then tell the story of the desk, which is now in the office. It was the desk that Richard Nixon used in the White House in which the infamous audio taping equipment was installed. In the kneehole, you could see the marks where the recording device was attached.

That presented me with the opening to tell a fascinating anecdote about American history. On the day Richard Nixon resigned, August 9, 1974, Vice President Ford escorted the Nixons out to Marine One, the presidential helicopter, to start their trip back to California. The helicopter still used the call sign "Marine One" since Nixon was still President. His resignation would not take effect until noon. That is when Nixon flashed the double V for victory sign that was so pathetic. He was getting run out of town, and the victory sign was in ironically poor taste.

As the helicopter lifted off, soon-to-be President Ford's turned to his Chief of Staff (none other than Donald Rumsfeld) and said to him, "Get rid of that goddamn desk". It was immediately removed from the Oval Office and now sits in the Vice President's office in the Senate. I do not know how it got there, or who decided that is where it should reside.

Another story I would relate was about Nixon's flight to California. The

Boeing 707 that was the presidential jet was always referred to as Air Force One, but it was officially "Special Air Mission (SAM) 27000". It only became Air Force One when the President was on board. At noon, the time when Gerald Ford was sworn in as President, the pilot, Colonel Ralph Albertazzie, radioed air traffic control: "Kansas City, this was Air Force One. Will you change our call sign to Sierra Alpha Mike 27000?" Back came the reply: "Roger, Sierra Alpha Mike 27000. Good luck to the President."

The crypt in the U.S. Capitol which houses the catafalque

While we were visiting the Capitol, I took the class on the Freeman tour, which included some things that tourists usually do not get to see. Along with all the more frequently visited areas such as the main Rotunda, the House and Senate Chambers, we would go downstairs to the basement to see the catafalque that is used to bear the caskets of heroic Americans who lie in state in the Capitol Rotunda. This honor is reserved for very few. It was kept in a small nook in the basement. It had borne the caskets of Abraham Lincoln and John F. Kennedy, among others.

I would explain to them about the catafalque being lent to the Supreme Court for the funeral of Justice Thurgood Marshall as his body lay in repose in the Great Hall of the Supreme Court. For the Court to use the catafalque, which is the property of the Congress, both houses had to pass a concurrent resolution permitting the loan.

Other sites we visited

See Appendix 4 for a list of sites around the city which my class visited for programs and/or meetings with guest speakers. We wore out our Metro cards each semester.

Washington Semester Program Faculty

One of the good things about having my office in the same building as our classrooms (Dunblane Hall on the Tenley Circle campus), was that students were able to drop by to talk. They came in to discuss legal issues related to class, legal issues unrelated to class, and frequently to discuss whether law school was a good option for them.

The other thing I enjoyed about Dunblane Hall was the proximity of the other professors. All the faculty offices were in there, so I would get to see colleagues in the hallways, in the copy room, in the coffee room, or in their nearby offices. If ever I had a problem, there was almost always someone around who had dealt with it before. I was the rookie, and I counted on the veterans. I met some fantastic people that way.

Two of my favorite faculty members were, like me, known to have a sense of humor, Rick Semiatin, who taught American Politics and was the driving force in getting me on board, and John Calabrese. We got to be known as the "Three Stooges". We all believed if you were not having a good time, you were probably doing something wrong. I was known as the "master punster" and lived up to that sobriquet whenever I gave guest lectures. John's regular classroom was next to my office, and I would occasionally walk in during his class without saying a word. I would enter, shake his hand, and walk out. Other times, I would silently bring him a cup of coffee (I knew he took it black) and leave. There were a few times when I asked his students how they rated having the best teacher on the faculty. When I did that, he would get out his wallet and pay me ten bucks for the plug.

✦✦✦✦✦✦✦✦

One of the nicest events involving a colleague took place at the Supreme Court. Jeff Crouch, who was a member of the faculty, had decided he wanted to be admitted to the Supreme Court. To qualify for admission, you need to be in good standing with your state bar for three years and have two current members of the Supreme Court bar sponsor you. You can get admitted by simply submitting the proper paperwork, or, as my family had, you can choose to have someone formally move your admission during a public session of the Court.

Jeff chose to have it done in person and asked me to make the motion. It was a professional milestone for him, and I was happy to do it. He is a fabulous teacher, a scholar and a terrific colleague.

On the morning of Jeff's admission, students from three different WSP classes were in the courtroom to watch the oral argument, but none of them knew about Jeff's pending admission. The students were elated to be there. Once the Marshall called the Court into session, Chief Justice Roberts announced they would receive motions for admission. The Clerk, my friend Bill Suter, then stood up and called my name.

From what I heard later, the students were stunned. I got up and made the formal motion, "Mr. Chief Justice, and may it please the Court. I move the admission of Jeff Crouch of the bar of the State of Michigan. I am satisfied he possesses the necessary qualifications". The Chief Justice is always gracious in these situations and granted my motion and warmly welcomed Professor Crouch to the bar of the Court. Bill Suter joined the three WSP classes later in the Great Hall of the Court and told the students the motion was granted, but it was a 5-4 decision!

As we left and were walking down the front steps of the Supreme Court, I was surrounded by students. I heard someone exclaim, "Wow, Professor Freeman, you rock". It was a splendid occasion.

Much to the dismay of most of the faculty, Dean Brown decided to retire in 2010. The new Dean was not much of a factor in my day-to-day life. There were occasional "all hands" meetings, but they were rare and inconsequential. I mostly avoided her, but I did make sure she got a packet of information about my seminar, the kind of speakers we had, the topics we covered and the types of exercises we engaged in. I wanted her to know about my course in case she was ever asked about it by a representative from a school that sent students to us. She never said anything about my courses, my guest speakers, or my students. I do not think she knew anything about them, or that she was interested in finding out.

Except when I bumped into her on campus or in the building when I was visiting other staff, I had almost no interactions with her. I did begin to hear a lot of grumbling about the way she was running things. She was into new-age management techniques. She liked holding so-called "standing meetings" that were supposedly more efficient because people did not blather on. I also heard disturbing reports about her abusive behavior towards some of the staff. I was told there had been several complaints made to the Human Resources Office at AU.

In December of 2011, she was called into the Provost's office, introduced to a campus police officer, who was there to escort her to her office and supervise while she packed up her things and left campus. That was how she got fired. Pretty brutal. All we were told by the Provost at an emergency faculty meeting the next day was she was "no longer employed by American University", and we were not authorized to say anything else.

A new Dean was appointed, and she took over in 2012. I made it a point to write her a note welcoming her. I also sat next to her during the first faculty luncheon she attended. I explained my course to her and told her a little bit about the guest speakers I had had in the past. I offered to give her some marketing materials about my class. She could not say no, so I gave her the same package I had given to her predecessor and each of the marketing gurus before and since. (Mostly without any results.)

The half-life of the marketing/recruiting staff was about six months. Every time someone would be named to that position, I would dutifully provide updated materials about my course. I also invited each of them to attend one of my classes. I did not think anyone would come to a session off-campus, but I did have hopes of a guest appearance to an on-campus class by someone responsible for recruiting students. My foolish expectation was that the experience of sitting in on my class might encourage them to talk it up when recruiting.

In the decade I taught at AU, only three WSP staff came to watch a class; the fabulous intern coordinator Amy Morrill-Bijeau, one man who was relatively high up in the hierarchy and was temporarily doing "marketing" (he was just passing through), and a faculty peer reviewer. I even invited the new Dean on several occasions, but she was just not able to "make it work". We regularly got complaints from the Dean about low registration and declining enrollments, but there did not seem to be a dedicated push to enhance recruitment.

One of the requirements for contract renewal was to have an evaluation of teaching by another faculty member, a peer review. I was doing my session on the legislative process, and I used the Brady Handgun Violence Prevention Act as the model. Professor Jeff Crouch sat in and submitted a very well-written and highly favorable evaluation. He wrote: "This was a lively, engaging--even entertaining, presentation on a notoriously dry subject. Professor Freeman has a very good rapport with students and showed mastery of the subject matter. Professor Freeman's style and his substantive knowledge together made for a very effective presentation". Jeff enjoyed the session so much he subsequently invited me on several occasions to present it to his classes. I still give this guest lecture regularly for him and other former colleagues.

One semester I was called into the Dean's office to meet with her, an Assistant Dean, and on the phone, the Associate Dean. I had been a guest speaker for the Associate Dean's classes for many years, and she was familiar with my style. I wanted to send out a letter to the coordinators from the various schools we drew from about my seminar. I convinced the three of them it might be a good idea, but they hesitated because "No one has the time to draft such a letter". Having been through this type of situation before, I said, "I have a hard copy for each of you, and I have a flash drive with the text on it to give to (the Dean's assistant)". I had inertia in my favor. If you want to get something done, and you need other people's approval, it is helpful if they do not have to do anything but say "yes".

I gave the flash drive to the Dean's assistant, confident, or at least hopeful, it would be sent out. Foolish me! Since this was "in the bailiwick" of yet another new marketing person, it was given to her to review.

When I called a couple of days later to make sure the letter had gone out, I was told the marketing manager "had not cleared it". I was getting irritated. The sooner the letter went out, the better. I called the marketer and wanted to know why it had not gone out; the three senior administrators had approved it. I was stunned with her reply, "I need to run some analytics on it first". I did not know what "analytics" were, how she was going to "run" them or what she was going to do with them when she finished. I told her to "just send the letter out". I went to the Dean's assistant and told her to send it. The administrative rigama-role continued, but the letter did go finally out. I could not understand why the marketing person would not be happy to accept something from someone who was doing part of her job for her. I think this was a sign of the "yellow editing", or marking of territory, that people do to flex their muscles and demonstrate their power.

I was somewhat surprised to find out the following week the new marketing whiz had submitted her resignation. She was there for less than a year. That meant I would have to start over yet again.

There were only two occasions when I was asked to contribute to recruiting. We used to get a good number of students from the University of Bergen in Norway. There was a large group from that school who came to Washington for a couple of weeks, and on their schedule was a meeting with people from the WSP. I was asked to speak to them. I was happy to do so and went into my professorial mode, replicating a mini-version of one of my constitutional law cases. I called on students and made them stand up and formally address me as a judge, "May it please the court". I was told I was a big hit, and several of the students expressed an interest in coming to WSP for my seminar. Three students did come the next semester.

Another time I got involved in recruiting was pure luck. I had stopped by to see one of the staff, Heather. She was not at her desk, and I was in the process of leaving her a note when I noticed her through the glass door of a nearby office. It was clear she was in a meeting, and I did not want to interrupt her.

When she saw me, she very animatedly waved me into the office. As I did not have classes that day, I was dressed informally. Whenever I was meeting with students, either on campus or downtown, I would always wear business attire. I did that for two reasons. I wanted to set a professional tone for my students, and also because after having worked on the Hill for all of those years, most of my wardrobe consisted of business attire.

I went in and was introduced to a prospective student and her parents, as well as her younger brother. Heather told them about my class, the kinds of speakers we had, and that it was taught in the Socratic Method used in law schools. She had been there during my presentation to the Norwegian students and liked what she saw. She encouraged me to give the student "a dose of what being in your class is like". So, I did. She was to become a lawyer in a courtroom and was to address me properly as a judge and make an argument. I even made her stand up even though there were only six of us in a WSP office.

Heather told me the student and her parents were impressed and excited about the prospect of her coming to Washington to be in my class. Things were unsettled at the time about my course load for the upcoming semester. I was tentatively scheduled to teach a new Honors Colloquium on main campus entitled "Bioethics and the Law". Because of that, we were not sure I would be teaching my Public Law Seminar. Heather told me the student's mother kept calling to find out if I was going to be teaching. As it turned out, I was, and the student came to WSP and was in my class.

✦✦✦✦✦✦✦✦

From the beginning of her tenure, it seemed to me the new Dean was not that interested in the Washington Semester Program. She was constantly announcing new programs, which never seemed to come to fruition. The administrative staff grew exponentially. When she left, the staff outnumbered the faculty by at least 2-1.

We moved to a building two blocks away on Brandywine Street, and it became much more difficult for students to drop by to chat. There were only a couple of classrooms in the building, so most of our classes were held on main campus. The building was locked, so students had to be buzzed in, or a professor had to go downstairs and let them it. It was too much of a hassle and did not lend itself to spontaneous visits. The Dean told us she was concerned for students' safety coming over to the Brandywine Building since they had to undertake the "dangerous trek" across a busy street—Wisconsin Ave. She seemed to be unaware of the fact our students navigated all over the city by subway, bus, and on foot. Wisconsin Avenue was not a significant hurdle.

I knew we were in for rough sledding when we were all "invited" to a mandatory faculty meeting one evening. This was going to be a touchy-feely session enhanced by a "facilitator" named Josie. I had a bad feeling about it from the beginning. We were going to be engaged in so-called "team-building". Spare me.

We were asked to sit in a circle and turn to the person next to us and tell them three things which he or she would not know about us. This was immediately after the Republican convention when Clint Eastwood had addressed an empty chair. He was pretending the chair was occupied by President Obama; it was dubbed by the press as the "invisible Obama" stunt.

I could not resist the temptation posed by this rather silly exercise. When I was recognized to reveal the three things I had learned about my friend and colleague Rick Semiatin, I did not play nicely. Instead of talking about Rick, I put an empty chair into the center of the circle and proceeded to reveal some things about the fictitious occupant of the chair. It got a huge laugh, but I could see the Dean and Josie were not amused. The last speaker in this exercise revealed something new he had learned about one of our colleagues; he was a magician. Again, I could not resist, and I asked him if he could "make us all disappear". And again, the Dean and Josie were not pleased.

As we broke for dinner, I was standing near the Dean, when my phone rang, or at least I opened it up as if it had rung. I still had a flip phone in those days. I spoke clearly enough so the Dean could hear my side of the "conversation". I then closed the phone to end the "call" and told the Dean I had to leave, with no further explanation. I did go over and whisper to my friend Dan Whitman that I was bailing out, and his response was, "You miserable bastard. I will never forgive you". I laughed at Dan's reaction and fled the scene.

Unfortunately, the Josie show was repeated the following year with the same type of Kumbaya exercises. This time we were all required to see how quickly we could pass a bean bag around and have everyone touch it. We started off tossing it around, but then some genius decided we should have one person hold it in the middle of the circle, and everyone could quickly lean in and tap it. I bailed early on this one, too.

The next one of these ridiculous sessions happened a year or so later. The faculty gathered in a room on the main campus to discuss what the name of the new school the Dean was creating should be. We spent over an hour exploring different combinations of words. It had to have the word "School" in it; that was part of the new empire the Dean was building. Lots of words were bandied about, and the Dean, as was her wont, would dutifully write them on a white-board. That was one of her favorite props. Among the words thrown out were "Adult", "Educational", "Continuing", "Studies" and "Progressive". The final result was, Ta-Dah… "The School of Professional and Extended Studies", to be known as "SPExS". Another waste of faculty time.

We would occasionally have "all hands" meetings, which meant all of the faculty and the entire administrative staff. These meetings were usually not helpful and were frequently incredibly boring. I took notice at one meeting; more than 50% of the attendees were on their electronic devices and not paying attention to what was going on.

The Dean was into sending out long emails, frequently with attachments. I learned early on not to read the first version because there would always be a follow-up with some corrections. One of the most memorable was the correcting email that said a word had been inadvertently left out of the last sentence. The missing word was "not".

I had an annual meeting with the Dean in January, simply to "check-in", she said. Nothing important ever came up in those meetings. There were no suggestions to improve my class, and there was never any constructive criticism she could offer because she knew practically nothing about my seminar. It was another waste of time.

✦ ✦ ✦ ✦ ✦ ✦ ✦ ✦ ✦

As time went by, I found it distressing how increasingly self-centered the students were. They believed that the world revolved around them and could not seem to fathom that people have other things to be concerned about. One of my students came up to me to complain about her internship supervisor. I asked her to describe the problem. She said, "My supervisor hates me". I was surprised to hear that, especially since it was the beginning of the semester, and I did not think that could happen so quickly. I wanted to know why. The answer surprised me. "I texted her over an hour ago and have not heard back", was the response. I had to enlighten the student that her supervisor had a real job above and beyond overseeing the interns in her office, and there were a lot of them. I suggested the student relax and give the supervisor time to get to her message. "You are not the only dish on her rather full table". That did not mollify the student since she wanted the answer to her question immediately. I reminded her that she did not have to be at her internship until later in the week and could resolve whatever issue she had with her supervisor face-to-face at that time. I am sure that was not satisfactory, but it was a good lesson for her to learn about priorities, and for me to understand the instant response students are used to in the cyber world.

✦ ✦ ✦ ✦ ✦ ✦ ✦ ✦ ✦

I had heard the term "helicopter parents", but I had never had to deal with one until the Fall semester of 2013. A student's mother called to say she did not think that her son was registered in the correct course number. She also told me that she was having trouble getting onto the American University Blackboard, which was how I sent out notices and posted reading materials for the students. Every Friday, I would post the schedule for the coming week and readings. These would include background materials on guest speakers, judicial opinions for cases we were going to be discussing, and materials in support of class exercises, such as the legislative hearing and debate.

I could not understand why this woman wanted to have access to her son's assigned reading material. This young man was a college junior, and I thought at that stage in his education, he should be able to get the materials and read them without his mother's help. I tried to mask my incredulity, and I told her that her son and I would make sure he was properly registered for the correct course. I then gently suggested to her that part of the reason her son was in Washington for the semester was for him to learn how to fend for himself, including getting assignments on his own. I do not know how much of an effect that had, but I did not hear from her again.

Wrapping up at WSP

As the semesters went by, I began to notice a diminution in the quality of the students. I found them to be increasingly entitled, complaining, and whiny. Many of them behaved as though they were here on a lark and were not comfortable with the demanding academic workload, internship supervisors, or me. I found this disheartening at first, and then frustrating. When I asked one student why she chose to come to the Program, she said, "I came to pad my grade point and have a good time". Certainly, some students were willing to work and were engaged, but I found a greater and greater proportion of lazy students. Inexplicably coupled with this laziness, came an expectation of high grades. This was a result, I expect, of grade inflation across academia, which led to dissatisfaction when students received their papers back from me with much lower grades than anticipated. I was getting more and more dissatisfied with their written work, which was sloppy, filled with grammatical errors, and incomplete sentences. It simply was not up to what I thought college students should be able to produce.

The WSP administration was becoming difficult and constantly in flux. The number of minutes per class we were allocated was diminishing, and the fundamental structure of the program transformed as well. Instead of three days with the seminar professor and two days on the internship, it morphed into 2 ½ days with me and 2 ½ days on the job.

Another significant modification was the "modularization" of several of the seminars. For my students, this meant combining the Public Law seminar with the Criminal Justice seminar. I resisted this change because I thought that the two somewhat diverse seminars would draw dissimilar kinds of students with differing interests. The Public Law seminar was aimed at students who were interested in going to law school. The Criminal Justice seminar drew a completely different type of student; those who were interested in criminology, prison reform and other related fields.

I had endured this combination of students for a couple of years before the formal switch to modules. The criminal justice students were not particularly interested in meeting with Members of Congress, Supreme Court Justices, or many of the other speakers relating to the legislative process, legal issues, or constitutional law. The prelaw students were frequently not interested in the criminal justice speakers. As I characterized it to one of my colleagues at the time, half of the students were unhappy every time the class met.

✦✦✦✦✦✦✦✦✦

While my wife and I were on vacation that December, I had fantasized about coming back to Washington while the University was still on Christmas break, submitting my resignation and packing up my office. I was not interested in going through another semester of dealing with a bunch of spoiled brats. My wife convinced me that it would not be professional to bail out so abruptly, and I should stick it out for one more semester and let the Dean know I would not be applying for renewal of my contract.

At the beginning of January, I was scheduled for my regular annual meeting with the Dean. I had not yet decided when I was going to tell her about my decision to leave, but I certainly had not planned to do it that day.

We were scheduled to meet at 2:30. I am an extremely punctual person. Her office was down the hall from mine, and the atomic clock I had on the wall said it was 2:24 when she appeared at my door and said, "I thought we were meeting at 2:30". I pointed to my clock and told her I would be there momentarily. In hindsight, I guess she was anxious to have this over with.

When we met, she asked me if I had reviewed my student evaluations of teaching. I told her when I joined the faculty, I was advised by one of my colleagues not to look at them because you would either be unnecessarily upset or inappropriately delighted. She then told me that she had reviewed my evaluations, and they were "off the charts" and that my "students loved being in your class". I said that it was nice to hear.

With that said, she told me she had just had a conversation with the University Provost, and they would not be in a position to offer me a renewal of my contract because of "budget considerations". I said, "Okay, fine", and we were done. No idle chit-chat. It was as simple as that. As I walked back down the hall to my office, I had mixed feelings. I was pleased with the result that this would be my last semester, as I had intended it to be, but I was a little irritated I was dismissed instead of resigning. That is a distinction without a difference, but I was denied the pleasure of submitting my resignation.

✦✦✦✦✦✦✦✦✦

There was to be a final aggravation as I began my last semester. I made it a practice to meet with each student individually at the beginning of the semester to find out a little bit more about them, about their internship search and to make them feel comfortable in Washington. Those sessions were usually pro forma, but I liked to establish an open avenue of communication. Our offices had moved to the Spring Valley Building. This was also the location for all of our on-campus classes. With a couple of glaring exceptions, I was able to have friendly relationships with most of the students.

One of my new students came in for her get-acquainted office visit. It was immediately evident to me that this was a hostile young woman. She did not make eye contact with me; her responses were monosyllabic, and my attempts to establish at least a friendly relationship did not seem to be going well. We discussed a couple of things about grading, and then she broached the subject of wanting to use her iPad in class. I told her that my policy was not to permit electronic devices in class and that my research on the topic has led me to the conclusion that it was not conducive to the learning environment. I told her that my policy was clearly outlined in both the course and the internship syllabi as well as in the "Greetings" email, which were sent to every student. Despite that, she rather forcefully said, "Yeah, I know that, but I want to use mine".

Since I had made it a point to talk about learning disabilities in the icebreaker, I asked her whether her desire to use the iPad was because of a learning disability. If she had a certification from her home school about a disability, I would be more than willing to make an accommodation. The Americans With Disabilities Act and other federal laws required me to do so. She said, "No, Professor, I just want to use my iPad". I did not think I was going to make much progress with her, so I decided to kick the can down the road and told her I would think about it over the weekend.

I had an uneasy feeling about this student, and I wanted to make sure that I had my bases covered. I decided to contact the Associate Dean of my program for assistance and advice. We had some back and forth emails. She asked me for copies of my syllabi as well as the text of my "Greetings" email. All of them contained the notice of my policy on electronic devices in class. I got those to her immediately and waited to hear any suggestions she might have on how to deal with this angry young woman.

I was relieved to get an email from the Associate Dean later that afternoon telling me she had spoken to the student and informed her that she would not be permitted to use her iPad in class. I thought to myself, "Well, that was simple". Unfortunately, it was not going to be that easy.

The following Monday, I had a rather angry confrontation with the student. She was extremely upset to have received the call from the Associate Dean instead of hearing from me. She then mischaracterized what I had said, which was I would think about her using the iPad. "No, you said we would discuss it", she countered angrily, and then she castigated me for not contacting her directly. "*You* are my professor, and *you* should be the one to communicate with me. *You* should have told me, not the Dean". I was uncomfortable and tried to extricate myself from this verbal altercation by telling her I went through normal channels and worked with my direct supervisor. She reiterated that it was my responsibility and said, "You should *not* have contacted the Dean". It was an unpleasant encounter.

I was relieved to find out the following week the student had transferred to another section. I did not think I would have to deal with her again. That was not going to be the case. A colleague asked me to give my talk on the Brady Bill to her class. Whenever I did such a guest lecture, I went around the room and asked the students to tell me their names and their home schools. I did not know the unpleasant student had transferred into that class. When I got to her, she, in a rather surly manner, mumbled her name and school. I smiled at her and greeted her warmly. "Nice to see you…" It was not, but I did say it.

Most of my students did not present any serious problems. Unfortunately, problem students seem to have an inordinate impact.

XX. Honors Colloquium
"Bioethics and The Law"

As I have no doubt already made clear, I have been interested in medicine since I was a kid. I watched television shows like "Ben Casey", "Dr. Kildare", "Marcus Welby, M.D.", "The Bold Ones", "Medical Center", "St. Elsewhere", "ER", "Chicago Hope" and many documentaries about medicine or surgery. My interest in medicine and bioethics never waned. I would frequently go to "mini-med schools" at Georgetown University, as well as public education events at the National Institutes of Health (NIH) (a fabulous place) and Suburban Hospital.

One of my friends with whom I played racquetball, Tony Gargurevich, was a urologist and surgeon. One evening many years ago, when we were getting ready to play, he showed me an x-ray of a patient of his using the plexiglass back wall of the court as a lightbox. The patient had two kidneys which looked normal except for the fact that they were perpendicular instead of parallel. Tony told me he was going to operate and asked if I would be willing to photograph the procedure because he wanted to write an article about it. He knew I was into photography and had my own darkroom. I enthusiastically agreed to participate. Since we were going to be in an operating room with incandescent lighting, I bought special film that was formulated to be used in tungsten light.

When the time came for the operation, Tony made sure I was gowned and gloved and filled me in on what was going to happen and what types of photographs he wanted. The patient had not yet arrived, but there were others present, including a surgical resident who was going to assist, an anesthesiologist, and several nurses. Tony stepped over to me and said in a quiet voice, "There are two things you need to do. First, if you are going to faint, faint backward *away* from the surgical field. Second, don't tell anyone you are a lawyer". I smiled beneath my surgical mask.

The patient was wheeled in. As the anesthesia was administered, I noticed Tony had his hand on the patient's shoulder. I thought that was very kind. I learned later, from my good friend Dr. Jim Evans, that one thing a doctor can do to minimize the possibility of being sued is to touch the patient.

The operation went well, and Tony talked me through each step. I also noticed he was treating this as an educational experience for the surgical resident. He was teaching throughout the operation. It was fascinating to see this human being opened up so I could see his heart, lungs and kidneys and even watch the aorta pulse with each heartbeat. Later, a pathologist came up from the lab to take a look at the renegade kidney to check for disease. He and Tony decided to remove it since you only need one functioning kidney. It was a fascinating experience.

✦ ✦ ✦ ✦ ✦ ✦ ✦ ✦ ✦

I had another chance to sit in on surgery a few years later. I was visiting a friend who worked at the Texas Heart Institute in Houston, where the famous cardiac surgeon Dr. Denton Cooley reigned. My friend asked me if I was interested in seeing Dr. Cooley in action. "Yes", was the obvious answer.

This was going to be open-heart surgery, and I learned that Dr. Cooley would only be in the room for a short time. Younger surgeons would do the preliminary work of opening the chest, putting the patient on coronary by-pass, and setting the stage for Dr. Cooley to come in and do his magic. I was sitting above the operating theater, looking through the glass dome down at the surgical field. I could also view the operation through a TV screen hooked up to a camera directly above the patient. There was another guest present; she and I were talking about how interesting it was. The other visitor told me it was going to be a coronary artery bypass, probably involving several blood vessels. I was happy to learn that, but as the operation proceeded, I thought I was seeing something else. Dr. Cooley had arrived and was cutting into the heart, not any arteries. I was confused. I said to the woman next to me, "I am not a doctor, but that looks like he is taking out some of the heart itself". She called down into the operating room to check, and lo and behold, I was correct; it was not a bypass. The operation was to repair a ventricular aneurism, which is a thinning of the wall of the ventricle. Dr. Cooley was excising the defective tissue and sewing the wall of the heart back together. The other guest was impressed that I knew that, and I was stunned.

Since I was fascinated by the complex problems posed at the intersection of bioethics and law, I made it a point to attend relevant seminars and courses on them whenever possible. One summer, I spent a week at the University of Virginia Center for Bioethics. I was the only lawyer in the class. The rest of the students were healthcare professionals, including one who was a prominent neurosurgeon from Little Rock. He said he was glad I was there because it gave him a different perspective on some of the challenging cases we discussed.

I recall one case vividly. A couple in rural Virginia, who had been married for a few years, split up in a bitter and acrimonious manner and went their separate ways. They did not bother to get a divorce. Several years later, each had a new partner with whom they lived. The man was involved in a terrible propane gas explosion that left him on death's door with third-degree burns over a large part of his body.

He was taken to the UVA hospital, which has an exceptional burn unit. It was touch-and-go for several days. His wife showed up at the hospital, and so did his partner. The doctors, and finally, the hospital general counsel, were confronted with the legal issue of who was the appropriate surrogate healthcare decision-maker for the patient. It was clear under Virginia law that the wife was legally entitled to act in that capacity. The new partner, under the law, had no standing. When the doctors proposed an experimental treatment for the patient, the wife asked, "Will it be very painful?" The doctors told her it would be, and with bitterness in her voice, she said, "Do it". The partner had no legal right to have any input.

When I got back to Washington, with that story clearly in my mind, I called up a good friend who was involved in a rancorous divorce. At the time, he was living with another woman. I told him he had better change his advance directive about his surrogate decision-maker, pronto!

A couple of years later, I decided to take some bioethics classes at Union College in Schenectady, New York. Union has a strong bioethics curriculum, and its pre-med students who do well are guaranteed admission to the Albany Medical College. There was a broad range of students in the bioethics class, and once again, they were mostly healthcare professionals. This program was different from others I had attended because it included a lot of time in the Albany hospital talking with doctors and patients.

I found being in the hospital to be emotionally challenging but rewarding. I spent a lot of time talking with potential transplant recipients who had agreed to speak to students. Being on the waiting list was stressful, and that came out in our conversations. It was difficult to speak with patients who had been approved for a transplant, been prepared for surgery, only to find out the prospective organ was not suitable. It was also hard to talk with parents of babies and children who were on the list, but not high enough to have any real hope of getting a new liver, heart, or lungs for their child.

My dear friend, Eric Easton, was teaching at the University of Baltimore Law school. He would always do the freedom of the press segment for my WSP students. We had frequently discussed some of the legal implications of the debates about bioethics which land in the courts. He called to let me know the adjunct professor who taught the "Law and Medicine" course was not going to be available for an upcoming semester. That course dealt with the bread and butter issues of any civil lawyer's caseload, medical malpractice. Since there was going to be a hole in the schedule, and it was during the evening, he wanted to know if I would like to teach a class on bioethics and the law. I decided this was an excellent opportunity, even though it would require me to work a full day on the Hill and then drive to Baltimore for an evening class.

I was able to compile a lot of the necessary reading materials from my friend Paul Lombardo who I had met when I attended the bioethics course at UVA. The rest of the materials came from contemporary sources, including, in many instances, newspaper articles about pending cases. It was a hell of a lot of work, but I managed to stay one small step ahead of the students. Evening students are a special breed. They are there because they want to be. They took the class seriously and, for the most part, were well-prepared. It was an exceptional learning experience for me, and I got excellent reviews from the students.

Teaching that course, coupled with my extensive public speaking experience, led me to believe that I might want to consider teaching bioethics in the future. I followed bioethics education seminars on the web and attended many lectures and symposia. Those sessions, together with the EINSHAC meetings where I would get the chance to interact with judges from all levels of courts and a wide range of jurisdictions, continued to fuel my desire to teach.

✦✦✦✦✦✦✦✦

About three years before I left the WSP, good fortune struck most unexpectedly. When the Dean hired a new administrative assistant, I made it a point to go by and welcome her. The Dean was in her office and said she wanted to talk to me. I do not know how she knew I had an interest in bioethics, but out of the clear blue, she asked if I would be interested in teaching such a course. I was excited about it and said I would be thrilled. I thought that it was going to be part of this new school she was trying to develop. Where the course was situated administratively was not important to me.

I heard nothing else about the course for a long time. So, it came as a surprise when I received a phone call from Doctor Michael Manson, who was the Director of the American University Honors Program on main campus. He invited me to chat about teaching an Honors Colloquium on bioethics. Dr. Manson was personable and friendly. I did not know what an Honors Colloquium entailed, but I was hopeful that it would give me the chance to deal with bright, inquisitive students in the subject matter area that I found fascinating. I was not to be disappointed. After our meeting, he offered me the chance to design and teach a course which was entitled "Bioethics and the Law".

The first time I taught the course, I had ten students. The upbeat and enthusiastic nature of the class discussions were a professor's dream. It was a good mix of men and women with varying backgrounds and a real thirst for knowledge. While it took them a while to get used to me, and me a while to get used to them, it ended up being one of the most rewarding experiences that I have ever had in the classroom. The students were all excited to be there and were always well-prepared.

They adapted quickly to the pulse of the course, the rapidly changing landscape of the discussion, and to my peculiar sense of humor. They took seriously the challenge that this was supposed to be a colloquium, and that meant there would be a lot of discussion in the class. I was constantly changing the facts and was pleased to see how they took that in stride. Occasionally a student would stop and ask for clarification because the scenario had changed so rapidly; "Wait, am I the patient, or the legal advisor?"

After the first couple of classes, one of the students asked if they could sit in a circle rather than in rows. I thought that was an excellent idea because it enhanced the ability of the students to engage each other as well as me. Making eye contact and reading the non-verbal body language of their classmates enhanced the quality of the classroom discussions.

One of the cases that we dealt with was a paternity action that involved a husband, his wife, and the biological father (not the husband) of a child born to the woman. Role-playing is always part of my classes, and I would randomly pick students to play one role or another. For this case, I needed one woman to play the wife/girlfriend/mother, one man to play the husband, and another man to play the biological father of the child. The legal question in the case was, "Who was the *legal* father of the child under California state law?"

I put three chairs in the front of the room where I was going to place the three parties. First, I had to choose the woman. I walked up to one of the students and said, "Mary, do you want to get married?" This was before the Supreme Court had ruled on same-sex marriage making it legal nationwide. Mary looked at me and said, "Professor Freeman, I am gay". As I reached out my hand to formally escort her to the middle chair, I replied: "Not for the next 20 minutes you're not". While that may have been politically incorrect, Mary was not flustered and took my hand as I escorted her to her seat. To make the visual more obvious, and for the fun of it, I had Mary hold hands with the student to her right, her "husband", *and* with the student to her left, the biological father of her child.

Everyone laughed at the set-up, and then we had an excellent discussion of the legal issues posed by the case. This class was chock-full of flexible students who responded well to both the educational challenges posed by the controversial and complex subject matter and to the relaxed and open atmosphere in the room.

I am pleased to say I am still in touch with Mary. Since she graduated from AU, she got married and became a Senior Account Manager at a media relations firm. She is now attending law school. It is a joy to spend time with her.

Another scenario we discussed in class was one that I made up out of whole cloth. It involved a "mature minor" who has a fatal illness who wishes to donate her kidneys for transplant while they are still viable. Students were assigned to be a nephrologist, a psychiatrist, the possible donor, her parents and her siblings. I posited the parents would be opposed to the donation, and the siblings would be in favor of it. The student I picked to be the donor was an extraordinarily bright young woman, who loved intellectual challenges. She got into her role with vigor and did a fantastic job. Outside of my class, she was a primate interpreter at the National Zoo, a chemistry lab assistant, and an all-around star. She is an impressive, happy, and warm young person. She was one of the best students I ever had the pleasure of working with. She went on to Columbia Law School, with a gentle assist from my recommendation. It was her first choice.

I was saddened for the semester to come to an end. I had enjoyed this class more than any other. I did something I had not done previously. I had a photograph taken of the whole class and me and asked each of the students to sign it. I kept that on my office wall for the rest of my teaching career at AU.

I taught the class again the next spring semester. This time I only had five students, all men. Having such a small class can be challenging, especially if one of the students is absent. This was also a bright group of students who were adept at the role-playing exercises. One of the students, Martin, I called on regularly when I needed a woman. He said he was "adept at chromosome changing". I laughed at both the comment and his comfort in making it.

Sometime during the next semester, I was having brunch with Renee, a former Public Law student. Surprisingly, our waiter was Martin, my "chromosome changer". I did not know he was working there. After explaining how I knew him, I introduced him to Renee as the "brightest girl in the class". I knew he would not be offended.

The third time I taught the bioethics class, I had seven women. There were two fairly shy ones, three very assertive voluble students, and two somewhat reticent ones who I was able to draw out during the semester. One of the students told me she never spoke up in any of her other classes, but she was very active in this one.

My wife came up with the solution to my single-sex student conundrum when I needed a male for a particular case. She went to the hardware store and bought me a couple of **Y** address sign letters, the **Y** representing the male chromosome. Whenever I needed a man, I would ask one of the women to put on the lanyard with the **Y** on it and presto we would have a male for the session.

I enjoyed this class immensely. One of the first exercises was to deal with advance directives. I asked each student to fill one out before discussing the right-to-die cases. Most of those cases dealt with young people, so the argument that these students did not have to think about those things did not hold much water. Teri Schiavo, Nancy Cruzan, and Karen Ann Quinlan were all in their 20s when they and their families were confronted with the question of terminating life support. While I required the students to fill out advance directives, I promised them I would not read them. I simply wanted them to think about what they would want if confronted with that scenario.

I did suggest they discuss the issue with their parents and even go so far as to ask their parents if they had advance directives. Most reported their parents did not want to talk about it. No surprise. One student's father was a college professor who taught public health, and he was delighted I had assigned this exercise. However, when I asked my student if she knew what her father had provided in his advance directive, and who, after her mother, was the surrogate decision-maker, she did not know. I suggested she had a bit of educating to do within her family.

Over the three semesters I taught the course, I found it challenging and very rewarding. The students lived up to my expectations. Dr. Manson was an enthusiastic supporter and was very complimentary about how well-received the course was. He wrote an exceptional recommendation letter for me when I was applying for reappointment in the WSP program.

XXI. The Students

Difficult Students

The most difficult student I ever had was actually two students, Elizabeth and Tara. I should have known immediately Elizabeth was going to be a problem. Before she arrived, she complained resentfully about having to go through what she called "the hassle" of getting the photograph I had requested in the "Greetings" email. She did not think her mother would pay for a formal portrait sitting. I told her all I wanted was a "selfie", so I could recognize her on the first day. I asked the incoming students to submit photos without sunglasses or hats so that I could see their faces. Elizabeth told me she always wore sunglasses because she lived in Florida. I told her to take them off for the 10 seconds needed for the picture. She was still miffed but somehow was able to get it done.

When she got to the city, our first exchange was about my "ridiculous policy" about electronic devices. Her "mommy" bought her a new iPad, and she wanted to use it. I told her my policy, which was clearly spelled out in the syllabi for both the seminar and the internship in bold letters as well as in the "Greetings" email, was that electronic devices were not permitted. She whined that since her mother bought it for her, she should be able to use it. I did not understand why that mattered, but I saw trouble ahead.

Elizabeth and Tara came to the program from the same school and were joined at the hip. I told them early on I wanted them seated separately in class. They tended to chat when sitting together, and it was disruptive. Whenever we were traveling in the city, they were always together and not interacting with the rest of the class.

Near the beginning of the semester, when the students were in the process of securing their internships, we were on the Metro on the way to a meeting on Capitol Hill. I asked Tara how her internship search was going. She told me her answer was going to "make you angry". They were both going to be working at the same internship organization. By this time, I knew any criticism I had for either of them would land on deaf ears. I responded that it did not make me angry. I did tell her that their working at the same internship would further isolate them, and it could diminish their experience in Washington. I reluctantly approved their internships since I did not want to put up with their complaining if I had not.

I spoke to the organization's director about them later in the semester. He had had my students in previous semesters, and I found him to be a good supervisor and one who demanded a high level of performance. He thought they did acceptable work but seemed to insulate themselves from the rest of the staff. They were horrified when he recommended they each receive a B grade for the internship. They were expecting As, of course.

I tried to keep my disappointment and negative feelings about them to myself. Still, I did find myself talking to colleagues about them whenever the issue of difficult students came up. They were an irritant all semester long, from complaining about the robust schedule to whining about having too much reading to do.

They were always contrary. We sat in on part of a federal civil trial, presided over by my friend U.S. District Judge Ricardo Urbina. A woman was suing for damages for an unlawful dismissal from her job based on an allegation of race discrimination. The judge's law clerk promised to call me when there was a verdict. The morning she called, I announced to the class that I had the jury's verdict, which I was prepared to reveal, but I wanted to poll the class first. I asked for a show of hands. The entire class, except for three students, felt the defendant should win; discrimination had not been proven. Elizabeth and Tara were the only two who felt the plaintiff should prevail. The only other holdout was my best student, Rose, who said she could not vote since she had not heard all the evidence. I thought hers was a particularly thoughtful answer. The defendant prevailed.

In the student evaluations of teaching, which the students complete at the end of the semester, there is a series of questions, and students rate the professor on a scale of 1-7, 7 being the best. One of the questions is how you would rate this professor from "one of the best" to "one of the worst". Throughout my teaching at AU, I had always received high marks on this question (and others), usually averaging in the mid-to-high 6s. That semester, when looking at the ratings, I noticed all the students rated me as a 6 or 7 except for two students who rated me as one of the worst. Although the ratings are done anonymously, I certainly knew who those two were.

Tara came in to complain about my behavior on another topic. In class that afternoon, we were discussing written requests in the context of physician-assisted suicide. I frequently use humor in the class, even on some serious subjects. When I was discussing Oregon's physician-assisted suicide law, I pointed out who would not be permitted to be a witness to the signing of such a request letter. No one who has an interest, or a potential interest is allowed to be a witness. You do not want any treating physician or anyone who might benefit from the requester's death being a witness. I then said, "You do not want someone who is a beneficiary in the will signing a request to knock off Aunt Sadie".

Tara complained because she thought my facetious comment was "terribly inappropriate and offensive", and that I should not even be discussing suicide in a college class. She said that someone at her home school had committed suicide, and she did not think I should be making light of the topic. I asked her if she was close to that student, and she said no. I explained this was a controversial public policy question, which was before the courts, and many of her classmates were interested in it. I was not going to poll the class before discussing every potentially sensitive topic and give any student the ability to veto it. If I did, there would be very little to discuss.

✦✦✦✦✦✦✦✦✦

After hearing from Kerry Kircher about the DOMA lawsuit, in a subsequent class on campus, we discussed the legitimacy of the Executive Branch deciding not to defend a statute passed by Congress. While this was supposed to be a debate about separation of powers, many of the students could not focus on that issue but chose to discuss/argue the inappropriateness of same-sex marriage. The conversation got a little heated, and several of the students from conservative religiously affiliated colleges were adamant that same-sex marriage "was just wrong". I tried to steer the conversation back to the institutional authorities question, with minimal success.

After the class, one of the students came into my office to complain indignantly that we were even discussing this matter. She had been very animated during the semester about "all these liberal ideas", which many of her classmates had. She regularly complained about my allowing students to talk about that "left-wing garbage". She was not willing to discuss ideas which she opposed. Although I would often try to get her to take the "other side", she always refused. "I can't make that argument because it is wrong" was her frequent response. She was vehemently against same-sex marriage, and I asked her why. "The Bible says it is an abomination". I did not want to respond to her flippantly, but I did ask her a serious question. "Since we discussed the fact that federalism dictates that most matters are reserved to the states, marriage being one of them, in what states is the Bible, the Torah or the Koran legally binding?" She spluttered, "That doesn't matter...I just know it is immoral and just plain wrong".

✦✦✦✦✦✦✦✦✦

An interesting thing happened as we were leaving Judge Urbina's courtroom after watching part of a trial. Judge Urbina is a dear friend and somebody I admire. When the testimony was completed for the morning, and the jury was excused for the lunch break, Judge Urbina came down from the bench. We greeted each other affectionately. Judge Urbina then spoke to the class for a while about the Federal Courts, and then we left. As we were walking down the hall outside of the courtroom, one of the students, a rather straight-laced conservative young man from a school in the deep South, came up to me and said, "Professor Freeman, I think it was inappropriate for you to be seen kissing another man." Before I had a chance to respond, one of the delightful young women in the class said to him, "What planet are you from?" There was nothing for me to say since she had made the point rather eloquently.

✦✦✦✦✦✦✦✦✦

In what was to be my penultimate semester, two incidents occurred that were representative of the problems I was dealing with. One of my students had complained with indignation that she was not being treated with the proper esteem at her internship. She said they were "not giving her credit for who she was". She was horrified to be tasked with answering telephones, making copies, and providing clerical support to a Member of Congress. I assisted her in changing internships because she was so unhappy with the first one. Little did I know she would end up switching not once but twice more. I only found this out when she was giving her final internship presentation the last week of the semester. She rather proudly announced to the class, "I didn't tell Professor Freeman this, but I quit two more internships because they were not treating me with the respect I deserved". I was astounded, but since it was already done and the semester was almost over, there was nothing I could do.

This student was very self-centered and did not believe the normal rules applied to her because she was "special". Her assignments were frequently not on time, and I had the feeling she was somewhere else when we were in class. One afternoon we were going over a Supreme Court opinion in a search and seizure case. The classroom was set up in a big double U, so there were two rows of students. This student was in the front row. I normally walk around the room when I am teaching. As I moved towards her, I could see she was not taking class notes but was writing out what was obviously a birthday card. I stood directly in front of her and stopped talking. She was so engrossed in the card it took her a full 10 seconds to recognize I had gone silent. She looked up at me with a start and said, "Oh, I am paying attention". "But not to me", I replied to a bit of laughter from the rest of the class. I did not feel bad about disturbing her correspondence.

✦ ✦ ✦ ✦ ✦ ✦ ✦ ✦ ✦

One day we were in the Capitol Building, waiting for our escort to the House when I saw a familiar face walking towards me, surrounded by people who looked like security; big, burly men with lapel pins on. The protectee and I made eye contact, and he recognized me. I pierced the bubble and went over to shake his hand and greet him. It was Paul Ryan, the Speaker of the House. I had known him when I was on the staff. He was first elected to the House in 1998. "Mr. Speaker, how nice to see you". "Dan, nice to see you too. What are you doing up here?" he replied. I explained I was visiting with my Washington Semester Program students. Since he was a graduate of the Program, I asked him if he had a few minutes to chat with them. I knew he was always running to one meeting or another, and I was surprised when he said: "Sure, I would be happy to". He spent about 5 minutes speaking with them fondly about his semester in the Program and about what being the Speaker of the House entailed. It was a bit of good fortune, and I hoped the students were pleased with that bit of serendipity. Most of them were, but later in the semester, a couple of them came to complain to me. It was the same two who had been difficult all semester. They wanted to know why they only got 5 minutes with the Speaker. They said I should have arranged a full session with him. At first, I simply could not believe it. Then when thinking about this spoiled, entitled group, I did.

✦ ✦ ✦ ✦ ✦ ✦ ✦ ✦ ✦

Another example of the arrogance of students happened the same semester with a different student. She was very opinionated and would not listen to anyone who did not agree with her. She refused to learn the lesson of "know both sides". When asked during an exercise to be the attorney for the government, she refused since she "did not believe in their side of the argument". I insisted she at least articulate the argument for the government. She was very irritated and did not do a good job. On a subsequent Wednesday afternoon, she approached me to announce proudly, "I was not in class yesterday". On the slim chance she had a good excuse for not being there, I asked her if she had been unwell. "No, I wanted to send a message to the speaker that I do not agree with him". I did not say what I was thinking; "I am sure Justice Scalia will be devastated to hear that". What I did say was, "You decided to skip a chance to meet with a Supreme Court Justice because you do not subscribe to his views of constitutional law?" "Yes, I boycotted him". There was nothing I could say.

International Students

Foreign students posed some issues on both ends of the educational spectrum. Students who were not native English speakers sometimes had problems, especially with American political terminology, and with American colloquialisms. For example, when I was talking about two extremely poor plaintiffs in a civil rights case, I said: "They did not have two nickels to rub together". That did not make any sense to a lot of foreign students since they did not know what a nickel is. I tried to encourage those who did not comprehend the colloquial language I had used to make a note and ask me about it after class.

I had a student from Brazil who was not sufficiently fluent in English to keep up. She and I had an arrangement that I would give her my notes before class so that she could follow along. That worked out well for the first 20 minutes of class, but I rarely followed my outline for long and just let the discussion flow. From that point on, my notes became useless to her. I always tried to meet with her after class to make sure she understood everything.

The other "problem" I had with foreign students was with the Norwegians and the Germans. I frequently had students from the University of Bergen in my class. I also had several German students. The difficulty was they always spoke and wrote English better than my domestic students. I rarely had to correct one of these foreign students about grammar or anything else in their writing or oral presentations. It was embarrassing to listen to one of the Americans following a Norwegian.

Students Where I made a Difference

People often ask me what the best part of teaching at AU was. That is an easy question to answer. Sure, we met with a lot of important people, Members of the House and Senate, Supreme Court Justices, Cabinet Officers and many others. But for me, the best part was being able to make a positive difference in the lives of some of the students. In my faculty profile on the AU web site, there is a question about my favorite place on campus. My answer is, "In the classroom with students".

I have written about the value of finding a mentor and being a mentor. In a good relationship, there are benefits to be gained by both parties. In academia, there are simply more opportunities to establish this kind of connection than in the working world. I would like to think I mentored many students while they were here. I worked with them to help sift through their post-graduate options. Most frequently, this included whether to go to law school at all and if they did decide they wanted to do so, whether to go directly to law school or take some time off and enter the working world first. I rarely made concrete suggestions, but instead, I would ask questions to help them think through their options.

I am still in touch with a number of my former students. I do take some pride in knowing I helped many of them while they were here and have continued to do so after they have scattered to the corners of the globe.

There are several students for whom I genuinely feel I made a difference in their lives. To protect their privacy, I will use pseudonyms.

✦✦✦✦✦✦✦✦

Zoe was a student from a small college who came in to talk about a paper she had written. I had gone over it very carefully and made extensive comments in pencil. When I joined the faculty, one of my colleagues told me to use a regular pencil and not red or blue. He told me that making comments in color was too "in your face" and frequently upsets the students.

With every paper, I would correct or point out spelling, grammatical, syntax, and word choice errors. I spent a lot of time going over them word-for-word. I was sometimes appalled with the lack of writing ability and even the lack of desire to produce a good product.

Zoe's paper was abysmal. It was filled with incomplete sentences, grammatical errors, misspelled words, and inappropriate language. I had spoken to her before about elevating the level of her writing and getting help in doing so. We went over it together, line-by-line. I explained what each fault or error was and how to correct it. We discussed the fact that the poor quality of her paper reflected on her lack of effort to do good, careful work. I thought she understood why her grade was lower than she expected (or at least hoped for). In another context, I might have simply returned the paper with no grade and required her to resubmit it in at least an acceptable form. I always emphasized that if it has your name on it, it should be letter-perfect.

She seemed to understand every criticism I made. She did not challenge any error I pointed out. I told her I thought she could do better, and she should spend more time on her papers. When we had finished the review, I thought she got the message. It turns out I was wrong. She proceeded to ask me if I was going to raise her grade! I must admit I was a little stunned by that. I said, "After I showed you all the deficiencies in the paper, why would I raise your grade?" Her response was, "At my home school if you go in and kiss up to the professor, they will raise your grade". I kept my cool but was appalled both that it might be true, and that she would tell me about it! I simply said, "That does not happen here".

This student also had difficulty with her oral presentations. She would mispronounce words such as "pitcher" for "picture", "aks" for "ask". She would speak quickly and swallow her words, so it was hard to understand her. I had tried to convey to her how important it was to speak professionally. I asked her if she wanted me to help her by pointing out errors or did she feel that would be too embarrassing. She said she came here to learn, and she wanted to improve. I told her we had a deal, but if it ever became too difficult, she should tell me, and I would stop correcting her.

I got a delightful thank you note from her after she returned to her home school. She said, "You impacted me in ways I never imagined, and I am honored I was given the chance to be one of your students. … I wish more of my professors taught in the fashion you did. If it had not been for you, I do not think I would have ever been comfortable enough to know who I was. I now know in order for me to receive a good grade, I must work for it, and I thank you for that".

She told me she went in to see her academic advisor to discuss her WSP experience. After about 20 minutes, he stopped her and said, "Who are you? Where is the student I knew before?" He was impressed by the change in her and could not believe it was the same young woman. Zoe was pleased her progress was so evident, and so was her advisor.

✦✦✦✦✦✦✦✦

One of my students, Denise, came from a small Midwestern town. She grew up on the family farm, and her parents' expectations for her revolved around being a farmer's wife and a mother. The parents were not very understanding about why she wanted to go to college. I got the impression they felt it was not worth the time or the money.

I had seen this situation a couple of times previously. In this case, I was convinced that this young woman truly wanted a future markedly different than her parents envisioned for her. She was having a difficult time wrestling with this divergence of expectations, and she came in to ask my advice.

The specific question she wanted to talk about was whether she should take a preparatory course for the Law School Admissions Test (LSAT). I think the real question she wanted to discuss was whether she should even dream of going to law school. It was clear to me that she did not think her parents could comprehend that goal.

I knew very little about her family, but I did perceive in her the ability to go to law school and her strong desire to do so. Based on what I had seen of her writing and oral presentations, I thought it was something she should at least consider. While the specific focus of our conversation was about the prep course for the LSAT, the overriding question in the background was her suitability for law school. As I usually do with students who are conflicted, I encouraged her to sit in on some law school classes while she was in Washington.

I frequently recommend this practice. I suggest the student find out who some of the better law school instructors are and to contact them about sitting in on a class or two. If you approach a professor and tell them you have heard that they are a good teacher, that usually does the trick. Most are flattered and readily agree. I would also suggest they tell the professor they want to get a feel for what law school is like and will not attempt to participate.

We did not come to a conclusion about her taking the prep course, but I let my actions speak louder than my words. After our conversation, I went over to the University bookstore and bought a copy of the LSAT study guide. I dropped it off at her dorm, feeling that I had done a good deed.

The next week I received a nice thank you note which said, "After receiving an anonymous gift on Friday, I concluded that you were the most likely source (from our conversation on Wednesday and the fact that my parents don't know what LSAT stands for). This is probably one of the most meaningful and encouraging gifts I have ever received…knowing you believe in me enough to help me take my first steps toward law school…I will remember your words of encouragement".

At the end of the semester, I received another note from her. She said, "I can honestly say that your class has given me the confidence and the beginning skills I will need for law school". I was pleased to find out she did go to law school and is now a public defender near St. Louis.

✦✦✦✦✦✦✦✦✦

Michelle was a student from a small Christian liberal arts school in Southern California. She was studying to be a nurse anesthetist. She came to Washington because her fiancé was working on a temporary assignment here. She was a terrific student but was a bit intimidated about dealing with the legal and constitutional issues. Early in the semester, I spent some time with her, familiarizing her with the way we were going to examine the court decisions. I also explained how to brief a judicial opinion for use in class. This was something unfamiliar to her.

She took to it like a fish to water. She was diligent in her preparation for each class and each guest speaker. She regularly came by my office to talk about things that were unclear to her, or to examine some of the issues in greater depth.

It was what she referred to as a "life-changing experience". I was pleased the following semester to receive a call from her asking if I would be willing to write her a letter of recommendation for law school. Her career choice had taken a dramatic turn, and she had decided to become a lawyer. She was admitted to the Washington College of Law at AU, and we met regularly for coffee during her law school career.

During one of our get-togethers, she asked me what I had planned for the students the following week. I told her we had several guest speakers scheduled, including one of my heroes, former Congressman and former Secretary of Commerce and Secretary of Transportation, Norm Mineta. Norm had spoken to her class, and I was sure she had been there. She then reminded me she had not come to class that day. She called me from an ambulance on the way to the hospital with a severe infection!

I asked her what she was doing the following Tuesday morning, and she said she had a law school class. I told her to skip the class and come downtown with us to meet with Norm. She jumped at my invitation and agreed to join us.

I made a big fuss over her Tuesday morning and introduced her to Prof. Semiatin, whose class was joining mine for the meeting. I had her sit up front, next to Norm. When he came in carrying the baseball bat I had given him, I made sure to introduce Michelle to him and tell him the story about why she had missed the previous meeting. He was very gracious and chatted with her about law school. I took a photo of them as a memento.

She invited my wife and me to her law school graduation party. It was a very moving event, and she gushed over me, especially when she introduced me to her parents. I did not know until that night that her parents had come to the United States illegally, and her father was illiterate. Quite a story from a young woman who was graduating from law school!

I am pleased to say we have stayed in touch. Like many young lawyers, she has changed jobs a couple of times. She comes to Washington regularly and considers me a mentor. She often asks for career advice. I will soon be proud to move her admission to the Supreme Court bar.

✦✦✦✦✦✦✦✦

One morning, another student, Emma, came in to see me. She was not a happy person, and I could tell she was troubled. She simply asked me if I was willing to talk with her about something unrelated to class. I said, "Certainly".

She sat in the chair across my desk and wrapped her knees up to her chest inside her sweatshirt. I had the feeling this was not going to be easy for her or me. I had not had much experience in dealing with the non-scholastic problems of college students. I was a bit wary and somewhat uncomfortable since I did not know what was coming.

She had started drinking heavily around the time she was sixteen after she came to grips with a "big issue", which had been extremely troubling to her. She did not tell me what it was, but I had a suspicion she was talking about abuse of some kind. She described her drinking pattern. Every Thursday night, she would start. She would get blind drunk and stay drunk until Monday morning. She did not remember what she did, how much she drank, or who she was with. I was utterly stupefied. She did most of the talking, although I asked a few questions.

She and I talked for almost three hours. I know it was stressful and gut-wrenching for me, and I can only imagine how difficult it was for her. We discussed possible options, including counseling, AA, detox, and in-patient treatment at a substance-abuse facility.

She started going to AA the next day. We would occasionally talk during the rest of the semester, and she seemed to be improving. I tried to walk a fine line between being concerned about her and not being intrusive. On the last day of class, when I was saying my individual goodbyes to each student, I asked her the one question which had been on my mind. Once she had decided to get help, why did she choose me to talk with about her problems? Her answer came without hesitation and surprised me. She said, "I felt you cared about me as a person and would listen". It was stunningly simple and yet incredibly profound. I was deeply moved.

Several years later, I heard from her. She had been on a difficult personal journey since she left Washington but was proud to tell me she had been clean and sober for three years. She also told me she had broken her pattern of abusive personal relationships and had achieved a level of happiness. One of my mantras for each semester was to try to get the students to understand they were going to be confronted with decisions for the rest of their lives. Most people do not make bad choices on purpose. You get the best information you can from people you trust and then select what you perceive to be the best option. Your choices may not always work out well. However, I told students the only irrevocable decision they ever make would be to have a child. Everything else can be changed; where you live, what you do for a living, who your friends are, who you marry, and how you choose to care for yourself. Emma told me she repeated that mantra to herself regularly, and it helped put things in perspective every time she had to make a decision. I felt privileged to have had such a positive effect on this young woman.

She continues to stay in touch and has overcome many obstacles to create a rewarding life. She has dedicated herself to being successful in her career and her personal relationships. I am proud for her and of her. I admire her courage and tenacity. I recently got an email from her. She wrote, "Years and years of working on my mental health have paid off - and big time". I was very pleased.

✦✦✦✦✦✦✦✦✦

My favorite student encounters happened regularly in my office. One of the brightest students, Rose, used to drop by my office and ask, "Do you want to fight?" That was her way of inviting me to engage in a debate. My response was to ask her what the topic would be. She would pick something, such as hand-gun control, and I would ask her which side she wanted to take. Whatever side she chose, I would say, "No, I will take that side". This went on for the whole semester, and I enjoyed these stimulating sessions thoroughly.

She asked me to write her a recommendation for law school, and I was pleased to do so. My practice when writing such letters was to ask the student to do the first draft, then I would "Freemanize" it. Most students found this difficult to do. Rose wrote a superb draft, which I tweaked a bit and submitted it. She took the LSAT and got an almost perfect score of 179 out of a possible 180. She was "over the moon" when she got into Yale Law School.

She continued to stay in touch while at Yale. She had a crisis during her first year and called me to discuss it. She asked, "When you were in law school, did you ever feel you were the stupidest person in the world?" At the beginning of each semester, I regularly discussed how challenged I felt in law school, and in that context, would reveal my learning disability; dyslexia. That was my way of encouraging any students who had any kind of learning disability to let me know so I could provide whatever accommodation was appropriate.

In responding to Rose's question, I said the period of time when I felt stupid only lasted three years (which, for those of you who do not know, is the number of years that law school lasts). She said she took some solace from that. I am glad to say she graduated from Yale Law School with flying colors and went on to be named a fellow at the prestigious Yale Center for Public Interest Law.

✦✦✦✦✦✦✦✦✦

Another student who I believe I helped was Judy. In the second week of the class, when she came in to see me, she was distraught. She told me she did not think she could handle the rigors of the class. She felt it was way above her, and most of the students were, at least in her mind, much better prepared to deal with the types of complex legal issues we would be covering. These concepts were unfamiliar to her. She also said other students made fun of her because of it, and they made her feel like a "loser". I was angry about that, but she would not tell me which students were bullying her. This was my first exposure to this problem at AU. However, I could empathize because I knew exactly how she felt since I had experienced many of the same things. There are always students who are braggarts and who love giving others a hard time.

I thought she was a bright, hard-working student, and I believed she could handle what the semester was would bring. I knew from our correspondence before the semester began, she had dreams of becoming a lawyer. Those dreams were in tatters that morning.

I decided to prepare her for the next day's class with a little bit of extra tutoring. We were going to be discussing the famous case of *Loving v. Virginia*. This case involved the anti-miscegenation law in Virginia. In dealing with judicial opinions in class, I would get the students to explain the facts first, and then to identify what the legal question was. She had her materials for the next day with her, including the Supreme Court opinion I had posted. I told her I was going to call on her, and she would have to act as if she were an attorney in court addressing the judge. The question was going to be, "What statutes were the Lovings charged with violating?" I told her the answer was on page 2 of the opinion, and she needed to be able to cite the specific sections of the Virginia Criminal Code. She had to know the relevant facts; a white man and a black woman had left the Commonwealth of Virginia to get married in Washington, D.C., where interracial marriage was legal, with the intent to return to Virginia where such marriages were not permitted and live as man and wife. As we carefully went over the material, her spirits lifted a bit, although I think she was still a little bit uncomfortable. She promised me she would be ready.

The next morning, I "randomly" called on Judy to stand and present the case. As the judge, I inquired, "Counsellor, what are the crimes the Lovings were accused of committing?" She took a deep breath and said, "May it please the court. Your honor, the two statues are section…" She did it with poise and precision. I was delighted.

She told me later that her self-confidence "soared" after that one exchange. Many of the other students were impressed with how well she had mastered both the formal manner of addressing a judge in court, her proper citations of the law, and her understanding of the legal issues. Magically, the bullies in the dorm backed off. There was a dramatic change in how she felt about herself. At the time, I was not aware of how significant it was, but having overcome her initial self-doubt, she became a star in the class and a leader in subsequent class exercises. I selected her to be the judge in another role-playing session, and she became known as "Judge Judy" by the class.

I am pleased to report she, too, went on to law school and became a public defender. She contacted me when she won her first case. She wrote, "…all I could think about was how you continue to make what are dreams of mine become realities. You are truly one of the greatest gifts that life has sent my way thus far. I can only hope to one day be half of the mentor, role model and friend that you are to me". It does not get any better than that!

✦✦✦✦✦✦✦✦✦

Mathew was a young man who was having some difficulty with both writing and public speaking. He came from a small college that did not have a reputation for high academic standards and was not as well-prepared for the program as many of the other students. However, he was always talking about his Congressman who "had nominated him to attend West Point".

Nominations to the five service academies are extremely competitive and difficult to get; 90% of cadets at West Point were in the top 20% of their high school class. Nominations are made either by one of the student's 2 Senators, their Member of Congress, or the Vice President. The competition is fierce for two reasons. First, these are rigorous programs, both academically and physically. Second, attendance at any of the military academies is entirely free.

I thought there was a disconnect between Mathew's pride at being nominated to go to West Point and the glaring fact that he did not attend. We had a couple of discussions about his poor performance in class. He was a strong kid, and I believed he could take a "tough love" approach. During one of our meetings, when I was reviewing his latest paper with him, he was pacing back and forth and somewhat angrily brought up the fact again that he had been nominated to West Point. My response was, "Matt, why didn't you attend West Point? Did you think you couldn't cut it?" He was utterly deflated and dejectedly sat down. He said with deep emotion, "I have never admitted that to anyone, but you are absolutely right. I did not think I could make it". We sat there for a moment, gathering ourselves. I believed we had had a breakthrough. We then talked for a long time about what he could do to improve both his writing and oral presentations.

As he left my office, he gave me a warm hug and thanked me for pushing him and for understanding. He promised he would work harder to improve his performance. I returned the hug and told him I believed in him and his commitment. From that day forward, even though it was at times difficult, I felt he was giving it his best. I told him I was proud of him.

I got a heartfelt thank you note from him after he left Washington. He said: "There are many people who have doubted my success, and to this day still doubt my capabilities. I have never run from a fight, I came close in your office, but you forced me to rise to the occasion. I respect and love you for that". I was deeply affected by his words.

✦✦✦✦✦✦✦✦✦

A student I will always think of as the most resolute person I know came to AU from a small college in the Mid-West. Renee was well-prepared to be in my class. I think she was one of the very few students who had read "The Federalist Papers". She had a tremendous thirst for knowledge and was thrilled about being in Washington. She was interested in government but also felt the city had a lot to offer her outside of class. She had a long bucket list of things she wanted to do when she was here. Most of them related to cultural and historical sites.

Renee came in to see me the second week and told me she had a genetic condition that required her to get body scans regularly. She said she would try to schedule them around class times, but she could not afford to miss any of them. I told her any classes missed for those were an excused absence, and her priority should be her health. I did not know what the condition was, and I did not ask her. I thought she would tell me if she felt like sharing it. After a few minutes discussing some of the upcoming "road trips" we would be taking all over the city, she described her condition to me. She had a very rare genetic mutation which caused her to develop tumors. I had never heard of it, but from what I understood, it could be severely debilitating and even life-threatening.

She had come to terms with this malady since she had been aware of it her whole life. Her mother died from it. Renee was very matter-of-fact in describing the condition and how she continued to cope. We talked about it, and she was astoundingly at peace.

Her attitude was upbeat and cheerful. We got through the description of her condition rather quickly, and then she said, "Enough about that, let's talk about all of the amazing things we are going to do this semester". My reaction was to say, "You certainly have blood type B positive". She looked at me quizzically and asked, "How would you know that?" My response was that even with her medical problems, it was evident to me she had a "be positive" outlook.

She was my "Freeman's First Law" student that semester and was always on the ball. I knew I could count on her for that, and everything else. Her class participation was always excellent and well-reasoned. She had no difficulty in arguing the other side. Her written work was outstanding, and she was a leader in class activities. In other words, she was the kind of student any teacher would love to have in class. Her internship went well, which was no surprise to me. Her supervisor commented Renee was "a joy to have in the office and became a valued member of our team".

Since leaving Washington, we have been in regular communication. She went back to her home school, graduated with honors, and went on to a top law school. She did well there and continues to keep in touch. I occasionally remind her of her "B positive" blood type. After graduating from law school, she took a job in Washington that combined her legal training with her leadership skills. She has since moved on to another position where she utilizes her legal training more actively.

I know she will continue to do well wherever she goes. I am proud of her and grateful to have had her as a student and to have her as a friend.

✦ ✦ ✦ ✦ ✦ ✦ ✦ ✦ ✦

One of the students I had a positive impact on was not in my class. I would often give the presentation about the passage of the Brady Bill to colleagues' classes. It is a lively session that involves a lot of role-playing, and the students usually get into it. My colleague, Rick Semiatin, who teaches American Politics, would frequently ask me to do this for his students.

One semester about a week after I did it, one of his students came in to see me. She had come to the WSP from a small school in Maryland. She had played one of the roles in the Brady Bill scenario, and I had pushed her fairly hard on some of the issues which she would have to confront as that hypothetical person. Joyce was thoughtful about her answers and was intellectually flexible enough to roll with the ever-changing fact pattern which I threw at her.

She was participating in a moot court at her home school, and she asked me if I would be willing to work with her to enhance her presentation and self-confidence. I readily agree to help her. There was a classroom next to my office which had a lectern and was big enough for us to use for practice sessions. She did well the first time she gave her argument. For that initial run-through, I let her finish without interruption. Afterward, we sat down and went over it in detail. I had several suggestions for improvement, which included not using superfluous words and eliminating overly complicated or repetitive words such as "heretofore", "aforementioned", and "as I previously stated". Not surprisingly, she was not aware of these. I suggested the Earl Dudley practice of recording her practice sessions. She found it to be an excellent way of catching these bad habits and using that awareness to eliminate them.

We agreed to meet again to give her a more realistic experience. This time, playing the role of a judge, I would interject questions. These disruptions can be extremely difficult to deal with. Taking questions in the middle of your presentation can be unnerving, and it often interferes with the flow of your thoughts. It also takes up precious time allotted for your argument. You have to be able to answer a question, which may not be relevant to an essential part of your case and, without getting flustered, get back to your point.

The combination of her diligence in learning the arguments both in support of and against her position, as well as her frequent practice sessions, put her in good stead. I know she felt the time we spent was well worth it. I thought she made tremendous progress during her semester in Washington.

She kept in touch when she went back to her home school. She excelled in the moot court, and partially based on that, she decided to go to law school. I was happy to write her a glowing recommendation. She got into her first choice, which was the University of Virginia; the same school Earl Dudley and Leonard Braman had attended. I was pleased for her. She did very well in law school and was an editor of the *Virginia Law and Business Review*. She is now practicing law.

+ + + + + + + + +

One night during the Spring semester of 2012, I was walking down the hall in our home when I slipped and fell. I hit a door jamb hard, and I was in a significant amount of pain. Mimi wanted to call 911, but I talked her out of it. I took some Tylenol and went to bed thinking I would be a bit sore in the morning. I was not just sore; I was in a whole lot of hurt! It was the worst pain I had ever experienced. We went off to our doctor's office. The doctor told me she thought I had either cracked or broken a rib. The drive from her office to the x-ray lab was excruciating. It felt like we hit every bump and pothole on Wisconsin Ave. We went home and waited for the results. Dr. Kaufman called later to tell me she was wrong. I did not crack or break *a* rib; I broke 7! She prescribed some heavy-duty pain medication and told me there is no treatment for broken ribs. All she could suggest was to make sure I was doing breathing exercises to keep my lungs clear. When it hurts to inhale, one tends not to.

I had classes scheduled the next day, and there was no way I was going to be able to get to campus, much less teach. I had a repeat guest speaker for the morning session, my old friend Professor Eric Easton. He had done this session on *Times v. Sullivan* for me before, so he agreed to do it without my being there. I did some schedule juggling and was able to get everything I had planned for that week completed in my absence.

On the following Sunday morning, my wife was looking out of our front window when she saw three squeaky-clean young people walking up the cul-de-sac where we live. We occasionally get religious proselytizers visiting on Sundays, so this was not completely surprising. However, Mimi told me they were not stopping at any other house and were headed straight for ours. I did not feel like receiving visitors, but they came to our door and rang the bell. Mimi answered, and I heard someone say, "We are Professor Freeman's students, and we came to see how he is doing". It was a sweet gesture, but I did not know how they knew where I lived. It seems one can find out anything online. We talked for a while, and then I asked Mimi to drive them to the Metro. On the way there, one of them asked her a question about something we had discussed in class. Mimi did not take the bait; she said she did not know enough about the subject to answer. The student responded, "You have definitely been living with Professor Freeman!"

It is hard to decide which student I had the most significant impact on, and I expect there have been some I do not know about to this day. However, I am certain about Ashleigh.

As a new member of the faculty, I told Dean Brown that if he needed any help during the summer session, I would be happy to pitch in. The only program he had in the schedule was the Lead America Summer Study Program, which was designed for students who had just graduated high school, as a pre-collegiate immersion program. The section I taught was focused on law. Another essential part of the immersion program was exploring DC, meeting with lawyers, and understanding the legal process. It was to serve as a transition for them into their collegiate experience.

I figured since I had dealt with Members of Congress for years as well as undergraduate students in my first semester, I could probably handle a group of high school kids. They were somewhat like my Washington semester students since they came from all over the country and were here to learn about government. They had a broad range of skills; some were well-prepared, others were in over their heads.

One of the students, Ashleigh, was extremely bright, had a dynamic personality, and I could tell she was going to be a leader. She was always ready for class, was extremely articulate, and had something most people her age did not seem to possess, the ability to listen. She was also a student who availed herself of the chance to discuss a whole range of public policy issues with me, as well as talk about personal matters.

One day she came into my office to tell me that her parents were coming to town and that she would be grateful if I would be willing to meet with them. I said that I would be pleased to. She told me that she had an ulterior motive. She was doing a lot of thinking about what she wanted to do after she graduated from college and was considering law school. Her parents were not so enthusiastic about that career path. They thought that she should pursue a career in accounting. I asked her why that was their choice for her. It came as no surprise to find out that both of her parents were accountants, and they were disappointed Ashleigh was not thrilled about following them into their profession.

She wanted her parents to meet me, and also have me make clear to them that their daughter had a wide range of career options available to her, including, among other things, going to law school. She thought that kind of observation, coming from me as a lawyer, would have an impact on them. I agreed to be her co-conspirator. The most important thing I could tell them was that I thought their daughter was extremely bright and could do anything she turned her mind to, becoming a lawyer being just one of those things. I planned to explain to them that having a law degree did not necessarily mean that you had to be a practicing lawyer. Many of the people I know who have law degrees are doing a wide range of other things that utilized their legal training, but they were not practicing law.

When her parents came in a couple of weeks later, we had a friendly discussion. I was impressed by how proud they were of their daughter and how supportive they were. I bragged on her mercilessly to them, tiptoeing around the career choice issue gingerly. As the conversation turned to the possibility of her going to law school, I could see Ashleigh was getting a little nervous. I think she was afraid I was going to lay it on too thick.

After her successful summer at AU, Ashley attended college there and graduated with her degree in political science. It was nice to have her on campus and to watch her grow. She continued to be a star during her undergraduate years. Interestingly, she decided not to go to law school or get a degree in accounting. She got a case of Potomac Fever and chose to pursue a career in government relations. I heard from her occasionally after her graduation. I always considered her to have been one of my best students.

Several years later, I received an email from her which brought tears to my eyes. Although it is rather lengthy, I am going to include the majority of it because it demonstrates what an exceptional young woman she is and the fact that she feels I had a positive impact on her life.

*"Last week I started a new job at a defense firm called ****. I am handling all their internal and digital media strategies for their executives in the Crystal City office. I wouldn't say it's my dream job, but it's pretty darn close. During my interview process, one of the questions was who in my life other than my parents, had the biggest impact on me, whether professionally or personally. Without even hesitating, I answered with your name. I went on to explain that you impacted my life in one of the best ways I could imagine. Growing up in a very small town in Cleveland, where I wasn't exposed to much, you opened my eyes to a bigger and better world. You allowed me to think outside of the box, question things I might not have done previously, and pushed me to think about what I really wanted to pursue in my professional career, while always reminding me the sky is the limit. You believed in me and supported me throughout my college decision days on where to apply. I can say full heartily that without having met you Professor Freeman, I know I wouldn't have come to Washington, DC for school, and thus wouldn't be where I am today. You pushed me out of my comfort zone intellectually to remind me that I need to always prepare for the other side of things. That has helped me*

tremendously throughout my career. Whenever preparing for a presentation, I'm always considering what cons the other side might bring up.

You taught me to think strategically. You taught me to always "squeeze" everything I could out of every opportunity I was given. Most importantly, you taught me that being different and stepping out of my comfort zone was okay. You have no idea how much that meant. While everyone back home was going to local colleges, I, as Robert Frost once said, "took the road less traveled", and that has made all the difference. You assured me it was ok to want bigger and better things out of this life, to have a career in Washington that would have a real impact on people's lives.

Whenever my father tells me he's proud of me, which he does constantly, I always reply that there are many, many people to thank who helped me along this journey. This was no easy feat. You, Professor Freeman, have been one of those people I have to not only thank but show a tremendous amount of gratitude towards. John Kennedy once said, "As we express our gratitude, we must never forget that the highest appreciation is not to utter words but to live by them." I live by all your words and wisdom you have taught me, Professor Freeman.

Thank you, --it is a simple phrase, but full of meaning.

Fondly,

Ashleigh"

I was simply speechless. It was the most moving letter I had ever received from a student.

American University Washington Semester Program Guest Speakers

Class with Associate Justice Samuel Alito

Class with Senator Richard Burr

Introducing 9/11 Fund Arbitrator Kenneth Feinberg on campus

Cong. John Conyers (D-MI) speaking to class after having "sworn them in" as Members of the House in the House Judiciary Committee Hearing room with me as "his counsel"

Class with Senator Jeff Flake

Class with Congressman Barney Frank

Class with Associate Justice Ruth Bader Ginsburg

Class with Former Congressman and Secretary of Agriculture Dan Glickman

Class with Congressman Alcee Hastings

Class legislative hearing and debate--House Judiciary Committee hearing room

Class with EEOC Acting Chairman Stuart Ishimaru

Class with Secretary of Transportation and former Congressman Ray La-Hood

Class with then-Congressman Mike Pence

Class with Federal Judge Barbara Rothstein

Class with Speaker of the House Paul Ryan--a WSP alum

Class with Associate Justice Antonin Scalia

Class with House Rules Committee Chairman Pete Sessions

Class with House Science Committee Chairman Lamar Smith

Class with Associate Justice Sonya Sotomayor

XXII. Final Thoughts

Over the years, as I have regaled people with the strange and exciting tales of my career, many have urged me to "put them down on paper". I have enjoyed the process. Many incidents that had faded in my memory began to surface as I wrote. One memory would trigger another. Due to my sense of humor, and how much I enjoy a good yarn, a lot of them relate to amusing happenings. Often during intense situations, something funny would come up that would release the tension and allow everyone involved to relax and refocus.

One of the fantastic things about writing about your life is that it provides an opportunity to reflect on the interesting people you have met and the effect they had on you, and in many cases, the effect you had on them. I had the good fortune to experience a broad, multifaceted career; I was able to function in many different capacities. I have been a practicing attorney, which I loathed, a part of the White House staff, which was fascinating for the insights it gave me, a lawyer who got to work on complex legal and constitutional issues in Congress, and an educator both in the Science and the Courts program and in two different subject matter areas in academia; government and bioethics. All of these were learning experiences, mostly good ones, but not all. I have tried to describe them clearly, knowing my perceptions may be somewhat colored. Others may have viewed the same situations differently. As the author, I have the prerogative to call them as I saw them.

My takeaway from writing this book is that positive interactions with others are the most important factors in a successful life journey. For the most part, I was able to tiptoe gingerly around what I refer to as the "human land mines" who, unfortunately, seem to populate everyone's life. I enjoyed working with a plethora of dedicated, caring professionals, many of whom taught me significant life lessons. I learned the power of being an honest broker, and how that would put me in good stead with most people. I also learned the corrosive effects that angry, insecure, and unhappy people can have on any environment.

Some days I was not fully conscious of the importance of the magnificent places where I was working. I would look at the White House when I walked onto the grounds and take a moment to feel the atmosphere of simply being there, but often lose that as I got busy doing my job. When I entered the House Chamber, I would also take in the majesty of the place which was my working environment. But that, too, would evanesce as I began to concentrate on the legislation we were working on.

I got to interact with famous people. I was on speaking terms with many who appeared on the national news, but I tried not to let their fame prevent me from completing my mission for the day. Many people thought I was a true professional, and that made me feel good. Conversely, the fact that some of them castigated me, while uncomfortable to take at the time, did not devastate me.

When reflecting on the incredibly varied tableau of people who I have encountered during my life, I have often thought of the books by the British veterinarian, James Herriot entitled "All Creatures Great and Small". Many of those people were great, and many of them were small. Often, the ones who were considered great by the outside world were, in my view, not, and some of those who were considered small were, in my estimation, great.

I have been a witness to history, in both my professional life and in the activities I chose to engage in outside of the office. My life was definitely made richer by not being a specialist in one particular field. I took pride in being well-read and knowledgeable about a wide range of subjects. This left me deficient in the views of some of the deep well-drillers who were contemptuous of people who were conversant with both the infield fly rule in baseball and the concepts embodied in the First Amendment, but not with section 1103(b) of some part of the US Code. Maybe it was my restless mind, and maybe it was my dyslexia that made me intellectually omnivorous and/or unable to stay focused on one area for too long, but my voracious appetite for learning enhanced my ability to have a rich and fulfilling life.

Senator Sam Ervin once said, "No man's search for knowledge should end on this side of the grave". I took that to heart. Being in Washington, with its plethora of continuing education venues, was extraordinarily beneficial. I took courses and attended lectures at the Smithsonian Institution, Georgetown Medical School, the National Institutes of Health, the Newseum, and scores of other places. These enriched my life, and in some cases, but not all, were linked to my professional activities. More often than not, they were not relevant to my career, but they were fascinating and educational. I encountered a broad range of people in these settings and expanded my horizons and worldview.

Speaker Tip O'Neill used to say, "It never hurts to be nice". I found that to be true. Not only did it not hurt, but it was also frequently advantageous. I seemed to get more out of people with whom I was working by being nice to them. Sprinkling in a kind word or a compliment served as lubrication in the gears of human interactions. Cynics accused me of being Machiavellian, but it was never done to take unfair advantage of others. It simply made life more pleasant, and resulted in other people being easier to work with.

In retrospect, I believe I have been successful in accomplishing the goal I described in the introduction; I have lived my life "on the Eagle's wing". I have been a dedicated public servant, and of that, I am immensely proud.

Thank you for joining me on my trip down memory lane.

Daniel M. Freeman

Appendix 1

Joint Sessions of Congress

The following is a list of Joint Sessions I had the privilege of attending:

Boris Yeltsin, the First President of the Russian Federation, June 17, 1992
This address took place after the breakup of the Soviet Union when it looked like there was going to be a significant rapprochement between our two countries. The Chamber was overflowing for this historic event.

Corazon Aquino, the 11th President of the Philippines, September 18, 1986
President Aquino's trademark was to wear bright yellow. She did so on this day, and the Chamber was full. Many of the women Members wore yellow, and there were a lot of men wearing yellow ties in her honor. She talked movingly about her late husband, who was assassinated.

Lech Walesa, Chairman Polish Solidarity Union, November 15, 1989
Mr. Walesa later became the second President of Poland and won the Nobel Peace Prize in 1983. He went from being a union worker in a shipyard to becoming the President of his country. An inspiring story.

Margaret Thatcher, Prime Minister the United Kingdom February 20, 1985
Mrs. Thatcher and President Ronald Regan were close allies, and she was the first woman prime minister in Europe. She was a dynamo.

Nelson Mandela, Deputy President, African National Congress, June 26, 1990
Mr. Mandela had spent 27 years in jail for fighting the apartheid policies of the South African government. He got a rousing reception. Every seat in the

Chamber was occupied.

Nelson Mandela, President of South Africa, Oct 6, 1994

This was the most moving Joint Session I ever attended. To consider what Mr. Mandela had overcome to appear as the President of his nation was dramatic and awe-inspiring, and no Member wanted to miss it. Mr. Mandela's magnetic personality and joyful presence made it an extraordinary event.

Viktor Yuschenko, President of Ukraine, April 6, 2005

I considered this session a special event because I was able to get my friend and colleague on the International Relations Committee, Doug Seay, to join me. Doug had been actively involved in the Ukrainian political evolution and was delighted to be there. He knew both President and Mrs. Yuschenko.

Elizabeth II, Queen of England, May 16, 1991

The context here was splendid. The week before the Queen spoke, General Norman Schwarzkopf, who was the Allied Commander in Chief during the Gulf War, was given a special honor to address a Joint Session in what was called a "Homecoming Address". As he walked down the center aisle of the House, he was greeted with handshakes and vigorous slaps on the back.

However, when the Queen walked down the same aisle a week later, there was none of that. No one touches the Queen! Members kept a proper distance as she was escorted to the Rostrum.

She had spoken the day before at a White House event. Unfortunately, the lectern which was provided was too tall for her. The Queen is only 5'4", and it was difficult for her to be seen. The "Washington Post" had a photograph on the front page of the Queen wearing a large-brimmed hat. Her face was partially obscured by the lectern, and the caption was "Talking Mushroom" because her hat looked like a giant mushroom. At the beginning of her remarks before the Joint Session, she said in her very proper English voice, "I hope you can all see me properly". It brought the house down! This was especially nice for me since I was able to get a seat for my wife, a Brit, to sit in the gallery. She had never seen the Queen in person.

Former Soviet President Gorbachev, May 14, 1992

He addressed both houses of Congress in Statuary Hall (the old House Chamber). Since he was not a head of state, a Joint Session was not appropriate from a protocol perspective. In 1987, during his summit with President Reagan, he had been tentatively invited to address a full Joint Session. There was a lot of resistance about bestowing such an honor on a man who was deemed by many to be an adversary. It was an unusual setting for this type of event, but it was an historic occasion, and I was glad to have been able to get in.

Appendix 2

Topics/Exercises for Public Law Seminar

Constitutional Issues

    Article I Congress and the Legislative Process

        Congressional Legislative Documents

        The Passage of the Brady Handgun Violence Prevention Act

        Mock Congressional Hearing and Debate on Gun Control Bill

        Intellectual property—copyrights, patents and

        trademarks

    Article II—The Executive

        Rules and Regulations--rulemaking process including the promulgation of rules related to food safety, prescription drugs and other issues.

        Take Care to faithfully execute laws—Defense of Marriage Act

    Article III-The Courts

        First Amendment

            Free speech: Symbolic Speech

                Students—*Tinker, and Morse*

                Flag burning—*Eichman/Haggerty*

                Funeral Protests—*Snyder v Phelps*—Westboro Baptist Church

                False Statements: "Stolen Valor"—*Alvarez*

                Obscenity—*Miller*

             Separation of Church and State—*Lemon*, Pledge of Allegiance--*Newdow "Under God"*

Freedom of the press—*Times v. Sullivan*

Second Amendment—*Heller* and *McDonald*

Fourth Amendment—Search and Seizure

GPS case—*Jones*

"Fruit of the poisonous tree"—*Wong Sun*

Sixth Amendment—Right to Counsel—*Betts v. Brady* and *Gideon v. Wainwright*

Tenth Amendment

Physician-assisted suicide—*Gonzalez v. Oregon*

Same-sex marriage—*Windsor, Obergefell*

Fourteenth Amendment—Equal Protection—*Loving v. Virginia*

Genetic Information Nondiscrimination Act (GINA)

"Right to die" *Glucksberg* and *Vacco, Quinlan,* and *Cruzan*

Other Subjects:

Immigration Reform

The Affordable Care Act

On-the-Job Sexual Harassment

The Family Medical Leave Act

The Americans with Disabilities Act

The Electoral College

Appendix 3

Guest Speakers

Public Law Seminar

Samuel Alito	Associate Justice U.S. Supreme Court
Tom Allen	Gauludette Univ./ Americans with Disabilities Act
Shawn Arbrus	Death Penalty Project
Dick Armey	Former Majority Leader U.S. House of Reps
Jennifer Knowles	AU/Americans with Disabilities Act
J. Gresham Barrett	U.S. House of Representatives
Judith Bartnoff	Federal Judge
Elizabeth Bazan	Congressional Research Service
Xavier Becerra	U.S. House of Representatives
Mark Begich	U.S. Senate
Joanne Benica	AU/Americans with Disabilities Act
Howard Berman	U.S. House of Representatives
Mary Bono Mack	U.S. House of Representatives
John Boozman	U.S. House of Reps/ U.S. Senate
Victoria Botvin	Office of House Employment Counsel
Karlyn Bowman	Poll Analyst
Chuck Brain	Lobbyist
Jess Bravin	Wall Street Journal
Stephen Breyer	Associate Justice U.S. Supreme Court
Daniel Bryant	Walmart Co.
Richard Burr	U.S. House of Reps-U.S. Senate/Chair Intel Com

Steve Buyer	U.S. House of Representatives
Chris Cannon	U.S. House of Representatives
Andrew Card	Former White House Chief of Staff
Ben Cardin	U.S. Senate
Glen Caroline	National Rifle Assn.
Ricardo Carvajal	Hyman Phelps/Former FDA attorney
Amy Caspari	D.C. Attorney General's Office
Steve Chabot	U.S. House of Representatives
Howard Coble	U.S. House of Representatives
John Conyers	U.S. House of Reps--Chair House Judiciary Comm
Bill Corr	Deputy Secretary Health and Human Services
Jeremy Cubert	Dickstein Shapiro--Intellectual Property Attorney
Andre Davis	Federal Judge
Bill Delahunt	U.S. House of Representatives
Kristen DeWire	D.C. Attorney General's Office
John Doll	U.S. Patent and Trademark Office
Dipu Doshi	Dickstein Shapiro--Intellectual Property Attorney
Bob Dove	Former U.S. Senate Parliamentarian
David Dreier	U.S. House of Reps--Chair House Rules Com
John Dudas	U.S. Patent and Trademark Office
Eric Easton	University of Baltimore Law School-Libel
Jo Ann Emerson	U.S. House of Representatives
Ladd Everitt	Everytown--gun control organization
Ken Feinberg	Arbitrator/Mediator--9/11 Fund, BP Oil Spill Fund
George Fishman	Staff U.S. House of Representatives--Immigration
Jeff Flake	U.S. House of Representatives/ U.S. Senate
Michael Flannigan	U.S. House of Representatives
Vito Foscella	U.S. House of Representatives
Barney Frank	U.S. House of Representatives
Leslye Fraser	Food and Drug Administration--food safety
John Frazer	National Rifle Assn.
Alan Frumin	U.S. Senate Parliamentarian
Agnieszka Fryszman	Private Practice--Human Trafficking
Phil Gingrey	U.S. House of Representatives
Mitch Glazier	Recording Industry Association of America
Dan Glickman	U.S. House of Reps, Commerce Sec., MPAA, BPC
Colin Goddard	Brady Center--handgun control
Bob Goodlatte	U.S. House of Representatives
Trey Gowdy	U.S. House of Representatives

Lindsey Graham	U.S. House of Reps/U.S. Senate
Jon Grossman	Dickstein Shapiro--copyrights
Scott Harris	Clerk U.S. Supreme Court
Amanda Harrison	AU/Americans with Disabilities Act
Alcee Hastings	U.S. House of Representatives
Jim Howe	Nuclear Power Lobbyist
Ellen Huvelle	Federal Judge
Stuart Ishimaru	EEOC/ Consumer Finance Protection Bureau
Darrell Issa	U.S. House of Representatives
Jesse Jackson, Jr.	U.S. House of Representatives
William Jackson	Judge D.C. Superior Court--Case of MB
Charlie Johnson	Parliamentarian U.S. House of Representatives
Marcy Kaptur	U.S. House of Representatives
Tim Keating	Boeing
Peter King	U.S. House of Representatives
Rufus King	Chief Judge, D.C. Superior Court
Kerry Kircher	General Counsel U.S. House of Representatives
Sarah Klein	Center Science in the Public Interest--food safety
David Lachmann	House Judiciary Committee Staff
Ray LaHood	Fmr Member U.S. House of Reps—DOT Sec.
Sy Lazarus	Carter White House Domestic Policy Council
John Lewis	U.S. House of Representatives/ Civil Rights Icon
Jon Liebowitz	Chairman Federal Trade Commission
Blanche Lincoln	U.S. House of Representatives/ U.S. Senate
Ron Lindsey	Religious Freedom Institute
Jose Lopez	Judge D.C. Superior Court
Dan Lungren	U.S. House of Representatives
Jennifer Luttman	FBI DNA expert
Ed Markey	U.S. Senate
Shana Matini	Office of D.C. Attorney General
Muftiah McCartin	Covington & Burling
Betty McCollum	U.S. House of Representatives
Jim McDermott	U.S. House of Representatives
Jim McGovern	U.S. House of Representatives
Mack McLarty	Former White House Chief of Staff
Edwin Meese	Former U.S. Attorney General
Scott Michelman	Public Citizen
Norm Mineta	U.S. House of Reps, Commerce Sec. DOT Sec.
Jim Moran	U.S. House of Representatives

Jerry Nadler	U.S. House of Representatives
Nicole Nason	Head Nat'l Highway Transportation Safety Admin.
Sandra Day O'Connor	Associate Justice U.S. Supreme Court
Michael O'Leary	Motion Picture Assn of America--Copyrights
Mike Pence	U.S. House of Representatives
Jay Pierson	U.S. House Floor Staff
Ted Poe	U.S. House of Representatives
Adeen Postar	AU Law Library--Administrative Procedure Act
David Price	U.S. House of Representatives
Deborah Pryce	U.S. House of Representatives
William Pryor	Judge D.C. Court of Appeals
Jim Ramstad	U.S. House of Representatives
David Rifkin	USA Patriot Act
Ann Rogers	U.S. House Employment Counsel
Chuck Rosenberg	U.S. Attorney Northern VA
Morton Rosenberg	Congressional Research Service
Ileana Ros-Lehtinen	Chair House of Reps. Foreign Affairs Com.
Steve Rothman	U.S. House of Representatives
Barbara Rothstein	Federal Judge
Ed Royce	U.S. House of Representatives
Lee Satterfield	Chief Judge, D.C. Superior Court
Antonin Scalia	Associate Justice U.S. Supreme Court
Bob Schieffer	CBS News
Aaron Schock	U.S. House of Representatives
Bobby Scott	U.S. House of Representatives
Rick Semiatin	Professor Washington Semester Program
Marlisa Senchak	Federal Deposit Insurance Corporation
Jim Sensenbrenner	U.S. House of Reps-Chair House Judiciary Com
Pete Sessions	U.S. House of Representatives Chair Rules Com
Ilya Shapiro	Cato Institute--healthcare
Katy Siddall	U.S. House of Representatives Staff
Chris Smith	U.S. House of Representatives
Lamar Smith	U.S. House of Reps-Chair Science/Judiciary Com
Caroline Smith DeWaal	Food and Drug Administration--food safety
Sonia Sotomayor	Associate Justice U.S. Supreme Court
Suzanne Spaulding	Dept. of Homeland Security/U.S.A. Patriot Act
Mark Stanley	National Institute of Standards
Cliff Stearns	U.S. House of Representatives
John Paul Stevens	Associate Justice U.S. Supreme Court

Malcolm Stewart	Deputy Solicitor General
John Sullivan	Parliamentarian U.S. House of Representatives
William Suter	Clerk U.S. Supreme Court
Tom Tancredo	U.S. House of Representatives
Todd Tatelman	House General Counsel's Office
Bill Thomas	U.S. House of Representatives
Laura Thrift	U.S. House of Representatives Staff
Nina Totenberg	National Public Radio-Supreme Court
Ricardo Urbina	Federal Judge
Dan Vice	Brady Center to Prevent Handgun Violence
Reggie Walton	Federal Judge
Eric Washington	Chief Judge, D.C. Court of Appeals
Debbie Wasserman-Schultz	U.S. House of Representatives
Mel Watt	U.S. House of Representatives
J.C. Watts	Former U.S. House of Representatives
Henry Waxman	U.S. House of Representatives
Tom Wickham	Parliamentarian U.S. House of Representatives
Kim Williams	Office of House Employment Counsel
Wayne Witkowski	District of Columbia Attorney General's Office
Buck Wong	National Institutes of Health
Bob Woodward	Watergate reporter/Author
John Yarmuth	U.S. House of Representatives
Chris Zealand	National Rifle Association
Joan Zeldon	Judge D.C. Superior Court

Appendix 4

Site Visits for meetings/programs

Public Law Seminar

Brookings Institution

Cato Institute

Center for Science in the Public Interest (CSPI) for a discussion about food safety

Congressional Research Service (CRS) in the Library of Congress for a discussion of search and seizure law

Department of Health and Human Services for a session on healthcare

District of Columbia Court of Appeals for oral arguments

District of Columbia Superior Court for meetings with Judges

Federal Trade Commission (FTC) for a discussion of consumer rights

Food and Drug Administration (FDA) for a discussion about Administrative Law and food safety

Heritage Foundation

Major law firms on various topics but for the students who were considering law school to discuss law practice: e.g., Covington & Burling, Hyman Phelps, Dickstein

Motion Picture Association of America (MPAA) for a meeting on copyrights National Archives

National Institutes of Health (NIH) for a meeting on Genetic Information Discrimination and a discussion of stem cells

Newseum for a session on the First Amendment

Recording Industry Association of America (RIAA) for a meeting on copyrights

United States Patent and Trademark Office (USPTO) for a discussion of trademarks and patents

U.S. House of Representatives Chamber—visit to the floor

U.S. Senate Chamber—visit to the floor

U.S. Supreme Court (Meeting with the several Justices, Clerk and oral arguments),

U.S. Court of Appeals, Federal District Court, D.C. Superior Court, D.C. Court of Appeals

The White House

Index

CPSIA information can be obtained
at www.ICGtesting.com
Printed in the USA
LVHW021357310720
662069LV00007B/458